Can Hong Kong Exceptionalism Last?

Can Hong Kong Exceptionalism Last?

Dilemmas of Governance and Public Administration
over Five Decades, 1970s–2020

Anthony B.L. Cheung

香港城市大學出版社
City University of Hong Kong Press

ISBN: 978-962-937-591-1

Published by
        City University of Hong Kong Press
        Tat Chee Avenue
        Kowloon, Hong Kong
        Website: www.cityu.edu.hk/upress
        E-mail: upress@cityu.edu.hk

Printed in Hong Kong

This book is dedicated to the four generations of Hongkongers in the contemporary era—Chinese and non-Chinese—whose hard work, daringness, and pride have cumulatively created the Hong Kong we know today.

The first generation—born before the Second World War and mostly migrants—suffered war and social strife and went through the toughest times amid poverty and insecurity. They laid the foundation for Hong Kong's subsequent reconstruction and industrialisation.

The second generation—the post-War baby boomers—grew up at a time of economic and social change, and seized new educational opportunities and affluence to cultivate a middle-class dream. They laid the foundation for Hong Kong's vibrant institutions, professionalism, and core values.

The third generation—born during the prosperous 1970s–1980s—embody the new Hong Kong identity and folklore, their future being shaped by the transition from British to Chinese rule. They are now the mainstay of our community.

The fourth generation—largely born near or after the 1997 reunification—have continued with the journey first started by previous generations. Enjoying better education and material conditions, they are at the same time growingly anxious about coping with the new challenges from regional integration, globalisation, technological revolution, and the implementation of 'One Country, Two Systems'. Many of them harbour strong anti-establishment sentiments and are compassionate about preserving the Hong Kong identity.

Hong Kong's future is in jeopardy. It is as much in the hands of the policy-makers in Beijing as in the hands of the latest generation in the city. May the younger generations be inspired by the experience and wisdom of their predecessors!

Table of Contents

Preface

The purpose of this book is to help explain Hong Kong's path of governance and public administration over the last five decades—a path which has seen many twists and turns, ups and downs, and pride and anxieties, as the city transformed from a British colony into a Special Administrative Region (SAR) of China in 1997 and grew under the principle of 'One Country, Two Systems'. At a time when confidence in Hong Kong's future seems to be ebbing away again, especially among the younger generation who bemoan the loss of autonomy under a strong yet non-democratic China, it is particularly critical that we do not lose sight of the evolving historical context by just lamenting the present problems and tensions. Nowadays, political jitters and pessimism abound, which could easily drive populist sentiments about the fall of the Hong Kong system. However, is this a fair assessment of Hong Kong's accumulated institutional strength or its social and economic achievements both before and after 1997? What is meant by the 'Hong Kong' system and values over the decades, where exceptionalism and hybridity seemed to have symbolised the city's potential as well as vulnerabilities?

I completed the first draft of this manuscript in mid-2019 when the anti-extradition protests against the Fugitive Offenders and Mutual Legal Assistance in Criminal Matters Legislation (Amendment) Bill 2019 were beginning to explode. Since then, Hong Kong has entered a tumultuous period of political unrest and violent confrontations causing the central government in Beijing to respond harshly. The final manuscript was revised in July last year just as the National People's Congress Standing Committee (NPCSC) passed the National Security Law in Hong Kong. Then, in March 2021, Beijing announced major changes to Hong Kong's electoral system to revamp the local political order and rid it of 'unpatriotic' elements. Such a highly volatile situation makes it challenging for any writer to comment on Hong Kong's politics and governance because new developments continue to unfold. It is not yet the time to form any definitive observations on how Hong Kong will evolve into the future. However, the trajectory of the past five decades will inevitably be relevant to the next phase of transformation, for better or worse. The statistics and references cited here are those available up to mid-2020, but new statistics will have come out since then. A Postscript has been added just before publication to give readers a provisional assessment of Hong Kong's latest overall governance situation.

The year 2019 marked not only the 70th anniversary of the establishment of the People's Republic of China (PRC), to which Hong Kong reverted on 1 July 1997, but was also the centenary of the May Fourth Movement which had inspired generations of Chinese students and revolutionaries seeking to build a strong and modern China free from feudal baggage and foreign subjugation in pursuit of 'democracy' and 'science' (respectively symbolising participatory governance and social progress sustained by scientific development). China today is keen to embark on another era of Chinese renaissance—the 'Chinese Dream'.[1] However, despite achieving rapid economic growth, there exists wide concern whether its politics and society have been sufficiently liberalised in accordance with the ideals championed by the May Fourth pioneers, some of whom took part in the founding of the Chinese Communist Party (CCP) that later won the civil war in 1949 and has governed the nation ever since. China's future forms the larger set in which Hong Kong evolves and transforms.

The May Fourth ideals also inspired student activists in Hong Kong during the 1960s–1970s, who were the core of the first generation of the pro-democracy movement in the 1980s, to which I also belonged. Based on an anti-colonial foundation, this movement fought for building a liberal and democratic Hong Kong where power was no longer concentrated in the hands of a synarchy of colonial rulers and business elites. The democrats at that time supported Hong Kong's return to China in 1997 out of nationalist principle and articulated a narrative of 'democratic reunification' (民主回歸) which was initially the subject of scorn by many sceptics and critics of communist rule. The quest for democracy has since been a long journey full of disappointment, frustrations, and setbacks. The post-1997 performance of the SAR government has been bumpy, to say the least. Mainland-Hong Kong relations have not been stable. Because of the lack of progress in democratisation, popular trust in the government has been deteriorating, resulting in a vicious cycle of local politics and executive-legislative gridlock. The prospect of the initially innovative 'One Country, Two Systems' framework has also been cast in doubt as 'Two Systems' tensions intensify, especially in the aftermath of the 2014 Occupy Central and Umbrella Movement protests.

I had my first contact with the inside workings of colonial Hong Kong's government machinery upon joining the civil service in 1974 fresh from university. That was an unusual move for a former student activist like me who denounced colonial rule and imperialism, and it was eye-opening.[2] After switching to academia in 1986, I focused on the study of public administration and governance in Hong Kong, as well as comparative public administration in Asia. My research sought to identify the political agendas and administrative motives behind managerial pursuits, distinguishing real-world concerns from reform rhetoric. I also took an active part in local politics, public service, and civil society activities, including think-tanks.[3] Then, as a major departure in my career, I joined the government as Secretary for Transport and Housing in July 2012 for a 5-year term. Therefore, I am used to looking at governance both from the outside in and from the inside out. Practical involvement certainly shapes one's perspectives. I may have been biased in some ways but have also become enlightened in others.

The last half-century has witnessed not only some of the glorious times of Hong Kong but also periods of anxiety, turbulence, and uncertainty. One of my first readings about Hong Kong as a university student in 1971 was *Hong Kong: The Industrial Colony*,[4] a fierce critique of the colonial administration for catering to big business and commercial interests at the expense of the Chinese masses whose labour and skills were the driving force behind the British colony's post-War industrial transformation. The analysis underlining this anthology of essays pointed to the dilemmas and paradoxes of the complex urban society which Hong Kong had already developed into, as the starting point of subsequent social, economic, and political development. In 1980, as Sino-British talks on Hong Kong's future were about to begin, another significant volume of essays under the title *Hong Kong: Dilemmas of Growth* provided an illuminating snapshot of the city's growth experience, by now already a financial centre with the potential of becoming a cultural entity and regional hub.[5] It was such a shining metropolis that it made China value its special status and made the international community concerned about its post-1997 future and impact.

A Hong Kong 'as is' to be reunited with the motherland but allowed to keep its economy and way of life as well as existing British institutions intact would seem to be the best of both worlds. However, the dilemmas were not confined to growth in the economic or general sense. How the city was to be governed under Chinese rule was heatedly debated during the 1980s and 1990s when the Sino-British Joint Declaration and the Basic Law of the post-1997 SAR were consecutively finalised. Issues outstanding from the Basic Law, notably constitutional development and national security legislation, have continued to haunt the new Hong Kong. At the same time, the practice of 'One Country, Two Systems' was subject to tension and stress. The possibility of preserving a Hong Kong system distinct from the Mainland system within one unified nation was once cherished as a blessing not to be taken for granted, yet the dominant transition ideology about minimal change so as to extend a 1980s-style modus operandi was highly conservative and not conducive to much-needed reforms to the city's politics, society, and economy.

Keeping Hong Kong's relevance and significance to both China and the world has since been at the centre of academic and political discourse. The clock of history did not stop in 1997. Institutions, economics, politics, and popular sentiments evolved, both in Hong Kong and on the Mainland. 'To change or not to change'—that seems the perennial question facing the Hong Kong community after 1997 under the impact of external and internal challenges. New generations of central government leaders and policy officials might have harboured rethinking and new concerns about the SAR amid the changing national picture. Within the polarising local polity, some people tend to either wholly negate the existing system or fully embrace the status quo without question. Such single-dimension approaches do not account for the complexity of governance in the historical context of Hong Kong.

Having been both outside and inside the establishment has enabled me to be critical of the system and yet cognisant of the progress and achievements made despite systemic limitations, human misjudgements, and challenges of the times. The story told in this book is, of course, only part of an unfolding historical drama. In the face of old and new dilemmas, Hong Kong still needs to search for a future beyond 2047 when China's promise of '50 years no change' will nominally expire. Hopefully, how well we understand the past and present will prepare us better for the future. Over the decades, I have written numerous academic papers and media commentaries on local political development and public policy. In preparing this book, I have taken the opportunity to revisit those past writings. Previous assumptions are reviewed, past conclusions reconsidered, and new questions asked. With some post hoc insight, the narrative of events and changes has been re-organised to tease out updated significance.

It is a process of interpreting and reinterpreting Hong Kong's administrative history. Hong Kong as a polity has long been embedded in ambiguities and sometimes contradictions, within a kind of 'neither here nor there' dilemma. Yet, the city had persisted in a most utilitarian and pragmatic manner to produce a strikingly successful case of 'administrative state' prior to British departure. After 1997, it has continued to thrive as a relatively resilient city-state still known for efficiency and effectiveness despite all the doomsday talk of failure attributed to the lack of progress in democracy, increasing challenges to governmental authority by society, and growing tensions with the Mainland. Against the rising agitations and sentiments of despair, I have tried to adopt a more cautious long-term view both about Hong Kong and China as a whole.

I completed the draft manuscript of this book in May 2019. At that time, none would have anticipated that an *annus horribilis* awaited Hong Kong in months of grave unrest. As if things have to become worse before they might get any better, the year since then saw the worst political crisis since the 1967 anti-British riots. It stemmed, unexpectedly, from the controversial *Fugitive Offenders and Mutual Legal Assistance in Criminal Matters Legislation (Amendment) Bill* (dubbed by the local and international media as 'the extradition bill' and is referred to as such hereafter in this book). Hundreds of thousands of protesters took to the street in territory-wide as well as district-based mobilisations, agitations, and violent confrontations that increasingly disrupted everyday life and business, with immense implications on SAR politics, governance, and 'Two Systems' relations. Political animosities spread, and violence escalated. An anti-establishment movement by the younger generation was born.

The unprecedented unrest is still ongoing at the time of writing (mid-2020), though slightly subdued because of the COVID-19 pandemic[6] that has shifted public attention and has also created new anxieties about the global economic depression ahead. As harsher challenges unfold, the dilemmas in governance will become more disturbing. The central government has taken the political crisis seriously, up to the level of national security, suspecting a foreign conspiracy in regime change that ultimately targets the Mainland. On the other hand, local sentiments about deviations from the original 'One Country, Two Systems' promise and the weakening of Hong Kong's freedoms and autonomy seem to be gaining force. When the National People's Congress (NPC) decided in late May 2020 to impose a national security law on Hong Kong, there was local and international shock. Like similar laws around the world, the national security law is harsh and gives sweeping powers to law enforcement. A different legal regime and operational logic is taking root which most Hongkongers are not used to. While the principle remains to strike a balance between protecting the nation and personal freedoms, new anxieties and more repercussions have emerged as the media, civil society groups, and some ordinary people begin to worry about restrictions on freedom of expression and dissenting views. Fear of the unknown is the greatest fear of all, keeping us in the comfort of the past and preventing us from envisioning a better prospect, reminding one of the ominous atmosphere of the early to mid-1980s when there was also much talk about migration.

Looking from any angle, the future of Hong Kong is at stake. Will Hong Kong from now on be pushed by circumstances towards a wholly alien pathway which would defy past wisdom? If so, what is the point of reviewing its historical and contemporary experience in governance? Even the purpose of this book would be in jeopardy. Hong Kong may well not be the same after 2019, but that should not necessarily mean the end of Hong Kong exceptionalism. The city has seen turbulent times before — the 1967 riots, the 1982–1984 Sino-British talks, the 1989 Tiananmen upheaval in Mainland China, and the last years of transition before 1997. We have now come to a crossroads and a trying moment not only for Hongkongers but also for the national leaders. All seem still keen on maintaining Hong Kong's special status and the broad concept of 'One Country, Two Systems'. Such an unspoken consensus should be valued. While the full implications of the still-evolving turbulence cannot be appraised at this stage, some initial conjectures are made in the context of discussion in the relevant chapters as well as in the Epilogue and Postscript.

The writing of this book is supported by a research grant from the Education University of Hong Kong. In the course of completing the manuscript, I was provided with competent research assistance from the university's Academy of Hong Kong Studies (in particular Dr Lee Ka-man), which is much appreciated. The chapters on public sector and civil service reforms as well as on government capacity, policy system, and state interventions are partly based on my previous research writings duly updated. The analysis behind the chapters on the nature of the SAR government and the 'Two Systems' was first presented in my Policy Dialogue Series co-hosted by the Department of Asian and Policy Studies, Education University of Hong Kong, and the Division of Public Policy, Hong

Kong University of Science and Technology, during the 2018–2019 academic year. It has benefitted from the exchange with the audience.

The support from the then heads of the two units, Professor Darryl Jarvis and Professor Wu Xun, for the Policy Dialogue series, as well as the administrative assistance rendered by Miss Molly Cheng and Mr Victor Lee, is thankfully acknowledged. The initial manuscript was first read by Mr Lam Woon-kwong,[7] Professor Lui Tai-lok, and Professor Darryl Jarvis. I thank them, as well as the anonymous external reviewers, for offering me valuable feedback and questions, in response to which improvements were made in the final version. The book would not have been produced without the strong encouragement and support of the City University Press Hong Kong, especially its Director, Professor Zhu Guobin, and its English Editor, Abby Manthey.

Finally, I thank my wife, Evelyn, and daughter, Charmaine. Both have endured my frequent absences from home ever since the 1980s as Hong Kong first entered the transition and then reunification, when I became so embroiled in politics and other heavy public service commitments, especially during my stints as a legislator, party vice-chairman, executive councillor, and then minister in the government. Without their immense patience and empathy, I would not have been able to muster enough strength and confidence to carry on my political and academic endeavours over the decades. One of my regrets in life is not having given my family more time.

Anthony Bing-leung Cheung
August 2021

About the Author

Professor Anthony Bing-leung Cheung (張炳良教授) is currently the Research Chair Professor of Public Administration at the Education University of Hong Kong (EdUHK) and Adjunct Professor of the Division of Public Policy at the Hong Kong University of Science and Technology. He was Secretary for Transport and Housing of the Hong Kong Special Administrative Region Government from July 2012 to June 2017. As Secretary, he was also Chairman of the Hong Kong Housing Authority, Hong Kong Maritime and Port Board, and Hong Kong Logistics Development Council, as well as Board Member of the Airport Authority and Mass Transit Railway Corporation Limited.

Professor Cheung graduated from the University of Hong Kong in 1974 with a BSocSc (Hon) degree in Sociology and Economics. He later obtained his MSc in Public Sector Management from the University of Aston, United Kingdom, and PhD in Government from the London School of Economics and Political Science, United Kingdom. He was awarded an Honorary Doctorate of Science by the University of Aston in 2016 and an Honorary Doctorate of Education by the EdUHK in 2017.

In the 1970s, Professor Cheung joined the civil service, and in 1986, he commenced his academic career at the Department of Public and Social Administration of the City University of Hong Kong, where he subsequently became Professor and Head of Department. From 2008 to 2012, he was the President of the Hong Kong Institute of Education, the predecessor of the EdUHK, laying the foundation for its transformation into university through an 'Education-plus' strategy.

Professor Cheung has researched extensively in governance, public policy, Asian administrative reforms, civil service issues, para-governmental organisations, and privatisation. Over the years he has published more than 100 refereed journal articles and book chapters, over ten authored/edited books, as well as numerous conference papers. He co-founded the Asian Association for Public Administration in 2010 and served as its President in 2011–2012.

Throughout his career, Professor Cheung has been active in public affairs, having served on the legislature and various government advisory and statutory bodies since the 1980s. Major positions include: Member of the Legislative Council and Chairman of its Education Panel (1995–1997); Non-Official Member of the Executive Council (2005–2012); Chairman of the Consumer

Council (2007–2012); Chairman of the Pay Trend Survey Committee (2007); and Board Member of Hong Kong Mortgage Corporation (2007–2017). He was Chairman of the political group Meeting Point (1990–1994), founding Vice-Chairman of the Democratic Party (1994–1998), and founding Chairman of the independent policy think-tank SynergyNet (2002–2005).

After stepping down from ministerial office, he was appointed Chairman of the Committee on Self-financing Post-secondary Education, and has been a Member of the Education Commission and University Grants Committee since November 2017. He also led a government task force to review self-financing post-secondary education in 2017–2018 in addition to being an adviser to the Steering Committee of the Hong Kong International Aviation Academy.

List of Acronyms and Abbreviations

AA	Airport Authority
AIIB	Asian Infrastructure Investment Bank
AO	Administrative Officer
BBC	British Broadcasting Company
BPA	Business and Professional Alliance for Hong Kong
CBA	Central Budget Agency
CCP	Chinese Communist Party
CDO	City District Officer/Office
CE	Chief Executive
CEPA	Closer Economic Partnership Agreement
CFA	Court of Final Appeal
CIQ	customs, immigration, and quarantine
COMAC	Commissioner for Administrative Complaints
COVID-19	Coronavirus disease 2019 (SARS-CoV-2)
CPF	Central Provident Fund
CPG	Central People's Government
CPPCC	Chinese People's Political Consultative Conference
CS	Chief Secretary/Chief Secretary for Administration
CSSA	Comprehensive Social Security Assistance scheme
DAB	Democratic Alliance for the Betterment and Progress of Hong Kong
DC	District Council
DMC	District Management Committee
DO	District Office/Officer
EfU	Efficiency Unit
EPP	Enhanced Productivity Programme
ExCo	Executive Council
FCO	Foreign and Commonwealth Office
FS	Financial Secretary
FSTB	Financial Services and Treasury Bureau
FTU	Hong Kong Federation of Trade Unions
GATT	General Agreement on Tariffs and Trade
GDP	gross domestic product

GST	goods and services tax
HKPORI	Hong Kong Public Opinion Research Institute
HKPR	Hong Kong Permanent Resident
HKUPOP	Public Opinion Programme of the University of Hong Kong
ICAC	Independent Commission Against Corruption
I&T	innovation and technology
IMF	International Monetary Fund
KCRC	Kowloon-Canton Railway Corporation
KMT	Kuomintang
LegCo	Legislative Council
MPF	Mandatory Provident Fund
MTR	mass transit railway
MTRC	Mass Transit Railway Corporation
NGO	non-governmental organisation
NIMBY	not in my backyard
NPC	National People's Congress
NPCSC	National People's Congress Standing Committee
NPM	New Public Management
OECD	Organisation for Economic Cooperation and Development
OMELCO	Office of Members of the Executive and Legislative Councils
OMLECO	Office of Members of the Legislative Council
PA	Political Assistant
PAC	Public Accounts Committee
PICO	Policy Innovation and Co-ordination Office
PLA	People's Liberation Army
POAS	Principal Officials Accountability System
PRC	People's Republic of China
PSB	public service broadcasting
PTI	pay trend indicator
PWD	Public Works Department
QE	quantitative easing
R&D	research and development
REIT	real estate investment trust
RMB	Renminbi
ROC	Republic of China
RTHK	Radio Television Hong Kong
SAR	special administrative region
SARS	severe acute respiratory syndrome
SCS	Secretary for the Civil Service

SEZ	special economic zone
UDHK	United Democrats of Hong Kong
UK	United Kingdom
UMELCO	Office of Unofficial Members of the Executive and Legislative Councils
UN	United Nations
US	United States of America
VFM	value-for-money
VRS	Voluntary Retirement Scheme
WKCD	West Kowloon Cultural District
WTO	World Trade Organisation
XRL	Guangzhou-Shenzhen-Hong Kong Express Rail Link

Introduction

Exceptionalism and Hybridity

1969 and 1979

The years 1969 and 1979 were both critical to Hong Kong's contemporary governance, public administration, and political development. In 1969, two years after the outbreak of anti-British riots in 1967 by local pro-Communists, which lasted for eight months, the British administration introduced the City District Officer (CDO) scheme in urban areas, modelled on District Offices (DOs) that had long existed in the leased New Territories. This marked a change of governing strategy by the colonial administration to reach out to the predominantly local Chinese population. The new-style CDOs, accommodated mostly in rented commercial premises easily accessible to the local communities, were tasked with monitoring and reporting community opinions and sentiments, as well as handling public inquiries and explaining government policies and measures.

The new scheme was preceded a year earlier by another move — the change of name of the then Secretariat for Chinese Affairs to Secretariat for Home Affairs, within the ambit of which CDOs were to function.[1] Such a change in nomenclature was significant as it marked the beginning of a gradual process to re-orient a government that had hitherto adopted indirect rule over the local Chinese population, treating them as a residual part rather than the mainstream of the community. Later, under a new Governor, Murray MacLehose, who assumed office in 1971, Hong Kong entered a golden-era decade of social and administrative reforms,[2] which served to modernise and transform the government, taking away many of its colonial wrappings.[3]

In 1979, in the aftermath of the devastating Cultural Revolution (1966–1976) that ended after the death of Mao Zedong in September 1976 and the subsequent fall of the 'Gang of Four', the old guards led by Deng Xiaoping (鄧小平) returned to power. At the Third Plenum of the 11th Central Committee of the Chinese Communist Party (CCP) in December 1978, it was decided that China would launch economic reform and opening-up, which eventually transformed the whole of the country. Hong Kong's industrialists and businesses were the first batch of external investors into the Mainland, proving to be a key element of China's process of modernisation that extended from economic to social life, paving the way for the present rise of China in the global arena.

Also in March of 1979, Governor MacLehose made his first official visit to Beijing, partly to gauge the latest economic development of the Mainland and restore Hong Kong-Mainland links which were either broken or made uncertain by the anti-foreign fervour of the Cultural Revolution, but more importantly to find out the attitude of the new leadership towards the future of Hong Kong when the 99-year lease of the New Territories expired in 1997. He met with Deng Xiaoping and returned with Deng's message to ask investors in Hong Kong to put their hearts at ease as the Chinese leaders attached great importance to the value of the city in China's modernisation. What MacLehose did not disclose was Deng's insistence that China would resume sovereignty over Hong Kong in 1997 as a matter of national policy. That encounter alerted the British government of the need to prepare for negotiations between the two governments. After his Beijing trip, MacLehose began to hasten the pace of district administration reform by establishing partially elected District Boards with advisory functions at the local community level to shore up the colonial government's people base.

The best of times, the worst of times

There were divergent objectives and strategies between Britain and China over the future of Hong Kong. Initially, the British government aimed at persuading the Chinese side to allow Britain to continue to govern Hong Kong under alternative arrangements, such as an extension of the New Territories lease, returning sovereignty in exchange for administrative power, or British presence and link of some kind (including the possibility of trustee administration).[4] However, Chinese leaders under Deng Xiaoping were determined to resume sovereignty over Hong Kong by 1997, and for them, sovereignty and administration were inseparable. The British side engaged a strategy of insisting on the international legality of the treaties (deemed by China as 'unequal' treaties) whereby Hong Kong Island and Kowloon Peninsula were ceded to Britain after the two Opium Wars in the nineteenth century (1839–1842 and 1856–1860), while also seeking from the Chinese side clarifications and reassurances on how to maintain Hong Kong's post-1997 stability and prosperity (including the protection of local and foreign business interests) before finally conceding on the matter of sovereignty in 1984.

For China, taking back Hong Kong was to end a history of national humiliation since the First Opium War. In addition, it wanted to take advantage of recovering Hong Kong, then already a booming metropolis and financial centre, to help support the Mainland's modernisation. As such, preserving Hong Kong's status quo would kill two birds with one stone. Before Sino-British negotiations formally commenced after British Prime Minister Margaret Thatcher visited Beijing in September 1982, the Chinese Government had already begun sounding out local business leaders and social notables about their concerns and ideas on a 1997 solution for Hong Kong. By January 1982, the Chinese leadership was able to promulgate a novel 'One Country, Two Systems' formula for both Mainland-Taiwan reunification (known as cross-strait reunification) as well as the return of Hong Kong to the motherland.[5] The Sino-British negotiations on the future of Hong Kong lasted for two years. At first, both sides stuck to their respective positions on the issue of 'unequal treaties' and failed to reach an agreement despite five rounds of talks. In March 1983, the British government finally recognised that China had sovereignty over Hong Kong all along. A consensus on all issues was reached after 22 further rounds of talks, leading to the initialling of the Sino-British Joint Declaration on 26 September 1984.[6]

Those two years were a tumultuous period. Paraphrasing the famous quote from Charles Dickens's *A Tale of Two Cities*, the 1980s 'was the best of times [and] it was the worst of times'. China reiterated its intention not to upset Hong Kong's existing way of life as it highly valued the city as a golden goose that laid golden eggs, an economic force to help the motherland reform and modernise, and a model to learn from especially in economic and public service management.[7] Later, Deng even called for the building of more 'Hongkongs' on the Mainland. Hong Kong's success as a thriving market economy with a small yet efficient government was regarded as key to maintaining its unique capitalist system different from the socialist system of the Mainland even after 1997. As China gradually rejoined the world market, Hong Kong's instrumental role in terms of capital intermediation (including the raising of capital for Mainland economic development and the facilitation of the Mainland's external trade) was deemed invaluable by Beijing.

However, Hong Kong people were caught in anxiety and worry over the prospect of handover to a communist regime from which some of them had fled in earlier periods. There was a crisis of confidence, not only among businesses, the professions, and the civil service but also ordinary people who questioned if returning to China in 1997 would mean the erosion of Hong Kong's long-enjoyed freedoms and rule of law. On 24 September 1983 ('Black Saturday'), upon rumours that Sino-British talks had come to the verge of a breakdown because of strong disagreement, the local currency fell to an all-time low of HK$9.6 against the US dollar (compared to about HK$6 a year earlier) and caused great panic.[8] Facing both a currency run and nervousness about the soundness of several banks, Black Saturday induced the colonial government to quickly adopt a currency-board system on 15 October 1983 of pegging the Hong Kong dollar to the US dollar at a fixed exchange rate of HK$7.80 = US$1 in order to stabilise the market and restore business and public confidence. This 'Linked Exchange Rate' has since become the basis of Hong Kong's monetary system.[9]

In the run-up to the reunification, what China wanted from Hong Kong was an 'economic city' with minimum political disruptions. Yet Hong Kong on its part had already become, by default if not by design, a city of politics, embroiled not just in agitations for a democratic system after 1997 but also mass sympathy for the 1989 pro-democracy movement in China that ended in tragedy with the

Tiananmen crackdown in June. Political backlash and pessimism quickly set in. However, the fatalist sentiments accompanying the handover had proved to be unnecessary though they underlined the vulnerability of the local psyche. When Hong Kong came closer to its return to China, the international magazine *Fortune* ran a report predicting 'the death of Hong Kong' after 1997.[10] In 2007, it had to openly admit it was wrong—Hong Kong was hardly dead.[11]

By the time of its restoration to Chinese sovereignty, Hong Kong was a developed economy and affluent society, with advanced legal and administrative systems, and active media and civil society, yet bound by a rather anachronistic political system originating from the nineteenth century even though it gradually liberalised during the transition. Here laid the inherent contradiction, or to put it more positively, the 'hybrid' nature of contemporary Hong Kong—the co-existence of the colonial and the modern and that of the Chinese and the English. Under British rule, Hong Kong had not lost its Chinese cultural heritage and ethnicity while acquiring British institutions and the English language. In the words of the last Governor, Chris Patten, Hong Kong 'is a Chinese city, a very Chinese city with British characteristics'.[12] Some had expected such hybrid charm to continue after 1997 to make it an 'English' city under Chinese rule. Despite the wish from all sides to have minimal change and maximum continuity, no society and polity could stay put for a prolonged period. The regime change was followed by new social and political dynamics not seen before under colonial suppression and management. Institutional incompatibilities began to unfold. Mainland-Hong Kong relations also underwent shifts not fully anticipated in the 1980s.

The Asian financial crisis that occurred immediately after the handover was also alarming, indicating that Hong Kong's economic prosperity should not be taken for granted. Hong Kong was destined for more turbulent times. Identity anxieties and growing frustrations over the slow progress of democratisation led to more government-society tensions, all contributing to a steady decline in political trust. In recent years, there have been increasing media commentaries and academic writings alleging more restrictions over civil liberties and regression in the implementation of the 'One Country, Two Systems' principle. Criticisms and suspicions abound, premised on China as a communist authoritarian regime that disliked democracy and sought to tighten its grips over the special administrative region (SAR), thereby reducing the promised scope of autonomy.

Since the 'Occupy Central' rallies and Umbrella Movement in 2014, suggestions revived of Hong Kong dying a slow death.[13] More pessimism and fatalism have emerged during the still unending governance crisis emanating from the 2019 anti-extradition protests. The decision by the National People's Congress (NPC) in May 2020 to enact a special national security law for Hong Kong (subsequently passed and implemented in July 2020) drew desperate outcries from the pan-democrats and some critical media outlets, who forecasted that it would mean the 'end of Hong Kong'.[14] The 'Two Systems' relations have never seen such stressful moments, with no clear way to break the political deadlock. Will history prove such soothsaying wrong once again? Let us put things into context by taking a historical and long-term view and re-examine how contemporary Hong Kong has made its way forward in governance and administration through the past five decades, confronting multiple dilemmas and challenges due to endogenous and exogenous factors.

The evolving political economy

Politics cannot be divorced from economics. Understanding governance necessitates an appreciation of the political economy, which evolves over time. In the academic and theoretical literature, there have been incessant and inconclusive debates and contestations about whether and how politics and economics (or the state and market) could be taken together, leaving the perennial question of whether the economic foundation (infrastructure) determines the superstructure (including politics and the state system) or whether the state defines the sphere and operations of the market.[15] Without delving into such debates, suffice it to say that one cannot fully appraise the functions of the state and the challenges faced by governance if detached from the economy.

In the case of Hong Kong, its economic significance has been closely tied to China since early British colonial times, first serving as a strategic outpost of British imperial expansion into Far Eastern trade. In the 1950s, its mercantile role faced challenges posed by the closed-door policy of a new Communist China and the imposition of a trade embargo on it by the West during the Cold War, lasting until rapprochement in the 1970s. Hong Kong experienced its first economic transformation in the 1950s–1960s, when it was forced by geopolitical circumstances to transit from entrepot trade to manufacturing industries. The industrial take-off took advantage of the arrival of industrialists and cheap migrant labour escaping economic and political turmoil on the Mainland. It was also a time when Southeast Asia was embroiled in anti-communist armed conflict (in Vietnam, Thailand, Indonesia, Malaysia, and Singapore), and the situation in Northeast Asia was far from stable (the Korean War, military dictatorship in South Korea, and martial law in Taiwan). Under British colonial rule, Hong Kong was considered peaceful and stable for foreign investment, giving it a unique historical advantage.[16] Hong Kong's de facto intermediary role between China and the external world had not been diminished during these transitions.

The second economic transformation during the late 1970s–1980s had benefitted from China's open-door and economic liberalisation policy after the end of the Cultural Revolution. With the bulk of manufacturing activities relocated to the Mainland in pursuit of cheaper and more abundant labour and land, Hong Kong turned to expanding its service industries to serve the Pearl River Delta area as an extension of the domestic economy. It quickly transformed into a service hub, enhancing its position as a financial, trading, and transportation centre in the Asia Pacific Region. Such restructuring fitted well the economic change of Mainland China. Over the next two decades, the industry sector halved from 31.7% of gross domestic product (GDP) to 15.2% in 1998 (with manufacturing down sharply from an average 22.6% in the first half of the 1980s to only 6.6% during 1996–1999); in contrast, the service sector rose rapidly from 67.5% of GDP in 1980 to 84.7% in 1998.[17] By 2017, the service sector's share of GDP was 92.4%, while manufacturing was only a dismal 1.1%.[18] There remains a cluster of industrialists in Hong Kong, but their production and investment are all outside the city—mostly on the Mainland and in lower-cost economies of Asia such as Myanmar.

As Mainland China's economy took off in the latter part of the 1990s, becoming both the world's largest factory and consumer market, and with economic restructuring and upgrading a major goal of the central government to turn the nation into a global economic power, Hong Kong faced opportunity as well as threat. Henceforth, the economic future of Hong Kong could only be found within an expanding and globalising Chinese economy, a prospect described by Stephen Chiu and Lui Tai-lok as (re)embeddedness in order to position as 'a Chinese global city' with competitive advantage.[19] The key to continued success lies in its balance of being both global and Chinese.[20] Hong Kong's interests would be best served if it could display its distinction from the Mainland as well as its closeness to the Mainland and other parts of a booming Asia.

Hong Kong today is connected to a world supply chain supported by an international banking system of which it is a crucial player, being one of the top global financial hubs (after New York and London). However, the 1999 Asian financial crisis also exposed Hong Kong's vulnerabilities as having too narrow an economic base with its pre-1997 growth boosted by an overheating property market that finally burst during the crisis. However, this does not mean Hong Kong should return to manufacturing industries. Instead, given its relatively high land and labour costs, it should seek to groom new high-value industries with a competitive edge, which can provide better employment opportunities for its educated workforce.

In the face of globalisation, the rapid advancement of information technology and the growing integration of the Mainland into the world economy, Hong Kong has entered its third transformation towards a knowledge economy. There are advantages to support such transformation, including its institutional vibrancy, world-class professional standards, excellent infrastructure and connectivity, hub status, and free flow of capital and information, all guaranteed by the Basic Law. If successful, though, it would only create more jobs for professionals and specialists, with some services outsourced to lower-cost locations. An unavoidable outcome is income stagnancy for other sectors (most acutely among the lower-skilled and downstream occupations) even as wealth accumulates and the cost of living increases.

Such structural contradictions have already become evident. While economic growth continues, the income/wealth gap and social disparity have widened, deepening social discontent not only among the grassroots but also the young middle class who increasingly distrust a non-democratic government suspected of only favouring big business (property developers and financial capital). A continuous property boom has pushed up housing prices and rents, not only making the lives of ordinary people harder but also undermining Hong Kong's competitiveness as a financial and services hub. At the same time, the lack of government readiness to step out of the conventional policy mindset to address such structural imbalance (through more ground-breaking social reforms in housing, social security, and retirement protection) has also aggravated domestic tensions.

These different stages of economic transformation demand different roles for the government. The early mercantile and entrepot period saw a small laissez-faire government facilitating free trade, law and order, and the protection of property rights. Once Hong Kong entered the industrial era, the government had to ensure the proper supply of land, labour, and capital flow as key factors of production and accumulation. The colonial administration began to assume a role in education, vocational training, social housing, healthcare, and welfare, accompanied by some regulative controls over land use and the banking system. Into the 1970s, a more active and regulative state, still within the official ideology of small government and non-interventionism, was required.

As the economy moved upward to focus on tertiary services, there was an increasing need for a more regionally and globally looking government to promote trade facilitation and investment. To grow an international trading and financial services centre demanded government-directed planning and infrastructure development, underpinned by extensive global connectivity and economic and trade links, as well as participation in international organisations and agreements. All this could not be achieved by just relying on private business initiatives. The government had to work in close collaboration with business and industry in securing bilateral cooperation and reciprocity in the regional and global arenas.

This was especially crucial in relation to the opening-up of the Mainland since the 1980s. After reunification in 1997, to leverage the new and expanding opportunities for local businesses and professionals, more government-to-government consultations and cooperation have taken place, especially within the Greater Pearl River Delta and, more recently, the Guangdong-Hong Kong-Macao Greater Bay Area. In tandem with such development, the role of government is no longer limited to the conventional sense of trade and investment facilitation, but it must be a more proactive state with steering and planning capacities. Today, Hong Kong's embeddedness in the Chinese economy and its role of financial and services intermediation have become even more prominent. Thus, this book examines how the evolving political economy of Hong Kong and its changing interface with the Mainland has shaped the government's role, functions, and links to the economy and society.

Conceptualising Hong Kong exceptionalism

History matters, as historical institutionalists like to say.[21] Hong Kong under British rule was exceptional in many aspects—economic, political, and social. It was neither entirely traditional/colonial nor fully modern, and neither solely Chinese nor British, but rather a special kind of hybrid created by historical circumstances. Such exceptionalism was supposed to be preserved after restoration to Chinese sovereignty in 1997. The Basic Law of the Hong Kong SAR was drafted with a considerable scope of compromise, flexibility, and ambiguity. Taken very rigidly and legalistically, it could impose a straitjacket on Hong Kong's further institutional development. However, a pragmatic approach based on the same Basic Law would also find it possible to chart innovative paths to meet new challenges and support new innovations. It is all a matter of practice. Hong Kong's governance is not susceptible to narrow conceptualisation by some conventional stereotypes such as colonialism, post-colonialism, democracy, authoritarianism, libertarianism, and autonomy. Hong Kong has a bit of all these and has always been a hybrid (hence its exceptionalism), displaying capabilities as well as vulnerabilities under both previous British rule and present-day Chinese central state authority. When someone sees pitfalls and limitations, others may also discover strengths and possibilities.

Before moving on, it is important to explain what is meant by 'exceptionalism' here because the theoretical notion of exceptionalism has a rather loose meaning in the literature depending on the context of the discussion. In common vocabulary, to be exceptional means to be different from others or unique. However, that alone cannot support an exceptionalism thesis because every country or culture can be said to be unique and special to an extent. It all depends on the level of granular description. At the lowest level (i.e., the highest level of generality), no country is unique.[22] What is seemingly exceptional in one country may sometimes be found in other countries as well, and some similarities between exceptionalist arguments about different countries may be derived from various factors which are peculiar to each country.[23]

As argued by Daniel Rogers: 'Exceptionalism differs from difference. Difference requires contrast; exceptionalism requires a rule.'[24] As institutions, practices, and values are so intrinsic to history, and no nation could be said to share the same historical trajectory, it would be difficult if not impossible to apply any common yardstick to measure similarity as opposed to exceptionalism. After all, as Marcel Mauss wrote in *On Civilization*: 'The domain of social life is essentially a domain of differences.'[25] Keith Dowding thus considers exceptionalism as a rhetorical device to make a country feel like it stands out and which 'can be used to justify either exuberance or despair over difference'.[26] As such, it is a kind of pride-conferring or awareness-building expression.

The United States was probably the first to assert its American exceptionalism, on the grounds of its institutional checks and balances, separation of powers, federalism, and reliance on regulation and volunteerism.[27] Subsequently, other countries have also been regarded as displaying exceptionalism in different domains including political, institutional, legal, foreign and domestic policy, economic, cultural, and ideological — hence, European exceptionalism, Australian exceptionalism, French exceptionalism, Japanese exceptionalism, and so on. Exceptionalism may be understood (in a broad and weak sense) as a matter of comparison of unique features, but some detect an articulation (in a strong sense) of hegemonic assertion or 'missionist' exceptionalism (that unique circumstances apply and therefore ordinary rules do not apply),[28] sometimes rooted in a cultural, historical, or even religious legacy which defines a country's sense of nationhood or collective awareness. Thus, it is argued that American exceptionalism is more than the US merely being special but implies an exceptionalist attitude or ideology within the global context.[29]

Hong Kong exceptionalism, as the term is used in this book, does not follow entirely the above framework of understanding that has emanated from the construction, extension, and critique of the notion as in American exceptionalism. Hong Kong is exceptional because its historical path had been very unique — born as a British outpost, from a 'borrowed time, borrowed place',[30] left to its own imagination and local formula of growth quite distinct among the Anglo-Saxon system, towards economic and social prosperity as one of the four Little Dragons of East Asia (but distinct and an exception, again, from the state developmental path pursued by the other three — South Korea, Singapore, and Taiwan), and then becoming an SAR with a different political and social system from its motherland. Culturally, Hong Kong has been described as a city of hybridity (雜種城市) (alongside cosmopolitanism) by local cultural critic and writer Chan Koon-chung (陳冠中).[31]

Hong Kong was designed to be exceptional post-1997, within a highly centralised/unitary and supposedly homogenous communist party-state, given rights and autonomy unparalleled in provincial and municipal polities on the Mainland, nor states and major cities of developed democracies whether federal or unitary. Constitutionally, Hong Kong (as a city with SAR status, which is free from most national legislation and conducts its own external and trade affairs as 'Hong Kong, China') is more autonomous than New York and London within their respective national structure. This makes it special and unique internationally. Today, over two decades after reunification, Hong Kong remains a geopolitical hybrid, both within the broad People's Republic of China (PRC) jurisdiction and yet outside its specific jurisdiction in terms of the application of the national system, law, and related institutions, thus creating tensions and ambiguities from time to time.

Hong Kong's unique culture has been depicted as a 'cultural fault-line' in shaky geographical terrain, a 'translation space' between Chinese-ness and Western-ness, a 'cultural hub' that joins vernacular culture with cosmopolitanism, a 'multifaceted, polyphonic culture that resists easy homogenization', a 'transmission zone', and so on.[32] Hong Kong Chinese culture can be clearly distinguished from Mainland Chinese culture, and the city is probably the only part of China where Cantonese is the dominant language, not Putonghua (Mandarin). Hong Kong's hybridity and its associated dilemmas have not disappeared in substance despite the journey of political reunification and social and economic integration over the years. What makes the Hong Kong case relevant to the wider exceptionalism discourse is that Hong Kong people like to articulate their uniqueness as 'Hongkongers' (香港人, *hoeng gong yan* in Cantonese pronunciation), defining their identity (whether locally, on the Mainland, or overseas) so as to stand out as a matter of collective pride, bearing Hong Kong memories and core values, especially during the recent years of rising local assertiveness.

In its governance, Hong Kong has historically never been the pure-form laissez-faire free market that some classical and neo-liberal economists (notably Milton Friedman) liked to portray, but fluctuated between non-intervention and intervention during the post-War decades until the 1997 handover, and then between reactive intervention and proactive intervention afterwards. Its administration pursued public sector reforms in the 1990s in tandem with the global trend despite the lack of big government, administrative inefficiency, or nationalised industries, and at a time of legitimacy crisis and political change and turbulence. Throughout the 1970s–1990s, Hong Kong was an unconventional case of bold reform of the bureaucracy by bureaucratic modernisers, which again made it exceptional within the context of how the world expects traditional 'small-governments' to function.

As an SAR, Hong Kong has been finding its narrow way forward between local autonomy and central authority under 'One Country, Two Systems', and between executive government and various institutional checks and balances, to strike a delicate balance in the form of 'durable' governance that could work in the circumstances and amid various constraints. The end of its colonial status meant an unavoidable degree of de-institutionalisation, but new institutions with clear functional logics have yet to be groomed. Such messy context and ambivalent identity of Hong Kong are fundamental to its present dilemmas in governance.

Some prevailing discourses

All big cities rise and fall, as history around the world has shown. Just what is represented by Hong Kong that we seek to preserve? This is part of the historical dilemma that needs to be tackled in any serious discourse about the city. Inasmuch as the past has determined and configured the present essence and interpretations, the present experience also reinterprets and even reconstructs the past. It has been pointed out that liberal-modernist historiographies of Hong Kong often tell a romanticised story about its growth from a barren rock to a capitalist paradise that, thanks to colonial non-interventionist rule and its liberal frameworks, had flourished, and ultimately created the Hong Kong 'miracle'.[33] It was this idealised Hong Kong which was sought to be preserved in its return to China but is considered by some critics to have been 'lost' after 1997 due to the incompetence of the successor SAR regime and the allegedly predatory Chinese central state in usurping the autonomy of a free Hong Kong. To them, the Hong Kong narratives could only be construed and embedded in the past dynamism and glory that gave its population pride as Hongkongers.

The positive role played by British colonial mandarins ('colonial benevolence') need not be ignored or belittled because of any politically correct anti-colonial sentiments or post-colonial critique, but it is equally important not to gloss over the ills of colonial rule and the accompanying economic exploitations and political repressions which formed part of British governance. The regretful thing is, in order to assert Hongkong-ness and the social imaginary of an indigenous Hong Kong history or origin and to be entirely detached from the China Mainland, some are attempting to beautify or even glorify the colonial past (focusing on the Patten era when colonial rulers finally moved to rapidly liberalise their regime) to establish the raison d'état of their actions. Indeed, their narrative about the demise of Hong Kong fails to fully understand regime change and evolution as part of an extended historical journey shaped and reshaped by internal and external factors.

Following the logic of their critical argument, if we can allow for British colonial benevolence, why can we not also recognise (realistically and historically) the benevolence of those Mainland officials given the task to handle Hong Kong's smooth return to the motherland without upsetting its stability and prosperity in the 1980s–1890s? Why can we not appreciate the benevolence of those post-1997 SAR government officials steering their course forward within historically and institutionally imposed constraints to safeguard Hong Kong's better interests? Yet, sentiments run high, especially among the younger generations, about Hong Kong's freedom and way of life being increasingly endangered by an 'external' CCP regime. Such feelings have been fully played out during the anti-extradition movement and subsequent political confrontations where young protesters call for 'liberating Hong Kong' (光復香港), a slogan that Beijing finds provocative. SAR government leaders are seen by the doubting public as Beijing's puppets, in much the same way as the anti-colonials during the 1960s–1970s saw British administration officials as only serving the interests of their home government in London. Polarisation may well reflect some inherent tensions but is not conducive to mutual accommodation under 'one nation'.

Reviewing the academic literature, most of the general texts on Hong Kong's government and public administration since the pre-1997 transition period focuses on constitutional and political changes as Hong Kong entered a period of uncertainty, anxiety, and even turbulence. For example, Ian Scott pointed to a legitimacy crisis and provided a political management perspective in understanding the challenges to and responses of the colonial government.[34] Lau Siu-kai, who later became an adviser of Beijing, wrote about the constraints on political reforms during the transition because of Hong Kong's unique constitutional path towards 'decolonization without independence'.[35] He further discussed the city's 'ungovernability' in the twilight of colonial rule.[36] Others have identified the nascent executive-legislative tensions accompanying the belated advent of legislative politics in the 1990s which have since shaped Hong Kong's governance.[37]

After 1997, the SAR government has continued to suffer from legitimation and governability problems, and the gap between rising community expectations on democratisation and the reality of constitutional reform (the pace and scope of which are dictated by Beijing). In much of the academic discussion, the democratic deficit has been an ongoing theme.[38] Related problems and issues highlighted include: the disarticulation of the political system,[39] institutional incongruity,[40] institutional incompatibility,[41] government capacity and public-sector difficulties,[42] the hollowing-out of executive power,[43] a crowding and differentiated polity,[44] failure in building a governing coalition,[45] fragmented authority,[46] and even a general governance crisis.[47] These observations and analyses capture the full variety of images and aspects of a weakening executive government which has been unable to assert its authority and leadership in the absence of a clear public mandate and effective links with the legislature. Others have contrasted the 'political leadership' of government before and after 1997[48] and have alluded to the erosion of local autonomy under 'One Country, Two Systems'.[49]

The prevailing discourses have mostly attributed problems of Hong Kong's political development to its incomplete journey of democratisation, accompanied by growing frustrations, conflicts, and uncertainties affecting the city's governance within the 'One Country Two Systems' constitutional framework. Executive-legislative gridlock, failure to build a viable governing coalition, and the poor political leadership of the non-partisan Chief Executive (CE) and their ministerial team are considered responsible for misgovernment, policy failure, and disappointing crisis management. These defects certainly present causes for concern. However, with a few exceptions such as Ian Scott, John Burns, and myself, insufficient attention has been paid to the significance of administrative restructuring, public sector organisation, service delivery, institutional building, and management reforms dating from the 1970s, to cope with rising public demands for accountability and responsiveness. The result of such reforms — which can be interpreted as 'administrative' solutions to political problems[50] — has been an evolving system of governance that is at the same time old-fashioned (in political design) *and* pioneering (in terms of policy management and service delivery).

Looking back, the bulk of governance has been too easily reduced to an issue of democratisation, while government functioning and operations in adapting to external changes (whether incrementally or in a more drastic manner) tend to feature less in the discourses. We need to be more alert to and reflective of democracy at work elsewhere. As Francis Fukuyama has observed of the international discussion:

> Since the onset of the Third Wave of democratizations [...] the overwhelming emphasis in comparative politics has been on democracy, transitions to democracy, human rights, transitional justice, and the like. Studies of nondemocratic countries focus on issues like authoritarian persistence, meaning the focus still remains on

the question of democracy in the long run or democratic transition. In other words, everyone is interested in studying political institutions that limit or check power—democratic accountability and rule of law—but very few people pay attention to the institution that accumulates and uses power, the state.[51]

He defines governance as a government's ability to make and enforce rules, and to deliver services, regardless of whether it is democratic or not (i.e., 'infrastructural' power).[52] Such infrastructural aspects have seldom caught the eyes of local or foreign observers of Hong Kong's governance in recent years because it is so easy to blame everything on the lack of democratic progress or the negative impact China's authoritarian rule has had on the extent of local autonomy.

Though Hong Kong's administrative efficiency and effectiveness, as reflected by the World Bank's Global Governance Indicators, remains highly rated internationally, some local literature has continued to doubt if its governance is too dominated by the longstanding bureaucratic culture which has survived colonial rule and been increasingly subject to Mainland influence (some would even say contamination) and central-state interventions and control.[53] The 2014 'Occupy Central' protests and Umbrella Movement have brought a new dawn of social and local awareness to younger generations at large, whose strong (and radical) expressions of local identity and autonomy are increasingly at loggerheads with a central state which is getting more nervous about the spread of separatism in much the same way as pro-independence ideology in Taiwan. The hardening of mind and position is mutual. Beijing becomes harsher because of some locals drifting further away from national identification, while some locals become more separatist in orientation because of Beijing's alleged 'hegemonic' actions.

Such confrontations come at a time when China's rapid rise in global power and assertiveness, accompanied by the display of stronger doses of party-state authoritarianism, is more widely perceived by the Western world as a major threat to international order.[54] This has made Hong Kong a focal point of attention within the context of structural tensions between hard state-authoritarianism and popular aspirations for freedom and democracy, and between tightening-up central control (re-centralisation) and local autonomy.[55] Near-doomsday theses abound, breeding fatalism and fear about the imminent collapse of Hong Kong's unique system and institutions under the central-state's huge pressures and forces of subjugation.[56] Hong Kong-Mainland tensions and local-central state relations have also attracted more academic discussion, both within Hong Kong and internationally.[57]

Governing Hong Kong

Against the above historical and contemporary background, how has Hong Kong been governed all these decades, in terms of achievements and failures? How has

Hong Kong's governance and growth fared amidst the institutional constraints, political turbulence and uncertainties, and other risks and challenges which all governments in the present world face? It is an appropriate time to ponder these questions not only in terms of enriching and deepening our conceptual understanding of governance and public administration, but also for the sake of appreciating Hong Kong's exceptionalism and hybridity despite limitations and scepticism—a nominally 'free' market with administrative pragmatism and emphasis on proactive government, a semi-democratic polity with plenty of checks and balances, a still-performing government (in a broad sense) without popular mandate and facing rising distrust, and an open society within a centralised party-state national system. In the eyes of many, Hong Kong exceptionalism is coming to a crossroads. Amid the current upheaval, pessimists would say it is reaching an end as they believe the Mainland now seeks to absorb and subdue Hong Kong.

Confronting the ascendency of separatist sentiments, the central government has been emphasising its 'comprehensive jurisdiction' (全面管治權) over the SAR, causing many political and academic commentators to predict a decline in local autonomy and the rise of authoritarianism within Hong Kong, especially when police power was expanded and emergency law resorted to in handling the 2019 anti-government confrontations. Such worry and fear are partly premised on a fatalist view of the future of China as it pushes for a form of state-directed capitalism ('socialism with Chinese characteristics') and consolidates a fused party-state regime. Political or rhetorical reductionism of simplifying complexities, conundrums and contentions into the inherent wrongs and evils of the CCP-ruled state would not help ordinary people gain confidence but would only amplify despair and fear. One needs a historical perspective to understand why and how China has evolved to today's form and to conjecture how it might develop and transform in the future, premised on a more realist rather than ideologically loaded assessment.[58] Unavoidably, Hong Kong as an SAR will be constrained and, to an extent, shaped by China's evolving reality. Yet at the same time, it could be strategically allowed to remain an outlier if it is able to play its card of exceptionalism well under 'One Country, Two Systems'.

Instead of reaching fatalist conclusions based on what Hong Kong is not and cannot do constitutionally, it serves better to look for what Hong Kong can and should do to sustain its vibrancy and resilience in practical circumstances. The 'Two Systems' context has resulted in 'two identities' and even 'two existentialisms'. Hong Kong's exceptionalism in governance had been nourished and reinforced over the decades, historically underpinned by a critical role in intermediating (and financing) the Mainland's modernisation and economic liberalisation, a role now less prominent after the Mainland's subsequent economic takeoff and rapid growth since the late 1990s. It could be construed as both a force and a threat—a force in that it has given Hong Kong people and the government some space and opportunity to evolve, and a threat because there is indeed no standard or clear modus operandi to rely upon as Hong Kong evolves. Such exceptionalism hinges not just on the formal institutional arrangements and historical inheritance, but also on the statecraft and art of administration of the day.

Exceptionalism comes hand in hand with dilemmas. Opportunities coexist with threats. Mutual trust between Hong Kong society and the Chinese central government is deteriorating as fundamental constitutional reform has repeatedly failed. More animosities are bred due to clashes in institutional practices, cultural expressions, and politics. Where locals fear losing autonomy, Beijing fears regaining possession of Hong Kong only in name. Many Hongkongers, explicitly or implicitly, see democracy as instrumental to withstanding Mainland intrusion, hence their growing despair about the democratic deadlock. The notion of a high degree of autonomy promised under the Basic Law has been seized upon by some local politicians and nativist/separatist activists to mean the total exclusion of any central government role in Hong Kong's governance. On the other hand, an economically stronger Mainland could be tempted to play down the importance and vitality of Hong Kong, especially as the central state becomes politically wary of local activism displaying separatist slogans and has been responding with harsher assertions of central authority.

The danger to Hong Kong's exceptionalism lies in such polarising positioning and head-on confrontation, which leads to a 'zero-sum' game. More Mainlanders have become resentful of Hongkongers due to the latter's 'anti-China' expressions and acts, a far cry from the early days of reunification when Hong Kong was held up as the crown jewel given its economic success. The two-systems equation has been fast changing, with Hong Kong's economic importance to China on the decline and Hong Kong having to find a longer-term engine of economic growth and employment in more competitive and complex global and regional environments. Both politics and economics seem to be working to Hong Kong's disadvantage. However, it is still the contention of this book that such a scenario does not need to be the logical finale.

Taking all the emerging tensions and controversies which are clouding Hong Kong's political future and its state of governance as givens, and arguing that Hong Kong has always been operating in a contentious and uncertain environment, it would be more instructive and constructive to explore the *what* and *how* of Hong Kong's governance in a less normative perspective (i.e., Hong Kong 'as is' with its real-world politics and administration). Ultimately, the ability to deliver performance and foster a sense of pride is what counts most in effective governance. Hong Kong exceptionalism is indeed facing threats and challenges. 'Governing Hong Kong' requires an intelligent and pragmatic realisation and interpretation of constitutional limitations, political constraints, historical opportunities, and institutional possibilities to carve out autonomous space for administration and growth. At this juncture, we may be experiencing setbacks due to uncertainties and sentiments of despair arising from months of political standoff and worsening relations with the Mainland, but we are still far from having to talk about managing the demise of Hong Kong.

PART I
THE LEGACY

Chapter 1

The Making of an Administrative State

Introduction

Two main factors have shaped Hong Kong's governing structure and administration. First, the institutional legacy of British rule under path dependence[1] provided the organisational framework, logic of governance, and modus operandi of the administrative system inherited at the point of transfer to Chinese rule in 1997. Second, the 1984 Sino-British Joint Declaration that laid the foundation for Hong Kong's future after British departure on 30 June 1997[2] and the Basic Law of the Hong Kong SAR promulgated on 4 April 1990, both enshrining the principle of continuity and minimal change in the transition.[3]

Every governmental system in the world has been subject to exogenous and endogenous factors of change. Thus, the present is always not just a projection from the past, nor is the future simply an extension of the present. Both the present and future can never be fully understood outside the historical context of the evolution of the system. In the case of Hong Kong, it was run as a British colony until its return to China in 1997. As a colony, all powers were concentrated in the hands of a London-appointed Governor. Significant changes began to be made starting in the 1970s as the British administration tried to address social issues of an expanding domestic population with rising expectations and demands, and as Britain entered into negotiations with China in the 1980s. Subsequent to the 1984 Joint Declaration, Britain pursued its plan of decolonisation, while China's objective was to take over a Hong Kong largely 'as is', with a full inheritance of the pre-existing organs of power and administrative institutions which were deemed to have delivered effective governance.

Still, the fact that British colonial governance was to be replaced by 'Hong Kong people governing Hong Kong' (self-administration) with a high degree of autonomy under China's newly proclaimed principle of 'One Country, Two Systems' meant that changes were unavoidable, not just during the transitional years leading up to 1997, but more prominently afterwards due to a growingly assertive local society, regional and global economic turbulence, and a different sovereign authority. Internal political aspirations and cleavages, as well as tensions arising from the exercise of Hong Kong's autonomy vis-à-vis a centralised and authoritarian national regime, have shaped the articulations and practice of politics and governance. The Joint Declaration represents a political bargain between

China and Britain, while the Basic Law represents a political bargain between the Chinese central government and the Hong Kong community at large. This chapter traces Hong Kong's legacy of British administration and the fundamental elements of colonial governance before we explore the new cleavages and challenges in subsequent chapters.

Atypical colony

Hong Kong was formally occupied by the British in 1841 and became a Crown colony after the conclusion of the Treaty of Nanking (Nanjing) in 1842 marking Manchu (Qing) China's defeat by Imperial Britain in the First Opium War. It was initially dismissed as a barren rock by London but eventually rose to become the most strategic British outpost in the Orient.[4] The territory was later enlarged to include the Kowloon Peninsula in 1860 under the Convention of Peking (Beijing) following the Second Opium War and then the New Territories, which was leased for 99 years under the 1898 Convention for the Extension of Hong Kong Territory (also known as the Second Convention of Peking) following the invasion of Beijing by Western powers in the wake of the anti-foreign Boxers Uprising. However, neither the subsequent Republic of China (ROC) (from 1912) nor the PRC (from 1949) accepted such cession of Chinese territory at gun-point as legitimate. Both regarded the treaties concerned as 'unequal treaties'.[5]

After the PRC assumed membership in the United Nations (UN) and its Security Council in 1971, it explicitly demanded that British-ruled Hong Kong be excluded from the purview of the UN's Special Committee on Decolonisation.[6] The preamble of the Basic Law of Hong Kong SAR clearly states:

> Hong Kong has been part of the territory of China since ancient times; it was occupied by Britain after the Opium War in 1840. On 19 December 1984, the Chinese and British Governments signed the Joint Declaration on the Question of Hong Kong, affirming that the Government of the People's Republic of China will resume the exercise of sovereignty over Hong Kong with effect from 1 July 1997, thus fulfilling the long-cherished common aspiration of the Chinese people for the recovery of Hong Kong.[7]

Thus, whereas Britain considered the situation a handover of sovereignty in 1997, China has maintained that sovereignty over Hong Kong had never been 'transferred', though for historical reasons the territory had been under British administration until its 1997 reunification with the motherland.

Nonetheless, Beijing had hitherto admitted de facto British jurisdiction over Hong Kong and had been willing to deal with London on Hong Kong-related matters under the so-called 'internal matters being handled externally' (內事外辦) principle. Hong Kong Chinese were regarded as Hong Kong 'compatriots' so far as their legal status was concerned.[8] For the British, according to George Endacott, an authority on the study of early colonial rule, Hong Kong was founded originally as a military, diplomatic, and trading station, rather than a settlement.[9] With this strategically located trading outpost in South China, together with its foothold in Shanghai and the Strait Settlements in Malaya and Singapore, Britain was able to dominate the profitable China trade and establish a formidable imperial presence in the Far East that complemented its empire in British India. At the beginning, there was only a tiny local Chinese population in Hong Kong. However, as the Qing Dynasty weakened further, marked by political and social turbulence, more Chinese from the Mainland came to British Hong Kong to seek refuge and economic opportunities, but they mostly treated it as just a transient place, still retaining close affinity with and loyalty to the Mainland.

From the late 1890s, anti-Manchu elements began to use Hong Kong as a base for organising subversive and revolutionary activities. The founder of Republican China, Sun Yat-sen, was educated in the College of Medicine in Hong Kong.[10] Even after the establishment of the ROC in 1912, Hong Kong's position did not change. The CCP's underground elements used it to connect to liberal and anti-Kuomintang (KMT, the then ruling Nationalist Party) circles and launch cultural and propaganda movements in support of Communist revolutionary uprisings. Throughout this time, Mainland Chinese could freely come to the colony. Under the Second Convention of Peking that leased the New Territories, Britain was required to respect and preserve Chinese customs and allow the free movement of Chinese between Hong Kong and the Mainland.[11]

Strategic considerations would have normally demanded a greater degree of imperial control, but in practice, administrative absolutism was constrained by a style of indirect rule over the local Chinese population. From the very beginning, the colonial government had adopted a policy of economic as well as political laissez-faire operating within a restricted range covering little more than the maintenance of law and order and the raising of taxes to meet the cost of the civil establishment and necessary public works. Britain was not keen to fully 'colonise' the territory to the extent of moving a large British and European population to this Far Eastern outpost and assimilating local Chinese into the European 'mainstream'. The local Chinese were essentially subject to Chinese law and customs and were looked after by their community leaders acting as intermediaries between them and their British rulers. Within the colonial government, a special department known as the Secretariat for Chinese Affairs was established as if the rest of the government would have little to do with the local Chinese population. A selected few rich, influential, and often British-educated Chinese leaders were, however, appointed to government bodies like the Legislative Council and Urban Council to advise the Governor.

Upon the Communist victory against the KMT and the establishment of the PRC in 1949, circumstances began to change. Border control measures were imposed in Hong Kong in 1949 with travel documents required from 1950, in order to contain the large influx of political and economic refugees from the

Mainland. After it became clear that the Communists were not keen to take back Hong Kong by force, the British Government had to develop an administration to face a fast-expanding Chinese population who would now regard Hong Kong as their home. Under the CCP's policy since the 1950s of 'long-term planning and making full use' (長期打算、充分利用) of Hong Kong's exceptional status quo, British Hong Kong had to be tolerated until such time when the question left behind by history could be properly resolved.[12] This, in turn, provided an alternative basis of political stability such that Britain was able to exercise effective rule and preserve its economic interests without undue challenges, upon an understanding not to allow any constitutional change to devolve power to the local people. Therefore, when Britain embarked on an active decolonisation agenda after the Second World War for many of its colonies, including India, Malaya, and Singapore in Asia, Hong Kong was excluded.

In terms of constitutional design, Hong Kong was no different from other British colonies. Under the *Letters Patent* and *Royal Instructions* issued by the British Crown, regarded as colonial Hong Kong's constitutional documents, the London-appointed Governor (as the Crown's representative) personified the combination of executive, legislative, civil, and military powers. The system of government was based on three main institutions: the Governor, the Executive Council (ExCo), and the Legislative Council (LegCo).[13] The Governor enjoyed both constitutionally supreme powers almost like an autocrat within the colony,[14] as well as de facto autonomy on a day-to-day basis from the home government in Britain which exercised oversight through the Colonial Office until the 1960s and then the Foreign and Commonwealth Office (FCO).[15] Although matters of defence and foreign affairs were within the control of London which dispatched a Commander of British Forces and a Political Adviser (seconded from the FCO), the Governor was concurrently Commander-in-Chief of the British garrison, and the Political Adviser's office was part of the colonial establishment under the Governor's oversight. In the years after the Second World War, the colonial administration secured a relatively high degree of autonomy in domestic affairs from London. Fiscal autonomy was achieved in the 1950s, and independence from Britain in trade relations and negotiations was achieved in the 1970s. Hong Kong was one of the early participants (first through British membership and then as a separate contracting party in 1986) of the General Agreement on Tariffs and Trade (GATT), renamed the World Trade Organisation (WTO) in 1995, well before the PRC was granted accession to it in 2001.

Bureaucratic autocracy

The local literature has variously described the colonial system of governance as 'an administrative state' and 'bureaucratic polity'. Such descriptions point to the fact that the government was dominated by administrator-bureaucrats who governed in the absence of accountable politics. Separation of executive, legislative, and judiciary powers did not exist. The Governor had ultimate direction of the government and presided at the meetings of ExCo and, until 1995, LegCo.[16] All appointments, promotions, transfers, and dismissals within the civil service were made by the Governor or in his name. A Public Service Commission advised him on these matters, but he was constitutionally entitled to reject its advice. Principal officials, however, were formally appointed at the pleasure of the Crown as conveyed through the Secretary of State in-charge in London. The Governor could give directives to all civil servants as to the policy they had to follow or the actions they had to take. He also appointed all judges (including the Chief Justice) and magistrates and could ignore the recommendations of the Judicial Services Commission. In addition to his unlimited powers of appointment and patronage, he could pardon any convicted criminal or remit all or part of the sentence. He could also make grants of any Crown lands that had not already been legally transferred.[17]

The ExCo consisted of four ex-officio members—namely the Colonial Secretary (later renamed Chief Secretary, CS), the Commander of British Forces, the Financial Secretary (FS), and the Attorney General—together with other members (both official and unofficial) appointed by the Governor formally on the instruction of the Secretary of State.[18] It considered all major policy matters and all principal legislation before tabling at the LegCo. It also made subsidiary legislation and considered appeals, petitions, and objections under certain laws. The Governor alone determined the agenda of the ExCo. He was empowered to disregard its members' views and act according to his own judgement; in so doing, he had to report to the Secretary of State in London. The LegCo comprised the three senior secretaries as ex-officio members, and both official and unofficial members appointed by the Governor with the approval of the Secretary of State. Apart from the powers to enact legislation and approve taxation and the appropriation of public funds, it could question the Administration on matters of public interest and debate questions of policy. The number of unofficial members was increased during the 1970s under a reformist Governor, Murray MacLehose. Until 1985, when some elected members on a limited franchise were introduced after the signing of the Joint Declaration (see Chapter 4), the Governor had the power to appoint civil servants to form a majority of the LegCo.

As unofficial members of both the ExCo and LegCo were groomed by the bureaucracy and appointed by the Governor, they owed their allegiance to the government and considered themselves to be performing a supportive and supplementary role (rather than a check-and-balance role). The more senior and experienced members of LegCo were concurrently appointed to the ExCo, which was seen as political promotion. The result was a fused model of executive-legislative collaboration underpinned by consensus and trust. The unofficials rarely obstructed the Administration in opposition. An Office of Unofficial Members of Executive and Legislative Councils (UMELCO) existed to provide a secretariat manned by civil servants to support appointed unofficial members of both the

ExCo and LegCo and their joint working panels in monitoring government work in different policy areas.[19]

Such was the kind of executive-led government much cherished during colonial rule until the 1980s. It was an Administration dominated by civil servants under the directive of the Governor, with the top posts almost exclusively filled by the upper tier of the elite 'Administrative Class', operating in effect as 'ministers'. There was a close government-business linkage. Heads of prominent British *hongs*, like Jardine Matheson, Swire, and the Hongkong and Shanghai Bank, were always given ExCo and LegCo seats. Appointees to LegCo were also drawn from professional sectors such as medicine and law, and later accounting, engineering/architecture, and education which became necessary as post-War Hong Kong embarked on economic, social, and infrastructure development. In political terms, the ExCo symbolised elites-integration and government-business 'synarchy' at the highest level.[20] An elaborate system of statutory and advisory bodies enabled elite participation in and legitimation of policy-making.[21]

Subdued society and politics

Lau Siu-kai has attributed the social acquiescence of colonial rule to the cultural ingredients of 'utilitarianistic familism' and a 'minimally integrated socio-political system' within the local Chinese community, relying on the presence of social 'resource networks' to help meet the needs of the lower strata and prevent their grievances and claims from becoming overt political demands.[22] Norman Miners similarly suggests that Hong Kong's early political tranquillity was a result of the paternalistic, authoritarian nature of the colonial government which the Chinese had been culturally accustomed to, as well as the latter's refugee mentality.[23] However, such cultural explanations have been challenged by John Rear who argues that it was more the population's sense of political impotence ('an acceptance of the inevitable necessity of British rule') that had rendered them apathetic.[24] What ensued was a system in which local politics was discouraged if not suppressed.

Although Endacott has credited the system as 'government by discussion', whereby interested opinion would be consulted continuously before any important government decision was made,[25] the colonial administrators had until the early 1970s adopted a 'hands off' approach towards the indigenous Chinese population whose views were not factored into 'interested opinion' save some selected views of prominent Chinese community leaders appointed to government boards and councils. Ambrose King explains this process as the 'administrative absorption of politics' by which the government co-opted forces of socio-political influence, often represented by elite figures and groups, into an administrative decision-making body, thus achieving some level of elite integration.[26] Such an interpretation of the 'administerisation' of politics, long held as the key to understanding colonial governance, was a rather generous one because in both constitutional and real-power terms, the administrators had monopoly over Hong Kong's governance, and ultimately neither business elite interests nor local Chinese elite interests would be allowed to override government interests and preferences. A cultural critique would argue that the Chinese elite rose to prominence because of their wealth and sought official recognition from the coloniser, as traditional Chinese gentry did from the emperor, resulting in a kind of 'collaborative colonialism' that ensured a politically under-developed bourgeoisie and a weak civil society.[27]

Because of the above organisation of the administration, colonial rule was often equated to corruption, which was rampant in both government and private business—most notably the Police Department (which at that time was also responsible for hawker control), Public Works Department (PWD; with monopoly over all government construction projects), Fire Services Department, and public utilities companies, like the Hong Kong Telephone Company. Kickback payments were rife in the commercial sector. It was difficult for any ordinary resident to get by in daily life without paying bribes or being demanded for bribes, even in passing a driving test, securing a school place, getting a telephone line, or in applying for low-cost or resettlement housing. After the suppression of the 1967 riots, the Police Force was awarded the 'Royal' title for its loyalty; however, police corruption worsened as the bureaucratic clout of the Force grew further, to the extent of defying other parts of government as if it was a separate empire. Eventually, controlling corruption became the most daunting challenge to the administration (see Chapter 2).

The colonial regime, therefore, did not enjoy any legitimacy in the eyes of the local Chinese population who only accepted it out of acquiescence, if the regime could provide law and order as well as social stability, as a form of 'palliative politics'.[28] The small group of expatriate officials (mostly British) enjoyed much more favourable employment conditions and an exclusive lifestyle detached from the plight of the ordinary people whose language they did not speak.[29] Some ad hoc initiatives might be put in place, not necessarily out of any long-term policy plan but instead as contingent measures under pressing circumstances.[30] From the 1960s onwards, the colonial administration created a unifying ideology around two 'principles'—the rule of law and laissez-faire—to give it a sense of moral strength.[31] If not for the demise in trade following the CCP's victory on the Mainland and subsequent economic embargo on China by the West, Hong Kong would not have turned to manufacturing industries facilitated by the arrival of cheap migrant labour and Shanghai industrialists. Thus, the so-claimed good administration of British rule needs to be more critically examined and qualified in a proper historical perspective.

As Hong Kong entered the phase of transition in the 1980s on the path towards reunification with China, more social cleavages and political conflicts became visible. Writing at the time, Ian Scott argued that Hong Kong's political history had been punctuated by many crises, most remarkably during the 1967 anti-British riots and then political uncertainties and anxieties during the transition period.[32] Such crises directly or indirectly challenged the British administration's claim to the right to rule or its authority over the territory. In contrast to the pre-War population of transients seeing Hong Kong as only 'borrowed place, borrowed time',[33] the post-War population, many of whom born or raised locally, regarded Hong Kong as their home and expected to have some say and participation on how it was governed. As the next chapter explains, the legitimacy stake in the aftermath of the 1967 riots was regained by the colonial government through the adoption of a somewhat corporatist strategy in the 1970s under Governor MacLehose. This saw the move from a 'hands-off' minimally integrated approach towards a relatively more proactive and inclusive style of political management involving social reforms, government interventions, and an increase in the supply of public services, in an attempt to reinvent the colonial regime.

Arguably, the legitimacy crisis could have been averted by more fundamental political reforms to give the local population the right to choose their government so as to ensure accountability and responsiveness. In practice, the colonial government had chosen not to pursue that route until the 1980s when the future of Hong Kong was to be negotiated with China.[34] The only significant proposals for political reform in the post-War period, in 1946 and 1966 respectively, were packaged as municipal council reforms, but even such moderate reforms were eventually rejected. As the only public body with elected members supervising the work of a government department, the Urban Council had long been the primary vehicle for local government reform.[35] The 1946 reform, known as the Young Plan after then Governor Mark Young who pushed for it, failed to take off because of immense opposition from the appointed unofficial members of the LegCo who saw it as eroding their powers and instead demanded direct election to the LegCo, something that neither the colonial government nor London expected.[36] By 1949, the new geopolitical realities following the establishment of the PRC made the British government hesitant about any substantive constitutional change in Hong Kong. The proposal was eventually dropped in 1952.

By the mid-1960s, there was a new wave of enthusiasm for local government reform, particularly from local political groups such as the Reform Club, riding on the tide of reforming local government in Britain at the time. The new attempts for change centred on the role and function of the Urban Council. Two sets of reform proposals emerged in 1966. An ad hoc committee of the Urban Council recommended an enlarged municipal council (to be renamed 'The Hong Kong City Council' modelled very much on the then Greater London Council) with extended powers in housing, education, social welfare, traffic and transport, medical and health services, and town planning, to be underpinned by a new tier of district councils.[37] The government's working party (the Dickinson Report) proposed a less ambitious two-tier system with the government at the top and the lower tier to comprise several local authorities, resulting in the dismemberment of the Urban Council whose functions would be devolved to new local bodies plus additional functions in housing estate management as well as the provision and management of schools and certain social welfare services.[38]

Such rather daring reforms were, however, disrupted by the outbreak of political disturbances and riots in 1967. Sensing a crisis of governance, the colonial administration backtracked. Instead, the Urban Council was reorganised in 1971, given financial autonomy (through full control over an earmarked portion of the urban rates) and made separate from the government with the withdrawal of all officials from its membership (though half of the members would remain to be government-appointed) and a chairman elected among its members. However, at the same time, the Council's functions were reduced to environmental public health, recreation and amenities, markets, libraries, and certain cultural services. Its previous involvement in public housing came to an end with the establishment of a Housing Authority in 1973 to take over both resettlement and low-cost housing. In 1986, a Regional Council was set up to cover the New Territories with similar powers.

Language hegemony was an inseparable part of colonial politics. The local language did not enjoy any status until the 1970s after a lengthy campaign for recognising the Chinese language as official language led by educationalists, university students, and some Urban Councillors, in what *The New York Times* at the time described as 'a stirring of latent Chinese cultural nationalism'.[39] Indeed, the campaign represented the first social movement for decolonisation.[40] Along with the new political strategy to cultivate a sense of belonging for the local Chinese population, the British administration finally passed the Official Languages Ordinance in 1974 declaring both English and Chinese to be official languages. From then onwards, important government announcements, reports, speeches, and papers became available in both languages, and simultaneous interpretation was introduced for meetings of the LegCo and later District Boards. In the judiciary, however, the law still mandated English as the sole language for use in the higher courts (including the Court of Appeal, High Court, and District Courts) until 1995.[41] The situation only improved gradually after the signing of the 1984 Sino-British Joint Declaration and the promulgation of the Basic Law in 1990. In 1987, the Official Languages Ordinance was amended to require all new legislation to be enacted bilingually in both English and Chinese.

The Administrative Service

Colonial governors used to come from a civil service background—with the rare exception of the last governor, Chris Patten (1992–1997), a former British cabinet minister and politician. Since the time of Murray MacLehose (1971–1982), as the question on the future of Hong Kong began to loom large on the British agenda vis-à-vis China, diplomats had taken up the Governorship, the others following him being Edward Youde (1982–1986) and David Wilson (1987–1992).[42]

The backbone of the government mandarinate was the Administrative Service (the Administrative Class officers or Administrative Officers, AOs), which was instituted only in 1960 to replace a previous cadet scheme started in 1861 to supply career officers recruited from Britain for various British colonies.[43] These officers operated as 'a miniscule band of officials with the same values and from the same social backgrounds'.[44] Following the tradition of the British civil service, AOs occupied most of the senior posts within the administration, including the Colonial Secretariat and top positions of Secretaries and Directors/Commissioners, to ensure the security of colonial rule. Until the mid to late 1960s, when a small number of local Chinese began to be recruited to the Administrative Service, AOs were predominantly expatriate officers recruited from 'home' (i.e., Britain) or seconded from other overseas British colonies. In a colony, cadet officers and later AOs were expected to act as 'political officers' to keep full control over the indigenous population with the assistance of locally co-opted community and tribal leaders, under a regime of indirect rule.[45] In a way, they functioned like the mandarins of Imperial China.

Understanding the ethos and esprit de corps of the Administrative Service and how it worked in practice—over domestic affairs, and vis-à-vis the British home government as well as regional politics, particularly after the establishment of the PRC in 1949 when CCP-KMT rivalries became a major source of local political confrontations—can provide the key to the nature of colonial governance during British rule.[46] Steve Tsang's book on AOs from the nineteenth century until 1997, largely based on interviews with retired British AOs and relevant archives and publications, offers useful insight into how Hong Kong was governed in the eyes of colonial mandarins.[47] According to his portrayal, AOs in the colonies, being not filled with the brightest graduates from the best British universities, would actually frown on those of their peers who sought to only engage in arguments to satisfy their intellectual curiosity. They were able to form an 'uninhibited political centre' in the absence of democratic checks and balances, prizing collegiality and pragmatism above all in making policies based on what they believed to be in the best interest of the colony, not necessarily identical to that of the home government in London.

Tsang claims AOs were 'not intellectually imaginative or arrogant enough to want either to challenge or to justify the assumptions behind the existing political system, or to seek to remove the gap between the constitutional provisions and the political reality in the exercise of power, or to change society in line with any intellectual or ideological belief'.[48] Their commitment to fair-mindedness, even-handedness, and integrity, as part of their esprit de corps, made the need to exert considerable self-restraint in the exercise of power acceptable.[49] Such ethos was forged and perpetuated by serving AOs seeking to recruit people like themselves. While hugely self-confident, AOs were also highly flexible. Being posted to a wide range of government functions and responsibilities helped groom them to become competent when taking up top positions later in their career. Yet, AOs also faced tensions with and resentment from some professional officers who were equally well-educated and considered themselves more knowledgeable in professional matters than the amateur administrators.

Tsang goes on to argue that the AOs could deliver good governance because they remained politically neutral, seeing themselves as guardians of the public interest,[50] a point somewhat resonating Leo Goodstadt's view that the colonial government had its own 'public interest' in mind and was thus not just abiding by the interests of the 'private profit' of the business tycoons.[51] It was said that while the colonial government had to routinely and ultimately defend British interests, the Hong Kong AOs would 'uphold the interests of British Hong Kong, rather than advance those of [Britain] at the expense of Hong Kong'.[52] During the days when professional politicians were absent from the scene, AOs took up the role of political officers representing the government and seeking support for the government. They formed a de facto 'government party'. During the final years of British rule, Governor Chris Patten helped turn the administrative state into an administrative-political hybrid machine somewhat comparable to an elected government of a democracy, with Policy Secretaries expected to behave as full-fledged ministers skilled in legislative manoeuvring. He left behind a political modus operandi that the successor SAR regime would have to follow.[53]

Contrary to Tsang's assertion, the colonial mandarinate could not be described as simply bright civil servants displaying political neutrality in the classical sense of party governments. Their images varied depending on one's perspectives and interpretations like the three blind men touching different parts of an elephant and each describing it as a different kind of animal.[54] Anson Chan, upon stepping down from the post of CS in 2001, summarised the civil service legacy as one where 'speak[ing] truth unto power' and maintaining political neutrality were the core values; while her successor Donald Tsang similarly alluded to the so-called 'culture of talking back'. It was Regina Ip, then Secretary for Security, also an AO, who contradicted her two colleagues and bluntly admitted that senior AOs were never politically neutral but had always had their political stance.

Some critics questioned the overall competence of the previously British-dominated Administrative Class. Some local officers, in private, did not think too highly of their expatriate superiors whom they felt were senior to them mainly because of race. Historian Ming Chan had very harsh words about expatriate officials, stating that

> the expatriate domination of the civil service top echelon is not only racially discriminatory but raises serious doubts about the integrity of the entire system as a genuine meritocracy in which recruitment, posting and promotion should be based solely on rational criteria of ability, skills, performance and overall effectiveness and contribution to the local community.[55]

He also pointed out that with some well-known exceptions, 'most of the expatriate top officials are illiterate or only semi-literate in Chinese'. Without doubting their devotion, their effectiveness as Hong Kong administrators and policy-makers was unavoidably handicapped by their limited understanding of the local Chinese community and developments in China.

Extending government by AOs after 1997

The AOs proved to be the loyal backbone of British rule; their professionalism, competence, and integrity were largely undisputed. Thus, there was no reason why the local AOs could not switch their allegiance to Chinese sovereignty once it was restored in 1997 and continue to be the new backbone of SAR rule. Indeed, after the signing of the Sino-British Joint Declaration, the British administration began to relax the restriction on the recruitment of local Chinese to the Administrative Service which until then was confined to those holding a British passport or naturalised to become British citizens. For a while in the 1980s, when democratisation of the political system seemed to be a logical move of decolonisation, it was thought plausible that the civil service might be relegated to the role of the politically neutral administrative arm of an elected government. During the drafting of the Basic Law, there was a suggestion from some quarters (myself included) that the post-1997 administration should be headed by a CE together with a ministerial system divorced from the civil service as in many other countries, in order both to articulate a new politics-based form of government and to safeguard the political neutrality of the civil service.

However, neither the Chinese nor British government was prepared to countenance such a prospect. Both argued in favour of extending the prevailing system of tasking top AOs as Principal Officials (i.e., the Secretaries), considering them to be safer pairs of hands, more experienced in and trained for ministerial responsibilities, and thus more conducive to a smooth transition of government. China's clear preference was for an 'executive-led' system with the civil service in charge of administration and legislative power appropriately restrained. Senior civil servants were led to believe that they would continue to maintain the same dominant position in the new SAR as they had enjoyed under the British Governor. Paraphrasing 'Hong Kong people governing Hong Kong' (港人治港), there was an expectation among some local Chinese AOs that come 1997, they would fly higher to become the new masters of the SAR under Chinese sovereignty in a kind of 'Hong Kong bureaucrats governing Hong Kong' (港官治港).

During the late transition period before the through-train arrangement was derailed following Governor Patten's political reform package (explained in Chapter 4), there was speculation that there could be Sino-British cooperation in grooming a candidate to be the first CE of the Hong Kong SAR. One possibility was that the most senior local Chinese AO under the British administration would be chosen as successor to the Governor if enjoying the trust and full confidence of both governments. He or she would first be appointed by Britain as Deputy Governor to understudy the top post before eventually being appointed by the

Chinese government as CE.[56] Instead, Tung Chee-hwa, a businessman with no previous political profile who joined Patten's ExCo but remained low-key, was selected as CE in December 1996. Still, Tung had to make sure the AOs were on side. Indeed, after he was appointed CE, CS Anson Chan was among the first to speak in his support to impress the local and international community that the civil service was firmly behind him.[57] Tung's inaugural ministerial team was often dubbed a 'Tung-Chan coupling' (董陳配), representing an alliance between a Beijing-chosen CE and the inherited British-trained civil service bureaucracy.

In the event, Tung retained all the incumbent local Chinese principal officials in his new administration and had essentially followed the colonial practice of government by bureaucrats.[58] The only exception was the appointment of Elsie Leung, a former private solicitor and Hong Kong deputy to the NPC, as Secretary for Justice to fill the vacancy left behind by the former Attorney General Jeremy Matthews who could not serve beyond 30 June 1997 because of his British nationality. She was regarded as highly trusted by the Chinese government. In August 1999, Tung also appointed Yeoh Eng Kiong (E.K. Yeoh), former Chief Executive of the Hospital Authority, as Secretary for Health and Welfare upon the incumbent's normal retirement. Then, in May 2001, he appointed private banker and Executive Councillor Antony Leung as FS to succeed Donald Tsang who took over from Anson Chan as CS upon her resignation. The appointment of these three 'outsiders' was justified on the grounds of professional expertise, and they were all appointed on civil service fixed-term contracts before the introduction of the new ministerial system (see Chapter 5).[59]

Same colonial architecture, changing institutional rules and practices

Although the system of governance in Hong Kong seemed to have maintained the same outer appearance throughout British rule, it had in fact undergone considerable reorganisation and various modifications (such as the composition of the appointed membership of the ExCo and LegCo), resulting in shifts in institutional 'rules' and practices. Two specific developments stand out. First, bureaucratic reformism in the 1970s–1980s had transformed the administrative state to make it more efficient and public service-oriented as well as more approachable for the local population, followed in the 1990s by measures to open up the administration in tandem with the international trend of modernising government. Second, the formalisation of district politics through setting up District Boards and of business and professional influence through new functional constituencies of the LegCo, as part of British decolonisation in the 1980s, led to the rise and consolidation of grassroots and elite populism. This, in turn, reshaped the political landscape and policy process of Hong Kong, the full impact of which was only felt well after 1997. Even though British attempts at implementing representative government were partially frustrated by the Chinese government, the various reforms accumulatively still managed to leave some lasting institutional footprints on public administration and governance inherited by the SAR regime. More will be said about such developments in subsequent chapters.

The power of the Governor also evolved during this time. Governors were not just constitutionally conferred with immense powers over the governance of the colony. They were also trusted by London to act and make decisions in Britain's best interests.[60] Despite possessing almost autocratic powers, the Governor was, over the years, subject to constraint by both the formal institutions (ExCo and LegCo, and civil service procedure) as well as established conventions which required him to consult and take advice from local community leaders. The making of policies by the Governor-in-Council, a practice obliging the Governor to share his policy-making prerogative with members of the ExCo, had become institutionalised and written into a range of local legislation. It was rare for the Governor to refuse to listen to the advice of his ExCo.[61] While colonial governors, as dispatched representatives of the Crown, ultimately had to do the bidding of their home government in London, in practice they often had strong views as to the priorities of the colony within overall British interests. Disagreement and resistance by governors to the Colonial Office/FCO was not uncommon, especially after the Hong Kong government began to 'localise' from the 1970s onwards.[62]

Since Governors came and went in much the same way as an elected government in a democracy, the colonial civil service became in effect an entrenched permanent career institution having continuous influence over policy formulation. Principal officials and heads of departments were the Governor's closest aides, whose commitment and competence were much depended upon to achieve effective rule. The Governor had to share powers with his top civil servants whose careers in the colony normally outlasted his. In western democracies, despite politics-administration separation, top bureaucrats grew in power and influence, not only in the formulation of policy but increasingly in the brokerage and articulation of interests, functions conventionally regarded as being within the exclusive province of elected politicians.[63] In stark contrast, Hong Kong's path was quite the reverse, with career bureaucrats monopolising such political functions all along until the late transition period when emerging local politicians and parties spurred by newly introduced electoral politics asked for a share of power.

The government remained a non-elected and non-party Administration, yet the bureaucracy began to feel agitated by legislative obstruction. Senior bureaucrats did not see legislators as political equals and detested the latter's politics of criticism and blame. It has even been said that in 1995 Anson Chan as CS

> led a powerful delegation of civil servants to Government House to urge Patten to redraft the constitution to reinforce the concept of an 'executive-led government' by forbidding the introduction of any private member's bills without the prior approval of the Governor.[64]

The pre-1997 LegCo Standing Orders (essentially retained and modified to become the Rules of Procedures of the SAR LegCo) were modelled on the formal rules, precedents, and practice of the British Parliament, some of which subsequently became written rules in the form of standing orders.[65] In a parliamentary system, various powers and room for participation and intervention are granted to Members of Parliament. Such powers were, however, more nominal than real as applied to Hong Kong during British colonial rule, posing no real threat to the supremacy of the Executive. It was only after the introduction of some elected seats in the mid-1980s, especially the directly elected geographical seats in 1991, that the LegCo began to make active use of those powers on the rule book and according to parliamentary conventions to check and challenge the Executive. Since 1985, when the Legislative Council (Powers and Privileges) Ordinance was enacted, the LegCo has also had the power to summon public officials, call for documents and evidence, and investigate matters of public concern through a select committee.[66]

By the 1990s, the era of executive-legislative fusion came to an end. The previous UMELCO system (later renamed the Office of Members of the Executive and Legislative Councils, or OMELCO) was replaced by a network of new policy panels established by an assertive LegCo to monitor and check the government independently. Panel meetings were opened to the media and public, both to increase transparency and to enable legislators to leverage media impact and exert more pressure on the government. Still, with the presence of some appointed members in the LegCo until 1995, the Governor was able to maintain a residual degree of 'control' over the legislature. Constitutionally, he had the right to refuse his assent to any legislation passed and to dissolve the LegCo and order fresh elections at any time. There was no intention to transfer power until the very end of British rule.

The supreme authority and wide discretionary powers of the Governor were key to the sustenance of the 'executive-led' system of governance in colonial Hong Kong, well beyond government-by-bureaucrats. Such authority and power were supposed to be inherited by the post-1997 CE, but as we shall see, in practice, this inheritance has been conditioned and sometimes disrupted by new political and institutional contexts.

Chapter 2
Administrative Modernisation

Introduction

The years 1966 and 1967 consecutively saw disturbances triggered by the increase in Star Ferry fare and the anti-British riots. The four-day April 1966 disturbances led to an official Commission of Inquiry which concluded that the main cause was the general lack of a sense of belonging to society among young people, along with social discontent and distrust of the colonial government.[1] The 1967 riots originated from a factory labour dispute in May and escalated into several months of large-scale social confrontations and street protests and violence (including bomb attacks) instigated by pro-communists under the influence of the Cultural Revolution on the Mainland.[2] The riots only subsided in December 1967 after suppression through curfews, closure of pro-communist newspapers, emergency regulations, and military-police joint operations.[3]

The 1966 and 1967 crises made the colonial government realise a looming legitimation crisis and the need to reform social policy and its style of administration. This marked a turning point in Hong Kong politics and governance—as seen in both a top-down shift in governing strategy by the colonial rulers and bottom-up expectations and demands for change from across society. Given its inability to organise society politically and establish an unquestioned mandate to govern within a colonial structure premised on low political mobilisation, the colonial government had no better choice than to resort to administrative actions to cope with social tensions and economic problems. The governing strategy moved towards the modernisation and localisation of public administration. More local university graduates began to be recruited into the British expatriate-dominated bureaucracy, including the elite Administrative Class and the commissioned ranks of the Royal Hong Kong Police Force. As the government expanded and the division of responsibility became more complicated and layered, efficient management posed a new concern.

As a longstanding tradition, the government was not held in custody by any specific philosophy of governance. Instead, the administrative logic had always been grounded in the often-repeated saying 'if it isn't broken, why fix it?' Such a minimalist 'hands-off' approach of laissez-faire doctrine was more a result of political expediency in a colonial setting. Having almost absolutist powers, the government did not find it difficult to augment policy interventions when the needs of governance so warranted, so long as it did not result in undue fiscal burden or explicit constitutional changes. The lack of any predetermined governing ideology allowed the government room for adjustment and growth within the boundary defined by the outer political perimeters and constraints. Exploiting that room, reforms of the bureaucracy through the bureaucracy provided the natural and safe solution to various problems of governance, whether administrative or political.

The colonial administrative configuration

Until the 1970s, the administrative configuration of Hong Kong had been relatively static, modelled essentially on the typical British colonial design. The internal structure of the administration had evolved around two types of organisations—the Colonial Secretariat and the Departments. The Colonial Secretariat, as the Colonial Secretary's department (run by the Deputy Colonial Secretary), oversaw the whole administrative machinery of government under the ultimate authority of the Governor. It formed what could be described as a 'miniature but very concentrated and comprehensive Whitehall'.[4] Sitting on the ExCo as an ex-offico member, the Colonial Secretary was the Governor's deputy and the de facto head of the civil service. He was, therefore, able to somewhat check the power of the Governor and gain the latter's ears at critical moments.

The Colonial Secretariat coordinated the work of various departments and acted as the link between the policy-making authorities, including the ExCo and Governor, and the administrative bodies which implemented the decisions made.[5] Heads of departments were generally responsible to the Governor through the Colonial Secretary. Although officials in the Colonial Secretariat had the responsibility of coordination, they were very often inferior in rank to the department heads, particularly those of super-departments like the Police, Medical and Health, and Public Works, a few of whom were appointed to the ExCo and LegCo. The authority of the Secretariat stemmed more from that of the Colonial Secretary as head of the civil service. In day-to-day interactions, Secretariat officials had to rely on persuasion and goodwill to secure the cooperation and support of the departments. Traditionally, the FS operated outside the control of the Colonial Secretary in economic policy and public finance. He reported directly to the Governor.

Growth in the work of the government, as well as the number and size of departments, was largely ad hoc early on. In the post-War years, problems arising from the need to govern a fast-expanding local population (doubling from about 2 million in 1950 to 4 million by 1970)[6] provided the main impetus for administrative growth to cope with pressing needs for housing, employment, and some basic welfare. Examples were the formation of the Resettlement Department in 1954 and the Social Welfare Department in 1958 (which initially started as a section of the Secretariat for Chinese Affairs in 1947). The immigration function was hived off from the Police Force in 1961 to form a separate Immigration Department to recognise the importance of immigration control in the face of the large influx from Mainland China. By the 1960s, the needs for economic growth, urban management, territorial and district planning, and infrastructure development became pertinent. New departments were set up such as the Transport Department in 1968 (by taking over relevant functions from the Police and PWD) and the New Territories Development Department out of the PWD in 1973. The Planning Branch within the Crown Lands and Survey Office of the PWD was also upgraded to be a full-fledged Planning Office in 1973, eventually becoming the Planning Department in 1990. By the early 1970s, there were already some 40 departments with a total civil service force of 112,800.[7]

Such scale of governmental growth was more a mixed outcome of political expediency and administrative incrementalism than any thoughtfully planned expansion given the colony claimed to have the classic minimalist form of government which left the market to private business unrestrained by administrative interventions.[8] However, being an absolutist administrative regime, the colonial government had never found itself inhibited from engaging in what could be regarded as 'state intervention' whenever it saw the political advantage or administrative necessity to do so (more discussion in Chapter 8). To that extent, government decision-makers were guided more by their bureaucratic rationale than any ideological or philosophical dogma. Indeed, bureaucratic reformism could be very efficient once the will for change was secured, as underscored by the modernisation of the colonial administration in the 1970s.

CDO Scheme

The 1967 riots and 1966 disturbances exposed deep-seated problems of government legitimacy and elite-mass integration.[9] Short of a political option to deal with the challenge (such as political reform by extending the franchise and powers of the Urban Council), the colonial government had no alternative but to pursue 'administrative' solutions that could absorb public demands for better government. Governor Murray MacLehose, a reformist, assumed office in 1971 and soon took up social and labour reforms, an ambitious 10-year public housing programme to accommodate 1.8 million people, and the development of infrastructure and new towns as his main policy agenda. In contrast to the previous colonial style of indirect rule, the new strategy was to relate government directly to the ordinary people and to inculcate among them a new sense of local identity.

Prior to that, in 1968, the Secretariat for Chinese Affairs was renamed Secretariat for Home Affairs, marking the beginning of a new era where the government would be prepared to face the whole population (which was predominantly Chinese) in its approach to governance. Under the newly introduced CDO scheme, young AOs, many freshly recruited from local universities under the localisation policy, were posted to various districts to better coordinate government activities and functions at the community level and to bring government closer to the people. CDOs were required to collect and report to the government centre any community opinions and sentiments through formal and informal feedback channels—known as 'Town Talk' and 'Flash Points'. A rudimentary two-way political communication mechanism was put in place which became the precursor of the District Administration Scheme of the 1980s. It is worth noting that the New Territories had long adopted a DO system, where the DO acted as the local representative of the colonial government with extensive powers and functions—including even police power (abolished in 1913), judicial and magistrative power (until the amendment of the New Territories Ordinance in 1961), and land disposal and control (until the establishment of the Lands Department in 1982 to unify lands administration across the whole of Hong Kong including the New Territories).[10]

Traditionally, the administrative absorption of politics was targeted at the elites. With the introduction of the CDO scheme and other related gestures of strengthening government links to the local communities, such absorption was gradually extended to incorporate elements down to the grassroots—through new Area Committees (within a district), mutual aid committees (in public housing blocks), and owners corporations (in private tenement buildings), all organised under the aegis of CDOs. The scheme was significant in laying 'the foundation for a new basis of legitimacy for the continued existence of a colonial regime whose senior officials were increasingly conscious that the territory was subject to political vicissitudes of a volatile China'.[11] The political subtext of such reform was: although the colonial government is not government *by* the people, it would listen to the people and seek to become a government *for* the people and *of* the people.[12] Community building was now deemed an essential part of the government's day-to-day work, supported by various public campaigns such as the Keep Hong Kong Clean Campaign and Fight Crime campaign.

Cleaning up the administration

By the early 1970s, syndicated and institutionalised corruption had become a major social disease eating into government and private business, even as economic growth and stability picked up. The escape of a Chief Superintendent Peter Godber from Hong Kong in 1973, while under investigation by the Anti-Corruption Branch of the Police Force over his wealth of over HK$4.3 million suspected to be amassed through corruption, caused a huge uproar and large-scale student protests calling for government action and the setting up of an independent anti-corruption agency. Many believed Governor MacLehose saw the political window of opportunity to act and was instrumental in the establishment of the high-powered Independent Commission Against Corruption (ICAC) in 1974 following the publication of the Blake-Kerr Report.[13] The move proved greatly successful in breaking up corruption syndicates within government departments (especially the Police) and detecting corrupt practices in both the public and private sectors.[14] MacLehose had managed to launch a 'silent revolution' and changed what many in Hong Kong at that time regarded as unchangeable.[15]

The success of the ICAC can be explained by both its three-prong strategy and the political purpose behind the anti-corruption campaign. The three-prong approach worked because it concurrently sought to: inculcate fear among the corrupt through vigilant enforcement and sanction backed by strong legislation; eliminate opportunities for corruption through preventive efforts in streamlining procedures and management processes to minimise the incentives to bribe in order to get public services; and alter the ordinary people's mindset in taking corruption for granted, through incessant public education and publicity, so that ultimately the tolerance of corrupt practices and the chain of 'reproduction of bribery' could be broken.[16] It was said that by grasping an anti-corruption agenda, MacLehose was able to demonstrate his authority and consensus-interpretation capacity by way of a major strategic response to a crisis no longer considered tolerable by all quarters of society.[17] The worth of the government was thus proven. Today, Hong Kong is rated as one of the cleanest societies in the world.[18]

Evaluating Hong Kong's integrity system over the years, two significant features stand out.[19] The first is the ICAC's institutional strength, which eventually made it one of the largest anti-corruption agencies in the world and a role model emulated by other countries.[20] Its statutory investigative powers were extended in the 1980s to election-related offences to uphold a clean election culture. The second notable feature is that there were supporting conditions and institutions—the integrity system did not solely rely on the ICAC. In addition to the introduction of 'supervisory accountability' within the civil service in 1978 at the behest of the ICAC, wide-ranging measures had been implemented in terms of civil service modernisation and public sector reform during the 1980s–1990s around the themes of 'serving the community' and performance pledges (see Chapter 3), and later to promote ethics and good governance. Of equal importance was that the ICAC had functioned under an independent judicial system bearing the highest standard.

The McKinsey reforms of government machinery

With the government setting out on a path of expansion in public services and community building, there was a concomitant need to streamline the administrative machinery to cope with such changes, which opened the door for the rise of professional power (the so-called specialist grades) in service departments. In 1972, the international management consulting firm McKinsey & Company was commissioned to review the organisation of the government machinery. It was the first time in colonial history that the government looked outside for new ideas of administrative change. Engaging an external consultancy instead of in-house review also possibly indicated MacLehose's lack of trust in the colonial bureaucrats.[21]

McKinsey recognised the failure of the existing system of government coordination caused by the increase in the number and size of government departments to a point beyond the capacity of the Colonial Secretariat. The problem was made more acute given that Secretariat officials were often not ranked as highly as the department heads with whom they had to work. Whenever disagreements arose, the department heads would insist that issues be passed upward for decision by the Colonial Secretary or FS or their deputies, thus overloading the top echelon. Another defect in the system was the low priority given to long-range planning. Secretariat officials were so preoccupied with immediate difficulties and issues that they had little time for anticipating the needs and problems of the future. The 1973 McKinsey Report proposed not only a significant reorganisation of the administration but also a modernisation of the mode of operations in tandem with a rationalist approach to public administration which was gaining popularity in North America and Western Europe (including Britain).[22]

McKinsey's main recommendations for increasing the efficiency of the Colonial Secretariat and reducing overload at the very top were threefold: (a) that many decisions should be entirely delegated to department heads and lower officials, particularly for minor financial changes and matters involving technical expertise without any policy implications; (b) that programmes should be drawn up for all policy areas and be regularly revised and updated; and (c) that a number of high-level posts should be created in the Secretariat (known as 'Super-Secretaries'), directly below the Colonial Secretary and FS, to head different policy branches with the authority to plan and control programmes within major policy areas and be held responsible for monitoring progress and ensuring that targets were met. Apart from clarifying and rationalising the roles of Secretariat branches and departments, McKinsey also suggested new processes to improve the planning and control of executive activities performed by the 'decentralised' departments, emphasising performance monitoring and control, and management by results rather than by resources used as in traditional administration. The long-term possibility of 'hiving off' some departments (such as aviation, railway, waterworks, and the post office) was contemplated.

These recommendations, mostly accepted by the government, would set a new administrative configuration for the next two decades until the end of colonial rule. The Secretariat was quickly reorganised into two 'resource branches' (Finance and Civil Service) and six 'policy branches' (Economic Services, Environment, Home Affairs, Housing, Security, and Social Services) in late 1973.[23] To complete the process of modernisation and distinguish further the new administration from its colonial past, the Colonial Secretariat was retitled Government Secretariat, and the Colonial Secretary renamed Chief Secretary (CS) in 1974. Influenced by the prevailing rationalist management model of separating policy-making from execution, McKinsey had redesigned the central administrative structure by simply using the same colonial-style organisation units (i.e., the 'Branches') in the Secretariat and giving them a new image with enhanced power and status. It was a typical process of innovation through evolution, leading to deeper changes and unleashing a different systemic logic altogether.

The new (and more powerful) 'policy branches' of the Secretariat would now focus on long-term programme planning and policy formulation, while the day-to-day administrative decisions would be delegated to departments, complemented by the streamlining of programme planning, implementation, and resource allocation to achieve cost-effectiveness. A new 'McKinsey format' was introduced to serve as a template for policy submissions and resource applications. A five-year forecast of resource requirements was added to the traditional cycle of annual estimates of expenditure, again emulating the rational planning practice in Britain (especially in local government) and other Western countries at the time. Some were of the view that the British modernisation of civil service under the Fulton Reform had provided inspiration for Hong Kong.[24] During this period (the mid-1960s to 1970s), there was also growing influence on the public sector by business management thinking and practices, such as in management by objective, a Planning Programming Budgeting System, cost-benefit analysis, strategic planning, and corporate management.

The impact of the McKinsey changes can be further construed as a form of quasi-ministerialisation, by default if not by design. Indeed, the experience of independence of former British colonies involved the evolution of the colonial government structure taking various 'modes' of ministerialisation whereby the former Secretariat divisions became new ministries or ministerial secretariats after self-government and independence were established.[25] The full integration of departments within the ministries was not always an early feature of independence, but eventually, ministers would achieve effective control over departments coming within their portfolios. In the case of Hong Kong, though independence was not on the agenda, implementing the administrative reforms of the 1970s was a process of modernisation to 'reinvent' government administration and remove its colonial wrappings as far as practicable. The top bureaucrats taking up the newly created Super-Secretary posts were quickly identified—both within government and by the public—as being 'in charge' of major policy areas and were held responsible for policy delivery and performance, even when government power remained centralised in the Governorship as assisted by the CS and FS.

Changing power relationships and the generalist-specialist divide

The 1970s, post-McKinsey, was an era of administrative modernisation. Yet, like most reforms elsewhere, things were not always as exciting as what the reform rhetoric implied. In an effort to accommodate the conservatism of the civil service and the negative tenor of most public comments, the McKinsey recommendations were diluted as they were implemented.[26] Powers and relationships were subject to a process of internal competition and adaptation. At the same time, departments and quasi-governmental organisations proliferated, and the size of the civil service grew, along with the rapid expansion in the range of government functions, services, and policy commitments. New departmental grades were established, and more layers and ranks were added to existing grades—such as different engineer, architect, and surveyor disciplines, town planners, medical doctors, dentists and specialist consultants, transport officers, labour officers, social welfare officers, lands officers, etc. The disciplined services also snowballed in size and structure, with the Police Force being treated as the elite department in recognition of its role as the 'agency of last resort'. AOs (and government lawyers) were the highest-paid among the civilian grades, while Police officers were better paid than other disciplined services.

Diversification and specialisation, while unavoidable and to some extent necessary to cope with new functions requiring new expertise, had created sensitive problems of pay relativities within the enlarged civil service, as well as complex management issues in the interface between the so-called 'generalists' (mainly AOs and Executive Officers who could be posted to various departments to undertake general functions like policy, finance, and human resource management, with a broader service-wide outlook) and 'specialists' who were principally departmental grade officers with professional or expert advantage over the generalists and more protective of their departmental interests and turf. The McKinsey reforms of the 1970s had enabled the AO-dominated Secretariat branches to assert policy leadership over specialist departments, but from time to time the latter questioned the competence of the AOs in the more specialised domains of knowledge. As a result, such 'AOs on top, experts on tap' relationship often bred internal tension and conflicts.

The smooth functioning of the post-1973 system depended on the relationship between the branch secretary and heads of departments. Although the former was responsible for formulating policy programmes and monitoring their implementation and was answerable for policy results, the latter remained in charge of the day-to-day operations and budget allocations made to them. There had never been a simple superordinate-subordinate relationship between the two because most of the statutory powers at the beginning still rested with the heads of departments in existing legislation, and these department heads continued to be directly accountable to the Governor through the CS. In a few super-departments like the Police, Medical and Health, and Public Works, the Director was ranked at the same level as the Secretary, resulting in an even more ambivalent relationship. To overcome this organisational anomaly, the government began to break up the super-departments (notably the PWD and the Trade Industry and Customs Department), 'administrativise' some professional departments (i.e., replacing professional officers by AOs as heads of departments, who presumably could work better with their administrator counterparts in the Secretariat), and upgrade the Secretaries, all to make clear that the Secretary was the policy 'master'. Some of the new Secretaries were also appointed to the ExCo.

The historical independence of the FS who worked directly under the Governor was akin to the Chancellor of the Exchequer in Britain. Prior to the introduction of medium-term policy planning in the late 1970s advocated by McKinsey, policy and spending decisions were dominated by the Finance Branch of the Secretariat, whose predominant position was hardly diluted by the reforms.[27] Run by the Deputy Financial Secretary (retitled Secretary for the Treasury in 1989) on the day-to-day basis, the Finance Branch scrutinised departmental budget requests, prepared the government's annual budget, and cleared all submissions for funds to the Finance Committee of the LegCo. Being charged with the overall responsibility to control public expenditure and taxation, the Finance Branch in effect became *the* 'central agency' that counted most within the Secretariat. It was often able to override departments and their policy branches, playing 'a disproportionately large role in determining the government's overall policy priorities' according to a former Deputy Financial Secretary.[28]

As if to balance the undue influence of the Finance Branch and in an attempt to win some goodwill from the otherwise apathetic departments they oversaw, policy branches tended to be more protective of 'their' departments when negotiating with the Finance Branch. The tripartite relationship ensuing from these interactions (department, policy branch, Finance Branch) was delicate and intricate, to say the least, with the departments resisting influence from the policy branch but at the same time trying to make use of the latter's blessing to get their way through Finance Branch. Such an ambivalent relationship only began to change in the 1990s when policy branches were devolved budgetary allocation and control powers over those departments and agencies within their policy portfolio under financial management reform (see Chapter 3).

Until 1973, civil servants in the professional grades could not normally expect to rise higher than the headship of their own 'specialist' departments, and such eminence was not open to them in all cases.[29] The AOs occupied most department headships and Secretariat senior posts. McKinsey proposed that senior posts in the Secretariat should be open to all grades, a suggestion in common with the post-Fulton reform thinking within the British civil service for unifying the different grades.[30] However, the instances where professional officers were given the opportunity to work in the Secretariat and then transfer to the Administrative Grade were limited.[31] In 1982, the government decided to adopt an 'open directorate' system whereby positions at the directorate level—in both departments and the Secretariat—would be open to administrative as well as professional officers. In principle, it opened up promotion opportunities to the professionals, but in practice, it also allowed some professional departments hitherto headed by their departmental grade officers (such as the Trade and Industry group of departments and the Social Welfare Department) to be legitimately 'admininistrativised', in a subtle move to centralise power within the administrative elite. The rivalry between AOs and professional officers for influence over policy directions was a constant source of intra-bureaucratic conflict, reinforcing the already contentious Secretariat-department relationship.[32]

Reforming district administration in the 1980s

In June 1980, the government proposed the launch of the District Administration Scheme and confirmed it in a White Paper the following year.[33] Basically, the scheme provided for the setting up of two types of new district-level institutions within the government structure: District Boards and District Management Committees (DMCs). District Boards were to advise the government on any matters which might affect the well-being of those residing or working in the district. Initially, one-third of the members of the District Board were to be elected on universal suffrage (the first time such a notion was built into colonial Hong Kong's constitutional framework), the rest being government officials and appointed unofficial members. From 1985 onwards, District Boards only included unofficial members — two-thirds elected and one-third appointed, with the chairman elected from among members to replace the DO who was board chairman at the beginning. In 1994, appointed seats were abolished under the new electoral arrangements implemented by the Patten Administration. DMCs were a formalised inter-departmental platform to act as a focal point for coordination of various governmental activities and services at the district level and for improving government responsiveness to local community needs.

The official rationale for introducing such district administration was that it was a natural evolution of Hong Kong's unique systems of representation, participation, and consultation, which dated back to the DO system and the elected Rural Committees that had long existed in the New Territories as well as to the CDO Scheme implemented in 1969.[34] However, the District Administration Scheme carried both a political and administrative reform agenda. Politically, following MacLehose's 1979 Beijing trip the British government had to prepare for the forthcoming negotiations with the Chinese government over the future of Hong Kong, and in the absence of truly representative institutions, it would be difficult for any British position to claim to represent the interests of the local population. The British government also had to prepare for the possibility of having to return Hong Kong to China and hence to start decolonisation of some kind which would not disrupt its rule while the ultimate future of the territory had yet to be clarified. The establishment of District Boards with a partially elected membership would help to facilitate such a strategic move.

Being only advisory in nature, District Boards could not challenge the government's predominant position. Having an elected element, they were able to tap some degree of popular support. Furthering the process of administrative absorption of politics at the district level, District Boards also helped satisfy the growing demand for political participation and provide a local arena for a more orderly resolution of social conflicts; hence the very unusual practice of constituting nominally advisory bodies with the most political means, namely direct elections at the district level. Lau Siu-kai argued that the implicit goal of this reform was depoliticisation because providing district focal points around which the political forces could coalesce would eventually 'defuse these political forces locally without allowing them to spill over into larger political arenas'.[35]

At the same time, there was an administrative (or bureaucratic) logic of reform in the setting up of the DMCs. Although the DMCs were to work in parallel with District Boards and to follow up advice from the latter, they were not the executive arms of the District Boards per se. In other words, the District Administration Scheme was not about the creation of any form of district government or local authorities. DMCs merely served as a coordinating mechanism for governmental services at the district delivery level. By that time, the appeal and effectiveness of the urban CDO Scheme was worn out. In the name of decentralising administration as advocated by McKinsey, major service departments had set up their own 'district offices' staffed by upgraded professional officers in a process of 'districtisation' in the 1970s, overshadowing the role of CDOs, usually more junior AOs, as the sole local representatives of government. By introducing the DMC with inter-departmental representation and appointing a directorate level DO (AO Staff Grade C) as chairman, a more structured system of corporate management and coordination could be facilitated, in line with notions of local government reform made popular by the 'corporate revolution' in Britain at that time.[36] By subjecting local departmental officials to mild local pressure from the new district advisory machinery, it was also hoped that the problem of bureaucratic performance could be better tackled.

Institutional checks

Institutional checks on the administration had been gradually strengthened since the 1970s. Following the enactment of the Audit Ordinance in 1971, the Director of Audit had gained wide powers (such as accessing the records of departments and requiring any public officer to provide information and explanation). His independence was made more prominent after the establishment in 1978 of the Public Accounts Committee (PAC) as a standing committee of the LegCo to consider his reports, modelled on a practice long in existence in the British Parliament.[37] In 1986, again following Britain, a set of value-for-money (VFM) audit guidelines agreed between the PAC and the Director of Audit was accepted by the government. PAC hearings held upon receipt of the regular VFM reports became useful platforms to hold government officials to account. In the 1990s, additional independent institutions like the Ombudsman, Equal Opportunities Commission, and the Privacy Commissioner were set up.

It should be noted that the appointment of an Ombudsman was the result of years of arduous advocacy, since the 1960s, from the legal community and non-governmental organisations (NGOs). In 1989, the colonial government finally accepted the need to set up a Commissioner for Administrative Complaints (COMAC), retitled Ombudsman in 1996, taking Hong Kong ahead of many jurisdictions in Asia.[38] The COMAC operated under the Governor rather than the legislature and was initially confined to handling complaints referred to it by legislators who had the sole responsibility for the redress of grievances under the previous UMELCO system. In June 1994, the law was amended to enable the public to lodge complaints directly with the COMAC and to empower the Commissioner to initiate direct (own-motion) investigations when deemed appropriate; a power subsequently used frequently.[39]

The growth of quasi-government

Until the 1960s, governmental growth had mainly taken the shape of reorganisation and proliferation of departments. Despite a long history of having various advisory boards and committees (including the Sanitary Board in 1883, a precursor of the Urban Council), non-departmental public bodies vested with executive functions were rare before the Second World War. In 1954, a Housing Authority was established to provide low-cost housing, with executive functions discharged by civil servants seconded from the then Housing Division of the Urban Council which was given a limited public housing role until its reorganisation in 1971.

The scene began to see some change starting in the late 1960s. In recognition of the importance of export trade for the economy and the need to use a commercial approach in the required operations, the government set up the first batch of statutory public bodies, namely the Export Credit Insurance Corporation in 1966 and the Trade Development Council in 1968. The latter took over the function of trade promotion previously undertaken by the then Commerce and Industry Department and could therefore be regarded as the first phase of hiving-off in Hong Kong. Subsequently, more statutory bodies with executive functions were established: the Productivity Council (1974), the Consumer Council (1974), the reconstituted Housing Authority (1973, to merge the resettlement housing and low-cost housing functions), the Examinations Authority (1977, taking over the examinations function from the Education Department), and the Hospital Authority (1990, by breaking up the Medical and Health Department and corporatising its medical services). With the exception of the Housing Authority, which continued to be served by a Housing Department (by the merger of the former Resettlement Department and Housing Division of the Urban Council), all these statutory bodies employed their own staff even though they were initially managed by civil servants seconded from the government.

As to public corporations, Hong Kong was spared from the influence of post-War nationalisation of industries that occurred in Britain. Private companies operated most public utilities on government franchise. The establishment of the Mass Transit Railway Corporation (MTRC) in 1975 marked the beginning of the government's use of a public corporation as an instrument of public policy. The MTRC was somewhat a product of accident, set up by the government following the withdrawal from the underground railway construction project of a Japanese consortium originally awarded the contract in 1973.[40] Subsequently formed public corporations included: the Industrial Estates Corporation in 1977 to develop industrial estates for land-intensive industries (predecessor of the current Science Park Corporation); the Kowloon-Canton Railway Corporation (KCRC) in 1982 to take over the responsibility from the then Railway Department for managing the land rail system;[41] and the Land Development Corporation in 1988 to redevelop old urban areas (subsequently reconstituted as the present Urban Renewal Authority).

The corporatisation trend during the 1960s and 1970s, though driven by home-grown administrative needs, was in tandem with similar changes in the West, especially Britain which saw government expansion mostly in the form of quasi-non-governmental organisations or 'quangos', a collective term used to denote quasi-government.[42] The increasing use of quasi-governmental organisations represented a new approach to public administration in implementing government policies outside the traditional civil service structure, as encouraged by the McKinsey review, which had advocated decentralisation and hiving-off. The attraction laid in having non-governmental public bodies taking up public functions without expanding the civil service establishment or having the costs fully reflected in the government budget as some of these bodies operated on a fee-charging and hence self-financing basis (except for the initial injection of funds from the government). In the growingly politicised environment, the setting up of quasi-governmental organisations headed by 'non-officials' appointed from among community elites could also be seen as improving accountability to the public.

Until the 1980s, the government's controlling influence over public corporations and statutory authorities was largely exercised through its powers of appointment to their boards, as well as sending senior officials to sit on them as non-executive directors and board members. In addition, the government usually had the deciding say over the appointment of their chief executive officer or executive director. However, as a scandal over the KCRC's 'golden handshake' payments to two departing senior managers in January 1989 revealed, government directors in public corporations were not always able to play a very assertive role and override board decisions.[43] When Public Sector Reform was launched in 1989, Hong Kong's public sector had become much more diversified, comprising some 60 government departments and agencies, a host of non-departmental statutory bodies and public corporations, as well as numerous public or semi-public organisations heavily subvented by the government, such as universities and polytechnics, schools, hospitals, and social service organisations. The government also had equity interest in some companies (such as the Building and Loan Agency, Cross-Harbour Tunnel Company Limited, and Hong Kong Air Cargo Terminal Limited) which were first started with government initiative and participation. The next chapter describes how one result of public sector reform was to give this diversified configuration a new overarching organisational logic.

Chapter 3
Public Sector Reform

Introduction

Bureaucracy-driven administrative reforms in contemporary Hong Kong began in the mid-1970s with the McKinsey review of the core government structure and the policy and resource management processes. Quasi-ministerial 'branches' were set up in the Government Secretariat, each led by a 'Super-Secretary', to provide policy coordination among government departments, thereby creating a new two-tier government structure. Supported by continuous attempts at civil service improvement and modernisation, district administration, and the wider use of public consultation, the bureaucracy had become the main force of policy and management renovations to reinvent a colonial regime that would be closer to the people despite its authoritarian nature. Such bureaucratic reformism, sustained by fiscal surplus during a long period of steady economic growth, helped to secure some conditional public acceptance.

The next decade saw the government gradually venturing into a more vigorous phase of public sector reform inspired and encouraged by the New Public Management (NPM) trend that started in Europe and began to gain prominence across continents and countries.[1] According to Christopher Hood and Michael Jackson, there were five central administrative tenets of NPM, involving shifts from policy to management, from aggregation to disaggregation, from planning and public service welfarism to an emphasis on cutting costs and establishing labour discipline, from process-based approaches to output control, and from production towards the separation of provisions, with more outsourcing of public services to the private sector and outright privatisation.[2] The Organisation for Economic Cooperation and Development (OECD) put the key words of public management reform as: efficiency, productivity, competition, results, decentralised management, flexibility, and strategic capacity (at the centre).[3]

However, the public sector reform occurring in Hong Kong was not just a passive response to, or convergence with, this new global trend to improve the efficiency of the public service. Hong Kong had its own trajectory of administrative reform to modernise its public services and shore up the capacity of its administrative state.[4] The fact that NPM-type changes were already taking place in Britain (privatisation, the 'Next Steps' reform)[5] probably made the Hong

Kong government feel that public sector reform was 'safe' as there were British models to learn from.

Public sector reform from the 1980s to 1997

The journey of public sector reform can be divided into two phases: the 1990s reform phase until the British handover; and the post-1997 reform phase. Table 3.1 highlights the more significant reform initiatives introduced in the 1980s until 1997.

In February 1989, without much fanfare, the Hong Kong government launched a Public Sector Reform document. It was officially a programme of financial management reforms seeking to promote 'an increased awareness of what results are actually being achieved by the government and at what cost'.[6] However, it did not stop at financial management but went much further towards re-rationalising the structure of the public sector to enhance the McKinsey logic underlying its organisation. The Public Sector Reform document was drafted by the management consultants Coopers & Lybrand in the language of NPM. A new Efficiency Unit (EfU) was set up in 1992 under the Office of the Chief Secretary, modelled on the British government's EfU, to spearhead reform initiatives, promote business-like operations within government, and provide management advice to government departments and agencies.

Apart from the managerial initiatives echoing the NPM reforms in Western countries (such as budgetary devolution, contracting out, trading funds and customer-oriented initiatives), Hong Kong's public sector reform was significant in reconstituting the centre of policy management. Policy secretaries (i.e., heads of policy branches) were now given the powers and resources to become full-fledged policy managers, able to hold various executive agencies within their portfolio accountable for performance and policy outcomes. The enhanced role of policy secretaries not only followed the NPM logic of redefining the principal-agent relationship[7] between central policy agencies and line organisations, but it also further pushed the process of 'quasi-ministerialisation' first unleashed by the McKinsey reforms.

The following sections explain the various areas of reform, including financial management reform, reconfiguring the public sector, performance management reform, consumer focus, corporatisation and privatisation, and trading funds.

Financial management reform

In Hong Kong, as elsewhere, traditional budgeting was based on 'incrementalism' underpinned by bureaucratic negotiations.[8] As the government accumulated more fiscal surplus and adopted a less rigid 'positive non-interventionist' approach towards its functions and scope of activities, both the budget requesters and

Table 3.1: Significant public sector reforms in Hong Kong from the 1980s to 1997

Period	Reform measures
1980s	• Devolution of authority to heads of departments to create non-directorate posts subject to limits on staff numbers and salary value • Amalgamation of line items in the budget • Abolition of the 'block vote' arrangement for service supply departments • Introduction of inter-departmental charging • Launch of Public Sector Reform document (1989)
Early to mid-1990s	• Corporatisation of public hospital services under the new Hospital Authority (1990) • Introduction of performance pledges and customer liaison/user groups (1992) • Establishment of the EfU (1992) • Monitoring customer satisfaction • Contracting out • Setting up trading funds • Serving the Community Initiative (1995) • Code of Access to Information • Resource Allocation Exercise and Baseline Budgeting • Devolution of financial resource authority to policy branches and enhancement of policy management function • Devolution of some human resource management responsibilities to departments
Final years before the 1997 handover	• Managing for results • Performance review system • Improving productivity • Private sector participation (including contracting out, outsourcing and divestiture) • Fundamental expenditure reviews • New management frameworks • Reinventing front-line services

Source: Adapted from Table 2 of A.B.L. Cheung (2012a) 'One Country, Two Experiences: Administrative Reforms in China and Hong Kong', *International Review of Administrative Sciences*, Vol. 78, No. 2, pp. 261–283.

budget controllers learned to mutually accommodate each other and stabilise their negotiations within manageable limits.

Since the 1980s, a series of financial management reforms were rolled out—notably, the increased delegation of authority from Finance Branch to departments; amalgamation of line items; abolition of the 'block vote' arrangement;[9] introduction of inter-departmental charging; and a new output budget format to incorporate policy objectives, programmes, and performance targets of departments as part of the Controlling Officer's Report. Riding on the tide of NPM into the 1990s, budget reforms in favour of one-line budget allocations and 'budgeting for results' became prominent.[10] Another innovation in the 1990s was the setting up of self-accounting 'trading funds', with full operational autonomy within financial and performance parameters set by the relevant policy secretary in the form of a framework agreement. Furthermore, departments were encouraged to make greater use of private providers through contracting out of services and outsourcing.[11]

Following the Finance Branch Review of 1993, more power over resource allocation and control was transferred from the Finance Branch to various policy branches of the Government Secretariat. Henceforth, policy secretaries could decide on the relative priorities of different policy programmes and departments and agencies within their respective portfolios, as reflected in the budget allocations they made out of the block budget received from the FS. In practice, though, the Finance Branch continued to advise them on the calculation of budget allocations to departments based on the 'baseline budgeting' model.[12] The budgetary process was revamped in the form of a new-style 'Resource Allocation Exercise' operating along the lines of baseline budgeting (known as 'baseline plus'). A new Star Chamber—chaired by the CS and composed of the FS, Secretary for the Treasury (now Secretary for Financial Services and the Treasury), and Secretary for the Civil Service (SCS)—was set up to scrutinise each department's baseline performance and determine the priority of new funding requests for the extension of services or introduction of new services.

Reconfiguring the public sector

A new public sector structure was configured, with the policy secretaries constituting the centre of policy management under the overall policy and resource control of the Governor, the CS, and the CS's Committee. Policy secretaries would hold their respective executive agencies (departments, statutory organisations, and public corporations) accountable for performance and policy outcomes. Government and quasi-government organisations were reclassified into four 'agency' types, based on three criteria: the type of service delivered, the degree of freedom from government control desired, and the pricing strategy applied to the service (see Table 3.2).

The new organisational typology was significant in shifting the public sector towards a more market- and private sector-driven approach. Although some strategic services remained to be classified as core services (such as law and order) requiring direct government control and provision to the public free of charge, most other public services were likely to fall within the other categories, thus necessitating an explicit cost-recovery strategy and, accordingly, a non-departmental mode of delivery. The underlying logic of public sector reform would ultimately pave the way for more 'hiving-off' and 'commercialisation' or 'privatisation' of one form or another.

Table 3.2: Typology of agency choices under public sector reform

Type of service	Degree of government control	Pricing strategy	Mode of agency
Core services	Direct control	Free	Traditional department
Core services	Direct control	Partial or full cost recovery	Trading fund
Core services	Arm's length control	Free or partial cost recovery	Non-departmental public body
Core services	Arm's length control	Full cost recovery	Public corporation
Support services	Direct control	Full cost recovery	Trading fund
Support services	Arm's length control	Full cost recovery	Public corporation
Commercial services	Direct control	Partial or full cost recovery	Trading fund
Commercial services	Arm's length control	Partial or full cost recovery	Public corporation

Source: Adapted from the table shown on pp. 7–8 of Finance Branch (1989), *Public Sector Reform*, February, Hong Kong: Finance Branch.

Performance management reform

Starting in the early 1990s, all departments were required to set performance targets and indicators, to show how well their operational objectives were achieved and with what degree of cost-effectiveness. Both qualitative and quantitative measures were designated.[13] Performance information had to be included in the Controlling Officer's Reports submitted by heads of departments, as a mandatory document accompanying their annual estimates of expenditure, to the Finance Committee of the LegCo for scrutiny each year in line with the new 'budgeting for results' orientation. Also, following a human resources management review conducted by the Civil Service Branch in 1993, a steady process of devolution of personnel authorities to line departments began, with emphasis on nurturing a performance-oriented culture.[14]

'Managing for Performance' had since become a key objective of the government, to be achieved by departments through various mechanisms, such as: refining performance measures; managing by programme; improving efficiency; managing public finances; managing human resources; managing support services; preparing departmental plans; and reviewing progress.[15] A programme management system was instituted to help policy branches and departments—entailing the setting of strategic objectives based on customer needs, identifying key result areas, formulating measurement criteria, gathering performance information, preparing an annual programme plan, and linking resource allocation to programme needs and performance results which would form part of a performance review. A shift from a process-oriented approach to a customer-oriented approach became apparent.

Despite the enthusiasm expressed in policy statements and management rhetoric, critical decisions in public sector management continued to be based on a broad-brush, across-the-board approach factoring in bureaucratic adaptation and negotiation.[16] Hong Kong was not alone in this. Over-claiming about best practices was found among various OECD countries.[17] The fundamental reality is the presence of both qualitative and quantitative aspects involved in measuring public sector performance (as opposed to just quantitative), making comprehensive and objective measurement a constant point of contention. There is also a danger of equating average performance to good performance.[18] Indeed, public sector work is generally less quantifiable, involves inter-departmental cooperation and teamwork, and is subject to more value-laden processes and a more politically charged environment, resulting in the so-called 'perverse effects' of performance measurement that cast doubt on its reliability and effectiveness and induce staff cynicism and resistance.[19] In practice, the use of performance measurement is often driven by a mix of different institutional logics—the logic of the professions, logic of public administration, and market-managerial logic, intertwined to a varying extent and contingent upon the organisational and institutional context.[20] Such complexity explains why linking staff remuneration or budget allocation to performance has proved so hard to meaningfully implement.

Customer focus

The 1990s also saw the growing recognition of the users of public services as consumers and customers. The adoption of 'performance pledges' in all government departments in 1992 (later extended to other public sector agencies and public corporations) was the brainchild of Governor Patten who borrowed the idea from the British Citizen's Charter movement to create a new 'culture of service'. In addition to publishing performance pledges, departments with a significant public interface also had to set up user committees and customer liaison groups, as a way to involve representatives of the public in the monitoring of performance and performance standards. In Britain and some other European countries, public service consumerism emerged concomitantly with the rise of NPM. Hence, performance evaluation of public services began to pay attention to dimensions like access, choice, information, redress, and participation from a consumer-centric perspective.[21]

Despite the consumerist rhetoric, the introduction of performance pledges during Hong Kong's late transition period had in effect strengthened managerial autonomy, helping to re-empower (and re-legitimate) public bureaucratic managers within a logic that played up citizens as service consumers rather than political voters.[22] There was limited knowledge on how performance pledges fared in practice though. Some past research using content analysis found that most of the pledges mainly served the purposes of management rather than consumers. The kind of information in performance pledges on alternative ways of access to service or choice in alternative services and delivery modes was at best sketchy. Performance targets and achievements were mostly presented in standardised formats with very few organisations providing year-to-year statistics, while redress mechanisms were only briefly stated, with less than half of the pledges providing evidence of designated customer relations officers or units. Furthermore, minimal importance was attached to customer participation or advice to users on how to join customer liaison groups.[23]

Like many customer service techniques and strategies elsewhere, the customer rhetoric of performance pledges quickly became routinised and domesticated to become no more than a public relations instrument. The fundamental difficulty in operationalising the notion of 'customer' within a public service environment in contrast to the private market had made the consumerist approach a misnomer. Thus, the mixed and uncertain outcome of transplanting something not intrinsically compatible with the public bureaucratic culture and public service operational logic, leading to cosmetic adherence and lip service, was only to be expected.[24]

Corporatisation and privatisation

Unlike many NPM-reform jurisdictions, privatisation and corporatisation did not feature significantly on Hong Kong's public sector reform agenda. Government activities were predominantly carried out by departments staffed by civil servants. Most public utilities, including public transport, were operated by private companies under government franchise or licence. The only exceptions were the railway, airport, and water supply which were managed by government departments. Due to the limited number of public enterprises, privatisation in Hong Kong had mainly taken the form of contracting out of public services, through service contracts (e.g., cleaning or security management contracts) and other types of outsourcing, management contracts (e.g., granting concession to a private company to manage car parks), and build-own-operate or build-own-operate-transfer schemes (e.g., granting concession to a private company to build, finance, and operate, or subsequently transfer to the government, a new infrastructure project such as a bridge or tunnel).

Early cases of corporatisation preceded the launch of public sector reform, notably the MTRC and the KCRC, and the setting up of the Export Credit Insurance Corporation and Trade Development Council and Examinations Authority (now Examination and Assessment Authority) during the 1960s–1970s, as discussed in Chapter 2. The Housing Authority, though set up in 1973 as a statutory authority, was not in the same category because it had continued to rely on a government department (the Housing Department) to act as its executive arm and thus did not gain any benefits of corporatisation.

The first corporatisation influenced by this wave of public sector reform was the establishment of the government-financed Hospital Authority in December 1990 to manage all public hospitals (both government-owned and government-subvented) under a single corporatised body, largely following the recommendations of the 1985 Scott Consultancy Report.[25] The reorganisation of hospital medical services was a mammoth exercise entailing extensive and sensitive institutional and staff interests. What made it significant and interesting was not the managerial thinking driving this reorganisation (which was typical in the heyday of the emerging NPM ethos), but the subsequent capture of the originally administrator-initiated reform by medical professionals embracing managerialist language and strategies, who succeeded in a reverse takeover of the policy agency and formed a new 'medical managerial' class.[26] Such medical managerialism has since dominated the Hospital Authority system.

In stark contrast, the attempt to corporatise the public broadcaster Radio Television Hong Kong (RTHK) to make it independent from the core government, like the BBC in Britain, was a failure. The original proposal for corporatisation was based on the recommendations in the 1985 Broadcasting Review, which was conducted when the political climate was focused on the transition and when some editorial and news staff at RTHK were becoming more concerned about editorial freedom after 1997.[27] Such corporatisation was less a managerial reform induced by NPM and more driven by a political agenda for an independent RTHK. A political policy 'window' was narrowly opened but proved to be short-lived.[28] The Chinese government, ever suspicious of Britain's decolonisation motives to cut down the powers of the future SAR regime, was opposed to RTHK corporatisation. Within Hong Kong, even if the departing British administration saw the political advantage of such corporatisation, the demands from the staff side for maintaining existing civil servant terms and conditions after corporatisation proved to be too much of a 'having your cake and eating it too' bargain to be swallowed by the administrative mandarins who were still concerned about fiscal and parity implications.

Lastly, in the final years of British rule, the government set up an Airport Authority (AA), first as a provisional authority to oversee construction work for a new international airport at Chek Lap Kok (which opened in July 1998), and eventually to take over the airport management function from the Civil Aviation Department, leaving the latter as a statutory authority on aviation safety and air traffic control. In a way, the AA was modelled on the MTRC, with commercial prudence being its primary objective. Because of Beijing's suspicions of a British conspiracy to create independent empires out of the core government and dilute the powers of the succeeding SAR regime, the setting up of the AA was debated by the Sino-British Joint Liaison Group, and the final AA was a hybrid with the nomenclature of an 'Authority' rather than a corporation even though it would operate as a fully commercial entity no different from a government-owned public corporation.[29]

Trading funds

One of the initiatives of the 1989 Public Sector Reform document was the introduction of a new mode of 'trading funds' operated on a commercial and self-financing basis, borrowing from an established practice in Britain.[30] Since the passage of the Trading Fund Ordinance in March 1993, six trading funds had been established: the Companies Registry (August 1993), Land Registry (August 1993), Sewage Services (March 1994), Office of the Telecommunication Authority (June 1995), Post Office (August 1995), and Electrical and Mechanical Services (August 1996). Of these, only the Sewage Services Trading Fund was not created out of an existing department. Although still run by a civil-service workforce, trading funds were empowered both legislatively and administratively to adopt a more flexible and market-oriented (as well as customer-oriented) management framework. This was meant to enhance the impact of the economic forces of demand on the production and decision-making processes, and to spearhead a new culture of cost-effectiveness.

However, right from the beginning, the question of how trading funds should set their fees (e.g., the new sewerage charges) dominated legislative politics and public discussion. While the managers might have welcomed the new flexibilities, staff members were mostly concerned about job security and advancement given the trading fund's self-sufficiency through revenue generated by fee-charging services. Due to the lack of real competition from the market and of the power to freely determine their price levels based on costs or customer demands, most trading funds continued to operate as monopolies or near-monopolies, not fully sensitive to 'market' disciplines other than the need to meet financial targets set by the Finance Branch. The exceptions, to some extent, are the Post Office, which began to face pressure from private parcel delivery services, and the Electrical and Mechanical Services Trading Fund, which shifted modes when the government relaxed restrictions on departments making use of private maintenance service providers after a protection period of three years. At the same time, trading funds did not have genuine control over their operating costs because their staff was still made up of civil servants whose salaries as well as terms and conditions were dictated by the core government.

While trading funds enjoyed less government accounting and financial restrictions, could keep their surplus, and were no longer required to look to central agencies for budget resources or funds to finance redevelopment and further investment, they were also put in a business situation with high levels of vulnerability and uncertainty when the initial gain from 'freeing up' began to evaporate. Thus, the claimed merits of such trading funds in terms of management flexibilities, competition, and effectiveness in cost control and pricing were in doubt.[31] After a Finance Branch review in 1996, the government indicated that no more new trading funds would be set up in the foreseeable future. The Sewerage

Services Trading Fund was terminated in March 1998, soon after the change of administration, because of persistent legislative objection to raising sewage charges.

Continuation of public sector reform after 1997

After the transition from British rule, the new SAR government by and large continued with the inherited path of public sector reform. Target-based management was emphasised, with the objective to 'manage for results, by results'.[32] All departments were expected to produce performance pledges and provide the best possible services to the public. While the bureaucracy was generally regarded as efficient and effective before 1997, it began to face increasing scepticism and doubts as the economic climate and social sentiments shifted.

The 1998–1999 Asian financial crisis triggered the worst economic recession in Hong Kong in 30 years,[33] causing widespread company closures, lay-off of workers, and wage cutbacks. Administrative and policy blunders deepened public discontent and distrust—notably in the handling of the economy, unemployment, and the outbreak of avian flu and the severe acute respiratory syndrome (SARS) epidemic. Cases of civil servants' sleaziness and misconduct, repeatedly exposed by Audit Commission reports, reinforced a negative picture of a workforce previously highly acclaimed. There was growing public perception that the civil service was overpaid, given its rigid pay structure with salaries and allowances taking up 70–80% of recurrent government expenditure, at a time when ordinary employees suffered massive pay cuts. This backlash against the bureaucracy induced public sector reform of a different brand and subsequently led to the introduction of a new ministerial system and reform of the civil service (to be discussed in Chapters 5 and 6).

In contrast to the previous phase, public sector reform in the post-1997 era was grounded in some genuine concerns within the upper echelons of government and the broader community about efficiency. Table 3.3 highlights the more significant reform initiatives introduced from 1997 until most lately. While public sector reform remained active under the first and second Tung Chee-hwa Administrations, it was toned down from the Donald Tsang Administration onwards because of reform fatigue within the civil service and attention being diverted towards the more controversial issues of constitutional development by the government, political parties, and society at large.

Efficiency enhancement and civil service downsizing

In his 1999–2000 Budget Speech, then FS Donald Tsang pushed for an Enhanced Productivity Programme (EPP) among government departments and subvented agencies to cut operating expenditure by 5% in three years by 2002–2003, hoping that 'the public sector should take full advantage of the recession to strengthen

Table 3.3: Significant public sector reforms and events in Hong Kong since 1997

1997–2002 **(Tung Chee-hwa Administration, first-term)**	• Target-based Management Process (1997) • Enhanced Productivity Programme (1998) • Civil Service Reform (1999) • Target to reduce civil service establishment by 5% over two years from 2000–2001 • Step-by-Step Guide to Performance Measurement issued
2002–2005 **(Tung Chee-hwa Administration, second-term)**	• New executive accountability system for principal officials (or ministers) (2002) • Amalgamation of some policy bureaus and subordinate departments (in Education, Environment, and Housing) • Civil service pay reduction by phases to 1997 level (2003) • Review of civil service pay adjustment mechanism • Targets set for reducing civil service establishment • Voluntary Retirement Schemes (VRSs) for civil servants • Use of non-civil service contracts • Private Sector Involvement — including outsourcing and public-private partnerships • Envelope budgeting • '3Rs + 1M' (Reprioritising, Reorganising, Reengineering, and Market-friendly) as direction for public management reform • Partial privatisation of MTRC (2000) • Privatisation of retail and car park facilities in public housing estates via public listing of a dedicated real estate investment trust (REIT) (2004–2005) • Public consultation on partial privatisation of AA (2005)
2005–2007 and 2007–2012 **(Donald Tsang Administration, first and second terms)**	• Merger of MTRC and KCRC (2007) • Shelving of partial privatisation of AA • Unfreezing of civil service recruitment in certain grades (2007) • Completion of pay level survey and pay trend survey, as well as starting salaries review • Resumption of civil service recruitment • Resumption of civil service pay rise (2007) • 'Public Sector Reform Conference — Public Service 2020' (2010)
2012–2017 **(Leung Chun-ying Administration)**	• Signature Project Scheme launched for the purpose of enhancing local engagement and bottom-up role of DCs (2013) • Social Innovation and Entrepreneurship Development Fund launched (2013), along with a 'Shared Value' Initiative, to drive innovations in business that would benefit local communities (2015) • 'Serving the Evolving City' Conference (2017)
2017–present **(Carrie Lam Administration)**	• Transfer of EfU from CS's Office to Innovation and Technology Bureau, and renamed the Efficiency Office (2018) • Establishment of the Policy Innovation and Coordination Office (PICO) (2018) • Establishment of Civil Service College being planned

Source: Adapted from Table 2 of A.B.L. Cheung (2012a) 'One Country, Two Experiences: Administrative Reforms in China and Hong Kong', *International Review of Administrative Sciences*, Vol. 78, No. 2, pp. 261–283; updated.

its fundamentals'.[34] In principle, the EPP aimed at achieving productivity gains through efficiency savings in operating expenditure. In other words, it sought to enhance productivity without affecting the quality of service and then to reinvest the savings thus gained in priority areas. Departments were assisted by new flexible measures in the procurement and virement of funds and given the incentive through setting up 'Save & Invest Accounts' to port part of the efficiency savings which they could subsequently use for innovation and development.

At the same time, the civil service was streamlined and downsized to reduce recurrent expenditure. A Voluntary Retirement Scheme (VRS) was introduced, and departments were encouraged to make greater use of temporary staff and staff on non-civil service contracts who would cost less. A target of reducing the civil service establishment by 10,000 posts or 5% over two years was announced in the 2000–2001 Budget.[35] Then, in his 2003 Policy Address, Tung Chee-hwa set a higher target of cutting down the civil service establishment by 10% (to about 160,000 posts) by 2006–2007, complemented by two initiatives—a general recruitment freeze with effect from 1 April 2003 and a second VRS.[36] All departments were expected to re-engineer business processes, streamline service delivery, and increase private sector participation in the delivery of public services. The restriction on civil service recruitment was only relaxed after Tsang succeeded Tung as CE in 2005, having seen for himself the uproar among civil servants and their unions about the problems of contracting out and the proliferation of staff on non-civil service terms (see Chapter 6).

One-line budgeting and budgeting for results

Following the new efficiency logic, and to facilitate expenditure capping and fiscal discipline, budgeting of expenditure in money rather than real terms was enforced and a new 'operating expenditure envelope' system (a form of one-line budgeting) was introduced in the 2003–2004 Budget by Antony Leung who succeeded Tsang as FS in 2001. Policy secretaries were now given flexibility 'to deploy resources within their operating expenditure envelope, and may retain for future use part of the savings achieved'.[37] In the same vein, lump-sum grants were introduced earlier in 2001 for the government-subvented social welfare sector to replace the previous system of earmarked fixed-item funding. 'Doing more with less' was the new catchphrase.

That seemed in line with the global trend of budget reforms driven by NPM, where the thrust of the budget exercise rested less in the traditional negotiations between departments or bureaus and the Central Budget Agency (CBA) (in Hong Kong's case the Financial Services and Treasury Bureau, FSTB) but more in the budget 'pre-preparation' stage.[38] The FS, with the assistance of the CBA, would first determine and allocate to various bureaus a 'provisional' operating expenditure envelope to guide their preparation of the annual estimates. Like budget reforms elsewhere, the new budget language emphasised linking resource allocation to performance and policy results. Despite these reforms, budgetary relationships had not moved towards control by performance as implied by the 'budgeting for results' objective. Some previous research indicated that a genuine results-oriented approach had never taken off, in Hong Kong or Singapore (which was another public sector reform pioneer in Asia).[39]

While the Controlling Officer's Report accompanying the annual expenditure estimates provided performance information, it was more for presentation purposes and was rarely used to reach the yearly central resource allocation decisions made by the FS as advised by the FSTB's Treasury Branch. There were no apparent links between the composition of budgetary allocations and the spending departments' various performance indicators. The provisional and final budget envelopes given to policy secretaries primarily followed the historical spending levels of relevant bureaus and departments as incrementally adjusted, depending on the overall fiscal situation of the government which would dictate either cutback or growth targets.

The hard reality remains that funding allocations are more geared towards meeting external demands for services and policy interventions as well as internal bureaucratic competitive pressures, than being driven by departmental or bureau performance outcomes. In practice, it would be politically difficult if not counterproductive to slash the budget of under-performing departments whose work and service provision are considered of higher priority and greater urgency in the eyes of the public and legislators.[40]

Privatisation, contracting out, and private sector participation

Because of the economic slowdown and increasing fiscal deficits, the government soon required departments to actively pursue contracting out and private sector participation measures (such as out-sourcing management and operations) to 'do more with less' and improve productivity. The 1999–2000 Budget identified the 'privatisation of public corporations' and 'rethinking the mode of delivering public services' as major reform directions.[41] In the event, there was only a narrow range of privatisations.

In 2000, the Housing Authority implemented a phased transfer of estate management and maintenance services to private firms or staff-initiated 'management buy-out' companies. Also in that year, the first divestment of public assets was launched with the partial privatisation of the MTRC, involving the sale of no more than half of its shares by stages through public offering to local and overseas investors.[42] In his 2003–2004 Budget Speech, to make up for the shortage of revenue, Antony Leung announced that the government would sell and securitise a total of HK$112 billion worth of public assets in the next five years.[43] Another major privatisation of government assets was the divestiture of the Housing Authority's retail and parking facilities in public housing estates. This involved the government setting up a new company, the Link Limited. Injecting such assets into the Link, which would own and manage the facilities, would allow them to then divest 100% of the government ownership by way of public listing as a real estate investment trust (REIT) to both institutional and retail investors. Because of some public housing tenants challenging the divestment through judicial review, the final listing of Link-REIT was delayed until mid-2005.

In the 2004–2005 Budget Speech, Henry Tang, who succeeded Leung as FS in 2003, also announced the intention to partially privatise the AA and the merger of the two railway corporations (MTRC and KCRC) within 2005–2006.[44] The legislation enabling the rail merger was eventually enacted in July 2007, but the plan to privatise AA was shelved partly because of the improved fiscal condition during the second Donald Tsang Administration (2007–2012) but more crucially due to the central government's concern about putting a strategic facility of immense importance to Hong Kong's as well as China's aviation and economic life in private hands.

The consequence of the rail merger was the monopolisation of Hong Kong's heavy rail, light rail, and underground railway systems by one company which was publicly listed (hence private in nature) though nominally controlled by the government as majority shareholder (with some 77% shares). A decade after the merger, what has been observed is that instead of securing the 'best of both worlds', Hong Kong might be experiencing the 'worst of both worlds'—a mammoth public transport monopoly majority-owned by government and favoured by the government's public transport policy, and yet beyond government control in fares (with automatic annual fare increases under a formula-driven fare adjustment mechanism even when making handsome profits).[45] In a similar vein, the privatisation and public listing of the bulk of retail and parking assets in public housing estates through the Link-REIT also resulted in unanticipated 'alienation', going against the originally rather innocent objective to create a commercially efficient operator of facilities still primarily geared towards serving the public housing neighbourhoods.[46]

The Donald Tsang Administration initiated another review on the status of RTHK in January 2006 through an independent committee on public service broadcasting (PSB). The option of corporatisation was again raised but suffered a similar fate as the pre-1997 attempt because of staff side insistence on keeping civil servant terms and conditions.[47] Many of the existing tensions between RTHK and the government have come from its status as a civil-service department, creating almost irreconcilable expectations on both sides—with government mandarins expecting it to behave like any other department and RTHK's managers and producers wanting more autonomy and freedom. Corporatisation would have provided a more sustainable solution to this dilemma but could not proceed without the buy-in of RTHK management and staff. However, it should be added that corporatisation cannot guarantee the absence of politicisation. As studies show, the independence of PSB has become a pressing issue even across European democracies. There is growing evidence of varying degrees of state-PSB tensions, political control, ideological interventions, or partisan domination, especially in less liberal Central and Eastern European states.[48]

Reform fatigue and slowdown in the 2000s

By the time of Donald Tsang's second term as CE in 2007, both the civil service as well as the wider public sector were dealing with widespread reform fatigue. The rebound in the economy and return to fiscal surplus helped ease the way for tuning down public sector reform. Softer forms of service improvement and innovation continued to be pursued—such as the emphasis on delivering higher quality, better value and citizen-centric services to the community; strengthening local engagement; improving public communication and handling public enquiries; and better use of public data at the level of individual bureaus and departments within the broad framework of 'serving the community'.

In the aftermath of the global financial crisis in 2008–2009, there was a suggestion that the previous supremacy of neo-liberalism hitherto driving globalisation and NPM had faced a collapse, with the world entering a post-NPM era where no new direction in administrative reform was in sight. Some have observed a growing trend to consider NPM as 'dead'.[49] So far, the post-NPM idea has been deployed more as an 'ideational weapon' to indicate a crisis of the NPM model than providing a specific blueprint for future reform. Others still see global capitalism (hence neo-liberalism) as an impactful force, particularly on global value chains.[50] Neo-liberal thought is far from being in retreat. Putting such debates aside, it seems clear that the downside of previous NPM reforms has been more widely felt in the current reform discourse—such as 'agencification' (resulting in more fragmentation of government), customer responsiveness (leading to less concern about citizens' political rights), and output-based performance (at the expense of process-based accountability). Emphasis has moved towards networks and citizen engagement, as well as better coordination, effectiveness, and responsiveness in governance.[51]

Against such a decline in NPM novelty, it is not surprising that there has been less interest in NPM and little enthusiasm for more public sector reforms in Hong Kong over the past decade, whether inside or outside the government. Instead, the whole of society has been embroiled in political reform debates and conflicts over the issues of democracy and election of the CE by universal suffrage. Politics, not public administration reforms, have dominated the public discourse. The changing focus of the EfU's work, before it was downgraded in 2018, reflected this shift.[52] The 'Public Sector Reform Conference—Public Service 2020' organised in November 2010 notably challenged participants to consider how the public service could adapt over the next decade to changes in demand from an ageing population, increasing automation and electronic business, expectations of improving services, and constitutional development.

To enhance local engagement as part of CE Leung Chun-ying's election manifesto, the government introduced the Signature Project Scheme in 2013. Under this scheme, a one-off grant of HK$100 million was earmarked for each district to implement one to two projects (works or non-works in nature), with the District Council (DC) responsible for advocating and deciding such projects, as well as spearheading their implementation. Also in 2013, a Social Innovation and Entrepreneurship Development Fund was established, with the EfU providing support to the Commission on Poverty to develop innovative approaches to creating opportunity and helping to address poverty and deprivation in the community. In September 2015, the Fund launched the 'Shared Value' Initiative to drive innovations in business firms that would bring business return while simultaneously advancing the economic, environmental, and social conditions in the communities where they operate. A growing emphasis was being placed on social innovation, trade facilitation, and partnership with business.

At the 'Serving the Evolving City' Conference organised by the EfU in January 2017, participants from across the public service, including ministerial officials, discussed how the public service could rise to the challenges faced by adapting to complexity and building up capabilities. Future prospective reform possibilities would focus on collective impact, knowledge sharing, and social innovation and capacity building.[53] Under the current Carrie Lam Administration, the EfU was transferred from the Chief Secretary for Administration's Office to the Innovation and Technology Bureau and renamed the Efficiency Office in April 2018, incorporating the Business Facilitation Division under the Economic Analysis and Business Facilitation Unit of the FS's Office. It will continue to be a change agent and catalyst for improving the management and delivery of public services, to make them more user-friendly and effective.[54] Similarly, Lam also revamped the Central Policy Unit into the Policy Innovation and Co-ordination Office (PICO).[55]

The politics and limits of public sector reform

Hong Kong's public sector reform experience in the 1990s did not fit the Western NPM route which spun off from an efficiency crisis of the state and related factors—such as government oversize, macroeconomic and fiscal crises, New Right ideology, and party-political incumbency in favour of cutbacks.[56] Hong Kong had not encountered any prolonged economic or fiscal crisis, nor did it face a collapse of the old public administration regime as observed in some Western countries.[57] Government overload was not a problem given the relatively low level of public expenditure (historically not exceeding 20% of GDP). On the contrary, there had been persistent demands for more public services provision and intervention over the years. The efficiency paradigm of public sector reform elsewhere did not appeal much whether to the local bureaucracy or the public at large because of the government's good reputation for being efficient and effective. Indeed, many in government were initially sceptical of reform.[58] Outside government, some criticised it for not pursuing political reforms and instead focusing on management reforms.

Any trace of following the global NPM fashion could at best be regarded as policy learning or 'bandwagoning' (i.e., using methods made popular by external practice to help achieve domestic ends or legitimise an agenda to address a domestic problem).[59] The domestic agenda was to do with the macro-political changes in the city's transition towards 1997, which resulted in the decline of the political authority and relative autonomy of the British administration. Meanwhile, the expansion and growing organisational complexity of the public sector, amidst a turbulent and pluralist environment of public policy and public services, had also created problems of policy leadership and coordination within the pre-existing structure last revamped during the McKinsey reforms of the 1970s. Public sector reform could be construed as a managerial strategy to restore the power of the policy centre through further devolution of management functions and 'letting go' to re-rationalise relationships in the changing context of both external and internal governance during the late transition period.[60]

A shift towards the microeconomic notion of efficiency in service provision as justified by NPM rhetoric helped to depoliticise performance evaluation of the public sector and enable a reinvention of bureaucratic power under the new managerial image.[61] In a sense, such reform represented a 'bureau-shaping strategy', as articulated by Patrick Dunleavy, in contrast with the hitherto assumption of 'budget-maximising' bureaucratic behaviour.[62] It would require policy bureaus to have their policy and resource-control powers fully legitimated as policy managers in exchange for granting managerial and micro-budgetary autonomies to departmental managers as executive agents. The re-delineation of the branch- or bureau-department relationship as principal versus agent under NPM also supported the further 'ministerialisation' of the administrative-class civil servants.[63]

Hong Kong was not the only exceptional case within the global NPM experience. In reality, the global trend had never been a simplistic journey of international convergence.[64] While there might appear to be some kind of commonality in terms of reform rhetoric and the generalised ends of reform (such as better performance and greater efficiency), the means employed to pursue these ends were of considerable variety in both locus and focus depending on the history, politics, and institutional features of the countries concerned. There was no single source of reform ideas and motives, and no single reform path or set of practices. Opportunities, expectations, agenda-crafting, and reactions vary among different systems. Even among the OECD countries, there was diversity in the emphases as well as main approaches to reform their public sectors in the 1990s.[65]

Reform terminology used across countries varies significantly, or sometimes similar terminology may disguise very different reforms.[66]

There existed two myths about NPM — that it was efficiency-driven and that it was anti-bureaucratic.[67] If one looks back into the history of public administration, we can in fact trace an over-a-century-long trajectory of pursuit of efficiency, from the Weberian mode of bureaucratic organisation and scientific management in the early twentieth century, through post-War nationalisations in Europe and the New Deal and Big Society reforms in the US, towards critiquing the pathologies of bureaucracies and government overload, and eventually a disowning of traditional government, with a replacement logic of privatisation as the key to better government.[68] The 'newness' of NPM was not its central themes of efficiency and managerial competence, but rather the 'new' political and ideological contexts in which such themes were being re-articulated and given new meaning and legitimation on the reform agenda for better governance. The first wave of onslaught on the bureaucracy that underpinned Big Government came in the 1970s in the form of privatisation in response to the then fiscal crisis of the state. By the time of NPM, the logic of reform had changed. As a reform strategy, NPM could be viewed as rather more pro-public sector than commonly presumed because it sought to transform the public sector into more commercial-like entities in the face of the attack by the New Right ideology and the logic of the market and privatisation ('if you can't beat it, join it'). In the US, this led to the advent of government 'reinvention'.[69] It was what Patrick Dunleavy explained as 'bureau-shaping' strategy.

As pointed out by some academic observers, NPM in practice continued to fall short of expectations and aspirations.[70] There were always tensions between politicians (presidents or prime ministers, political officials) and public servants and among agencies over the distribution of power, resources, and policy influence (as some agencies gain while others suffer from some reforms) — hence, the institutional and organisational politics of reform and the proliferation of various reform hybrids combining different theoretical and practical elements.[71] Obstacles and resistance to reform arise not just from pre-existing conditions but also from new arenas of contestations emerging from the way reform is agendised and implemented. Reforms induced by global trends cannot avoid being 'domesticated' by local institutional legacies and political and bureaucratic practice. In the real world, all reform junctures comprise elements of both preservation (hence resistance to change) and innovation or renovation, and the resulting reform journey has always been a process of rebalancing.[72] Incremental but accumulative reforms are less alarming than revolutionary mega-changes, thus more susceptible to strategic compromise and consensus-building.

In the institutional literature, two 'orthodox rhetorics' of administrative reorganisation can be identified — the rhetoric of administration (about the design of administrative structures and procedures to facilitate the efficiency and effectiveness of bureaucratic hierarchies) and the rhetoric of realpolitik (speaking of reorganisation in terms of a political struggle among contending interests).[73] Following the latter rhetoric, public sector reform in the pre-1997 Hong Kong context can be interpreted as a process of re-legitimation of public bureaucratic power, both for managerial and political considerations. Post-1997, reform can still be construed within the same administrative reform paradigm as that of the late colonial period, whereby administrative restructuring and redefinition of institutional relationships helped re-empower the administrative bureaucracy within a changing and socially more politicised setting.[74] The underlying political agenda of the bureaucratic elite was to strengthen its crisis-weathering capacity. Thus, it was, fairly or unfairly, criticised as a reform exercise targeted mostly at the bottom rather than the top. Such managerial solutions, however, failed to deal with a looming political crisis that underpinned the growing public discontent towards the government's overall performance.

Some have argued that NPM reforms in all countries were initiated in reaction to current political (and institutional) challenges, with NPM being packaged as modernisation strategies (from the NPM tool-box) in response to perceived challenges. Indeed, this kind of supply-and-demand explanation of NPM can be applied to Hong Kong.[75] During the pre-1997 transition, public sector reform was typical of reforms by bureaucrats for bureaucrats through bureaucrats, as was also the case in Singapore, for example, where a pro-state and pro-bureaucracy ethos continued to dominate such reforms.[76] Post-1997, new political crises confronting the SAR regime and the changing relationship between the CE and senior civil servants induced the advent of a different kind of 'public service bargain'[77] in stark contrast to the pre-1997 bargain dominated by the bureaucrats. Other interests, both inside and outside government, had their own motives in reforming the public sector, shaping the process and fate of civil service reform.

PART II

TRANSITION AND CHANGE

Chapter 4
Regime Transition and Institutional Changes

Introduction

In pursuit of Hong Kong's reunification with the motherland, Beijing's leadership went a long way to emphasise the preservation of Hong Kong's existing way of life and capitalist economy, and promised a 'One Country, Two Systems' framework whereby Hong Kong people could practice a high degree of autonomy and self-administration with freedoms and separate legal and other relevant jurisdictions protected.[1] It hoped to restore confidence among both investors and ordinary residents, rich and poor.

China also had to obtain British cooperation to reduce uncertainty and ensure a smooth transition. As said in the Introduction to this book, during Sino-British negotiations, Britain was at first keen to keep Hong Kong under British administration of some kind, explaining to the Chinese side the importance of retaining their administrative role in the system prevailing in Hong Kong. It was only when it became clear that the continuation of British administration after 1997 would not be acceptable to China in any form did Britain propose that the two sides discuss on a conditional basis what effective measures other than continued British administration might be devised to maintain the stability and prosperity of Hong Kong.[2] While Britain only agreed to enter into a joint declaration upon satisfaction that the essentials of the existing system would be safeguarded, there seemed no illusion on its part that returning Hong Kong to China under a negotiated deal was the only viable (and preferred) option on the city's future.[3]

In the name of continuity and stability, what the Chinese government would like to receive and retain, after reunification in July 1997, was an administrative state in Hong Kong that would: be executive-led, not legislature-led; ensure central-state supremacy similar to that of London under British administration; and continue to exercise administrative pragmatism unaffected by ideological or partisan inclinations or narrow class interests. To meet such expectations, the best form of government would seem to be a government by career bureaucrats selected on merit, not held ransom by political parties or sectoral interests.

Preparations for political and constitutional changes

Once China and Britain came to an agreement on the future of Hong Kong, by way of a Joint Declaration initialled by the two governments in September 1984 and signed in December that year, Hong Kong had officially entered the period of 'transition'. On its part, the British administration began to plan for decolonisation and the gradual devolution of power to local institutions. Apart from electoral changes in the attempt to develop representative government, other significant British moves included: the enactment of a Bill of Rights in 1990; the establishment of a COMAC in 1989 (as precursor to the future Ombudsman); and the (aborted) attempt to corporatise RTHK. It was ironic that while an Ombudsman and a Bill of Rights were considered unnecessary and inappropriate by the colonial administration in the past, they became accepted by the late 1980s as crucial to ensuring accountable governance and protection of citizen's rights.

The localisation of senior appointments was also sped up in the late transition period. However, the key posts critical to British administration remained held by British officers until the final years. The first local Chinese Commissioner of Police was appointed in 1989. Anson Chan was the first local Chinese appointed as the SCS in April 1993 and soon afterwards as CS in November 1993. In 1995, Donald Tsang was the first local Chinese appointed as FS and Peter Lai to the sensitive post of Secretary for Security. The post of Attorney General continued to be occupied by a British officer (Jeremy Matthews) until the last hour of British rule. While local AOs and other members of the senior civil service had served the British government loyally, this should not be taken to mean that racial prejudice had disappeared entirely from the colonial establishment.[4]

As the British decolonisation plan proceeded, the Chinese government started the process of drawing up the Basic Law of the future Hong Kong SAR, based mainly on Annex I of the Joint Declaration, which set out China's basic policies. Under such policies, the Hong Kong SAR would be vested with executive, legislative, and independent judicial power, including that of final adjudication. Both the government and legislature would be composed of local inhabitants. The CE would be selected by election or through consultations held locally and be appointed by the Central People's Government (CPG), while Principal Officials (equivalent to 'Secretaries') would be nominated by the CE for appointment by the CPG. The legislature would be constituted by elections, with the executive authorities accountable to it. Judges would be appointed by the CE acting in accordance with the recommendation of an independent commission; and judges from other common law jurisdictions could be invited as required to sit on the Court of Final Appeal (CFA).

The drafting of the Basic Law began in 1985 with the establishment of the Basic Law Drafting Committee and Basic Law Consultative Committee.[5] Between 1986 and 1990, seven versions of draft Basic Law provisions were considered by the Drafting Committee before the Final Draft was presented to the NPC for approval.[6] When approving the Basic Law on 4 April 1990, the NPC also made respective decisions on the establishment of the Hong Kong SAR on 1 July 1997, on the methods for the formation of the First Government and First LegCo of the Hong Kong SAR, and on the establishment of a Basic Law Committee under the Standing Committee of the NPC (NPCSC).[7] The formation of the First Government and First LegCo was based on the then consensus reached with the British side about the smooth transition, as if a through train, of the pre-1997 government and legislature to become the first-term government and legislature of the SAR.[8]

Between the Chinese and British governments, a Joint Liaison Group was set up in accordance with Annex II of the Joint Declaration, for the period from 1 July 1988 until 1 January 2000, to consult on and oversee the implementation of the Joint Declaration and smooth transfer of government in 1997 and to resolve any ensuing issues and problems. The Joint Liaison Group was an organ for liaison and not of power, and it could set up sub-groups to deal with specific matters. As Hong Kong got closer to the date of reversion to Chinese sovereignty, more issues and differences were requiring intensive consultations and proper resolution, such as major infrastructure projects straddling 1997, like the construction of a new international airport and the extension of Hong Kong's prevailing treaties and external relations. Under Annex III of the Joint Declaration, a joint Land Commission was also set up to provide consultations on land lease issues and the observance of an annual limit of 50 hectares of new land (excluding land for public rental housing) that might be granted by the British administration for terms beyond June 1997 but expiring not later than 30 June 2047. While there was never meant to be any 'co-rule' during the transition period, it was clear that significant issues affecting Hong Kong's future and well-being, including pertinent issues of convergence, would be subject to Sino-British consultations.

In the initial years of transition, there were frequent rows between the two sides, especially concerning constitutional development. Britain had initially sought to develop a form of representative government locally to whom power would gradually be transferred, but China insisted on any constitutional changes to 'converge' with the Basic Law to be drafted by China as its internal affairs. China also demanded that the power of rule (including administrative power) be first transferred to it as the sovereign authority, which would, in turn, be devolved to the future SAR government according to the Basic Law. Then Chinese leader Deng Xiaoping had categorically instructed the Drafting Committee at the outset that the Western doctrine of separation of power or parliamentary government was appropriate neither for China nor the future Hong Kong SAR.[9] He further insisted that the People's Liberation Army (PLA) had to station a garrison in Hong Kong as a symbol of China's sovereignty over the territory and to prevent any social unrest.[10]

The British attempt at a representative government

British decolonisation in other colonies had all worked towards devolving power to the local population and their elected leaders via self-government and then full independence. In the process, the British would groom the future local leaders. Hong Kong's unique constitutional development path, however, could only lead to 'decolonisation without independence'.[11] The impossibility of ultimate independence precluded the transfer of the Westminster model to Hong Kong. Indeed, it was observed that the successor regime (i.e., the Chinese government) would view any significant political change during the transition with suspicious eyes, and any major constitutional reforms initiated unilaterally by the departing British administration would be short-lived and replaced by another executive-centred system of government bent on 're-centralisation' and 're-dependence on the bureaucracy'.[12] In a way, the 'China factor' had always been the primary concern of British colonial rule whereby the local government had to respect China's political interests.[13]

Still, there were three rounds of political reforms by the British administration. The first round took place relatively early on as Britain prepared to enter into formal negotiations with China on the future of Hong Kong following Governor Murray MacLehose's trip to Beijing in 1979. As previously discussed in Chapter 2, in 1982, this took the rudimentary form of district-level advisory democracy through the introduction of District Boards.[14] The second round came just before the conclusion of the 1984 Sino-British Joint Declaration, in the form of the further development of representative government—now rationalised as a three-tier system (i.e., district boards, municipal councils, and LegCo)—under the Green Paper and White Paper of 1984.[15] The third round was the electoral reform package announced by Governor Chris Patten in his maiden policy address in October 1992, after the Basic Law was already promulgated, aimed at enlarging the range of LegCo seats elected by some form of popular franchise.[16]

The 1984 Green Paper on representative government aimed 'to develop progressively a system of government the authority for which is firmly rooted in Hong Kong'.[17] Drastic changes were proposed to the system of government, except the office of the Governor. Indirect elections were to be introduced to the LegCo through an electoral college comprising all elected and appointed members of the two municipal councils (Urban Council and Regional Council) and District Boards to represent geographical constituencies, as well as several functional constituencies to represent traditionally recognised business and professional sectors (law, medicine, engineering, architecture, education, and social service) plus a labour constituency of trade unions to represent grassroots employees. These indirectly elected members would, however, only constitute a minority of the legislature (12 out of 48 seats). Direct elections on universal franchise were mentioned but were not yet considered appropriate because they 'would run the risk of a swift introduction of adversarial politics, and would introduce an element of instability at a crucial time'.[18] Both appointed and official members would remain in LegCo, whose numbers would gradually dwindle. Table 4.1 gives the details of the proposals.

As for the ExCo, it was proposed that by 1991 at least eight of its unofficial members should be elected by the unofficial members of the LegCo, who would then form the majority. This was to extend the representative status of the ExCo and to establish a more direct relationship between the ExCo and LegCo. The possibility of allowing unofficial members of the ExCo and LegCo to assume ministerial functions was mentioned but not proposed to be pursued. It is obvious from such proposed arrangements that the British administration was keen to pave the way for some form of quasi-parliamentary government to emerge once power was transferred to the local people, along a route similar to post-War British decolonisation processes elsewhere. This alarmed the Chinese government, and they firmly insisted that there should be 'convergence' with the future Basic Law in any constitutional changes undertaken by the British side.[19] Later, at the meeting of the Sino-British Joint Liaison Group, the British side accepted the need for convergence.

The subsequent White Paper released in November 1984 presented a set of watered-down proposals. While still preserving the original aims of progressively developing a system of representative government more directly accountable to the people of Hong Kong and firmly rooted in Hong Kong, and agreeing to bring forward from 1988 to 1985 an increased number of elected seats in the LegCo, the British administration had dropped its more sensitive proposals regarding the ExCo, saying that 'no conclusions have been reached about the development of the Executive Council, nor about the introduction of a ministerial system and these matters will be considered at a later stage'.[20] Of the new LegCo membership of 57, there were to be 10 government officials, 22 unofficial members appointed by the Governor, 12 members elected by an electoral college of District Board members, and another 12 elected by functional constituencies of mainly conventional business and professional sectors. The officials together with appointed unofficials constituted a majority.

Nonetheless, the White Paper promised to undertake a review on the development of representative government in 1987, prior to the 1988 LegCo elections. The subsequent Green Paper on the review was issued in May 1987, regarding the functions and composition of the three tiers of representative government and whether the Governor should continue to be the LegCo president. The most eye-catching proposals related to the composition. Four options were put forward: no change to the existing number and relative proportions of official, appointed, and indirectly elected members; ruling out direct elections; some element of direct elections being desirable but not to be introduced in 1988; and direct elections desirable for 1988.[21] While the pro-democracy coalition campaigned hard for direct elections in 1988, the business sector was sceptical, worrying that direct elections would bring about welfare politics. Chinese government officials expressed grave reservations, insisting that any significant electoral changes should converge with the future Basic Law to ensure a smooth transition in 1997.[22]

Table 4.1: Proposed distribution of LegCo seats

	Existing	1985	1988	1991
Elected by electoral college	0	6	12	14 (20[a])
Elected by functional constituencies	0	6	12	14 (20[a])
Appointed by the Governor	29	23	16	12 (0[a])
Official members	18	13	10	10
Total	47	48	50	50

Source: Adapted from paras. 43 and 45 of Hong Kong Government (1984b), *Green Paper: The Further Development of Representative Government in Hong Kong*, Hong Kong: Government Printer.

[a] Subject to review in 1989, the number of appointed unofficial members might be reduced or completely removed, with the released seats distributed equally between the electoral college and functional constituencies.

Pro-Beijing groups suspected there was a British conspiracy and opposed the universal suffrage proposal, with the Hong Kong Federation of Trade Unions (FTU) saying that workers would 'rather want a meal ticket than a ballot ticket'.

A Survey Office was set up by the government to collect public opinion on the Green Paper.[23] The White Paper published in February 1988 concluded that while there was wide public support for the principle of introducing some directly elected members to the LegCo, the community was divided over the timing of such a move.[24] It thus proposed that 10 members of the LegCo would be directly elected in 1991, one from each of 10 district-based constituencies. It further acknowledged the necessity for continuing development between 1991 and 1997, and the need to enable Hong Kong's system of government to evolve in a way that was compatible with both the aspirations of the Hong Kong community and the framework to be set out in the Basic Law.[25] Later, in the aftermath of the 1989 Tiananmen crackdown on pro-democracy movement in China, which caused huge political anxieties and a crisis of confidence in Hong Kong's future, the British administration decided, with Beijing's tacit consent, to expand the number of directly elected members in 1991 from 10 to 18, to be returned by nine double-seat geographical constituencies.

As mentioned in Chapter 1, the LegCo was given more powers with the passage of the Legislative Council (Powers and Privileges) Ordinance in 1985. The LegCo Chamber was moved from Central Government Offices to occupy the former Supreme Court Building in the same year to underscore its independence from the Administration,[26] even though the Governor continued to be the LegCo President until 1993.[27] In 1986, with the arrival of the first batch of elected LegCo members, the former UMELCO was renamed 'OMELCO' or the Office of Members of the Executive and Legislative Councils. LegCo later decided to set up its own system of policy panels to monitor the Administration. In 1993, following the membership separation of the ExCo and LegCo, the OMELCO was further renamed 'OMLECO' (Office of Members of the Legislative Council), to reflect that the support services of the Secretariat were provided to LegCo members only. In 1994, the Legislative Council Commission was established under the Legislative Council Commission Ordinance, to provide administrative support and services to the LegCo through the LegCo Secretariat with its own recruited staff (replacing seconded civil servants).[28]

Patten's political reforms

The 1989 Tiananmen tragedy caused an international shock and induced a change in British strategy towards the return of Hong Kong to China. After losing his Bath seat in the 1992 British parliamentary elections, Chris Patten was given the Governorship by Prime Minister John Major. Upon arrival in Hong Kong, he announced a string of new electoral arrangements in his October 1992 inaugural policy address, presented as bold attempts at widening the electoral franchise and democratising Hong Kong as much as possible before an honourable British departure.

The more significant changes were: lowering the minimum voting age from 21 to 18; abolishing all appointed seats on the District Boards and two municipal councils; broadening the franchise of certain existing functional constituencies, mainly those of the professions, by replacing corporate voting by individual voting; creating nine 'New Functional Constituency' seats with much larger electorates of ordinary employees amounting to some 2.7 million people; and forming an Election Committee of all District Board members to return 10 members to the LegCo.[29] By granting franchise to employees of occupational groupings, Patten in effect sought to turn the 'new' functional constituencies into quasi-direct elections on popular franchise. No wonder once he came up with such idea, there were demands from the pro-democracy camp for allowing housewives, students, and the unemployed to have a vote as well.

Beijing was furious with Patten and adamant that his New Functional Constituencies were contradictory to the Basic Law and previous diplomatic understanding reached between the two governments via an exchange of letters. Hong Kong politics became deeply polarised, with some pro-democracy figures even calling for ignoring the necessity for convergence with the Basic Law provisions. Chinese officials warned that should the LegCo be elected according to Patten's proposals in 1995, then it could not enjoy a full four-year term straddling 1997 as originally envisaged under the 'through-train' arrangement to ensure maximum continuity and 'convergence'. Britain and China then entered into negotiations, but after 17 rounds of such talks, they failed to reach any agreement.

Eventually, Patten put his reform proposals to a vote in the LegCo, which were marginally passed with the support of pro-democracy legislators. Meanwhile, China decided to plan for unilateral actions (described as 'setting up a second stove', 另 起爐灶) in the face of British non-cooperation and the derailment of the 'through-train'.[30] Later on, China found it necessary to establish a Provisional LegCo to assume power under the Basic Law on 1 July 1997, using the same Selection Committee established by the SAR Preparatory Committee (set up by the NPC in January 1996) to select the first CE. During its one-year tenure, the Provisional LegCo annulled the most controversial elements of Patten's reforms, including the abolition of the nine New Functional Constituencies and restoration of corporate voting for some traditional functional seats. Appointed members were reintroduced to the district boards and municipal councils. Proportional representation was adopted as the method for LegCo multi-seat geographical elections, replacing the 'first past the post' method used for single-seat constituencies in 1995.

Other political changes introduced by Patten included: separation of membership between the ExCo and LegCo; Governor's Question Time in LegCo sittings modelled on Prime Minister's Question Time in the British Parliament; and driving policy secretaries to behave more like political ministers lobbying legislators and political parties to get policies and bills approved. During his term, a Code of Access to Information and Performance Pledges were also introduced to promote freedom of information and responsiveness in public services. British archival records recently declassified show that around 1994, Patten had considered setting up a Human Rights Commission which was supported by pro-democracy parties and legislators, but subsequently did not proceed further because of the concern about a strong reaction from the Chinese government.[31]

During the transition period, China co-opted more local business and professional elites and community leaders into its network of advisory bodies—such as the Chinese People's Political Consultative Conference (CPPCC) at both national and provincial/local levels, the SAR Preparatory Committee and the preceding Preliminary Working Committee, and Hong Kong Affairs Advisers. The pro-Beijing camp had become a formidable political force, especially with the establishment of their own political parties, notably the flagship Democratic Alliance for the Betterment of Hong Kong (DAB) in July 1992 (later renamed Democratic Alliance for the Betterment and Progress of Hong Kong after absorbing the Hong Kong Progressive Alliance, anther pro-Beijing party, in 2005). Meanwhile, in the tug of war for political affiliation and loyalty, the departing Britain administration under Patten sought to maintain some kind of political balance of power by courting and counting on the support of pro-democracy politicians and organisations.[32]

The Basic Law constitutional design

The political design for the future SAR governance was a major controversy between Hong Kong and Beijing as well as among different political camps within Hong Kong. Chapter 10 will give a fuller account of the intricacies and debates involved, while this section outlines the basic constitutional structure. Under the political design of the Basic Law approved by the NPC in April 1990, the CE (replacing the Governor) was to remain as powerful and dominating as in colonial governance, while the legislature was given an independent status constitutionally on the same level as the executive but with lesser powers of initiation and check-and-balance compared to a US-type presidential system. Judicial independence was enhanced with the power of final adjudication entrenched locally.

The CE

Under Article 43 of the Basic Law, the CE is the head of the SAR and its government, essentially inheriting all the powers of the previous colonial governor, and is accountable to both the CPG and the SAR. An Election Committee elects the CE.[33] The powers of the CE include those: to conduct external affairs on behalf of the SAR as authorised by the central authorities; to nominate principal officials for appointment by the CPG; to appoint members of the ExCo; to appoint judges subject to the advice of the Judicial Services Commission (while the appointment and removal of judges of the CFA and Chief Judge of the High Court are also subject to legislative endorsement); to appoint holders of all public offices, either directly or under delegation; to decide on government policies and issue executive orders; and to grant pardon to convicted persons.

The practice of the Governor-in-Council has continued as CE-in-Council, but the Basic Law also provides that the CE can ignore the majority advice of the ExCo (Article 56). If so, they have to put the specific reasons on record but do not have to report to the CPG, in contrast to the previous colonial requirement for the Governor to report to the Secretary of State in London when advice from the ExCo was refused. The previous system of establishing advisory bodies by the executive authorities is retained (Article 65), as is the system of 'District Organisations' (i.e., municipal councils and district boards) (Articles 97–98). 'Principal Officials' (all the Secretaries plus the heads of Police, Immigration, Customs and Excise, and the ICAC) are placed under the category of 'Public Servants' (Chapter IV, Section 6), underscoring the original intent of keeping them as civil service postings in line with colonial practice. Such wholesale inheritance of autocratic powers of the British period led some to conclude that the SAR system of government under the Basic Law political design was still a form of executive authoritarianism or at best a semi-democracy or authoritarian democracy.[34]

Although the separation-of-power doctrine was not enshrined in the Basic Law, one can argue that by emphasising the separate formation of the executive authorities (headed by the CE) and the legislature, with neither being subservient to the other, as well as the independence of the judiciary, there was, for the first time in Hong Kong's constitutional design, the essence of separation of power. Unlike the British Governor being concurrently the Commander-in-Chief of the British Forces, the CE has no command over the Chinese army garrison in the

SAR, even though they could request the central government for the garrison's assistance in the maintenance of public order and in disaster relief (Article 14).

The LegCo

The LegCo was to be constituted by elections—geographical direct election, functional constituency election, and (until 2004) electoral college election.[35] The idea of functional constituencies was borrowed from the British administration which first introduced such constituencies selectively in 1985 to give franchise to those traditional professions who in the colonial past were targets of co-optation through appointment into the ExCo and LegCo. With the central government resisting outright democracy on universal suffrage and desiring preservation of the more conservative functional interests as the mainstay of the SAR legislature, the logic of functional representation was played up as more conducive to economic prosperity and stability. Because of the large number of seats allotted to functional constituencies, such logic had to be further stretched so that more professional and occupational sectors would be identified outside the traditional elites, such as the tourism and retail industries.

Article 64 of the Basic Law confines how the government is accountable to the legislature in four specific aspects: implementing laws passed by the LegCo and already in force; presenting regular policy addresses to the LegCo; answering questions raised by the LegCo members; and obtaining approval from the LegCo for taxation and public expenditure. Article 74 curbs legislative power by disallowing legislators individually or jointly to move any bills affecting public expenditure or political structure or the operation of government, while the written consent of the CE is required before any bills relating to government policies can be introduced by them. The split-voting method, whereby the passage of any non-government bills and motions requires the double majority of both functionally and geographically elected legislators (as opposed to a simple majority of the whole membership for government bills and motions), makes it hard for legislators to exercise the power of initiation. The LegCo could still block government-initiated legislation or finance bills if legislators manage to act in unison. In other words, while the LegCo could not propose, it could exercise its veto power to force the government into compromise, unless the government commands enough legislative support from pro-establishment parties and legislators.

In stark contrast to the previous irremovable position of the colonial governor (who served at the pleasure of the Crown), Articles 49–52 of the Basic Law provide a mechanism to resolve any constitutional deadlock should there arise major disagreement between the CE and LegCo. If the CE considers a bill passed by the LegCo not compatible with the overall interest of the SAR, they may return it to the LegCo within three months for reconsideration. If the LegCo passes the original bill again by not less than a two-thirds majority of all the members, the CE must sign and promulgate it within one month. If the CE refuses to sign such a bill passed the second time by the LegCo, or when the LegCo refuses to pass a budget or any other important bill introduced by the government and if consensus still cannot be reached after consultations, the CE may dissolve the LegCo. However, such dissolution is confined to only once in each term of office. Should the new LegCo so elected still pass an original bill in dispute by a two-thirds majority of all the members or refuse to pass a budget or any other important bill in dispute, the CE must resign.

Such a mechanism to resolve executive-legislative deadlock has never been put to the test in real circumstances. For several years when some opposition legislators used filibustering to prolong Committee Stage proceedings on the annual budget (i.e., the Appropriation Bill) by moving thousands of amendments each of which (if accepted by the LegCo President as valid amendment) had to be debated, there was a risk that the budget would reach a so-called fiscal cliff.[36] In the event, the LegCo President managed to control the proceedings and have the budget put to the vote before further action had to be taken by the government. Once the filibuster was settled, there were enough votes from the pro-establishment camp to ensure passage of the budget.[37]

Another possibility of using the 'dissolution of the LegCo' mechanism is where a constitutional amendment bill on election methods fails to secure two-thirds majority support, as was the case when pan-democratic legislators managed to block government-initiated constitutional packages by using their critical minority (more than one-third of the seats) following the 2000 legislative election.[38] It would have been interesting to see how the general public as electorate might cast their vote in any new election of the LegCo called just to resolve the constitutional dispute, something like a referendum. The mechanism is there; whether the central government would support the CE in using it is, of course, another matter as the political gamble would be too big and might set an undesirable precedent in the eyes of Beijing.

A local impeachment mechanism is also built into the Basic Law. Under Article 73(9), if a motion initiated jointly by one-fourth of all the members of the LegCo charges the CE with a serious breach of law or dereliction of duty and if the CE refuses to resign, the LegCo may, after passing a motion for investigation, give a mandate to the Chief Justice of the CFA to form and chair an independent investigation committee. If this committee finds sufficient evidence to substantiate the charge, the LegCo may pass a motion of impeachment by a two-thirds majority of all its members and report it to the CPG for decision. Again, how such a mechanism might work in practice has never been tested.

The judiciary

Under Article 83 of the Basic Law, the structure, powers, and functions of the courts of the SAR at all levels are prescribed by local law. In effect, the pre-existing system of courts was retained in 1997, with the notable addition of the

CFA which may invite judges from other common law jurisdictions to sit on it as required. This arrangement was agreed by Beijing in order to reassure the local legal community and international businesses of Hong Kong's continued strong connections with common law jurisdictions.

However, in recent years there have been misgivings from time to time from some pro-Beijing quarters as to why foreign judges should sit in a Hong Kong court.[39] Another new feature is that the appointment or removal of the judges of the CFA and the Chief Judge of the High Court by the CE must obtain the endorsement of the LegCo and be reported to the NPCSC (Article 90). Such requirement for legislative consent had been non-controversial all along until most recently when some issues were raised by a few pro-establishment legislators who questioned the liberal views on same-sex marriage rights of certain foreign CFA judges.[40] Still, Hong Kong has never encountered the kind of political storm over the endorsement of candidates for judicial appointments as in other locations, such as the US.[41]

Relations with the central state

The PRC is a unitary state led by the CCP whose role and power as the permanent ruling party is prescribed by the constitution. Thus, all levels of local government derive their administrative power from the centre and can only legislate on local affairs within the confines of national policies and laws. Alongside the set-up of national and local governmental structures exists a corresponding network of party committees that mirror, monitor, and supervise the government-side departments and agencies, with the party secretary considered the 'number one in-charge' (第一把手), to realise the CCP's leadership over the state. However, under the principle of 'One Country, Two Systems', the CE in Hong Kong is entrusted by and accountable to the CPG in governing the SAR in accordance with the Basic Law. Unlike provincial or municipal party secretaries and governors or mayors usually sitting on the CCP's Central Committee (with some of them also members of its Politburo), the CE of Hong Kong does not have such party linkage and thus enjoys less political clout within national politics and policy-making.

In Beijing, the Hong Kong and Macao Affairs Office of the State Council (國務院港澳事務辦公室) is the central coordinating office with ministerial status, advising the State Council on national policies and strategies towards Hong Kong (and Macao) and maintaining a regular link with the CE of the SAR. Within Hong Kong, the Liaison Office of the Central People's Government in the Hong Kong SAR (中央人民政府駐香港特別行政區聯絡辦公室) was established in December 1999 to replace the previous New China News Agency Hong Kong Branch (Xinhua News Agency Hong Kong Branch, 新華通訊社香港分社) which hitherto operated as the de facto representative office of the Chinese government when the city was under British rule and doubled as the CCP's Hong Kong Work Committee — discharging both governmental and party functions. The Liaison Office Director, with ministerial rank, together with the Commissioner of the Ministry of Foreign Affairs and Commander of the PLA Garrison, attend official SAR ceremonies as principal representatives of central government institutions in Hong Kong. A most recent reorganisation of the two central organs on Hong Kong and Macao work, announced in February 2020, makes the Liaison Office report to the Hong Kong and Macao Affairs Office, with its director also made concurrently one of the deputy directors of the latter.[42]

Post-1997 structural changes in the governance landscape

The new SAR political order was supposed to be a continuation of the previous mode of executive-led and bureaucracy-based governance. By making it a statutory requirement that the holder of the CE post cannot belong to any political party,[43] the CE is theoretically above party politics and the only dispenser of political resources, patronage, and appointment. Tung Chee-hwa, the inaugural CE, introduced two major constitutional changes after 1997, both serving to recentralise executive power.

The first was the review of the two municipal councils (Urban Council and Regional Council) and District Boards in 1998, to decide whether such an inherited structure of district representative institutions would continue to ensure the efficient and responsive delivery of services. Eventually, it was decided to abolish the municipal councils and transfer their responsibilities to relevant policy bureaus. The dissolution took place in 2000. The 18 District Boards were retitled District Councils (DCs), with a slight increase in councillors' remuneration and the amount of funds for local works projects and district campaigns. Otherwise, their advisory nature remained intact. Some critics saw the abolition of the municipal tier as a move towards greater centralisation of authority in an 'executive-led' government'.[44]

In hindsight, the move backfired. Politically, such abolition was supposed to remove the room for local politics to coalesce. However, the emerging local politicians groomed by parties then turned to the DCs as new platforms of local activism to support legislative politics. Having elected district politicians with only advisory functions and no actual power in district management would not breed responsible politics at the community level, whereas the former Urban and Regional Councils had some power over municipal management. Henceforth, district politics across the partisan spectrum could only play the game of high-sounding advocacy and 'blaming and shaming' government departments for policy and service inadequacies.

The second change is related to the centre of government. Tung's first term was embroiled in the rivalry between two competing 'executive-led' paradigms — one riding on the constitutional supremacy of the CE and the other based on the traditional notion of bureaucratic polity.[45] In July 2002, with Beijing's blessing, Tung implemented a new Principal Officials Accountability System (POAS) whereby top civil servants were replaced by political appointees as policy secretaries (the ministers) even though some senior civil servants were allowed to retire to change track as political officials. In the name of enhancing accountability, the POAS had the effect of centralising policy powers in the hands of the CE and his ministerial team at the expense of the bureaucracy dominated by the Administrative Class of civil servants (more discussion in Chapter 5). Yet, despite these centralising measures on top of those powers inherited from the British Governorship, the experience after 1997 saw executive power continuously eroding or 'hollowed out'.[46] There were several structural reasons for that.

Colonial 'executive-led' governance was realised not just in a more powerful executive but also an executive that could subjugate other powers and, where necessary, override and unify elite interests. While the co-optation of professional elites gave them privileged representation and shored up their standing and influence within the system of governance, the colonial logic dictated that ultimately the will of the colonial rulers (meaning the Governor and his top officials) would prevail. The final years of British rule saw a quicker pace of politicisation, inducing the government to be more open and responsive to legislative scrutiny and local public opinion. Senior bureaucrats were no longer as predominant as before. The introduction of legislative elections spurred the growth of political parties and quasi-party groups (including trade union organisations) and elected legislators as new political actors. The LegCo was no longer at the service of the administration.

Such traumatic but unavoidable changes in the political landscape were not fully anticipated by the Basic Law drafters in the late 1980s, who had assumed it both possible and desirable to maintain business as usual after the handover. When the colonial rulers virtually formed a synarchy with the business and professional elites, the Governor was in full command of things given his near-autocratic constitutional powers. Such a relationship began to shift during the political transition as the advent of functional constituencies nurtured a new mode of institutionalised corporatism subsequently built into the Basic Law political architecture. As these functional elites were also targeted by Beijing for political co-optation and allegiance in rivalry with the outgoing British administration, they were accorded enhanced recognition and clout.[47] Narrow sectoral interests often became a new hindrance to SAR policy decision-making, such as over the reform of the Medical Council in 2016 to enlarge lay participation and the reform of the taxi industry to introduce a new type of franchised taxis.[48]

While the CE owed their position largely to the political blessing of the central government, they still had to secure a decent number of votes from the Election Committee, which means the CE had to make pledges and concessions through their policy platform as if in any political election. Local business and professional interests had become entrenched in a unique system of functional representation to elect both the CE and almost half of the seats of the LegCo. Their political power base was, in a way, created for them by government recognition since the late 1980s, but once recognised, these elites would seek the allocation of resources and benefits from the government as well as exploit opportunities at times for their 'reverse capture' of government. Facing an independent LegCo with substantial check-and-balance powers, the CE had to rely on pro-establishment camp politics in order to govern. Meanwhile, the Judiciary had been playing an increasing role in scrutinising the legality of government decisions and policies when the community became more active in seeking judicial reviews. The seeds for an unintended encroachment of executive power had been laid by default if not fully by design.

Politics at the district level had also gradually served to usurp government power. Although district councillors did not have any decision-making or executive powers over district administration, their influence should not be under-estimated. They formed the points of local networks of support (constituency 'vote captains') for the geographically returned legislators on whom they could exert pressure to adopt policy stances according to their preference. The DCs were also venues for the grooming of future election talent for political parties. In recent years, district populism has been on the rise, shaping legislative politics as well as reinforcing local community hurdles to planning and development decision-making, as seen in the rising not-in-my-backyard (NIMBY) sentiments.

The DCs were again reviewed in 2005–2006, when Donald Tsang at first sought to empower them, enhance the status of DOs and improve district-level work. Conceptually, DC reform should not be just about the transfer of management responsibilities over certain district facilities or services to these elected bodies or the increase of remuneration of councillors. It should be about making them a real focal point of district governance, which would call for a new brand of councillors. If the present 18 DCs could be reorganised into, for instance, five or six regional councils, the District (Regional) Management Committee, with enhanced councillor participation, could be upgraded into an executive arm of the new regional council, led by a District Commissioner politically appointed by the CE, who would be a district leader and not just a 'faceless' bureaucrat of the Home Affairs Department. Better-staffed secretariats and research arms could then be provided to the new councils.

In the event, however, the opportunity of amalgamation into larger but fewer local or regional councils with some executive authority was foregone. Again, the result of the review was not devolution of local administration powers or functions. The advisory nature of DCs remained unchanged although they were given more say in district management through participation via their chairmen and vice-chairmen in the DMCs.[49] Under the Leung Chun-ying Administration (2012–2017), DCs were allocated more funding, to the order of HK$100 million per district, for use in launching impactful district projects under the Signature Project Scheme introduced in 2013.

Institutional tension and incompatibilities

The British government considered it had handed over to China in 1997 a world-class city of prosperity and an institutional legacy, with civil servants of the highest probity and the most steadfast commitment to the public good.[50] Such an achievement was only possible under very unique historical and institutional circumstances. During the colonial era, several conditions and factors contributed towards government effectiveness. There was elite integration through the close linkage between administrative and business and professional elites, and among intra-government elites (within the bureaucracy). Once the colonial administrators were determined to go for reform, they could bulldoze bold (at times controversial) plans given the legislature was the handmaiden of the executive. The logic of colonial rule helped to induce public acquiescence so long as the rulers were able to provide basic freedoms and deliver economic affluence, social mobility, and some channels for public consultation and participation. Political mobilisation was limited, and civil society was relatively weak. Being mandated externally and autocratically, the government could enjoy the advantage of staying above privileged private interests, although it maintained a close alliance with British business interests most of the time.

Such conditions simply could not be replicated in the post-1997 era because both times and circumstances had changed. The colonial logic had been replaced by the logic of 'Hong Kong people governing Hong Kong'. The government's hitherto unchallenged policy power had to be shared with other domestic organised interests—the question was only to what extent and on what terms. Since the transition, the local population had begun to take their civil and political rights more seriously, and such rights had become part of the 'core values' of Hong Kong that the community strived to safeguard. Yet, public aspirations and enthusiasm could not be positively channelled into the system of governance because of the slow progress in constitutional reform and Beijing's hesitation to support democratisation and party government.[51] Policy powers remained in an executive at first dominated by administrative bureaucrats as in British days, and later a hybrid of bureaucrats and political officials, entrusted by Beijing but without a political mandate of their own, vis-à-vis elected legislators and their parties who could claim to represent and articulate public and sectoral interests and sought a de facto system of co-rule. This explained the more frequent executive-legislative and government-party rivalries and tensions over policy directions in recent years, sometimes resulting in policy impasse.

Soon after the handover, the growing incompatibility between the Basic Law institutional design based on extending the colonial executive-led system and the changing political environment was a fundamental source of the stress and uncertainty in institutional relationships.[52] In terms of the executive-legislative relationship, there was a widening fissure between the party-less administration of the CE and a legislature increasingly shaped by party politics. All parties, whether pro-establishment or pan-democratic, acted *as if* in opposition. Without their electoral base, the CE could not match with the legislature in the bottom-up mandate. Executive-legislative gridlock was not uncommon—a stark contrast with executive-legislative fusion in the heyday of colonial rule. In terms of the political executive-civil service relationship, there were now intra-elite rivalries, which were especially present in the initial SAR years under conflicting 'executive-led' paradigms.[53] In terms of the government-elites relationship, business and professional elites now enjoyed more institutionalised political power that could challenge the government's authority.

On the other hand, the role and impact of the co-opted advisory elites had become marginalised by the rise of electoral politics and civil society activism.[54] They had been pushed to the periphery of the policy circle, still honourable in the formal process but weaker in clout and substantive influence.[55] Finally, in terms of the government-society relationship, the colonial mindset of public acquiescence was no longer sustainable after 1997 when the general public expected the SAR government to be fully accountable and responsive, now that a government by a fellow Hongkonger rather than a foreign colonial was in charge. However, a government they played no part in electing would find it difficult to gain and sustain the political trust of the community at large, ever-suspicious that the administration would mostly do the bidding of Beijing or big business in Hong Kong. The social capital so necessary for policy capacity became hard to come by.[56]

Furthermore, the role of the central-state agencies in SAR governance had become ambivalent in recent years—more assertive in keeping stability and less prepared to face any risk that might arise from Hong Kong arguing about and making its own decisions on controversial issues under the principle of self-administration. In the aftermath of the 1 July mass protests in 2003, the central government became nervous about political developments in Hong Kong. An inter-ministry 'Central Coordination Group for Hong Kong and Macao Affairs' (中央港澳工作協調小組) was established under a top official with national leader status—first Vice-President Zeng Qinghong (曾慶紅, 2003–2007), then Vice-President Xi Jinping (習近平, 2007–2012), then Chairman of the NPCSC Zhang Dejiang (張德江, 2012–2018), and currently Deputy Premier and CCP Politburo Standing Committee member Han Zheng (韓正, from April 2018)—to strengthen central leadership and coordination over the two SARs. It was announced in February 2020 that this coordinating group had been reconstituted as the Central Leading Group for Hong Kong and Macao Affairs (中央港澳工作領導小組).[57] In 2013, the Chinese Association of Hong Kong and Macao Studies (全國港澳研究會) was established under the aegis of the Hong Kong and Macao Affairs Office to serve as a semi-official think-tank to the central government.[58]

The relationship between the SAR government and the Liaison Office has been a rather delicate one that attracts a lot of media and political attention because only the latter has the capacity to influence pro-establishment politicians and organisations. Today, the Liaison Office has a large staff complement, comprising 23 divisions and offices, including district work offices in Hong Kong Island, Kowloon, and the New Territories, reaching out to all sectors of the Hong Kong community (political, business, professional, labour, religious, and social services sectors as well as district organisations). Some critics even describe the situation as if a party committee is overseeing the operations of the SAR government.[59] While the Liaison Office certainly would be concerned about the overall political situation of the SAR, and can relay directives from the central government, it is not empowered to dictate preferences on its own to the CE and SAR government. However, in the most recent development following enhanced central oversight over Hong Kong due to the prolonged political unrest, the Liaison Office emphasised that it, along with the Hong Kong and Macao Affairs Office of the State Council ('the two Offices'), has the power to 'supervise' major affairs in Hong Kong.[60]

The institutional dilemma for Hong Kong is that there is no going back to the government by bureaucrats and government by consultation of the old colonial days. Neither is the position of the CE in relation to the CPG entirely comparable to that of the British Governor vis-à-vis London, not to mention the vast difference in the political system between China and Britain. Within Hong Kong, the genie has been released, and new politics (both local and national) have firmly taken over in the system of governance beyond what could have been anticipated before 1997. Lau Siu-kai was right to observe back in the 1980s that 'decolonisation without independence' in a unique Hong Kong way was the only feasible path. Yet, the possible modus operandi of such an alternative route had always been in the abstract. Lau initially saw the prospect in the promotion of a new political order whereby a bureaucracy loyal to the new sovereign (i.e., China) would form into a grand coalition of establishment forces, which could dictate politics and policies in the same fashion as in British times; and he had been using that as a benchmark to evaluate the success and drawback of the post-1997 SAR regime.[61]

According to Lau, a new political order had to be premised on, among other things, the wide acknowledgement of the authority and interests of the central government; all political forces accepting a common set of 'rules of the game' with the pro-democracy opposition parties willing to assume the role of a 'loyal opposition'; the SAR regime being fully competent in directing the executive authorities and securing majority support in the legislature and endorsement of a broadly representative governing coalition; and social and political cleavages mostly about material interests rather than irreconcilable ideological conflicts. It would be contingent upon stable and non-confrontational relations between the central government and local people, with the latter not allowing hostile forces to turn Hong Kong into an anti-communist base of subversion of the Mainland's socialist system. Writing in 2013, he lamented that the political realities were far from such an ideal scenario.[62] The situation since then has turned even worse (see Chapter 12), indicating that such an ideal political order is more a castle in the air.

Politics is about the realities, not ideal-types or wishful thinking. The challenge to all governments is finding their way forward (the practical solutions) amid imperfect if not adverse conditions. The realities in Hong Kong, as Lau too has somewhat alluded to, have been that there are widening social and political cleavages, with the relations between the central government and local pan-democrats fast deteriorating, especially in recent years amid the rise of separatist, anti-Mainland tendencies inducing hardline reactions from Beijing. Furthermore, pro-establishment forces are not entirely in unison, rendering the establishment coalition more an appearance than substance, vis-à-vis a united opposition camp capable of mobilising extra-legislative forces and the media to shape public discourses and gaining the upper hand in the political struggles.[63] The old executive-led orthodoxy and the colonial mechanisms of administrative domination and absorption have long faded in functionality, and in any case would be unable to cope with the new conditions, demands, and challenges. Ian Scott had very early on depicted the SAR's institutional crisis as 'the disarticulation of Hong Kong's post-handover political system' which was neither parliamentary fish nor presidential fowl.[64] Hong Kong is heading towards an increasingly fragmented and divisive polity.[65] The government simply cannot dictate its will on society, even if for the public good, unlike a colonial reformist administration in the MacLehose era.

Chapter 5
A New Ministerial System

Introduction

In the early days of the handover, the central government in Beijing made sure not to be seen in any way upstaging the senior civil service upon whom it relied to secure a smooth administration in Hong Kong. National leaders like then President Jiang Zemin and Premier Zhu Rongji openly praised the performance of top SAR officials such as FS Donald Tsang and Monetary Authority Chief Joseph Yam on the occasion of the annual meetings of the World Bank Group and International Monetary Fund (IMF) hosted by Hong Kong in September 1997. Beijing was confident that top public servants would be politically loyal to the new sovereign authority and hopeful that they would cooperate well with its appointed CE Tung Chee-hwa in keeping Hong Kong well-governed.

Whether the change of regime and government leadership had induced any shift in the attitude and competence of senior bureaucrats was something much watched by the local population and international observers.[1] While most would tend to agree that the civil service institution had remained intact, there also emerged a dose of scepticism among some. Writing about the post-1997 AO culture, a former expatriate AO observed that there was 'a reinforced paternalism, more "Confucian" but also "more colonial again"; less accountability downwards ("just as dedicated to our jobs, but forgetting what they are for"); more caution and conformity upwards'.[2] Such scepticism might be a bit harsh because most senior civil servants at the time would supposedly try to gauge the attitude and ethos of their new political masters (both the CE and CPG).

Beijing was keen to 'de-Pattenise' Hong Kong's politics and to revert the territory from a political city to an economic city. In so doing, there was a meeting of minds with the local business and bureaucratic interests equally concerned about the drastic political changes upsetting the status quo too much. Tung also openly blamed politics for the declining morale and efficiency of the civil service.[3] The bureaucracy might have tried to take advantage of the post-1997 conservative backlash to regain its supremacy under the previous 'executive-led' paradigm, which was challenged by elected legislators in the final days of British rule. What the senior mandarins did not anticipate was a political challenge from the new CE and his close advisers as to who was to 'executive-lead'.[4]

Two competing 'executive-led' paradigms

Two 'executive-led' logics seemed to be in competition—with the top mandarins or AOs still favouring a traditional civil service-dominated ministerial system, while Tung's supporters preferred a more presidential style of executive government to take back policy leadership from the senior civil service. Tung had the ambition to launch major policy reforms in housing, education, technology innovation, industrial policy, and the civil service. On the surface, this was but normal for any incoming administration, especially upon a historical change of rule in 1997. However, the rhetoric driving reform was often couched in a mindset suspecting the former British administration as laying too many policy landmines before its departure or that it had failed to do what it should in the last years of the transition out of ulterior motives. The urge to push for a quick fix on multiple policy fronts had resulted in insufficient public debates and more top-down initiatives, thereby alienating too many stakeholders as well as those senior bureaucrats associated with the inherited policy regimes.

A politically more competitive environment also affected bureaucratic performance or at least the perception of it. Elected and appointed politicians across the political spectrum seized the opportunity accorded by post-1997 economic crisis and policy blunders to question the hitherto seldom-challenged supremacy and invincibility of the senior civil service. During the first few years after the handover, many of Tung's close advisers and those in the pro-Beijing camp tended to blame the lack of competence and cooperation of senior bureaucrats for the many policy setbacks he faced.[5] They criticised the top civil servants under the leadership of Anson Chan for not giving him sufficient support and loyalty.[6] There began to be talk of introducing some form of ministerial system staffed by 'outsiders' as a means to augment the government's political capacity and to bring in new perspectives.

One of the key advocates of such a move was Chung Sze-yuen, a former Senior Member of the colonial ExCo in the 1980s much respected by senior civil servants under the British administration, who was invited by Tung to be the inaugural convenor of non-official members of his ExCo (until June 1999). Chung had on the record proposed party-nomination of the CE who should enjoy his party coalition's full support in the LegCo. He also advocated turning Principal Officials into non-civil service political appointees, who would constitute the CE's cabinet in the form of a new-style ExCo, while retaining only a few full-time non-officials as 'cabinet minister without portfolio'.[7] In that case, the ExCo would become a full-fledged cabinet with both power and responsibility while the civil service would revert to a politically neutral institution. If so, the meaning of an executive-led government could be made more apparent—a presidential style of government dominated by the CE and his political cabinet.

While the introduction of a ministerial system of political appointment in Hong Kong was intended to bring about undisputed political control over the bureaucrats who used to run the government, it is interesting to note that even among developed democracies practising such a political system, there has been ongoing tension between political ministers and bureaucrats, with the NPM-driven changes being packaged as an approach to strengthen political control over the civil servants.[8] In other words, politician-bureaucrat tension is a perennial feature of most political systems though in varying contexts. The question is how to manage such tension.

A layer with enhanced policy power and accountability

In his October 2000 Policy Address, no doubt with Beijing's blessing, Tung proposed to review the existing system so that the 'Principal Officials' at the rank of Secretary would assume an important role in policy formulation and implementation, different from that of other civil servants. Their accountability for policy outcomes within respective portfolios would be enhanced, together with a compatible system of appointment, while the existing principles of permanence and neutrality of the civil service would be preserved.[9] More details were disclosed in his 2001 Policy Address — to introduce a new system of appointing Principal Officials, who could come from within or outside the civil service. These officials would be appointed on terms different from those in the civil service, including remuneration and conditions of service. Their term of office would not exceed that of the CE who nominated them. Their responsibilities would include formulating and explaining policies, defending policies, canvassing support from the LegCo and the public, and being answerable to the CE for the success or failure of their policies.[10]

Differentiating the policy-making role of political executives from the policy implementation role of civil servants (bureaucratic executives) has firm ground in the long-held principle of politics-administration dichotomy prevalent in Western democratic systems though there exists a range of variants in practice.[11] That its adoption in Hong Kong had been so late and yet so controversial speaks volumes of the odd (or unique) conditions of governance in Hong Kong since colonial times. In July 2002, as his second term commenced, Tung implemented the POAS whereby political appointees replaced top civil servants as policy secretaries (the ministers).[12] The reaction of senior civil servants to the new ministerial system was mixed. Some senior AOs did not subscribe to the new system of political appointment which they worried might open up the top layers to only 'Beijing loyalists' or those 'outsiders' whose competence they lacked confidence in.[13] There were also those quite willing to accept the backseat role of a politically neutral mandarin.[14]

Yet, it was not necessarily consequential that the AOs would then become disempowered as suspected at the outset. The political ministers would have to rely on them for policy advice and execution in much the same way as ministers operated in a Westminster system.[15] As Joseph Wong, the first SCS under the new system, himself an AO, commented at the time:

> There are speculations that the shine of the AO Grade is fading away because some Principal Officials have come from the private sector [...] these speculations are unfounded. [...] At the practical level, Principal Officials in the Government were virtually alone by themselves. They do not have deputies and advisers. They have to rely on the civil service, particularly AOs within it, for the necessary policy analysis and for the smooth implementation of policies.[16]

The domination of government by AOs remained a feature. In mid-2002, over 90% of the directorate posts among the policy bureaus were filled by the AO grade. Out of the 16 Permanent Secretaries, 15 were AOs; and out of the 14 ministers, half of them, including the SCS, came from the AO grade.[17]

While the power of appointment of Principal Officials formally rested with the CPG, the CE's power of nomination was critical. In other words, the CE would now be able to form their own ministerial team, without being bound by civil service norms and procedures that determined who should be promoted within the hierarchy to Secretary rank as in the past. Henceforth, senior civil servants, including the new top rank of Permanent Secretaries who headed civil servants within the bureaus under the new ministers, were expected to change in three directions, as put by the EfU in 2004: vision delivery (to play a crucial role to help deliver the government's vision); productivity improvement (to improve public sector productivity to meet the community's expanding needs and rising expectations at a time of real budget constraints); and supporting ministers (to adjust to the new ministerial system and work in effective partnership with the politically appointed ministers).[18] The top layer of the administration became politicised and separated from the career civil service, paving the way for the possible formation of a new political class vis-à-vis the Administrative Class who had dominated the government for so long.

The politicians' response to Tung's idea of 'ministerialisation' was not particularly enthusiastic. Some legislators, though keen on enhancing policy accountability, believed that the political appointment of Secretaries would only be effective if the LegCo had a role to play in both their appointment and dismissal—such as through appointment hearings, as in the US Congress, or subject to no-confidence votes, as in parliamentary systems. Such a legislative role was ruled out given the constitutional requirement that the CPG appoint Principal Officials upon nomination by the CE. Pro-democracy parties were worried that instead of making the ministers more accountable to the legislature, the new system would render them loyal to the CE personally, resulting in the further concentration of executive power. In the absence of a democratically elected CE, they would instead prefer to see some internal checks on the CE's authority by meritocratic bureaucrats protected in their jobs by the civil service system. Pro-Beijing and pro-business parties hoped that the change would open up opportunities of political advancement to their affiliates beyond seats in the LegCo. If their members and nominees were appointed to head some policy bureaus, these parties would be more willing to enter into a formal or informal governing coalition with the CE, which, if in majority control of the LegCo, could ensure legislative support for government bills and policies.

Such thinking, however, failed to materialise. The subsequent Administrations continued to be partyless and remained essentially grounded in the bureaucracy. Looking back, the ministerial system of political appointment introduced was only half-baked. The ultimate source of supply of political appointees was not fully thought through within the context of longer-term constitutional development. Of all the ministers appointed to Tung's first political cabinet in 2002, none except Henry Tang were politicians.[19] Thus, there was limited enthusiasm from political parties for the change. The deliberate attempt to officially depict the new system as an accountability system had shifted much of the public and legislative attention to how political and policy accountability could be better enforced, driving the public to expect heads to roll whenever there was any policy failure or uncalled for incident.

Minister-bureaucrat relations

The appointment of 'outsiders' to policy portfolios was not magic in itself. While making an institutional distinction between the two streams of the executive branch, as common in many other political systems, whether the new ministerial system would bring about competent policy-making and policy delivery was highly dependent on how the two streams could work together effectively and who were recruited as the new-style ministers. Also, securing the civil servants' sustained cooperation was as crucial as bringing in new political blood. Retaining top bureaucrats at the Secretary-rank level as Permanent Secretaries, in line with the British and Commonwealth practice, was one way to assure them that they would remain key members of the executive government and their respective ministerial bureaus, and that there would still be an attractive career prospect for the Administrative Class.[20]

Ministers alone could not make effective policies without good and honest policy advice from their senior civil servants, in particular the Permanent Secretaries, and their faithful implementation of agreed policies—a high degree of mutual trust is essential to the minister-bureaucrat relationship. Though in theory subordinate to their political masters, Permanent Secretaries are not merely 'yes-persons'. There exists, in practice, a symbiotic relationship which, if handled properly, would facilitate policy work.[21] Unlike some systems such as in Europe, ministers in Hong Kong are not allowed to retain a small number of non-civil servant political aides and advisers to form their own ministerial 'cabinets'. At the start of the new ministerial system, there was only one layer of political appointees, namely the Secretaries. This rendered ministers even more dependent on the support from senior civil servants of their bureaus headed by the Permanent Secretaries who continued to be the designated Controlling Officers in charge of bureau personnel and financial management.

Unlike ministers supported by alternative policy advice from the ruling parties and party-linked policy think tanks elsewhere, Hong Kong's political ministers mostly lack such political linkage. Whereas those other systems might experience tension among competing sources of policy advice to the minister, the Hong Kong case places the minister at the mercy of the Permanent Secretary. The new modus operandi is subject to a 're-negotiated' bargain, so that while ministers are clearly in policy leadership, senior civil servants (especially the AOs who dominate Permanent Secretary posts) are left in no doubt that they would continue to play a crucial policy role. It thus all the more demands political and policy skills from the ministers in working with their senior civil servants, securing the latter's loyalty but without being captured or unduly manipulated by them.

Some hold the view that the 'strong belief of civil servants in the rule of law and in their role as guardians of the public interest' is conducive to the maintenance of rule-based governance, to provide 'an important constraint on the power of an unelected government'.[22] There seems a dose of myth about the neutrality of the senior civil service dating from colonial days despite their dominating role in making policies to decide who would gain and who would lose. By emphasising their neutrality, colonial mandarins could stand above sectoral politics as the final arbiters to fend off external pressures. Post-1997, given that the public at large has tended to trust bureaucrats more than political appointees of a non-democratic government, such perception of neutrality would reinforce their image as the 'conscience' of Hong Kong to check the ruling power of a Beijing-picked CE.[23]

Such belief in the better virtue of civil servants fails to appreciate the very different contexts in which political appointees and career bureaucrats operate. It has also glossed over the inherent conservativeness of those risk-averse civil servants who hesitate to bear responsibility, take action and initiate change, often hiding behind procedures, precedents and conventional practice.[24] Why career civil servants (e.g., AOs) as a whole are still held in better regard than political appointees by the public can perhaps be attributed to the varied performance of individual ministers as well as their perceived level of policy competence and political skills. The impression has been reinforced by the contrasting ethos between senior civil servants and political ministers, with empirical studies finding that the former tended to see themselves as loyal to the public interest and the law, displaying a kind of trusteeship mentality and values about 'fiscal prudence' and 'balanced interests'.[25]

Arguably, some ministers in overseas systems are equally non-experts in the portfolio given to their charge, and some are regarded as deficient in policy competence and skills.[26] Others may well be examples of political nepotism. Yet, by and large, their ministerial system has seldom faced a legitimation problem mainly because there exists a well-accepted constitutional and institutional ethos underpinning the practice of political appointment. For example, the US President is entitled to appoint anyone he deems fit for the top executive jobs subject to Senate endorsement, while the British Prime Minister is free to form their cabinet from among parliamentary members of the ruling party or coalition, sometimes on merit and at other times to reward supporters or facilitate political bargains. Such power of appointment is considered an executive prerogative of the head of government.

In recent years, there have been concerns among some European systems about the politicisation of senior civil service appointments, which to some extent exists in so-called Napoleonic countries and Central and Eastern European countries, especially as a 'compensation strategy' in the face of rising organisational and managerial autonomy of departments and agencies under NPM. While latent competition between political leadership and administrative leadership in policy-making is arguably longstanding, research so far has not found firm evidence of such politicisation.[27] Neither is it evident in the Hong Kong context where the key concern is about top civil servants overwhelming ministerial appointees in policy formulation and influence. Reflecting on Singapore's experience, Primer Minister Lee Hsien Loong expresses a more balanced view, saying:

> Ministers are responsible for getting the politics right, just as the civil service is primarily responsible for policy. [...] Even if ministers are diligent and well-intentioned, if they are not quite up to the mark or unable to play their roles properly, the public service cannot function well.[28]

In Hong Kong, because the CE is not democratically elected, it has been frequently alleged by pan-democrats and some critical media outlets that ministers are appointed indiscriminately, being cast in doubt as a 'black-box operation', 'political cronyism', and the 'adoption of affinity differentiation'.[29] For example, the appointment of Under-Secretaries and Political Assistants (PAs) by the Tsang Administration in 2008, contrary to strengthening government, was embroiled in an unexpected political controversy, inviting public suspicions that their appointment and remunerations were 'arbitrary, unlike the rigorous and transparent system in the civil service'.[30]

The ongoing comparisons between so-called amateur political appointees and the more experienced and elitist administrative mandarins at that time underscored the reality that the general as well as informed public mostly subscribed to the administrative logic of government dating from colonial rule. In contrast, there are also critics from a pro-regime change perspective, such as former Head of the Central Policy Unit (2002–2012) Lau Siu-kai who questioned if the CE and his political leadership team had been successful in reining in the inherited British-groomed civil service—especially the administrative mandarins who displayed 'homogeneity', 'corporate consciousness' and their own set of action ideas such as fiscal prudence, small government and procedural justice, so much so that they formed the block to bold visionary initiatives and caused frictions within government.[31]

The paradox for the ministerial appointees is that, on the one hand, they would need to impress upon their bureaucrats that they are in charge and possess the competence to do so, and on the other hand, to respect their bureaucrats sufficiently so that the latter would work faithfully as their partners. Otherwise, policy failure would be bound to appear, and constitutionally the ministers would take the largest share, if not the whole, of the political blame. At the same time, there should be a firewall to ensure that different lines of command would apply to the political tier and the permanent civil service, even though they are unified at the level of the minister. In other countries, civil service laws and respective codes for ministers and civil servants have been drawn up to provide legislative and regulatory guidelines for minister-bureaucrat interaction. Hong Kong has done the same. Table 5.1 compares key provisions of the Civil Service Code and the Code for Officials under the Political Appointment System.[32]

In other systems such as Britain and Commonwealth countries (e.g., Australia and Singapore), a top civil servant is appointed to be Head of the Civil Service whose role is to protect civil service neutrality, integrity, and other institutional interests of the civil service as a whole. Hong Kong should have adopted a similar practice. However, there was no clear arrangement in terms of system design when the new ministerial system was introduced in 2002, except the requirement that the SCS must come from a civil servant background, and if an incumbent civil servant, the Secretary could return to the civil service upon leaving ministerial appointment if not yet reaching retirement age.[33] This arrangement was unsatisfactory as it confused the political role of the Secretary with the Head of Civil Service role which should be politically neutral. Because the system has never properly designated a head of the civil service, many in the community as well as within the civil service continue to regard the CS, now already a political appointee with no necessary civil service connection (unlike the SCS who by design must come from within the civil service), as the head of the civil service.[34]

Ministerial accountability

An important impetus to the installation of the ministerial system of political appointment was the need to satisfy the public that there would be enhanced accountability of the Principal Officials for their performance and outcome within their policy portfolios. Discharging effective accountability requires two prerequisites: the mechanisms for providing information and the mechanisms for imposing sanctions.[35] In the Westminster-style of parliamentary government, individual ministerial accountability is a constitutional convention whereby a minister is required to resign by the prime minister or by parliament, if committing serious policy mistakes or grave personal misconduct. There are no hard and fast rules though. Conventions are set by a series of precedents, by agreements among the major political players, or by justified government principles like democracy

**Table 5.1: Key provisions of the Civil Service Code
and the Code for Officials under the Political Appointment System**

	Civil Service Code	POAS Code
Content	1. Introduction 2. Core values 3. Standards of conduct 4. Authority for the management of the civil service 5. Roles and responsibilities of civil servants in relation to politically appointed officials 6. Relationship between civil servants and politically appointed officials 7. Communication, complaint, and redress mechanism	1. Introduction 2. Responsibilities 3. Official secrets and security 4. Involvement in political activities 5. Prevention of conflict of interest 6. Travel 7. Others (reporting of criminal offences and attempted bribes, legal proceedings, sanction)
Management	The SCS is responsible to the CE for policies and management of the civil service. One of the SCS's major tasks is to safeguard the core values and define the standards of conduct of the civil service.[a]	Politically appointed officials shall note that civil servants shall report directly, and enjoy direct access, to them through their Permanent Secretaries, and that Under-Secretaries and PAs shall have no direct line of command vis-à-vis Permanent Secretaries. In their dealings with civil servants they shall have due regard to the Civil Service Code which sets out the framework within which civil servants are expected to work with politically appointed officials.
Core values	Civil servants are required to uphold the following core values, which are of equal importance — (a) commitment to the rule of law; (b) honesty and integrity; (c) objectivity and impartiality; (d) political neutrality; (e) accountability for decisions and actions; and (f) dedication, professionalism, and diligence.	Politically appointed officials shall at all times actively uphold and promote a permanent, honest, meritocratic, professional, and politically neutral civil service. In particular, they shall actively uphold and promote the core values of the civil service.
Responsibilities and accountability	Civil servants support politically appointed officials in formulating policies. They are responsible for executing policies, carrying out executive tasks, managing and delivering services to the public, and undertaking law enforcement and regulatory functions, in accordance with the decisions of the government of the day and the directions of principal officials.	Principal officials are responsible for their respective portfolios designated to them by the CE and lead the executive departments within their respective portfolios. They are responsible for formulating, explaining, and defending government policies as well as canvassing support from the public and the LegCo. They are accountable to the CE for the success or failure of their policies.

Table 5.1 Continued

	Civil Service Code	POAS Code
Responsibilities and accountability (*continued*)	Civil servants are accountable for the exercise of various statutory powers conferred on them by law. Those appointed as Controlling Officers under the Public Finance Ordinance are accountable for all public moneys, property, and expenditure under their charge, and the use of such resources in compliance with the directions and decisions made by their principal officials. They are responsible for the efficient and effective use of resources under their charge.	Politically appointed officials shall be bound by and collectively responsible for the decisions taken by the CE-in-Council.
Political loyalty and neutrality	Civil servants shall serve the CE and the government of the day with total loyalty and to the best of their ability, no matter what their own political beliefs are. They shall not allow their own personal party-political affiliation or party-political beliefs to determine or influence the discharge of their official duties and responsibilities, including the advice they give and the decisions or actions they take. In their official capacity, they shall not engage in party-political activities or use public resources for party-political purposes such as electioneering or fund-raising activities for political parties. Civil servants are disqualified from being nominated as a candidate at an election of the CE, LegCo, or a DC.	Politically appointed officials are disqualified from being nominated as a candidate at an election of the CE, LegCo, or a DC. They are also disqualified from being elected as member of the LegCo or a DC. They shall declare to the CE whether they are in any way affiliated with any political party, whether they are members of any political party and whether they hold any office in any political party. They shall declare to the CE if there is any change in their status in relation to any political party. When taking part in activities organised by political parties, there should be no actual or potential conflict of interest with the business of the government or the official duties of the politically appointed officials and their participation in such activities shall not cause any embarrassment to the government, the CE, or other politically appointed officials.
Relationship between civil servants and politically appointed officials	Civil servants shall follow the directives and work priorities determined by principal officials. They shall provide politically appointed officials their full, honest, and impartial advice, without fear or favour, and whether or not the advice accords with the views of politically appointed officials. To uphold their integrity and professionalism, civil servants shall endeavour to provide politically appointed officials with the best	Politically appointed officials shall give fair consideration and due weight to honest, informed, and impartial advice from civil servants and shall have due regard to Government Regulations which are applicable to civil servants or otherwise regulate the operation of the government.

Table 5.1 Continued

	Civil Service Code	POAS Code
Relationship between civil servants and politically appointed officials *(continued)*	advice they believe they can give and all relevant information they have access to. They shall work together with politically appointed officials in the spirit of partnership and foster mutual trust and confidence.	

Source: Civil Service Bureau (2009) *Civil Service Code*, 9 September, Hong Kong: Civil Service Bureau, www.csb.gov.hk/english/admin/conduct/files/CSCode_e.pdf; Constitutional and Mainland Affairs Bureau (2012) *Code for Officials under the Political Appointment System*, July, Hong Kong: Constitutional and Mainland Affairs Bureau, www.cmab.gov.hk/en/issues/PAO_Code_1.7.2012.pdf.

Note: In addition to the Civil Service Code, all civil servants are required to comply with Civil Service Regulations, Civil Service Bureau circulars, and circular memoranda, covering areas relating to conduct and integrity such as conflict of interest, acceptance of advantages and entertainment, investments, outside work, indebtedness, reporting crime and corruption, production by government officers of publications containing paid advertisements, public communications, public donations, participation in political activities, and avenues for complaint/seeking redress.

[a] According to former SCS Joseph Wong, the SCS was to be the guardian of civil service values and, under the original POAS, could handle complaints of political interference relating to all politically appointed principal officials, including the CS and FS. If the complaint could not be resolved satisfactorily, the SCS could bring the matter to the personal attention of the CE. However, under the 2009 Civil Service Code, SCS had to put the matter to either the CS or FS for resolution first before bringing it to the CE's personal attention should the complaint remain unresolved. See J.W.P. Wong (2013) 'Expanding and Destroying the Accountability System', in J.Y.S. Cheng (ed) *The Second Chief Executive of Hong Kong SAR: Evaluating the Tsang Years 2005–2012*, Hong Kong: City University of Hong Kong Press, p. 43. That might well be so. In practice, if the argument, as common among many former senior AOs, is that the new ministerial system has put all ministers working directly to the CE instead of via the CS/FS, there is nothing to prevent some ministers speaking directly to the CE on any matters of disagreement.

or constitutionalism.[36] In other words, they are not merely based on simple legal stipulations but created out of political practice or consensus honoured by political parties, whether in government or opposition. In Australia, for instance, it was observed that ministers frequently faced calls for resignation for departmental failure when they could be said to share at least some of the blame. However, actual resignation on these grounds was rare.[37]

In Hong Kong, some local academics had quite early on (after the introduction of the POAS) urged that some form of individual ministerial responsibility be developed, based on precedents clearly conveying the conditions under which the minister should be held partially or fully responsible for policy failure.[38] The independent think-tank SynergyNet suggested some guidelines to determine when a Principal Official should tender resignation to take responsibility, specifying that they should resign for: a major policy error or failure in policy administration within their portfolio which has caused significant damage to the public interest or the public's trust in the government; a serious failure in supervision over their bureau or subordinate departments or agencies in policy implementation, which has resulted in significant damage to the public interest or the public's trust in the government; or any act which has grossly harmed the reputation and integrity of the government.[39] However, apart from some general stipulations in the Code for Officials under the Political Appointment System, the new ministerial system has been silent as to when a minister has to take responsibility and accept sanctions including resignation.

Several defining moments, though, have seen varying reactions to public sentiment and legislators' demands for resignation or motion of no-confidence. During the Tung Administration, Fred Ma as a newly appointed Secretary for Financial Services and the Treasury had to openly apologise for the penny stock fiasco in July 2002.[40] In the aftermath of the 1 July mass protests in 2003, Antony Leung resigned as FS and Regina Ip as Secretary for Security, the former over his car purchase ahead of his 2013 Budget announcement on an increase in first registration tax and the latter for reason of pursuing further studies (after she became the principal target of political attack over the Article 23 legislation fiasco). Following the publication of the LegCo's investigation report on the SARS crisis the same month, in which he was severely criticised, Yeoh Eng-kiong resigned as Secretary for Health and Welfare. During the Tsang Administration, SCS Denise Yue was openly reprimanded by Donald Tsang for poorly handling the Leung Chin-man case where Leung, despite being a retired Director of Housing, was granted approval to take up post-retirement employment with a major developing company.

No minister resigned or was censured during the Leung Chun-ying Administration. However, two ministers faced a vote of no-confidence in the LegCo moved by pan-democratic legislators in 2012, which was not passed—namely, Secretary for Education Eddie Ng over the national education fiasco, and Secretary for Development Paul Chan over the involvement of his family in leasing subdivided units in private housing tenements and owning agricultural land in Kwu Tung in the New Territories that the government had plans to develop, which was perceived by opposition legislators and critics to be a conflict of interest. During the Guangzhou-Shenzhen-Hong Kong Express Rail Link (XRL) construction delay saga in mid-2014, Secretary for Transport and Housing Anthony Cheung publicly offered to resign should an Independent Expert Panel chaired by a retired senior judge find him personally or his bureau responsible for the delay. In the event, the panel did not establish any such responsibility.[41]

One notable consequence of the POAS is that some administrative mandarins (including Permanent Secretaries and Deputy Secretaries, as well as heads of departments) seemed to have somewhat retreated to the backseat, either voluntarily, out of deference to the Secretary (minister), or out of circumstances (where legislators would ignore them when pursuing the ministers as the prime target). Henceforth, the media, political parties, and legislators all quickly jumped to demanding ministerial heads to roll whenever any major incident happened, or an alleged scandal or failure was reported. Because some policy issues involved more than one policy bureau (or Secretary), it was often difficult to determinate which Secretary should be held accountable for the action or lack of action, or policy failure, under the principle of ministerial accountability.

These ever-changing accountability politics have not helped to strengthen performance or governance at large. Instead, policy bureau officials have become more reluctant to 'own' and 'lead' problems and issues where policy boundaries are less clear-cut, because once they have done so, the rest of the accountability burden would stay permanently with their bureau—including scrutiny by the LegCo, investigations by the Audit Commission and the Ombudsman, inquiries from the media, queries from politicians, and so on—and they are most likely to be sent to the firing lines of 'shame and blame' politics that could possibly result in career setbacks. Increasingly, Secretaries and Under-Secretaries as political appointees are expected to be the principal targets of accountability even if, at times, the matter has more to do with execution and day-to-day administration than policy decision and direction per se. In this light, it is debatable whether accountability in the government has been strengthened or conversely narrowed in terms of substance after the introduction of the POAS.

Recruitment of political appointees

The recruitment of ministers has been the most critical issue. To maintain some degree of continuity and because there was probably insufficient interest from a lot of 'outsiders' to cross into government to take policy jobs that carried political risk, some serving Secretary-rank civil servants had to be appointed as political ministers when Tung formed his first ministerial team in 2002 (6 out of 14).[42] As the political executive did not come from a party or established camp, there was no steady mechanism for the recruitment, training, or promotion of political appointees.

In a Westminster system (such as that in Britain), promising young political activists often join the party headquarters as operatives or become a personal aide to Members of Parliament or ministers before being nominated by the party to get elected to the Parliament, from there to embark on a career of political progression from parliamentary secretary to junior minister and then possibly minister and cabinet minister. In some countries like Japan, France, and Singapore, it is common to recruit ministerial appointees from among civil servants and administrators (even military officers in Singapore). Where ministers must constitutionally be Members of Parliament (not France where ministers must leave the National Assembly once appointed to the government), these political recruitees have to first leave the service and contest in parliamentary elections and win a seat.

In Hong Kong, since Donald Tsang's tenure as CE, there has been continuous reliance on appointing civil servants, even retired ones, as political ministers. Table 5.2 gives the ratio of politically appointed ministers from civil service background in successive Administrations. Having senior civil servants as political

Table 5.2: Number of politically appointed ministers from the civil service in successive administrations under POAS (as at July 2020)

Administration	Total number of ministers	Those coming from civil service (including retired civil servants)[a]	Percentage with civil service background
Tung Chee-hwa (2002–2005)	14	6[b]	42.9%
		7[c]	50.0%
Donald Tsang (2005–2007)	14	7	50.0%
Donald Tsang (2007–2012)	15	9	60.0%
		10[d]	66.7%
		9[e]	60.0%
		10[f]	66.7%
Leung Chun-ying (2012–2017)	15	8	53.3%
		7[g]	46.7%
	16[h]	7[i]	43.8%
		6[j]	37.5%
Carrie Lam (2017–2022)	16	7	43.8%
		8[k]	50.0%

[a] Those appointees who had served as civil servants quite some years ago but then moved to other public organisations such as the Hospital Authority and Hong Kong Monetary Authority are not included. Tsang Tak-sing, an outsider (deputy editor of *Tai Kung Pao*, a pro-Beijing newspaper) who first joined the Tung Administration as full-time member of the Central Policy Unit on civil service contract and later appointed as Secretary for Home Affairs in Donald Tsang's second-term Administration is not counted.

[b] Excluding Elsie Leung (Secretary for Justice) and Yeoh Eng-kiong (Secretary for Health and Welfare) who were appointed prior to the POAS on civil service contract, even though both were then 'outsiders'. Yeoh was previously a government doctor until he left the civil service to become Chief Executive of the Provisional Hospital Authority in 1989.

[c] After the resignation of Antony Leung (FS), Regina Ip (Secretary for Security), and Yeoh Eng-kiong, and various consequential appointments.

[d] After the resignation of Fred Ma (Secretary for Commerce and Economic Development) and appointment of Rita Lau (civil servant) to succeed him.

[e] After the resignation of Rita Lau (Secretary for Commerce and Economic Development) and appointment of her Under-Secretary Greg So (non-civil servant) to succeed her.

[f] After the resignation of Henry Tang (CS) to stand for the CE election, and consequential appointments.

[g] After the resignation of Mak Chai-kwong (retired civil servant) and appointment of Paul Chan (non-civil servant) as Secretary for Development.

[h] After the establishment of the Innovation and Technology Bureau.

[i] The new Secretary for Innovation and Technology Nick Yang was a non-civil servant.

[j] After the resignation of John Tsang (FS) and Carrie Lam (CS), both former civil servants, to stand for the CE election and consequential appointments.

[k] After the government reshuffling in April 2020 resulting in the replacement of Patrick Nip by the Director of Immigration Erick Tsang (both former civil servants) as Secretary for Constitutional and Mainland Affairs, the replacement of Joshua Law by Patrick Nip (both former civil servants) as SCS, the replacement of Lau Kong-wah by Under-Secretary for Labour and Welfare Caspar Tsui (both non-civil servants) as Secretary for Home Affairs, the replacement of James Lau by Christopher Hui (both non-civil servants) as Secretary for Financial Services and the Treasury, and the replacement of Nicholas Yang (non-civil servant) by the Director of Electrical and Mechanical Services Alfred Sit (civil servant) as Secretary for Innovation and Technology.

ministers does not necessarily help the minister-bureaucrat relationship because their former bureaucrat colleagues might treat them in the old light or resent them for having crossed the bench.

In the absence of party-based political recruitment, an unavoidable challenge to the CE is how to ensure that their nominees, coming from diverse backgrounds, work as a cohesive political team sharing common values of and approaches to governance.[43] In the pre-1997 civil service-monopolised system, senior mandarins coming from the Administrative Class shared a sense of esprit de corps and a common philosophy of administration inculcated through long years of service. The then CS, as head of the civil service and a long-serving bureaucrat, was also able to command fellow Secretary colleagues to provide a reasonable degree of consistency and collaboration. In the new ministerial system of political appointees, the CE has to play a strong steering role to integrate various portfolios and minimise policy clashes and inconsistencies as all ministers regard themselves as political equals only answerable to the CE and the CPG. As such, with the exception of Tung who was not known as an overly dictating leader, subsequent CEs have all increasingly behaved in a 'presidential' style.

The political executive should be strengthened by installing a junior ministerial layer and small ministerial teams to support individual Secretaries who otherwise would become 'lone fighters'. There was an attempt to do so in 2008 during Tsang's second term through the introduction of politically appointed Under-Secretaries and PAs, so as to shore up the government's capacity to reach out to the community and secure political support for policies and initiatives.[44] Under-Secretaries were responsible for assisting the Secretaries in undertaking the full range of political work and would deputise the Secretaries during their temporary absence while PAs were responsible for assisting the Secretaries in conducting liaison, lobbying, and other political work.

Tables 5.3 and 5.4 provide the backgrounds from which the additional layers of political appointees were recruited over the years. There was much less reliance on former or incumbent civil servants compared to the ministers (except in the current Carrie Lam Administration). PAs were almost all outsiders. However, though equivalent in rank to principal assistant secretaries in a bureau, PAs have often been seen as political liaisons with the working level of legislators and parties, thus unable to display a more visible role given that legislators still prefer to deal with the higher-ranking Secretaries and Under-Secretaries.

Compared to senior bureaucrats who had been exposed to various government functions through different postings, some Secretaries and Under-Secretaries did not have prior experience in either political work or public administration, which could be a handicap at the beginning given the very political nature of ministerial work. Based on the experience of the POAS so far, the CE's ministerial team (including Under-Secretaries and PAs) had not been entirely able to operate as a well-organised 'government party' with shared political vision, ideology, and strong inspirational and mobilisational capacity. Unlike party governments

**Table 5.3: Number of politically appointed under-secretaries
from the civil service in successive administrations under POAS
(as at July 2020)**

Administration	Total number of under-secretaries appointed	Those coming from the civil Service (including retired civil servants)[a]	Percentage with civil service background
Donald Tsang (2007–2012)	9	2	22.2%
Leung Chun-ying (2012–2017)	11	3	27.3%
	12[b]	3	25.0%
Carrie Lam (2017–2022)	12	5[c]	41.7%

[a]   Those appointees who had served in public organisations before are not included.

[b]   After the establishment of the Innovation and Technology Bureau.

[c]   Number remains unchanged after government reshuffling in April 2020.

**Table 5.4: Number of politically appointed PAs from civil service background
in successive administrations under POAS
(as at July 2020)**

Administration	Total number of PAs appointed	Those coming from the civil Service (including retired civil servants)[a]	Percentage with civil service background
Donald Tsang (2007–2012)	9	1[b]	11.1%
Leung Chun-ying (2012–2017)	13	1[c]	7.7%
	14[d]	1	7.1%
Carrie Lam (2017–2022)	14	1[e]	7.1%

[a]   Those appointees who had served as civil servants quite some years ago but then moved to other public organisations or the private sector are not counted.

[b]   Excluding Linda Choy, PA at the Environment Bureau, who was an AO from 1998 to 2004.

[c]   Excluding Patricia Woo, PA at Transport and Housing Bureau, who was a civil servant from 1990 to 2010. The PA of the CS (non-civil servant) later left the appointment and there was no replacement. Upon the appointment of Ronald Chan (non-civil servant) from PA to Under-Secretary of the Constitutional and Mainland Affairs Bureau in September 2015, the PA vacancy was unfilled.

[d]   After the establishment of the Innovation and Technology Bureau.

[e]   Number remains unchanged after government reshuffling in April 2020.

elsewhere, it could not depend on the pro-establishment parties for political mobilisation because those parties were not part of the government. The new political class much hoped for had failed to materialise. The small contingent of political appointees often had to face tougher times in the LegCo and a more inquisitive style of policy scrutiny from party legislators than senior civil servants who were regarded as politically more neutral. As if by default, executive-legislature relations under the new ministerial system became more frictional, as if a rivalry between two competing political parties existed.

A ministerial system of political appointment of 'outsiders' will work well if those outsiders have sufficient political and community standing (beyond narrow business or professional reputation), possess good prior political skills and acumen gained from the experience of interaction with politics (such as through public service work and links to political parties), and do not mind giving up their well-established private sector or non-government career, and sometimes higher incomes, in order to take up ministerial office. Top government appointments might well be prestigious and indicators of achieving power but carry only modest salaries compared to the corporate world, with no pensions or gratuities.[45] Their job satisfaction would come in the form of serving the community and achieving a position of public authority that would enable them to realise their vision and plan for a better society. Public office at the ministerial level should not be treated as just another career posting, an honorific appointment, or a place for someone who is only a political novice and detests politics.

One may argue that former or sitting legislators, or trade union and NGO leaders, who have accumulated rich political or social action experience would be ideal candidates for ministerial service.[46] However, the short tradition of Hong Kong's ministerial system has been biased towards recruiting 'outsiders' from members of the business and professional elites, an approach perhaps inherited from the pre-1997 British legacy of appointing these elites to major statutory and advisory bodies. The evolving reality now is that ministers are not well respected in the community, especially within the legislative chamber where they are often subject to verbal attack in the most derogatory manner. The opportunity for displaying political or policy performance, something that would be counted as a reward for a political career in other jurisdictions, has become limited because of Hong Kong's unique circumstances. If one does not find job satisfaction in ministerial office, and given the sacrifice one has to make in accepting political appointment such as the loss of privacy and dignity, the traditional recruitment pool of elite 'outsiders' would dry up, leaving incumbent or former senior civil servants the main source of candidates for ministerial posts. Even so, such alternatives might not always possess strong political skills and leadership demanded in a growingly turbulent polity.

Media outlets and commentators like to compare 'outsider' ministers with senior AOs and fault the former for lacking sufficient experience in public administration.[47] In Britain, ministerial office and the civil service are two distinct and seldom intermingled careers—with members of the former accumulating policy expertise and experience within a parliamentary career both as backbenchers and subsequently through appointments on the government bench or opposition frontbench handling different portfolios, and members of the latter spending a dedicated bureaucratic life as administrative mandarins posted to various departments or professional specialists of particular departments. Because of these separate career paths, there are different political ethos and expectations. In the US-style presidential systems, political appointments have long been a key feature at the upper echelons of government departments and agencies, not just at the cabinet level, and few would make a big issue out of such appointments which are at the sole discretion of the President. A 'revolving door' exists whereby movements between top government appointments and industry and think-tanks have become a norm among some OECD countries, but this has also raised concerns about policy favouritism and the regulatory capture of public policy by, for example, financial institutions.[48]

A new hybrid of 'political bureaucrats'?

In the aftermath of the 1 July 2003 mass protests, Tung was persuaded by circumstances (and his health) to leave the scene in March 2005 as Beijing opted for the return of government by AOs. Donald Tsang, who was previously perceived as being sidelined, was tasked by Beijing to replace Tung. In his June 2005 campaign during the CE election, while accepting that political appointments were to stay and that more 'outsiders' should be invited to join the governing team, Tsang also urged those civil servants who wanted to participate in politics to leave the civil service to take up political appointments.[49] Whereas Tung's project was to recruit outsiders into government and to retain former civil servants as ministers in charge of some portfolios as a transitional arrangement, Tsang, due to his bureaucratic background, seemed to go for a somewhat reverse approach—to have some outsiders in his administration but to principally rely upon the AOs as the source of ministerial talent. Those portfolios key to his new policy agenda were assigned to ministers of AO background, such as Finance, Constitutional Affairs, Education, Development, and Transport.

Under him, and now Carrie Lam, a kind of 'hybrid administrative state' based on 'government by political bureaucrats' (recruited from the civil service) is on the ascendancy. The AOs seem to have once again become the unifying and sustaining force of government, to help bring policy and administrative organisations together within more coherent structures and processes, although Lam has extended her selection of ministerial talent to some non-AO civil servants.[50] Singapore is arguably also a system keen on grooming bureaucrats for ministerial office, which has been working well over the decades. However, it pays to take heed of the reflections of former Singaporean Prime Minister Goh Chok Tong who warns against falling into a situation of 'group think' where there are less differing (and dissenting) views within the ruling party:

> [I]f they are unable to attract people from outside the civil service and armed forces, then you'll have some kind of civil service, public service thinking [...]. And then over time, if you're attracting only fewer and fewer top civil servants, you end up with many SAF [Singapore Armed Forces] officers, old generals; again the group is even narrower.[51]

Hong Kong's government, however, is not a parliamentary government like Singapore. In the absence of an institutional means to link the bureaucrat-dominated executive and parties-dominated legislature, the overall system of governance has remained disjointed. Besides, the administrative competence of the AOs has become somewhat demystified after several post-1997 crises, so much so that AOs can no longer command the same (high) level of adoration or respect whether by other civil servants or legislators and political parties as in the colonial days. Still, public attitudes have been conditioned by long years of government by bureaucrats. Many people view political appointments of 'outsiders' especially at the minister level with scepticism. Whereas 'political bureaucrats' can claim lineage to the civil service as an advantage and power base, the 'outsiders', even if themselves successful business or professional leaders, lack a proper political base of their own (particularly where party affiliation is not encouraged). Thus, they suffer an a priori disadvantage and would not take political appointment as rewarding in the prevailing political climate where ministers become easy targets of the 'blame and shame' politics of the legislature and media.

As far as the central state is concerned, apart from relying on the competence and loyalty of the hybrid political-bureaucrat ministers, as well as members of the CE's ExCo, for stable governance of the SAR, it also has to ensure that civil service leaders—namely, the permanent secretaries and the heads of disciplined forces—are made aware of national interests, concerns, and objectives especially when Hong Kong faces a more volatile political environment. Starting from the Leung Administration, whenever any national leaders have come to visit Hong Kong, an opportunity is arranged for the leader to speak to these top civil servants as well, both to demand their loyalty and to boost morale.

Chapter 6

The Civil Service System and Reform

Introduction

The Hong Kong civil service system is an institution inherited by the SAR as part of the British legacy. It now has a total workforce of some 173,700, with more than 400 grades and over 1,000 ranks, operating on 12 general pay scales.[1] As a unified service, all civil servants are subject to common appointment procedures and similar disciplinary codes.[2] Since colonial times, the civil service has been managed according to an internal set of government regulations known as the Civil Service Regulations. Following the introduction of the new ministerial system of political appointment in 2002, in response to public expectations to preserve a merit-based and non-partisan civil service institution, the government promulgated a Civil Service Code in September 2009, in which several core values were set out for all civil servants. These include: commitment to the rule of law; honesty and integrity; objectivity and impartiality; political neutrality; accountability for decisions and actions; and dedication, professionalism, and diligence.[3]

Discrepancies in employment terms and conditions between expatriate and local officers (such as in overseas leave, housing, and children's education allowances, etc.) were gradually removed in the 1990s as Hong Kong entered the late transition period. Prior to the Sino-British agreement on a new pension system in 1987, civil servants were not entitled to pension rights per se. The life pension awarded to them upon retirement at the age of 55 were at the pleasure of the Crown. Afterwards, pension became an entitlement with the 'pensionable' retirement age extended to 60 (55 for disciplined officers).[4] As of 2000, as part of civil service reform, new recruits are no longer eligible for retirement pensions. Instead, a provident fund with higher employer contributions than under the Mandatory Provident Fund (MPF) system for ordinary employees has been implemented.[5] From June 2015 onwards, all newly recruited civil servants enjoy an extended retirement age, at 65 for civilian officers and 60 for disciplined services. Article 102 of the Basic Law honours the commitments of the pre-1997 British administration to retired and serving public servants in respect of pensions, gratuities, allowances, and benefits due to them, irrespective of their nationality or place of residence. Article 100 reassures incumbent public servants that such payments would be 'on terms no less favourable than before' (i.e., before 1 July 1997).

The colonial system for managing the civil service had essentially followed the British home practice, which was kept intact after the transfer of rule in 1997 under Article 103.[6] A statutory Public Service Commission advised the Governor (now CE) on civil service appointment, promotion, and discipline matters, to safeguard the impartiality and integrity of the mechanisms concerned. It was by convention led by a retired top civil servant (an AO) as paid Chairman, a practice continued today. The Basic Law also provides for the employment of foreign nationals in the public service subject to certain restrictions. Under Article 101, only the top posts must be occupied by Chinese nationals among permanent residents of the SAR with no right of abode in any foreign country.[7] Otherwise, the SAR government may employ British and other foreign nationals previously serving in the public service (i.e., before the transfer of rule), or those holding SAR permanent identity cards, as public servants in government departments at all levels. In addition, foreign nationals may be recruited as advisers to government departments or to fill professional and technical posts. This should be perceived as a very liberal policy not just to keep the British legacy but to enable Hong Kong to continue to thrive as a cosmopolitan city.

Civil service training has become more emphasised, accompanied by a pronounced localisation policy, since the 1970s. With improved salaries and conditions of service, and thanks to vigorous anti-corruption efforts, the Hong Kong civil service was able to attain an image as an efficient, clean, and well-paid workforce by the 1980s, able to attract people from the highest calibre of society. During British rule, newly recruited AOs were sent to Oxford University for training and immersion programmes, and civil servants of various grades were supported by government scholarship to undertake further studies in Britain to acquire relevant professional qualifications.[8] This helped to inculcate a sense of identification with British systems and standards, and pride of elitism and esprit de corps through old-boys networks. From the 1990s, some senior civil servants including AOs began to be sent to national studies programmes run by prestigious Mainland universities and institutes (e.g., Tsinghua University and Peking University), a practice extended after the handover in 1997.[9] Apart from the provision of knowledge about the Mainland's policies and standard operations, such programmes also serve to enable local bureaucrats to build social networks which may facilitate their work when it involves interactions with Mainland authorities.

Civil service pay system and controversies

Pay and conditions of service were the most sensitive areas of civil service management and on a few occasions saw serious disputes between the staff and management. The traditional civil service system served British rule well as it treasured a life-long career with maximum job security, stable expectations, and minimum incentives to transfer out, through the operation of a retirement pension scheme which disadvantaged early departure before retirement age and other length-of-service-induced occupational benefits (such as housing), as well as favourable pay and conditions of service. Such a system was conducive to maintaining a devoted and stable workforce.

Colonial Hong Kong followed the British Priestley model (after the 1953 Priestley Commission).[10] It ran a civil service pay system according to the principle of 'fair comparison' with the private sector—on the grounds that the government did not intend to lead or influence the market in wage rates. Since it was impossible to determine pay for civil servants according to their market values, the only fair and efficient way was to link the pay levels of different categories (grades) of civil servants to their counterparts in the private sector, to ensure that the government only paid civil servants the prevailing market wages and maintained competitiveness vis-à-vis the private sector in recruiting and retaining staff of good calibre. When making comparisons with the private sector, the government normally used larger employers with better pay practices as the benchmark, to underscore government as a good employer. As a result, civil servants generally enjoyed better terms and conditions compared to the average private-sector employees.

Several key elements formed the foundation of the pay policy, namely: 'fair comparison' with comparable counterparts in the private sector; internal comparisons (known as 'internal relativities') within the civil service, particularly for those grades lacking comparable external counterparts; acceptability by the civil servants as being fair; acceptability by the public as being fair; ability to attract and retain candidates of good calibre; and paying lower-rank civil servants better salaries than their counterparts in the private sector.[11] As the civil service expanded in both size and complexity, pay issues became more intricate and politically sensitive, and also more susceptible to disputes.[12]

Prior to 1974, an ad hoc approach was adopted for the review and adjustment of civil service salaries. Every five years or so, a one-off Salaries Commission was appointed to conduct a comprehensive pay survey. In 1974, following the failure of the occupational class survey system adopted by the 1971 Salaries Commission, an annual pay trend survey of the private sector was implemented, with the findings—known as 'pay trend indicators' (PTIs)—used as the basis for determining annual pay adjustments for the civil service.[13] The advent of an inflationary economy in Hong Kong after the 1973 oil shock also rendered it pertinent to catch up with private sector pay levels on a more frequent basis than hitherto, but only one pay level survey was conducted because of methodological problems and difficulties in determining private sector analogues. In 1979, a Standing Commission on Civil Service Salaries and Conditions of Service (Standing Commission) was set up to provide independent advice to the government on such matters and to conduct pay reviews and surveys. Over time, three other independent bodies were also established: the Standing Committee on Directorate Salaries and Conditions of Service, the Standing Committee on Judicial Salaries and Conditions of Service, and the Standing Committee on Disciplined Services Salaries and Conditions of Service.[14]

In May 1986, after widespread agitations arose within the rest of the civil service for salary adjustments, following the government's award of a special pay rise to directorate staff based on a directorate pay survey, the Standing Commission tasked Hay Management Consultants (Hong Kong) Limited to conduct the first pay level survey for non-directorate staff. Its methodology and findings were, however, disputed by the staff, forcing the government to appoint an independent Committee of Inquiry (Burrett Committee) in 1988 to provide arbitration. The Burrett Committee recommended in 1989 that from then on, three-yearly pay level surveys should form the foundation of the civil service pay system, in order to keep closer track of private sector pay rates.[15] During the years between pay level surveys, pay trend surveys would provide the basis for annual pay adjustments in line with private sector trends.

The government did not explicitly accept such recommendations, but neither were they rejected. The Standing Commission also considered it practically difficult to identify enough private sector job analogues for making job-for-job comparisons and was concerned that frequent pay level surveys would cause inevitable disruption to internal relativities and upset civil service stability. In practice, since the 1989–1990 pay structure reviews and up until the end of British rule, the government had not asked for, and the Standing Commission had not initiated, any pay level surveys, although annual pay trend surveys continued to be conducted. As a result, pay relativities with the private sector became eroded, particularly after the outbreak of the Asian financial crisis in 1998, when severe economic downturn led to rapid pay cuts by many private companies whereas civil service pay rates remained untouched.

Although a pay system premised on a relatively 'objective' comparison with market rates and internal relativities could provide system stability and a regime of reasonable expectations, such stability and predictability came at a price. The 'fair comparison' principle could not guarantee comparable levels of performance. The fact that many civil service grades lacked private-sector counterparts also meant that their pay levels were not linked to the market, but instead sustained by historical internal relativities within the civil service, a process criticised by the private sector as subjective and bureaucratic. A pay system based on a centralised process of external and internal comparisons also deprived departmental managers of using pay adjustment as an important tool for inducing staff performance. The only tool available to these managers was promotion, which might not be the most appropriate reward for the satisfactory performance of employees in their present rank, as well recognised by the Peter Principle.[16] Relying on promotion as the key staff motivator would lead to an unnecessary proliferation of higher ranks.

Internal relativities became a potential source of pay grievances and disputes. Any disruption of historical relativities, perceived by staff as part of pay equity, would in effect mean a 'market devaluation' of concerned grades and ranks, thus causing morale problems.[17] While a pay system based on market surveys would obviate the need for tedious and even acrimonious negotiations with staff, as well as incessant agitations and pressure politics, pay issues could never be free of politics especially in more volatile economic circumstances. Raising pay was always easier than reducing it. In boom times, the PTIs tended to be favourable to civil servants. In a recession, when salary cuts would seem warranted, reductions would be strongly resisted by civil servants and were rare, leading to private sector criticism that civil servants did not share the pain of a shrinking economy.

During the 1990s, civil service pay reform was a trend among OECD countries driven by NPM strategies.[18] In the run-up to 1997, the government was keen to secure the stability and morale of the civil service as an important pillar of a smooth transition. Although the 1993 Civil Service Branch review had called for moving towards a performance-oriented culture, there was limited political desire to push for extensive management changes because of expected resistance from civil servants and their unions who also actively lobbied the Chinese government to keep the status quo intact.[19]

Civil service reform

As the Asian financial crisis gained momentum in 1998, Hong Kong had to endure an economic recession of a scale not seen in three decades. In the midst of economic uncertainties, the public was increasingly questioning whether the civil service still provided value for money. Private companies responded to changing market conditions quickly by means of downsizing and wage cuts, which further widened the pay gap between the two sectors. The civil service was under heavy fire from many sides. The business sector called for public sector pay cuts, echoed by some politicians. Media editorials and commentaries advocated civil service pay reform. Within the government, there was increasing fiscal pressure to cut costs in response to the worsening economic situation.

Feeling that reform was unavoidable, the new Tung Administration decided to introduce some fundamental changes to the civil service system. As then SCS Lam Woon-kwong remarked at a public forum: 'If we don't initiate the change ourselves, change will be imposed on us!'[20] The 1999 consultation document on civil service reform, under the theme 'Civil Service into the twenty-first century', acknowledged that the public was unhappy with the handling of several incidents by the government and that the efficiency of certain departments was in doubt. It set out three directions of structural change: an open, flexible, equitable, and structured civil service framework, with more flexible entry and exit mechanisms to take in talent and remove non-performers at all levels; an enabling and motivating environment for civil servants, with a competitive but performance-based reward system to attract, retain and motivate civil servants; and a proactive, accountable, and responsible culture, enhancing efficiency and quality of service and nurturing a performance-based and service-oriented management culture.[21] The keywords were: performance, flexibility, and accountability.

Various changes were contemplated—covering entry and exit arrangement, conduct and discipline, pay and conditions, performance management, and training and development. As far as pay and conditions were concerned, apart from reiterating the existing pay principles and committing to a starting salaries review, the consultation document promised to consider how elements of performance-based reward systems could be progressively introduced into the civil service and how the pay trend survey mechanism could be modified and improved to make it compatible with a performance-based system.[22] The Civil Service Reform package was bold and in tandem with the global reform trend. It was no surprise that it was met by strong reaction from the staff and even some departmental managers who doubted its practicability and were wary of the impact on staff morale. At a LegCo motion debate on 9 June 1999, Lam acknowledged the concerns regarding performance-related pay and promised to implement trial changes in selected areas to ensure that any new system was workable, practicable, and generally acceptable before extending them to other areas.[23]

With the replacement of Lam Woon-kwong by Joseph Wong as SCS in February 2000, civil service reform was toned down. The government gave up the proposal to eventually turn all basic ranks, representing two-thirds of the civil service, into contract posts. The three advisory bodies on non-judicial civil service pay were invited by the government to set up a Task Force in 2002 to review civil service pay policy and pay system (excluding judiciary salaries which were subject to a separate review). Phase I involved an analytical study of recent developments and best practices in pay administration in other countries. The Task Force examined civil service pay reforms in five countries—Australia, Canada, New Zealand, Singapore, and Britain—focusing on five aspects: pay policies, pay system, and pay structure; experience of replacing fixed pay scales with pay ranges; pay adjustment system and mechanism; performance-based rewards; and simplification and decentralisation of pay administration.

A Phase I Interim Report was published in April 2002 for public consultation, together with the findings of a consultancy study completed by PwC Consulting Hong Kong Limited.[24] The Task Force's final report, submitted to the government in September 2002, made a number of near, medium, and long-term recommendations. In the short term, they suggested to devise a practical framework and methodology for conducting a pay level survey, to review the pay trend survey methodology, and to consider appropriate interim measures for the annual civil service pay adjustment exercise pending the outcome of the above review. In the medium term, they recommended to consider the feasibility of introducing elements of performance pay and flexible 'pay ranges' to civil servants (at the directorate level initially, then throughout the civil service if proved feasible), and to consolidate job-related allowances within basic salary as part of a move towards a 'clean wage' policy in the long run. In the long term, they recommended to gradually decentralise pay administration to departmental managements, giving departments greater freedom to manage pay arrangements to suit their needs.[25]

These recommendations were, however, deemed too radical. Not unexpectedly, they were not well received by the staff who harboured immense suspicions about the government's pay policy intentions and questioned the feasibility of performance-related pay and flexible pay ranges. Even departmental managers were sceptical and worried that too much flexibility would create differential treatment which might have a detrimental effect on teamwork and staff morale. The government sat on the Task Force report for several months. When it finally accepted the Task Force's recommendations in February 2003, it decided that priority should be given in the short term to devising a practical framework and methodology for conducting a pay level survey and to reviewing the pay trend survey methodology. The other recommendations were put in abeyance.

In other countries, although linking pay to performance in the civil service had indeed become a growing trend in times of economic and fiscal adversity, strong resistance was still encountered from both management and frontline civil servants to any attempts to tamper with the existing pay system that was valued for its stability and uniformity.[26] According to a top executive survey of the public sector, performance-related pay was the least widely used reform tool among European countries.[27] In Hong Kong, the idea did not go far either and was soon withdrawn. A pilot scheme of team-based performance reward was experimented with by a few departments in 2001, which had to fund the reward scheme out of their own budget (e.g., by utilising their efficiency savings under the EPP). The scheme was eventually shelved because of the lack of broader interest within the government, in particular the larger departments.

It was clear that a full-fledged performance-related pay system would be complicated to implement. Instead, attention turned to reforming the system of annual salary progression to make 'increments' no longer automatic but linked to performance appraisal.[28] Such tightening up went some way in highlighting the importance of performance, but only among those staff not yet reaching the maximum point of their salary scale. There were other initiatives to streamline and downsize the civil service establishment, including enhanced efficiency drives, hiring of staff on non-civil service contract to cope with new services and increased workload, two rounds of general VRS in 2000 and 2003, targeted VRS for specific grades between 2000 and 2006, and the general freezing of open recruitment (from fiscal year 1999–2000 to 2006–2007, with breaks in 2001–2002 and 2002–2003). As a result, compared to around 185,800 in 2000–2001, the civil service establishment and strength were down to around 159,400 and 153,800 respectively by March 2007, a reduction of some 14–17%.[29]

Pay-cut disputes and settlement

Meanwhile, a major civil service pay dispute had culminated in staff protests and judicial challenge in 2002 and 2003. The 2002 annual pay trend survey indicated that net downward adjustments of 1.58%, 1.64%, and 4.42% for the lower, middle, and upper salary bands respectively would be warranted. Instead of merely freezing civil service pay as in the past when negative PTIs were obtained, the government decided to go ahead with pay cuts. Upon advice by its lawyers that pay reductions would lack sufficient legal force in the absence of legislation, the government opted to introduce pay-cut legislation. This triggered a strong reaction from the staff. Some union leaders were opposed to a pay cut of any kind, claiming 'reasonable expectations' of employees in a system where salaries were paid on fixed scales and had never been subject to reduction before. Others objected to using legislative means to reduce pay as this would create a precedent that might be applied to other civil service benefits such as pensions.

While the business sector welcomed pay cuts, trade unions and pro-grassroots political parties (including pro-establishment ones) were sceptical of such a move for fear that a downward adjustment of civil service pay might in turn trigger further depression in the overall wage level in a contracting economy. As the public sector included some 350,000 employees (about 180,000 in the civil service and the rest in other public-sector and subvented-sector organisations, such as schools, universities, and social services agencies, which were broadly linked to the civil service in pay and conditions), any pay cuts would likely significantly impact the community and even cause the deflation of consumption power of a considerable proportion of the working population. The room available for pay cuts was also constrained by legal and constitutional complications, especially Article 100 of the Basic Law noted above.[30] In the event, the pay-cut legislation was passed in July 2002 after heated debates in the legislative chamber and amidst protests by some civil servants and their supporters. Staff relations were under severe strain which threatened morale.

The pay adjustment legislation's constitutionality was challenged in court by a few individual civil servants with the support of staff unions. The Court of First Instance ruled in favour of the government, noting that the Executive had sought legislation to reduce civil service pay *not* to meet a 'target figure' unilaterally calculated as being fiscally prudent or entirely arbitrary in relation to the existing mechanism for adjusting pay, but they instead sought to reduce that pay entirely in accordance with the existing mechanism and with principles long accepted by both the Executive and the representatives of the civil service, a founding principle being the need for a 'broad comparability' between private and public sector pay.[31] The court concluded that Article 100 of the Basic Law was not worded in such rigid terms as to direct that pay, allowances, and benefits may not for any reason, in terms of specific figures, fall below those bestowed on 30 June 1997. So long as the previous 'system' of pay and conditions was not altered to be less favourable than before, the relevant constitutional provisions were not breached.

Upon appeal, the CFA ruled that Article 100 should be seen principally as ensuring the continuity of employment so that no civil servant suffered as a consequence of the handover itself. The Court upheld the plenary powers of the legislature to include the alteration of a term in civil servants' contracts and a reduction in pay. It said that Article 103 guarantees the continuation of Hong Kong's previous system of public service 'employment' and 'management', not any system of public service 'pay and conditions of service'.[32] Following this ruling, some civil service unions feared that the government would now have a free hand in fixing pay levels. Such worry should be qualified despite the lifting of judicial hurdles. Since colonial times, civil service pay had been as much a matter of legality as of politics and staff stability and morale. It had long been government policy that civil servants' remunerations should be broadly linked to the private-sector levels.

Following the decision to suspend the 2003 annual pay trend survey, the government was left with the alternatives of either waiting until a comprehensive pay level survey was completed before making any adjustment to civil service salaries, or negotiating with the staff on an acceptable rate of adjustment. Eventually, it opted for a negotiated settlement first, to be followed by a pay level survey, which could then be allocated more time to be completed. In February 2003, Joseph Wong reached consensus with the staff-side of the four central consultative councils[33] and representatives of major service-wide staff unions on civil service pay adjustments in 2004 and 2005, as well as the development by 2004 of an improved civil service pay adjustment mechanism in consultation with the staff-side and based on the existing mechanism. A steering committee under his chairmanship, together with a consultative group, was set up in April 2003 for such tasks. The Phase II study of the earlier Task Force was not pursued. The settlement reached—enabling civil service salaries to be frozen in 2003 and then cut in two stages, by 3% on average from 2004 and another 3% from 2005 (the so-called '0–3–3' package) to bring overall pay levels to those in 1997—was seen as a political climb-down by the government in the face of severe pressure from staff.

In mid-2007, following the completion of a pay level survey (which found civil service pay levels by and large not deviating from private sector levels by more than 5% one way or the other), a newly conducted pay trend survey and a starting salaries review, civil servants were given a pay rise for the first time in several years. Under the improved civil service pay adjustment mechanism adopted that year,[34] three sets of surveys would be conducted regularly to assess how the prevailing civil service pay compared with private sector pay and, having regard to the findings of the surveys, whether and how the civil service pay should be adjusted. The three sets of surveys were: the annual pay trend survey (with some smaller companies included in the survey field and a gross-up factor of 25% applied to these companies); the triennial starting salaries survey; and the six-yearly pay level survey comparing the prevailing salaries of different segments of non-directorate civil servants (categorised by job levels and job families) with their counterparts in the private sector. Apart from these surveys, grade structure reviews for selected grades would also be conducted as and when necessary. In addition to pay-related surveys, the fringe benefits and allowances provided to civil servants were also subject to review and modernisation.

The politics of civil service reform

The politics of public sector reforms could be understood in terms of a 'public service bargain' between politicians and bureaucrats, with the ultimate reform model being an outcome of political competition and negotiation.[35] Hong Kong in the 1990s did not yet have a politics-bureaucracy bargain per se because its government was run by bureaucrats who controlled agenda setting, including that for public sector reform (as explained in Chapter 3). Besides, the community at large did not doubt the merit of the civil service which was deemed a vital pillar of the Hong Kong system of governance. The bureaucrat-driven reform served to provide a new buffer of managerialism to shield bureaucrats from growing societal politicisation.

Post-1997, however, public sector reforms began to display some civil service-bashing connotations, with concurrent efforts to downsize the bureaucracy through extensive contracting out, outsourcing, non-civil service contract employment, and voluntary retirement. Because of economic and fiscal pressures in the aftermath of the Asian financial crisis and the public discontent about civil service performance, the Tung Administration was driven to more performance-oriented reform measures to restore efficiency and effectiveness. The attempts to overhaul the civil service pay system and implement other NPM practices, packaged as Civil Service Reform, marked a shift in the reform trajectory. The previous pro-civil service tradition gradually eroded. Instead of solely relying on bureaucratic excellence as the remedy to new political and policy shortcomings, Tung Chee-hwa opted for a political solution after the bureaucratic solution failed during his first term by introducing the political appointment of principal officials (as discussed in Chapter 5).

Civil service reform was poorly received by many rank-and-file and middle-level civil servants who saw it not as a source of rejuvenation and performance improvement but as a means to downsize and denigrate the civil service. Some of them blamed the top mandarins, alleging that the administrative elite had sacrificed their subordinates' interests in order to contain the impact of a larger political crisis not of the latter's making. A 'political' tug of war was played out between the staff and management. What was ironic was that while the government's crisis of efficiency and efficacy had opened the window of opportunity for civil service reform, the controversies triggered by the specific reform proposals and the way the reform process was managed had in turn fuelled anti-government action, thereby deepening the legitimacy crisis already suffered by the government. The pay-cut legislation in July 2002 led to the largest-ever protest by 50,000 civil servants, public sector employees, and their supporters, exposing a cleavage between the government and staff not seen during colonial times.

The original attempt to establish a performance-based culture and remuneration system had to beat the drum of retreat by late 2000. Still, the government had succeeded in impressing upon most civil servants that the days of permanent tenure were gone. VRS was put on the books, which gave the government greater flexibility in dealing with redundant and non-performing staff when proceeding with privatisation exercises or downsizing plans. The price for this partial success was a political one. As mentioned, new civil servants recruited from June 2000 onwards would no longer enjoy lifelong pension after retirement; a provident fund scheme was put in place instead. Job security and steady pay progression in the past, supplemented by generous job-related welfare and fringe benefits, had been instrumental in making the former colonial civil service one of the most loyal workforces in the world. This edge over private employment was gradually removed. Henceforth, civil servants would by default become less loyal in their career commitment and be more motivated by material gains than a sense of lifelong vocation. In comparison, the Singapore government, also pursuing similar reforms at around the same time, had preserved pension arrangements for its elite Administrative Class, Diplomatic Service, and Police and Military Services, even though these were abolished for the civil service at large.

Although linking pay to performance in the civil service was much talked about in the global NPM arena, it was easier said than done and not pushed wholeheartedly in many countries because of political and administrative complexities. Indeed, many middle managers tended to take a cynical view of a performance-related pay system, and junior civil servants feared they would be subject to arbitrary evaluation by those supervisors who favoured their protégés or were otherwise prejudiced.[36] Furthermore, performance-related pay may not be any more effective at motivating staff than other aspects of the work situation. For example, an OECD study conducted in the late 1990s found that, for many public sector managers, job independence, a sense of accomplishment, challenging work, and respect and fair treatment were deemed more important motivators than performance-related pay.[37] In terms of staff motivation, one should not lose sight of non-monetary incentives (such as better career development and improved working environment and practices) and other value ingredients (such as job satisfaction, sense of achievement, and social appreciation). To achieve an efficient, productive, and streamlined civil service, non-pay measures, such as structural changes, de-layering, modernisation of work procedures, and job reviews, would often have more impact.

In any case, to address the concern about VFM, it would be incumbent upon the government to embark on a more vigorous programme of performance evaluation to reassure the public that cost-efficiency and performance monitoring are indeed key elements of civil service reward management.[38] However, for any such flexible pay system to be implemented at all, there must be sufficient trust in changes within the civil service and among the community at large, as well as sufficient capacity of the government to push for reform. None of these conditions seems present in Hong Kong. Whereas civil service reform has ceased to be a focal point of administrative improvement since the Donald Tsang Administration (after the 2007 pay adjustment settlement), it is still an area of concern in public administration elsewhere. For example, as late as 2012, a Civil Service Reform

Plan was launched under the previous Conservative-Liberal Democratic coalition government in Britain aiming to make its civil service fit for the twenty-first century (CS21)—smaller, more efficient, more skilled, more open, and less bureaucratic.[39] That Hong Kong, whether within government or the community at large, has stopped talking about civil service reform (or public sector reform for that matter) speaks volumes of a polity increasingly embroiled in constitutional debates with no breakthrough and a civil service culture that is becoming more risk-averse and shying away from bold thinking.

Chapter 7
Government Capacity and Policy System

Introduction

Henry Kissinger once said:

> [B]efore I served as a consultant to [J.F.] Kennedy, I had believed, like most academicians, that the process of decision-making was largely intellectual and that all one had to do was to walk into the President's office and convince him of the correctness of one's views. This perspective, I soon realized, is as dangerously immature as it is widely held.[1]

Indeed, in the real world, the business of governing and policy-making is a complex and indefinite process not wholly dictated by the leader of the government, even in the most autocratic system.

In the literature, while it is not disputed that policy capacity is fundamental to public policy-making and implementation, there is a range of disagreements on how policy capacity can be delineated and operationalised, with some opting for a more expansive definition and some a more focused one.[2] Conceptual contestations aside, the policy capacity of a government can be defined in a more straight-forward manner as 'the ability of the state to organize its information-gathering and decision-making power to enable the making of intelligent collective choices about the allocation of scarce resources towards public ends', as ultimately determined by the general capacity of the state itself.[3] Such ability of government to achieve its targets and deliver results is shaped, constrained, and facilitated, as the case may be, by both structural factors (the architecture) and process factors (rules, conventions, dynamics, and circumstances) which are far from determinate according to formal power and authority.

When Hong Kong was under British colonial rule, the Governor was almost supreme in power, but that did not mean he could do whatever he wanted. He was still subject to constraints by past policy precedents, conventional practice, dominant policy thinking, his own bureaucracy, and elite interests safeguarded and represented by his appointees to major advisory bodies, including the ExCo. After the restoration to Chinese sovereignty in 1997, successive CEs—inheriting the former powers of Governorship and under the 'executive-led' principle—have embraced some bold policy visions and plans, but they have been mostly frustrated in the end because of the serious policy impasse and political and social divisiveness in the community due to various structural and contingent factors restricting state capacity. The term 'state' here does not mean a sovereign state per se, but rather the governing institutions in the sense of the 'state' versus 'society' and 'economy' common in public administration and governance discourse.

Foundation of government capacity

The scope of government determines how to get things done in pursuance of state-defined objectives and goals. However, as Linda Weiss has cautioned, the state is often a conglomeration of varied crystallisation exhibiting internal 'imbalances', parts of which may have more capacity than others.[4] The academic debates on state capacity, especially in Asia, have gained momentum since the 1982 benchmark study by Chalmers Johnson of Japan's previous Ministry of International Trade and Industry (MITI), illuminating a model of the developmental or 'plan-rational' state.[5] In his seminal study of Korea, Taiwan, and Japan, Robert Wade conceptualised an understanding of East Asian developmentalism as the 'governed market'.[6] In contrast to the earlier emphasis on the state-business relationship in the literature, Peter Evans advanced a concept of 'embedded autonomy' which expected the state to have the capacity to combine two contradictory aspects: 'Weberian bureaucratic insulation' and 'intense immersion in the surrounding social structure'.[7] Theda Skocpol similarly advocated state autonomy, highlighting the potential of state bureaucracies for autonomous operations and the notion of social embeddedness to give the state the legitimacy to act.[8]

The conventional discussion of state capacity tends to engage a notion of a 'strong' state with a high capacity to complete four critical tasks: penetrate society, regulate social relationships, extract resources, and appropriate resources.[9] However, a strong versus weak state dichotomy might not always help to delineate state capacity because the state does not always need to subdue the economy (industry) or society to achieve results and realise its goals. Besides, it is difficult to identify states with a high degree of capacity in all policy areas.[10] It has also been pointed out by some, as if rebutting Johnson, that Japan has achieved impressive economic growth since the 1960s despite its weak state and fractured centre.[11] Weiss's theory of state capacity took Evans's concept of embedded autonomy one step further by putting the preferred state as being insulated from undue special interests but firmly embedded in society, and as maintaining effective linkages with industry and other societal and economic actors to ensure the happening of things through what she theorised as 'governed interdependence', 'whereby the state exploits and converts its autonomy into increasing coordinating capacity by entering into cooperative relationships with the private sector, in order thereby to enhance the effectiveness of its economic and industrial policies'.[12] The state was still considered vital, but it had to shore up its capacity through extended embeddedness.

There has also been a contrasting stream of articulations resigned to the weakening or even hollowing-out of state power in Western countries due to the fiscal crisis and overloading of the state, triggering neoliberal efforts to roll back the frontiers of the state since the 1980s and justifying off-loading to the private sector through privatisation and to the non-government social sectors as the 'third sector'. Contrasting state-centred models, society-centred approaches have focused on transforming governance into 'governance without government'.[13] The surge in networks has been prompted by the persistent critique of traditional forms of governance around hierarchies and markets.[14] The 'new' governance discussion in the past two decades has paid more attention to the governability of society, going beyond institutions and actors within government and the formalities of politics, in favour of a more holistic interpretation of legitimacy and the exercise of power.[15] The new governance narrative recognises 'a differentiated polity characterized by relationships of co-dependence and reciprocity',[16] and advocated shifting from a unilateral (government or society separately) to an interactionist focus (government with society), with emphasis on inter-dependencies.[17] In other words, the state is realistically not only a static institution per se but a system or conglomeration of overlapping strategic linkages.

Inasmuch as the government's connectedness to economic and social sectors is regarded as critical to state capacity, the autonomy of the state from 'society' and 'particular interests' is equally pertinent (i.e., whether the state 'is able to *formulate* and *impose* policy upon them' and 'how […] a state so separate, so autonomous, from society, [can] obtain adequate information and get society to conform to its policies').[18] Connectedness and autonomy are thus two aspects of the dialectic, hence the structural tensions between state and society—even more so in a system where the state lacks political legitimacy. Critics of the new network and collaborative governance theorisations, while accepting the trend for governments to cultivate more links and partnerships with different sectors and to make greater use of market and social means in addition to hierarchical authority to pursue state goals and implement policies, have further questioned if the state has receded or could recede at all as it remains to be in charge and is expected to do so. To them, the state could not hand over ultimate authority and responsibility to non-state actors even though it could seek to boost its capacity by employing an expanding range of governance strategies and building closer relationships with relevant non-state sectors, culminating in a kind of fused state-centric relational approach.[19]

Grounded in these observations and approaches, an overarching conceptual framework has been developed to capture and link four specific dimensions—'bureaucracy' (organisational strength and insulation following the Weberian formulation), 'economy and industry' (government-industry linkages grounded in governed interdependence as articulated by Weiss), 'civil society' (Evans's notion of social embeddedness), and 'political society' (in terms of strong political leadership, legitimacy and authority) (see Figure 7.1).[20]

Figure 7.1: State capacity configuration

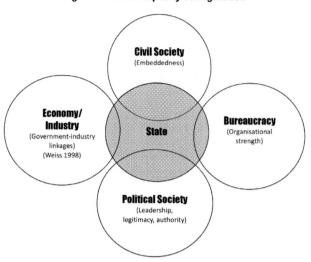

Source: Adapted from Figure 12.1 of A.B.L. Cheung (2005d), 'State Capacity in Hong Kong, Singapore and Taiwan: Coping with Legitimation, Integration and Performance', in J. Pierre and M. Painter (eds) *Challenges to State Policy Capacity: Global Trends and Comparative Perspectives*, Basingstoke: Palgrave Macmillan, pp. 225–254.

The 'autonomy' of the state from the economic, social, and bureaucratic forces, to avoid being reversely captured by them, and the ability of the state to connect (and 'steer') such forces through effective linkages in pursuit of what the state in its overall strategy considers to be vital to social and economic development would demonstrate the capacity of the state. However, the state, economy, and civil society are not discrete domains. They mutually influence and infiltrate one another. The exact dynamics depends on the specific domestic context, the nature of state, and the stage of development of the economy and society.[21] The policy capacity of a government, which determines whether and how it performs, cannot be understood in isolation from the state's capacity to secure support for and acceptance of policy measures, as well as its capacity to ensure effective policy implementation through the bureaucracy with the cooperation of social, economic, and political elites.

Evolution of government capacity in Hong Kong

In the case of Hong Kong, both the polity and civil society were underdeveloped during colonial times, leaving the 'state' firmly in the hands of the Governor-led bureaucracy which, through the synarchy forged with business elites, was able to govern somewhat effectively (and without too much restraint) in a period where the government did not need to step too much into society and economy. Apart from rationalisation by a laissez-faire or non-interventionist 'small government' ideology, the stage of development and colonial nature of the city also did not call for an active involvement of the state until the 1970s. Even though state capacity had not grown into a configuration embracing vital linkages to industry/economy, civil society, and political society, the colonial administration was able to keep things under control, delivering what some saw as 'exceptional' political and social stability.[22]

From the 1970s onwards, as the colonial government began to reform and modernise, both civil society and newly emerging local politics were given a role to play so long as they did not become too confrontational and threaten the power of the rulers. An enlightened but efficient form of authoritarian government was politically tolerated by society. The government had also gradually taken up a more interventionist strategy in social and economic development (see Chapter 8). In terms of state linkages, government-industry relations were strengthened through industry-related advisory boards and quasi-governmental bodies such as the Trade Development Council and Productivity Council. Short of instituting a democratic regime, the colonial government had managed to develop a level of state capacity grounded in an effective and autonomous bureaucracy, a more agile economic policy regime, some rudimentary state-society and state-industry linkages, and a partially inclusionary political system (from the 1980s).

The colonial logic of rule and the rather autocratic power of the Governor ensured that the state was autonomous from and above social forces, allowing a reformist bureaucracy emboldened by fiscal surplus to do things and perform to gain credibility and some sort of utility-based legitimacy. Still, the colonial administrative state maintained a tight grip on politics and society, and through 'administrative absorption' forged some form of elite integration and community support. This state model was a fused model of executive-legislative collaboration underpinned by a reasonably high degree of consensus and trust among the ruling elites. There was joined-up governance of an undemocratic kind.

As Hong Kong ceased to be a British colony in 1997 and transitioned into an SAR of China with self-administration by Hong Kong residents, one would have expected government capacity to strengthen based on more bottom-up participation. Yet, the old and new actors occupying the inherited institutional architecture, their interests and thinking, as well as both the internal and external habitats, had all undergone subtle but significant changes, with consequential impact and constraint on the exercise of governmental power and on policy-making and delivery. The style of cohesive administration as practised during colonial times could no longer be taken for granted. Chapter 4 has already discussed some institutional incompatibilities following the regime transition. Disconnected from legislative politics and lacking its own popular political base, the SAR's state capacity found it hard to command or steer the polity. Some disabling symptoms were observed even in the early years after the handover.[23]

The desire for preserving the status quo rendered the policy regime more stagnant than expected. The gap widened between the conventional government-centred ethos extended from the colonial administrative state and the new age of socially embedded 'governance' necessary for managing old and new cleavages within a more differentiated and polarising polity. The need for political bargaining eroded the traditional modes of government-by-bureaucrats and government-by-consultation. Policy-making became burdened by more uncertain partisan politics, sectoral interest negotiation, media intervention, opinion polls, and political agitations. While colonial mandarins were able to make policy mostly according to administrative pragmatism, the new SAR government faced more community mobilisations, social and cultural clashes, and class politics. Short of public support or policy consensus, it was difficult for the government to lead society and industry to go through major policy overhauls and the much-needed economic restructuring.

With both institutional and policy shortfalls persisting in the larger picture of governance, the belief in the previous Hong Kong 'growth miracle'—which the 'One Country, Two Systems' framework was supposed to sustain—was shaken. Old social and policy assumptions no longer seemed to hold. There was growing fragmentation of an initially fragile society cemented mainly by economic success in the past. The trajectory in state-capacity building and decline before and after 1997 could be depicted as a process of institutionalisation and de-institutionalisation.[24] The erosion of state capacity can be analysed using the above-mentioned four-dimension framework, as illustrated in Table 7.1.

In the SAR era, successive CEs have championed a pro-business economic environment, yet the fostering of state-business relations is often perceived and criticised as 'government-business collusion'. The behaviours of some business and industrial interests seeking to capture the government for their own gains do not facilitate the state's strategic role in economic development. State-society relations have worsened as the government has failed to deliver an inclusive style of governance and the progress in constitutional reform to secure bottom-up mandate and empowerment has been slow. Unrestrained populism reinforced by the SAR's precarious political system has also made it hard for a still fiscally conservative regime to pursue a proactive social policy for fear of opening a floodgate. With the rise of popular expectations and organised politics, government by consultation would have to give way to some form of government by consent. The new ministerial system has induced greater demands for accountability and responsiveness. The need to renegotiate some form of institutionalised political order (re-institutionalisation) that could function even if constitutional reforms lag behind has become pressing.

Attempts at reinventing an administrative regime with strong capacity

After succeeding Tung as CE in 2005, Donald Tsang promised to build a strong and efficient government, and a closer partnership between the executive and

Table 7.1: State capacity in Hong Kong before and after 1997

Dimensions	Before 1997	Post-1997
Polity	• From de-politicisation to limited accommodation of local politics • Government by discussion and co-optation • Legitimation by performance and acquiescence	• Disintegration of pre-existing political institutions following emergence of elected politicians and parties, and functional corporatism • Concurrent crises of performance, legitimacy, integrity, and confidence
Bureaucracy	• Administrative domination and modernisation • Using bureaucracy as means to achieve performance—bureaucratic reformism	• Decoupling of political and administrative elites • From government by bureaucrats to government by politically appointed ministers • Staff morale problems due to civil service reform and gradual erosion of previously unchallenged bureaucratic power
Economy	• From laissez-faire to 'positive non-interventionism', to more interventions • Prolonged period of economic boom providing necessary fiscal basis for policy performance • Belief in Hong Kong's 'growth miracle'	• Impact of regional and global financial crises on local economy • Government economic philosophy tossed between more or less intervention • Concern over losing competitiveness and slowdown in economic growth despite accumulation of fiscal reserve • Gradual erosion of faith in Hong Kong's growth model
Society	• From exclusionary corporatist system of elite-rule to partially inclusionary state • From 'hands-off' approach to integration approach in community building	• Growing disconnection between government and society as demand for political participation is not sufficiently accommodated • Social cohesion in jeopardy, as evidenced by escalating anti-government protests

Source: Adapted and updated from Table 12.2 of A.B.L. Cheung (2005d), 'State Capacity in Hong Kong, Singapore and Taiwan: Coping with Legitimation, Integration and Performance', in J. Pierre and M. Painter (eds) *Challenges to State Policy Capacity: Global Trends and Comparative Perspectives*, Basingstoke: Palgrave Macmillan, pp. 225–254.

legislature to facilitate consensus politics.[25] 'Consensus politics' was once attributed to the British colonial administration's governing style as a pragmatic substitute for an undemocratic system lacking popular consent. He also encouraged AOs to join the ministerial track and later extended political appointment to the layers of Under-Secretaries and PAs drawn from wider professional and social background to provide an enlarged political support team for his cabinet.

Tsang's political project was to reinvent a 'hybrid administrative state' essentially based on 'government by political bureaucrats', accompanied by a loose network of cross-sector and possibly multi-party links facilitated by political appointments to the ExCo and major statutory and advisory committees, including a new Commission on Strategic Development to tap community wisdom in policy-making.[26] Whether by necessity or by choice, he also started to embrace a more active and interventionist economic approach. In his 2007 re-election platform 'Statement on Progression', Tsang set out ten major relationships that he thought Hong Kong must tackle properly in order to rise to a new height and enter a new era.[27] By articulating his second-term vision in governance in such rhetoric, he had in a way identified some major dilemmas and fundamental cleavages in Hong Kong requiring strategic attention, or else a zero-sum scenario might ensue turning tensions into hostilities. Balancing these relationships was thus about reducing disparities and forging mutual trust and harmony.

Tsang's subsequent inaugural Policy Address of his second term was peppered with the 'new'-prefix—such as *new* era, *new* spirit, *new* opportunities, *new* Hongkongers, *new* goals, *new* miracle, and *new* journey.[28] In his 2008 Policy Address, he further talked about the importance of 'core values', balanced development, and the need for a 'third way', sounding more positive about government interventions when asserting that the market was not omnipotent and intervention was not necessarily evil.[29] However, in the absence of constitutional reform, he was unable to articulate a new discourse in governance that could excite the population and help rebuild a new 'common ground'. Nonetheless, for him to venture into such previously unthinkable narrative as 'the third way', given his bureaucratic upbringing in the non-interventionist dogma, it was a remarkable maturation into his political leadership role.

Still, Tsang's efforts to rebuild a strong administrative state were largely frustrated. Not having to win a popular election, government-by-AOs did not have any incentives to cultivate specific supporter constituencies with targeted benefits and deliverables, in contrast to political parties and unions which were always seeking to identify and consolidate their respective support base, even in Hong Kong's fragmented system. By increasingly relying on pro-establishment parties like the DAB to engage and mobilise the public at the local level, the bureaucrat-dominated government rendered its district administration machinery obsolete over time, a far cry from the CDO/DO days of the 1970s and 1980s.

As a result, despite its sometimes broad-based and generous economic relief packages and welfare handouts, the Tsang Administration remained isolated. Its policies and efforts failed to be translated into dependable and sustainable political support within the wider community. Executive-legislature relations remained under stress. When parties and legislators joined hands to oppose government proposals, a government without clear public backing would have no alternative but to back down. The re-planning of the West Kowloon Cultural District (WKCD) in 2005[30] and the shelving of the goods and services tax (GST) proposal in 2006 are cases in point.[31] More recently, the Carrie Lam Administration had to withdraw its proposal to adjust toll charges of the three cross-harbour tunnels for the sake of improving cross-harbour traffic flow.[32] The lessons from the Tsang or Lam Administrations were that there was no way out of Hong Kong's governance quagmire by just returning to the old paradigm of administrative state.

Many critics today like to point to the colonial era of the 1970s when Murray MacLehose, a reformist governor, could bulldoze major institutional and policy reforms short of democracy in order to achieve some form of instrumental legitimacy based on output performance. However, these critics ignore the crucial fact that MacLehose had almost autocratic powers to make policy, did not have to face an institutionalised opposition or a vibrant civil society, was free from the now elaborate and tedious planning and environmental impact assessment procedures, and could therefore just focus on overcoming internal bureaucratic inertia or recalcitrance. This form of enlightened colonial authoritarianism cannot be replicated in the SAR era.

The policy process: Old architecture, new actors and context

Public policy is whatever a government chooses to do or not to do in the face of social needs and demands.[33] It is both a science and an art. Policy is a science because it should be evidence-based to establish links between problems and solutions and should rely on hard data (statistics, demographics, data analytics, economic and financial analysis) to support different options. Policy-making should involve cost-benefit comparisons of different options and assessments of short, medium, and long-term implications. However, not all costs and not all benefits are quantifiable and tangible. Some measures are costly to the present generation but can give rise to benefits to future generations, such as education and infrastructure investments or efforts to fight climate change. Some measures bring pain to some local communities but may result in a larger community good, such as housing and land development projects.

Conceptually, there exists the so-called Pareto Optimum whereby a policy is preferred if it can bring welfare to some but no gains or harm to others.[34] However, it is not easy to find such solutions in the real world in which all sectors of the population perceive the changes as non-threatening to their entrenched values, interests, and welfare. This highlights policy-making as an art, where all policies are ultimately about politics and the balancing of interests and trade-offs. In practice, policy is always about 'who gets what, when, [and] how',[35] in terms of resource allocation or the distribution and redistribution of costs and benefits. The widespread sentiments of NIMBYism nowadays often sit uncomfortably with rising community expectations, to the extent that for the government and policy-makers, the dilemma is 'damned if you do, and damned if you don't'. The paradox of policy-making is often 'no pain, no gain'.

Policy advocates, social activists, and legislators may argue for the 'best' solution, as if there is one, but policy-making in the real world is mostly an outcome of compromise, negotiation, mutual accommodation, and incremental change (à la Charles Lindblom).[36] Policy is not wholly rational in the economic or administrative sense. What eventually matters is the policy result because there are so many unpredictable variables contributing to a particular outcome. The policy capacity of government has to address the 'real' question of what is possible and what is deliverable, in terms of resources availability, implementability, impact acceptability, risk control, public perceptions, and political acceptance, not to mention issues of ethics, morality and ethnicity, which can all be divisive. The recent rise of social media, populism, and post-truth politics has made the policy process even more complex and volatile worldwide—including in Hong Kong. Against this backdrop, there exist no ideal conditions for policy-making. Policy officials simply have to nudge and fudge their way along in a given set of conditions and dynamics within the policy environment.

Although the previous British colonial policy-making architecture was inherited by the SAR regime in 1997, its occupants and dynamics had profoundly changed, facing an increasingly crowded policy scene and a highly differentiated polity.[37] New institutional tensions and cleavages were partly responsible for upsetting the pre-existing modus operandi of policy-making. Table 7.2 highlights some salient changes.

Policy habitat and actors

Colonial policy-making went through three stages. Until the 1970s, the policy habitat was relatively stable, sustained by the refugee mentality of the local Chinese population, 'indirect rule' imposed by colonial bureaucrats, and the suppression of politics, resulting in low expectations on the government. The 1967 riots caused the colonial administration to rethink and re-orient its governance strategy, leading to a new era of reforms and government-society connection. The 1970s and early 1980s saw the second stage of a guarded opening-up of the policy process as public demands began to build up. Social conflicts surrounding livelihood issues such as public housing, redevelopment, and labour rights became common.[38] Gradual economic affluence strengthened the government's fiscal capacity to supply but also induced rising expectations.

After 1984, the colonial administration embarked on a limited form of representative government. This third stage resulted in the advent of local electoral politics. Initially, the government bureaucracy was still firmly in charge, able to maintain policy coherence. By the late 1990s, a more unsettling domestic policy environment took root because of political anxieties and agitations, the consolidation of trade union power and grassroots populism, the growing vocalness

Table 7.2: Policy-making in Hong Kong during the colonial and SAR eras

	Colonial era	SAR era
Policy habitat	• A relatively more submissive, acquiescent society, politically under-mobilised and less articulate • Environment began to change during post-1984 transition period	• Crowding because of the increase in the number of actors, higher mobilisation, and greater demand for participation • A more complex society and a more differentiated polity • Rise of active social media, NIMBYism, and populism
Policy actors	• Bureaucrat-led	• From bureaucrat-led to political minister-led, coupled with the rise of elected politicians, parties, and civil society activism
Policy process	• Policy consultation through advisory bodies as a means to achieve policy legitimacy	• Political consultation and bargaining with elected legislators and political parties, on top of interest-groups and community-level consultations
Policy philosophy	• 'If it's not broken, why fix it?' • Positive non-interventionism coupled with administrative contingency	• Towards a more interventionist administration • New cleavages over values and identity politics

Source: Updated and modified from Table 1 of A.B.L. Cheung (2007b), 'Policy Capacity in Post-1997 Hong Kong: Constrained Institutions Facing a Crowding and Differentiated Policy', *Asia Pacific Journal of Public Administration*, Vol. 29, No. 1, pp. 51–75.

and influence of professional middle-classes, and new legislative politics posing as a countervailing force to bureaucratic power in policy-making.

Into the SAR era, the government was persistently marred by internal cleavages and insufficient coordination and joining up. Strained politics-administration interface and the under-capacity of the political executive handicapped policy formulation and implementation. At the same time, the outer political environment had become more multi-actor, multi-factor, fragmented, and turbulent, resulting from political conflicts, mobilisations, and uncertainties, worsened by economic and other crises. Political cleavages, in terms of the pro-democracy versus pro-Beijing divide, as well as social and economic class conflicts and value differences, dominated the policy scene, making it less susceptible to consensus building and governability. The previous monopoly of bureaucrats was broken up. Conventional administrative absorption and advisory politics eventually gave way to outright political agitations, protests, and bargaining. Policy coherence became harder to achieve.

During the colonial era, bureaucrats made decisions and consulted social elites behind closed doors. The non-official chairpersons of major advisory bodies such as the Transport Advisory Committee, Social Welfare Advisory Committee, and Education Commission, and members of advisory committees at large were considered influential government advisors who played an important part in brokering public policies and acted as intermediaries between the government and community. As political representation deepened in the late 1990s, elected representatives like legislators, district councillors, and political parties came to prominence as the key players in influencing government policies. Whether pro-democracy, pro-Beijing, or pro-business, they have all demanded a share of policy power.[39] Nowadays, advisory committees no longer satisfy the escalating need for political participation by a more demanding and vocal public. Their expert advice does not carry sufficient political legitimacy for making hard policy choices. The policy scene has been transformed from a single- to multi-actor one, gradually disaggregating authority.

Civil society activism has also been on the rise in the SAR era, and civil engagement has been recognised, from both the government-led and society-led perspectives, as a necessary part of the process of policy-making and governance, though often with mixed agenda and results.[40] Activists and concern groups no longer simply organise campaigns and street actions to exert pressure on the government, they also take the issues to court and use judicial review as an extended political arena for agenda setting and bargaining, as frequently seen in planning, land use, and environmental issues to challenge pre-existing policy orthodoxy.[41] Post-Occupy Central, a new generation of civil society groups and community organisations have been born, positioning themselves in self-defence against the erosion of what they regard as the core values of Hong Kong, their professions, and their local districts.[42] Government initiatives and policy measures are increasingly perceived with great suspicion and scepticism, fuelled by social media challenges and rising sentiments of NIMBYism in local communities. Constructive mutual engagement has virtually collapsed. Civil society groups and activists are now more reluctant to join advisory institutions because of their distrust of the governmental system.

In addition, the sovereignty factor has become more significant. The final decade of British rule saw London in effect allowing the local bureaucracy much autonomy in deciding on domestic economic and social policy matters, retaining only residual control over constitutional, political, and diplomatic matters. In comparison, the influence of the Chinese central authorities over Hong Kong's development as an SAR seems to be gradually rising, especially after the 1 July mass protests in 2003, which alerted Beijing of a looming crisis of governance locally for the first time. The central government at first resorted to economic measures to support Hong Kong so as to stabilise the situation. However, when the pan-democrats became radicalised under the Occupy Central protests and Umbrella Movement in 2014–2015, the central state, wary of the rise of separatism, was set to tighten political control over the SAR. Such a tendency has become stronger in the wake of anti-government confrontations in 2019 (discussed further in Chapters 12 and 13).

According to an OECD study two decades ago, the capacity of government leaders to balance conflicting interests while maintaining a consistent line of action based on the government's agenda depends largely on the government's legitimacy to lead, the degree of political discipline which the leadership can command, and the extent to which the centre can translate its intentions into a corresponding degree of administrative discipline.[43] This observation remains valid today. In post-1997 Hong Kong, it seems quite clear that such capacity has been shrinking in successive Administrations. The government's formal executive power may well appear strong in constitutional terms. In policy practice, however, it has become increasingly vulnerable to various political hurdles, threats, and administrative disjunctions, resulting in an ironic scenario of 'strong executive, weak policy capacity'.[44] In the aftermath of the 2014–2015 protests, it was said the weak state was now accompanied by a highly polarised and 'weak society'.[45] Governmental authority and legitimacy have only been further eroded during the political confrontations since 2019.

Policy process and cleavages

The policy-making process under the previous British administration was essentially centralised and controlled, but it was at the same time adaptive enough to external and internal changes since its very existence was not under threat as the local population by and large accepted or acquiesced to colonial rule. Bureaucratic policy-making was by nature a combination of institutional inertia, administrative expediency, and professional disposition driven top-down. Strengthened by fiscal surplus and internal reorganisation and modernisation during the 'golden era' of the 1970s–1980s, before the handover to China and local politics began to loom large, the colonial regime was able to chart a reformist course of governance based on bureaucratic rationality and planning that helped to gradually ease tension between the government and society, and shore up its acceptability if not legitimacy. After the 1997 transition, the formal policy-making process has remained largely intact. In a sense it is becoming more mature and sophisticated, such as in seeking advice from statutory and advisory bodies, district consultation through DCs, formal public engagement exercises, and gazettal and planning hearings, as well as sounding out and lobbying political parties, business, and professional bodies, labour organisations, and interest groups.

However, the importance of advisory bodies has been overshadowed by the growing prominence of LegCo policy panels. Partisan bargaining has become the rule of the new game. Public consultation was repackaged into 'public engagement' under the Tsang Administration. With all the paraphernalia of a public consultation document, town-hall meetings, briefings for various stakeholders, opinion surveys, consultation reports, etc. during a prescribed consultation period (usually three months but could be longer or shorter at times depending on the topic), public engagement is now the standard practice for important policy reviews and the launch of new initiatives. Cumbersome and time-consuming, such exercises have not necessarily delivered the desired outcome of narrowing social differences to achieve a broad consensus that will enable the government to claim public support for particular directions.

Some academic and civil society critics might say that the same technocratic-cum-elitist attitude as in colonial times has remained entrenched in the post-1997 administrative culture, with senior civil servants not truly appreciating the merits of civic engagement.[46] The reality, though, is less one-sided. From the government side, both ministers and bureaucrats (including professional officers) might well find public engagement exercises increasingly 'politicised' or polarised and unable to produce acceptable compromises that could support practicable ways forward. Populism has often overridden professionalism, and public consultation sometimes becomes a delaying process and straitjacket rather than facilitator and enabler, particularly in the present distrustful and fragmented society where diverse views proliferate, thus breeding indecision and inaction. The new identity politics which have emerged in recent years have bred exclusion and divisiveness, especially regarding any issues involving the Mainland. For some controversial issues, such as land supply, public consultations might likely result in only more heated debates and the amplification of conflicting views and hostilities in the absence of a strong government to collate views, make hard decisions and take action.[47]

Critics frequently fault government officials for not listening to the experts. The notion of 'evidence-based policy' implies that the nature and dimensions of the problem being addressed are known, measurable, and unambiguous, and that appropriate monitoring will show the success of policy measures. It also suggests that the evidence 'speaks for itself' and that 'good evidence' is a conclusive guide to action.[48] Such cases are rare. On the contrary, expert knowledge is only one part (and often not the decisive part) of the policy process. At best, the mobilisation of evidence is part of an interactive but multi-voiced process, subject to other interventive and intermediary variables in real-world policy-making. Policy analysts have been in almost constant conflict with policy-makers across the world, reflecting a tense relationship between science-based expertise and political judgement. Pessimists and sceptics consider politicians as asking for advice only to support and legitimise their pre-formed political discussions and policy choices. In real practice, the relationship is probably more symbiotic varying in different contexts and boundaries of interaction.[49]

Within the SAR government, there are both top-down bureau preferences (and ideas and directives from the CE) and some bottom-up initiatives from departments. Appropriate assessments are conducted before policy proposals are formulated and taken further—such as environmental, traffic, and other impact assessments; legal, human rights, and Basic Law compliance considerations;

and equal opportunity, competition, and family and gender implications. For issues or policies with cross-bureau implications or requiring inter-departmental collaboration, there are inter-bureau discussions and top-level inputs and clearance at the 3C Meeting chaired by the CE[50] and the Policy Committee chaired by the CS (attended by all policy secretaries). Once intra-government consensus is reached, if the matter is of policy significance or involves legislation, it has to go to the ExCo for a decision to be made by the CE-in-Council.

Pertinent policy proposals, even without legislative or funding requirements, are put to the relevant policy panels of the LegCo for inputs from legislators as part of their policy supervision function. Major policy initiatives are normally highlighted in the CE's annual Policy Address and the government's annual Policy Agenda document. For those initiatives requiring financial resources, bureaus and departments concerned have to bid for the necessary funding through the annual Resource Allocation Exercise administered by the Treasury Branch of the FSTB, overseen by the Star Chamber chaired by the CS who would arbitrate and make the final decision over any disputes between the Treasury Branch and spending bureaus.

The influence of the mass media, as well as the 'commentariat' of academics, media columnists, and opinion leaders, has been on the rise. In recent years, some government officials have paid more attention to political communication, or 'political spin', to help garner support and positive public opinion feedback. Such tactics often fail to work once the initial excitement evaporates. More recently, innovation and technology (I&T)-minded ministers and officials have begun using internet-based social media platforms like blogs, YouTube, and Facebook to explain government policies and measures and to influence social opinion. However, given the anti-establishment and subversive nature of social media,[51] these efforts have not paid off. Meanwhile, messaging platforms (such as Telegram) have transformed the context for public perceptions, collective action, and political mobilisation, as evidenced in the 2019 anti-extradition protests and confrontations.[52]

As the next chapter discusses in detail, policy thinking in government has shifted quite significantly from the colonial to SAR period. The colonial administration did not adhere to any fixed political ideology but was guided by an inherent policy conservatism: 'If it's not broken, why fix it?' While the dominant orientation was that of 'small government' and non-interventionism, the bureaucratic elites could expand welfare and public services not out of pursuit of any clearly defined value preferences or ideological convictions, but to do something 'good' that government could afford as public finances improved and to cope with changing public expectations and circumstances, within the confines of administrative pragmatism and technocratic evaluations. The SAR government inherited this policy tradition under which the bureaucrats continued to resist extensive intervention, especially in welfare, for fear of reinforcing a dependency culture which they considered at odds with Hong Kong's proclaimed formula of success. However, in recent years, there has been more pressure for active social policies from populist legislative corners as well as some political ministers who aspire for change for ideological or short-term political reasons.[53]

Policy debates are now shaped by more values-laden community mobilisations and class and identity politics. In addition to the 'efficiency versus equity' concerns that characterised traditional social and public policy discussions, the post-1997 scene has seen the emergence of new non-institutional cleavages grounded in value-oriented interests, which not only impose greater demand on the limited political and policy capacity of the SAR government, but also poses new policy challenges which cannot be entirely met by simply spending more money or launching more public schemes and projects. Some of these cleavages centre on the so-called clash of values, as seen in environmental, heritage protection, democracy, freedom of speech, rule of law, fairness, and other issues over core values, as well as in the concern over government-business relations and, more recently, the perceived erosion of local autonomy and identity.

Policy instruments

In the literature, the importance of policy instruments has long been recognised.[54] Policy instruments are the means that the government has at its disposal to put policy into effect. They broadly belong to three families: regulatory/coercive, financial incentives, and information transfer. Christopher Hood's 'NATO' tool-kit categorises instruments or tools either as 'detectors' or 'effecters', according to the government's four basic resources: nodality, authority, treasure, and organisation.[55] The use of different instruments depends on varying policy domains—sometimes 'voluntary' instruments are used involving little role for government beyond advocacy and persuasion, while at other times 'mixed' instruments are used employing a greater role for the state (including information and exhortation, subsidies, taxes, and user charges) and 'compulsory' instruments such as regulation, public enterprises, and direct provision of services.[56] Other determinants include resource intensiveness, targeting and selectivity, political risk, government capacity, and the precedents and normal 'style' of policy instrument within a policy subsystem.[57]

In a consensual society, people tend to be more receptive to nodality and treasure. A conflict situation may call for orders or physical coercion. However, obedience to or compliance with government authority does not come automatically, hence the importance of 'legitimacy' which in a way sets the constraint on the use of authority. As consensus and acceptance decline, the government is increasingly unable to rely on its other effectors of persuasion alone. 'There comes a point at which government's official tokens and demands for payment are flouted, its messages fall on deaf or hostile ears, and its cheque-book fails to buy physical support'.[58] In such circumstances, the government has to turn to direct-action tools, making use of the more expensive kinds of instruments. Conceptually, nodality-based tools are the most efficient, followed by treasure- or authority-based ones depending on the government's financial and enforcement capacity. Organisation-based coercive tools are the most intrusive and bureaucracy-intensive.

Against such a model, the SAR government's tool kit seems to have increasingly depended on resources-depleting means in financial and organisational tools, particularly in dealing with the adverse political situation since 2019. The decline in government legitimacy has constrained its ability to inspire and steer social behaviours through voice and authority. While it has recently made more use of social media, it has not come out of the traditional one-way information dissemination mindset and style, which is less conducive to interactive communication and empathy building. The ability to strengthen authority by way of enacting legislation and tightening up regulatory regimes has become increasingly more difficult because of the volatile legislative process, in which legislators can take advantage of legislative procedures to make demands (the opposition, for example, has frequently resorted to filibustering and other procedural tactics to block or delay government measures and actions). The generally unfavourable social and political environment also hinders any expansion of government power (e.g., more planning objections and judicial challenges). As a result, the inclination among government officials is to use administrative means as far as possible (instead of enacting or revising legislation) to implement policy changes and new measures. Because of this, some legislation has become outdated over the years.

Other than the economic recession following the Asian financial crisis and SARS outbreak during the Tung Administration, as well as some temporary fluctuations caused by the global financial crisis in 2008–2009, Hong Kong's economy (and hence the government's fiscal performance) has been in good shape until 2019–2020 when social unrest, US-China trade tensions, and the COVID-19 pandemic collectively made the future more volatile and uncertain. This has had an unavoidable impact on government revenues. Fiscal reserves stood at about HK$1,100 billion, equivalent to 22 months of government expenditure at the beginning of the fiscal year 2020–2021; however, in that year's budget, these were estimated to drop to only 16 months of government expenditure at year-end because of a large deficit to support large-scale countercyclical fiscal measures (see the updated discussion in the Postscript of this book).[59] The Exchange Fund under the Hong Kong Monetary Authority had a balance of HK$4,094.6 billion as at end-March 2020,[60] which should be the envy of many governments worldwide. This has enabled and encouraged a kind of cheque-book government.

Indeed, for over a decade, successive Administrations have used one-off (non-recurrent) cash handouts in budget times (e.g., tax and rates rebates, public housing rent relief, exemption of fees and charges, electricity subsidies, extra social security payments, etc.) to pacify social discontent and gain public applause. Table 7.3 shows the levels of such cash handouts over the past 13 years since the second-term Tsang Administration. In addition, there have also been recurrent subsidy schemes, such as the means-tested Work Incentive Transport Subsidy

Table 7.3: Cash handouts announced in the annual budget, 2007–2008 to 2020–2021

Fiscal Year	Total amount of cash handouts (in HK$)
2007–2008	$14.8 billion
2008–2009	$42.61 billion
2009–2010	$8.38 billion
2010–2011	$19.07 billion
2011–2012	$60.8 billion (including $37 billion for a $6,000 one-off subsidy)[a]
2012–2013	$32.22 billion
2013–2014	$32.6 billion
2014–2015	$20.0 billion
2015–2016	$32.0 billion
2016–2017	$35.34 billion
2017–2018	$32.9 billion
2018–2019	$51.60 billion (not including $11 billion for $4,000 one-off subsidy under the Caring and Sharing Scheme introduced post-budget)[b]
2019–2020	$42.86 billion
2020–2021	$120.95 billion[c]
Total handouts, 2007–2008 to 2020–2021	$546.13 billion ($557.13 billion if including the '$6,000 scheme' in 2011 and the Caring and Sharing Scheme in 2018, but not including injections into the Anti-Epidemic Fund)

Sources: Adapted from Table 2.2 of The Academy of Hong Kong Studies (2017) *Public Finance Civilian Report*, March, Hong Kong: Education University of Hong Kong, available at: www.eduhk.hk/include_n/getrichfile.php?key=4fdbfd39f452215b3f4321e1cccc5c8b&secid=50197&filename=ahks/SSDL/Public_Finance_Civilian_Report.pdf; Budget Speech of Financial Secretary, various years from 2007 to 2020.

[a] The '$6,000 scheme' distributed HK$6,000 each to some 6.12 million eligible persons holding HKPR status of 18 years and above. It was rolled out in response to strong public and legislative demand for cash handouts in light of a budget surplus.

[b] The Caring and Sharing Scheme was announced in March 2018 whereby a person who met the relevant eligibility criteria could apply for HK$4,000 or the balance after deducting the relevant tax concession or rates concession. Although it was not announced as part of the budget measures, it was rolled out to pacify strong anti-budget sentiments demanding cash handouts in light of a big budget surplus. About 3.07 million applications had been approved at that time.

[c] Not counting the two rounds of injections into the Anti-Epidemic Fund amounting to some HK$150 billion.

Scheme introduced by the Tsang Administration in 2011 and a non-means-tested Public Transport Fare Subsidy Scheme implemented by the Lam Administration in January 2019, to reduce livelihood costs. In July 2008, to combat inflationary pressures in anticipation of global economic difficulties, the Tsang Administration also implemented a HK$57 billion relief package to ease hardships, especially lower-income households.

Such rebates and bonus payments, once introduced upon demand and pressure from political parties, would become almost legitimate expectations and be very hard to withdraw, thus adding to the long-term fiscal burden. Some of the subsidy schemes may well be necessary for targeted social and environmental needs, such as the Work Incentive Transport Subsidy Scheme, Old Age Living Allowance, elderly health vouchers, and the scheme in 2014 to support the trade to replace commercial vehicles to more environmentally friendly Euro-IV ones.[61] However, the financial resources for some tax rebates and relief measures (such as rent exemption for tenants of public rental housing),[62] and one-off cash handouts on a whole-population basis,[63] might have been better spent on other targeted areas to have a greater impact in addressing societal needs in education, healthcare, and elderly services.[64]

Extra-budgetary handouts have become even more frequent under the Carrie Lam Administration. Partly to anticipate growing economic difficulties and partly to appease a politically discontented population during the latest governance crisis, the government launched a series of relief measures in August 2019 for enterprises and residents amounting to HK$19.1 billion on the grounds of an austere economic environment.[65] Such sweetener measures, though, did not help ameliorate the worsening political situation. In her October 2019 Policy Address, Lam rolled out further spending and relief measures.[66] Because of the outbreak of the COVID-19 epidemic in February 2020, the government set up an Anti-Epidemic Fund of HK$30 billion to implement 24 support and relief measures. In addition to those budget handout measures which have by now become somewhat customary, further injections into the Fund totalling some HK$120 billion were announced in the 2020–2021 Budget, to cover a range of measures to support enterprises, safeguard jobs, and relieve people's burden, including a HK$10,000 cash payout scheme for all adult Hong Kong Permanent Residents (HKPRs) amounting to HK$71 billion (see the Postscript of this book for an update on the current fiscal situation).[67]

In strong contrast to cash handouts, financial means to manage social behaviours and give effect to reasonable policy objectives have often been frustrated by parties and legislators. The most recent years have seen the government fail to secure the LegCo's support to increase fixed penalty charges for illegal parking under traffic offences and toll charges of the central and eastern cross-harbour tunnels to rationalise vehicular traffic despite worsening traffic congestion. Legislators were also reluctant to support proposals to set up new agencies and expand the government machinery.[68]

A competitive habitat to continue

Some critics like to blame the present problems entirely on the incompetence of the SAR government which they accuse of only listening to the central government and doing the bidding of Beijing. They, especially those from younger generations who have little real-life experience under colonial administration, have rather nostalgic sentiments about the 'good old days' and the legacies and myths of British rule. Such nostalgia is not helpful in confronting the new era and new realities after 1997 under 'One Country, Two Systems', the challenge of globalisation, and the growing politicisation and polarisation of local society. A policy system tuned to the bureaucratisation of governance, both by design and by default, has rendered policy-making avoidably incremental, thus inducing continuous demands and bargaining on the part of various sectoral and popular interests. Such a competitive and at times acrimonious habitat makes the policy power of a legitimacy-deficient government even more untenable.

Looking around the world, it has become increasingly difficult to pinpoint the location of policy power and to determine who is to blame for political and economic catastrophes, which have led to escalating public disenchantment with politicians and bureaucrats.[69] These issues are arguably more common for a system like Hong Kong's, where there is an innate distrust of the government and other political institutions, including the LegCo. Meanwhile, political overload—with day-to-day government overwhelmed by various episodes and big and small crises—encourages neither bold attempts nor bold failures, inducing more risk aversion. Critics abound who simplistically attribute government or policy failures to either the arrogant AOs monopolising power or to the amateur political ministers sidelining the experienced bureaucrats. Neither is close to the truth. The reality is that the heyday of a paramount policy centre is gone. Policy impasse is becoming a worldwide phenomenon, dragging down the popularity of many presidents and prime ministers.

Chapter 8

From Positive Non-Interventionism
to Proactive Government

Introduction

To the extent that Hong Kong was cherished as a successful capitalist economy in the 1980s, which had to be preserved as the other 'system' under China's promise of 'One Country, Two Systems', the functional importance of the colonial state in the maintenance of Hong Kong-style capitalism requires further exploration. As the tasks of and challenges to governance are closely related to the political economy of the times, the role of the state in capitalist development is of inherent importance. Although conventional Marxist and neo-Marxist perspectives have fallen out of academic fashion since the demise of Soviet and Eastern European communism, it would still be insightful to borrow some of the Marxist state theories to help unravel some pertinent issues in Hong Kong.

According to such analysis, state power is a complex set of social relations reflecting the changing balance of forces in a determinate conjuncture, and it is capitalist when it creates, maintains, or restores the conditions required for capital accumulation in given circumstances; and political forces do not exist independently of the state but are shaped in part through its forms of representation and intervention.[1] The state, as a formation of institutions and various economic and social relations, ultimately serves to extend the capitalist order. Forms of representation (i.e., the political superstructure and related mechanisms and institutions) shape the ways in which the interests of capital in a given accumulation strategy are articulated and, through the structural selectivity inscribed in such forms, could privilege some strategies at the expense of others, a result of intra-capitalism competition such as between emergent and declining industries and between strategies favouring international capital and those more protective of domestic capital interests. Different forms of intervention similarly could have diverse implications for the pursuit of specific accumulation strategies.

State intervention is, therefore, not a test of a capitalist economy. An interventionist state would be no less capitalist than a minimalist state or what classical economists portrayed as the 'night watchman' state. Further, a state with strong autonomy (vis-à-vis industry and society) or strong social links only marks the different stages of capitalist development and different demands on an effective state formation. Observed in such an evolutionary perspective, the Hong Kong colonial state was closely coupled to the process of capitalist accumulation of its time, with the concomitant modes of political representation and intervention, contributing to the non-classical East Asian economic miracle.[2] The notion of non-interventionism, undergoing semantic changes over the years, had existed to some extent in substance but most of the time only as rhetoric. In practice, the colonial government had been more interventionist than some dogmatists would like to believe.

Upon reversion to Chinese rule in 1997, demands and support for more active and explicit forms of state intervention emerged as a combined result of the reconstitution of rulership, shifting political powers and social expectations (among both the elites and grassroots), and changes in the internal and external environment of the economy.[3] More intensified global and regional competition since the turn of the century had necessitated extensive and deeper state interventions worldwide, even more so in the aftermath of the 2008 global financial crisis. Against such a backdrop, the evolution in state form from an original 'small government' to institutional reforms and contractisation since the 1980s, then towards an extended public sector and an entrepreneurial and public-service state, is a logical trajectory of the Hong Kong state irrespective of governmental changes. There has been growing acceptance of the need for state support to various social sectors and classes in the process of capitalist accumulation and development, or in response to a serious crisis, such as the global financial crisis and COVID-19 pandemic.

Hong Kong's traditional minimal state and mode of capitalist development

During colonial rule, Hong Kong was held highly as an exception to East Asian developmentalism,[4] purportedly an almost pure form of laissez-faire capitalism. Milton Friedman was so impressed with it as to remark:

> In today's world big government seems pervasive. We may well ask whether there exist any contemporaneous examples of societies that rely primarily on voluntary exchange through the market to organize their economic activity and in which government is limited to [...] four duties. Perhaps the best example is Hong Kong.[5]

Alvin Rabushka, another admirer of its free economy, claimed Hong Kong as having the most classical minimalist form of government that left the market to private business unrestrained by administrative interventions.[6] John Cowperthwaite, FS from 1961 to 1971, was a believer in Adam Smith and limited government, and also fought against Keynesian economics. It was said that to ensure temporary fluctuations in business conditions were not used to justify government controls, he even banned the collection of macroeconomic statistics.[7]

The observations of both Friedman and Rabushka might have been more valid of the colonial government up to the 1960s. Indeed, the early colonial state was an 'exclusionary corporatist state' which only incorporated local social and business elites but provided for minimal interaction and integration between state and society.[8] As discussed in Chapter 1, regime stability was built on a low level of social mobilisation and participation, with the suppression of political activities concurrent with the transient and refugee mentality of the early Chinese population, thereby inducing a sense of political apathy and impotence. The ends of government were generally accepted without cleavage, with 'an efficient administration within an accepted social and economic framework, bound up with a laissez-faire economy'.[9] Such style of governance changed drastically after the 1967 pro-communist riots. The 1970s–1980s were a period of expansion in favour of bureaucratic growth and performance.

Under Governor Murray MacLehose's ground-breaking administrative and social reforms, Hong Kong began to embark on a different development path, though dissimilar to the state-driven industrial policies of Singapore, South Korea, and Taiwan at the time.[10] Towards the end of the 1970s, the government even established an advisory committee on industrial diversification in recognition of the narrow manufacturing base of Hong Kong and the rising competitiveness in wages and labour supply of the surrounding region, made acute by growing import restriction on textile goods by the US and Europe—a major source of export income for Hong Kong.[11] This review indicated the need for the government to assist the industry in coping with external economic shocks, fluctuations, and trade restrictions. It might have triggered an overhaul of Hong Kong's export-led industrial strategies if not for the opening up and economic reform in Mainland China in 1979, which provided a new lease of life for declining local industries by moving their production northward. In Singapore, which faced similar pressures, the government decided to mandate a wage increase to induce industrial upgrading through a better educated and trained workforce.[12]

Unlike the post-War growth of Western European welfare states, Hong Kong did not move into welfare expansion in pursuit of any ideological or social policy consensus. The process was administratively driven. For example, the introduction of public assistance in the early 1970s (later repackaged as the Comprehensive Social Security Assistance scheme, CSSA) was an administrative discretion subject to fiscal affordability, rather than a mandatory social entitlement. Yet, CSSA has been in existence ever since, with continuous incremental improvements in both the scope and level of financial assistance, and is well-entrenched as a major pillar of social welfare. In explaining its way of capitalist development, Jonathan Schiffer argued in the 1980s that although Hong Kong was not of a Western welfare state form, the colonial administration was nonetheless active in regulative controls and had extensive involvement in education, housing, healthcare, social and community services, relying on land revenue instead of heavy taxation as the principal means of supporting these services, thereby producing a rather unique growth model.[13] As a result, Hong Kong's market forces operated upon 'an infrastructural support system' of non-market regulation of economic activities, administration of key prices (such as in rice and other reserved commodities, public transport, and public utilities), subsidisation of the 'social wage' (notably public housing, universal education, and healthcare), and ownership of land (one of the two factors of production).[14]

Despite the absence of macro-economic planning and subsidisation of faltering industries as observed in some Western economies at the time, such a system of non-market forces made Friedman's portrayal of Hong Kong as 'the modern exemplar of free markets and limited government' somewhat a myth.[15] Though without dirigiste policy controls as in neighbouring East Asian authoritarian regimes at the time, the Hong Kong system was underpinned by a government by bureaucrats who were not unduly constrained by local politics and individual business interests and could pursue policies more conducive to longer-term economic growth and accumulation, as observed by Leo Goodstadt.[16] Some also argued, within the conceptual framework of globalised cities, that despite its laissez-faire reputation, Hong Kong had a long history of urban entrepreneurship, adapting its accumulation strategies to the changing circumstances of the region and global economy subsequent to the Mainland's reform and market liberalisation and the onset of globalised competition.[17]

Colonial Hong Kong's growth in welfare and other public services coincided with a similar path towards a welfare model in East Asian states. Such experience, however, was distinct from the Euro-American welfare models.[18] Besides, there were clear variations even among countries in Europe and North America.[19] Some portrayed East Asian models in terms of the 'Confucian welfare state',[20] or 'developmental state'.[21] Ian Holliday used the term 'productivist welfare capitalism' which could not be fully explained by a unique East Asian social base of political superstructure.[22] It was a result of bureaucratic politics that drove social and economic policy development—notably by those technocrats and elite policy-makers staffing key East Asian economic agencies. The Hong Kong case seemed to vindicate the lines of his argument.[23]

The 1970s saw the government reinterpreting its non-interventionist policy. The colonial state had long been fiscally limited and conservative. Even during the expansionary period of British rule, public spending was broadly capped at no more than 20% of GDP, compared to an average of some 46% among Western countries and Japan by the mid-1990s.[24] Some attributed such low public expenditure to a range of historical-contextual factors—the volatile export-led economy of Hong Kong in the post-War years, making government revenue unstable; the doctrine of self-dependence of a colonial government; and the proclaimed non-interventionist economic philosophy of the governing bureaucrats.[25] To these should be added the exercise of indirect rule and a minimally integrated socio-political system within the local Chinese community, as noted in Chapter 1, inducing a culture of self-reliance rather than active demands for social goods and services from the state.

By the time Sino-British negotiations commenced in 1982, the share of government expenditure in GDP had already reached 19.1%, tripled from only 6.5% in 1900.[26] Indeed, the government had a direct impact on economic growth through its investment in physical capital (infrastructure, land production, and housing) and human capital (education, training, and healthcare), as well as promoting technical change (through setting up institutions such as the Productivity Council). Between 1949 and 1984 (just before the political transition), government capital formation at current prices grew 222 times (or 16.7% on average per year), while total capital formation grew 160 times (15.6% per year). Government capital formation as a percentage of GDP rose from 1.6% to 5.0%. During the same period, government expenditure on education and healthcare expanded 403 times and 228 times (18.7% and 16.8% annually), respectively.[27] There was clear evidence of active state intervention at work; non-intervention only applied to the micro-level of market operations. Significant interventionist policies and measures included: free basic education, public rental housing, assisted home ownership scheme, development of new towns, large-scale transport infrastructure projects (including the cross-harbour tunnel and an underground railway), regulating the stock market, and setting up industrial estates—all for economic and social development.

'Non-interventionism' had become a façade. Not bound by any ideological dogma, the bureaucrats could choose to expand welfare and public services to meet rising expectations as long as the government could fiscally afford it, thanks to the economic takeoff and growing affluence since the 1970s despite the low tax regime. A quasi-welfare state began to take shape. By the early 1980s, FS Philip Haddon-Cave claimed that the government's stance towards the economy was that of 'positive non-interventionism' rather than 'laissez-faire'.[28] Though maintaining no attempt to plan the allocation of resources available to the private sector or to frustrate the operation of market forces, he said the government would recognise a responsibility on its part to respond when industries with social obligations ran into trouble and when an institution needed regulation to prevent inequity. The prefix 'positive' was to signify a more proactive and less laid-back form of the practice of non-interventionism. The government would weigh up arguments for and against an act of intervention and come to a positive decision as to where the balance of advantages laid.

There was an epilogue to such redefinition of economic philosophy as the colonial administration entered its final years. In February 1992, then FS Hamish Macleod uttered an even more proactive interpretation by writing in the *South China Morning Post*:

> I have never liked the phrase 'positive non-interventionism', which outlived its usefulness years ago. What we should recognize is that Hongkong has become more

sophisticated. The government is doing more and more, and that is very much a fact of life. We have to walk a tightrope. We believe in the market mechanism, but you only have to look at the way the market works in some areas — property [speculation] is a good example — to realize you cannot always leave it to the market.[29]

He later described his approach as the Hong Kong style of 'consensus capitalism'.[30] Whether that was mere media rhetoric or indicative of a mindset-change among the AOs, the scene seemed set for a more watchful state with explicit objectives to intervene through public policies, services, and regulations.

Still, under British administration, polity and bureaucracy were one, and only a moderate degree of state-society interface and state-economy linkage was necessary because of the relatively low level of social expectations and mobilisations and the prevailing non-interventionist ideological wrappings. Accordingly, there was 'fit' between structure and demands. The colonial state's raison d'être was legitimated by economic performance and affluence and sustained by gradually proliferating services and outputs as well as moderate interventions. Taking into account administrative and public sector reforms in the 1980s–1990s, it is fair to say that the evolution of the state form during the late colonial period pointed to the considerable capacity of state managers (bureaucrats) to self-reform and actively adjust to changing endogenous and exogenous conditions. Table 8.1 highlights the key elements of that evolutionary journey.

Post-1997 state interventionism versus old orthodoxy

By the time of the transfer of rule in 1997, in addition to the accumulation and legitimation strategies that constituted part of the inherited state policy trajectory, the state form in Hong Kong had also evolved to embody political representation of recognised functional interests, supplemented by some limited elements of territorial representation. The specific forms of articulation of functional and district (grassroots) interests within the SAR political architecture had together induced and sustained the expansion of the role and functions of the state in support of a more directive interventionist strategy. This development seemed natural for a new administration keen on regime-building tantamount to nation-building of a post-colonial independent state. In contrast to the colonial form of state interventionism largely driven endogenously by bureaucratic reformism, post-1997 state interventionism was often triggered by exogenous forces embedded in the new SAR political system, as well as changing global and regional economic conditions prompting the government to deliver extensive relief and support measures.[31]

Tung Chee-hwa's 1997 inaugural policy agenda — with housing, education, elderly care, and industrial reinvigoration as priority areas — initially gained him much support. His popularity rating was close to 70% at the beginning of his

Table 8.1: Evolution of state intervention and state form in Hong Kong during British colonial rule

Period	State role and mode of intervention	State form
Until late 1960s	• Laissez-faire • Low-expenditure regime • Minimally integrated socio-political system	• Colonial indirect rule • Low participation • Administrative absorption
1970s to early 1980s	• Positive non-interventionism • Growth in public services, quasi-government, and regulatory functions • Active intervention in physical and human capital investment	• Provider state • Response to legitimacy crisis • Towards high outputs and inclusionary state
1990s	• Beyond positive non-interventionism • Consensus capitalism	• Emergence of electoral and legislative politics • Widened inclusion of societal interests — functional and popular

Source: Adapted from Table 2 of A.B.L. Cheung (2000b), 'New Interventionism in the Making: Interpreting State Interventions in Hong Kong after the Change of Sovereignty', *Journal of Contemporary China*, Vol. 9, No. 24, pp. 291–308.

term.[32] In his second Policy Address in October 1998, when the Asian financial crisis had yet to fully unfold and Hong Kong was at its economic height, he launched several 'strategies for growth', such as I&T development, a teleport, and promotion of the film industry and Chinese medicine.[33] In his 1999 Policy Address, when the backlash from the economic slowdown was growing, Tung seemed more cautious about the role of his government in the economy by emphasising that only when the market mechanism was not working properly would the government step in with some necessary and limited interventions. The prolonged Asian financial crisis and subsequent collapse of the property market led to deteriorating recession and unemployment. However, the government was constrained by fiscal contraction to deliver economic and social investments. By his 2001 Policy Address, Tung had to talk about economic restructuring, in order to move up the value-added ladder and spur economic growth by making the best use of Hong Kong's competitive edge and encouraging creativity.[34]

The ideological contentions between government intervention and non-intervention became more acute. When Tung's newly appointed FS Antony Leung (an 'outsider') advocated in his maiden Budget Speech in March 2002 a 'proactive market enabler' approach,[35] it instantly drew an uproar from established interests while the influential free-market economists suspected he might embark on a path of state planning, which was a deliberate misreading of his intentions.

Subsequent pressures and circumstances forced Tung to retreat to a 'small government, big market' articulation a year later, which was further underscored by Henry Tang, who succeeded Leung in August 2003.[36] Meanwhile, harsh measures to cut down fiscal deficits had angered bureaucrats and taxpayers alike, and prolonged budget deficits reduced the government's capacity to meet growing service demands and the expectations from enterprises, large and small, for government relief actions during the economic crisis.

By 2003, because of SARS and widespread opposition to Article 23 national security legislation, discontent towards the government reached a new peak. Eventually, Tung was forced to retreat and then resign in March 2005. Before his departure, he was persuaded to set up a Commission on Poverty to formulate measures to alleviate poverty, a breakthrough step in itself. Looking back, some of the Tung Administration's policy ideas and initiatives were indeed pertinent to Hong Kong's long-term development, such as in I&T, education reforms, and the grooming of new industries. However, these sectors all suffered collateral damage because of the adverse politics at that time.

The next CE, Donald Tsang, was determined to be more proactive in the face of economic challenges from globalisation and domestic political pressures, despite coming from an AO background and being a disciple of Philip Haddon-Cave. After an economic summit in September 2006, he commented that positive non-interventionism was no longer a relevant factor in government policy, though 'big market, small government' would remain the overriding principle. Like Antony Leung before, his remarks immediately caused a big row in society, with severe criticisms from both free-market ideologues and some opposition politicians who suspected there would be more government intervention without a public mandate.

Tsang was forced to issue a long statement to articulate his new approach, comparing the situation with that back in the 1970s and 1980s, when positive non-interventionism was the key, and then relating current needs and issues to the new economic and social environment of the SAR government.[37] He alluded that 'positive non-interventionism' from the outset had been an ambiguous term, and said even Haddon-Cave himself agreed. Some claimed this was just a fancy term for laissez-faire, while others equated it to a 'do-nothing' approach. Tsang explained that in an era of globalisation, the ability to attract and retain talent had become a defining factor in global competitiveness, and technological innovation and creativity were vital for a knowledge economy; besides, environmental issues were economic 'externalities' to be addressed with gusto. All these challenges would require new initiatives.

The economic principles of successive Financial Secretaries including himself were recalled by Tsang to have demonstrated a degree of consistency over the years:

> Sir John Bremridge (Financial Secretary during 1981–86) said, 'your Government remains committed to support of the free market economy'. Sir Piers Jacobs (1986–1991) said, 'the economy will normally be most efficient if market forces are relied on

and government intervention in the private sector is kept to a minimum'. Sir Hamish Macleod (1991–95) said, 'Hong Kong's economic philosophy is not difficult to describe. It is a commitment to enterprises, a commitment to low taxation and a commitment to free markets and free trade' and he described this commitment as 'what might be called consensus capitalism'. When I was Financial Secretary (1995– 2001), I emphasized 'maximum support, minimum intervention and fiscal prudence'. Antony Leung (2001–03) saw the government's role as 'a proactive market enabler'. Our current Financial Secretary Henry Tang upholds the principle of 'market leads, government facilitates'.[38]

He added that the externally oriented nature of Hong Kong's economy dictated that in the face of rapid changes in the world and on the Mainland, the government had to take a proactive but at the same time pro-market approach to provide a platform and foster an environment that would best support economic development.[39]

Subsequently, in his 2007 campaign manifesto for another term, Tsang advocated more government leadership and intervention.[40] After re-election, he outlined a rather visionary and balanced policy agenda in his new Policy Address, setting out three 'guiding principles' — namely, promoting economic development as a primary goal; promoting sustainable, balanced, and diversified development; and enhancing social harmony to facilitate social mobility, help the poor, create job opportunities, and promote a caring culture in the community.[41] He described his governing philosophy as 'progressive development', to embrace sustainable, balanced, and diversified development, rather than economic development alone, so that every citizen had the opportunity to share the fruits of prosperity and progress.[42] He also urged enterprises to look beyond their economic role in society and shoulder social responsibility in areas such as wage protection, environmental protection, heritage conservation, and building a caring society.[43]

In his 2008 Policy Address, as the signs of a global financial meltdown began to be felt following the US sub-prime mortgage crisis, Tsang emphasised the importance of 'strong governance' by pointing to the rising uncertainties and risks to the economy, society, and everyday life.[44] He also rolled out new infrastructure projects to create jobs. Among his major initiatives were: ten major infrastructure projects including new rail and road links to boost connectivity with the Mainland and enhance Hong Kong's internal transport network; the WKCD; a new cruise terminal at Kai Tak; enhancing heritage protection and revitalising historic buildings; promoting cultural and creative industries; and introducing new food safety laws and standards.

Tsang was also under pressure to respond to the trade unions' demands for minimum wage protection. The government had long resisted the mandatory minimum wage and considered it a nightmare for the free market, where wages should be set by supply and demand. He first announced in his 2006 Policy Address the launch of a wage protection movement with voluntary participation by employers, hoping this could help obviate the need for legislation. However, he also said that should voluntary action fail, he would have to accede to the demand for minimum wage legislation. In the event, he had to go the legislative route when there was little enthusiasm for voluntary action by employers. In a similar vein, he introduced a fair competition law in 2012, overturning the long-standing resistance within the bureaucracy since colonial times.[45]

In the aftermath of the 2009 global financial crisis, Tsang feared the worst might happen to bring Hong Kong's economy down again. He therefore set up the Task Force on Economic Challenges to discuss strategies and ways to cope with economic change. His 2009 Policy Address was partly devoted to the Task Force's recommendation that six 'new pillar industries' should be groomed to form a broader base for growth and help weather economic headwinds — to open up new economic opportunities and create jobs. These 'pillars' were education, medical services, testing and certification, I&T, environmental industries, and cultural and creative industries. At the same time, he launched dedicated funds and loan schemes to help small and medium enterprises. However, the new industries did not have much success. John Tsang, who served as FS (2007–2016) under both Donald Tsang and Leung Chun-ying, later warned in December 2012 against blindly pursuing new industries to drive growth, maintaining that 'conventional economic pillars [still] have their edge'.[46] The traditional pillars he was referring to are finance, trade, tourism, and professional services.

Amid the controversy about government intervention, John Tsang sounded a note of caution. Emphasising a commitment to society, sustainability, and pragmatism as the three guiding principles, he said in his 2007 maiden Budget Speech that he would uphold the principle of 'big market, small government' because a big market could increase the share of the private sector in the economy and allow market forces to allocate the limited resources in the most efficient way for the maximum benefit of the community as a whole, while a small government could prevent the public sector from acquiring excessive resources (thus reducing allocative efficiency) and minimise regulation, thereby facilitating business operations and attracting overseas investment.[47] This was safe liberal economic language. Despite his tenure witnessing Hong Kong's economic rebound and boom, Donald Tsang's final years saw his popularity decline amid political difficulties (especially with the pan-democrats) and a looming housing affordability crisis due to property price escalation.[48] He left the CE office in June 2012 somewhat as a politically dismayed and defeated man, just like Tung Chee-hwa.

Towards 'proactive government'

Leung Chun-ying came to power with an ambitious policy agenda that sought to break the inertia of the past, especially in terms of housing provision and land supply, poverty alleviation, economic restructuring, promoting I&T, and expanding Hong Kong's external economy on the Mainland and overseas based on his 'super-connector' vision for the city. Later, he actively advocated Hong Kong's participation in the national Belt and Road Initiative and the Guangdong-Hong Kong-Macao Greater Bay Area development plan. Some critical commentators faulted him for only being interested in partaking in national economic initiatives. However, this was not altogether a fair observation. He cared as much about empowering Hong Kong's economic capacity and competitiveness as taking advantage of new opportunities offered by national economic development, and not letting other rising Mainland cities overtake Hong Kong.

In his inaugural Policy Address in January 2013, Leung stated that the government must be 'appropriately proactive' (適度有為). To realise the government's appropriate role in the economy, he chaired an Economic Development Commission to study the overall strategy and policy to enhance long-term development and pushed for deepening and expanding the financial services industry (including offshore Renminbi business), legal services (arbitration and mediation), high-value maritime services, I&T-related new industries, and testing and certification services. He worked hard to attract new I&T multinationals and start-ups to set up in Hong Kong. His term saw the final resolution of the territorial dispute between Hong Kong and Shenzhen over the Loop in New Territories North, declaring the area, now confirmed by the central government as within the SAR's boundaries, to be the silicon valley of Hong Kong in developing an Innovation and Technology Park via a Hong Kong-Shenzhen collaboration.[49] Leung was persistent in securing the support of the LegCo in establishing a new Innovation and Technology Bureau towards the end of 2015, to spearhead I&T development as part of what he conceptualised as 'Re-industrialisation' as well as to facilitate industrial diversification and transformation and foster high-value-added new technology and manufacturing industries.[50] He also championed a New Agriculture Policy to promote the modernisation and sustainable development of local agriculture.[51]

However, Leung's term was marred by rising political hostilities, incessant confrontations with the pan-democrats over constitutional reform, the 2014 Occupy Central protest movement that briefly paralysed the city, the central government's hardline reaction to this movement, and worsening Hong Kong-Mainland tensions. His aggressive housing agenda was derailed because of opposition and sabotage from different quarters (political parties, green groups, local community interests) towards the government's land supply efforts. Although the introduction of controversial demand management measures (in the form of additional stamp duties) during his term was able to restrain the momentum of property price hike to some extent, compared to other major cities also experiencing the property bubble,[52] he was unable to turn around the housing affordability crisis caused by the global economic environment of ultra-low interest rate and easy credit. Ultimately, it was adverse politics that dragged down his Administration, despite his new economic initiatives and measures to improve elderly support and reduce poverty.[53] He had also pledged to legislate on minimum working hours and resolve the longstanding practice by employers of 'offsetting' MPF contribution payments by the mandatory severance payments or long-service payments, which the trade unions found unfair to employees. However, strong business and labour disagreement made any policy breakthrough unobtainable.[54]

Carrie Lam, who succeeded Leung as CE in July 2017, has continued the emphasis on promoting I&T.[55] In May 2018, she managed to secure President Xi Jinping's support to Hong Kong being developed as an international I&T centre, in addition to its traditional positioning as an international finance, trading, maritime, and aviation centre. She has also given priority to efforts to increase land and housing supply to solve the housing affordability problem, as underscored by setting up a high-profile Task Force on Land Supply in 2017 (which reported in December 2018) and announcing a large-scale 'Tomorrow Lantau Vision' reclamation plan in October 2018.[56] In her maiden Policy Address in October 2017, she said her administration would continue to respect the rules governing the economy and market operations and promote free trade. With what she described as 'a new style of governance of being proactive, [with] a strong sense of commitment embodied in the new roles of the Government, as well as a new fiscal philosophy to manage our finances wisely', she said she would inject new and continuous impetus to Hong Kong's economy.[57] Again, it was a policy declaration towards becoming a more proactive government.

Somewhat like Donald Tsang's September 2006 statement, Lam as a former AO in charge of public finances defended her thinking on 'proactive government' at considerable length in her 2018 Policy Address.[58] Describing her government as a 'facilitator' and 'promoter' as well as more proactive in handling economic and livelihood issues, she denied that the government's proactive-ness would deviate from the market economy upheld by Hong Kong, or from the principles of fiscal prudence by allocating public resources more robustly to improve people's livelihood. She explained that with its ample fiscal reserves, it is the government's responsibility to use these resources derived from the community for the good of the community, invest for the future, relieve people's burdens, and enable people from different walks of life to share the fruits of economic growth. While bold on education spending,[59] on cash subsidies and relief measures as sweeteners, on actions to promote I&T and economic cooperation and integration with the Mainland, and on the related planning processes, Lam remains constrained by conventional fiscal conservativeness and the resistance to more fundamental social policy reforms (see Chapter 9).

Apart from domestic demands and external economic challenges and crises, the rapid rise of the Mainland economy on the global scene has also imposed a new sense of urgency for Hong Kong to shape up or else become marginalised. In September 2006, the Tsang Administration hosted the first-ever government economic summit on 'China's 11th Five-Year Plan and the Development of Hong Kong', clearly marking a new departure in economic policy thinking. In ensuing years, successive Administrations have put a strong emphasis on consolidating and enhancing Hong Kong's strategic role within the context of national development. This is especially critical as Hong Kong faces fierce competition from other cities and provinces on the Mainland, especially Shanghai, Shenzhen, and the Guangdong province, which in the past learned from Hong Kong but have now become mature economies themselves and have established their own path of growth. To illustrate, Shenzhen, a long-time beneficiary of Hong Kong's investment and knowledge transfer, is now much larger than Hong Kong in population size (12.5 million versus 7.4 million), with nominal GDP slightly exceeding or close to Hong Kong in 2019, depending on the prevailing exchange rate,[60] something probably inconceivable at the time of reunification, not to mention the 1980s when Shenzhen started as a special economic zone (SEZ).

The introduction of the Closer Economic Partnership Agreement (CEPA) in 2003 conferred 'free-trade' treatment to Hong Kong-based enterprises. However, the details and conditions of such access to the Mainland market had to be negotiated industry by industry and service-sector by service-sector. Sometimes, practices varied from province to province and from city to city, thus requiring a leading role of the SAR government in helping open the doors for local enterprises. More recently, the active participation of Hong Kong business and professional sectors in the Belt and Road Initiative and Guangdong-Hong Kong-Macao Greater Bay Area development plan has also demanded that the government steer, support, and facilitate, especially in inter-governmental discussions and consultations with relevant central and provincial authorities.[61]

Advent of a quasi-developmental state?

Since the turn of the century, economic challenges like globalisation and regional and global financial crises, coupled with political challenges resulting from regime change (with or without democratisation) have together induced public policy rethinking among East Asian governments.[62] This notwithstanding, any readjustments in policy have not fundamentally digressed from the original policy path — being still essentially productivist and conforming to the East Asian model of state developmentalism. Hong Kong's social and economic policy twists and turns could be partly understood within larger East Asian developmentalism, not just as an economic management strategy but also historically path-dependent, embracing the need for sustained growth (or 'accumulation' in the Marxist sense) and political legitimacy ('legitimation') despite a cultural and social tradition of assigning welfare functions to the family, the clan, and the corporate sector.

Hong Kong may well be moving towards only a mode of 'soft' developmentalism compared to East Asian developmental states, but its need for transformative capacity is just as pertinent. Such a state would display features of a public-service state[63] as well as a regulatory state, as the public would expect the government to exercise more vigilant regulatory controls over private sector activities affecting public well-being, privatised or contractised public services, banking, financial services, public transport, food safety, and even universities and schools.[64] The government would also be urged to assume the purposefulness of an entrepreneurial state.[65] As state involvement progresses towards a medium and high level, a diverse set of incentives and coercive instruments is required—such as subsidies, regulation, direct provision, and the use of state organisations.[66]

A proactive and steering government needs legitimacy, innovative thinking, and strong links with society and industry. Given the constraints imposed by the existing political system on its policy capacity (as discussed in the last chapter), the SAR government might not possess sufficient political power or strategic capacity, or the right administrative tools for effective intervention. Unlike Singapore, for example, bureaucrats in Hong Kong are reluctant to play the role of 'picking the winner' in an active industrial policy regime. Most of them lack experience in running enterprises and managing markets and are too risk-averse in facing economic transformation and restructuring, where business risk is unavoidable when nurturing new industries. Historically, Hong Kong's corporate sector and even the community at large have shunned bureaucratic planning. Sometimes innovative ideas failed to bear fruit because of a weak state and inadequate bureaucratic competence, as in the case of Cyberport which turned out to be more of a property development project than a Hong Kong silicon-valley as initially envisaged by the first Tung Administration. In a political climate where citizens are ever sceptical and suspicious of the government's intentions, the SAR government has frequently been caught in a 'Catch 22' situation as best illustrated by the persistent row over positive non-interventionism. Attempts to collaborate with Mainland institutions and businesses are often perceived as sidelining domestic interests or 'being planned' by the Mainland.

Internationally, different countries and governments have found the need to cultivate an entrepreneurial state both to promote new technologies and their application (big data, artificial intelligence, etc.) and also to tap new opportunities by nurturing start-ups and attracting new I&T multinationals to achieve a cluster or hub impact. A new fundamental role of the state in this process of riding on technology-driven innovation capitalism is to recognise the 'collective' character of innovation which has to depend as much on state investment in research and development (R&D) and education as private sector initiatives. The transformative evolution of modern I&T (such as the Internet, iPhone, digital medicine, and green technology) would not have been possible without state investment in the initial research, often in connection with defence technology as in the US.[67] Similarly, China's very rapid technological advancement in recent years would not have been possible without a state-directed strategy linking up both state-owned and private conglomerates involving heavy R&D investment.[68]

Arguably, the state could play a crucial role in building the necessary ecosystem as well as in de-risking in a world full of uncertainty. Government intervention in this context is not just about correcting market failures or providing some supportive funding. The state as a collective is an essential or even steering part of innovation. The Leung Administration initiated a start in this strategic direction, and the Lam Administration has also embraced the vision of forging a 'Smart City' and promoting an international I&T hub. Bold rhetoric and generous public funding aside, the government has to be ready for shouldering greater investment and de-risking responsibilities not experienced before. It is questionable whether the SAR government possesses the necessary competence, links to industry and research institutions, and capacity to direct and intervene strategically. The paradox is that while the shift towards some form of soft developmentalism and entrepreneurialism seems logical and almost unavoidable, the conventional wisdom and longstanding social discourse on the role of state may remain incompatible with it, not to mention the institutional restrictions on government capacity and instruments for a stronger role (unlike those historically more interventionist and entrepreneurial states, such as Singapore and Israel).

Chapter 9
Government Performance and Trust

Introduction

Despite the institutional and political constraints highlighted in previous chapters, and the policy dilemmas and impasses faced in governance, the performance of the SAR government, as a semi-democratic and semi-authoritarian regime, has by and large still been capable of delivering economic and social progress and stable administration, while confronting growing social and political divisiveness and decline in public trust. Indeed, in the years after 1997, Hong Kong continued to thrive as a resilient city-state known for efficiency and effectiveness according to international benchmarks. Two considerations can explain this. First, Hong Kong still had a comparative advantage in terms of institutional vibrancy accumulated over long years, which would not disappear easily despite all the anxieties and threats. Second, critical local and international observations on the Hong Kong SAR had at that time tended to over-focus on its political difficulties and democracy deficit and ignore the day-to-day effectiveness of its government machinery and public service delivery. Across the world, every country or city has faced its own set of social and economic problems as well as its own governance challenges. In comparison, what Hong Kong achieved in the two decades after reunification could well be envied by many others.

This chapter explores such achievements as well as vulnerabilities and limitations in order to put the overall governance situation in proper perspective. It is recognised that the situation in Hong Kong has become more volatile following the extradition bill controversy (see Chapter 12 for more details). The time since June 2019 has been very unusual because of both political unrest and the outbreak of the COVID-19 pandemic, causing economic slowdown, social conflicts, and changing perceptions worldwide about the city in terms of safety, opportunities, and the degree of freedom and autonomy. Some analysts even suggest that its status as a premier Asian financial hub may ebb because of persistent political tensions, both domestic and international.[1]

Steady and positive performance since 1997

Based on the World Bank's global governance indicators released in September 2019 (see Table 9.1), in 2018, Hong Kong was close to the top

**Table 9.1: World Bank Global Governance Indicators, 2018:
the Hong Kong SAR compared to other countries and Mainland China**

	Voice and Accountability	Political Stability and Absence of Violence/ Terrorism	Government Effectiveness	Regulatory Quality	Rule of Law	Control of Corruption
Hong Kong	62.1	74.8	98.1	100.0	95.2	92.3
Singapore	41.9	98.6	100.0	99.5	97.1	99.0
South Korea	73.9	65.2	84.1	82.2	86.1	72.1
Japan	80.3	88.1	94.2	88.0	90.4	89.4
Taiwan	78.8	75.7	88.5	89.4	83.2	82.2
China Mainland	9.9	36.7	69.7	48.1	48.1	45.7
USA	81.3	61.9	92.3	92.8	89.4	88.5
Britain	93.6	48.1	88.0	96.2	91.8	93.3
Australia	95.6	82.9	92.8	98.1	92.8	92.8

Source: World Bank (2019) *Worldwide Governance Indicators 2018*, http://info.worldbank.org/governance/wgi/#home.

of the list in terms of government effectiveness (98.1 out of 100), regulatory quality (100), rule of law (95.2), and control of corruption (92.3), while its political stability (74.8) was rated ahead of the US, Britain, and South Korea. The only drawback was in 'voice and accountability', but with a score of 62.1, it was considerably higher than Singapore (a parliamentary democracy) at 41.9 and not far behind South Korea (a third-wave democracy in Asia) at 73.9. Despite the lack of full democracy, these data indicate that in 2018 the government was to a degree still held accountable for performance and responsiveness because of an active and demanding legislature elected partially by universal suffrage, a critical media and civil society, and various institutions built over time that together helped to ensure meritocracy, rule of law, efficiency, integrity, clean government, transparency, and fairness in administration. However, the outbreak of political unrest in 2019 and the subsequent violent confrontations have affected how the world views Hong Kong. Because of the worsening political situation, a decline in certain aspects, especially political stability, is to be expected (see the Postscript to this book).

Though having been affected by serious challenges since the 1997 reunification—notably the Asian and global financial crises, the bursting of the dot-com bubble, the outbreak of the avian flu and SARS epidemic, and political tensions of recent years—economic growth and progress achieved during the first two decades across a broad range of areas according to some indicators used by the government had been impressive (see Table 9.2).

Table 9.2: Key economic indicators of growth and progress over the two decades since 1997

Indicators	1997 *(as at)*	2016 *(as at)*
GDP	HK$1,373 billion	HK$2,491 billion
Per capita GDP	HK$211,592	HK$339,531
Fiscal reserves	HK$370.7 billion (1997/1998)	HK$935.7 billion (2016/2017)
Monetary reserves	US$92.8 billion	US$390.5 billion
Exchange Fund total assets	HK$637 billion	HK$3,630 billion
Government total expenditure	HK$194 billion (1997/1998)	HK$491 billion (2017/2018)
Government recurrent expenditure	HK$149 billion (1997/1998)	HK$371 billion (2017/2018)
Tourism—no. of visitors	10.41 million	56.65 million
Airport throughput—passengers	28.5 million	70.5 million
Airport throughput—cargo	1.80 million tonnes	4.52 million tonnes
Container throughput	14.57 million TEUs	19.81 million TEUs
No. of Hong Kong-based regional headquarters and offices of overseas companies	903 + 1,611 = 2,514	1,379 + 2,352 = 3,731 (mid-2016)
Foreign Direct Investment – total Direct Investment inflow – Direct Investment liabilities	HK$114 billion (end of 1998) HK$1,744 billion (end of 1998)	HK$1,404 billion (2015) HK$13,697 billion (2015)
Hong Kong Direct Investment in Mainland	US$20.6 billion	US$81.5 billion
Mainland Direct Investment in Hong Kong	HK$142.4 billion	HK$3,270.3 billion (end of 2015)
Total market capitalisation of stock market	HK$3,202 billion	HK$24,761 billion
No. of listed companies	653	1,973
Bilateral agreements signed	46	198

Source: Hong Kong Special Administrative Region Government (2017) '20 Years of Growth and Progress: The Facts', *20th Anniversary Fact Sheets series*, Hong Kong: Information Services Department.
Note: TEUs = Twenty-foot equivalent units.

Contrary to some doomsday predictions prior to 1997, Hong Kong's way of life by and large continued as usual after its reunification with the Mainland. Until 2019, the city was the world's freest market economy, third top global financial centre (after New York and London), busiest cargo airport, and third busiest international passenger airport (after Dubai and London Heathrow). In 2020, because of political unrest and the perceived uncertainties regarding its future autonomy and freedom, it has lost its top place to Singapore in the

Index of Economic Freedom of the Heritage Foundation and dropped to sixth place in the Global Financial Centres Index (overtaken by Tokyo, Shanghai, and Singapore).[2] Still, Hong Kong remains a regional and global hub in trading, aviation, and maritime services. Among major cities, Hong Kong has one of the largest clusters of world-class higher education institutions, with four of them among the world's top 50.[3] It is ranked third in the World Economic Forum's 2019 Global Competitiveness Index (after Singapore and the US), moving up four places from 2018.[4]

Hong Kong's fiscal health has been in good shape except in the aftermath of the 1998–1999 Asian financial crisis. Since the economic rebound around 2005, both the annual fiscal surplus as well as the overall financial reserve of the SAR government have been on a continuous upward trend, with the latter at over HK$1,170 billion in 2018–2019 (see Figure 9.1) — which many developed economies, including those in the OECD, would envy. Such a strong fiscal position could well support government policy initiatives in a wide range of areas. Based on the World Bank's data, Hong Kong's per capita GDP in 2018 was about US$48,675.6, among the more affluent in the world and ahead of developed economies like Britain, Germany, France, Canada, and Japan,[5] which should help to nurture a contented population on the basis of the wealth effect should there be no serious income or wealth disparity across society.

Of course, one must not equate wealth creation as denoted by GDP to either economic welfare or general welfare. The UN, through its Sustainable Development Goals, has been pushing for the measurement of economic and social progress 'beyond GDP', by assessing a country's wealth with a broader range of indicators that would reflect the distribution of well-being in society and its sustainability across social, economic, and environmental dimensions.[6] A 'beyond GDP' approach would review the distribution of household income, consumption, and wealth (both vertical inequality and horizontal inequality);[7] economic security; access to education and training; access to healthcare; living conditions, subjective well-being, and even people's trust in others and institutions. Under such an approach, Hong Kong would have a mixed scorecard.

In many respects, Hong Kong society has progressed steadily. Life expectancy, reflecting improving healthcare, rose from 77.2 years for men and 83.2 years for women in 1997 to 82.4 years and 88.2 years in 2018, respectively—the highest in the world.[8] According to the Bloomberg Health System Efficiency Index, Hong Kong had been almost continuously ranked number one in the world since 2012, only losing once to Singapore in 2014.[9] The post-secondary education participation rate of secondary school graduates already reached the government's target of 70% by the 2015–2016 academic year, with about 45% at university undergraduate degree level.[10] Real wages of ordinary workers have been on a steady increase,[11] especially for the lowest-paid jobs, thanks to the introduction of the statutory minimum wage in 2011 (see Figure 9.2). The overall unemployment rate had been at a low level of less than 3.18% on average for the five years from 2014

Figure 9.1: Annual fiscal surplus or deficit and closing financial reserve balance since 1997 (in HK$ million)

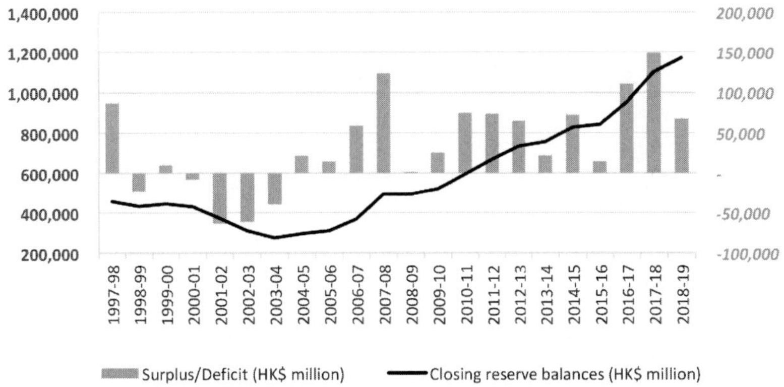

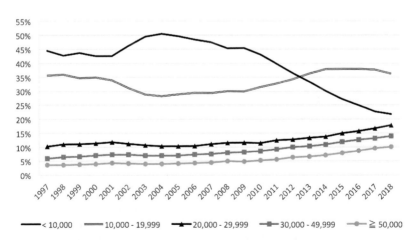

Surplus/Deficit (HK$ million)   ———Closing reserve balances (HK$ million)

Source: Census and Statistics Department (various years) *Hong Kong Annual Digest of Statistics*, Hong Kong: Census and Statistics Department; the data were specifically retrieved from the tables for 'Government's reserve balances (General Revenue Account and the Funds)'.

Note: Figures for 2018–2019 are subject to audit by the Director of Audit.

Figure 9.2: Employment income in Hong Kong since 1997 (monthly in HK$)

———< 10,000   ———10,000 - 19,999   —▲—20,000 - 29,999   —■—30,000 - 49,999   —●—≧ 50,000

Source: Census and Statistics Department (various years) *Hong Kong Annual Digest of Statistics*, Hong Kong: Census and Statistics Department; the data were specifically retrieved from the tables for 'Employed persons by monthly employment earnings'.

to 2018.[12] The unemployment rate in early 2019 was only 2.9%, though subsequently going up during the year mainly due to political unrest which greatly affected the retail and tourism sectors, resulting in an annualised rate of 3.63%.[13] The youth unemployment rate stayed at 5.4% for the 20–29 age group and 10% for the 15–19 group in 2019,[14] outperforming many developed economies.[15] Also, Hong Kong is among the safest cities in the world.[16] The Hong Kong SAR passport is recognised by 170 countries and territories for entry without a visa, putting it at 19th in the Henley Passport Index.[17]

The above performance scorecard is by no means unimpressive, putting post-1997 Hong Kong well-placed on various fronts and the envy of many other developed countries and cities. Of course, some of the achievements have been pulled down most recently by a double whammy of political troubles and the COVID-19 pandemic. While Hong Kong's performance in combating coronavirus is astounding compared to other developed nations, its international reputation has been too much overshadowed by the ongoing political unrest.[18] The economy has slowed down since mid-2019, resulting in its worst contraction in a decade, with an annualised –1.2% in 2019.[19] As the threat of the COVID-19 pandemic crept in, economic recession deepened in the first quarter of 2020, with real GDP contracting sharply by 8.9% from a year earlier, the steepest for a single quarter on record. Areas affected the most include tourism, aviation, accommodation and food services, retail, and import/export trade.[20]

The global economic forecast is gloomy. Amidst high uncertainties, the government has revised the real GDP growth forecast for 2020 downwards from –4% to –7%.[21] The unemployment rate has gone up to 5.2% as at end-April 2020.[22] Fortunately, the government's fiscal and Exchange Fund reserves remain at a high level (at some HK$1,100 billion and HK$4,100 billion respectively in early 2020), enabling it to use countercyclical and other measures where necessary to tide the community and enterprises over the difficult times,[23] unlike some other economies facing the challenge of COVID-19, which have to go into more public debt.[24]

Concerns and vulnerabilities

Since reunification, despite overall economic affluence, steady growth in wealth and wages, and improvements in education and training opportunities, social disparity has worsened, as indicated by the continuous rise in the Gini-coefficient—from 0.518 in 1996 to 0.539 in 2016 (see Figure 9.3), suggesting that although some have benefitted from the expanding global financial services and cross-boundary economic integration, many others were left out of the fruits of affluence[25] and bear the brunt of capacity constraints (for example, in more congested transport and overheated property prices and rents). Social mobility has slowed down, especially among the young and lower-middle class.[26] Hong Kong people are by and large unhappy about their well-being. The annual World

Figure 9.3: Gini-coefficient in Hong Kong since 1996

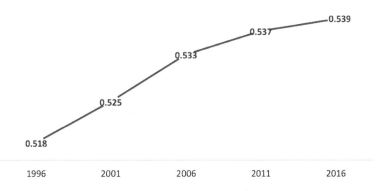

Source: Census and Statistics Department (2002) *Hong Kong 2001 Population Census Main Report*, Hong Kong: Census and Statistics Department, p. 19; Census and Statistics Department (2017a) *Hong Kong 2016 Population By-census Thematic Report: Household Income Distribution in Hong Kong*, Hong Kong: Census and Statistics Department, p. 11.

Happiness Index ranked Hong Kong at 76th in 2019 (64th in 2013), compared to Taiwan at 25th, Singapore at 34th, and Mainland China at 93rd.[27]

Housing has been an ongoing policy challenge for the SAR government ever since the regime change in 1997. In the aftermath of the Asian financial crisis, Hong Kong's economy quickly entered a prolonged recession, causing the property market to plummet by as much as 70%. Tung Chee-hwa's ambitious housing supply agenda (the so-called '85,000 housing units' policy, which was his original new annual housing supply target) was blamed for the crisis which resulted in widespread negative equity. The challenge at that time was how to 'rescue' the market. The housing market began to pick up as the economy rebounded from around 2006.[28] Since 2009, ironically right after the outbreak of the global financial crisis, property prices (and rents) have been on a continuous upward trend. The challenge, swinging to the other end of the pendulum, has been how to suppress market exuberance and increase affordable supply.

Housing affordability has been the most serious social problem haunting successive Administrations from the time of Donald Tsang. With private housing prices going up by 2.2 times and domestic rentals by only 80% over the past decade, it is easy to understand the social discontent generated (see Figure 9.4). It has to be pointed out, however, that Hong Kong is not alone in facing the housing affordability crisis. Other big cities like London, Sydney, San Francisco, Toronto, Vancouver, Tokyo, and even Munich, not to mention Shenzhen, Shanghai, and Beijing on the Mainland, have all experienced serious property bubbles over the past decade or so, primarily due to an extremely low interest-rate and easy credit environment induced by quantitative easing (QE) measures adopted by major

Figure 9.4: Hong Kong private domestic price and rental indices since 1997
(1999 = 100)

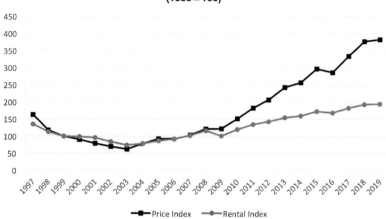

Source: Rating and Valuation Department, *Property Market Statistics: Private Domestic Price Indices by Class (Territory wide) (since 1979)*, www.rvd.gov.hk/en/property_market_statistics/index.html; Rating and Valuation Department, *Property Market Statistics: Private Domestic Rental Indices by Class (Territory wide) (since 1979)*, www.rvd.gov.hk/en/property_market_statistics/index.html.

developed economies led by the US, and supported by China, to help 'rescue' the financial market in the aftermath of the global financial crisis in 2008–2009. In comparison, the impact on Hong Kong was not as devastating as that on others thanks to the demand management measures (mainly through extra and heavier stamp duties) targeted at non-local buyers and investment purchase, inducing housing prices to come down by almost 10% for a limited span between the third quarter of 2015 and mid-2016.[29]

However, since the interest-rate normalisation process of the US Federal Reserve Board had not materialised as the market previously anticipated, property prices re-escalated in the latter part of 2016 and were further reinforced by strong domestic investment demand when local buyers expected a prolonged period of extra-low interest rates and found they had no better way to invest their money than in bricks and mortar.[30] So far, despite recent political troubles, housing prices have been holding relatively firm in Hong Kong and remaining very high against employees' wage levels.[31] The government estimated in 2017 that some 91,800 households and 209,700 persons lived in sub-divided units.[32] As at March 2020, there were about 153,500 general applications for public rental housing, and another 103,600 non-elderly singleton applications under a separate 'quota and points system', with an average waiting time for general applicants of 5.4 years.[33] Meanwhile, shortage in land supply has continued to handicap the objective of the Long-Term Housing Strategy promulgated under the Leung Administration in 2014, to provide more affordable and adequate housing (both rental and ownership units) to meet the aspirations of the grassroots and middle class alike.[34]

Another challenge is the growing disillusion of the educated young generation. Despite being better educated than their parents and grandparents, many youths feel that they lack a bright and upwardly mobile future, largely because of the present relatively rigid employment structure. The government has been spending a handsome proportion of public expenditure on education (including vocational education)—20.6% in 2019–2020 (revised estimates) and over 19% per year on average in the previous few years[35]—but the outcome in terms of improved employability and employment income still lags behind expectations. For example, the new associate degree introduced in 2000 by the Tung Administration to boost post-secondary participation rate was originally intended to provide a terminal qualification other than a university degree, but it has become mainly an interim qualification for articulation to undergraduate degree programmes, with 80% of associate degree graduates opting for further studies instead of immediate employment.[36]

According to a 2018 survey, a fresh university graduate earned a median monthly salary less than what they made ten years ago,[37] while housing prices went up by 2.2 times, as mentioned above. It has become increasingly common for middle-class parents to help their adult children to acquire homeownership by providing them with either a considerable down-payment or the bulk of the purchase price. Expectancy theory[38] could explain why some young people are getting more frustrated and disillusioned with the middle-class dream which had motivated their predecessor generations in the golden years of the 1970s–1990s, coinciding with the heyday of British rule. Again, Hong Kong is not unique in having to face such a dilemma. Management guru Kenichi Ohmae pointed out as early as the 1990s the M-shape society phenomenon of an economically stagnant Japan where the middle class began to confront a downward mobility challenge that overturned previous dreams and presumptions.[39]

Even across OECD countries, the middle class is being squeezed, with only 60% of millennials being part of the middle class in their twenties compared with 70% of the post-War baby-boomers. Over the past 30 years, middle-income households have experienced dismal income growth or even stagnation in some countries, fuelling perceptions that the current socio-economic system is unfair and that the middle class has not benefited from economic growth in proportion to its contribution.[40] In other countries experiencing a discontented young generation and disenchantment with major social and political institutions, inter-generation conflicts have increased, and politics become more polarised, resulting in the rise of radical right-wing populism.[41] Here in Hong Kong, a similar populism can be observed in recent years which puts the blame not just on the government and mainstream parties but also the Mainland and the 'One Country, Two Systems' model as well.

The other demographic challenge faced by Hong Kong is its fast-ageing society, with about 30% of the population forecasted to be aged 65 or above by 2039.[42]

This, together with a rising dependency ratio,[43] will see a heavier burden on retirement security and various care and support services. In the final period of British rule, there were increasing calls for a fundamental improvement of Hong Kong's retirement protection system, accompanied by a widely supported proposal to set up a Central Provident Fund (CPF) similar to that of Singapore or other comparable schemes.[44] Governor Chris Patten, however, made a strategic decision for Hong Kong in 1993 by rejecting the CPF idea which had by then actually gained cross-party consensus.[45] Instead, he first advocated a compulsory contributory old-age pension scheme which was considered too radical for diverse stakeholders to stomach and was opposed by many mainstream free-market economists.[46] Eventually, he opted for a privately managed MPF scheme that was neither here nor there, with insufficient accumulated contributions to enable retirees to have proper elderly security, and only benefiting the insurance (and banking) industry.[47]

After the implementation of the MPF scheme, most employees have not found their investments generating good enough returns but have instead seen administrative fees eating into their hard-earned savings.[48] There has been widespread demand for MPF reform, including regulating administrative fees and the possibility of the government launching public options vis-à-vis private products offered by banks and insurance companies.[49] Because of the failure of the MPF, the old-age retirement protection issue has continued to haunt successive SAR governments. At the outset of the Leung Chun-ying Administration, an Old Age Living Allowance was introduced.[50] The government also undertook a review of the retirement protection system but concluded that a non-means-tested universal old-age pension system supported by public funds and employees' contributions would not be financially sustainable.

Apart from retirement security, medical services have also become stretched by an ageing population. Since the 1990s, successive Administrations have contemplated fundamental health care reforms mainly to reduce dependence on the public hospital system funded by tax revenue and to encourage private health insurance, especially by the middle class. The Harvard Consultancy Report in 1999 advocated the introduction of mandatory universal health care insurance, which did not find support from the Hospital Authority, private doctors, patients groups, or even the government.[51] Since the Tsang Administration, policy consideration has focused on a voluntary health insurance scheme with some government financial support to contributors under mandated terms, on top of eligibility for public hospital care, hoping to induce more higher-paid middle-class families to opt for private insurance. After over a decade of twists and turns, and repeated modifications to address concerns from the insurance industry, the government finally announced the implementation of the Voluntary Health Insurance Scheme from April 2019 whereby consumers may choose to purchase 'Certified Plans' as offered by the participating insurance companies.[52]

Like the discontented young generation, an expanding elderly generation poses an equally challenging problem to the government both demographically and politically. The elderly problem is not just a welfare issue as traditionally classified by both the colonial and post-1997 SAR governments. Putting the Elderly Commission under the purview of the Labour and Welfare Bureau might be a kind of misnomer reflecting the lack of an enlightened perspective. A third of the population being 65 and above in two decades should not be conservatively construed as a welfare and fiscal burden. The elderly create demand for more care and medical services. At the same time, however, their potential contribution as assets of the society (and not just as supplementary labour) should be more widely explored. The way the city is run should be underpinned by a more progressive 'ageing' policy and management regime that cuts across different policy domains.

Many critics, particularly from academia, social service, and NGO sectors, and various civil society and livelihood concern groups, have blamed the government for not doing enough to raise the standard of living despite accumulating abundant fiscal reserves. Among them, Leo Goodstadt, Head of the pre-1997 Central Policy Unit, accused successive SAR Administrations of 'mismanaging the city's prosperity'.[53] Apart from past neglect under British colonial rule, he argued that there was a new poverty due to the continuing pro-business and welfare-sceptic policy mindset of top SAR officials, alleging that government hostility towards social expenditure had intensified, reinforced by boundless obsession with economic vulnerability despite Hong Kong's financial strength and economic prowess.[54] Granted there is some validity in various critiques of the government's still residualist social policy thinking and fiscal conservatism, one cannot deny the significant expansion in public and social services (including policy interventions such as the mandatory minimum wage) since reunification.

The government's dominant policy mindset or ideology has not been pro-welfare, which can be explained by path-dependent factors in both the political power structure (from bureaucrat-business synarchy under British rule to functional corporatism of the SAR era) as well as a policy regime being sustained historically by a popular psyche in favour of personal efforts and unsympathetic to welfare dependency. A fundamental breakthrough in the policy regime will not happen quickly or easily where adherence to the fiscal prudence principles is still regarded as sacrosanct. Nonetheless, deeper reforms could be possible in some selected areas (e.g., elderly programmes and retirement protection) if there is a clear vision and strong political will at the top level, supported by the society at large and adequately mandated by the political process (such as cross-party consensus and legislative support). Such vision is lacking, especially for a government that cannot secure a clear political mandate from the local community.

At the same time, there are also real concerns about the long-term sustainability of Hong Kong's competitiveness as other cities in the region (especially on the Mainland) surge in their capacity in I&T and infrastructure development. Land and labour supply have become major bottlenecks that constrain the city's further growth and development.[55] Compared to other big cities, Hong Kong lags in the race towards becoming a 'smart city'. Its 'Innovation Capability' pillar is rated as the weakest aspect of competitiveness by the World Economic Forum. Although a lot of effort has been devoted to fostering a greener environment, the achievements made are still behind expectations.[56] The city's public transport system remains one of the most efficient in the world,[57] yet it is experiencing worsening capacity constraint partly due to the huge influx of visitors.[58]

On the economic front, while Hong Kong's GDP has continued to grow over the past few decades with only short-term disruptions due to external economic circumstances, the pace of growth has slowed down since the 2000s. Unlike Singapore, Hong Kong has missed major opportunities to diversify its industrial base, first in the late 1970s because of the Mainland's post-Cultural Revolution opening-up and reform. Hong Kong's industrialists suddenly discovered a new lease of life by moving their production lines to the Mainland to exploit the abundance of cheap land and labour there, subsequently taking advantage of a fast-expanding consumer market on the Mainland for their products. Many Hong Kong business firms also managed to make huge profits out of property investments as the Mainland opened up its land market.

After 1997, there was a bold attempt in industrial upgrading through I&T under the Tung Administration. However, this opportunity to get away from domination by property business and move into technology-based new industries failed to take off partly because of the lack-of-fit with the pre-existing economic structure and party due to the unexpected outbreak of the Asian financial crisis forcing the government to rescue the property market (and hence the banking system which had overextended loans on properties). The collapse of the dot-com market at the turn of the century also dampened any remaining enthusiasm for technology-focused industry until more recently.

Once the overall economy began to rebound in 2005–2006, the government's economic philosophy and policy returned to business-as-usual, making big developers the chieftains of the economy as before. The 'high-tech 揩嘢, low-tech 捞嘢' wisdom of doing business in Hong Kong (meaning in local Cantonese parlance: 'those pursuing high-tech activities would lose and those pursuing low-tech ones would gain') became the unchallenged paradigm again. There was a short spell of aspirations under the Tsang Administration, in the aftermath of the 2008–2009 global financial crisis, in grooming six new industries. In the event, it turned out to be more of a rhetoric (with the government lacking pursuable strategies and private businesses not seeing any advantage in investing in them instead of the familiar old industries including property) and was soon off-track because of the economic recovery and a return to another decade of property boom.

Later, Leung Chun-ying put forward reindustrialisation as a key part of his economic restructuring agenda with I&T very much at the forefront. Carrie Lam has continued with this strategic direction, with the central government's blessing, to develop Hong Kong into an international I&T centre.[59] Efforts are being focused on: increasing resources for R&D; pooling technology talent; providing investment funding and technological research infrastructure; reviewing legislations and regulations; opening up government data; bettering procurement arrangements; and popularising science education.[60] Hong Kong's start-up scene is fast changing, with over 2,200 start-ups in 2017, a growth of 16% compared with 2016; and venture capital investing in local start-ups expanding 14 times from about HK$624 million in 2012 to HK$9 billion in 2017.[61] A start-up survey in 2019 reports a significant increase over 2018 on all key parameters, with a total of 3,184 start-ups (+21%) employing some 12,480 employees (+31%) across 92 co-working spaces, incubators, and accelerators.[62]

It is still an open question as to whether renewed government efforts will succeed this time. The Hong Kong economy, unlike that of the Mainland or other state-directed economies, is still very much market-driven. Thus, strengthening the organic connection between government, enterprises, and research institutions (such as universities) must receive priority policy attention (as discussed in Chapter 7 over state linkages). Furthermore, any reindustrialisation strategy should be built around the comparative advantage already unleashed by Hong Kong being a financial centre to amplify synergy, rather than seeking to de-emphasise it. A sophisticated economy spearheaded by financial services — plus the related professional and management capabilities — should also be a global hub for transport, knowledge (education), and culture, helping to extend the city's economic base beyond its physical boundary.

Intra-government reluctance and constraints

Government exists to solve problems. However, where the government's political and administrative capacities come under heavy stress and its mandate to govern is fundamentally questioned, where it is blamed as the cause of every social failure, it would become difficult for the logic of government intervention, no matter how justifiable, to square with the political reality. Thus, the government's capacity to deliver in this era of distrust and distortion should not be over-estimated. 'Satisficing', à la Herbert Simons,[63] may well be a more realistic objective. Still, to do this, the administrative mindset needs to be adjusted. The key to effective governance across different political systems is always the capacity to reflect, learn, correct, innovate, and change in tandem with the times. Once such capacity is depleted because of institutional disconnect or gridlock, there is no way for the government to lead even administratively.

Macro political and socio-economic conditions and the associated challenges aside, intra-government behaviours and modus operandi might also determine the government's capacity to act and solve problems.[64] During British rule, the colonial government was less 'administrative' in mindset than many would like to assume. When it confronted real problems, its solutions could well be quite ground-breaking, never bound by dogma, such as setting up the ICAC and MTRC and launching an ambitious public housing programme in the 1970s. However, compared to the 1970s–1990s, when 'reform' and 'review' were the catchwords of the government, the post-1997 SAR regime was overly cautious and slow in policy and administrative innovation, raising questions as to whether it would open up debates on new issues it felt unable to contain, or which some officials found too risky, and whether it would step out of its policy comfort zone in the face of inquisitive legislative and media politics. The government gradually became a victim of its past success.

Any small policy change or new project could easily take several years to implement because of bureaucratic hesitation, extensive but often less fruitful consultations, and numerous planning and impact assessment requirements. An increasingly lengthy administrative and policy cycle simply could not catch up with the much faster political cycle, and the even speedier social media cycle, resulting in public impatience and frustrations building up against a slow-in-action administration. Officials have also become reluctant to legislate, fearing that any legislative move might open a can of worms to invite more scrutiny of government actions or questioning of existing policies and practices. Difficulty in legislating, due to the deterioration in executive-legislature relations and unconstructive party politics, also discourages policy reviews and changes that require legislative scrutiny and approval. This has resulted in many laws being behind the times and outdated.[65] During colonial rule, local legislation was relatively straightforward when administrative-legislative fusion was in place, and the government lorded over the legislature, so much so that a lot of administrative details were written into the legislative regime which was ultimately controlled by the government. After 1997, in a grossly different political environment, this practice of detailed legislation has created hurdles for the government and curbs its ability to act.[66]

In addition, administrations have relied too much on external consultants, partly because of inadequate in-house capacity caused by difficulty in increasing the staffing establishment[67] and partly by the reluctance to directly bear the responsibility for 'risky' policy proposals and measures. It has also become too judicial review-averse. Without denigrating consultancy or legal advice, government-by-consultancy or government-by-legal advice would not help to shore up government capacity because ultimately it is not the consultants or lawyers who would face political scrutiny — the government still has to make difficult decisions in balancing diverse demands, interests, and perspectives. Indeed, sometimes using consultancies could, whether by design or default, become another way of delaying action.

Meanwhile, public consultations have not always helped to narrow differences or reduce conflicts in a distrustful and fragmented society where disagreements would remain intact or become even aggravated due to the mobilisations and confrontations during the process. The land supply consultation in 2018 is a case in point. Consultation might also fail when the government finds it hard to accept the outcome of consultation, either because of the cognitive gap between how the critical issues are understood respectively by government and the various stakeholders, or where the consultation mechanism and tools are not properly employed, or at times if some government officials are being too arrogant and obstinate about their long-held views.

Division of responsibilities and specialisations is unavoidable in any large organisation, but most countries also find it necessary to promote more joined-up government, less compartmentalisation and greater alignment of different minds. In Hong Kong, bureaus and departments sometimes spend a lot of time arguing over where policy responsibility should lie for different issues and problems (e.g., which bureau should be the 'lead' bureau?). There is a logic in this because once a particular bureau or department has taken up the leading role, it will be held responsible for handling legislative and audit questions, and accountable for any administrative shortfalls and policy failures. Yet the demarcation of responsibilities among bureaus and departments is such that often no single bureau or department can, on its own, competently deal with the issues. As a result, the process sometimes gets dragged on, hindering action-taking and making it harder to pinpoint accountability.

Intra-government hurdles and constraints reduce the government's ability to perform, which is further conditioned by its capacity to connect and communicate with the public. In the new social media era, communication is essentially anti-establishment and works against all governments and established institutions (public or private). Things sometimes become worse when some officials in the government prefer to communicate as minimally as possible so as not to let others (the media, critics, and legislators) grab more issues to attack them. Their tactic tends to be one of containing issues rather than proactive framing and agenda-setting. In media battles, the government often loses out not because it could not technically use the latest social media platforms, but because it dares not reach out with more and to-the-point information. Too often, officials use administrative and technical language only familiar to bureaucrats and professionals, failing to appreciate what ordinary people are puzzled or angry about. In this information age, if the government responds too slowly and too sparingly, the sceptical public will be inclined to believe the critics' allegations whether right or wrong. Leading and shaping public discourse during incidents and crises, backed by sufficient information and explanation, so as to communicate effectively, is of paramount importance in any crisis management.

Deficit in trust despite government performance

In overall governance, while Hong Kong used to be rated highly in the World Bank's global governance indicators, second only to Singapore in terms of 'government effectiveness' and 'regulatory quality', policy-making has been subject to more frequent contentions and political controversies especially over the past decade, with diverse interests all too keen to assert themselves, making consensus and trade-offs harder to achieve. The community has generally turned more cynical and sceptical of both government and opposition. The lack of democratic progress since 1997 has induced a form of 'democracy by substitutes'—like protests, rallies, media monitoring, judicial reviews, and the politics of opinion polls and mobilisations. Apart from the government, the LegCo, political parties, and the media (the so-called fourth power) are also suffering from declining credibility—the only public institution still retaining a decent degree of credibility is the judiciary.[68]

Some critical citizens, especially among the younger generation, like to compare the currently complex and at times dysfunctional system of governance with the much simpler but more top-down approach used during British colonial rule, which they now view with nostalgia. They tend to blame most problems on the 1997 return to China and the SAR's partially democratic political system within the 'One Country, Two Systems' context, regarding them as the cause of setbacks and failures in local administration. Pan-democratic parties and many civil society groups are highly distrustful of the central and SAR governments. The more distrustful they become, the less willing they are to support the government in dealing with harsh social and economic problems that demand consensus. The level of distrust creates a gap ultimately too large to be filled by the positive day-to-day performance of the government.

Figures 9.5 and 9.6 show the level of people's net trust (i.e., trust level minus distrust level) in the SAR government fell sharply from 54.3% in June 2008 to only 7.9% in June 2018, –13% in June 2019 and then –38.4% in December 2019; while net trust in the central government dropped from 41.4% in June 2008 to –39.9% in December 2019. The trust level plunged in 2019 because of the extradition saga and subsequent political confrontations, which saw young people getting increasingly hostile towards those in power. This slump in trust continues even now.

As for the CEs, Tung Chee-hwa, Donald Tsang, Leung Chun-ying, and Carrie Lam all started from a decently high point at the beginning of their terms in office—at 64.5%, 72.3%, 52.5%, and 61.1%, respectively (with Leung comparatively more marginal probably because of the controversy surrounding 'unauthorised structures uncovered' in his private residence prior to his inauguration) (see Figure 9.7). The CEs all experienced steadily declining popular ratings over the rest of their term—with Tung finishing at 47.9%, Tsang at 39.3%, and Leung at 38.1%. Although Lam fared better than Leung in her first two years, her mismanagement of the 2019 extradition bill has resulted in the worst political crisis since the 1967 anti-British riots. Her popularity rating dropped to 19.6% by the end of 2019. Figure 9.8 indicates that her net hypothetical support vote was already well into the negative at –18.6% by mid-June 2019, plunging to –61.2% by December 2019.

Figure 9.5: People's trust in the Hong Kong SAR government since 1997

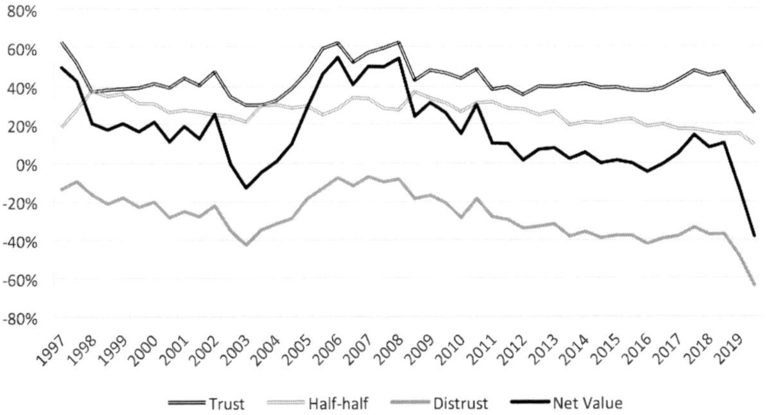

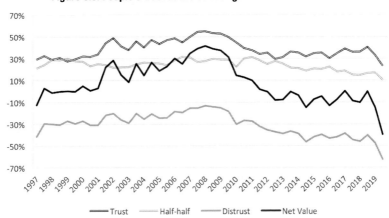

Source: Public Opinion Programme of the University of Hong Kong (HKUPOP) (n.d.) *People's Trust in the HKSAR Government*, www.hkupop.hku.hk/english/popexpress/trust/trusthkgov/index.html; Hong Kong Public Opinion Research Institute (HKPORI) (n.d.) *People's Trust in the HKSAR Government*, www.pori.hk/pop-poll/government-en/k001.html?lang=en. The HKPORI has continued conducting the polls from July 2019 using the same survey methodology as the HKUPOP.

Note: Figures on half-yearly basis up to December 2019.

Figure 9.6: People's trust in the central government since 1997

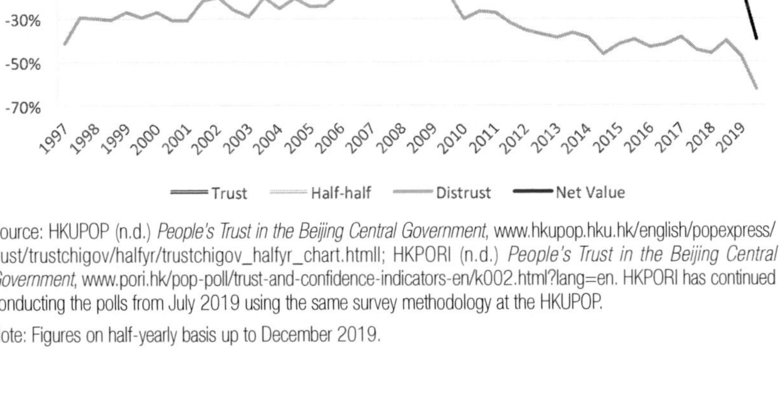

Source: HKUPOP (n.d.) *People's Trust in the Beijing Central Government*, www.hkupop.hku.hk/english/popexpress/trust/trustchigov/halfyr/trustchigov_halfyr_chart.htmll; HKPORI (n.d.) *People's Trust in the Beijing Central Government*, www.pori.hk/pop-poll/trust-and-confidence-indicators-en/k002.html?lang=en. HKPORI has continued conducting the polls from July 2019 using the same survey methodology at the HKUPOP.

Note: Figures on half-yearly basis up to December 2019.

Figure 9.7: Popular rating of the CE (full mark = 100)

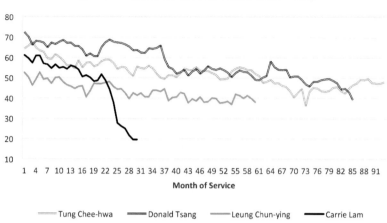

Source: HKUPOP (n.d.) *Ratings of Various Chief Executives*, www.hkupop.hku.hk/english/popexpress/ce2017/cl/cecomparison/datatables.html; HKPORI (n.d.) *Comparison between Ratings of Chris Patten, Tung Chee-hwa, Donald Tsang Yam-kuen, Leung Chun-ying, and Carrie Lam*, www.pori.hk/pop-poll/chief-executive-en/a-rating-combined.html?lang=en. HKPORI has continued conducting the polls from July 2019 using the same survey methodology at the HKUPOP.

Note: Figures on half-yearly basis up to December 2019.

Figure 9.8: Hypothetical voting on Carrie Lam as the CE

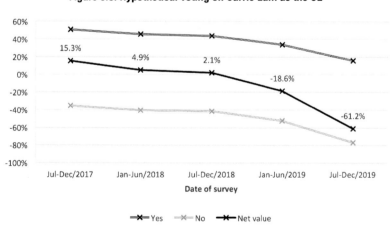

Source: HKUPOP (n.d.) *Hypothetical Voting on Carrie Lam as the Chief Executive*, www.hkupop.hku.hk/english/popexpress/ce2017/vote/poll/cl_vote_chart.html; HKPORI (n.d.) *Hypothetical Voting Results for Carrie Lam as the Chief Executive*, www.pori.hk/pop-poll/chief-executive-en/a003-app.html?lang=en. HKPORI has continued conducting the polls from July 2019 using the same survey methodology as the HKUPOP.

Note: Figures on half-yearly basis up to December 2019.

Looking around the world, most democratically elected leaders of developed nations have faced fluctuations in approval ratings and have at some stage experienced high levels of dissatisfaction and distrust while in office. To illustrate, former British Prime Minister Theresa May's net approval rating dropped to –49% when she announced her departure in June 2019 after she failed to strike a 'Brexit' deal acceptable to the Parliament.[69] French President Emmanuel Macron's popular approval rating was only 26% (with 73% disapproval) in December 2018 because of the 'yellow vest' protests, a sharp fall from the 66% approval rate upon his election in May 2017.[70] Some pro-democrats in Hong Kong talk highly of democracy in Taiwan, but its previous president Ma Ying-jeou left office in May 2016 with only 23% approval rating and 58% disapproval (i.e., net approval of –35%).[71] The incumbent president Tsang Ing-wen began her term in May 2016 with a 47% approval rating but her popularity plummeted to only 26% approval against 60% disapproval (i.e., –34% net approval) by May 2018, though subsequently rebounding to 61% approval against 25% disapproval (i.e., 36% net approval) by the time of her second-term inauguration in May 2020, following a landslide election victory.[72]

Of course, these scores should not be compared as if like with like because the survey methodology and public attitudes across countries and regions do vary. What can be drawn from these comparative trends is that all government leaders suffer from popularity decline after assuming office, which has become a reality of being in power. Hong Kong's non-democratically elected CEs have fared no worse than their overseas counterparts who are popularly elected. Although the local media have been painting a negative picture of government performance and the competence of officials, Hong Kong has been doing well (or at least 'good enough') by international comparison, despite the lack of full-fledged democracy. To say this is not to dismiss the importance of democratic institutions.

Democratic governance is generally regarded as conducive to building political trust and giving the government the legitimacy to rule. Trust helps to induce behaviour among the public to accept sacrificing some short-term interests in support of hard decisions to implement policy or structural reforms with long-term benefits to the society, such as pensions and taxation reforms. Democratisation is at the same time seen as a positive institutionalisation of distrust as embodied in the principle of separation of powers, and various institutions of accountability, audit, and scrutiny. The argument is that if the people are over-confident in their rulers, it may lead to government arrogance or even autocratic rule. Therefore, a democratic design should strike a balance between trust *and* distrust, in order to function well in practice.[73] In Hong Kong, the fundamental constitutional flaws have put the government in almost permanent legitimacy deficit and uncertainty. That said, as argued by Russell Hardin, it may suffice for a government not to be generally distrusted.[74]

The challenge to the SAR government is how to overcome the rapid accumulation of distrust in society. Conceptually, two different sources of 'trust' can be delineated—instrumental/functional and integrative/value-oriented, denoted in

Table 9.3 as respectively Type A and Type B trust. During British rule, the colonial administration essentially relied on Type A trust. The changing political context and rising public expectations after 1997 have affected the level of Type A trust even though there continues to be a comparable degree of performance as in the colonial past. Type B trust is arguably what the SAR government is most lacking, partly due to the democratic deficit and partly the absence of a sense of common identity and shared values within the political community and society at large. Type A trust can reinforce Type B trust, but only to a certain extent. On the other hand, at some junctures Type B trust will become more crucial in helping generate performance capacity, which can, in turn, enhance government performance and thereby strengthen Type A trust. The two are interactive. Type B trust is what should be cultivated by the SAR regime, and yet it is very hard to achieve given the present constitutional and political realities. Here lies the major paradox of governance in Hong Kong.

According to the OECD Trust Framework, trust in government is ultimately determined by a range of government mandates and drivers, as summarised in Table 9.4. A constitutionally democratic government that lacks in some or, worse, most of these elements would not be able to deliver good governance. By the same logic, a government system that is competent and effective in these elements, though not fully 'democratic', can still inspire and sustain public trust.

Strong governance is impossible to pursue in any habitat of widespread distrust. Political prejudice and reductionism can easily simplify policy debates into talk of an original sin about the lack of democracy and people power, a theme harped upon by many in order to avoid facing hard policy realities.[75] Even if bureaucratic competence could be maintained, it would not necessarily deliver the values-driven moral force that is so essential to governing in crisis. Political distrust breeds greater pressure on accountability on a day-to-day basis as people become more suspicious and sceptical of government intentions. Such distrust is naturally reciprocated by some government officials wary of critics and dissenting voices. Ministers might feel inhibited in being too unconventional in policy thinking. Civil servants might become more uptight about being flexible in the application of policies and the exercise of discretionary power because they know public and legislative reaction is unlikely to be sympathetic if anything goes wrong. In the end, the government's overall capacity to make hard policy choices under these circumstances will only become even more minimised.[76]

An uncertain prospect

Across the world, there has been a growing crisis of trust in government as well as in business, NGOs, and the media, as noted by the 2020 Edelman Trust Barometer.[77] The masses tend to be more distrustful of government than the

Table 9.3: Different sources of trust

Instrumental/Functional (Type A trust)	Integrative/Value-oriented (Type B trust)
Performance trust • Based on government performance or satisfaction with government performance **Strategic trust** • To exchange citizens' trust with performance of public officials and their institutions [a]	**Paternalistic trust** • Trust in moral obligation of those in power to care for and protect those less powerful and are in need of help [b] • Accepting the authorities' power in confidence that it will be used to fulfil the caring responsibility and not do harm or hurt the interest of the people [c] **Moralistic trust** • Based on normative values of trust and on culture and disposition as the foundations of trust (e.g., a sense of shared humanity or altruistic concern for the community) [d] • Trust as a 'moral good', so that social cooperation is made possible [b] **Symbolic trust** • Trust in those values as represented by institutions, to create solidarity and integration [b]

Source: Adapted from Table 3 of A.B.L. Cheung (2010b), 'In Search of Trust and Legitimacy: The Political Trajectory of Hong Kong as Part of China', *International Public Management Review*, Vol. 11, No. 2, pp. 38–63.

[a] R. Hardin (1998) 'Trust in Government', in V. Braithwaite and M. Levi (eds) *Trust and Governance*, New York: Russell Sage Foundation, pp. 9–27.

[b] J. Tao (2006) 'A Confucian Way Out of the Paradox of Trust in Democracy?' paper presented at an International Workshop on Governance for Harmony organised by the Governance in Asia Research Centre, City University of Hong Kong, 9–10 June, Hong Kong.

[c] A. Baier (1986) 'Trust and Anti-Trust', *Ethics*, No. 96, pp. 231–260.

[d] E.M. Uslaner (2002) *The Moral Foundations of Trust*, Cambridge: Cambridge University Press.

Table 9.4: OECD trust framework

Government mandates	Drivers
• Provide public services • Anticipate change, protect citizens • Use power and public resources ethically • Listen, consult, and explain to citizens • Improve living conditions for all	**Competence:** • Responsiveness • Reliability **Values:** • Integrity • Openness • Fairness

Source: OECD (2017) *Trust and Public Policy: How Better Governance Can Help Rebuild Public Trust*, Paris: OECD.

informed public (47 compared to 59 out of 100). In Hong Kong, the level of trust in government stands at 42 (down from 55 before the political unrest in 2019), putting it in mid-stream among the 26 economies surveyed, on a par with Japan (at 43) but still higher than some OECD countries like Britain, France, Spain, and Italy. In Asia, several countries have scored much higher in the trust barometer, including Singapore, Malaysia, Indonesia, India, and Mainland China, ranging from 58% to 90%. Other available international data also suggest a similar pattern of public distrust. For example, in 2016, on average, only 42% of citizens had confidence in national government among the OECD countries.[79]

Thus, democracy alone does not guarantee public trust among developed democratic economies. As early as the 1990s, US scholars have argued that Americans have been asking the impossible of their government, giving it 'inconsistent, contradictory, and hence unachievable goals and tasks',[79] resulting in citizens not being sure about when and where to trust the government.[80] While Hong Kong's problem in public trust is not unique, it cannot be ignored. The democratic deficit is certainly a structural factor that has been driving the political confrontations since 2019. Despite showcasing relatively impressive economic indicators and competitive international rankings, the issues of a slowdown in social mobility, worsening housing affordability, widening wealth gap, wage stagnation for many young people, and a rapidly ageing society without adequate retirement protections have all added up to an embarrassing discrepancy between economic performance and the quality of life. Economic wealth has not filtered down as expected. The general population perceives the lack of social policy breakthroughs by successive Administrations as an outcome of an entrenched political system that is unfair, enabling collusion between government and big business to the detriment of ordinary wage-earners and small enterprises.

Without a bottom-up political mandate or pressures for change from a reformed system of governance, the present quagmire will only persist, leading to more social discontent and a collapse in political trust. Can Hong Kong still tread on such a paradoxical path? At present, this prospect seems uncertain given the all-out political opposition by younger generations who have displayed a total loss of trust in and respect for the government, resulting in more vocal dissent and 'uprisings'. The suppression of such uprisings by force does not mean the end of the governance crisis. Inasmuch as the lack of performance breeds distrust, it would be equally right to say that incessant (and rising) distrust will ultimately hamper performance because the necessary capacity to take a risk and make innovative and necessary changes will dwindle in the face of new and increasing challenges. The vicious cycle needs to be broken to avert the risk of ungovernability.

PART III

TENSION AND CHALLENGES

Chapter 10

The Quest for Democracy

Introduction

In January 1984, as Sino-British negotiations progressed over the political future of Hong Kong, the Student Union of the University of Hong Kong wrote to then Chinese Premier Zhao Ziyang insisting on the principle of 'democratic administration by Hong Kong people' (港人民主治港), with the future head and government of the city to be popularly elected by its residents. In his official reply dated 22 May 1984, Zhao praised the students for supporting the resumption of sovereignty over Hong Kong by the motherland and reassured them that it would be a matter of course that the future Hong Kong SAR would implement a democratic political system, which is the same as 'democratic administration' as advocated by the students.[1] Such top-level promises have been driving the quest for democracy in Hong Kong ever since. In a way, 1997 presented a historical opportunity for democratic vision-building among many Hong Kong people, especially the post-War generation who felt politically debilitated by a colonial system that seemed impossible to change.[2]

The reality, however, was that the Chinese leadership, represented by Deng Xiaoping, did not believe in Western-style democracy. Beijing was also wary that a democratically elected CE might allow Hong Kong to become too autonomous (or too 'independent') from central government authority. Locally, the business sector and other established interests supporting the colonial government were essentially conservative and elite-minded. They worried about democracy falling into the hands of the grassroots who would only demand 'free lunch' welfare. The British administration was neither a champion of electoral democracy but had all along considered benevolent bureaucratic rule a cornerstone of Hong Kong's hitherto success. It only reluctantly realised the political necessity to pursue 'representative government' of some kind after the 1984 Sino-British Joint Declaration was agreed, both to respond to local demands and to pre-empt the political intrusion of the incoming sovereign power. That left the newly emerging indigenous pro-democracy movement as the leading force to campaign both for political reform in the transition period and for the installation of a fully democratic political system after 1997 under the new Basic Law.

The post-1984 years could be likened to a period of 'spring and autumn' and 'warring states' for the great political debates of Hong Kong.[3] In the beginning, the pro-democracy movement only had a small following in the community.[4] However, their support base began to expand after the pro-democracy student rallies in Beijing during April and May 1989. The Tiananmen suppression on 4 June of that year triggered mass demonstrations in Hong Kong by over a million people, spurring a fast-growing voice among the local population in favour of a democratic system in the future Hong Kong SAR. Many of the locals now saw democracy as a safeguard to protect their freedoms and check authoritarian power and as a bulwark against direct communist rule.

Different forces and political models

Broadly speaking, there were five main forces at play during the drafting of the Basic Law which had a stake in the design of the future political system: the Chinese government, the British government (and British administration in Hong Kong), the pro-Beijing patriotic camp, the pro-democracy camp, and the business and professional camp. Chinese leaders had from an early stage insisted on an 'executive-led' system and ruled out a 'separation of power' model. Thus, any proposal grounded in making an elected legislature the root of governmental power, such as a Westminster system, would not be accepted.[5] The concept of 'residual powers'—that the Hong Kong SAR should be given authority over all affairs except those specifically vested in the central government—was also firmly rejected as being incompatible with its status as a local administrative region of a unitary sovereign state. Indeed, the principal controversies in the debates were about the methods of election of the future CE and LegCo members, and to a lesser degree, the power relationship between the executive and legislature.

The pro-democracy movement advocated a fully democratic political system based on election by universal suffrage. The business and professional sectors which were accustomed to colonial consultative politics feared that a democratic system would disempower them and allow the grassroots (and welfare politics) to take over. They therefore favoured a system of indirect elections on a more limited franchise. The pro-Beijing camp, comprising the so-called 'leftist' patriotic organisations (including some trade unions and district residents associations), pursued an approach within the broad perimeters set by Beijing but also found it necessary to take advantage of Hong Kong's transition from colonial to SAR rule to give the ordinary people greater say in governance. They thus toed the line somewhere between the pro-democracy camp and the business and professional camp.

Early on in this process, in June 1985, Cha Chi-ming, a business-background member of the Basic Law Drafting Committee much respected by Beijing, made a submission to the Committee to propose that an advisory council should nominate a single candidate as the CE for the first three terms to be considered by the central government for appointment, and that after 2010, this advisory council could nominate two or three candidates for approval by the central government before direct election by universal suffrage. That was the first sign of local business interests accepting a conditional direct election of the CE though in the more distant future. As to the legislature, he proposed that one-third of its members should be constituted by the same advisory council, one-third by functional organisations (similar to functional constituencies introduced by the British administration), and one-third by District Boards or district direct-elections. Cha also suggested that the ExCo, as the executive authority, should be headed by a chief minister (i.e., the CS) to be elected by the LegCo and, upon the CE's agreement, appointed by the central government. The CS would nominate other Secretaries with the principal ones preferably being legislators. Under such design, akin to a parliamentary system of government, the CE would become head of the SAR, while the CS would head the government.[6] Such a Westminster model would not have found favour with Beijing, which preferred a 'controlled' nomination of the future CE.[7]

By 1986–1987, the major local camps had all put forward their main proposals—as summarised in Table 10.1. It is worth noting that the pro-democracy camp at that time was sufficiently sensitive to the need for balanced participation in the LegCo by different sectors and interests, and hence despite their preference for universal suffrage, was prepared to accept a quarter of the LegCo members to be returned by functional constituencies. On the other hand, the pro-Beijing camp was hoping for Beijing loyalists to play an important role in the future political system. During this time, they also advocated the substitution of 'functional sector' elections (on limited franchise) by 'occupational sector' elections so that all registered electors would have a vote according to their occupation. In the ensuing period, more ideas and proposals came from different groups, sectors, and notable individuals in the community, including academics. Meanwhile, the consultative process undertaken by the Basic Law Consultative Committee had stimulated extensive public discussions and lobbying.[8] By the latter part of the drafting process in 1988–1989, both establishment and pro-democracy advocates further refined their main proposals, with some seeking to provide compromised options.

In November 1988, the Hong Kong convenor of the Political System Sub-group of the Basic Law Drafting Committee, Louis Cha, jointly with Cha Chi-ming, put forward a 'mainstream option' (dubbed the 'double-Cha proposal' by the media) which was said to have incorporated the major features of various competing proposals across the political spectrum. Under this package, both the CE and LegCo members could be directly elected by universal suffrage from 2012 earliest if so agreed by a local referendum. Before that, the CE would be elected by an 800-member election committee, while functional seats would dominate the LegCo versus directly elected seats until reaching a balanced proportion

Table 10.1: Positions of main political camps on the methods for constituting the CE and the LegCo of the SAR, 1986–1987

	Business and professional sectors (Group of 89)[a]	Pro-democracy camp (Joint Committee on the Promotion of Democratic Government)[b]	Pro-Beijing camp (Group of 28)[c]
CE	Elected by a 600-person electoral college	Directly elected after nomination by the LegCo	Directly elected after nomination of 3 candidates by a 128-person nomination panel, with 92 members from occupational sector elections (32 from each of three main categories), 16 members elected by the LegCo and 16 members by local NPC deputies and CPPPC national committee members
LegCo	Half elected by functional organisations, one-quarter by CE electoral college, and one-quarter by direct election after nomination by members of various tiers of representative institutions	Half directly elected, one-quarter by functional organisations, and one-quarter by district representative bodies (namely urban and regional councils and district boards)	48 (i.e., two-thirds) of the proposed 72 members elected by 'occupational sectors' and 24 elected by district constituencies of 2–3 seats each

Source: Meeting Point Basic Law Committee and Information Centre (1988) *A Collection of Basic Law Commentaries* [in Chinese, 《基本法評論匯編》], May, Hong Kong: Meeting Point.

Notes: Direct election = popular election by universal suffrage; Occupational sectors = occupations to be grouped under three main categories: (a) trade, industry, banking, and employers; (b) professional and administrative; and (c) labour and those not taking part in economic activities.

[a] In August 1986, the business and professional sectors formed a coalition of '57 Members' (of Basic Law Consultative Committee members from these sectors) led by Vincent Lo, to oppose the direct election of the CE and instead advocate election by an electoral college. The Group of 57 was subsequently enlarged to become the Group of 71 and then the Group of 89 Members.

[b] The pro-democracy groups initially formed a coalition of 190 individual and organisation signatories, which was later formalised into the Joint Committee on the Promotion of Democratic Government led by Szeto Wah and Martin Lee. Many core members of the Joint Committee later became founding members of the United Democrats of Hong Kong (UDHK) and then the Democratic Party.

[c] In March 1987, a Group of 28 Basic Law Consultative Committee members and educationalists, mainly from the pro-Beijing camp, was formed (labelled by the media as the 'middle camp'). Key spokespersons of this Group were Tsang Yuk-sing and Cheng Kai-nam, who later became the founding Chairman and Secretary-General respectively of the pro-Beijing DAB in 1992.

in 2007.[9] The pro-democrats were greatly disappointed with the mainstream model and staged protests against it.[10] The proposal laid the foundation for the second Draft Basic Law issued in April 1988 for public consultation. When consulting some local groups, Mainland members of the Drafting Committee explained their preferred approach as a 'timetable compromise solution' such that the political system would commence from a starting point closer to the business and professional sectors' model and ultimately reach the more ideal model advocated by the pro-democrats.[11]

In the aftermath of the Tiananmen crackdown in June 1989, a consensus quickly gained momentum in Hong Kong for a faster pace of democratisation. Earlier, at the end of May 1989, amid the heat of pro-democracy rallies at Tiananmen, the unofficial members of the ExCo and LegCo agreed on an OMELCO consensus proposal, under which one-third of the LegCo seats should be directly elected in 1991, no less than half in 1995, and (after the handover) two-thirds by 1999, so that by 2003 the LegCo would be fully directly elected, while the CE should be directly elected by universal suffrage from 1997 onwards. Meanwhile, in August 1989, Lo Tak-Sing, a former appointed ExCo and LegCo member and now Vice-chairman of the Basic Law Consultative Committee, championed a bicameral model of functional seats and geographical (directly elected) seats for the future SAR LegCo such that any motions and legislation had to be passed by both 'chambers', on the grounds that they represented different kinds of interests in society.

In the midst of post-Tiananmen political uncertainties, local establishment and business leaders as well as the pro-democracy camp sped into action to reach a consensus model broadly acceptable to major forces in October 1989, hoping that such consensus could have more influence over Beijing. The resulting '4:4:2 compromise option' provided that directly elected seats should take up 40% of the LegCo by 1997 (with 40% functional seats and 20% electoral college seats), to rise to 60% in 2001 (versus 40% functional seats), and then the whole of LegCo by 2005 if so decided by the preceding LegCo; while the CE would be nominated by the electoral college for direct election by universal suffrage from the third term (i.e., 2007) onwards.[12] Xiao Weiyun (蕭蔚雲), the Mainland convenor of the Political System Sub-group of the Basic Law Drafting Committee, later commented that the political system design was achieved after arduous efforts. He said there was no firm option on the part of Beijing, but that the bottom line was to abide by the 'One Country, Two Systems' principle, be advantageous to Hong Kong's stability and prosperity, cater to the interests of various social strata, and develop democracy in a gradual and orderly manner.[13]

Both the 'double-Cha' mainstream option and bicameral proposal were eventually taken on board to form the basis of the SAR political structure design in the final Draft Basic Law endorsed by the NPCSC in February 1990 and then approved by the NPC at its plenary session on 4 April 1990. Under the Basic

Law, although universal suffrage was prescribed as the ultimate goal (Articles 45 and 68), it was stipulated that until 2007 the CE was to be elected by an Election Committee formed primarily by representatives of functional organisations, while only up to half of the LegCo's members would be elected by universal suffrage (with the remainder by functional constituencies and, up to 2007, the same Election Committee that elected the CE) (see Table 10.2).[14] If no amendment was made to these methods in 2007, which would require two-thirds majority support of all members of the LegCo and consent of the CE, and reporting to the NPCSC for approval (in the case of the CE) or record (in the case of the LegCo), the default constitutional design was for a CE elected by an Election Committee and a LegCo membership elected in equal proportion by functional and graphical constituencies.

Debates on constitutional development after 1997

After reversion to Chinese rule, the Hong Kong SAR's constitutional development journey essentially followed the arrangements set out above in the Basic Law and subsequently elaborated in local legislation.[15] Reforming the election methods in 2007 became a principal cause of the pro-democracy camp that believed there was a 'promise' by Beijing to implement universal suffrage ten years after reunification so long as there was wide support for it in Hong Kong.[16] The gradual reduction of Election Committee seats in the LegCo and their replacement by geographical directly elected seats also gave a sense of democratic progression, with the pro-democracy parties and politicians making some inroad in the legislature, winning over one-third of the seats from the second term (2000–2004) onwards, thus achieving a critical minority that could veto any constitutional development proposal coming from the government. Such a critical minority is, however, double-edged. It would confer on them political clout in the negotiation with the government but also burden (or liability) in that no constitutional reform involving the change of election method of the CE and formation of the LegCo could be passed without a degree of support from them (in order to forge a two-thirds majority of all members).

Riding on the strong public sentiments expressed during the 1 July 2003 mass protests against Article 23 national security legislation and in support of universal suffrage, the pro-democracy parties and groups demanded the implementation of election by universal suffrage of both the CE and the whole of the LegCo (dubbed as 'double universal suffrage') without delay.[17] Tung Chee-hwa had earlier opted for a public consultation in 2004 before his duty visit to Beijing in December 2003 to meet with President Hu Jintao and senior central government officials. The central government was determined to exercise full control over Hong Kong's constitutional development.[18] Indeed, in both constitutional and real-politics terms, Beijing held the key to constitutional reform.[19] Without its nod, the CE (being accountable to the CPG) would unlikely give consent to any

Table 10.2: Methods for the selection of the CE and formation of the LegCo according to the Basic Law

CE (5-year term)	LegCo (4-year term)
First term:	**First term: (2 years)**[a]
Selected, in accordance with the NPC Decision on the method for the formation of the First Government and First LegCo of the Hong Kong SAR, by a 400-member Selection Committee with the following composition:	Formed in accordance with the NPC Decision on the method for the formation of the First Government and First LegCo of the Hong Kong SAR:
• Industrial, commercial, and financial sectors: 25%	• Functional constituency seats: 30
• The professions: 25%	• Geographical constituency seats through direct elections: 20
• Labour, grassroots, religious, and other sectors: 25%	• Election Committee seats: 10
• Former political figures, Hong Kong deputies to the NPC, and representatives of Hong Kong members of the national committee of the CPPCC: 25%	**Second term:**
	• Functional constituency seats: 30
	• Geographical constituency seats through direct election: 24
	• Election Committee seats: 6
Subsequent terms:	**Third term:**
Election by an 800-member Election Committee comprising:	• Functional constituency seats: 30
• Industrial, commercial, and financial sectors: 200	• Geographical constituency seats through direct election: 30
• The professions: 200	
• Labour, social services, religious, and other sectors: 200	
• Members of the LegCo, representatives of district-based organisations, Hong Kong deputies to the NPC, and representatives of Hong Kong members of the national committee of the CPPCC: 200	
Terms subsequent to 2007:	**Beyond 2007:**
Method for election of the CE can be amended with endorsement of a two-thirds majority of all members of the LegCo and consent of the CE; such amendment to be reported to the NPCSC for *approval*	Method for formation of the LegCo can be amended with endorsement of a two-thirds majority of all members of the LegCo and consent of the CE; such amendment to be reported to the NPCSC for record

Source: Hong Kong SAR Government (n.d.) *The Basic Law of the Hong Kong Special Administrative Region of the People's Republic of China*, Annexes I and II, www.basiclaw.gov.hk/en/basiclaw/index.html; NPC (1990) *Decision of National People's Congress on the Method for the Formation of the First Government and First Legislative Council of the Hong Kong Special Administrative Region*, 4 April, Beijing.
[a] Assuming 'through-train' arrangement.

constitutional changes as part of the mandatory local process. The pro-democracy legislators could not move constitutional amendment bills unilaterally because under the Basic Law, any bills affecting the political structure of the SAR must come from the government, not legislators. Legislators could at the most move and pass a non-binding motion to put pressure on the government.

Beijing's position was subsequently made clear in April 2004 when the NPCSC interpreted the provisions of Annexes 1 and 2 of the Basic Law to require a 5-step process to affirm its veto power over any changes in the election methods.[20] It also passed another resolution to disallow the implementation of universal suffrage in 2007 and 2008 for electing the CE and the whole LegCo, respectively.[21] The 5-step process required: (1) the CE to first make a report to the NPCSC as to whether there is a need to amend the two electoral methods (for the CE and LegCo); (2) a determination to be made by the NPCSC as to whether the electoral methods need to be amended; (3) the resolutions on the amendments to be introduced by the SAR government to the LegCo and be endorsed by a two-thirds majority of all the members of LegCo; (4) consent to be given by the CE to the motions endorsed by the LegCo; and (5) the relevant bill to be reported by the CE to the NPCSC for approval or record as required by the Basic Law.[22] Before the implementation of election of the whole LegCo by universal franchise, there has to be an equal proportion of geographical and functional seats — in other words, there is no possibility to just add geographical seats to increase the directly elected membership.

The pan-democrats (as the pro-democrats were called by now) staged counteractions against the NPCSC decisions. At the beginning of the new LegCo session in November 2004, they sought in vain to pass a motion at the Constitutional Affairs Panel to propose a public referendum to seek the people's mandate on universal suffrage, but no vote was taken because of the ensuing chaos at the panel meeting. Both the pro-establishment camp and the central government's Liaison Office in Hong Kong rejected the call for referendum as an attempt to encroach on national sovereignty or to turn Hong Kong into an independent polity.[23] Beijing knew too well what the majority of Hong Kong people would want but was reluctant to take universal suffrage forward for various political and strategic reasons. Apart from its innate distrust of Western-style democracy by the ballot box, Beijing was also suspicious of some pan-democrats seeking to use democratisation to 'usurp power'. Therefore, working out how to constructively engage the central government to remove its worries and concerns would make better political sense than just getting embroiled in a prolonged but fruitless referendum debate.

Constitutional reform aborted in 2005

Following the 5-step procedure, the Tung Administration set up a Task Force on Constitutional Development, comprising the CS, Secretary for Justice, and Secretary for Constitutional Affairs (now Secretary for Constitutional and Mainland Affairs after government reorganisation in mid-2007), to gauge public opinions and come up with a reform proposal.[24] Soon afterwards, in March 2005,

Tung resigned and was succeeded by Donald Tsang. The Fifth Report of the Task Force published in October 2005 proposed to expand the 800-member Election Committee to 1,600, to include all 529 DC members (of whom 102 were government-appointed or ex-officio members from Rural Committees in the New Territories) (known as the 'District Council' model) to widen the base of the still limited electorate.[25] This expanded Election Committee would then elect both the CE in 2007 as well as half of 10 additional seats in the 2008 LegCo (with the remaining half by direct geographical elections)—thus maintaining an equal split between geographical directly elected seats and functional (plus Election Committee) seats in line with the 2004 NPCSC decision.

The proposed reform could not be passed without the support of at least some of the pan-democratic legislators who together held the critical-minority veto power. Initially, the mainstream democrats such as the Democratic Party and Article 45 Concern Group seemed willing to consider supporting the proposal should the appointed members of the DCs be excluded from the expanded Election Committee, although hardliners in the pan-democratic camp refused to make any concession.[26] Later, the more radical forces won the upper hand and were able, through signature campaigns and protest rallies, to steer the camp towards a firm opposing stance—demanding the abolition of all DC appointed seats and a clear roadmap and timetable for 'double universal suffrage', despite public opinion polls indicating willingness to accept the proposal.[27] Tsang repeatedly appealed to the public for support on television and radio programmes to put pressure on the pan-democrats. It was rumoured that at some point he was almost able to persuade a small number of pan-democratic legislators to accept the proposal, but nothing materialised from this. Ultimately, the vote in the LegCo on 21 December 2005 failed to secure the requisite two-thirds majority because of the en bloc veto by the pan-democrats.[28]

Given a solid level of public support to the reform package, Tsang could have opted, if granted Beijing's blessing, to dissolve the LegCo under Article 50 of the Basic Law in the hope that re-election would allow the popular electorate to put pressure on the candidates especially those from pan-democratic parties and groups. There is a catch, though, under Article 52 which states that if the new LegCo still refuses to pass the original bill in dispute, then the CE must resign. The political gamble would have been a huge one. Besides, the central government would unlikely consent to allowing the public, through a re-election of the LegCo tantamount to a referendum, to decide on the fate of constitutional development.

Roadmap and timetable

Everything was back to square one. A further amendment to the existing election methods could only be considered for the next term (i.e., 2012) for both the

CE and LegCo. Beijing still considered the mainstream democrats (such as the Democratic Party, the new Civic Party evolved from the Article 45 Concern Group, and pro-democracy think tanks and academics) a moderate force with whom it could continue to engage. In March 2007, the pan-democrats launched a 'mainstream transitional proposal' supported by 21 of their legislators, calling for the 800-member CE Election Committee to be expanded into a 1,200-member Nomination Committee by incorporating all the 400 or so elected district councillors, with a low threshold of 50 members in nominating candidates for election by universal suffrage. The abolition of the nomination committee mechanism was to be the ultimate long-term goal. As for the LegCo, all its members should be elected by universal suffrage, half through geographical single-seat direct elections and half territory-wide through proportional representation.

After rounds of listening to the views of different sectors, the NPCSC resolved on 29 December 2007 that the election method for the fifth-term CE in 2017 might be by universal suffrage, and that after the CE was elected by universal suffrage, all members of the LegCo might then be elected by universal suffrage.[29] It also decreed that appropriate amendments conforming to the principle of gradual and orderly progress might be made to the specific method for selecting the fourth-term CE and forming the fifth-term LegCo, both in 2012. Although the pan-democrats strongly criticised such decisions as 'democratic regression', it was the first time that Beijing was willing to commit to a clear roadmap and timetable for universal suffrage (i.e., 2017 the earliest for the CE and 2020 the earliest for the LegCo). That election by universal suffrage for the CE should precede that for the LegCo underscored the central government's concern about maintaining an executive-led government unimpaired by legislative power.[30]

Breakthrough in 2010

In November 2009, in accordance with the 5-step process, the Tsang Administration published a consultation document proposing to enlarge the Election Committee for the fourth-term CE from 800 members to 1,200 and increase the number of LegCo members from 60 to 70, allowing elected district councillors both to have more seats on the Election Committee and to elect five of the new LegCo seats, with the remaining five to be returned by geographical constituencies on universal suffrage, thus in effect enlarging the legislature's 'democratic' base (i.e., through direct and indirect elections by the general electorate).[31]

The pan-democrats had mixed views about this package. The more radical legislators (including Wong Yuk-man and Leung Kwok-hung from the League of Social Democrats) called for the concurrent resignation of one pan-democratic legislator in each of the five multi-seat geographical constituencies, so as to trigger territory-wide by-elections which could be turned into a de facto public referendum on universal suffrage. The Civic Party joined this move while the Democratic Party ultimately decided not to.[32] This marked the first split of the pan-democrats. Both the SAR government and central government condemned such 'strategic' resignations as wasting public resources.[33] The pro-establishment parties resolved not to field any candidates for the by-elections, and the five resigned pan-democratic legislators got re-elected easily in May 2010, thus diluting any claim of a mandate of referendum.

The final government proposal presented to the LegCo in April 2010 was essentially the same as that in the consultation document, which CS Henry Tang described as striving for 'maximum latitude to enhance democratic elements of the two elections in 2012'.[34] The responses from the pro-democracy camp were negative. The Civic Party considered the five additional 'DC' functional constituency seats regressive in principle, and the Democratic Party initially counter-proposed that these seats be elected among all elected district councillors by proportional representation instead of block voting for fear that the pro-establishment majority among these councillors would take all five seats in a winner-takes-all voting system. The moderate pan-democrats, including some academics, formed the Alliance for Universal Suffrage which demanded a guarantee to abolish functional constituencies by 2020 before it would accept the new seats. In return, the government said it would consider abolishing appointed district councillors if pan-democratic legislators would support the passage of the reform package.

There was a stalemate for a while as both sides sought to find a breakthrough in order not to repeat the 2005 fiasco. In May 2010, representatives of the Democratic Party and the Alliance for Universal Suffrage were invited, for the first time since the regime change in 1997, for formal discussions with a team from the central government's Liaison Office led by Vice-Director Li Gang (李剛), hoping to 'seek consensus while maintaining differences' (求同存異). On the other hand, the Civic Party sided with the radicals in the League of Social Democrats and People's Power to reject any proposal short of universal suffrage. On 21 June 2010, two days before the LegCo sitting to debate and then vote on the government motion, the Tsang Administration indicated a willingness to revise its proposal further following the Democratic Party's latest idea to let the five 'new' DC functional constituency seats be returned by all registered voters even though only the elected district councillors could nominate candidates and be nominees.[35]

These new seats have since been dubbed 'Super-District Council' seats because of their whole-territory electorate.[36] With the eight support votes from the Democratic Party (one of its legislators refused to toe the line and left the party), the revised government package was passed in the LegCo on 25 June 2010 by 46 to 12 votes. It was history-making in achieving a political reform consensus between government and part of the pro-democracy camp.[37] The new 2014

LegCo composition for the first time had a majority elected based on universal suffrage (40 out of 70 seats). The Democratic Party did Hong Kong a service but was shortly after accused by some radicals as being political 'turncoats'.

Constitutional reform aborted again in 2015

When Leung Chun-ying came to office as CE in 2012, he had the job of working out the electoral arrangements for 2017, with most pan-democrats expecting a package on the election of the CE by universal suffrage. Leung declared in a radio interview two days prior to winning the election (by Election Committee) on 25 March 2012 that he would hope to win his second term by universal suffrage.[38] In his remarks upon election, he said that '[a]lthough the election was by the 1,200-member Election Committee, the community also participated through diverse channels, thereby laying the foundation for universal suffrage in the CE Election in 2017'.[39] It seemed he had hoped for a constitutional breakthrough during his term. However, the subsequent political climate for the constitutional reform debate was very much marred by growing cautiousness of the central government and the radicalisation of the pro-democracy camp.

Some Beijing officials began to emphasise the need to rely on balanced cross-sector participation in a Nominating Committee to nominate a small number of candidates for direct election by universal suffrage and that the central government's power to appoint the winning candidate as CE would be substantive, not just symbolic. They also said that the CE candidates had to be persons who 'love the country and love Hong Kong' (愛國愛港) and not be confrontational to the central government.[40] Albert Chen, a Hong Kong member of the Basic Law Committee, observed that precisely because of the SAR's high degree of autonomy, the central government could not afford to let it be governed by someone who might be ideologically opposed to or otherwise unable or unwilling to adopt a cooperative attitude towards the central government.[41] Many pan-democrats suspected that the central government was backtracking on its promise of universal suffrage in 2017 and launched a campaign for 'genuine universal suffrage' (真普選). In early 2013, Benny Tai, a pro-democracy law academic, openly advocated the use of an 'Occupy Central [District]' movement as non-violent civil disobedience to exert pressure on the central government. He quickly gained wide support from pan-democratic parties and activists, fanned by the 'government-hostile' media like *Apple Daily*.[42] By 2014, there were campaigns for and counter-campaigns against the Occupy Central movement.[43]

In June 2013, the student activist group Scholarism, who successfully spearheaded the campaign against national education earlier in July to September 2012, demanded the use of civic nomination by ordinary electors for the CE election, probably borrowed from the practice in Taiwan, which was immediately ruled out by the government and pro-establishment camp as not in accordance with the Basic Law provisions. The main pan-democratic parties were hesitant to distance themselves from the student radicals' demands, and the looming radicalisation of the pro-democracy camp did not bode well for a possible compromise on constitutional development as in 2010. In December 2013, the Leung Administration issued a public consultation document to seek views on future election methods.[44] In January 2014, the pan-democratic coalition Alliance for True Democracy, supported by all 27 pan-democratic legislators, proposed the inclusion of three nomination channels: civil nomination, political party nomination, and nomination by the Nominating Committee.[45]

Some moderate pro-democracy academics advocated a middle-ground proposal (the '18 Scholars Proposal') in April 2014, so that an eligible person receiving signatures of support from 2% of registered voters could become a potential candidate for consideration by the 1,200-member nominating committee, while political parties and nominating committee members could also put forward candidates. Those potential candidates supported by one-eighth of the members of the nominating committee would enter direct election by universal suffrage. On the pro-establishment side, the DAB proposed in April 2014 that a 1,200–1,600-member CE nominating committee should be constituted with reference to the composition of the existing CE Election Committee comprising four primary sectors, with additional subsectors to be included to broaden representation. A CE candidate should have nomination by at least one-tenth but not more than one-eighth of the members of the nominating committee so that several candidates could be endorsed for direct election by universal suffrage.

Amid escalating political tensions caused by mass mobilisations for and against Occupy Central, Leung Chun-ying submitted a formal report to the NPCSC in July 2014 in accordance with the 5-step process, on the need to amend the methods of the CE election in 2017 and LegCo formation in 2016.[46] In August 2014, meetings were arranged between some pan-democratic legislators and Zhang Xiaoming (張曉明), Director of the central government's Liaison Office in Hong Kong. A delegation of legislators including 15 pan-democrats also met with Wang Guangya (王光亞), Director of the Hong Kong and Macao Affairs Office of the State Council, and Li Fei (李飛), Deputy Secretary-General of the NPCSC and Director of the Basic Law Committee, in Shenzhen. These were the last attempts for both sides to try to convince each other before the NPCSC would make up its mind on the way forward.

The NPCSC Decision on 31 August 2015 came as a bombshell for the pan-democrats. Dubbed as the '8.31 Decision', it required the CE to be a person 'who loves the country and loves Hong Kong' and that the method for selecting the CE by universal suffrage had 'to provide corresponding institutional safeguards for this purpose'.[47] A Nominating Committee similar to the present Election Committee composition would nominate two or three candidates, each supported by more than half of the members of the nominating committee. The method for forming the 2016 LegCo would remain unchanged. The pan-democrats, full of disappointment and anger, saw the 8.31 Decision as Beijing breaking its promise of universal suffrage and vowed to veto any proposal based on it. The Occupy Central organisers decided to stage the civil disobedience protest as planned in early October.

In the event, the protest rally was hijacked by the pre-emptive actions of radical activists from the Hong Kong Federation of Students and Scholarism to surround the Central Government Offices at Tamar in Admiralty, forcing them to kick it off earlier, on 28 September 2014, resulting in 79 days of large-scale street-camping protests branded as the 'Umbrella Movement'.[48] The script for failure in constitutional reform was more or less written. After the police finally cleared the protesters' camps in December 2014, the SAR government launched the second-round consultation for two months in January 2015. It proposed the election of the CE in 2017 by universal suffrage based on the nomination of two or three candidates each obtaining endorsement of at least half of all members of a Nominating Committee modelled on the 38 subsectors (and any new subsectors added) within four main sectors of the existing Election Committee, with the subsector electorate base remaining unchanged.[49]

The pan-democrats boycotted the consultation. On 22 April 2015, the government published the consultation report keeping the original proposal essentially intact except refinement regarding the Nominating Committee member recommendations and Nominating Committee nominations.[50] According to the upper and lower limits for the 'entry' threshold, the system could allow 5–10 persons to be considered for nomination by the whole committee through voting by secret ballot, with 2–3 candidates finally nominated.[51] The government also launched a '2017 Make It Happen!' campaign to garner public support for its reform package. Public opinion polls conducted by university units during May–June 2015 indicated that close to half of the respondents supported passing the package by the legislature, with a relatively less but still considerable proportion supporting a veto vote.[52] Before the vital LegCo vote took place, Wang Guangya, Li Fei, and Zhang Xiaoming jointly met with a LegCo delegation comprising pan-democratic members in Shenzhen at the end of May 2016. Any hopes for concessions from Beijing were dashed. The government motion was ultimately defeated in the LegCo on 18 June 2015.[53]

Thereafter, Leung Chun-ying declared that his Administration would henceforth focus on economic development and livelihood issues instead of constitutional reform.[54] When Carrie Lam assumed office in mid-2017, she also stated that she would not restart the constitutional development process until conditions improved.[55] The central government's position was that the NPCSC's 31 August 2014 decision would remain the basis for any future reform proposal, a bottom-line that pan-democrats could not possibly swallow. Things are now in a quagmire with no foreseeable breakthrough. Without first implementing the election of the CE by universal suffrage, the formation of the LegCo wholly by universal suffrage cannot proceed. The 2007 roadmap and timetable have been made redundant.

Is the quest for democracy futile?

The political window of opportunity for constitutional reform in Hong Kong towards a full electoral democracy has always been very narrow, though not entirely unavailable. Beijing's conservative stance on universal suffrage is not sudden or a new development under the more hardline President Xi Jinping as the media prefer to perceive.[56] From day one during the 1980s, central leaders like Deng Xiaoping were not convinced of the merit of or need for Western-style democracy by the ballot box. That Beijing was pushed and induced into a position that allowed the inclusion in the Basic Law of an ultimate goal of selecting the CE and forming the whole of the LegCo by universal suffrage was in itself a significant breakthrough at the time, which was a result of the good sense and efforts of all sides concerned (including some central government officials) when there existed sufficient mutual trust and respect.

Even then, as underscored by the debates during the Basic Law drafting process, the central government and those drafters close to it had always favoured restrictions over both the nomination process and the number of candidates, even if universal suffrage was to eventually apply to the CE election, in order to prevent any direct election getting out of control and turning Hong Kong into a 'political city'.[57] Thus, this path dependence has existed for several decades. When the pro-democracy camp and Beijing were engaging constructively, such as in the 1980s before the Tiananmen crackdown and for a short spell in negotiating a deal in 2009–2010, it was possible to persuade the Beijing leadership that democratic progress in Hong Kong, though not without political risk from its perspective, was more conducive to political consensus-building and stability, and would not necessarily lead to anti-central government consequences (i.e., the 'One Country' consideration).

However, Beijing has been alarmed at the radicalisation of the pro-democracy movement by localist sentiments in recent years. These have deteriorated into separatist and even pro-independence tendencies, and mainstream democrats have found it politically expedient not to condemn them. Central government officials seem convinced that the risks and costs of democracy in Hong Kong would outweigh any possible benefits. They also suspect that activists supported by foreign politicians and organisations are using democracy as a rally cry against CCP rule and China's jurisdiction over Hong Kong. Such suspicions work against constructive dialogue and mutual accommodation in finding a way out. The situation was further aggravated in the 2019 mass confrontations that saw young protesters taking their fight for a 'free Hong Kong' to the international arena (see Chapter 12).

For a political breakthrough to occur, it is crucial to match Beijing's power of appointment with the local people's right to elect their leader. The balancing point lies in the nominating committee and the nomination threshold and mechanism. Abolishing the existing functional seats in the LegCo would involve balancing interests within Hong Kong. One way of compromise to achieve balanced representation would be to have registered functional-sector bodies and members nominating candidates from among their own ranks for election territory-wide by universal suffrage, like the 'Super District Council' elections.[58] Conceptually, any constitutional reform could take a range of steps—the move towards election of the CE and the whole of LegCo by universal suffrage according to the original 2007 roadmap, reform of district administration with more devolved powers to the local communities, and the fostering of more constructive party politics.

Four key players possess veto power over constitutional reform. The central state, through the NPCSC, has the final say over whether there is a need to commence consideration of and consultation over such reform, and ultimately approves any constitutional change. The CE holds the key to initiate the 5-step process. The pro-establishment legislators together have the majority of LegCo votes, but the pan-democratic legislators, if they continue to secure more than one-third of the seats based on the existing electoral system, will continue to hold the critical minority.[59] In other words, if the pan-democrats are unwilling to engage with the other three parties and accept some strategic compromise, then the process will go nowhere. A crucial precondition is that any sub-national democracy within a unitary state cannot be adversarial to the CCP central government's sovereign authority. Any side could halt progress on universal suffrage. Therefore, a give-and-take strategic compromise is unavoidable in order to move forward.

At present, political trust is slim if not non-existent between the central government and pan-democrats (even the moderate ones). It remains doubtful if the central government would risk reopening old wounds and controversies and paving the way for the pan-democratic opposition to grab more political power by relaunching constitutional reform along the original roadmap. Trust between the pan-democrats and the CE has dropped even further since the extradition bill fiasco. At the same time, the pan-democrats are no longer a unified camp. Neither is the pro-establishment camp, because of diverse backgrounds and interests among its component parties and individual legislators. As political polarisation and fragmentation deteriorate, it will only become harder, if not impossible, to reach any political consensus between the two camps on constitutional reform, which can easily be perceived as a zero-sum game.

After four decades of a traditional pro-democracy movement by signature campaigns, rallies, protest march, hunger strikes, and even LegCo walkouts and 'mass resignations' from legislative seats to trigger pseudo-referendums, the pan-democrats have been politically discredited within their usual support base for failing to achieve any meaningful deal. The failure of the Occupy Central campaign and Umbrella Movement in forcing the central government into major concessions clearly shows that the pan-democratic parties and newly radicalised activists had run out of strategies for a breakthrough. Their desperate actions only served to instil an atmosphere of despair and fatalism. This paved the way for the mass confrontations in 2019, led by young radicals who do not subscribe to strategic compromise and are ready for sabotaging Hong Kong and causing maximum reputational damage to China internationally in a kind of fatalistic uprising resorting to escalating violence and vandalism.

That their actions have gained sympathy from many in the population who have been frustrated by years of Beijing's stubbornness towards democratisation may well give them new moral momentum. However, such moral force could not be translated into a real capacity for negotiation. The central leaders are unlikely to succumb to such new pressures just as they had refused to concede in 2014 in the face of the Occupy protests. The hardline approach taken by Beijing towards the ongoing political standoff and international intervention is underscored by the NPC's decision in May 2020 to impose a national security law on Hong Kong (more on this in the Epilogue).

Political reform may now be considered as a risk rather than an accomplishment by the central government. The latest crisis of governability is presenting Beijing with a huge dilemma. It might opt for a harder line of suppression and freezing the current political system for fear of the worst or gradually becoming persuaded of the need for another pragmatic attempt at a constitutional breakthrough. Either way, it would see the costs as excessively high. Factors working against pragmatism include the high-profile interventions by some Western governments, particularly the US, which feed into the hardliners' conspiracy theory about a 'colour revolution' to turn Hong Kong into a counter-CCP bridgehead. A prolonged period of constitutional stagnancy might ensue, putting further stress on the existing defective political system which still has to deliver practical governance amidst widening political divides, rising public frustrations, and falling expectations.

Chapter 11
A Government without Parties or Votes

Introduction

As Thomas Dye once put it:

> Governments do many things. They regulate conflict within society; they organize society to carry on conflict with other societies; they distribute a great variety of symbolic rewards and material services to members of the society; and they extract money from society, most often in the form of taxes.[1]

In other words, governments are in the business of problem-solving, organising actions, distribution, redistribution, taxation and expenditure, and social regulation and law enforcement, to provide social and economic stability. To function well, all governments need to have credibility, authority, power, resources, and organisational capacity (as discussed in Chapter 7).

Previous chapters have explained some of the contextual and path-dependent factors which have shaped the evolution of the system of government and policy architecture in Hong Kong, including the British colonial legacy, Chinese central government preferences, and design of the Basic Law. Inherited from the colonial administration, the Hong Kong government structure at the point of transition in 1997 was essentially a government by bureaucracy with features of centralised power as well as executive-led and top-down administrative dominance, a fiscally driven policy regime, consultative politics, and institutional autonomy relatively unrestrained by outside forces. The colonial government was able to govern effectively because of its autocratic nature and monopoly of appointments, resources, and patronage, and from the 1970s onwards, its brand of authoritarian reformism pursued to gain popular acquiescence if not active support. The more classical colonial era (until the late transition period in the 1990s) was de facto a period of 'when there is a will, there is a way'.

Such government effectiveness was what the Chinese government had in mind in the 1980s when it opted for keeping the executive-led system intact and extended beyond 1997, subject only to some unavoidable modifications because of the restoration of Chinese rule and the need to accommodate newly emerging aspirations for democratisation and local autonomy. However, Beijing did not intend to promote Western-style democracy and separation of power; rather, it preferred to maintain a strong executive and a weak legislature. To prevent any capture of the legislature by grassroots populism, thus upsetting the interests of capitalism, the LegCo would function as a quasi-bicameral system through 'split voting' between an equal proportion of geographical and functional seats, whereby the functional votes could exercise veto power over motions, bills, and amendments introduced by individual legislators.[2]

Chapter 4 reviews the growing incompatibilities between such institutional design and the changing political environment. In terms of function, the SAR political system may be better understood not for what *it is*, but rather for what *it is not*. It is not entirely presidential or parliamentary, nor is it entirely executive-led. It is not a party government or entirely a cabinet government. It is not just any local government of the PRC. It is a government without party support or votes — neither the popular vote nor legislative votes. Given such features, it is not easily susceptible to conventional political science typology, nor direct comparison with other existing systems of government around the world, democratic or otherwise. This does not necessarily mean the government is unable to carry through any policy initiatives or legislative amendments. However, a 'government without votes' has to rely all the more on popular trust and acceptance, which was the route taken with the brand of consultative politics practised by the previous colonial administration. Once these conditions are short in supply, the government's ability to govern becomes vulnerable.

Representation and mandate

The absence of electoral democracy by universal suffrage in the formation of the executive (the CE) and the whole of the legislature has lent much credence to the argument that there is insufficient popular mandate to the government. Yet, there exist some forms of elections to these two governance institutions. The legislature is already a partial democracy in the sense that a slight majority of the LegCo membership is elected on the basis of universal suffrage — 40 seats (35 of which are geographical seats plus the 5 'super DC' functional seats) out of 70 seats (although this has changed following the election reforms enacted in March 2021; discussed further in the Postscript). As for the 1,200-member Election Committee that elects the CE, while not a democratic electoral college and constituted essentially through functional subsector elections, some of such elections have been based on individual voting.[3]

The presence of these partially democratic configurations, concomitant with the full string of institutional and procedural checks mentioned in earlier chapters, should not be equated to any other authoritarian regime as if the government could easily ignore the demands and sentiments of the community. Of course, one may argue that even though there is a degree of representation in the system, the style of government is still authoritarian because of the inherited colonial autocratic culture and the Basic Law political design to vest undue powers in the non-democratic executive at the expense of a semi-democratic legislature. Granted, it is still fair to say that the present SAR political system is formally more open and subject to more checks and balances compared to the pre-1997 colonial regime. A simplistic democratic versus authoritarian dichotomy does not appreciate the capacity, complexities, and drawbacks of the present system.

The fact that only the LegCo enjoys some degree of democratic mandate, while the CE is widely perceived and criticised as the product of a 'small circle' election or, worse, alleged to be a 'puppet regime' of the central government in Beijing, means that the CE, a priori, suffers from a legitimation inequality vis-à-vis the legislature. The structural division between functional and geographical constituencies—with the former returning more members tending to be pro-establishment in political orientation, and the latter adopting proportional representation—has produced a more fragmented legislature steadily split between the pro-establishment and pan-democratic camps.[4] Over the years, the pan-democrats have managed to secure enough seats to form a critical minority of the LegCo, thus holding veto power over any constitutional development bills which require approval by a two-thirds majority of all legislators.

This split is not the same as that in a two-party system because neither legislative camp could aspire to government office. Meanwhile, the fragmentation of the LegCo has been made worse by the emergence of small parties or groups within both the pro-establishment and pan-democratic camps, making it difficult for the executive to work and negotiate with a clear majority party or political alliance within the legislature. While parties and independents of either camp would likely vote in unison on major issues of constitutional and political significance often related to central-state positions or interests, they tend to have more of their own political and electoral calculations as a party or individually on other issues (particularly livelihood as well as district and profession-specific issues) given they have to compete with one another within the same camp in legislative elections. Such strategic behavioural differences between the parliamentary and electoral arenas have long been recognised in Western democracies.[5] The partisan distribution of the LegCo since 1998 is given in Table 11.1.

Executive domination

Executive dominance is not just a feature of an authoritarian system or a colonial system like Hong Kong in the past under British rule. In fact, it underscores both a parliamentary and presidential system (or a quasi-presidential system like France) in order to enable the government of the day to govern effectively. The difference among various systems is but a matter of degree of such dominance.

During the drafting of the Basic Law in the 1980s, there was a debate early on about whether the future political system of the SAR should be based on an 'executive-led' or 'legislature-led' principle, with some pro-democracy activists

Table 11.1: Partisan distribution of the SAR LegCo from 1997 to 2020

	1998–2000	2000–2004	2004–2008	2008–2012	2012–2016	2016–2020[a] (until July 2020)
Democratic Party	12	12	9	8[b]	6	7(7)
Civic Party	–	–	6	5	6	5(5)
Labour Party	–	–	–	–	4	1(1)
Other pro-democracy groups and independents (including League of Social Democrats, People's Power, etc.)[c]	6	9	11	9	11	16(10)
Pan-democrat	**18**	**21[d]**	**26[d]**	**22[d]**	**27[d]**	**29(23)[d]**
DAB	8[e]	8[e]	10[f]	10	13	12(13)
FTU	2	2	3	4	6	5(4)
Liberal Party	10	9	11	3[g]	5	4(4)
Business and Professional Alliance for Hong Kong (BPA)	–	–	–	–	7	7(8)
Other pro-establishment groups and independents (including New People's Party)	15	12	5	12	10	13(14)
Pro-establishment	**35**	**31**	**29**	**29**	**41**	**41(43)**
Non-affiliated independents[h]	7	8	5	9	2	0
Broadly pro-establishment	**42**	**39**	**34**	**38**	**43**	**41(43)**
Total	**60**	**60**	**60**	**60**	**70**	**70(66)**

[a] The figures in brackets reflect the change in membership following two LegCo by-elections held in March and November 2018, respectively, as a result of 6 pan-democrats and localists elected in the September 2016 general election being disqualified by the court from assuming office over the oath-taking controversy (see Chapter 12). While the pan-democrats were able to win back two of the seats falling vacant, three other seats were snatched by pro-establishment candidates. A CFA ruling in December 2019 upheld the judgment of the Court of First Instance of the High Court that the two pan-democratic legislators returned in the March 2018 by-election were 'not duly elected' because of a problematic disqualification by the returning officer of two other pro-democracy candidates from entering the election. A pro-establishment legislator, Ho Kai-ming of the FTU, resigned to join the government on 1 June 2020 as Under-Secretary for Labour and Welfare. In June 2020, the effective membership of LegCo was only 66. See Legislative Council (n.d.) *Changes in Membership of the Sixth Legislative Council (2016–2020)*, Hong Kong: Legislative Council, www.legco.gov.hk/general/english/members/yr16-20/notes.htm.

[b] Including Emily Lau whose political group, The Frontier, merged with the Democratic Party in November 2008. Lau was then elected chairman of the party in December.

[c] There have been frequent movements of pan-democratic legislators from one party to another, or to form new party groups.

[d] Critical minority (i.e., over one-third of the total LegCo membership).

[e] Including Tam Yiu-chung who was also a leader of the FTU.

[f] The DAB merged with the Hong Kong Progressive Alliance in 2005.

[g] Some legislators left the Liberal Party to form Economic Synergy, one of the predecessors of the BPA in 2012.

[h] Most of these members, though not affiliated with any party or pro-establishment group, were broadly pro-establishment business-professional elites returned by functional constituencies. Some occasionally vote against the government on certain issues affecting functional interests but otherwise support the government.

campaigning for the latter in support of holding the CE fully accountable to the legislature along the notion of parliamentary supremacy as in the Westminster model. Beijing reacted strongly that any departure from the 'executive-led' system was an attempt to weaken the future SAR government, the top echelon of which would be subject to central government appointment. Some pro-Beijing critics even ventured to suggest that a parliamentary system, as advocated by some in the pro-democracy camp, such as Meeting Point, would result in a legislature-led system. This was a total misunderstanding of the real dynamics of a parliamentary system in which the cabinet, through the majority control of parliament by the ruling party or coalition, actually commands and leads the parliament, thus delivering an executive-led outcome.

A simplistic binary debate fails to grasp the reality of government under a specific political design. According to Arend Lijphart, there exists a variety of executive-legislative relationships in modern democracies across different political systems.[6] The capacity of the executive to command legislative majority support is a result of both constitutional design and political practice in party competition. The British Westminster model tends to ensure executive dominance, complemented by a 'first past the post' voting system which is more likely to turn out a party with a clear majority in the Parliament. The continental European systems, often accompanied by a 'proportional representation' voting system that enables small parties to gain seats (thus reducing the possibility of dominant parliamentary parties to emerge), tend to see an executive-legislative balance. Presidential and semi-presidential systems might tip either way, depending on the specific party-political environment and constitutional conventions. The strength and cohesion of the president's party in the legislature decides the relative power of the executive and legislature. For example, despite being the earliest to embrace Montesquieu's doctrine of separation of power, the US system has tended to allow the President to have more sway in power, though at times Congress can make significant policy changes difficult.

Conceptually, if we are to ensure an executive-led or dominated system, the British parliamentary system is the best model to follow. Unless there is a backbench revolt and the party whip fails to impose political discipline, the governing party continues to command a legislative majority and can ultimately pass any laws, taxation, and public expenditure no matter how marginal the majority is. However, the political environment has been gradually changing even among parliamentary systems. The fragmentation of party politics in recent years has sometimes led to a 'hung' parliament, necessitating the formation of a coalition government (as in the Conservative-Liberal Democrat coalition government in Britain during 2010–2015) or a government relying on cross-bench support by a few 'independents' (as in Australian federal governments under the previous Liberal-National coalition or Labor administration).[7] In typical majoritarian party politics today, there is seldom a government formed solely by a single majority party of the legislature. Coalition governments thus formed, sometimes with a thin majority or involving several parties, are often at the mercy of shifting alliances among parties and legislators.

On the contrary, a presidential system like the US guarantees the stability of the government as it is not subject to any vote of confidence in the legislature. Still, given that the House of Representatives and Senate can initiate and pass their own laws and appropriations of funds, subject to checks and balances between the executive and legislature as well as between the House and Senate, it accords the legislature (Congress) room for political clout even though the President is constituted separately with a popular base through an electoral college. This notwithstanding, intense executive-legislature negotiations and frequent showdowns have become the norm of partisan politics.[8] Most democratic political systems now find it common to endure more negotiations between the executive and legislature, and in parliamentary systems, between the government frontbench and the backbenchers within the ruling party. Therefore, executive dominance should not be taken for granted even in Westminster systems.

In Hong Kong, although preserving the executive-led system was an important official principle for the post-1997 system of governance, such a principle was not explicitly stipulated in the Basic Law. In his address on the Draft Basic Law at the NPC on 28 March 1990, Ji Pengfei (姬鵬飛), Chairman of the Basic Law Drafting Committee and Director of the Hong Kong and Macao Affairs Office of the State Council, only stated that the SAR's political system had to 'preserve those elements of the original political system which have been working effectively, and also orderly and gradually develop a democratic system that suits Hong Kong's circumstances', and that 'the executive and legislature should check and complement each other while the judiciary should be independent'.[9] Henceforth, the central government has been describing the SAR system as an executive-led system, a point repeated by the SAR government. At a forum to commemorate the 10th anniversary of the implementation of the Basic Law, Wu Bangguo (吳邦國), Chairman of the NPCSC, emphasised that the most significant feature of the SAR's political system was that of being executive-led.[10]

Given that the CE is separately elected and constituted, their power is not derived from the legislature, and they form their own cabinet of ministerial officials (subject to central government appointment) and executive councillors, and given that the Basic Law design has curbed the LegCo's power to initiate bills and policies freely, the SAR has in effect a kind of quasi-presidential system complemented by some of the powers enjoyed by a parliamentary government (notably over the legislative agenda). This has prompted the suggestion that Beijing established the functional constituencies and proportional representation system for installing business elites and the traditional pro-Beijing patriotic forces in the SAR LegCo in order to form a stable pro-government majority.[11] Irrespective of any such inclination, it should be pointed out that the concept and design of 'functional constituencies' came from the British administration when implementing representative government in the 1980s, and proportional representation is a common voting method in Europe to encourage small parties to exist to cover the interests of a more pluralist society. As things stand, unless the government's authority is politically strengthened by a CE elected with a popular mandate or an executive in strong alliance with major political parties in the LegCo beyond the notion of a nominally pro-establishment label, its command over local politics will not materialise as originally expected of an executive-led government by the Basic Law drafters or the central government.

Neither presidential nor parliamentary

The CE's government is often mocked as 'having power but no votes', whereas the partially democratic LegCo enjoys an electoral edge but lacks power in policy-making ('having votes but no power'). Without a clear or reliable pro-government (instead of just pro-establishment) majority in the legislature to help deliver government bills, appropriations, and policy proposals, the big question is whether the prevailing system that is neither presidential nor parliamentary can still broadly achieve *good enough* executive-legislative relations, with sufficient cooperation amid tension, even if the pan-democratic opposition does not spare the government from procedural hurdles and political sabotage.

In a presidential system, while there are constitutional checks and balances between the executive and legislature, the president as chief executive derives their mandate from a popular election (whether directly on universal suffrage or indirectly via an electoral college as in the case of the US) and does not have to be held ransom by the legislature. Elected with a clear manifesto, the president is expected by the electorate to deliver it. Such expectation, backed by popular political support, can help the president in the negotiations with legislators when it comes to enactment of laws, taxation, or appropriation of public funds. In a parliamentary system, the power of initiation rests in the executive which enjoys a virtual monopoly over public business and the enactment of public bills as typical of the Westminster model. However, there also exist conventions in British-style adversarial politics whereby there is a constitutional and political role to play by the official opposition (i.e., the largest opposition party) in parliament, often seen as government-in-waiting, whose views would be given due regard by the government.

Inheriting a British-shaped form of government premised on the LegCo as the principal theatre of government and politics, the SAR government has continued to play by the rules of procedure, conventions, and modus operandi of the LegCo in terms of policy-making, legislation, reorganisation of government, establishment control, and managing public business. The former political architecture of colonial rule, while enabling the governor to be almost autocratic, had at the same time endowed a lot of formal though seldom-used powers in the LegCo modelled on the British Parliament. In keeping with the practice of parliamentary government, the power of initiation of policies and laws had firmly remained in the custody of the executive, a feature retained in the Basic Law, thus depriving legislators, in a group or individually, the same degree of legislative power as in the US Congress. Still, the rules of procedure enable legislators to cause various hurdles (especially over directorate establishment and public works proposals, as well as government reorganisation). Indeed, day-to-day politics have become defined by the LegCo's sittings and debates, and the activities of its committees and panels including inquiries and public hearings.

During the early part of his first-term Administration, Donald Tsang attempted to position himself as a 'whole people' CE above partisan politics, but he failed. His cultivation of goodwill with the pan-democratic legislators did not help deliver their support for his constitutional reform package in 2005, marking a major political setback after assuming office with high popularity. From then onwards, Tsang had to accept the pro-establishment/pan-democrat divide, officially referring to the pan-democrats as 'the opposition' and having to rely on the pro-establishment parties and legislators for the passage of government bills, funding proposals, and the budget. The present CE Carrie Lam who, like Tsang, was originally perceived to be on friendly terms with some moderate democrats, has to follow his footsteps in forging a closer working alliance with the pro-establishment camp especially after the 2019 extradition bill controversy when all the pan-democrats demanded her removal. There exists no alternative because the pan-democrats, as an opposition, see their role as finding fault in the administration and challenging the government whenever possible just like the political opposition in other systems. Besides, they do not trust the central government and suspect the CE to be under Beijing's undue influence and directive.

One way of evaluating executive-legislative relations is to examine how 'cooperative' the LegCo has been in passing government bills. Brian Fong previously examined the SAR government's capacity to convert its annual legislative agenda (as expressed in the CE's Policy Address and the government's Legislative Programme) into bills that were ultimately passed by the LegCo, as a measure of 'legislative success rates'.[12] He observed that all the three CEs before Lam experienced similar difficulties in steering legislative changes, achieving a success rate of only 55.33%, 57.47%, and 57.41%, respectively. Fong did not just look at government bills formally put to the LegCo but also proposals originally on the annual legislative agenda that were subsequently shelved or postponed (on average some 40%). He surmised that this was due to executive-legislative tension and that the government was simply staying away from controversy.

This may be somewhat an over-speculation. Some of the postponed cases had little to do with the LegCo but the delays were a result of policy bureau or law drafting backlog, or even caused by the unforeseen complexity of the bill itself which required more internal scrutiny and deliberations before the bill would be ready for submission to the LegCo. Thus, a more realistic assessment is that the 'legislative success rate' was well above 50% but less than the very high 'passing rates' of 91.9% (from 1998 to 2000) and 97% (2000 to 2004) noted by Ma Ngok simply based on those bills formally introduced to the LegCo for first reading.[13] Nonetheless, Fong did raise a relevant question: 'Why does the pro-government majority in the Legislative Council, contrary to the constitutional design of the HKSAR executive-dominant system, fail to function as a stable support base for the Chief Executive's legislative agenda?'[14]

The irony is that pro-establishment parties and groups do not feel they are part of the government, as in the case of a ruling coalition or there being any lineage to the government, such as how Republican lawmakers view a Republican President in the US. While the pro-establishment camp has, by and large, to abide by the central government's line to support the SAR government in governing according to the Basic Law, electoral competition dictates that even legislators of this camp have to challenge the government and blame and shame government officials from time to time in order to discharge their role as legislators in checking the executive. So the relationship between the government and pro-establishment camp is at best ambivalent—with government stability resting on the support of the pro-establishment camp in the LegCo and yet an underlying instability also existing between the two sides because they are not a formal governing coalition in pursuit of a common policy or political agenda (despite a few pro-establishment figures and former legislators joining the government as political appointees in recent years).

Furthermore, the CE does not enjoy the favour of either a parliamentary or presidential system. Worse, the CE is prevented by design and by law from belonging to any political party. Such prohibition stems from the decision of the Hong Kong SAR Preparatory Committee which drew up the rules for the selection of the first CE in December 1996 through a 400-member Selection Committee formed under its aegis. The CE was supposed to be a leader above party politics as in the colonial administrative state before. When the restriction was written into local legislation in 2001 prior to second-term CE election held in March 2002, the only relaxation made was to permit a party-affiliated candidate to stand for election, but once elected that person has to resign from the party. As such Hong Kong's CE is politically handicapped in terms of building strong party links, even with the pro-establishment camp. Some observed that the dysfunction of the executive-dominant system in post-colonial Hong Kong is the result of Beijing's resistance to the development of party government, resulting in the uneasy partnership between the non-partisan CE and the pro-establishment parties.[15]

Another political consequence is that political parties do not see it as a realistic prospect to achieve the power of government through the formal process. Even though pro-establishment parties can still regard aligning themselves with the incumbent CE as a second-best option and can actively lobby the CE to appoint their members to the ExCo, important statutory and advisory bodies, and certain ministerial posts (mostly at Under-Secretary and PA levels), their overall political ambitions remain capped by a legislative career path. Since parties cannot position themselves as the government-in-waiting as in a Westminster system, they essentially operate as government-critical and sometimes government-bashing voices to attract public and media attention and thus popular votes in legislative and district elections. Pro-establishment parties do not feel they owe their allegiance to the CE because their future mainly lies in winning electoral seats driven by a wholly different political logic. As a result, political elections see parties contesting for seats on a manifesto of demanding the government to do more and blaming the government for not doing enough, rather than what they, upon winning the election, would be able to deliver themselves. In practice, all parties across the political spectrum are 'in opposition' towards the sitting government.

The fragmentation of the LegCo and its partisan politics has further rendered any stable support to the government difficult to achieve and sustain. Examples of policy impasses abound in recent years (such as those over government reorganisation, tightening up copyright protection, and opening up the Medical Council to more lay-member participation) because of the executive-legislative gridlock.[16] The government has increasingly viewed some legislators and parties as unconstructive and frequently blocking government initiatives. On the other hand, many legislators tend to distrust the government and perceive officials as bureaucratic and deaf to the representatives of the people and functional sectors. It takes two to tango. Dancing between two unavoidable partners in a political system with different logics of sustenance and mindsets only results in missteps, but this has already become a fact of life in SAR politics. In parliamentary systems, ministers are members of parliament who could enjoy peer support or sympathy from some fellow legislators. In presidential systems, though ministers cannot be members of the legislature, they enjoy political support through the popular mandate gained by the president. Hong Kong's political executive is neither here nor there and still in search of coherent institutional logic.

Two factors are pertinent in the debate over whether party government will be possible in the long term. First, the present legal restriction over the CE's party affiliation has to be removed. This is feasible as it is based on a local law that can be changed. However, it is doubtful if the central government would support such a change because of the difficulty to square party government in Hong Kong with the PRC's constitutional stipulation of the CCP as the ruling party over the whole of China including Hong Kong. Beijing needs to have a more holistic view of the overall constitutional development of the SAR and adopt a more flexible and imaginative interpretation of the PRC constitution in much the same way as central leaders led by Deng Xiaoping did in the early 1980s to come up with the novel concept of 'One Country, Two Systems'. Second, should this restriction be lifted, which party or party-coalition will likely emerge as a ruling party within a system of self-administration? Some local political parties might worry that once fielding a CE, their check-and-balance role vis-à-vis the government will diminish, which will erode their support base in LegCo elections.

Also, there might not be enough institutional or political incentives for pro-establishment parties to see holding office in the government as a rewarding and risk-free political achievement. Pan-democrats would rather be in 'opposition' than in government which would necessitate compromises with the establishment forces and the CCP central state, which they might find it hard to reconcile with their longstanding ideology and political dogma. Short of formal party government, there is still conceptually the possibility of a hybrid model whereby a non-partisan CE forms a formal coalition with those parties constituting a majority of the LegCo. However, such a model would be difficult to operate under the check-and-balance ethos. In different ways, Tung, Tsang, and Leung all tried to accomplish this but in vain.

Collective responsibility without cabinet government

The principal ministerial officials are all nominated by the CE for the CPG's appointment and are concurrently members of the ExCo. Non-official members of the ExCo are appointed by the CE and serve to support the administration. Both the ExCo and the CE's ministerial team are regarded as a cabinet, bound by the doctrine of 'collective responsibility' and 'secrecy' carried over from the Governor-in-Council practice of colonial times. However, this is only the surface of it. In reality, the SAR government does not fully operate like a cabinet government elsewhere.

According to Jean Blondel, cabinet systems have served Western European countries well, with the cabinet government usually linked to parliamentary rule.[17] A cabinet government should, first, reflect the political spectrum of the parliament or national assembly and, second, enjoy majority support from the parliament or assembly. It can remain in existence so long as it enjoys parliamentary confidence. The success of Western European cabinet systems has varied according to the size of the cabinet, the role of the prime minister, the turnover of ministers, and ministerial competence. Depending on the actual political convention and practice, there can be a 'representative' or 'administrative' (bureaucratic) cabinet, and a 'majoritarian' or 'consociational' cabinet to embody the nature of party politics ranging from majority government to coalition government of similar or diverse partisan orientations.

Such political features are simply absent in the case of Hong Kong. The previous British administration operated as the Governor-in-Council, seen by many as a form of cabinet decision-making under the principle of 'collective responsibility', whereby the ExCo members could not openly speak contrary to the decisions already made and could not reveal any dissenting individual views. However, there was a difference in policy power and influence between the official and unofficial (non-official) members of the ExCo at the time. The non-officials' prominence partly stemmed from their role as 'outsiders' and as the Governor's trusted policy advisors. As ExCo members, they scrutinised proposals and submissions from top bureaucrats, holding the latter somewhat accountable and providing a community and political perspective in formal deliberations. Key ExCo non-officials also headed important statutory and advisory bodies, displaying policy influence and political clout.[18] At times they were given the role of publicly defending government policies in certain areas.[19]

Immediately after 1997, the Secretary posts continued to be monopolised by career civil servants, mostly AOs. The logic was there for maintaining an ExCo whereby non-official members could have reasonable input as leaders from various walks of life in order to give government decisions the necessary community flavour. Since the introduction of the new ministerial system (i.e., the POAS) in 2002, the ExCo has included all politically appointed Secretaries (ministers), together with leaders of major pro-establishment parties as well as, at times, selective individuals from the pan-democratic camp, all appointed ad personam.[20] However, such composition is not linked in any way to coalition government as in the Western European sense. The colonial ExCo culture had carried on into the SAR regime. Most ExCo members, even those from political party backgrounds, have to defer to the will of the CE. Non-officials are not supposed to speak against government policies openly (whether having been discussed at ExCo meetings or not) or, in the case of those members who are also legislators, vote against government positions in the LegCo.[21] The practice of tasking some ExCo non-officials to head key bodies continued after 1997.[22]

During the more enthusiastic times of representative government development in the late 1980s, the government had considered turning ExCo non-officials into quasi-ministers by appointing them to head major policy advisory commissions and statutory authorities and in effect to lead policy formulation (a 'half-ministerial system' as advocated by Lydia Dunn, a Senior Unofficial Member of the ExCo during the transition period). However, this idea was never fully debated. Post-2002, the new ministerial system has obviated the need to make ExCo non-officials semi-ministers given that Secretaries are now no longer civil servants but sit on the ExCo as full-fledged political ministers. Even though ExCo non-officials rank just below the Secretaries according to the official protocol and list of precedence, their actual influence has been gradually declining.

After the installation of the ministerial system, the CE and the appointed team of ministers constituted the *real* cabinet. However, not all major policy and political decisions are made collectively as such. Internally, the government has continued to function strictly according to portfolio lines as in the previous administrative regime, such that ministers, as well as their senior civil servants, are not supposed to intrude into or partake in the decision-making process over any policy matters outside their portfolio unless in the case of cross-bureau issues or until the time some major policy proposals are at the final stage discussed in the Policy Committee chaired by the CS prior to consideration by the CE-in-Council. In theory, one can imagine that important business would be debated and decided upon collectively as in cabinet governments elsewhere through formal or informal intra-cabinet debate and sometimes through special cabinet committees. This has not been the practice in Hong Kong, where line authority remains a stronger element of the decision-making process than horizontal collective authority, due partly to the inherited legacy of government by bureaucracy.

While all ministers are members of the ExCo which approves all proposed legislations and policies, from the Tsang Administration onwards (since June 2005), those ministers whose items are not on the agenda of an ExCo meeting can be excused from that meeting though they still have access to all the ExCo papers concerned. The exceptions are the three senior Secretaries: the CS, FS, and Secretary for Justice. Thus, it is not common for all ministers to be present at an ExCo meeting. However, under the principle of collective responsibility, whether or not a minister is present in the ExCo discussion leading to a decision, once a decision is made by the CE-in-Council all ministers have to abide by the official line. Between officials and non-officials in the ExCo, there might well be heated debates on various policy issues, but the officials (i.e., ministers) concerned are the ones to publicly explain, defend, and be held accountable for the policies. As a result, most non-officials have tended to be less vocal and generally take a backseat on specific policy matters in the name of secrecy and collective responsibility. Should they comment in public, they have to follow the government's line-to-take.

Constitutionally, the CE can act more like a president to impose their will as far as the Basic Law allows, subject only to restraint by the central government. Since Donald Tsang's time, the CE has certainly behaved more presidentially, but whether or not the CE's power is allowed to be unbounded depends very much on the behaviour of their ministers—whether they hold strong views and are willing to put them forward even when facing a dominating CE. This contrasts with the operation of cabinet government under a prime minister in the Westminster system, where interdependence between the prime minister and other ministers is supposed to be crucial, and the former is obliged to follow the collective advice of cabinet colleagues.[23]

However, even in Britain, there have been suggestions over the past decades that the power of the Prime Minister has grown to such an extent that it has supplanted cabinet government with a system of almost presidential government or an elected monarch. Such views have been challenged by George Jones, a leading academic authority on British premiership, who remarked in 1964 that

> [t]he Prime Minister is the leading figure in the cabinet whose voice carries most weight [...]. A Prime Minister who can carry his colleagues with him can be in a very powerful position, but he is only as strong as they let him be.[24]

He again concluded in 2016 that

> the premiership is like an elastic band that can be stretched to accommodate an assertive prime minister and relaxed for a less dominant figure. […] Above all the prime minister remains only as powerful as the cabinet colleagues let him or her be.[25]

Central-state support

During British rule, no one doubted London's trust in and support for the Governor, although at times local elites (especially the British tycoons) would try to influence or put pressure on the Governor by way of lobbying the Colonial Office or FCO and Members of Parliament. Suppose the CE of the Hong Kong SAR was directly dispatched by Beijing and was held solely accountable to the State Council. In that case, they might enjoy a more privileged position beyond any local challenge politically. That, of course, would imply an authoritarian mode of governance as under British rule. Whereas the Governor was the undisputed representative of the Crown and home government, assuming concurrently the role of Commander-in-Chief of British forces in Hong Kong and having authority to handle foreign affairs with advice from the FCO-seconded Political Advisor, the CE is not designated as the sole representative of the CPG. A triumvirate now represents central-state power in Hong Kong: the Director of the Liaison Office of the CPG, the Commander of the PLA Hong Kong Garrison, and the Commissioner of the Ministry of Foreign Affairs. Moreover, once the national security law is implemented, the Director of the central government's Office for Safeguarding National Security in Hong Kong will become another prominent figure representing central authority in the SAR.

Often perceived by the public as being subordinate to the Director of the Hong Kong and Macao Affairs Office of the State Council, and with the central government's Liaison Office seemingly having the real power to steer and command the pro-establishment camp (including pro-Beijing patriotic forces), the CE lacks overwhelming political clout. Unless empowered by a strong affiliation to or command over parties in Hong Kong, so as to forge a steady majority coalition in the LegCo, relying solely on the formal stipulated powers under the Basic Law does not take the CE or politically appointed ministers very far in terms of policy leadership and authority. Although the current process of electing the CE by the Election Committee (with limited franchise) for substantive appointment by the CPG more or less ensures that the CE must have Beijing's blessing to get elected and appointed, this is not the same as someone dispatched by the central state.

The central government can always distance itself from the CE's policies and only support them when governing effectively according to the Basic Law. Indeed, while the central government has become active in commenting on matters affecting national security and national interests—such as the issue of 'Hong Kong independence' and the direction for constitutional development—its officials are normally reluctant to be seen as getting involved in the domestic affairs of the SAR. However, it has become common for Liaison Office officials to be invited to events organised by community organisations and be conferred growing prominence.[26]

Sizing up dysfunctional governance

Given all the limitations mentioned in this chapter, it would be easy to conclude that Hong Kong has a political system not conducive to nurturing strong governance, nor truly responsible politics. As they have no part in electing the SAR government, ordinary people inherently do not trust it and tend to elect district councillors and legislators only to maximise demands for benefits and bash (not just 'check') those in power. The media and civil society tend to stand on the side of the 'eggs' against the 'high wall' (to them, the government), using the analogy made famous by Japanese writer Haruki Murakami (村上春樹).[27] Executive-legislative disjunction means permanent contestation between the capacity to contain and solve problems and the capacity to create and amplify problems. Legislative proceedings have been frequently filled with filibusters and delay tactics by the opposition, and legislators across the political spectrum are keen to blame and embarrass government officials, playing to the gallery of critics and sceptics. Declining public trust in the government serves to encourage such negative politics.

Political quagmire easily breeds public scepticism, administrative inertia, and policy immobilism. Society becomes a headless chicken in the absence of effective political leadership. Given the rather messy hybrid regime, which looks set to continue unless there is any breakthrough in constitutional reform, the SAR government has to get real and learn how to govern amidst adversity and instability, drawing lessons from minority governments elsewhere. It pays to get out of the outdated 'executive-led' orthodoxy and learn to seek compromise solutions within a crowded and pluralist polity that is the 'new normal' in politics here and elsewhere. Executive-legislative tension and gridlocks are the price to pay for zealous checks and balances. The US is notoriously known for this kind of disconnect. Yet, even though the President under the constitution enjoys rather dominant executive powers, few Americans seem to have lost confidence in the US political system just on that count.

While 'blaming and shaming' has certainly become the game in legislative and media politics, inducing further distrust in governance institutions, it is not a phenomenon unique to Hong Kong. Most Western democracies are facing a similar onslaught on government authority and legitimacy in the rise of populism, social polarisation, and distrust in the political establishment and mainstream parties. That alone, or a disarticulate SAR political system as analysed above, would not necessarily produce ungovernability or administrative chaos *if* other institutional safeguards can still function well enough to maintain government effectiveness and social and economic order by and large. However, the situation has been getting very precarious in the SAR and could easily turn vulnerable. Despair and pessimism also feed into a self-fulfilling prophecy. When people and the government lose their belief in the possibility of moving forward, no matter how incrementally, they are placed in the trap of fatalism. This is what they must strive to resist.

Chapter 12

Two Systems, Two Existentialisms

Introduction

The Hong Kong SAR was founded as a separate system under the principle of 'One Country, Two Systems' first mooted by Chinese leaders in 1981 and later elevated into a basic national policy in 1985.[1] Prior to that, the PRC Constitution was amended in 1982 to incorporate a brief new Article 31 stipulating that the State when necessary can set up SARs, the system of which shall be prescribed by the NPC in law according to the specific circumstances. Because of the vague and broad-brush way of expression, one might argue any possibilities could be accommodated and facilitated under the 'One Country, Two Systems' concept. Apart from allowing a different socio-economic mega-system to thrive (i.e., capitalism versus socialism), the political formula for reunification also provided for 'a high degree of autonomy' and 'self-administration by the residents of Hong Kong'. The three elements were intertwined and supposed to be mutually supporting.

The new 'SAR' incarnation differed sharply from the new SEZs established on the Mainland in the early 1980s to pilot market-based and profit-oriented economic reforms in selected locations (namely, Shenzhen, Zhuhai, Shantau, and Xiamen).[2] While the SEZs would still be an integral part of the Mainland's socialist system which later evolved to become a socialist market system in the 1990s according to official parlance, an SAR would be both economically and politically subject to an entirely different regime, the perimeters of which were to be spelt out in a separate set of legal instruments in the Basic Law mandated by the NPC.

The brevity of Article 31 was also in stark contrast to the more detailed prescriptions for the ethnic minorities autonomous regions entrenched in Chapter III of the PRC Constitution (a total of 11 articles under Section 6).[3] Despite the more specific constitutional stipulations, grounded in the macro-policy to respect the minorities' cultural traditions, customs, and religion, their autonomy has remained construed as an integral part of the same system of governance. Besides, these autonomous regions in practice depend heavily on financial and personnel assistance from the central government—and without economic and fiscal powers, autonomy is more nominal than real. The high degree of autonomy granted to Hong Kong as an SAR is very substantive, almost on a par with a sub-national state in a federal system. Some even observed that such autonomy was larger than that enjoyed by member states of federal countries.[4]

Relationship with central authorities and SAR autonomy

As the Basic Law sought to preserve Hong Kong's status quo at the time of transition, the pre-existing autonomy in fiscal, trade, and certain external relations matters were all maintained to form the starting point of the constitutional design for the new SAR. The CPG would retain some final and veto powers as previously available to the British government—mainly the power of executive appointment (of the CE and Principal Officials), the power to veto local legislation and to extend national laws, control over foreign affairs and defence, and the exclusion of acts of state from the courts' jurisdiction in line with common law practice.

The relationship between the central authorities and the Hong Kong SAR was defined in Chapter II of the Basic Law. The SAR comes directly under the CPG (i.e., the State Council), thus giving it para-provincial status. The Ministry of Foreign Affairs has established a Commissioner's Office to deal with and advise on foreign affairs, while the military garrison is commanded by its own Commander and Political Commissar. Under Article 14, the garrison 'shall not interfere in the local affairs' although the SAR government may, when necessary, ask the CPG for assistance from the garrison in the maintenance of public order and in disaster relief.[5] No central government department, and no province, autonomous region, or municipality, may interfere in the affairs within the SAR's autonomy (Article 22). If there is a need for these organs to set up offices in Hong Kong, they must obtain the consent of the SAR government and the approval of the CPG. All such offices set up in Hong Kong and their personnel have to abide by SAR laws.[6] The Hong Kong SAR may also establish an office in Beijing.[7]

Under Article 17, laws enacted by the SAR legislature have to be reported to the NPCSC for the record. Such reporting shall not affect the entry of the laws into force. However, if the NPCSC decides any of these laws are not in conformity with the Basic Law, it may return the law in question but shall not amend it. A returned law is immediately invalidated but without retrospective effect. Such provisions are arguably more generous compared to British rule where the Crown enjoyed reserve powers in addition to the power of disallowance of colonial legislation.[8] Since the establishment of the SAR, no local law has ever been 'returned' by the NPCSC. While the SAR is vested with independent judicial power, including that of final adjudication, SAR courts have no jurisdiction over acts of state such as defence and foreign affairs (Article 19). Nonetheless, they are authorised by the NPCSC to interpret on their own, in adjudicating cases, those provisions of the Basic Law within the limits of SAR autonomy. Should any such interpretation by the courts relate to provisions concerning affairs within the central government's responsibility or the relationship between the Central Authorities and the SAR, and if such interpretation will affect the judgments on the cases, the courts shall, before making their final judgments which are not appealable, seek an interpretation from the NPCSC. Before giving an interpretation, the NPCSC has to consult its Basic Law Committee which comprises both Mainland and Hong Kong members.

The application of national laws to the SAR is restricted. Article 18 stipulates that national laws shall not apply in the SAR except those listed in Annex III to the Basic Law, coming into effect locally either by way of promulgation or local legislation. Such national laws are confined to those relating to defence and foreign affairs as well as other matters outside the limits of SAR autonomy, such as relating to the national flag, national emblem, national day, territorial sea, and nationality, which apply to the nation as a whole. This is somewhat similar to the application of Acts of Parliament to Hong Kong as a British colony in the past. However, in the event that the NPCSC decides to declare a state of war or, by reason of turmoil within the SAR which endangers national unity or security and is beyond the control of the SAR government, decides the territory is in a state of emergency, the CPG may issue an order applying relevant national laws in the SAR (presumably including the laws relating to the imposition of martial law). Article 23 requires the SAR to enact laws on its own for three additional purposes: to prohibit any act of treason, secession, sedition, subversion against the CPG or theft of state secrets; to prohibit foreign political organisations from conducting political activities in the SAR; and to prohibit local political organisations from establishing ties with foreign political organisations.

Under Article 21, SAR residents who are Chinese nationals are entitled to participate in the management of national or state affairs. In accordance with the selection method specified by the NPC, a prescribed number of deputies to the NPC are elected locally every five years by an electoral college.[9] The current 13th NPC has 36 Hong Kong deputies. By convention, a senior Hong Kong deputy would be elected to the Standing Committee.[10] In addition, prominent Hong Kong residents have been appointed to serve on the CPPCC—at the national, provincial, and city levels, as well as in special designated sectors.[11] Also, it has become a convention that retired CEs are appointed to the CPPCC as a vice-chairman (which has been the case for both Tung Chee-hwa and Leung Chun-ying).[12] The central government's Liaison Office briefs local NPC deputies and CPPCC members from time to time on central government policies and positions regarding Hong Kong. Because of the restricted franchise for the selection of local NPC deputies, those elected tend to be mostly Beijing loyalists active in pro-Beijing and pro-establishment circles. As such, NPC deputies are often seen by the public as the loyal troops of the central authorities instead of bottom-up representatives to articulate the concerns and aspirations of the local Chinese population on national affairs.

Chapter V and Chapter VII of the Basic Law on 'Economy' and 'External Affairs', respectively, spells out Hong Kong's autonomy in economic, finance, and trade affairs as well as in related external relations. Briefly, the SAR enjoys independent finances and an independent taxation system, with its own separate currency and monetary and financial policies. It maintains its free port status and pursues free trade policies. As a separate customs territory, it may participate in relevant international organisations and international trade agreements using the name 'Hong Kong, China'. It also maintains and develops its own relations and concludes and implements its own agreements with foreign states and regions and relevant international organisations with regard to economics, trade, finance, monetary affairs, shipping, communications, tourism, culture, and sports.[13] It can establish its own official or semi-official economic and trade missions in foreign countries.[14]

Intentions and context

It is clear that the degree of autonomy envisaged by the central government for Hong Kong as an SAR is, first of all, no less than that already enjoyed by Hong Kong under British rule in the 1980s when the Sino-British Joint Declaration was signed, as a manifestation of China's 'no change' policy under 'One Country, Two Systems'. Furthermore, this level of autonomy is greater than that granted to autonomous regions for ethnic minorities on the Mainland. However, to the local population and some foreign observers, the fact that the 1997 settlement was largely premised on political expediency to ensure a smooth transition meant that the full implications of SAR formation within the PRC's constitutional framework were yet to be tested.

Moreover, as it is stated in the Basic Law that Hong Kong's status as an SAR was to be valid for 50 years after 1997, sceptics have always suspected that such expediency might not last forever.[15] An arrangement grounded in political expediency enabled its application with suitable flexibility and moderation despite the constitutional provision granting the central government considerable residual powers. Still, some worry that in a state system such as the PRC, leaders' preferences sometimes outweigh constitutional logic or generally worded legal provisions. Thus, such flexibility also creates indeterminacy and uncertainties.

When Hong Kong was under British rule, the home government never felt any political threat from the colony towards London— it was more concerned with China's reaction to local happenings.[16] Now, as an integral part of China and being an important southern gateway, the Hong Kong SAR carries significant security implications for the whole country. Ever since the overwhelming demonstration of support by the local population for the pro-democracy movement in Beijing in 1989, Beijing has been worried about Hong Kong being exploited by foreign powers (and Taiwan) as a base for subversion of the Mainland's socialist system—hence the repeated exhortations in the 1990s that Hong Kong's 'well water should not interfere with [Mainland China's] river water' and vice versa.[17] In recent years, emerging separatist and pro-independence sentiments in Hong Kong have alarmed Beijing further. To central government officials, this is a serious issue of national sovereignty, territorial integrity, and national security, and not just a matter of freedom of expression protected by Article 27 of the Basic Law. When some locals actively seek to erode the Mainland's communist political order or campaign for Hong Kong's independence, the red line is crossed, which naturally triggers strong central-state reactions.

'One Country' in Chinese (一國) also refers to 'one state' as the Chinese characters (國家) can be used interchangeably between 'country' (as a geographical territory) and 'state' (as a sovereign jurisdiction). The 'capitalist system' of Hong Kong is not supposed to be fully on a par with the mainstream 'socialist system' on the Mainland because the state constitution of the PRC, which covers the whole country, is premised on the practice of socialism under the leadership of the CCP. In other words, it cannot be argued that the state constitution does not apply to Hong Kong despite the provision under its Article 31 for exceptional (flexible) institutional arrangements as an SAR. Following constitutional logic, the national constitution prevails should there be a fundamental political disagreement between the two systems, which therefore should be avoided.[18] That said, the central leadership has reiterated that 'One Country, Two Systems' will be implemented comprehensively without distortion or wavering.[19]

The practice and operationalities of SAR autonomy versus a centralised communist party-state hinge on a host of constitutional, historical, institutional, and real-political factors—namely, constitutional safeguards as stipulated in the Basic Law; historical and sociological conditions; local pre-existing institutional factors helping to sustain the Hong Kong system and its modus operandi; and real-political considerations such as Hong Kong's strategic importance and its contribution to national development.[20] The 'real' autonomy depends on the dynamics of SAR-central state interactions as well as the evolving circumstances and contexts, rendering it ultimately a negotiated space.[21] The two principal limitations under the 'One Country, Two Systems' framework, as observed by Basic Law Committee member Albert Chen, are that the constitutional and legal guarantees for autonomy are less secure than in federalism and that there is only a limited extent of democratisation in the SAR.[22] It is thus incumbent on the central government under a unitary state system to exercise self-restraint when invoking its constitutional powers on the SAR.

Controversies and tension

Over the past two decades, the implementation of 'One Country, Two Systems' has been tested in several major controversies, especially over national security, constitutional issues, the NPCSC's interpretations of the Basic Law, application of the national anthem law, and, most recently, extradition. Protests and confrontations ensued which intensified tensions between the two systems and between the central government and SAR. Chapter 10 has already discussed the key controversies and rounds of negotiations and confrontations on constitutional reform. The national anthem law, in the same category as the national laws on national flag and emblem applied to the SAR as symbols of Chinese sovereignty on 1 July 1997, should not have been controversial. However, given the rising anti-Mainland sentiments in the last few years, where some Hong Kong people have shown disrespect to the national anthem at official ceremonies and major events (including soccer matches), the passage of this law locally was treated by Beijing as a test of loyalty to the nation and by the pan-democrats as a test of how much freedom of expression could be tolerated.[23]

Here we focus on other major controversial incidents.

National security legislation

Every nation has national security laws which apply to all of its constituent parts. At the time of the drafting of the Basic Law, it was widely considered unacceptable by the Hong Kong community to apply the PRC's relevant national security laws to the future SAR via Article 18, bearing in mind that such laws were then still couched in terms of combating counter-revolutionary activities and any acts challenging the socialist system. Furthermore, China made its first set of national security law only in 1993. The eventual compromise was for the SAR to enact relevant laws on its own under Article 23.[24]

When the Tung Chee-hwa Administration presented the Article 23 legislation package at the beginning of its second term in mid-2002 as a constitutional duty, the proposal was widely interpreted as a test of Hong Kong's political autonomy and freedom. As some laws already existed to protect the interest of national security and prohibit the theft of state secrets, both in common law and written law, some legal critics questioned the legislation and identified them as extended restrictions on personal freedoms. As the debates intensified in 2003, the specific provisions of the government bill were perceived as not only being targeted at 'subversive' political activities but, more seriously, as limiting the degree of political freedoms and access to information as well as posing a threat to ordinary people in different ways and circumstances.[25]

The Article 23 controversy, together with other social grievances such as economic recession, unemployment, and collapse of the property market which drove many people to negative equity, eventually led to mass uproar and protests on 1 July 2003 by over half a million people. The protests reflected a serious government-society gap. Immediately afterwards, Tung made major concessions in a revised bill.[26] However, public sentiments against Article 23 were so strong that the pro-establishment Liberal Party felt it politically expedient to desert the government, forcing it to withhold the proposal for want of the necessary legislative votes. By September 2003, with a new Secretary for Security in post and following reassessment of the political situation, Tung finally withdrew the bill from the legislative process.[27]

It was not as though most Hong Kong people would object to any national security legislation, but the devil is in the details. Looking back, if the Tung Administration had proceeded more carefully, issued a White Bill for in-depth consultation as widely demanded, and secured the advice and hopefully acceptance of the legal community at large, things might have turned out differently. Instead, the politics of Article 23 were grossly under-estimated.[28] In recent years, there have been strong hints from Beijing that the Hong Kong SAR should fulfil its constitutional duty without undue delay since the Macao SAR already passed national security legislation in 2009. Such rhetoric indicates that the legislation (at least in some form) could not be stalled permanently. The question is not 'whether' but 'what' and 'how'. Proper legislation would give reassurance to the central government which has frequently doubted if sufficient safeguards exist in SAR law for 'One Country'. Yet, successive Administrations have shied away from making any attempts to revive Article 23 legislation.[29]

Recently, some hardliners have begun to see the need for the central government to impose national security requirements on the SAR by applying national legislation or an NPCSC Decision. Yet, even as late as 2015, when the NPC passed a new national security law, it was not extended to Hong Kong as Beijing was still concerned that the cons might outweigh the pros despite the impact of the Occupy Central protests. However, the political upheaval since the extradition saga in 2019 has altered Beijing's policy calculus. With pan-democratic legislators and localist activists calling for international intervention and lobbying the US and Western countries to 'punish' China, Beijing's patience is wearing out. The central leaders are wary of Hong Kong being used as a Trojan horse by external forces to destabilise China, and so they are determined to strike back at all costs.

National security in Hong Kong is now a top priority, but Beijing doubts the Lam Administration's capacity to push for another highly controversial legislation. Quite unexpectedly, the 13th NPC at its third session held in May 2020 decided to establish and improve a legal framework and enforcement mechanism for safeguarding national security in Hong Kong. The NPCSC was authorised to draft and enact a tailor-made national security law, to be applied to the SAR via inclusion in Annex III of the Basic Law as for a few other national laws. The purpose of the law is to prevent, stop, and punish any act occurring in the SAR to split the country, subvert state power, organise and carry out terrorist activities, and other behaviours and activities that seriously endanger national security, as well as activities of foreign and external forces to interfere in the affairs of the SAR. In addition, the CPG has established a national security agency in Hong Kong (known as the Office for Safeguarding National Security of the Central People's Government in the Hong Kong Special Administrative Region) and the CE is required to submit periodic reports on national security.[30]

The NPC's move and the new National Security Law have caused local and international repercussions, though they were seen by Beijing, the SAR government, and the local pro-establishment camp as necessary for stopping protest violence and subversive activities. The bone of contention lies not in the need for national security, but how a law made by Beijing can be compatible with Hong Kong's rule of law and preserve all those rights and freedoms protected by the Basic Law. Former Chief Justice Andrew Li, echoed by his pre-1997 predecessor Yang Ti-liang, considered Beijing's move understandable and openly called for such a law to conform to Hong Kong's common law principles. He also suggested that offences should be limited in scope, trials openly conducted, and defendants presumed innocent.[31] Details of the law were not disclosed for public discussion prior to enactment in light of their sensitivity despite the provision of the PRC Legislation Law (立法法).[32]

NPCSC interpretations of the Basic Law

The Basic Law expressly vests the power to interpret the Basic Law with the NPCSC, in line with the constitutional practice of the PRC where 'legislative interpretation' of enacted laws is fully recognised, unlike the British system which the Hong Kong legal community had long been accustomed to. The difference in legal traditions and values aside, political distrust and suspicion have driven many local lawyers and politicians, especially those in the pan-democratic camp, to be sceptical of the impartiality of the NPCSC. They tend to see NPCSC interpretations as politically motivated and eroding the authority of the SAR judiciary to interpret the law in the course of adjudication. Mainland officials and legal experts consider this an arrogant overreaction and not respecting the national legal system on which the Basic Law was based. Since 1997, there have been five occasions of NPCSC interpretation of the Basic Law provisions resulting in varying degree of public reaction and controversy:

(1) The right of abode in Hong Kong (June 1999);
(2) Amendments to election methods for the CE and LegCo (April 2004);
(3) Defining the term of a CE (April 2005);
(4) Diplomatic immunity of the Democratic Republic of Congo (August 2011); and
(5) Taking the oath of office by the CE, Principal Officials, and members of the LegCo (November 2016).

The 'right of abode' case stemmed from the request of Tung Chee-hwa to deal with the confusion over the right of abode in Hong Kong of Mainland-born children of HKPRs. The NPCSC ruled that, contrary to the CFA's judgment which it deemed not consistent with the legislative intent, children born outside of Hong Kong would only qualify for the right of abode if at least one of their parents had earned HKPR status at the time of the child's birth, and that they applied for permission from Mainland authorities before migrating to Hong Kong.[33] Because the NPCSC rebutted the CFA, it triggered an extreme reaction from the legal community who staged the first-ever demonstration (silent march) by lawyers dressed in black, lamenting 'the death of the rule of law'.

The 'term of CE' case was more an interpretation on a legal point,[34] while the Congo case was upon request from the CFA in the adjudication of an appeal case from the Democratic Republic of Congo.[35] In the remaining two cases, the NPCSC took the initiative to interpret the Basic Law where matters of constitutional significance to central-state authority were deemed to be involved—to mandate a 5-step process for the amendment of election methods (see Chapter 10) and to require the solemn and proper taking of oath by top SAR officials and legislators to uphold national dignity, respectively.[36]

Inasmuch as many people in Hong Kong, especially the legal community, worry about the NPCSC actively using its power of interpretation, such power has not been used frequently over the past two decades and is only supposed to be exercised in order to clarify any constitutional doubt and legislative intent. However, in the two cases where the NPCSC took the initiative to interpret the Basic Law, it is unavoidable that it has been perceived by the pan-democrats as a move to limit their seats in the legislature. The issue is not whether the NPCSC can interpret the Basic Law as a matter of its constitutional power, but under what circumstances and how. As such, in order to reduce future controversies, there is a need to institutionalise the interpretation procedure and enhance the transparency and accountability of how the Basic Law Committee's advice to the NPCSC is formed, such as allowing legal experts to present evidence and arguments on points of law before a decision is reached by the Committee.[37]

White Paper on 'One Country, Two Systems'

As the pan-democrats geared up for the Occupy Central protests in 2014, putting pressure on the central government to respond to their demands for democracy and autonomy which were gaining increasing international attention, Beijing released a White Paper on the policy and practice of 'One Country, Two Systems'.[38] The White Paper emphasised in its Foreword that '"one country, two systems" is a new domain in which we constantly explore new possibilities and make new progress in a pioneering spirit' and that 'a comprehensive and correct understanding and implementation of [this] policy will prove useful for safeguarding China's sovereignty, security and development interests, for maintaining long-term prosperity and stability in Hong Kong, and for further promoting the "one country, two systems" practice along the correct track of development'.[39]

The central state's power vis-à-vis the SAR was underscored by reasserting several policy principles: the central government's 'comprehensive jurisdiction' over the SAR; the high degree of autonomy of the SAR being neither full autonomy nor a decentralised power, but 'the power to run local affairs as authorised by the central leadership'; and 'loving the country' being the basic principle for Hong Kong's administrators who have the responsibility to safeguard the nation's sovereignty, security and development interests, as well as to ensure the long-term prosperity and stability of Hong Kong.[40] The White Paper also declared the necessity to stay alert to the attempts of outside forces to use Hong Kong to interfere in China's domestic affairs, and prevent and repel such attempts made by a 'very small number of people who act in collusion with outside forces' to interfere with the implementation of 'One Country, Two Systems' in Hong Kong.

These principles were not entirely new ones. Beijing's repeated constitutional logic during the drafting of the Basic Law was that as a unitary state, China's central government had comprehensive jurisdiction over all local administrative regions, with the high degree of autonomy of the SAR subject to the central leadership's authorisation. The White Paper reiterated there was no such thing as 'residual power' for the SAR, a point already made in the 1980s. Even before the signing of the 1984 Sino-British Joint Declaration, Deng Xiaoping had made it clear that the SAR should be governed by 'patriots' who would stand for the national interest. While such policy positions had always been part of the official thinking since the 1980s, they were not emphasised, to avoid making Hong Kong people uncomfortable. The need to utter them so bluntly now indicated how gravely Beijing viewed the evolving political situation and challenges. The central state was keen to convey its red line on Hong Kong in no ambiguous terms. As expected, the White Paper triggered strong local reaction, especially from the pan-democratic camp who then expedited the launch of the Occupy Central protests.

In a way, this sharp and harsh assertion of central authority over the SAR had evolved from the 1 July mass protests against national security legislation in 2003. Before that, under the 'well water should not interfere with river water' articulation, Beijing was quite happy to leave Hong Kong alone to grow as an economic city so long as it did not pose any threat to the Mainland's socialist system and the national communist regime. When national security legislation failed in 2003, the central government not only faulted the Tung Administration for its inability to command over the local situation but also decided to comprehensively revamp its policy and strategy towards Hong Kong, resulting in a 'new' Hong Kong policy which marked a reversal of the previous largely hands-off approach.[41] Henceforth, the central government would emphasise more engagement and involvement in Hong Kong's political development and governance.[42]

A more aggressive and assertive central-state strategy on all fronts had nurtured not only a sense of 'encroachment' and subjugation among the pan-democrats who portrayed everything within a conspiracy theory of political regression and suppression, but also a change of heart among more moderate academics and intellectuals who, though supportive of democracy, had still been sympathetic to the 'One Country' principle. The 2014 White Paper was a dividing line that marked their loss of trust in Beijing and overwhelmingly turned them to the cause of the Occupy Central campaign.[43]

Co-location of border checkpoints in Hong Kong

The implementation of the co-location of Mainland- and Hong Kong-based customs, immigration, and quarantine (CIQ) checkpoints at the West Kowloon Terminus was part of the plan for the new XRL commissioned in September 2018. The intent was to facilitate smooth and speedy CIQ clearance at a one-stop point, both for passengers taking this train service northward from Hong Kong to Mainland destinations and vice versa. Without such arrangement, the XRL would lose its transport and economic advantages as it would be unrealistic to expect separate checkpoints to be set up in every major city on the Mainland connected to the network.[44] However, pan-democratic legislators and some lawyers considered the permission for Mainland CIQ officials to enforce relevant Mainland laws within the designated 'Mainland Port Area' inside the terminus as in breach of Article 18 of the Basic Law which generally prohibits the application of national laws in Hong Kong except in connection with defence, foreign affairs, and those matters outside the SAR's autonomy. They alleged that the expensive rail was forced upon Hong Kong for the sake of integration with the Mainland, failing to recognise that it was in Hong Kong's strategic interest not to be marginalised from the rapidly expanding national high-speed railway network.[45]

Furthermore, legal opinions differed regarding the application of Mainland criminal laws within the Mainland Port Area—which is now deemed as outside SAR jurisdiction for CIQ clearance while remaining as SAR territory where Hong Kong's civil and commercial laws still fully apply. Whether the arrangement is in breach of Article 18 is a debatable legal point. The NPCSC, in its resolution on co-location in December 2017, considered allowing the enforcement of relevant Mainland laws within the Mainland Port Area only for CIQ control as a power within the SAR's high degree of autonomy when reaching a mutual agreement with Mainland authorities (represented by the Guangdong provincial government).[46] As such, the agreement had to be endorsed by legislative process on both sides (by the NPCSC on the part of the Mainland and by LegCo enactment of co-location legislation on the SAR side).[47] This seems on a par with the concept underlining co-location agreements overseas involving two sovereign states with separate jurisdictions.[48]

As a kind of mini-constitution, it can be argued that the Basic Law should not be interpreted too literally but instead as a 'living constitution' to be read 'in totality' in keeping with the spirit of 'One Country, Two Systems'.[49] It is ultimately a test of mutual political trust grounded in reciprocity of benefits. Upon judicial review, the court ruled the arrangement consistent with the Basic Law. In its 13 December 2018 judgment, the Court of First Instance of the High Court agreed with the government's position that neither the establishment of a Mainland port for carrying out CIQ clearance in the heart of the city (instead of at the boundary) nor the delineation of jurisdiction at such port for facilitating CIQ was prohibited by the Basic Law.[50]

Extradition bill

The Fugitive Offenders and Mutual Legal Assistance in Criminal Matters Legislation (Amendment) Bill was proposed in February 2019 to establish a mechanism for the transfers of fugitives to Taiwan, Mainland China, and Macau, which are not covered in the SAR's existing laws.[51] The lack of such a mechanism has a long history dating from British colonial rule because of political and legal complications. The government justified its move to 'plug the loopholes' in current legislation because of an urgent need to deal with a case from 2018 involving the murder of a Hong Kong resident by another Hong Kong resident while in Taiwan (the Chan Tung-kai case). Initially criticised by the pan-democrats as ignoring the risk to Hongkongers, the bill eventually drew widespread opposition from the legal community and even local and international business chambers who had reservations about the prospect of Hong Kong residents (and foreign nationals passing through Hong Kong) to be sent for trial on the Mainland where the courts are perceived to be subservient to the CCP's political control. There were similar murmurings even within the pro-establishment camp.

The Lam Administration grossly under-estimated the political sensitivity of extradition between the 'Two Systems'. This was further exacerbated by cross-strait tensions over 'one China' in Taiwan's election year, which eventually saw a landslide victory by incumbent President Tsai Ing-wen (of the pro-independence Democratic Progressive Party) who played up Hong Kong people's fear of being subject to extradition to the Mainland to discredit China's Taiwan policy. Limited time was spared for public consultation on this complex and politically charged bill or for securing stakeholder buy-in, especially from the legal sector. When the pan-democrats used delay tactics in electing the chairman of the bills committee to scrutinise the proposed law, the government, with the high-profile support of central government officials, decided to bypass normal legislative procedure and immediately resume second reading debate at the full sitting of the LegCo, thus fuelling the suspicion that there was a hidden agenda to expedite legislation.[52] As opponents and critics played up the bill as a major threat to freedom and judicial integrity, some foreign governments and international media joined the chorus to 'protect' Hong Kong, a trend which was perceived by Beijing as a conspiracy to demonise China. A perfect storm was thus formed.

Fear over the possible loss of freedom began to sink in. Multiple protests against the extradition bill organised by the Civil and Human Rights Front (which spearheaded the 2003 mass protests against Article 23 legislation and the subsequent annual 1 July protests) eventually culminated in a large-scale demonstration on 9 June 2019, with the organisers claiming a historical turnout of 1.03 million people (270,000 according to the Police count). Bloody clashes followed on 12 June between the Police and young protesters who surrounded the LegCo complex to prevent legislators from entering it to hold a sitting to pass the bill. There was a huge outcry against this alleged police violence. On 15 June, Carrie Lam was forced to announce that the proceedings relating to the bill would be suspended. However, the Civil and Human Rights Front was not satisfied with the bill only being suspended and made five demands—that the bill be formally withdrawn; that an independent inquiry be set up to investigate police violence; that the previous depiction of the protesters' confrontations on 12 June as 'riots' be annulled; that those arrested be released or otherwise granted amnesty; and that Lam step down.

Despite the suspension of the extradition bill, protests did not stop. Instead, the subsequent mass demonstration on 16 June attracted an even larger turnout, claimed to be 2 million by the organisers and 338,000 by the Police. Although Lam then formally apologised for the government's failure in handling the extradition bill, the opposition would not halt the protests because she had not acceded to the 'five demands' (by now the demand for her to step down was substituted by a new one on immediately implementing full electoral universal suffrage). Some protesters launched an online crowdfunding campaign to finance full-page 'Stand with Hong Kong' advertisement in major international newspapers before the G20 summit on 28 June in Osaka as a campaign to raise global awareness and appeal for world leaders' intervention for a 'free' Hong Kong. For Beijing, it was tantamount to 'internationalising' the Hong Kong issue.

On 1 July, another protest march took place, with the organisers claiming the participation of 550,000 people (190,000 according to the Police estimate). Separately, hundreds of young radical protesters stormed into the LegCo chamber without police obstruction, not only destroying various meeting facilities but also desecrating the SAR emblem and displaying the old British colonial flag—a deliberate challenge to the SAR's constitutional order in the eyes of Beijing. The 1 July attack was a dividing line that saw the anti-extradition movement being turned into an anti-government and anti-China onslaught. Mass protests continued in various districts with increasing frequency and severity, especially during the weekends, each time attracting tens of thousands of participants with escalating violence in protester-police confrontations. Protesters accused anti-riot police of excessive violence and alleged police-triad collusion in an incident on 21 July in Yuen Long where white-shirt clad individuals suspected of being triad members assaulted protesters and bystanders.

After that, protesters engaged in tactics of disrupting public transport, blocking vital roads and the cross-harbour tunnels. Violence, arson, and attacks on mass transit railway (MTR) stations and other public properties became common. There were also actions to block the airport and to boycott and disrupt shopping malls owned by the MTRC and those shops of known pro-Beijing owners. The objective of the radical activists was to sabotage the city to force the government and Beijing to succumb to their demands, chanting 'If we burn, you burn with us'[53] and engaging in the 'politics of fear' seen in right-wing populism elsewhere.[54] Their slogan of 'Liberate Hong Kong, the revolution of our time' (光復香港，時代革命) became popular among ordinary people and students who opposed the government. Separatist sentiments were running at an all-time high. Young students were quickly radicalised and mobilised. Class boycotts and human chain actions in solidarity with the protesters spread on university campuses and secondary schools after the summer break.

Beijing's worries about the situation in the SAR getting out of control were not ungrounded. On 21 July 2019, protesters surrounded the CPG's Liaison Office in Hong Kong and desecrated the national emblem. Many Mainlanders were horrified by scenes of Hong Kong protesters shouting anti-China slogans, defacing the national emblem and flag, and attacking Mainland organisations and visitors. In a rare move, the central government held media conferences and briefings in Beijing on several occasions in August 2019, warning that the violent protests had begun to show the 'signs of terrorism'.[55] On 7 August, the Director of the Hong Kong and Macao Affairs Office of the State Council Zhang Xiaoming (張曉明) told an assembly of some 500 pro-establishment figures and business leaders in Shenzhen that the central government was highly concerned about the Hong Kong situation and that the most pressing and overriding task was to 'stop violence, end the chaos' (止暴制亂) and restore order, so as to safeguard the homeland and prevent Hong Kong from sinking into an abyss.[56] It was made clear that should the situation get out of control, action would have to be taken according to the Basic Law (speculated by many at the time to be referring to the possible use of military force to deal with a state of emergency under Article 18 of the Basic Law).

Although Lam finally announced on 4 September that the extradition bill would be formally withdrawn in October and introduced additional measures to help calm the situation, including the holding of social dialogues,[57] her concession was greeted by opposition legislators and protesters as 'too little, too late'. She still refused to set up an independent inquiry as widely demanded.[58] On 1 October (national day), Hong Kong experienced one of its most violent and chaotic days up to that point. On 4 October, the CE-in-Council invoked the Emergency Regulations Ordinance to impose an anti-mask law to ban wearing face masks in public gatherings, attempting to curb the ongoing protests. This triggered even worse confrontations. During a state visit to Nepal on 13 October, President Xi Jinping spoke openly about the demonstrations for the first time and warned against separatism.[59] Worse was to come in the weeks from 11 to 29 November with standoffs between students barricaded on university campuses (the Chinese University of Hong Kong and then Hong Kong Polytechnic University) and anti-riot police (who alleged the presence of 'weapon factories' on those campuses), blocking major thoroughfares and attracting international spotlight.

In the subsequent DC elections held on 24 November, pan-democratic and localist candidates, many of whom were young and without experience in district work, won a landslide victory, securing 87% of the seats (392 out of 452, though with only 57% of the total votes) and the control of 17 out of 18 DCs. These poll results served as a barometer of the rising public discontent. Space here does not allow a detailed account of the hundreds of incidents and episodes occurring since June 2019 in the political turmoil even though the scale of mass protests has gradually subsided because of the outbreak of the COVID-19 pandemic in February 2020 that discouraged mass gatherings. A delayed report of the Independent Police Complaints Council (IPCC) published in May 2020, while much criticised by the pan-democrats and protest organisers because it did not investigate into the alleged police violence and abuse of power given its confined statutory powers, provides an overview of the 'public order incidents' between June 2019 and February 2020.[60] According to Police information, of the 8,981 persons arrested from 9 June 2019 to 29 May 2020, over 3,660 or 40.8% were students (about 1,970 college level and above, and over 1,600 secondary school students).[61] Almost 20% of the arrested were aged below 18.[62]

The year of demonstrations and confrontations is described by the *South China Morning Post* as a year of 'water and fire', with both peaceful protests and street violence.[63] With the wisdom of hindsight, things might have evolved differently if the Chan Tung-kai case had been decoupled from the extradition bill. Legislative scrutiny could then have had additional time in which to iron out disagreements and consider pragmatic revisions. When mass protests broke out in June 2019 accompanied by violent confrontations, Lam did not act fast enough to take the heat out of the looming conflict. The reluctance to withdraw the bill until September 2019, when violence had become the norm, and refusal to launch an independent inquiry left her government with little room to manoeuvre. The opportunity for post-tragedy closure and reconciliation in the immediate aftermath was lost. The undue dependence on police suppression to end the conflict proved to be counterproductive. More ordinary people became persuaded by circumstances to side with the protests. The events of 2019 were a significant watershed in the SAR's trajectory in governance with immense implications (see the Epilogue).

Cooperation and integration

The 1997 reunification should have been the beginning of another journey for Hong Kong to achieve a new identity and new opportunities as (then) the most advanced city of China. However, local sentiments at the time were resistant to integration or even collaboration. In the early years, attempts by Guangdong Province and Shenzhen for a closer link to Hong Kong in economic and infrastructure cooperation were essentially cold-shouldered by the SAR officials, who were still grounded in a self-sufficiency mindset. Even developments on the Mainland were not factored into Hong Kong's strategic planning until recently. Thus, once the Mainland economy entered a high-growth phase in the 2000s, with impressive advancement in infrastructure and I&T, Hong Kong began to feel the sudden threat of being dwarfed and marginalised.

The year 2003 was a turning point. Hong Kong ran into both economic and political troubles. The outbreak of SARS, following the impact of the Asian financial crisis and economic stagnation, almost made Hong Kong a dead city. Then, the 1 July mass protests brought the government nearly to a standstill. It was against this background that the central government found it necessary to save the SAR from economic collapse and decided to push for more economic integration to ensure it would not fall either economically or politically. This strategy can be interpreted as an 'economic absorption of politics'.[64] While Beijing was all along very firm and at times harsh on constitutional, political, and national security matters, it displayed flexibility and a softer approach to economic and social affairs—by supporting Hong Kong businesses' access to the expanding Mainland market and facilitating Hong Kong residents retiring, investing, working, and studying on the Mainland through various schemes.[65]

Such support first came in the 2003 CEPA agreement and the Individual Visit Scheme. The CEPA now covers four areas: trade in goods, trade in services, investment, and economic and technical cooperation. All goods of Hong Kong origin enjoy tariff-free treatment, while Hong Kong service suppliers enjoy preferential treatment in entry into the Mainland market in specified service areas.[66] Many of the preferences surpass the concessions made by China upon its accession to the WTO. Professional bodies of Hong Kong and the regulatory authorities on the Mainland have also signed several agreements or arrangements on mutual recognition of professional qualifications.[67] For a long time, ordinary Mainlanders could only travel to Hong Kong in group tours organised by the state-run China Travel Service and their numbers were small. The new Individual Visit Scheme introduced in July 2003 opened the door to droves of Mainland outbound tourists in support of the local economy, benefitting downstream sectors like tourism and retail.

Then, Hong Kong's role and importance were formally acknowledged and incorporated in the national Five-Year Plans.[68] Various regional platforms for cooperation and integration had been established where Hong Kong, along with Macao, were invited to play a part, such as the '9+2' Pan-Pearl River Delta Cooperation and Development Forum in earlier times,[69] and the latest Guangdong-Hong Kong-Macao Greater Bay Area.[70] Hong Kong was also included within national and regional transport infrastructure development, notably the Hong Kong-Zhuhai-Macao Bridge and the XRL which have now drastically reduced travel times between Hong Kong and the rest of the Pearl River Delta region (Greater Bay Area), facilitating speedier and smoother interflow of people and goods and helping to forge a so-called one-hour sphere of living in the region.[71] Government-to-government cooperation conferences have also been established with Guangdong Province, Shenzhen municipality, Shanghai municipality, Beijing municipality, Fujian Province, Sichuan Province, and Guangxi Autonomous

Region, to promote mutual dialogues and the formulation of common agendas and cooperation plans.

All these efforts are aimed at bringing Hong Kong 'back into the family' and at enabling easier access to the Mainland for Hong Kong businesses and population. To further boost Hong Kong's global financial hub status, and in turn strengthen mutual stocks investment, the Shanghai-Hong Kong Stock Connect and Shenzhen-Hong Kong Stock Connect were launched in November 2014 and December 2016, respectively. While the central government has been keen to internationalise the Renminbi (RMB) currency and thus promote RMB offshore transaction centres in various overseas cities including Singapore and London, Hong Kong remains the largest offshore market of RMB payments.[72] Hong Kong was also invited to play an active role in the national Belt and Road Initiative and the Asian Infrastructure Investment Bank (AIIB) pioneered by China.[73] In support of the Belt and Road Initiative, professional bodies and some corporations (such as the AA and government majority-owned MTRC) have responded by showcasing Hong Kong's strength in professional services and management and operations expertise.

There are, however, growing worries that Hong Kong might become overshadowed by Shanghai and Shenzhen as the central government is keen to support their further transformation into major international metropolises to the extent that China would no longer need Hong Kong's economic contribution as much as it did in 1997.[74] As a growing global economic power, China needs a range of metropolises with diverse economic advantages. Hong Kong's status as a global market, a financial and business hub supported by excellent transport and information connectivity, and a world-class professional services cluster cannot be easily replicated on the Mainland simply by policy diktat. Whether Hong Kong can continue to sustain and even enhance such unique advantages, vis-à-vis Mainland cities, is ultimately in the hands of Hongkongers.

Hong Kong would certainly benefit from economic integration with the Mainland in terms of market and business opportunities. However, as a prominent economist has pointed out, one should be sensitive to some major asymmetries (e.g., in the level of economic development, economic size, and degree of openness) that do not make it easy to install a truly competitive relationship and might yet create potential problems — such as worsening local income distribution and the possibility that the Mainland market demand will overwhelm supply capacity in Hong Kong — which need to be duly recognised and properly managed by the government.[75] Whereas Hong Kong-Mainland economic cooperation in the past was premised on complementarity between developed and developing economies, now that the Mainland economy has matured and expanded, such a relationship would unavoidably shift towards complementarity among equals with relative strengths and advantages in different niche areas. Hong Kong has to identify and strengthen such niche areas — such as finance, professional services, aviation, and legal services.

Regional planning in the context of integrating 'Two Systems' is not as straightforward as official pronouncements put it. Historically, planning on the Mainland had been a top-down, centralised, bureaucratic process of resource allocation (in economic and spatial division of labour), in contrast to Hong Kong's market-led, government-facilitated process. Although the market has now played a more important role on the Mainland after economic reform and open-up, that market is still largely state-directed and subject to national planning. Hong Kong as an SAR has also seen a gradually more proactive government with regard to planning (see Chapter 8). However, the pace and dynamics between the two systems remain quite at variance, such that further cross-boundary collaboration and co-development must factor these issues into the equation.

The changing Hong Kong-Mainland equation

Reunification in 1997 was not just a natural return to the motherland after 150 years of alien British colonial rule. The process was a hard-fought battle for the 'hearts and minds' of the local population by the CCP regime who knew that deep in their hearts, the local Hong Kong Chinese did not embrace communist rule. From this was born the unorthodox 'One Country, Two Systems' framework that would allow the co-existence of two distinct, and ideologically even conflicting, systems of life within the communist party-state. Social existence determines consciousness, as Marxists like to say.[76] The two 'existentialisms' were supposed to continue on their own, without intervention or erosion by the other side.[77]

Looking back into history, it should be noted that earlier generations of Hong Kong Chinese had strong links to Guangdong Province, where a large majority of them originated. Until the 1950s, the term 'Province-Hong Kong-Macao' (省港澳) was a popular expression among the locals, treating south China as a regional collective they could identify with. The actual separation of Hong Kong from the Mainland only took place in the 1960s–1970s as China underwent an era of ideological and political fanaticism under Mao Zedong's Cultural Revolution, in addition to the geopolitical consequences of the Cold War. Economic and political refugees escaping from Mainland turmoil and chaos rejected communism, and some of them eventually made their fortune in British-ruled Hong Kong. That period saw Hong Kong increasingly defined by its difference from Mainland China as 'the Other'—coinciding with the British administration's attempt to inculcate a strong local identity (to be discussed in the next chapter).

During the 1950s–1970s, Hong Kong was able to prosper because of the turbulence in China, which suppressed the growth of some Mainland cities previously more advanced than Hong Kong (such as Shanghai and Guangzhou) and supplied the colony with industrial entrepreneurs and cheap labour fleeing the Mainland. As the Mainland gradually opened up its economy and border in the 1980s, Hong Kong businesses returned to the Mainland in pursuit of new opportunities, spurring an era of the mutually beneficial 'front shop, back factory' (前店後廠) business model for cooperation with Mainland production units, many of which operated at the township and rural levels. Visits by the local Chinese to the Mainland, especially Guangdong, became a feature. Both socially and culturally, the Chinese populations on both sides had already been engaging in frequent interactions despite the formalisation of the 'Two Systems' to maintain distinction and separation between the two. That constituted the *real* basis for co-existence and interchange between the two existentialisms.

Now, over two decades after reunification, Hong Kong is again at a crossroads. The scenario of an economically strong Hong Kong vis-à-vis an economically backward and underdeveloped Mainland has been turned around. While Hong Kong's GDP represented nearly one-sixth of the Mainland's GDP in the early 1980s and 27% (peak) in 1993, it was down to about 2.54% in 2019.[78] Large state-owned enterprises such as China Petrochemical Corporation (Sinopec), China National Petroleum Corporation, State Grid Corporation of China, China State Construction Engineering Corporation, and CRRC Corporation Limited have emerged as multi-national conglomerates actively expanding worldwide, together with some successful private companies like Alibaba, Huawei, ZTE Corporation, and Lenovo. In stark contrast to the initial reform period of the 1980s, Hong Kong no longer seems to be the economic role model for the Mainland, which has now found its own model of development (more discussion in Chapter 14). According to the 2019 Asia Power Index of the Lowry Institute of Australia, China netted the highest gains in overall power in 2019, for the first time narrowly edging out the US in the assessment of economic resources.[79]

Economic realities can transform the social and political balance of power, as well as people's expectations. Hong Kong's economic prospect has become much more dependent on its links to the Mainland, even though its global and regional profile remains equally important. Major professions—notably engineering, architecture, accountancy, legal, and property management—all yearn for a foothold in the Mainland market. Since 2003, thanks to new schemes to attract investments as well as educated and professional talent from the Mainland,[80] more Mainlanders have come to settle in Hong Kong and acquire HKPR status.[81] Better-off Mainlanders have also been buying local properties. At the same time, more middle-class Hongkongers are acquiring second properties on the Mainland, in the Pearl River Delta cities as well as their home provinces outside Guangdong. Large numbers of Mainland students have been coming to Hong Kong for higher education at its world-class universities.[82] Similarly, the number of Hong Kong students studying at Mainland universities has been on the rise.[83] Most Hong Kong universities have or are planning to set up campuses on the Mainland.[84]

Owing to the new Individual Visit Scheme, inbound tourism from the Mainland is now an important source of economic income. In 2018, out of 65.14 million external visitors to Hong Kong, 51.04 million (or 78.4%) were from the Mainland.[85] However, such an overwhelming number of Mainland tourists has also caused a looming capacity crisis—in commuter and pedestrian traffic, and shopping (with some outlets and shopping areas gearing towards Mainland customers at the expense of the locals and other non-locals). Feeling overwhelmed by a huge number of Mainland visitors in real-life experience has fed into the anti-Mainland sentiments of some Hong Kong residents in recent years because of cultural and behavioural differences as well as concern about 'losing control' of their city.[86]

All these developments could not have been envisaged before 1997, and certainly not in the 1980s when the Basic Law was drafted. Geo-economics aside, one must also be aware of the changing political context in which 'One Country, Two Systems' is being practised. In the run-up to reunification in 1997 and for the first several years afterwards (until the 1 July mass protests in 2003), Beijing essentially pursued a 'leave Hong Kong on its own' approach assuming that the preservation of previous institutions would enable the new SAR to continue to thrive to benefit the Mainland's modernisation. Post-2003, the central government sought to bring Hong Kong closer through economic integration and to give the SAR a new impetus for growth. Politically, it called for strengthening national identity and reiterated the importance of entrusting SAR governance only to 'patriots'—those who 'love the country and love Hong Kong'.

After reunification, it is only natural that the Mainland would start to look towards more integration of Hong Kong into the national family, while Hong Kong as an SAR would become more sensitive about preserving its pre-1997 legacy and distinctiveness. Over the years, there have been growing tensions between the national narrative and the Hong Kong-centred narrative on the city's role and development. The former is based on how the central government factors the SAR into national strategies and plans and how it fits the SAR into the national governance architecture while accommodating the Basic Law-guaranteed differences, in the interest of whole-nation development. The latter has been grounded in the perspectives to safeguard local freedoms; to enhance local economic, business, and elite interests; and to maintain separate governance institutions outside the CCP party-state framework.

Today, China is a strong economy looking forward to a national renaissance in the context of a China order that will not be subordinate to the Western-defined global order. Thus, the way central leaders and officials interpret 'One Country, Two Systems' will not be of the passive 'hands-off' mode of the past. After the 19th CCP Congress in October 2017, Mainland academics conversant in Hong Kong affairs urged there to be an understanding of China's Hong Kong policy within the new national scene of the Xi Jinping era, with some suggesting that 'One Country, Two Systems' has entered version 2.0.[87] Such interpretations of central policy thinking point to a more dominating national agenda over the SAR's governance and development, a far cry from the minimalist strategy of the 1980s and 1990s.

Towards a *third* existentialism?

During British rule, Hong Kong's 'Englishness' and insulation from the Mainland gave it a historic opportunity to develop and modernise, sheltered from the political and economic turmoil that plagued the Mainland under Maoist fanaticism. However, the city can no longer continue to thrive in such an insular position. Hanging on to the past formula of success may hinder its ability to see new variables and perspectives. Hong Kong is already in China. Taking a realist and pragmatic approach, the SAR cannot afford to stay passive and be at the margin; instead, it should strive to play a more active role at the frontier of national growth while still maintaining a status distinct from other Mainland municipalities. Maintaining 'Two Systems' should not preclude cooperation and reciprocities. The Basic Law, rather than becoming a straitjacket reinforcing an inward-looking mindset, should be used to enable new possibilities and ventures.

Apart from serving 'national needs where Hong Kong is the best' ('國家所需，香港所長'),[88] Hong Kong should also continue to embrace a global vision.[89] Its cosmopolitanism, flexibility, adaptability, and overall competitiveness allow it to display a less parochial and more international outlook, fully using its 'Hong Kong, China' status under the Basic Law to engage in inter-city diplomacy and play an active part in the international arena (including non-governmental bodies) to showcase its areas of strength and fields of excellence. Hong Kong should not view its relationship with the economically booming Mainland as a 'zero-sum' game.[90] Avoiding such a negative mindset requires more mutual trust and self-confidence between the two systems and an ultimate sense of national belonging, conditions presently short in supply. Still, the 'One Country, Two Systems' framework remains essential for the SAR's future. The challenge is to learn to construct a third existentialism upon and transcending the two pre-existing existentialisms, as a kind of cross-over synergistic existentialism that does not seek to annul the original ones and yet can bring about an additional identity that can accommodate the complex realities and aspirations of a city moving between 'Two Systems'.

Against such a backdrop, the Greater Bay Area could well provide a test of compatibility, complementarity, and connectivity.[91] The more interflow there is, though, the more conflicts might ensue due to the possible clash between different cultures, behavioural modes, and institutional practices, which in turn could expose risks that have to be properly and patiently addressed. Some Mainland planners might well focus on the positive side of full integration, while sceptics and pessimists in Hong Kong suspect the aim as total absorption of the two SARs. Leaving political doubts aside, true regional integration is more than adding up populations and GDPs, or industrial investment opportunities and the flow of goods, services, and people. It also involves developing a sense of shared fate, identity, and strategic partnership. How such a broad collectivity can be solidly grounded in the supporting institutions, law, and cultural and social interface, is a much greater challenge.

Chapter 13
The Rise of Identity Politics

Introduction

Hong Kong exceptionalism has historically nurtured a local identity that is neither British nor Chinese even though it was ruled by Britain as a crown colony for 156 years and at the same time has always essentially been a population of ethnic Chinese who, until the 1960s, would see their origin in the Mainland of China, with political allegiance to China's regimes (whether of the CCP or KMT) rather than the foreign British administration. The resulting Hong Kong identity is a hybrid, with features coming from both British influence and Chinese culture, and some from more home-grown sources over the decades, rooted in the existential life of the specific history and context of Hong Kong as it has been squeezed between two dominant state systems.

A typical 'identity' experience of the post-War generation of local Chinese illustrates such hybrid and ambiguity. During the formative years, there was a feeling of being a second-class citizen because both the government and society were organised with the English-speaking expatriate class very much on top, thus dominating officialdom and business. Only those English-educated Chinese elites could aspire to be incorporated into this 'respectable' social circle. On their Hong Kong identity card, they could claim to be Chinese or British (if born locally). If they claimed their Chinese nationality, they had to get a Certificate of Identity when travelling overseas, which without exception required application for a visa.[1] Starting in the 1970s, if they held a British passport issued by the Immigration Department, it was not considered a full British passport—in other words, they were treated similar to 'aliens' when entering Britain.[2] When visiting Mainland China, they had to use a home-return permit (回鄉證) issued by the China Travel Service on behalf of the Guangdong public security department and were officially classified as a 'Hong Kong and Macao compatriot' (港澳同胞).[3]

It was only after reunification in 1997 that local Chinese (now holding an official entry/exit permit for Hong Kong and Macao residents known as '港澳居民來往內地通行證') could enter the Mainland as Chinese nationals. However, when travelling abroad using their Hong Kong SAR passport, they are still classified as 'Hong Kong SAR' rather than 'Chinese' by foreign immigration officials. This kind of identity trilogy has underpinned the 'Hong Kong identity' which carries significant history as well as contemporary political and cultural connotations.

Borrowed time, borrowed place

Richard Hughes' 1968 book made famous Hong Kong's status as a borrowed place in borrowed time during colonial rule.[4] Early generations of local Chinese regarded Hong Kong as a transient place, to escape from the chaos and wars on the Mainland, or to make a fortune through trade relationships with foreigners. Many still had roots in the Mainland and ultimately planned to return there. Before the imposition of immigration control at the Sino-British 'border' in 1949, Chinese people could freely enter the colony. While some upper-class Chinese families might have acquired English education, language, and etiquette, with some working as compradors for British and other European companies (or the *hongs*), the majority of the local population remained distant from (or even alien to) the dominant elites despite experiencing varying degrees of Anglo-Chinese hybridisation in social and economic life.

The first awareness of the Hong Kong identity emerged during the period of detachment from the Chinese Mainland following the communist takeover, especially after the colony's economic takeoff in the late 1960s, which gradually brought with it an indigenous sense of achievement and self-worth, something cherished as home-grown. Many new post-War migrants sent their children (the baby-boomer generation) to Anglo-Chinese schools, and these children later became beneficiaries of the economic boom. Politically, the cutting-off of Hong Kong from China was a result of both the new CCP regime's close-door policy as well as a deliberate attempt by the Western powers, led by the US, to surround and contain Chinese Communism as part of the Cold War. Hong Kong had henceforth been portrayed as the free world's enclave confronting a tyrannical Communist China.

Those industrialists and intellectuals fleeing from communism to find refuge in British Hong Kong, together with waves of ordinary urban and peasant folks escaping from war and political struggles, nurtured a Hong Kong Chinese psyche that was fiercely anti-communist but still China-oriented. For them, Hong Kong was the only place where the cultural legacy of China could be preserved without political intrusion. The 1950s and 1960s witnessed clashes between rival ideological camps—supported by the CCP and KMT regimes on the Mainland and Taiwan, respectively—competing for allegiance from the (by now largely refugee) local Chinese population. Inasmuch as the local Chinese desired to embrace a strong China that could give them a sense of national belonging and pride, many found it hard to relate to either the CCP or KMT regimes, both of which they considered repressive. The default option was thus to accept British rule out of acquiescence. Thus, after the colonial administration began to launch social reforms and more public services in the 1970s, and as rapid economic growth served to bring general affluence to the masses and groom a new middle class, it was able to gradually win the hearts and minds of some in the community.

Formation of the Hongkonger identity

The 1967 riot was a significant dividing line in this process of indigenisation. The violence of anti-British pro-communist rioters turned most of the local Chinese population against them (dubbed as 'lefties', 左仔) and in defence of the colonial administration that maintained law and order. As discussed earlier, Hong Kong entered a golden era of social and administrative reforms in the 1970s to reinvent the colonial government as one that cared for the people and, through community building and campaigns, to nurture a new local identity independent of British or Chinese links. The official attempts to establish a 'Hong Kong Belonger' identity coincided with the further detachment of Hong Kong from an increasingly radicalised and chaotic Communist Mainland during the Cultural Revolution and a calculated move by the British government to refine British nationality and its rights to pre-empt any exodus of Hong Kong Chinese to Britain. After the passage of the British Nationality Act of 1981, prior to the commencement of Sino-British talks, only British Dependent Territory Citizen passports with no right of abode were issued to those Chinese born or naturalised in Hong Kong.[5]

During the 1970s, for economic reasons, the Hong Kong dollar was un-pegged from the British pound sterling.[6] Hong Kong was allowed to have its own voice (though still within the British delegation) to represent and articulate Hong Kong interests as opposed to British interests in international trade negotiations, such as over textile trades and export quotas under the Multi-Fibre Arrangement and within the GATT and subsequently the WTO.[7] Increasingly, Hong Kong had acquired self-standing status in the international arena. At the same time, popular culture with unique home-grown Cantonese influence emerged, through Hong Kong movies, Canto-pop music, television soap operas, and even Hong Kong-style cuisine and café food, all of which greatly influenced Chinese diasporas, particularly in Britain, North America, and Southeast Asia. As a result, a kind of Hong Kong pride began to take root vis-à-vis the political and economic turmoil on the Mainland and martial law and political suppression in Taiwan.

Among the three authoritarianisms (i.e., Mainland China under CCP rule, Taiwan under KMT rule, and Hong Kong under British colonial rule), Hong Kong was considered to be the most liberal, with a prominent economic edge and better protection under the rule of law, enabling many Hong Kong Chinese to perceive themselves as representing the only free Chinese community. Being rejected by both Britain and China as full-fledged British or Chinese nationals, the Hong Kong Chinese had no alternative but to embrace a Hong Kong 'self', grounded in the city's economic success and international image. While multiple elements were contributing to the formation and consolidation of a self-sustained Hong Kong identity, it was ultimately the 'political' aspect that conferred legitimacy to such identity. The Sino-British talks, officially a process of finding a smooth formula for Hong Kong's reunification with China, had ironically paved the path for acknowledging and legalising a separate Hong Kong identity.

A separate Hong Kong identity under the Basic Law

During the Sino-British negotiations, the Chinese government insisted on only talking to Britain on Hong Kong's post-1997 future, rejecting the so-called 'tripod chair' notion to include the separate representation of Hong Kong locals (by the Governor of Hong Kong supported by his local Chinese officials) as urged by Britain. At the same time, it went to great lengths to reassure the local population that Hong Kong would be left alone to continue as usual under the 'One Country, Two Systems' principle. Back then, Mainland China was viewed by many Hong Kong people as an economic backwater. The Mainland, too, was wary that its socialism should not become eroded by fully absorbing an enclave known for its carefree capitalism. Strategic 'separation' thus seemed to serve the purposes of both sides. The underlying tone was: 'you go your own way, and we go ours'.

At the time, Hong Kong enjoyed an institutional edge over the Mainland and offered a role model for its economic reform and development. For a while in the 1980s, Hong Kong-style Cantonese was dubbed 'the language of economics' because the prominent external investors were Hong Kong businesspeople few of whom could speak Putonghua fluently. Hong Kong movies, television dramas, and Canto-pop songs also became attractive to the new-age post-Cultural Revolution generation who regarded Hong Kong as representing modernity with an international outlook. Deng Xiaoping even urged that more 'Hong Kongs' should be built in China and that Mainland cadres should learn about the external world and its modus operandi through the window of Hong Kong. This created an odd combination of Hong Kong's economic superiority and its political inferiority vis-à-vis the Mainland.

It was under these exceptional historical circumstances (and based on its economic advantage) that Hong Kong was able to secure a future as an SAR with a separate economic identity ('Hong Kong, China') within the highly centralised PRC. Hong Kong people were granted a new citizenship status as 'HKPRs' under the Basic Law, with a full string of constitutionally defined civil and political rights that befitted some kind of sub-national identity, even though HKPR was not the same as and could not supersede national citizenship (i.e., Chinese citizenship). Henceforth, Hong Kong would be a city of 'permanent residents' and 'residents', with the former having the right to elect and to be elected to government positions, and to enjoy certain social benefits. To give substance to the symbolic importance of Chinese sovereignty, the Basic Law requires key officers of the three branches of government to be Chinese citizens with no right of abode in any foreign country. They include: the CE, all Principal Officials, and members of the ExCo; the President and at least 80% of the members of LegCo; and the Chief Justice of the CFA and Chief Judge of the High Court.[8]

Citizenship denotes a sense of collective meaning and destiny for a community. It is ultimately about where one belongs to. Following T.H. Marshall's logic, the concept of 'citizenship' is traditionally premised on civil, political, and social aspects.[9] Constitutionalising the HKPR identity makes Hong Kong people (both Chinese born or in permanent residence locally, as well as Chinese and non-Chinese being legally resident in Hong Kong for at least seven years) a community of common interest with shared rights and obligations, to the exclusion of others, including Chinese on the Mainland.[10] Such legally conferred identity was both historically specific and contingently convenient. Hong Kong would revert to China's sovereignty without becoming part of mainstream China, and Hong Kong Chinese could travel inside and outside China not as PRC passport holders, but as Hong Kong citizens holding a special entry permit (previously 'home return permit') and SAR passport. Legally defined citizenship aside, Hong Kong would also constitute the foundation of a local identity concurrently carrying cultural meaning as the other 'system' within China, encompassing different institutions and legacies (such as English common law system and the rule of law). Reunification (and nationalisation) without being absorbed (or fully nationalised) seemed to be the underlying logic. Yet, such expectations had proved to be too simplistic to be sustainable. Tensions arose even during the pre-1997 transition period and became more complicated and pronounced after the regime change. Decolonisation and reunification with the motherland should have solved the identity problem, but the question of 'Who am I?' persisted—Hongkongese, or Chinese, or Chinese Hongkongese?[11] The answer has never been straightforward or clear cut.

Identity anxiety during the transition

The Hongkonger identity crisis was further exacerbated during the 1989 pro-democracy movement in China and the subsequent Tiananmen suppression. Over a million Hong Kong people marched on the streets in May and June 1989, first to express support for democracy, then to mourn the victims of the military crackdown on 4 June. While Hong Kong was at first excited over its solidarity with the Mainland (highly symbolic of its national identification), this emotional outburst was relatively short-lived. The Tiananmen crackdown shattered many locals' confidence about returning to China, induced their resentment towards the Mainland authorities, and strengthened their desire and determination to shore up Hong Kong as a self-sufficient economy and polity. Such sentiments sowed the seeds for an inward-looking form of localism that would loom larger in the subsequent decades. Beijing's warning that Hong Kong should mind its own business ('well water should not interfere with river water') and not become a base of subversion of Mainland socialism installed yet another paradoxical wall between the two sides.

The national identification journey was disrupted. Large numbers of Hongkongers, mainly from the rich and middle-class, resorted to migration to Western countries like Canada, the US, Australia, and Britain, either permanently or to secure a safe exit pass (i.e., foreign passport) for themselves and their families before returning to Hong Kong to earn money while the economy was still doing well. In 1990, the British government was persuaded by circumstances to agree to grant full British nationality to 50,000 local families (mainly senior civil servants, business people, and professionals).[12] Among those who were prepared to stay in Hong Kong and accept life under Chinese rule, many had become more hostile to the CCP regime and wanted to keep Hong Kong 'immune' from the Mainland system. As it was not uncommon for members of Hong Kong Chinese families to have acquired foreign nationality, the Hong Kong identity issue became even more complicated as dual nationality had to be considered. The Chinese government was induced by pragmatic considerations to allow those Hong Kong Chinese holding foreign passports to retain their HKPR status and be treated as Chinese nationals, by deeming their foreign passports as only travel documents.[13]

Post-Tiananmen, there were concerns as to the political threat Hong Kong could pose to the Mainland. Historically, Hong Kong had played a disproportionately significant part in both the Republican and Communist revolutions, by providing a base for some revolutionaries. As a piece of Chinese soil under foreign rule and beyond the effective control of the Mainland authorities, colonial Hong Kong had thrived as a source of new ideas and as a safe haven for political dissidents and economic refugees alike. Perceived threats and opportunities together continued to shape the Hong Kong psyche and identity during the transition towards the handover, with rising uneasiness over the threats from both sides.

Reasserting the 'local' after reunification

The final years of transition saw a growing discourse on identity issues, with some tracing a link to the Sino-British struggle over 'decolonisation' — 'a dual struggle over the politics of identity and the social basis for a new economic and political regime in the approach to 1997', as some put it.[14] Immediately after reversion to Chinese sovereignty, an early expression of identity politics was witnessed in a clash over language, when the new SAR government decreed to enforce the use of the mother tongue (meaning traditional Chinese in written form and Cantonese in spoken form) in place of the English language as the medium of instruction at the junior secondary level. Such pedagogically sound and politically correct policy had, however, proved to be highly unpopular with schools and parents alike. Some critics saw the school language policy as not just a pedagogical matter but a political one because 'the English language has not only become a habitus of society; it also serves to distinguish Hong Kong people from Mainland Chinese'.[15]

Contrary to the widespread conspiracy theories, the SAR government did not seem to have a coherent national identity project back then. The irony of the new language policy was that it permitted over 100 schools to be exempted and continue to be English-medium schools, thus creating a two-tier system actually in favour of English.[16] In 1999, following the interpretation of the Basic Law provisions by the NPCSC such that children born on the Mainland of HKPRs were denied their right of abode in the SAR for the sake of protecting Hong Kong's economic and social interests, there was concern that it deepened the cleavage between the people of the two places.[17] Economic self-interest aside, there were constant anxieties about a contraction of the city's political sphere as the perceived unavoidable convergence of two different political structures could one day curb the articulation and development of local identity.

The dominant national discourses during the political transition might have nurtured a favourable atmosphere for re-nationalisation. However, as soon as the political transition was over, Hongkongers re-adhered to their own label in their struggle for cultural autonomy as they began to worry that assimilation into the national culture and identity would place the indigenous Hong Kong culture in danger of 'disappearance'.[18] Resistance to surrendering the local identity soon became visible and vocal in the political, cultural, and discursive arenas. The post-transition politics of identity were subsequently fully played out in the public debates over Article 23 legislation and constitutional reform, as well as in the growing movement to preserve Hong Kong heritage and the Cantonese language, underlining more deep-seated concerns about the loss of autonomy, freedom, and legacy. Beijing's renewed exhortations on patriotism—which some suspicious locals interpreted as in deference to the Mainland's definition of national interest—made them more sensitive to the perceived threat to Hong Kong's political space and more demanding of democratisation.

Another impetus to the uneasiness over Hong Kong identity came rather unexpectedly from the economic front. Into the transition and reunification, the Hong Kong Chinese had believed that they were different from and superior to their Mainland compatriots because of their more advanced economy and affluence. Immediately after 1997, the serious recession triggered by the Asian financial crisis shattered their confidence. Meanwhile, the Mainland economy had grown steadily and rapidly, so much so that by the mid-2000s some in both government and business began to worry if Hong Kong might risk losing its competitive edge as Shanghai and even Shenzhen were fast catching up. Instead of leading China's economic development, Hong Kong now seemed to be turning around to ask the central government for economic favours and support—a great irony for Hong Kong exceptionalism.

The mass protests of 1 July 2003 were the first show of force in safeguarding the 'local' culture as well as a demonstration of 'people power'. They also marked the rise of middle-class social activism and collective action.[19] Issues of identity began taking centre stage in local politics, as exemplified by new waves of political demands for democracy, freedom, and autonomy, and a campaign by a group of 300 professionals, academics, and NGO activists to uphold Hong Kong's 'core values'.[20] The surge of pro-heritage sentiments since the early 2000s, accompanied by nostalgia (described as 'collective memory'), was not an entirely cultural outburst, but it was also indicative of an underlying political assertiveness for a locally rooted Hong Kong identity in preservation, planning, and development processes.[21] The post-transition generation, like their jittery parents during the Sino-British talks and prior to reunification, were worried about losing the city's local worth and identity, something that could only be traced to its past colonial legacy if unable to be established by a future vision and mission.

The raison d'être of the Hong Kong system (or 'Hongkong-ness') rested on the city's ways of living, institutions, core values, and cultural forms all inherited from the past under British rule. Hong Kong did not undergo a proper process of decolonisation during the pre-1997 transition to give birth to any new identity (as in an independence movement following decolonisation elsewhere like India or a post-revolution nation such as China in the 1950s). Yet it was not immune from a trend that many new and post-colonial societies had experienced in their transition from a nationalist to a post-nationalist stage, with classical nationalism giving way eventually to a search for cultural identity. Given the 'Two Systems' reality and mindset, there was no nationalism per se for Hong Kong people to aspire to but only a quest for being distinct and different from the Mainland, hence reinforcing the formation of a local identity grounded in past (colonial) history, campaigns for democracy and core values, and a new movement of local awareness around environmental, heritage, cultural, and civil society issues.

That said, until recently, the emerging local identity concerns were not necessarily confrontational towards the national identity. As late as June 2005, a civic education survey conducted by the government's Committee on the Promotion of Civic Education found that 73% of the respondents were proud to be Chinese while at the same time displaying a strong sense of belonging to Hong Kong, with high correlation between the two. If indeed that was the case, Hong Kong would have achieved the best of both worlds under 'One Country, Two Systems', which might be put as 'one nationality, two identities'—a kind of new hybrid. Even the SAR government had found it necessary to articulate local identity. When Donald Tsang was the CE, he sought to foster a new era for Hong Kong and cultivate 'new Hongkongers', a project quite akin to nation-building in other post-colonial societies, with 'progressive development' being his new catchword.[22] Leung Chun-ying, who succeeded him in July 2012, did not deploy any similarly bold expressions, but had quite early in his term emphasised that he would put Hongkongers' (i.e., HKPRs') interests first, as seen in his housing policy and the measures to end the birth of babies in Hong Kong of non-HKPR Mainland parents.[23]

The new century has seen the rapid and drastic rise of China. Business and professional sectors now wonder if Hong Kong is being left behind in this Mainland boom. The sense of boundary between the SAR and Mainland is being transformed, with the two sides more intermingled than before—economically, socially, and culturally. Nonetheless, despite a good degree of economic integration and social interaction, political suspicion and scepticism remain on both sides, at the risk of breeding hostilities. Some pro-Mainland patriots see Hong Kong as devoid of national identity because of its 150 years of British colonial rule and urge national (re-)education. They harbour the logic that before full democracy is to be introduced Hong Kong people should learn to be patriotic first. However, things need not be dichotomised this way. Hong Kong Chinese people can take pride in the nation's economic, social, cultural, and sports achievements while at the same time be critical of its political system and policy and legal shortcomings. On the other hand, there is no reason why singing the national anthem, displaying and respecting the national flag, or learning more about the Mainland should be made a subject of political controversy and ridicule by some pan-democratic supporters.

In terms of how local people have expressed their identity, it would be useful to refer to the regular polls conducted by the HKUPOP since 1997 (see Figure 13.1). Random samples of respondents were asked to choose one of the five identity categories: Hongkonger, Hongkonger in China, Chinese in Hong Kong, Chinese, or mixed identity. If we take 'Hongkonger + Hongkonger in China' as a more pro-local identity, and that of 'Chinese + Chinese in Hong Kong' as more pro-national identity, it can be observed that the proportion expressing a pro-local identity has indeed been on the rise, but this increase has been moderate, at least until the outbreak of the 2019 political confrontations. During the two decades since reunification, pro-local identity rose from around 60% in 1997 to around 67% by 2018, while pro-national identity has been on a proportionate decline from about 37% to 30%. The 'Chinese' articulation peaked in 2008, the year China hosted the Beijing Olympics, which presumably brought national pride to many local people, with the 'Hongkonger' expression bottoming in the same year.

The 'Hongkonger' expression peaked in early 2012 for the first time (at about 45%) but then declined to only 27% by mid-2012. The subsequent Occupy Central campaign and Umbrella Movement might have triggered more localist and nativist sentiments, yet the 'Hongkonger' identification still fluctuated between 34% and 42% from 2014 onwards, reaching a level no higher than that in 1999 (42%) when Hong Kong suffered a serious economic setback in the aftermath of the Asian financial crisis. However, this pattern changed drastically in 2019 because of the extradition controversy, with the 'Hongkonger' identification escalating to some 53% by June 2019. Subsequent polls conducted by HKPORI, following the same methodology as HKUPOP upon the latter's closure in July 2019, showed a continuing upsurge in pro-local identity (77.8% by year-end, comprising 55.4% 'Hongkonger' and 22.4% 'Hongkonger in China').

Figure 13.1: How Hong Kong people express their identity

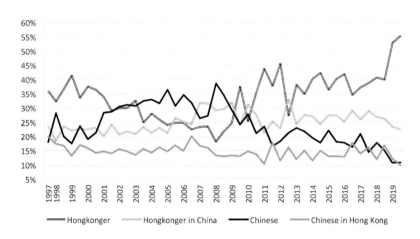

Sources: HKUPOP (n.d.) *You would identify yourself as a Hongkonger/english/Chinese in Hong Kong/Hongkonger in China*, www.hkupop.hku.hk/english/popexpress/ethnic/eidentity/halfyr/datatables.html; HKPORI (n.d.) *Categorical Ethnic Identity: You would identify yourself as a Hongkonger/english/Chinese in Hong Kong/Hongkonger in China*, www.pori.hk/pop-poll/ethnic-identity-en/q001.html?lang=en.

The new politics of identity

Beijing's emphasis on the need to strengthen national identity and national education in Hong Kong stemmed from the Article 23 controversy, which it considered as a failure to fulfil a constitutional duty under the Basic Law. Afterwards, the central government began to adopt a more hands-on policy towards a defiant Hong Kong, complemented by the call to nurture patriotism among Hong Kong people, particularly students and youngsters. On 30 June 2007, during his visit to Hong Kong to officiate the inauguration ceremony of Donald Tsang's second-term government, President Hu Jintao (胡錦濤) urged the fostering of a strong sense of national identity among young people.[24]

The consultation document on National Education was published in May 2011 for extensive stakeholder and public consultations before a revised plan was released in April 2012, just before the end of the Tsang Administration.[25] Despite already taking on board a range of suggestions from the teaching and other sectors (including the influential pro-democracy Hong Kong Professional Teachers Union), the implementation of the revised national education package was met with strong protests led by Scholarism (a group formed by senior secondary students) in July 2012, catching the incoming Leung Administration by surprise. The Anti-National Education Movement saw some pan-democrats, teachers, and students surrounding the Central Government Offices at Tamar for 11 days, playing up the issue of identity and inculcating anti-communist and anti-Mainland sentiments among many students and parents in opposition to alleged brainwashing.

National education, though controversial, should not be simplistically equated to political brainwashing or promoting narrow nationalism or patriotism, or only an official definition of national identity. Properly conducted national education should allow room for reflecting on the 'nation' from multiple perspectives—appreciating national achievements while not ignoring national failures, deficiencies, constraints, and baggage. Knee-jerk reactions with deep political prejudice, as displayed during the protests against national education, will not help facilitate a better understanding of the nation but will instead induce more mutual suspicions and hostilities. The 2012 revised curriculum guide highlighted that 'Moral and National Education' should provide students with a more systematic, holistic, and sustainable learning experience that could cater for their developmental needs and cultivate their moral and national qualities through a value-based curriculum. It is difficult to fault such reformulations as 'brainwashing' or imposing any particular preconception of China on the students. Yet, in the heat of political agitation and mobilisation, any rational discussion became futile.

The new identity politics reached another peak in the 'Occupy Central' movement that started as a mass campaign for electoral democracy, intending to use the tactics of civil disobedience as a moral call to inspire the masses and force the central and SAR governments into concession. The campaign backfired in two ways. First, instead of persuading Beijing into political compromise, it hardened the central government's stance towards Hong Kong, resulting in the 2014 White Paper that emphasised 'comprehensive jurisdiction' over Hong Kong and the 31 August 2014 decision of the NPCSC, a major setback in Hong Kong's democratisation process. Second, the campaign was quickly hijacked by student radicals and separatist groups and turned into the so-called 'Umbrella Movement' that pursued a fiercely nativist and separatist campaign to resist any compromise or engagement with Beijing.[26] Identity politics to the new generation of pro-democracy campaigners is becoming tantamount to rejecting China as a way to assert Hong Kong's autonomy (independence), free from any authority and control of the central state.

Reacting to the new anti-Mainland and separatist tendencies, the central and SAR governments came up with firm stances and harsh measures, including the NPCSC's interpretation of the Basic Law on oath-taking by top officials and legislators.[27] Meanwhile, there has also emerged a vocal pro-Beijing nationalist force in support of national identity and putting pressure on the SAR government to take tougher actions on separatist elements to protect the national interest. Society is becoming more polarised between the so-called 'yellow camp' (those critical of the central government and the Mainland, comprising the mainstream pan-democrats and the more radical separatists in favour of 'self-determination' or even independence) and the 'blue camp' (those who are pro-establishment, pro-law and order, nationalistic, and supportive of the central government's policy).[28] In between the two camps, other local people are becoming disillusioned and frustrated.

Less noted in the local 'identity' discourse is the economic factor. As pointed out previously, Hong Kong's wealth creation had historically been closely tied to the Mainland—from the 'China trade' in pre-War years to early industrialisation thanks to China's chaos following the Communist regime change and the Cultural Revolution, and then to a role in financial intermediation and trade and services facilitation in the Mainland's initial process of economic reform and outreach to the world. As Mainland China completes this process and is better able to chart a more indigenous course of growth sustained by domestic consumption and expansion of large state-owned and private enterprises (some of which have already turned multinational and opened up new overseas markets and production sites), the reliance on Hong Kong has become reduced, raising the possibility of economic 'marginalisation'.

Hong Kong may still have an important role to play in an economically strong China, but of a different nature that requires new means of connection and articulation. Meanwhile, a new economic imbalance has taken root, reversing the pre-1997 perspective of Hong Kong leading the Mainland economy, making Hong Kong people all the more anxious, especially when they see Mainland companies becoming a dominant player in the local financial market and Mainlanders coming in droves to spend on brand goods and consumables alike and to buy up properties. Within big local corporations and multinational companies based in Hong Kong, more Western-educated Mainlanders are taking up the middle to senior positions. All this feeds into the identity uneasiness and uncertainty that first started with the cultural and political factors highlighted above.

Opposing identity discourses

By the time the 2019 extradition saga and subsequent political unrest broke out, the local identity discourse had several variants. The more moderate conventional pro-democracy discourse, articulated by mainstream pan-democratic parties like the Democratic Party and Civic Party, took the line that to safeguard Hong Kong's autonomy and self-administration under the Basic Law and 'One Country, Two Systems', Hong Kong should implement self-determination.[29] These parties did not support Hong Kong independence but maintained that only self-determination could ensure that the local community would keep the right to determine its form of democratic self-administration, social system and way of life. This discourse was rejected by their younger supporters as being too compromising in the face of what they perceived as Mainland encroachment and central government pressure or diktat.

The more radical separatist wing was represented by Demosistō (a party of young activists mainly coming from the student action group Scholarism and the Hong Kong Federation of Students). Though short of openly advocating

Hong Kong independence, it argued that under the principle of 'sovereignty in the people', Hong Kong people have the right to decide their political future by referendum in which the options should include independence and local self-rule.[30] Still further to the extreme were the pro-independence groups such as the Hong Kong National Party which treated China as a coloniser of Hong Kong and called for establishing an independent Hong Kong nation-state.[31] At present, openly pro-independence activists are small in number. However, separatist tendencies, in varying degrees depending on circumstances, are getting more entrenched and shaping 'yellow camp' narrative and politics, especially following the polarisation since 2019. In a way, the traditional pro-democracy era has gone, replaced by more militant and populist activism in favour of de facto self-rule.

As to the nationalist discourse, it can be divided into the official government positions and the discourse embraced by parties and groups within the 'blue camp'. The central government's position is straightforward and clear. It does not tolerate any advocacy for or activities supporting Hong Kong independence and is firm on matters involving the cardinal principles of integrity of national sovereignty, territorial integrity, and national security.[32] The SAR government, with some local sensitivity, understands the concerns about putting Hong Kong's interests first while enforcing the central government lines on matters of sovereignty and national security. Present CE Carrie Lam has made it clear in her 2018 Policy Address that:

> the HKSAR Government and I will not tolerate any acts that advocate Hong Kong's independence and threatens the country's sovereignty, security and development interests. We will fearlessly take actions against such acts according to the law in order to safeguard the interests of the country and Hong Kong. To nip the problem in the bud, we have also reinforced the understanding of all sectors of the Constitution, the Basic Law and national security and fostered an awareness of 'One Country' in the community.[33]

Her rival in the 2017 CE election, former FS John Tsang, representing another voice within the establishment, similarly opposed any move for Hong Kong independence. However, he believed that localism was not necessarily the same as pro-independence and could be an expression of 'loving Hong Kong'.[34]

Among the pro-establishment parties and groups, the traditional patriotic camp (represented by the DAB and FTU) maintains that 'Hong Kong independence' is unconstitutional. It makes a distinction between separatism and local sentiments to put Hong Kong first and to preserve local characteristics.[35] However, newly emerging forces — such as the Alliance for Peace and Democracy (保普選反佔中大聯盟), Alliance in Support of our Police Force (撐警大聯盟), and Defend Hong Kong Campaign (保衛香港運動), all formed in opposition to the Occupy Central movement — have called for stronger legal action and firmer enforcement against pro-independence advocacy and activities, as well as for the pro-democracy movement to be identified as being disloyal to the nation.[36] Pro-business parties like the BPA and Liberal Party broadly follow the government lines but were otherwise less vocal towards localist concerns until 2019 when BPA has toughened its stance. Similar to the yellow camp, there exist both moderate and hardline voices within the blue camp, but these have been increasingly radicalised by the ongoing political confrontations.

Most post-war decolonising states in Asia have displayed identity politics and conflicts that in some cases led to community violence and even war — in India, Pakistan, Bangladesh, Singapore, and Malaysia. In a way, Hong Kong was spared from such conflicts and violence under British rule except during the 1967 riots. Until the question of Hong Kong's political future beyond 1997 was raised in the early 1980s, the sensitive identity issue had been suppressed not simply because of the will of the colonial rulers,[37] but also as a result of voluntary preference on the part of the local Chinese population at large who took a rather instrumental approach to their identity — seeking protection from the British buffer against an overspill of political turbulence on the Mainland, taking advantage of British institutions like education, rule of law, and business and professional practices, and yet mostly indifferent to the hoisting of the British flag or playing of the British national anthem 'God save the Queen'. Stability was also in some ways influenced by China itself (whereby the local population would not want to rock the boat causing the CCP government to take back the city even before it considered the situation ripe for reunification) and the positioning of Hong Kong as an international city where the local Chinese lived in harmony with an international expatriate community in an English-dominated society.

Identity began to loom large as a defining political issue from the 1980s onwards as the Hong Kong community sought to bargain for a future that would be distinct from the Mainland system. Their experiences under British rule seemed to give many local Chinese a frame of reference, to the extent that they would hope for replicating such experiences under China with unchanged rules of the game. In a way, many people would still like to continue with an instrumental approach to their way of life, treating reunification as no more than a formality or symbolic change — which could be loosely depicted as a notion of 'decolonisation without nationalisation'. Thus, when it comes to national security, the national flag, and the national anthem, and even national education, many Hong Kong people tend not to take them seriously, unlike their fellow Chinese on the Mainland or indeed citizens of other countries they consider advanced.

For those who perceive the Mainland system as a threat to their local existentialism, they will only become increasingly assertive as if fighting for the rights of 'nationhood'. Indeed, some younger generations have harboured thoughts of being separated from the Chinese nation, sometimes using derogatory descriptions in social media like '支那' (pronounced in local Cantonese as *gi-na*, the way the Japanese called China during the war of aggression in the 1930s–1940s) or '北方強國' (*bak fong koeng gwok*) or simply '強國' (*keong gwok*) (meaning 'that strong country in the north'/'strong country') to refer to the Mainland, as if Hong Kong was not part of China. A small segment of young radicals even seek to promote the forging of some kind of 'Hong Kong nation', underpinned by independence discourses borrowed from and inspired by separatist and pro-dependence movements elsewhere, such as the Catalonia independence movement in Spain and Scottish independence in Britain.[38] Not surprisingly, this trend has triggered a corresponding rise in fierce nationalism identified with China and the CCP government within the blue camp.

The inherent clashes between central-state-preferred nationalisation (or patriotism) and the moderate to radical expressions of Hong Kong-centred nativism have become more visible and antagonistic, leading to two opposing politics of identity. The central government has been concerned about Hong Kong's political system divorcing from the national orbit and has thus repeatedly reiterated that 'Two Systems' can only function within the context of 'One Country' and that democracy should not be at the expense of national security and integrity. It is also sceptical of the pro-democracy camp getting too close to the US and other Western powers which see the rise of China as a threat to the Western-defined global order.[39] On the other hand, many pan-democrats and their supporters consider the local electoral contests not just as a competition among alternative policy platforms on how to govern Hong Kong better domestically, but ultimately as a political crusade against an SAR government and its allies deemed as puppets of a CCP regime that they do not trust. Mutual prejudice and confrontations have turned local elections into a kind of perennial proxy war between Beijing and pro-democracy diehards.

Polarisation has further extended beyond local political and ideological rivalries to feed into new tensions at the national level between local Hong Kong populism and the escalating Chinese populism on the Mainland.[40] Local resentment towards Mainlanders is often a knee-jerk reaction to the huge influx of Mainland visitors and tourists whom the locals perceive as taking away the city's resources from its residents. Narrow-minded anti-Mainland groups have used racist language in calling these visitors 'locust' (meaning they were like locust coming in vast swarms eating up the harvest and vegetation within a short time). Such sentiments could perhaps be better understood within the wider global context if reference is also made to the new form of identity politics looming large in Europe and North America, which has led to a new radical populism with a political style performed, embodied, and enacted across different political and cultural contexts.[41] The growing popularity of right-wing (and sometimes left-wing) nationalist forces, at the expense of more moderate mainstream political parties, are indicative of an anti-establishment, anti-migration, and anti-globalisation psyche. Many young people find themselves less 'possessed' and more 'disenfranchised' in the present age. Such populist identity politics (which are also exclusivist and nativist) often come hand in hand with the 'politics of nostalgia',[42] a 'new age of anger',[43] and a 'new tribalism' which has led to a crisis of democracy.[44] Hate-mongering against immigrants, minorities, and various designated 'others' has gone mainstream.[45]

In the case of Hong Kong, the 'others' are the Mainlanders, on whom every social ill tends to be blamed by the nativists, especially given the 'Two Systems' tensions of recent years where some locals see the Mainland as an overpowering force. Hong Kong's educated young generation feel they are earning less and cannot aspire to affordable housing compared to the previous generation. Many of them blame it on the 1997 return of Hong Kong to China, the influx of Mainlanders buying up Hong Kong properties, and the undemocratic political system working only for the benefit of the business-bureaucrat ruling class. Some are anti-development, not just out of environmental concerns but because of their belief that large development projects only make the rich even richer and put the city's prospect in the hands of big developers with close links to Beijing. They see major cross-boundary transport infrastructure projects such as the XRL as only serving the Mainland interests at the expense of Hong Kong taxpayers. Without the real experience of British rule and the sense of national identity of their parents' and grandparents' generations, the post-1997 younger generation is easily susceptible to ideas of separatism fuelled by rising suspicions of an alleged erosion of the Hong Kong system and its core values under China.

Hong Kong identity reconsidered

It has been argued that identity builds on a cultural construct that simultaneously establishes commonness and difference, and in the case of Hong Kong, a variety of identity claims have existed based on some intersecting and competing discourses or narratives, such as 'localness', 'Chineseness', 'nationalism', and 'globalness'.[46] Indeed, identity has ethnical, political, social, economic, and cultural dimensions, which create a distinct mosaic that differentiates a person or group of people from the 'others'.[47] In a way, the clash of identities has been central to how Hong Kong people have discovered and articulated their sense of relatedness — to their habitat, their motherland China, and to the world given the city's international connections. Therefore, it can be said that the Hong Kong identity has always been somewhat fused and contested.

It was only in the late 1960s to 1970s that a more distinguishable Hong Kong identity emerged, riding on the then colony's economic takeoff and against a backward and inferior 'other' — the Mainland.[48] A subsequent global identity articulation (including the branding in 2001 as 'Asia's world city' under the Tung Chee-hwa Administration) was construed to somewhat demarcate Hongkongers from the Mainlanders. The official Hong Kong identity was the creation of a unique segment of history. Underneath that identity has been the constant concern over what Charles Taylor has called 'the politics of recognition'.[49] In the early years after the handover, there was conjecture that the parallel processes of decolonisation from Hong Kong's past and its future psychological reunification with Mainland China might produce a new biculturalism to characterise Hong Kong people.[50]

Decolonisation for Hong Kong should have entailed both a process of national reunification and identification with China, as well as a process of reconstructing a new distinct cultural identity, partly rationalised by the 'One Country, Two Systems' logic and partly sustained by its historical experience (or existentialism). The anxieties and conflicts emanating from the cognitive gap between the Mainland and the Hong Kong community have been as much an outcome of institutional differences as an outgrowth of decoupled cultural identities. In the initial decade of reunification, there seemed no dispute with identifying with China as the nation—though the sentiments then were more inclined towards identifying with a 'cultural and historical China' than a 'political China'. At the same time, anything embodying Hong Kong's past would be deployed as an expression of a collective sense of belonging and pride, as underscored by actions in heritage and core value issues to articulate a separate 'cultural' Hong Kong. There were moments of sharing national pride such as during the Beijing Olympics in 2008 and when China's spacecraft *Chang'e 3* made its first successful landing on the moon in December 2013, but the trend had been more to re-narrate and re-empathise local aspects especially as closer integration with the Mainland economically and socially created social and cultural clashes.

After the Occupy Central campaign and Umbrella Movement protests, the whole scene of identity tensions and politics was transformed. 'Anti-China' sentiments have been on the rise and have crept into electoral politics.[51] There are variants of academic interpretation of such politics—ranging from the more conventional narrative of resistance against the Mainland's intervention in Hong Kong's democratisation, freedoms, and social and economic development, to a centre-peripheral conceptualisation of Hong Kong localism or sub-nationalism.[52] Such academic discourses, while reflecting some public discourses and media representations and seeking to understand the emerging localism in a new light, have also reinforced the logic and even legitimacy of separatism and self-determination. As put by a young scholar, although the term 'localism' denotes that Hong Kong is a distinct entity, 'it obscures the explicit cultural declaration that the Hong Kong polity is independent from China'.[53] Cultural autonomy has now replaced the previous identification with a cultural China. Such was the inherent dilemma between the local and national identities, in addition to the political differentiation between centre and periphery and geopolitical division between 'Two Systems'.[54]

As political polarisation worsened and hostilities escalated in the 2019 confrontations, seeing frequent bloody clashes between protesters and the police and a rising number of protesters arrested, some of those in the middle have shifted towards sympathy with the younger generation-led protests, while radicals started to dictate the action agenda of the pro-democracy movement.[55] Surveys conducted from May to September 2019 produced some illuminating findings, which are indicative of a growing trend.[56] The proportions of respondents claiming to be localist, radical democrat, moderate democrat, in the middle, without political inclination, pro-business, pro-establishment, or pro-China were respectively 11%, 4%, 36%, 22%, 19%, 1%, 4%, and 3%. Discounting those in the middle, people opposing the government were in an overwhelming majority. There was also a significant decline in respondents still insisting on the peaceful non-violence principle in protest actions, from about 80% to 70%.

Even more alarming is that the proportion of localists and radical democrats went up during this 5 month period, from less than 10% to 15%, of whom three-quarters were in the 15–39 age bracket. Overall, among students aged between 15 and 24, 38% claimed to be localist, 14% radical democrat, and 30% moderate democrat; only 16% considered themselves in the middle and 3% pro-China or pro-establishment. If the 2014 Occupy movement marked the origin of nascent localism and separatism, the 2019 confrontations have seen the radicalisation of the younger generation who now embrace more rampant ideas of self-determination and perceive the Mainland as a threat rather than part of the larger 'national' family. Such outbursts, often expressed as sentiments of fear of losing Hong Kong's freedom, opportunities, and other defining values and institutions,[57] are no different from 'the politics of fear' found among the rising currents of radical populism in Europe and the US laying bare the normalisation of nationalistic, xenophobic, racist, and anti-semitic rhetoric.[58]

On the other hand, central government officials and think-tank strategists also believe it may be too risky to put too many eggs in Hong Kong's basket for China's next phase of intensive and deeper economic restructuring. They, too, are being captured by a reverse politics of fear (national security being threatened). Anti-Mainland sentiments are being reciprocated by widespread hostile feelings towards Hong Kong on the Mainland, especially after some violent protesters defaced the national emblem and other symbols of national sovereignty over the SAR. Hong Kong-Mainland relations have come to a low ebb. Hong Kong is no longer a shining star in the eyes of previously admiring Mainlanders. Maintaining distinctness is one thing, but separateness could easily become separation that could lead to marginalisation, with Hong Kong being cast to the periphery of China's rapid development.

Big cities rise and fall over the course of history. Geopolitical and geo-economic conditions change over time, and new pressures of global and regional competition are continually unfolding. Hong Kong cannot afford to be complacent, or else it risks becoming yesterday's city. During British rule, its 'Englishness' (and connection to the West) and insulation from the Mainland gave it the historical opportunity to develop and modernise without being affected by the political and economic turmoil inflicting the Mainland before reform and opening up in the 1980s. However, Hong Kong cannot continue to thrive in such an insular position. Hanging on to past success may hinder it from seeing new vulnerabilities and possibilities. If the present predicament cannot be overcome, the identity crisis will only persist and become destructive to the body politic of the SAR. Hong Kong will find its confidence only when immersing more in China does not amount to so-called 'Mainlandisation' and maintaining strong links with the Western world does not mean a deficit in national identity.

Instead of focusing on how Hong Kong has been transformed by China, as many critics and sceptics do, a new discourse should shift towards how Hong Kong can contribute to China's evolving transformation into a modern and civic polity, the power of which should go beyond the economic. To do that, Hong Kong has to be *relevant* to China—now and in the future—to help define Hong Kong's prospect and self-worth.[59] As a metropolis, Hong Kong should strive to become a melting pot of China (like New York in the US), open to and attracting Chinese from anywhere within the country, as well as talent from other nations, who come for creativity, entrepreneurship, professionalism, freedom, and good governance. Only by maintaining multi-cultural and multi-lingual features can Hong Kong truly turn into a city of growth, diversity, respect, and opportunity. Neither a narrow sense of nativism or localism nor an overly racial expression of nationalistic patriotism is conducive to such cosmopolitanism, a concept which Beijing still values in Hong Kong.

Chapter 14
The Wider Governance Debates

Introduction

The foregoing chapters have traced and analysed Hong Kong's trajectory in governance, political development, and public administration from a more Hong Kong-centric perspective, in terms of internal structures, institutional change, political dynamics, and social and economic transformation. The replacement of British colonial rule by self-administration as an SAR of the PRC, as well as regionalisation and globalisation in the world environment, have brought in new exogenous factors with increasing impact on the domestic scene. Indeed, Hong Kong's transition towards 1997, apart from the political controversies about the Basic Law and the pace and extent of democratisation, also saw extensive administrative and public sector reforms influenced by international trends and ideas, notably NPM. As argued, such reforms could at the same time be interpreted as administrative solutions to larger political problems of the times—a longstanding approach in Hong Kong's public administration history.

This chapter ponders the future of Hong Kong's governance within a wider context of the changing global prospect of governance, where the hitherto dominant liberal democracy paradigm that emerged after the collapse of the Soviet Union and Eastern European communism, along with the Third Wave of democratisation,[1] has been facing various challenges and doubts, not least the rise of China and the alternative developmental path it represents. Emerging tensions between China and the West led by the US for leadership on the world stage are presently reshaping international politics, as well as impacting Hong Kong's position in the national and global arenas.

The situation has been made more acute by the political confrontations since 2019 where some local protagonists (including pan-democratic politicians) sided with the West in its clash with China and lobbied the US and other Western countries to put pressure and sanctions on Beijing. The US and some Western governments have made high-profile comments critical of China's handling of Hong Kong. In a recent tug of war, the then US Secretary of State Mike Pompeo openly called China's ruling CCP a central threat of the times.[2] At the time, the US was close to staging an all-out offensive on China in the name of fighting for Hong Kong after the NPC decided to impose a national security law on the SAR, and in doing so, building an anti-China front through the 'Five Eyes' intelligence alliance.[3] Tension has been running high ever since.

Hong Kong re-entering China's orbit

During the 150 years of British colonial rule, Hong Kong was considered part of the Western world, being an important outpost of its Far Eastern trade. After the communist victory in 1949, which some US politicians and media depicted as 'the loss of China', China became encircled by the US-led economic and political containment within the context of the Cold War. British-ruled Hong Kong found itself at the forefront of the so-called Free World confronting the 'Bamboo Curtain'.[4]

Hong Kong's attitude towards Mainland China was then shaped by British foreign policy and the changing geopolitical realities of the Cold War in the region (the Korean War, Vietnam War, and later US-China rapprochement). Its administrative and governance trajectory was basically outside China's orbit and heavily influenced by developments and ideas in the Anglo-Saxon world of Britain and the US, from which institutional practices and policy lessons and models were derived. Political turbulence and economic and social chaos on the Mainland resulting from incessant 'class struggles' and mass campaigns during the 1950s–1970s gave many local Chinese little to look up to in their motherland. Gradually, the Mainland had become for them a symbol of backwardness and political repression. In contrast, thanks to economic growth and a more benevolent administration of British rulers since the 1970s, the locals found Hong Kong's self-esteem and identity more appealing.

This developmental trajectory began to change after reversion to Chinese sovereignty in July 1997, partly due to politics and partly to economics. Politically, Hong Kong is now part of the PRC under 'One Country, Two Systems'. While it enjoys self-administration as an SAR with a high degree of autonomy, it has returned to China's orbit and will duly be subject to influence from national policies one way or another. Foreign countries, including the US, Britain, and other Western states that in the past treated Hong Kong as part of their ranks would henceforth view the city as an extended part of Communist China and situate it as such in the context of their strategic moves towards China and Asia.[5] Geopolitics have been turned around. Economically, Hong Kong cannot afford to not be integrating into the Mainland market and economy now that China has emerged as the world's second-largest economic power after the US. As a hybrid and intermediary between East and West, Hong Kong's role was predisposed towards Western interests until 1997 and then has unavoidably become more geared towards China's national interests and foreign policy directions afterwards.

Hong Kong's future now rises and falls with that of China. It would therefore be unrealistic to contemplate governance and administrative development issues in Hong Kong in complete isolation from the national and wider Asian contexts bearing in mind the rapid transformation undergone by both China and other major Asian countries in recent decades. As an international metropolis, Hong Kong has never stopped drawing inspiration and borrowing good practices from the Western developed world. At the same time, Hong Kong's gradual but steady economic and social integration with Mainland China—driven by market forces as well as, more recently, a degree of national planning—would facilitate exchanges of administrative and institutional experiences. In the 1980s and 1990s, interactions were mostly a one-way street, with the Mainland emulating the Hong Kong model. Now, as Mainland provinces and cities have been developing rapidly, with local innovations, especially in municipal management, there are possible opportunities and incentives for mutual learning. This could well be positively seen as enrichment and extension of Hong Kong's hybrid journey, but sceptics and pessimists tend to perceive it as Mainland encroachment of the Hong Kong system.

Globalisation, administrative thought, and governance

Globalisation has facilitated and even induced the crossing of borders of 'foreign' ideas and practices—in policy transfer and convergence—although the success of such transfers and lesson-learning is not without question.[6] The real world, as an ever-evolving environment, is inextricably more complex and paradoxical than what can be neatly conceptualised by some grand designs. Sometimes, what seems to have worked in other countries and cultures might not fit the domestic institutional climate and habitat, and, paraphrasing Graham Allison, what appears similar could well be 'fundamentally alike in all unimportant respects'.[7] As an ancient Chinese philosopher Gongsun Long (公孫龍) of the 'School of Names' (名 家, somewhat akin to the school of logic) put it some 300 years BC, 'a white horse is not a horse' (白馬非馬).[8]

Administrative thought in modern times has been swinging like a pendulum. The reason for this is that, like *yin* and *yang*, there are always two sides of the same humanity, and two traits or tendencies of an organisation or social structure—viz., collaboration versus contestation, coordination versus autonomy, centralisation versus decentralisation, globalising versus localising, collectivism versus individualism, market freedom versus government intervention, inclusiveness versus exclusiveness, and so on. It is not always a choice between good and bad in the moral sense, as choices and inclinations are contingent upon interests and circumstances. Thus, understanding the cultural and historical contexts is critical in institutional and policy design. Public administration needs to 'get real'—to manage diverse private needs (even excessive wants) sometimes consolidated or championed as 'public' interests and to contain unending desires, because all governments have limits in capacity, power, and resources.

As Christopher Hood asks:

> What are the effective limits of taxable capacity in the modern state, as debt-ridden governments seek to reduce debt levels and budget deficits after the financial crashes and economic recession of the late 2000s? What are the limits of safety and security that can be realistically achieved by administrative structures and procedures in a so-called risk society? What are the limits to the achievement of

ambitious social engineering to improve the human lot by conventional organisations and bureaucracies?[9]

Yet, inasmuch as government action is repeatedly demanded as if it were an instant solution, the government is concurrently bashed as wicked and blamed as the cause of social failure. Here lies the greatest paradox of public administration. Policy is politics, and 'all politics is local'.[10] Thus, grand theories and ideal types of governance and administration may only help to set some benchmarks but would be of limited relevance to real practice on the domestic ground in a society of complexity, diverse self-interests and constraints.

Every era has its 'new' grand designs and movements. Many of these fads are in effect reactions (as solutions) to problems of an earlier era. Looking at things more philosophically, the administrative world feeds on actions and reactions, sometimes resulting in synergy and sometimes in disconnects and even chaos, but never short of 'new' or reinvented approaches to inherently 'old' questions which have persisted as if part of human nature. What appears new may well be just reincarnations of the old in the long river of human civilisation. Every government has to go back to the basics and understand factors accumulatively shaping its path dependence. It is to such extent that the administrative and governance experience of all countries and eras, in both the West and East, North and South, could become something educational, with lessons to be learned by others but not in a copycat manner.

Ancient and traditional administration was governed by ethos and ethics in much the same way as rules and constitutions regulate modern public administration. Organisational wisdom and logic of the past (the 'traditions'), whether Western or Oriental, might have informed modern-day theories and praxis. Thus, to understand the logic of contemporary Western political systems, one has also to go back to Christian or even Greek statecraft and philosophy. In China, under the traditional Confucian design of the imperial court across the dynasties, some notions of separation of power—with nascent executive, legislative, and judiciary functions, plus a remonstratory institution somewhat like the modern-day Ombudsman, all unified under the emperor (embodying the mandate of heaven to rule as if modern-day sovereignty)—had existed long before Montesquieu published his treatise that helped transform political systems in the modern era.[11]

Governance reforms at the turn of the millennium within the larger global context were partly spurred on by the onset of new-age globalisation, the preceding collapse of the Soviet and East European communist system in 1989–1990, the end of the Cold War, and then, for a while, the proclaimed final victory of liberal democracy cheered by Francis Fukuyama as 'the End of History' from a somewhat Euro-centric perspective.[12] The outbreak of the Asian financial crisis in 1997–1998 had for a decade reinforced the US-led Western belief in the superiority of the free market cum liberal democratic institutions—the so-called 'Washington Consensus' which was imposed as political and economic prescriptions for Asia and other developing and underdeveloped nations.[13] To the sceptics of Asian growth, that crisis exposed the 'myth' around the East Asian economic miracle sustained by state-led markets.[14] Such a sense of post-Cold War Western triumphalism, however, proved to be short-lived.[15]

The contemporary understanding of globalisation and its impact was essentially grounded in Western civilisation, institutions, and values which were regarded as universally applicable to all nations and societies in their quest for development, a process extending the twentieth-century logic of 'modernisation'. Since modernisation was essentially Westernisation in the nineteenth to the twentieth century, globalisation had been equated to benchmarking against and convergence towards Western (mostly Anglo-American) capitalism and its institutional off-springs, with such logic also permeating the subsequent 'Good Governance' discourse. Despite the preaching and pressures for global convergence with the Western development model, recent history is full of examples of divergence and deviance from strong world trends.[16]

Samuel Huntington was arguably the first intellectual in the West to point to a clash of civilisations, between the force of indigenisation and that of Westernisation seeking to impose a 'universalist' regime of global order and modernity.[17] John Gray, too, was articulate in demystifying and deconstructing so-called global capitalism by arguing that there had never been one mode of 'Western' capitalism.[18] While many today would credit Huntington for his foresightedness prior to the 'September 11th' terrorist attacks of 2001 and the subsequent Western-Islamic conflict, his thesis was in a way not entirely novel. History tells us that the 'learning from the West' experience of modern China and Japan from the nineteenth century onwards had amply displayed cultural tensions between the domestic and foreign. Jonathan Spence observed in these two Asian countries a tradition of emulating the West to 'catch up' and accelerate their national development, regarding imitation as part of a process of external legitimisation for renewed domestic momentum still constrained by internal institutional and cultural factors.[19] The longer the civilisation and more entrenched the traditions and institutional heritage (or baggage), the more turbulent such tensions are expected to be.

In the contemporary period, despite China's enormous and strenuous reform process in pursuit of a modernisation agenda grounded in learning from the West, there has all along been no intention among the leadership to dismantle or dilute its pre-existing CCP rule, or to transplant the Western liberal democratic model as the preferred form of governance.[20] This is not just out of the fear of a US-led 'peaceful evolution', but a more innate concern about preserving China's own cultural and national uniqueness (and self-worth). One may point to China's importation of Soviet-inspired communism in the last century as evidence of giving up its traditional political system. Still, Chinese communism has always been more Chinese than communist or soviet. The importation of 'Western' tools and systems would be allowed and encouraged so long as these served the best interests of the party-state, to re-empower it rather than to erode its authority and minimise its capacity to govern. Such instrumentalist reform thinking is reminiscent of the notion of 'Chinese study as the essence [substance], Western study as the tools [application]' (中學為體，西學為用) espoused by imperial modernisers in the late Qing Dynasty during the second half of the nineteenth century, whereby the 'tools' were considered subordinate to the 'essence'.[21]

While many Asian countries might defer to the instrumental superiority of Western-created institutions and practices, once they reach a developed stage, they will typically consider themselves to have mastered the weapon and then resort to embedding such instrumentality within their own indigenous cultures and values and reconnect them to their past traditions, so much so that the imported ways would become indigenised and transformed (into some form of hybrid systems). The 'Western' would no longer be as Western as before. As Seymour Lipset remarked about Japan in the early 1990s:

> Japan [...] has challenged the assumption that technological development leads to convergence with the cultural models that emerged in western industrialized societies. It seemingly is now rejecting aspects which it appeared to accept during the post-war decades. [...] As a defeated economically 'backward society', many Japanese consciously took America as a model to be emulated. Now that Japan thinks of itself as 'number one', it can return to its own traditions.[22]

The 'Asian Values' discourse of the 1990s, championed by then Singapore leader Lee Kuan Yew and Malaysian leader Mahathir Mohamed, represented a political desire to go back to Asian traditions to rediscover a nation's moral strength and cultural identity and pride, a dimension often missed by some Western critics who only took 'Asian Values' as a political rhetoric by Asian authoritarian leaders to justify their less liberal-democratic practice.[23] Today, President Xi Jinping's 'China Dream' vision could similarly be interpreted as a national project to restore lineage to several millennia of past Chinese civilisation and glories.

Asia's rise and Asian governance reforms

The 2008–2009 global financial crisis shattered the hitherto superpower-domination of US capitalism, with China quickly emerging as a real rival. In the twenty-first century, internationalisation is no longer just Europeanisation or Americanisation. The rise of Asia has helped draw attention to Asian ways and Asian values as being relevant to the global governance discourse. For example, Kishore Mahbubani argues that in the same way the rise of the West transformed the world, the rise of Asia will bring about an equally significant transformation.[24] He foresees a new historical epoch with an enormous renaissance of Asian societies. Indeed, by the 1990s as some affluent Asian countries (notably Japan and then Singapore and South Korea) sought to play a role in global affairs, there was already talk of the 'Asianisation of Asia' (i.e., with Asians interpreting and reinterpreting Asia through Asian instead of Western eyes).[25] A later and similar observation of

Asia's rise is Gideon Rackman's Easternisation thesis, which argues about Asia's transformation and the gradual collapse of the post-War global order previously dominated by the US-led West (and for a few decades the Soviet Union).[26]

Asia has already reached a stage where Asians have their own stories (both success stories and hard lessons) to tell, including their institutional paths, achievements, and pitfalls in governance. Whichever way one looks at it, we are witnessing the advent of Asian modernity that is going to have a significant impact on the rest of the world.[27] Against this backdrop, Hong Kong's journey in governance may henceforth become more a part of the Asian modernity than of the Anglo-Saxon system of the pre-1997 past, and be unavoidably caught in the East versus West debates and rivalries. In addition to reflecting on Western developmental and institutional experiences, as common in current governance discourse, one may also ask: 'Can Asian ways and values offer lessons for the pursuit of effective governance?'[28] The present international literature to help answer this question is scant. More empirical and historical studies, as well as theorisations, need to be conducted which can connect Asia's present to its past and its administrative and governance traditions, as well as rigorous cross-cultural comparisons with Western systems.

Even as Asianisation is emerging as the newest sedimentary layer in the geology of global civilisation, it does not necessarily mean that American or European influence has lost its glamour across the globe. However, there are new perspectives under the Asianisation paradigm that challenge some of the conventional wisdom from Western-dominated eras (e.g., the views that '[some] Asians practice neo-mercantile industrial policy rather than free-market capitalism, […] Asia is also highly bureaucratized and multilateral, but via new Asian-driven institutions that both complement and compete with incumbent Western ones').[29] The launch of the AIIB spearheaded by China in 2015 is one good example though its impact on world finance has yet to be demonstrated. It is important to remember that China and India were the two largest economies until the early nineteenth century, and now the world is seeing the resurgence of these two giants in the twenty-first century after economic and social liberalisations.[30]

When it comes to governance reforms, it is increasingly recognised that a culturally diverse public administration landscape at the global level tends to be the norm rather than the exception, with the Asian countries' distinct and varied governance experiences and trajectories attesting to such diversity. Preserving and enhancing state power and capabilities has all along been a principal concern and feature of Asian governance. The pursuit of governance reforms in contemporary Asia has encountered multiple paradoxes and dilemmas induced by their political economy and strong bureaucratic traditions, as well as previous reform trajectories and constraints which created their own path dependence distinct from Europe and North America. East Asian public administration has displayed a combination of state-led development strategies and the instrumentalities of Western-inspired public administration, where developmentalism remains the foundation of public governance with policy-making dominated by a developmental bureaucracy keen on state-building.[31]

While the bureaucratic elites might inherently be obstacles to fundamental change, they have been paradoxically depended upon to deliver economic and social reforms and modernisation. Reforms have at times been 'captured' by the bureaucracy for rent-seeking purposes. Indeed, the politics of some Asian administrative reforms have been portrayed in terms of 'political nexus triads' of politicians, bureaucrats, and citizens interacting and attempting to protect and enhance their respective political and administrative power.[32] Therefore, reforming the state and the state's relationships with society and the economy is no simple task as it touches on the complex web of interests of the state system, not to mention ideological resistance. In future reforms, a delicate balance has to be struck between the forces for change and those for stabilisation and authority. Granted, it would be unrealistic to presuppose the breakup of the pre-existing state power configuration just to achieve reforms and some governance results, as shown by the political and administrative reforms of China and Hong Kong.[33]

China's experiment

China is now arguably the most internationally noted, though also controversial, player of the emerging Asian modernity. Within barely four decades since opening-up and reform at the end of the Maoist era in the late 1970s, it has been transformed from a centrally planned economy into a thriving market economy with the private sector accounting for more than 60% of GDP,[34] under the name of 'socialism with Chinese characteristics'. In the 1960s, China's share of world GDP was below 5%; today, it has risen to over 18%.[35] This is no small achievement. In the process, both domestic motivations for modernisation and for keeping the socialist party-state largely intact, as well as external influence from Western market ideas, good-governance concepts, and administrative innovations (including NPM) have together shaped the country's zigzagging reform journey.

In a way, the early CCP reformers had tried to embrace Lenin, Confucius, Weber, and Thatcher all at the same time. Indeed, they were modernising a socialist regime by preserving its Leninist traditions, and hence emphasising party control and democratic centralism, while also rediscovering the Confucian ethos of paternalistic governance and social harmony (and resisting Western-style adversarial politics). Reforms also focused on rebuilding some form of rational-legal 'bureaucracy' (re-establishing hierarchy and order after the chaotic Cultural Revolution) and learning from Anglo-American managerialism and the pro-market logic of the 1980s and 1990s (in order to revive the economy).[36] These goals were concurrently complementary and contradictory, leading some to summarise the arduous process of reforms as 'creative incrementalism'.[37] Because of the lack of a clear ideological break with the past, reforms were pursued as a cautious balancing act ('feeling the stones when crossing the river' [摸著石頭過河] as vividly put by Deng Xiaoping in the 1980s), without unduly upsetting pre-existing institutions and interests.

Nonetheless, administrative reforms were extensive — ranging from government restructuring and downsizing; ending permanent tenure; cadre management reforms; the establishment of a national civil service system; decentralisation, reform, and privatisation of state-owned enterprises; to fiscal reforms; anti-corruption reforms; and so on.[38] In the 1980s, Zhao Ziyang, the short-lived party General Secretary disgraced during the 1989 Tiananmen crisis, even advocated a fundamental reconfiguration of the party-state: with the separation of party and government, government and enterprises, and government and society; putting the armed forces under the state rather than the party; and the establishment of a more independent legislature and judiciary. Post-Tiananmen, however, such political reforms became taboo, though economic reforms were given a free run.[39]

With China's rapid rise over the last decade, the CCP leadership has become more confident (critics might say arrogant) of its approach to economic growth, administrative modernisation, and governance at large. The dominant role of the party in all spheres of life has been re-emphasised under President (and CCP General Secretary) Xi Jinping, who has also removed his presidential term limit and has written the 'Xi Jinping thought' into the PRC constitution in 2018. Today, the market economy has thrived further but under party-state steering.[40] Government organs have been brought once again within tight party control, with party-state separation — a major objective of political reform in the 1980s — now finally terminated and replaced by wholesale party-state reintegration.[41] Such a looming governance picture of China, perceived by the international media and liberal-democracy promoters as institutional regression and therefore disconcerting, is expected to stay in the foreseeable future, though the broader logic of reform and transformation should remain essentially on course.

China's achievements and experiences are no longer confined to catching up with Western developed economies or to the simple emulation of their policies and methods. It is already officially proclaimed and now widely recognised internationally that China has established its own unique method and model, inviting vastly contrasting reactions to and perceptions and interpretations of its rise. Most Western media see China as a new breed of state-authoritarian capitalism. Some Western powers had previously bet on China becoming part of the Western-led and defined global political order after entry into the WTO. This has led to nervousness that today's China, under a highly nationalistic CCP regime, is both economically and technologically strong enough to ignore the West in pursuit of its own interests. The US and some Western powers are increasingly talking about a clash of systems where the West would be threatened by an assertive Communist China keen to redefine global order.[42] Sceptical of such views, Jeffrey Sachs has observed that China is doing what any country in similar circumstances should do and that it has followed the same development strategy as some Asian economies before it.[43] Whereas the use of influence through culture and values to augment a country's strength and global leadership is affectionately seen as 'soft power',[44] China's similar use of foreign friendship, educational, and cultural means to nurture global opinion in its favour is criticised as infiltration and coercive and manipulative 'sharp power',[45] just because it is an authoritarian regime now capable of threatening US supremacy (the so-called 'Thucydides trap' as depicted by Allison Graham).[46]

At the other end of the intellectual spectrum, there have been theorisations appreciative of the merit of the China model. Joshua Ramo coined the term 'Beijing Consensus' to portray China's alternative model of development in contrast to the Washington Consensus, which could inspire other developing countries.[47] Daniel Bell described the system in China as a 'political meritocracy'—meritocracy at the top, experimentation in the middle, and democracy at the bottom.[48] One way or another, the influence of the China model of authoritarian reformism (or authoritarian 'resilience') at the international level should not be discarded casually, despite the current US-led strategic containment and ideological negation of China. Even Andrew Nathan, a renowned China scholar and critic, previously admitted that China's new hybrid authoritarianism had worked, although it was not at that time sufficiently understood.[49] Others have also taken a realistic view, arguing that the China model is essentially a system of adaptability.[50]

It is clear that the CCP leadership does not believe in Western democracy and has been keen to pursue its own path, in much the same way as it did not believe in the Soviet model of communism. This resulted in the Sinicisation of Communism under Mao Zedong in the 1940s emphasising the virtue of the peasantry in socialist revolution, in contrast to the preaching by the Communist International on urban proletarian uprising. Such strategic disagreement finally culminated in Sino-Soviet ideological conflicts in the 1960s and 1970s and later the launch of 'Socialism with Chinese characteristics' under Deng Xiaoping in the 1980s, which is often simplistically mistaken as 'Westernisation'. Today, Xi Jinping's revival of the 'China Dream' and return to China's centuries-old traditions are just another demonstration of similar efforts to pursue an indigenous (nativist) route to modernity, progress, and order.[51] Some academics on the Mainland see this as the second-phase (i.e., after Deng's first-phase) of the reconstruction of Chinese socialism guided by Xi's thought.[52] China's developmental model has seen a vital role played by both entrepreneurs and the state—the state directs and the market operates, to an extent reminiscent of the state developmental model of East Asia in the 1970s–1990s, only that the CCP party-state possesses even stronger dirigiste power and capacity to steer and mobilise social and economic resources.[53]

In Hong Kong, Britain used to provide models and practices for the colonial administration, whether in policy or management. Legal and institutional practice remains an extension of the British legacy. British professional and occupational standards (e.g., in engineering and construction) have been written into law and regulatory guidelines. As a global city, the SAR has continued to be alert to international trends and ideas, especially in the English-speaking world. At the same time, the rising importance and impact of China will not go unnoticed among SAR government leaders, officials, and the professions who have an interest in understanding how and why that model works. Inter-governmental exchanges and cooperation with the Mainland at central as well as provincial and municipal levels, especially through participation in national planning and major schemes (such as the Greater Bay Area Development), also facilitate the mobility of ideas and practices, lesson learning, and mutual influence no matter how subtle these might be. Whether this leads to greater acceptance of influence from the Mainland (reluctantly or enthusiastically), as many Hong Kong-centric critics worry, will depend on the merit and vibrancy of the Hong Kong system and practices as well as how the central state views the strategic importance of keeping and even strengthening a Hong Kong outlier. Should Hong Kong lose its self-worth and institutional excellence, the more dominant national factor will gradually weigh it down.

The search for good governance

The word 'governance' is derived from the classical Greek term *kybernan*, meaning to pilot, steer, or direct.[54] Thus, the litmus test of governance is the government's ability to lead and steer. All governments and public administration systems seek good and effective governance as a natural course. In recent years, China has also sought to enhance its level of governance as a national goal.[55] However, 'good governance' remains a fluid notion. It is easy to prescribe some essential features and ingredients of governance or good governance, but it is more problematic to decide how and whether such good governance can be realised. Good governance often defies objective, straight-forward, and non-controversial measurement as governance is a concept 'of many proprietors and many varieties of definition and explanation'.[56] In the real world, just as a perfectly competitive economy is hardly found, good governance may more be an illusion than an achievable reality unless one adopts a 'satisficing' approach. In the post-Cold war era, the call for 'good governance' was most often made by international organisations like the IMF and World Bank in an ideological drive to promote convergence towards a global economic order supportive of a neo-liberal agenda represented by the Washington Consensus. Because it was believed that the most 'successful' (as opposed to 'fragile') states were those liberal democratic states in Europe and North America, good governance was often equated to promoting liberal democracy (hence the term 'democratic governance').

In 1996, the World Bank began to measure over 200 countries and territories using its World Governance Indicators, focusing on six aspects: accountability, political stability and absence of violence, government effectiveness, regulatory quality, rule of law, and control of corruption.[57] Right after the 1998 Asian financial crisis, which exposed economic cronyism in authoritarian regimes around the region, the Asian Development Bank championed some core qualities of governance, namely accountability, transparency, openness, predictability, and participation.[58] In a 2005 guide, the IMF stressed the importance of 'promoting good governance in all its aspects, including ensuring the rule of law, improving the efficiency and accountability of the public sector, and tackling corruption, as essential elements of a framework within which economies can prosper' and made the presence of certain good governance policies and practices a condition for countries to receive IMF loans.[59] At around the same time, the United Nations Economic and Social Commission for Asia and the Pacific set out eight areas in which to measure governance: accountability, responsiveness, consensus-oriented, effectiveness and efficiency, equity and inclusiveness, participation, rule of law, and transparency.[60]

Notwithstanding these broadly similar benchmarks of good governance, as Merilee Grindle observed in 2002,[61] good governance is deeply problematic as a guide to development because it entails calling for improvements that touch virtually all aspects of the public sector—from institutions that set the rules of the game for economic and political interaction to organisations that manage administrative systems and deliver goods and services to citizens, from human resources that staff government bureaucracies to the interface of officials and citizens in political and bureaucratic arenas—essentially opening up a can of worms beyond easy management and measurement to deliver results. Others contested those standards presumed common to Western democracy as measures of 'goodness' in government, claiming that cultural differences would result in conflicts with the standards of the international community.[62] It has been argued that instead of pursuing an absolute state of 'good governance', countries should go for a contingency-theory notion of 'good enough governance' that could deliver reasonable results.

The conventional wisdom under the neo-liberal agenda took the view that improved governance was conducive to economic growth, a goal much treasured by Asian and other developing countries, with the corollary that economically more affluent nations would in turn be better able to afford the costs associated with a competent bureaucracy and strongly entrenched institutions of good governance, thereby inducing a virtuous circle. This causal relationship was challenged by Daniel Kaufmann and Aart Kraay based on some empirical studies.[63] First, when the institutions of the state were 'captured' by vested interests, those entrenched elites could benefit from a worsening status quo of misgovernance and could successfully resist demands for change even as income rose. Second, economic growth could sometimes be achieved despite the lack of what neo-liberals defined as elements of good or democratic governance—China and Singapore often being cited as examples. This led to the suggestion of the possibility of 'growth without governance'.[64] Most advocates of 'good governance' take democracy as definitionally intrinsic to good governance, yet the relationship of democracy to state performance has yet to be thoroughly evaluated empirically.[65]

The last decade saw the demise of the one-size-fits-all notion of governance reform. The global financial crisis emanating from the most advanced economies in the US and Europe had exposed the intellectual and practical vulnerabilities of any singular 'good governance' model grounded in the Western reform agenda. The superpower domination of US capitalism was seriously eroded, leading to the questioning of not just its economic might, but also its cultural superiority. There has been growing acceptance that 'good government means different things in different countries'.[66] The globalisation discourse has since been challenged by post-neoliberal thoughts advocating emancipatory, inclusive, and re-regulatory roles for the state,[67] opening up debates for a refashioned 'bring the state back in' paradigm and lately a 'new socialism' with a democratised economy.[68] Some developing countries look to the China model (Beijing Consensus) for reform inspiration. It is time to explore governance in terms of 'effective government' that can deliver social and economic results, as well as political and policy stability, as all governments are supposed to achieve. Even Francis Fukuyama has turned to such missing dimensions of 'stateness' (or state power and capacity) in his reflections on governance and the world order of the twenty-first century.[69]

Democracy at a crossroads worldwide

As Hong Kong entered the early stages of the transition pre-1997, its politics had predominantly been embroiled in the issue of democratisation, partly because of the British schemes for decolonisation, the Chinese central government's promise of self-administration, and the local population's urge for greater say over the future of their city, and party because of the worldwide impact of the Third Wave of democratisation.[70] Closer to Hong Kong, the democratisation experience of Taiwan since the 1990s also provided a showcase of how a Chinese society, long presumed to be historically and culturally more accommodating towards authoritarian or even autocratic rule, could be transformed into a highly participative democratic polity. Sceptics of the CCP considered a bottom-up democratic political system crucial to withstanding any intrusion by the central regime into Hong Kong's freedoms and way of life. For social activists, democratic rights in the hands of the citizenry would be essential to prevent government-business collusion which, to them, was characteristic of colonial rule.

Chapter 10 has reviewed the long and winding road in Hong Kong's quest for democracy and the many twists and turns of the journey in constitutional reform. The political impasse and hostilities resulting from the 2014 Occupy Central and Umbrella Movement confrontations and the harsh response from the central state, now made worse by the political standoff starting in 2019, have meant that any real breakthrough in Hong Kong's democratisation is at best a distant goal and not an achievable outcome anytime soon. This political winter seems to have hardened the radicalism of some in the pro-democracy camp, particularly the separatists and 'self-determination' activists, and reinforced a sense of impotence even among the mainstream population, which further undercut the government's legitimacy and breed political polarisation and instability. Against this larger picture, even if government performance in policies and services could arguably help to mitigate the legitimacy deficit, it will not make the government's life easier.

Inasmuch as it is necessary to reconsider the broader strategy for securing political compromises in the arduous process of constitutional development, it is opportune to critically reflect on the future of democracy now that there is increasing scepticism about the functioning of electoral democracy following the rise of populist and radical politics in the US, Europe, Latin America, and Asia. The new wave of populism stemmed from the 2008–2009 global financial crisis. Because of the rescue packages and stimulus strategies adopted by major developed economies and followed by China, such as QE policies, the big crash did not materialise as many worried. However, the reality has been less simple. That crisis was the greatest one to have struck Western societies since the end of the Cold War, with immense consequences.[71] Languishing wages and incomes, QE-induced speculative financial capital riding on easy and cheap credit, property bubbles in major cities, and austerity policies in many Western countries are together responsible for uncertainties, social anxiety, and class anger that have fuelled the growth of previously fringe politics whether on the right or the left of the political spectrum.

History might repeat itself as nations hasten to return to QE and launch generous spending packages to bring a temporary boost to a rapidly contracting economy in the wake of the COVID-19 pandemic, which by the end of July 2020 had already caused some 749,000 deaths with 18.2 million confirmed infections across the world. Most governments (including Hong Kong) have focused on stringent suppression and mitigation measures against the pandemic and have prioritised the implementation of massive economic relief and stimulus packages.[72] Because of city and country lockdowns and other bans on close contact and travel, social and economic activities have been significantly constrained and adversely affected. To illustrate, in June 2020, the OECD expected world economic output to plummet by 7.6%, with the future prospect depending on whether there would be a second wave of the pandemic.[73] It seems likely that the longer-term implications on social and economic life as well as political attitudes will be of a scale larger than the 2009 global financial crisis.

The increasing backlash against neo-liberalism and globalisation, as well as the mainstream democratic political system underpinning them, has spurred the steady rise of anti-establishment populism with a vicious kind of identity politics (extreme nationalism, new tribalism, and nativism).[74] Anti-elitism and antiglobalism jeopardise international organisations like the WTO, even putting at risk meaningful international cooperation such as fighting climate change.[75] Social media in search of sensations, exaggerations, and radicalisation have served to amplify divisions and conflicts, undercutting compromises and political subtleties and feeding such populism in distrust of institutions.[76] Younger generations seek immediacy, self-expression, emotional connection, and authentic relationships, which explains why social media platforms are so attractive to them. Yet they find most governments and bureaucratic agencies are only used to one-way information dissemination and response, and are poor in emotional bonding during micro-encounters, except perhaps in the course of election campaigns.[77] They see mainstream parties and politicians only minding the next election and focusing on their and special-groups' near-term interests.[78] A similar trend of distrust in conventional politics and pro-democracy actions is also evident in the current radicalisation of Hong Kong, accompanied by an escalating hostility towards the CPG or the 'One Country, Two Systems' political order.

Democracy is in crisis, but not for the first time in history. Epitaphs for democracy were also in fashion in the 1930s.[79] For a period, some intellectuals in Europe and the US wondered if democracy could survive the challenge of Nazism, Fascism, and Communism. Before the Third Wave of democratisation in the 1990s, out of alarm by anti-establishment social discontent and protests in the West during the 1960s and early 1970s, the Trilateral Commission published a report in 1975 which examined the changing context of democratic government and the dysfunctions of democracy (such as the de-legitimation of authority, overloading of government, and disaggregation of interests) in the US, Europe, and Japan.[80] It can therefore be argued that democracy has never been devoid of structural instabilities and functional problems, just like the market economy which is subject to cycles that need to be corrected from time to time by suitable policy and institutional measures. The collapse of Soviet communism in the early 1990s had, somehow, created such an illusory image of the infallibility of the liberal democratic order (best represented by Fukuyama's 'End of History' thesis) that inherent instabilities (or symptoms of ungovernability) were casually ignored.

While Fukuyama was proved to be over-idealistic, Huntington's 'clash of civilisations' articulation, which appeared to be more realistic, had not gone far enough into reflecting on the fundamentals of the Western liberal democratic order. During the post-Cold War decades, riding on the triumphalism of liberal democracy, the US and other leading democratic states had often pointed to the importance of democracy-building for weak and failed states in the Third World which were suffering from political conflicts and the lack of legitimacy, stability, and capability. Democracy promoters were optimistic that all states would become 'democratic' one day while accepting softer authoritarian states (such as those having 'elections without democracy') as a transition state, though cautioning that it would be possible that a new authoritarian regime might emerge.[81] So much so that even today, many Western leaders and politicians, as well as academics and commentators, gloss over the structural defects and systemic failures of liberal democracy and fail to see any merit in alternative or modified political models.

Yet an ailing democracy is plain to see. According to Larry Diamond:

> Support for authoritarianism has risen steadily around the world, including in the West: 18% of Americans would back military rule today [2019] compared to just 8% in 1995. Distrust of public institutions continues its relentless slide. And the voting share of extremist parties continues to grow in most democracies.[82]

Formal processes and institutions of democracy are becoming a façade as politicians increasingly engage in empty rhetoric but fail in the substance of governance while the populace increasingly loses its faith in the political system and its ability to deliver equality and better life. Some new democratic states in Central and Eastern Europe have reverted to semi-authoritarianism and illiberalism. Therefore, the spread of political disaffection and the rise of populism is essentially an outcome of democratic failure.[83] Many in the West have recently shifted the blame to China as a major culprit in the erosion of an international order that has outlasted its good old days.[84] To face the crisis of democracy, some consider it important to unpack not only the normative presumptions one has in relation to what democracy is and should be but also the recent transformations in the way politics is understood and practised in contemporary societies.[85]

To Francis Fukuyama now, state building on the output side is as crucial as the building of democratic elections, accountability, and checks and balances on the input side.[86] It has only been more recently that some in the leading democratic states started to question if their own democracy is failing and giving way to political extremism and demagogues. As Steven Levitsky and Dianiel Ziblatt have warned lately, 'elected autocrats' are subverting democracy.[87] These autocrats are not confined only to former military rulers, communist party apparatchiks, or hard-core socialists in post-communist or weak states. Demagogues and 'autocratic' leaders, with the former US President Donald Trump epitomising the phenomenon,[88] as well as nativist political movements, can also come from within old established democracies long-held as role models for the democratising nations. Mainstream parties in Europe are being discredited and fringe radical parties are coming to centre stage, such as those in Southern Europe like the Podemos (radical left) in Spain, the Five Star Movement (radical right) in Italy, and the Syriza party (radical left) in Greece, to name a few.

This book is not the place to discuss the full list of pros and cons of democracy. Suffice it to say that the less we view democracy as a perfect system or a simplistic universalist framework, the less we risk becoming over-presumptive about what it can deliver in practice and underplaying the limits of a democratic system in the real world. In a similar vein, if we do not label a non-liberal democracy as necessarily out of place or even evil, allowing more room for the co-existence, mutual engagement, and competition of diverse political systems and regime types internationally according to a common set of rules on the grounds of reciprocity, it would be more conducive to teasing out those fundamental elements of governance, public services, economic growth, social cohesion, environmental sustainability, and political stability that all states and societies could share and should aspire to achieve. The fact that Hong Kong is not a full-fledged democracy does not mean we should ignore or disparage what has been achieved and what is important in delivering the real results of governance, and should not drive us into total despair about the city's future. At the same time, the quest for democratisation, while important to promoting bottom-up participation and a popular mandate for the government, should not lead us into a blind faith that once we have established universal suffrage and other formal democratic institutions, then all problems will be solved.

Hong Kong's autonomy and way of life remain protected by the Basic Law even though the actual space of autonomy needs to be negotiated and renegotiated amid changing geopolitical and geo-economic equations, as discussed in Chapter 12. Many states across the world—in particular transitional states—are hybrid regimes of some kind,[89] and some see Hong Kong within the conceptualisation of a 'hybrid state' too, where the rulers use various mobilisation and electoral strategies to suppress dissent and opposition.[90] As argued at the outset of this book, Hong Kong under British rule was an atypical colonial regime. After 1997, the Hong Kong SAR has operated as a special and therefore atypical local administration of an authoritarian Chinese central state—with a free economy, free society, separate legal jurisdiction, and a polity subordinate to and yet somewhat detached from the central system. The central government prefers Hong Kong to be more integrated into the motherland, and Hong Kong people want their own way of life (or existentialism) fully safeguarded. Between 'national security' (from the central government's perspective) and 'local freedom', the balancing point for a mutually acceptable degree of local autonomy and democracy must be found. Right now, both sides are still in the process of searching for such a delicate point.

Can a polity long conditioned by colonial authoritarianism, and now under the jurisdiction of an authoritarian central state growingly nervous about the SAR becoming a runaway enclave, ever evolve into a de facto near-democratic system? This has been a thought-provoking question for both the local population and observers of Hong Kong governance. Or will there be democratic backtracking in the aftermath of the 2019 crisis because of Beijing's heightened distrust of popular elections which it regards as only favourable to the pan-democrats? The political future remains volatile amid an uncertain state of trust. Given that Hong Kong has already developed a rather sophisticated system of legislative and DC elections, yet with restrictive functional representation dominating the election of the CE and a sizable component of the legislature, it has become tempting to perceive and analyse the SAR regime in terms of 'electoral authoritarianism' (i.e., the use of unfree competition by the forces in power to subdue the opposition and civil society).[91]

Some have conceptualised Hong Kong politics within the notion of liberal authoritarianism with the possibility to change in ways paralleling Singaporean electoral authoritarianism.[92] There has also been the suggestion that the SAR regime falls in between liberal authoritarianism and electoral authoritarianism.[93]

It is too early to form any firm classification lest it confines the scope of imagination and actions. The real world entails much more than a simple binary choice between democracy and authoritarianism. As 'a white horse is not a horse', any form of hybridity is not exactly of the same property as the generic or semi-generic description. If there is more mutual goodwill and more respect for history and realism between the SAR and central state, Hong Kong could well become a new hybrid local regime that practises a decent degree of accountable politics grounded in both popular mandate and central authority. What counts most is how any such regime relates to the local society, economy, the nation, and the world to deliver its best in policies, regulations, and services, to enable the population to enjoy safety and affluence and thus to have pride in the city and its government. That is what politics is ultimately about for all nations and municipalities.

Epilogue
Hong Kong Exceptionalism at a Crossroads

Understanding the administration and bureaucracy has always been the key to understanding Hong Kong's governance and politics. Throughout the colonial era, the Governor-led senior bureaucracy operated as the unchallenged rulers supported by the cooperation of business and professional elites. Major reforms of the bureaucracy (the McKinsey reforms in the 1970s, then public sector reform in the late 1980s–1990s) helped modernise the colonial administration but did not alter its bureaucratic nature. In the name of continuity when entrenching an executive-led system, the administrative mandarins (the AOs) were originally prepared for running the new SAR as a successor administrative-state after reversion to Chinese sovereignty on 1 July 1997.

The 1984 Sino-British settlement was essentially premised on a strategic expectation on both sides that the city's status quo, and the stability and prosperity it was deemed to represent, could be extended at large. This expectation was also widely shared by the local population—both elites and grassroots—who felt anxious about an uncertain future. Thus, Hong Kong did not go through a proper process of decolonisation and national reunification. Because of this, there was no opportunity to critically reflect on the deficiencies and wrongs of a political order dominated by British colonial rulers, nor to passionately ponder and embrace the prospect of nationhood (as part of China). In the actual process of negotiations between Britain and China in the early 1980s, the former got what it wanted by keeping 'British' institutions intact in the new Hong Kong SAR, while the latter secured a clear recognition of its sovereignty and 'national' authority over the city. The future of Hong Kong seemed largely frozen in a 1980s-like state. Such an incomplete journey of reunification, in a way, paved the path for subsequent contradictions, tension, and distrust within the local society and between the city and the rest of the country.

The old framework of governance ('executive-led', government by bureaucrats) was regarded as unproblematic. The pre-existing financial, business, and professional elites were allowed to hold sway in the new SAR regime through constitutional design under the Basic Law which was interpreted as mandating 'business as usual' and the continuing separation between China and Hong Kong as in British days. Some pertinent issues (notably, executive-legislative relations and the roles of political parties and the civil service) were simply swept aside presuming that the old framework would still function beyond 1997. The understanding of 'One Country, Two Systems' was initially in favour of mutual non-intervention such that Hongkongers would expect and presume Beijing to leave Hong Kong alone to mind its own business save defence and foreign affairs.

Such presumptions, however, failed to anticipate new contexts and new interpretations and dispositions arising in the post-1997 environment. While the handover logic of maximum continuity and minimal change had worked to pacify doubting minds and bring about a relatively smooth and peaceful transition, it also sowed the seeds of instability and discontent after reunification when internal and external crises served to expose the more deep-seated political, administrative, economic, and social anomalies. In a way, Hong Kong has become the victim of its success by setting 'minimal change' as a condition for reunion with China. It is still very much in a transitional mode of de-institutionalisation without replacement by properly functioning new political institutions displaying a coherent logic. There exist gaps of institutionalisation to be filled, failing which political uncertainties and disorder are but expected, and if these are allowed to persist, then they will likely feed into a new path dependence that will hinder necessary reforms.

Local politics began to loom large even during the pre-1997 transition period. Administration and politics became entangled, which was probably 'normal' for a modern and pluralistic society. The challenge to both the Chinese central government and Hong Kong SAR government was how to cope with the changing political environment while maintaining a high degree of continuity and stability. The hitherto administrative-cum-political path dependence was shifted because of economic setbacks and social upheaval in the initial years of regime change, leading to an unanticipated crisis of the civil service that in turn induced the unfinished 1999 civil service reform and the introduction of a half-baked ministerial system of political appointments. Given that the ministerial system has proved insufficiently attractive to outsiders to pursue a political career, the senior bureaucrats, especially the AOs, have soon regained prominence with the installation of government-by-political bureaucrats under Donald Tsang and continued under Carrie Lam.

Political parties (pro-establishment or pan-democratic) have all failed to establish themselves as viable alternatives to the bureaucracy as the mainstay of government and stability. In the absence of a clear commitment on the part of the central state in Beijing to promote electoral democracy as the principal logic of governance in the SAR, these parties remain under-developed. Short of any real opportunity in forming government and delivering what they advocate in their manifestos, political parties tend to be high-sounding but vague in policy ideas and engage in 'blaming and shaming' politics, but would otherwise shy away from supporting the making of hard policy choices. The unenviable responsibility of the government falls back on the bureaucrats as the remaining pillar of effective rule and administrative stability. There is no route for grooming 'responsibility' politics through elections.

Things have turned into a vicious cycle. Multiple structural disparities have become obvious: using a traditional administrative regime to govern an increasingly pluralistic and vocal society; relying on a centrally blessed and appointed CE lacking popular mandate to exercise 'executive-led' authority over legislative politics that are backed by district and functional sectoral interests; keeping political parties that seek only to expose government ills and raise public expectations but never having the chance or obligation to deliver what they preach; and persisting with a largely administrative culture when dealing with political or politicised problems. Government is inherently weak rather than strong as constitutionally implied, increasingly dragged down by executive-legislative disconnect and gridlock. Policy deliberations now take longer cycles yet result in more limited decisions and actions.

Starting in the 1970s, the former colonial laissez-faire approach gradually gave way to a more positive mode of non-interventionism. The advent of social activism and electoral politics during the 1980s–1990s brought about more willingness to intervene through social and economic measures, especially after the outbreak of the Asian financial crisis. Among the post-1997 CEs, both Tung Chee-hwa and Leung Chun-ying, as outsiders, were known for embracing proactive government. For the two former civil servants brought up in the tradition of fiscal conservatism, Donald Tsang had formally discarded positive non-interventionism after becoming CE while Carrie Lam is also noted for more proactive steering and policy intervention. A kind of soft state-developmentalism seems to be taking root despite the still fiscally conservative administrative mindset prevailing within the bureaucracy.

In contrast to an administrative superclass able to command, direct, and take risks with a 'can do' spirit in the colonial past, present-day bureaucrats are often handicapped by multi-institutional checks and constraints as well as various political challenges to their authority. The institutionalisation of functional sectors has enabled business and other vested interests to entrench and proliferate their rent-seeking tendencies to the extent of sometimes obstructing even mild social reforms, thereby precipitating the discontent of the masses and their perception of a grossly unjust political system cemented by government-business collusion. The cost of being daring has become too high for the government. A conventional administrative mindset is also ill-equipped to respond to ever-changing national and international politics all serving to define Hong Kong's autonomy and political manoeuvrability.

The limitations and defects of bureaucratic government are well known. They need to be accepted as the price for the lesser evil of a non-democratic yet somehow professional administration. Unlike many former British colonies becoming independent after the Second World War, with the notable exception of Singapore, Hong Kong's civil service as inherited from British legacy has continued to thrive as a meritocracy disposed towards respecting efficiency and procedural justice. The independent judiciary is another inherited pillar of fair rule. Whereas judges largely stay above politics, the upper echelons of the civil service cannot do so. It is incumbent upon their political masters and our politicians and media to protect them from over-politicisation, otherwise such a final pillar of fair and effective administration might become eroded. After the 2019 crisis, which saw the political demise of Carrie Lam, once acclaimed as a highly competent administrator, the credibility of this pillar has been seriously tarnished.

The quest for self-administration under 'One Country, Two Systems' has been accompanied by four decades of slow democratisation in Hong Kong. By now, it is clear that Beijing's interpretation of self-administration and its attitude towards democracy are quite at variance with the aspirations of many locals. History and experience across nations and societies tell us that there is no one single mode of democracy. The same ideals of democracy, freedom, and equality have driven successive social and political revolutions and the establishment of democratic states since the late eighteenth century. In the real world, democratic systems vary in structure and practice, and are mostly a mixture of new formal institutions and inherited traditions and practices as well as logic from the ancien régime, resulting in different hybrids all in the name of democracy. The Hong Kong SAR regime is no longer the near-autocratic bureaucratic regime of the colonial past; neither has it been transformed into an electoral democracy. Its state form is not a replication of the party-state on the Mainland even though some diehard critics like to denigrate it as the agent or puppet of an authoritarian central regime.

The decline in trust in government institutions and the rise in executive-legislative gridlock are not problems unique to Hong Kong. They are now prevalent in Western democracies as well. Policy reforms have become less easy to push in many countries and regions because of growing social divisiveness and political polarisation. The middle ground is fast giving way to right-wing and left-wing populism. Younger generations everywhere have become disillusioned. There is a global crisis of governance. Old democracies are seen cracking, while some of the new democracies born out of old dictatorships and autocratic or authoritarian regimes (such as in Central Asia, Eastern Europe, and the Middle East) have reverted to old practices in new institutional wrappings. For instance, political cronyism has not disappeared in Taiwan after democratisation.[1] Over-emphasis on the distribution of power and checks and accountabilities in the global democracy discourse has led to less attention being given to the essence of governance (i.e., the capacity to deliver effective policies, economic growth, and social stability for the well-being of ordinary people). Hong Kong should learn from the lessons of such failure in democratic transitions.

The practice of 'One Country, Two Systems' has unleashed various dilemmas for Hong Kong exceptionalism. This should not come as a total surprise. Contradictions are part of the historical compromise. It demands mutual trust and accommodation, plus a sense of realism, for the political compact to work. Grievances and uneasiness have loomed large on both sides. As the Mainland becomes stronger economically and more assertive politically, Hong Kong people feel their own identity and perceived freedoms and autonomy dwindling, displaying the politics of 'fear of losing' in the national security, national education, and extradition debates. Beijing, on the other hand, questions why many Hongkongers do not care about national security and identity as much as nationals in other countries. The rise of localism and nativism is a worldwide trend. However, as localism in Hong Kong evolves into separatism that negates the Mainland and disrespects central-state authority, it has, not surprisingly, led to a strong reaction on the part of Beijing. An SAR that only looks introvertly and ignores the larger national connection and context will not assure the Mainland that it adds value to the nation. As a result, both sides are easily prone to feelings of being 'under threat'.

The relationship between the two systems is not the same as between two equal partners, but is instead a delicate balancing act between the superordinate and subordinate within a unitary party-state system, requiring mutual respect, compatibility, and accommodation in order to facilitate smooth coexistence. It demands political wisdom, good common sense, pragmatism, and mutual empathy on both sides to make things work. There exist both pessimistic (even fatalist) and cautiously positive views about Hong Kong's political future, with probably more of the former at this juncture in time. Pessimistic sentiments are driving pan-democrats towards the more aggressive and confrontational end of the political spectrum, which in turn triggers and reinforces Beijing's perception of a growingly hostile local polity that must be tamed by whatever means available. This explains the move in recent years by the central state to (re)assert its constitutional authority and jurisdiction over the SAR—officially justified as correctly implementing 'One Country, Two Systems' but framed by many local critics as tightening its grips over the territory.

After the disruptions caused by the 2014 Occupy Central and Umbrella Movement protests, and then the escalated political confrontations starting in 2019, opposition politics have become dominated by anti-Mainland radicals who champion separatism and self-determination. Even moderate pan-democrats now believe that under President Xi Jinping, the central government has been less flexible and more high-handed towards Hong Kong, especially over the issue of democratic reform. Hostilities towards Beijing from those with pan-democratic and localist views also gained added impetus from former US President Donald Trump, who fanned the flames of hate to portray China as a global public enemy, resulting in a hardline reaction from Beijing to counter foreign conspiracies.[2]

Out of despair, many among the radicalised younger generation and within the pro-democracy camp bet Hong Kong's future on the prospect of the fall of the CCP regime in China. They either engage in a doomsday rhetoric of mutual destruction or refuse to entertain incremental reforms, as common in the colonial period, to make the Hong Kong system function better. This is tantamount to wishful thinking and strategic sleaziness. The realist approach is to have China's party-state system factored in as a larger given, within which to map out the city's strategic future. As ultimately the tail cannot wag the dog, Hong Kong has to try to thrive in the narrow geo-political and geo-economical lanes it has been given.

The changing parameters of 'One Country, Two Systems' due to shifting perceptions and sentiments on both sides and the intensification of Mainland-Hong Kong interactions have together generated new problems that need to be properly addressed and turned into new opportunities, rather than hostilities and threats. Under the Basic Law, with dual loyalty and accountability to both the CPG and SAR, the CE is supposed to serve as an intermediary between the two systems and political domains. However, the experience since reunification indicates that the dual loyalties and accountabilities are difficult to reconcile, to the extent that a CE gaining Beijing's confidence tends to lose the trust of many in the local population. The higher such distrust becomes, the more likely the CE will be perceived as merely a Beijing-loyal official instead of a leader able to coalesce and articulate local interests and aspirations while safeguarding national dignity and interests. The resulting tension does not serve Hong Kong well.

It is unlikely the coming years will see the end of the tunnel in democratisation, but they will certainly determine if Hong Kong's administrative governance will remain functional as the SAR approaches 2047. Hong Kong today can no longer replicate the story of 'governing without democracy' of the colonial past because some seeds of democracy have already been sown to curb the power and autonomy of the bureaucracy. Furthermore, the CE's power and autonomy cannot match those of the British Governor, and the conditions for nurturing and sustaining self-confident and relatively liberal and compassionate bureaucratic leaders without popular support are wearing thin. The fact is that society is growing more and more fragmented and polarised, and more people seem to be losing faith.

Hong Kong's past glory was achieved through creative adaptability and an entrepreneurial spirit. Today, Hong Kong people have to search for opportunities and windows of change within the geo-political realities of the nation and the region. The ultimate risk is the loss of a sense of purpose and pride in Hong Kong's hybridity and willingness to make the best out of given constraints, some of which are beyond domestic control. Hong Kong exceptionalism can be pessimistically viewed as a neither/nor situation or more positively contemplated within an either/or mindset of strength, pragmatism, and possibilities. However, even for a solution short of full democracy and autonomy, a lot more effort needs to be made by all political players concerned to allow such exceptionalism to work.

Such a relatively positive note to end this book may well be questioned given the tragic series of recent anti-government confrontations and disruptions, which have brought Hong Kong to the brink of ungovernability. The deterioration of US-China relations will only make the international geopolitical environment worse for Hong Kong. Even though the government machinery still seems to be functioning smoothly in a business-as-usual manner, deep-seated incompatibilities within the system of governance have been laid bare. The extradition bill controversy has served to explode a series of time bombs. The ensuing mass protests have transformed into a movement that both challenges the political order and casts doubt on the 'One Country, Two Systems' model. More people have become convinced that it is necessary to take radical action against the government to safeguard what they regard as Hong Kong's core values and way of life.[3]

Largely in response to the above shift, Beijing has proceeded to overhaul its policy and strategy regarding Hong Kong. The fourth plenary session of the 19th CCP Central Committee in October 2019 concluded it would take responsibility for the city's governance seriously, pledging to 'govern [the SAR] in strict accordance with the constitution and the Basic Law' and to 'establish a sound legal system and enforcement mechanism for safeguarding national security'.[4] Shen Chunyao (沈春耀), Chairman of the NPCSC Constitution and Law Committee (previously known as the Law Committee) and Director of the Hong Kong Basic Law Committee, further said that the system for the appointment of the CE and Principal Officials would be improved, implying a more proactive exercise of central authority. In early 2020, the two central organs on Hong Kong affairs were restructured and top personnel reshuffled.[5]

Both the Lam Administration and CPG are most concerned about the collapse of law and order, with the latter particularly wary of foreign manipulation and intervention. Heavy-handedness in suppressing disruptions and violent protests, in order to end the unrest, seems unavoidable. However, it is questionable if that alone can restore Hong Kong to order and normalcy. Because of this continuing unrest, together with the lingering impact of the COVID-19 pandemic, Hong Kong's economy has suffered its worst contraction in a decade and is expected to undergo steeper recession in the months ahead. Major credit rating agencies have downgraded their rating of Hong Kong, although it still maintains a 'stable' outlook.[6] The added impact of the new national security law and US measures to terminate Hong Kong's separate trade status should not be under-estimated. Meanwhile, the pandemic is likely to weaken many Western powers and see the further rise of China.[7]

Although the protest movement has lost some steam over time, pessimism and fatalism abound about the demise of Hong Kong given the damage done to Hong Kong-Mainland relations, the loss of hope of many in the younger generation in 'One Country, Two Systems', and the tightening of sovereign control by Beijing.[8] Does that leave any room for change for the better? Is there a way for Hong Kong to get out of this conundrum? Arguably, Hong Kong is not alone in this world of social unrest, mass protests, and bloody clashes.[9] Other large cities have seen similar trials recently, leaving some to wonder why certain cities rebel. One suggestion is that they are all facing a crisis of social mobility and grievances over inequality.[10] Hong Kong has no shortage of such frustrations, and the lack of democratic progress has reinforced stronger sentiments of disillusionment and political discontent that feed into a growing process of radicalisation, first germinated during the 2014 Occupy Central protests. Escalating violence and disorder since 2019 have alarmed many. As commented by a newspaper editor, Hong Kong is locked in a death spiral of 'hatred, narrow-mindedness and a lack of compassion'.[11]

To find a breakthrough, hope in the future has to be re-cultivated. After the 1967 anti-British riots, when the narrative of this book begins, the British administration first used military-police joint operations to end the riots. Thereafter, it underwent a transformation in governance strategy and established a new brand of government-people relations, supported by successive administrative and social reforms. Simply relying on police suppression cannot be the only means used to break the cycle, as the prolonged protests show. Law enforcement must go hand in hand with political reconciliation and reform. There needs to be a major paradigm shift in governance. Is the SAR government capable of learning from the wisdom of the previous colonial rulers half a century ago to unleash an era of institutional renewal and hope? Is the national leadership in Beijing willing to embrace a more flexible and constructive interpretation of the 'One Country, Two Systems' policy to let Hong Kong shine as an atypical metropolis of the nation and give the younger generation a stronger sense of stake in Hong Kong, China, and the future? Can the young people of Hong Kong become more receptive towards national concerns while asserting their local identity?

Across the boundary, politics aside, every step forward by Mainland cities is mostly a step of progress. With Beijing less trusting of Hong Kong, and both Shanghai and Shenzhen becoming more innovative and competitive than Hong Kong in many aspects, it begs the question whether there is still a prominent place for Hong Kong in the national landscape. Building on its pre-1950s industrial foundation, Shanghai has quickly learned and added new elements to become China's pre-eminent metropolis leading the Yangtze River Delta megalopolis. Today, Shanghai is more self-confident than Hong Kong and aspires to plan big, whereas Hong Kong is bogged down in internal strife and despair despite its still impressive performance scorecard. Shenzhen, once a Hong Kong satellite, has outgrown the Hong Kong model. Having found its unique high-tech route after being rejected for integration by Hong Kong in the 1990s, Shenzhen now has the capacity to be a close rival in several areas given its ability to attract talent and investors from all over the country.

During a visit to London in early 2017 as Secretary for Transport and Housing, I asked to hold a sharing session with leaders and international experts of the maritime services sectors there. The question from them that disturbed me most was: 'Why do you say Hong Kong is so special and attractive as a hub when Singapore is closer to Asia and Shanghai is at the heart of a booming China?' Their undertone was that Hong Kong might find itself at the margin of major happenings in this region. Thus, Hong Kong people must honestly ask themselves where Hong Kong's comparative advantage lies and what kind of hybrid would serve Hong Kong best, both inside and outside China. Hong Kong exceptionalism ought to be redefined and reinvigorated under the new circumstances and realities.

'Can Hong Kong exceptionalism last?' The answer hinges on how Hong Kong people at large can assure Beijing that the SAR will not become a threat to the national system (sovereignty or national security) or a political burden (diminishing economic benefits and increasing political costs), but will instead deliver stable and effective governance different from and yet complementary to the Mainland system. Otherwise, there is no strong incentive for China to keep Hong Kong exceptional. Any thought of the city under US or international 'protection', as championed by some radical activists and pan-democratic politicians, is illusory and leads nowhere. In response to such interference, Beijing will only harden its political judgement that they refuse to accept that Hong Kong today is China's Hong Kong. While the national security law implemented in Hong Kong in July 2020 is a start to helping Beijing feel less insecure about the SAR, it is still unclear if central government officials will begin to encourage some necessary reforms to improve the SAR's governance and standing in order to enable 'One Country, Two Systems' to continue.[12]

These are times of uncertainty and volatility, of despair to some and of hope for change to others. With enough mutual goodwill and big-picture courage, Hong Kong's exceptionalism could continue to thrive because it defines its political, cultural, and economic distinctness (and therefore its sense of purpose) within the context of a renaissance of the Chinese nation. The substance of that exceptionalism will not stay stagnant. Whether or not it will be as vigorous as before and sustainable is the major litmus test of China's 'One Country, Two Systems' mega-project, which does not seem likely to end abruptly in 2047 even though it might assume a readjusted form based on the experience and lessons learned since 1997 and the changing local, national, and geopolitical conditions.[13] If indeed it is an appropriate juncture now to begin contemplating the longer future of Hong Kong, and if 'One Country, Two Systems' is destined to become a more permanent feature of China in this century, then the events since 2019 may only be a small wave in the long river of history.

Both Beijing and Hong Kong should reflect on the frustrations and tensions since reunification, come away from past mindsets, prejudice, and myths, and proceed from a new set of realities and aspirations to breathe new life into a novel constitutional framework originally born out of contingency thinking. A major historical choice is waiting to be made, with no less significance than the choice made for 1997.

Postscript

By the time this book was externally reviewed, revised, and finalised in July 2020, Hong Kong was entering a new era upon the promulgation of a new national security law. Beijing's post-2019 responses to Hong Kong's tumultuous crisis did not stop with this law, however. In March 2021, the NPC approved an 'improved' electoral system for the SAR to ensure that only 'patriots' will administer the city.[1] The NPCSC promptly amended Annexes I and II of the Basic Law in the same month, followed by the speedy passage of local SAR legislation to implement the changes in May 2021.[2] The full implications of the new national security law and revamped electoral system are not covered in the present text. Thus, this Postscript briefly considers if the latest situation warrants any adjustments to the fundamental analysis in this book.

China interpreted the events and turbulence in Hong Kong over the past two years as a separatist attempt tantamount to a 'colour revolution' instigated by some external forces and was determined to nip it in the bud. The harsh backlash from Beijing was beyond the expectation of many pan-democrats, some of whom had previously got too close to the *laam chau* (or 'mutual destruction') strategy of those extremists who harboured the illusion of an international crusade to bring down the Chinese communist regime. Immediately upon the NPCSC's enactment of the national security law, then US President Donald Trump signed the Hong Kong Autonomy Act in July 2020 to impose sanctions on foreign individuals and entities for 'contributing to the erosion of Hong Kong's autonomy' as well as an executive order to end its special status under the 1992 Hong Kong Policy Act that previously accorded special treatment to the SAR different from the rest of China. Other Western countries followed suit with various restrictions and sanctions and annulled their extradition agreements with Hong Kong. Critical foreign commentators similarly decried the so-called demise of the 'One Country, Two Systems' framework.[3]

After the NPC approved the new electoral rules for Hong Kong, the pan-democrats labelled the move as an unprecedented political regression.[4] British Foreign Secretary Dominic Raab asserted that 'Beijing's decision to impose radical changes to restrict participation in Hong Kong's electoral system constitutes a further clear breach of the legally binding Sino-British Joint Declaration'.[5] The G7 countries and European Union expressed grave concerns at the decision to fundamentally erode the democratic elements of the electoral system in Hong Kong and called on China to act in accordance with the Sino-British Joint Declaration and its other legal obligations as well as to respect fundamental rights and freedoms as provided for in the Basic Law. The European Union High Representative in Hong Kong even stated that 'China is consciously dismantling the "One Country, Two Systems" principle in violation of its international commitments and the Hong Kong Basic Law'.[6]

Hong Kong's national security law, like similar laws around the world, is harsh and gives sweeping powers to law enforcement. It has imposed an entirely new set of legal perimeters which Hongkongers are not used to and do not fully understand. The urgency of the law stems in part from the city failing to enact local legislation in accordance with Article 23 of the Basic Law for over two decades, such that Beijing could no longer wait. It was also driven by the worsening geopolitical environment that has alerted Beijing to a looming national security crisis in Hong Kong.[7] In the 'new cold war', the US and its close allies are on an all-out offensive against China and the communist party. For Beijing, an 'open city' like Hong Kong is a significant risk in terms of national security. The new law provides for a parallel enforcement and procuratorial mechanism outside the jurisdiction of the SAR for special circumstances through the central government's national security office in Hong Kong.[8] Should the US-China conflict escalate, Beijing will likely become even more concerned about national security in the city and further precautionary actions might be taken.

A law induces behavioural adaptations and cultural shifts. While the new national security law maintains the importance of respecting human rights and those rights and freedoms protected by the Basic Law as well as those stipulated in two international covenants as applied to Hong Kong, ordinary people will be more affected by how the law is applied and enforced in practice. Any attempts to maximise the punitive impact of the law, or to 'weaponise' it for other reasons, are bound to lead to extending its scope, by default if not by design, to various spheres of civil life, thus triggering the public's concern about exercising their conventional freedoms in expression and action. The challenge to the central and SAR governments is how to keep national security enforcement in proper judicial check and minimise the risk of creating new grievances, increasing political distrust, and lending further ammunition to international hostility. At the time of writing, 117 people have been arrested on national security offences, with more than 60 charged so far.[9]

The NPCSC's latest rewriting of the SAR's electoral rules has essentially derailed the original track of constitutional development according to Beijing's December 2007 roadmap based on a gradual expansion of the democratic base. A new path is to be set while the 'double universal suffrage' target remains unchanged in the Basic Law. The proportion of directly elected seats on universal suffrage is more than halved from 40 (including 5 'super-district council seats' officially defined as functional constituencies) out of 70 seats (i.e., 57%) to 20 out of an expanded legislature of 90 seats (or 22%) with the super-seats abolished. The bulk of the legislative seats now goes to the CE Election Committee—40 out of 90 seats (or 44%). A fifth sector of 300 local NPC delegates and CPPCC members as well as local branch representatives of national organisations will join the present four-sector 1,200-member Election Committee to make it more attuned to safeguarding 'national interests'.

Corporate voting by designated organisations, ex-officio or nominated seats, and election by members of government-appointed district-level committees, such as Area Committees and Fight Crime Committees (in lieu of elected DC members) have replaced individual voting in Election Committee sub-sector elections. For the LegCo, proportional representation has been replaced by a 'double seats, single vote' method in geographical constituencies. Of the 30 functional constituency seats, only 7 are to be elected by individual electorates (not counting the seats from the Heung Yee Kuk and the constituency of representatives of national institutions and local branches of national organisations), while the rest will be determined by corporate electorates. These changes will likely return more legislators whose mode of operation is less aggressive than that of previous (especially pan-democratic) legislators mandated by popular geographical or functional votes. In addition, all legislative candidates must obtain nominations from the Election Committee in addition to the electorate of their respective constituencies. A new Eligibility Review Committee will vet all candidates for public office to ensure they meet the 'patriot' requirement, supported by investigations of the Police's national security branch and recommendations of the national security committee chaired by the CE.

Post-2019, the loyalty of the civil service to the Basic Law constitutional order, especially among young civil servants, has been questioned by the central government and the local pro-establishment camp. Civil servants have been reminded that they form part of the national governance system of the PRC. They now have to take a mandatory oath of allegiance or sign a declaration to uphold the Basic Law, swear allegiance to the Hong Kong SAR, and be responsible to the SAR government. Those who refuse to sign will be asked to leave the service.[10] The replacement of Matthew Cheung (an AO by background) by John Lee (formerly Secretary for Security and a police officer by background) as CS in late June 2021 was widely perceived as a signal of Beijing's displeasure with the performance of the AO-turned-political bureaucrats during the 2019–2020 political crisis. The undertone calls for resolute political loyalty from the AOs.

Backed by the new national security law, the SAR government likely feels empowered and even obliged to investigate suspected subversive activities by individuals and organisations (including media outlets critical of the government), to provide stricter guidance for schools, and to enact laws against 'fake news' and 'doxing', etc., measures which will tranquilise the social and political environment. While this will naturally give Beijing more political reassurance that Hong Kong will not become a rebel city again, the national security law cannot by itself turn political impasse into harmony. Electoral changes can minimise the pan-democrats' presence in the legislature, but the changes will not turn their large base of supporters within the population into government enthusiasts. The tension over maintaining 'two systems' and the divisive politics of identity are too deep-seated. They call for a process of reconciliation to win hearts and minds, and demand a political solution involving major stakeholders.

This book is about the nature and characteristics of Hong Kong exceptionalism in governance since the 1970s when Hong Kong was under British rule. Such exceptionalism survived the reversion to Chinese sovereignty in 1997 and the advent of a new constitutional context under China's 'One Country, Two Systems' framework, though not devoid of dilemmas, stress, and conflict between the two existentialisms. Witnessing what has transpired during the past two years, it is clear Hong Kong has entered yet another era. The big question at this most critical juncture is whether 'One Country, Two Systems' will remain on track and whether Hong Kong can continue to be exceptional and, if so, in what sense. The answer to this depends on what happens next, but understanding the past will also help explain how we have arrived at this point and why.

Hong Kong under British rule grew into one of the 'four little dragons' of the East Asian economic miracle despite the absence of democracy. It was the city's free economy, open society, rule of law, cosmopolitan status, and international connectedness which together made it tick and impressed the then Chinese leaders so much. Beijing's belief back in the 1980s and 1990s was that by respecting Hong Kong's then status quo and consolidating (or 'freezing') it under the constitutional safeguards of the Basic Law, the city's long-term future and prosperity would be ensured. There was no evidence of Beijing agreeing to such a blueprint with the intention of not delivering on it. Since then, however, interpretations and understandings have changed, and perceptions and sentiments have shifted. The post-1997 path of Hong Kong's exceptionalism has never been smooth.

On the surface, the 1997 handover did not alter much in terms of social and economic institutions. Politically, the pre-existing bureaucratic and business elites continued to run the new SAR, joined by the Beijing-coopted loyalists. However, there were two major points of departure from the British colonial setup. First, under the post-1997 notion of 'self-administration' as promised by the Basic Law, achieving electoral democracy by universal suffrage has become a unifying political cause for the majority local population, whereas Beijing does not believe in Western-style democracy. How to develop local democracy within an authoritarian party-state gaining increasing self-confidence upon China's rapid economic rise is a thorny problem to tackle. The deteriorating mutual trust in recent years has made this even more difficult, not to mention Beijing's growing conviction that the pan-democrats and separatists are using democracy for usurping power and forcing a regime change.

Second, in 1997, Hong Kong exited the Western 'free world' and reunited with a motherland with a historical legacy that is significantly different from Western civilisation. The long-term significance of Hong Kong's return to China's orbit was little noticed initially, but its return has increasingly shaped the city's future under 'One Country, Two Systems', where the 'one country' implications are as pertinent as the 'two systems' features. Hong Kong people as well as central government officials have been experiencing uneasiness in different ways about the 'two systems' interactions. The political controversy in 2019 was unanticipated, but when it came, it quickly led to an implosion because of the accumulated tension and distrust.

The more specific cause was the *laam chau* actions of the radical protagonists seeking foreign intervention to force Beijing to succumb to their demands. Facing polarising and hostile global geopolitics, Beijing is now determined to rid the SAR of any threat, real or potential, of regime change and destabilization. It seems clear that Beijing hopes to suppress the electoral power of the pan-democrats who are believed to be obstructing and even sabotaging the regime. With some of their leading figures facing trial for public security and national security charges, the pan-democrats are in a great dilemma: 'To be or not to be [within the revamped political order]?' They can still win some (though much fewer) legislative seats thanks to their popular support base, but their participation would be accused by the radicals as whitewashing an 'unfair' system. They must re-frame the narrative of political opposition to impress on their supporters that being 'inside' rather than 'outside' a legislature, even with reduced popular representation, will still be meaningful. All this requires some serious soul searching and reflection on past strategies, successes, and failures.

With one stroke by the central state the local political landscape has been significantly redrawn. Even the present pro-establishment parties feel the pressure to deliver 'constructive' politics instead of simply counter-balancing the pan-democratic force in the legislature as in the past because the latter will only have a marginal presence, if felt at all. By extensively reconstituting the sector-based Election Committee as a key political vehicle to elect both the CE and the bulk of the legislative seats, Beijing seems to be hoping that the future LegCo will be more disciplined and supportive of the government and that the local polity will not fall into impasse again. Gone will be the days of incessant filibusters and procedural delays by pan-democratic legislators. However, the Election Committee is not a closely knit caucus. If not properly managed, given the proliferation of small segments within its structure, the Election Committee might risk leading to further fragmentation of the SAR polity.

There is growing international concern that Hong Kong has had many of its past freedoms curbed and its autonomy and rule of law reduced.[11] The independence of the judiciary has been called into question even though the courts continue to adhere to common law principles while also upholding the new statutes enacted locally or by the NPCSC. The 'fall of Hong Kong' has become an eye-catching depiction not just among foreign media outlets but also in academic circles. Considering these pessimistic sentiments, it is easy for many to conclude that the new national security restrictions and electoral rewriting, along with any future corrective actions in other arenas such as education and the media,[12] would together amount to a death knell for democracy and for Hong Kong.

Democratic progress may be stalled, at least for now. However, it will not evaporate if a new breed of committed politicians and civil society leaders can keep the faith and work to make the best out of the current circumstances within the confines of the national security law. They need to be strategic and pragmatic, and to engage better with the Mainland. It is not the end of the beginning but the beginning of a new end. The challenge remains to strive for a sustainable political future for Hong Kong as part of China despite all odds. The pro-democracy movement started in the 1970s and 1980s from almost nothing, when a subdued colonial legislature was entirely appointed by the British administration. Many early democrats supported reunification with China and were fully prepared to work for democracy within an as-yet uncertain post-1997 system with hope that China would modernise and liberalise. Despite the serious setback due to the faulty strategies and miscalculations by many pan-democrats, which resulted in the undoing of previous achievements in political reform, it may still be possible to start anew if there exists the long-term will and commitment. However, a new path must be recognised, one that is defined by some reinforced ethos as well as newly introduced features: executive-led, central-state control, political screening based on the 'patriots to administer' principle, selective electoral franchise, an Election Committee-dominated legislature, and a largely marginalised pan-democratic opposition. The post-1997 logic of governance relying on administrative competence and conventional (i.e., business and professional) elite support has come to a turning point. New institutional logic will emerge with an uncertain (and yet-to-be tested) modus operandi carrying constraints, risks, and opportunities. The political culture of the city will also change.

Crucially, Hong Kong will not have a stable future if it continues to be perceived as a threat by China. At present, mutual trust is fragile, and rebuilding this trust will be a painstaking process. Conditional trust is still possible so long as circumstances are not simply considered as zero-sum and there is better mutual understanding of opportunities and limitations for the city. The central leadership should still value the merits of Hong Kong's plurality, freedoms, common law system, and judicial independence, *so long as* the city functions within the boundary (or so-called 'red line') of 'patriotism' and duly safeguards national security. This boundary is not entirely rigid—the more trust there is from Beijing, the more room for Hong Kong's autonomy and plurality. It is also affected by the global geopolitical environment. The extreme turbulence of the past two years has created a perfect storm of distrust, ultimately resulting in Beijing losing its patience with Hong Kong. All sides have to learn a hard lesson.

According to the World Bank's 2019 global governance indicators, released in September 2020, while Hong Kong continued to rank high in all other aspects, it suffered a severe fall in terms of political stability and absence of violence and terrorism—from 74.8 to 36.7 out of 100. There was also a considerable decline in 'voice and accountability' from 62.1 to 54.2.[13] These changes can mainly be attributed to the escalating political unrest and violence as well as Beijing's response measures. With the outbreak of the COVID-19 pandemic, Hong Kong's economy has plunged enormously, with GDP for 2020 down by 6.1% and unemployment more than doubling to 7% in February 2021,[14] though the latter figure subsequently moderated to 6.4% in May 2021. By July 2021, the government has already spent some HK$320 billion on anti-epidemic support and relief, but its coffers are not unlimited despite the hefty reserves accumulated over the years.[15]

Hong Kong's future is under multiple threats—notably those stemming from Beijing's distrust, Western boycotts and marginalisation, and uncertainties in national integration. Hong Kong desperately needs to be reinvented in the new era, to see regional integration (such as the Greater Bay Area) as an opportunity (not a threat), and to effectively play its role in 'serving national needs where Hong Kong is the best' (國家所需,香港所長). However, one sure route to Hong Kong's demise is the evaporation of its relative value to a rising China. The sanctions and other restrictive measures imposed on Hong Kong by the US and its allies serve to erode its international hub status, inducing the departure of capital and professional talent. Hong Kong leaders must find ways to respond.

While many people in Hong Kong (especially the younger generation) may lack self-confidence, they need to learn how to distinguish between the real and perceived aspects of losing institutional vibrancy. Hong Kong is not facing an imminent collapse of its social, economic, administrative, or judicial institutions which have taken generations to build—not yet anyway. Hong Kong's civil society still compares favourably with other open societies. Local politics will hopefully revive to some extent (albeit in a new, limited form) after the electoral changes settle. Whether such politics can support a reasonable level of democratic representation and checks on government actions, of course, has yet to be tested and largely depends on the praxis of a new generation of politicians and activists. Under the 'One Country, Two Systems' framework, Hong Kong must learn how to display its visibility and assert its voice *within* the nation, not *against* the nation.

Despite the economic boom of Mainland metropolises such as Shanghai and Shenzhen, Hong Kong is still given special status under the Basic Law. It enjoys more civil freedoms, a different legal system, entrenched judicial independence, more extensive international connectedness, and a more cosmopolitan outlook. Such features and their underlying core values will only dwindle if Hong Kong people do nothing to preserve them and grow them further. Hong Kong must keep both a national face and an international face. Without its Mainland affinity and advantage, Hong Kong cannot sustain its global impact. However, only looking inward and relying solely on 'internal economic circulation' within China may also weaken its international advantage. The challenge lies in finding a balance and establishing a mission for the city.

A Hong Kong without China's trust cannot go far. The city is undergoing a bigger test than what it faced in 1997. If it cannot pass this test, the prospects for the next phase of the 'One Country, Two Systems' model and of Hong Kong's exceptionalism will become dimmer and less certain. Paraphrasing Charles Dickens in *A Tale of Two Cities* (1859), it is the best of times, it is the worst of times, it is the age of wisdom, it is the age of foolishness, it is the epoch of belief, it is the epoch of incredulity.[16] It is a crucial time for Hong Kong people to reflect on the way forward and not let themselves fall into a self-fulfilling prophecy.

Anthony Cheung
August 2021

Notes

Preface

1. The Chinese Dream, targeting the goal of 'great renewal of the Chinese nation' (to realise a prosperous and strong country for the well-being of the people and to revive national glory) is attributed to State President and Party General Secretary Xi Jinping's agenda of making China strong after his ascendency to supreme power in 2012. See *Xinhuanet*, 'Chinese Dream — Special Report' (in English), www.xinhuanet.com/english/special/chinesedream/; see also *The Economist* (2013) 'Xi Jinping and the Chinese Dream', editorial, 4 May, p. 11.

2. As a civil servant from 1974 to 1986, I worked in Customs and Excise (then known as Preventive Service), the Commerce and Industry Department, the Finance Branch of the Government Secretariat, the Public Works Department, a District Office in the New Territories, and the ICAC.

3. I was one of the founders of the Democratic Party and served on both the LegCo (1995–1997) and the ExCo (2005–2012), as well as a wide range of statutory and advisory boards and committees (including civil service pay bodies). In 2002, I co-founded an independent policy think-tank SynergyNet. During the 1980s and 1990s, I had the opportunity to be involved in the discussions and debates with Mainland officials and academics over the drafting of the Basic Law and political development.

4. K. Hopkins (ed) (1971) *Hong Kong: The Industrial Colony — A Political, Social and Economic Survey*, Hong Kong: Oxford University Press.

5. C.K. Leung et al. (eds) (1980) *Hong Kong: Dilemmas of Growth*, Hong Kong and Canberra: Centre of Asian Studies, University of Hong Kong, and the Research School of Pacific Studies, Australia National University, Canberra.

6. The COVID-19 pandemic is an ongoing pandemic of coronavirus disease 2019, which is caused by severe acute respiratory syndrome coronavirus 2 (SARS-CoV-2). See World Health Organisation, 'Naming the coronavirus disease (COVID-19) and the virus that causes it', www.who.int/emergencies/diseases/novel-coronavirus-2019/technical-guidance/naming-the-coronavirus-disease-(covid-2019)-and-the-virus-that-causes-it.

7. Lam Woon-kwong is a former senior civil servant who has risen to the ranks of Director of Education, SCS, and Secretary for Home Affairs. He has also served as the Chairman of the Equal Opportunities Commission (2010–2013) and Convenor of Non-Official Members of the Executive Council (2012–2017).

Introduction

1. In the New Territories, DOs were of a senior rank (at the directorate level of the civil service) and operated as a separate system under the Secretary for the New Territories, previously known as District Commissioner New Territories. In 1981, the two systems of DOs were merged under a new department named City and New Territories Administration headed by a

Super-Secretary (first known as Secretary for City and New Territories Administration and then Secretary for District Administration).

2. Local academic work on Hong Kong's post-war social and economic development mostly highlights the achievements of the MacLehose era, notably T. Lin et al. (eds) (1979) *Hong Kong: Economic, Social and Political Studies in Development*, New York: M.E. Sharpe; A.Y.C. King and R.P. Lee (eds) (1981) *Social Life and Development in Hong Kong*, Hong Kong: Chinese University Press.

3. For example, the former Colonial Secretariat which coordinated the whole of the government machinery was renamed Government Secretariat in 1976, with the Colonial Secretary (who deputised the Governor) retitled Chief Secretary.

4. In the Introduction to its White Paper on the 1984 Sino-British Joint Declaration, the British Government revealed that: 'In the course of the negotiations, Her Majesty's Government explained in detail the systems which prevail in Hong Kong and the importance for these systems of the British administrative role and link.' See British Government (1984) *White Paper: A Draft Agreement between the Government of the United Kingdom of Great Britain and Northern Ireland and the Government of the People's Republic of China on the Future of Hong Kong*, 26 September, Hong Kong: Government Printer (reproduced), para. 10.

5. Ye Jianying (葉劍英), Chairman of the NPCSC, delivered *An Address to Taiwan Compatriots* on 30 September 1981, spelling out nine principles to facilitate peaceful national reunification (known as 'Ye's Nine Principles'). See Permanent Mission of the People's Republic of China to the United Nations (1981) 'Chairman Ye Jianying's Elaborations on Policy Concerning Return of Taiwan To Motherland and Peaceful Reunification', 30 September, New York: United Nations (UN), www.china-un.org/eng/zt/twwt/t28922.htm. On 11 January 1982, Deng Xiaoping for the first time put the 'nine principles' into a specific concept — 'One Country, Two Systems' — under which two different systems would be allowed to co-exist and the relevant policies might be applied, not just to Taiwan but also Hong Kong. See Hong Kong SAR Government (n.d.) Publication on the 15th Anniversary of Reunification, Ch. 1, www.basiclaw. gov.hk/en/publications/book/15anniversary_reunification_ch1_1.pdf (accessed in June 2019, but the link is no longer active).

6. With the stalemate over the sovereignty issue removed in March 1983, the two sides moved on to the second stage of negotiations focusing on more detailed issues. In early June 1984, China and Britain established a working group at the ambassadorial level to draw up the agreement. On 18 September 1984, the two sides made concessions to each other on issues regarding the military garrison, social security, the formation of the legislature, the draft of the agreement and so on, reaching consensus on all issues. On 26 September 1984, the heads of the Chinese and British delegations, representing the two governments, initialled the Sino-British Joint Declaration and its three Annexes. On 19 December 1984, in the Great Hall of the People in Beijing, Chinese Premier Zhao Ziyang (趙紫陽) and British Prime Minister Margaret Thatcher signed the Sino-British Joint Declaration.

7. Hong Kong subsequently provided a model for China in establishing stock exchanges in Shenzhen and Shanghai, and in land and housing administration reforms (including the disposal of state lands through auctions and the privatisation of collective housing).

8. In panic some people raided local supermarkets for all kinds of items, including toilet paper, in anticipation of the collapse of the economy and subsequent chaos.

9. J. Yam (1999a) 'The Creation of the Linked Exchange Rate', *Viewpoint*, Hong Kong Monetary Authority, 4 November, www.hkma.gov.hk/eng/publications-and-research/reference-materials/

viewpoint/19991104.shtml. Joseph Yam was the former Chief Executive of the Hong Kong Monetary Authority (1993–2009).

10. L. Kraar (1995) 'The Death of Hong Kong', *Fortune*, 26 June, http://archive.fortune.com/magazines/fortune/fortune_archive/1995/06/26/203948/index.htm.

11. S. Prasso (2007) 'Oops! Hong Kong is hardly dead', *Fortune*, 28 June, http://archive.fortune.com/magazines/fortune/fortune_archive/2007/07/09/100122332/index.htm?postversion=2007062816.

12. C. Patten (1997) 'Governor's Speech at the Farewell Ceremony of the Hong Kong Handover 1997', 30 June, www.americanrhetoric.com/speeches/chrispattenhongkonghandoverceremony.htm.

13. For example, P. Bowring (2018) 'A slow death for Hong Kong's separate identity in China', *South China Morning Post*, 24 October. Philip Bowring is a journalist who has been based in Asia since 1973.

14. R. Wong (2020) ' "This is the end of Hong Kong": Reactions pour in as Beijing proposes security law', *Hong Kong Free Press*, 22 May, https://hongkongfp.com/2020/05/22/this-is-the-end-of-hong-kong-reactions-pour-in-as-beijing-proposes-security-law/.

15. For a good discussion of this, see J.A. Caporaso and D.P. Levine (1992) *Theories of Political Economy*, New York: Cambridge University Press. Surveying different political economy traditions — from classical to neo-classical and Marxist approaches, and their later-day extensions — Caporaso and Levine argue that politics and economics are not reducible to one another.

16. Hong Kong's port city status continued throughout the industrial period. Indeed, Hong Kong was the world's busiest port until the turn of the century (about 2005), before the rise of Singapore, Shanghai, and then Shenzhen as Asia's new container port cities. Aviation transport also expanded rapidly during this time so that by the mid-1990s, Hong Kong had already surpassed Tokyo Narita as the world's busiest international cargo airport.

17. E. Chen and R. Ng (2001) 'Economic Restructuring of Hong Kong on the Basis of Innovation and Technology', in S. Masuyama et al. (eds) *Industrial Restructuring in East Asia: Towards the 21st Century*, Singapore and Tokyo: Institute of Southeast Asian Studies and Nomura Research Institute, pp. 209–238.

18. Census and Statistics Department (2020e), *National Income*, 'Table 036: Gross Domestic Product (GDP) by Major Economic Activity — Percentage Contribution to GDP at Basic Prices', www.censtatd.gov.hk/hkstat/sub/sp250.jsp?tableID=036&ID=0&productType=8.

19. S.W. Chiu and T. Lui (2009) *Hong Kong: Becoming a Chinese Global City*, London: Routledge.

20. *Ibid.*

21. See, for example, S. Steinmo (2008) 'Historical Institutionalism', in D. Della Porta and M.J. Keating (eds) *Approaches and Methodologies in the Social Sciences: A Pluralist Perspective*, Cambridge, UK: Cambridge University Press, pp. 118–138. Historical institutionalists believe history matters because political events happen within a historical context which has a direct consequence on decisions and events. Furthermore, actors or agents can learn from experience, and behaviours, attitudes, and strategic choices all take place inside particular social, political, economic, and even cultural contexts. Expectations are also moulded by the past.

22. K. Dowding (2017) 'Australian exceptionalism reconsidered', *Australian Journal of Political Science*, Vol. 52, No. 2, pp. 165–182.

23. N. Matsuda (2003) 'Exceptionalism in Political Science: Japanese Politics, US Politics, and Supposed International Norms', *Electronic Journal of Contemporary Japanese Studies*, Vol. 3, Paper No. 4.

24. D.T. Rogers (1998) 'Exceptionalism', in A. Molhol and G.S. Wood (eds) *Imagined Histories: American Historians Interpret the Past*, Princeton, NJ: Princeton University Press, pp. 21–40 (quote at p. 22).

25. Quoted in M. Lamont and M. Fournier (1992) 'Introduction', in M. Lamont and M. Fournier (eds) *Cultivating Differences: Symbolic Boundaries and the Making of Inequality*, Chicago and London: University of Chicago Press, pp. 1–17.

26. K. Dowding (2017), op. cit., p. 178.

27. S.M. Lipset (1996) *American Exceptionalism: A Double-Edged Sword*, New York: W.W. Norton.

28. B. Humphrey (2016) 'Russian Exceptionalism: A Comparative Perspective', *Politics in Central Europe*, Vol. 12, No. 1, pp. 9–20.

29. G. Nolte and H.P. Aust (2013) 'European exceptionalism?' *Global Constitutionalism*, Vol. 2, No. 3, pp. 407–436.

30. R. Hughes (1968) *Hong Kong: Borrowed Place, Borrowed Time*, London: Andre Deutsch.

31. K.C. Chan (陳冠中) (2005) *My Generation of Hongkongese* [in Chinese, 《我這一代香港人》], Hong Kong: Oxford University Press, preface. Chan is my contemporary — we were in the same class at the University of Hong Kong in 1971–1974. He formed his articulation on Hong Kong hybridity based on his personal experience growing up in the city since the 1950s.

32. K. Louie (2010) 'Introduction — Hong Kong on the Move: Creating Global Cultures', in K. Louie (ed) *Hong Kong Culture: Word and Image*, Hong Kong: Hong Kong University Press, pp. 1–8.

33. W.S. Law (2009) *Collaborative Colonial Power: The Making of the Hong Kong Chinese*, Hong Kong: Hong Kong University Press. Law was critical of such interpretations which implied that 'the British never exploited Hong Kong economically, and Hong Kong remained not an imperialist-dominated terrain but a neutral arena where both Western and Eastern cultures could intermingle' (p. 1).

34. I. Scott (1989) *Political Change and the Crisis of Legitimacy in Hong Kong*, Hong Kong: Oxford University Press.

35. S.K. Lau (1987) *Decolonization without Independence: The Unfinished Political Reforms of the Hong Kong Government*, Occasional Papers No. 19, Hong Kong: Centre for Hong Kong Studies, Chinese University of Hong Kong.

36. S.K. Lau (1994) 'Hong Kong's "ungovernability" in the twilight of colonial rule', in Z.L. Lin and T.W. Robinson (eds) *The Chinese and Their Future: Beijing, Taipei, and Hong Kong*, Washington, D.C.: AEI Press, pp. 287–314.

37. C.K. Choy (蔡子強) and S.L. Lau (劉細良) (1996) 'The Executive-Legislative Relations in Hong Kong before 1997' [in Chinese, '九七回歸前夕的香港行政與立法關係'], *Hong Kong Journal of Social Sciences* (《香港社會科學學報》), No. 8, Autumn, pp. 237–266.

38. See, for example, S.K. Lau (2002a) 'Hong Kong's partial democracy under stress', in Y.M. Yeung (ed) *New Challenges for Development and Modernization: Hong Kong and the Asia-Pacific Region in the New Millennium*, Hong Kong: Chinese University Press, pp. 181–205; M. Sing (2006) 'The Legitimacy Problem and Democratic Reform in Hong Kong', *Journal of Contemporary China*, Vol. 15, No. 48, pp. 517–532; I. Scott (2005) *Public Administration*

in Hong Kong: Regime Change and Its Impact on the Public Sector, Singapore: Marshall Cavendish; I. Scott (2007) 'Legitimacy, governance and public policy in post-1997 Hong Kong', *Asia Pacific Journal of Public Administration*, Vol. 29, No. 1, pp. 29–49; J.T.H. Tang (2008) 'Hong Kong's continuing search for a new order: Political stability in a partial democracy', in C. McGiffert and J.T.H. Tang (eds) *Hong Kong on the Move: 10 Years as the HKSAR*, Berkeley, CA: University of California, Berkeley, pp.18–36; N. Ma (2011) 'Value Changes and Legitimacy Crisis in Post-industrial Hong Kong', *Asian Survey*, Vol. 51, No. 4, pp. 683–712.

39. I. Scott (2000) 'The disarticulation of Hong Kong's post-1997 political system', *The China Journal*, No. 43, pp. 29–53.

40. W.Y. Lee (1999) 'Governing post-colonial Hong Kong: Institutional incongruity, governance crisis and authoritarianism', *Asian Survey*, Vol. 39, No. 6, pp. 940–959.

41. A.B.L. Cheung (2005b) 'Hong Kong's post-1997 institutional crisis: Problems of governance and institutional incompatibility', *Journal of East Asian Studies*, Vol. 5, No. 1, pp. 135–167.

42. J.P. Burns (2004) *Government Capacity and the Hong Kong Civil Service*, Hong Kong: Oxford University Press; I. Scott (2010) *The Public Sector in Hong Kong*, Hong Kong: Hong Kong University Press.

43. A.B.L. Cheung (2007a) 'Executive-dominant governance or executive power "hollowed-out": The political quagmire of Hong Kong', *Asian Journal of Political Science*, Vol. 15, No. 1, pp. 17–38.

44. A.B.L. Cheung (2007b) 'Policy capacity in post-1997 Hong Kong: Constrained institutions facing a crowding and differentiated polity', *Asia Pacific Journal of Public Administration*, Vol. 29, No. 1, pp. 51–75.

45. S.K. Lau (劉兆佳) (2000) 'The executive-dominant system of governance: Theory and practice' [in Chinese, 〈行政主導的政治體制：設想與現實〉], in S.K. Lau (ed) *Blueprint for the 21st Century Hong Kong* (《香港21世紀藍圖》), Hong Kong: Chinese University Press, pp. 1–36; S.K. Lau (2002a), op. cit.; B.C.H. Fong (2014a) *Hong Kong's Governance under Chinese Sovereignty: The Failure of the State-business Alliance After 1997*, Abingdon, Oxon: Routledge; B.C.H. Fong (2018b) 'Executive-legislative Disconnection in the HKSAR: Uneasy partnership between Chief Executives and pro-government parties, 1997–2016', in B.C.H. Fong and T.L. Lui (eds) *Hong Kong 20 Years after the Handover: Emerging Social and Institutional Fractures after 1997*, London: Palgrave, pp. 45–71.

46. N. Ma (2017a) 'From Executive Dominance to Fragmented Authority: An Institutional and Political Analysis', in B.C.H. Fong and T.L. Lui (eds), op. cit., pp. 21–43.

47. T.L. Lui and S.W.K. Chui (2007) 'Governance crisis in post-1997 Hong Kong: A political economy perspective', *The China Review*, Vol. 7, No. 2, pp. 1–34.

48. Such as L. Goodstadt (2013) *Poverty in the Midst of Affluence: How Hong Kong Mismanaged Its Prosperity*, revised edition, Hong Kong: Hong Kong University Press; L. Goodstadt (2018) *A City Mismanaged: Hong Kong's Struggle for Survival*, Hong Kong: Hong Kong University Press; P.K. Lee (李彭廣) (2012) *Governing Hong Kong: Lessons from Disclosed British Archival Records* [in Chinese, 《管治香港：英國解密檔案的啟示》], Hong Kong: Oxford University Press. Leo Goodstadt served as the Head of the Central Policy Unit under Governors David Wilson and Chris Patten.

49. I. Scott (2017) '"One country, two systems": The end of a legitimating ideology?' *Asia Pacific Journal of Public Administration*, Vol. 39, No. 2, pp. 83–99.

50. A.B.L. Cheung (1996a) 'Efficiency as the Rhetoric? Public Sector Reform in Hong Kong Explained', *International Review of Administrative Sciences*, Vol. 62, No. 1, pp. 31–47;

A.B.L. Cheung (1996b) 'Public Sector Reform and the Re-legitimation of Public Bureaucratic Power: The Case of Hong Kong', *International Journal of Public Sector Management*, Vol. 9, No. 5/6, pp. 37–50.

51. F. Fukuyama (2013a) 'What Is Governance?' *Governance*, Vol. 26, No. 3, pp. 347–368.

52. M. Mann (1984) 'The Autonomous Power of the State: Its Origins, Mechanisms, and Results', *European Journal of Sociology*, Vol. 25, No. 2, pp. 185–213.

53. For example, B. Chou (2015) 'New Bottle, Old Wine: China's Governance of Hong Kong in View of Its Policies in the Restive Borderlands', *Journal of Current Chinese Affairs*, Vol. 44, No. 4, pp. 177–209; P.T.Y. Cheung (2017) 'Beijing's Tightening Grip: Changing Mainland-Hong Kong Relations amid Integration and Confrontation', in B.C.H. Fong and T.L. Lui (eds), op. cit., pp. 255–286; B.C.H. Fong (2017b) 'In-between liberal authoritarianism and electoral authoritarianism: Hong Kong's democratization under Chinese sovereignty, 1997–2016', *Democratization*, Vol. 24, No. 4, pp. 724–750.

54. For example, J.P. Cardenal et al. (2017) *Sharp Power: Rising Authoritarian Influence*, National Endowment for Democracy, International Forum for Democracy Studies, Washington, D.C., www.ned.org/sharp-power-rising-authoritarian-influence-forum-report; A. Bowe (2018) *China's Overseas United Front Work Background and Implications for the United States*, US-China Economic and Security Review Commission, Washington, D.C., www.uscc.gov/Research/china%E2%80%99s-overseas-united-front-work-background-and-implications-united-states. Anti-Chinese sentiments have escalated since the outbreak of the COVID-19 pandemic in 2020. See M. Santora (2020) 'Pompeo Calls China's Ruling Party "Central Threat of Our Times"', *The New York Times*, 30 January; S. Manavis (2020) 'Covid-19 has caused a major spike in anti-Chinese and anti-Semitic hate speech', *New Statesman*, 29 April.

55. B.C.H. Fong (2017b), op. cit.; A. Lecours and J. Dupré (2018) 'The emergence and transformation of self-determination claims in Hong Kong and Catalonia: A historical institutionalist perspective', *Ethnicities*, Vol. 20, No. 1, pp. 3–23.

56. Such as W.M. Lam and C.Y. Lam (2013) 'China's United Front Work in Civil Society: The Case of Hong Kong', *International Journal of China Studies*, Vol. 4, No. 3, pp. 301–325; B.C.H. Fong (方志恒) (ed) (2015) *Hong Kong Reformation Thesis* [in Chinese,《香港革新論：革新保港，民主自治，永續自治。為香港前途而戰], Taipei: Azothbooks (漫遊者文化), pp.18–36; K. Bradsher (2017) 'Once a model city, Hong Kong is in trouble', *The New York Times*, 29 June, www.nytimes.com/2017/06/29/world/asia/hong-kong-china-handover.html.

57. B.C.H. Fong (2017c) 'One Country, Two Nationalisms: Center-Periphery Relations between Mainland China and Hong Kong, 1997–2016', *Modern China*, Vol. 43, No. 5, pp. 523–556; R.C. Bush (2016) *Hong Kong in the Shadow of China: Living with the Leviathan*, Washington, D.C.: Brookings Institution Press; P. Preston (2016) *The Politics of China-Hong Kong Relations: Living with Distant Masters*, Northampton, MA: Edward Elgar.

58. While some people harbour preconceptions about the 'evil' of communist regimes, there is an alternative analysis that seeks to organically connect today's Communist China with Ancient China. For example, Wang Fei-ling has argued that the Chinese ideation and tradition of political governance and world order — the China Order — is based on an imperial state of Confucian-Legalism as historically exemplified by the Qin-Han polity, which the present communist regime has picked up. See F.L. Wang (2017) *The China Order: Centralia, World Empire, and the Nature of Chinese Power*, Albany, NY: State University of New York Press.

Chapter 1

1. J. Mahoney (2000) 'Path Dependence in Historical Sociology', *Theory and Society*, Vol. 29, No. 4, pp. 507–548; S.E. Page (2006) 'Path Dependence', *Quarterly Journal of Political Science*, Vol. 1, No. 1, pp. 87–115; T.C. Boas (2007) 'Conceptualizing Continuity and Change: The Composite-Standard Model of Path Dependence', *Journal of Theoretical Politics*, Vol. 19, No. 1, pp. 33–54.

2. Hong Kong Government (1984a) *Joint Declaration of the Government of the United Kingdom of Great Britain and Northern Ireland and the Government of the People's Republic of China on the Question of Hong Kong*, September, now accessible from the Constitutional and Mainland Affairs Bureau, www.cmab.gov.hk/en/issues/jd2.htm.

3. *The Basic Law of the Hong Kong Special Administrative Region of The People's Republic of China* [widely known as simply the Basic Law], passed by the NPC of the PRC on 4 April 1990. Article 5 stipulates that 'the previous capitalist system and way of life shall remain unchanged for 50 years'.

4. When Admiral Charles Elliot seized Hong Kong island for Britain during the First Opium War, the Foreign Secretary, Lord Palmerston, was not pleased and dismissed the island as 'a barren island with hardly a house upon it'. What he had hoped to acquire was Zhoushan (Chusan), an island at the mouth of the Yangtze River south of Shanghai. For this and more, see F. Welsh (1994) *A History of Hong Kong*, London: HarperCollins, pp. 104–109. In 2020, Zhoushan-Ningbo was the fourth largest port in the world ahead of Hong Kong, while Shanghai was number one.

5. After its establishment in Nanjing in 1927 following the Northern Expedition, the ROC government launched a movement to annul old (unfair) treaties and conclude new ones with some foreign powers, especially in relation to so-called 'international settlements', leased concessions, and extra-territorial arrangements. In 1930, it was able to get back Xiamen and Weihaiwei (now Weihai) from Britain through diplomatic negotiations. See *Daily Headlines* (《每日頭條》) (2017) 'Attempts by Republican Government to recover Hong Kong' [in Chinese, 〈國民政府試圖收復香港始末〉], 26 July, https://kknews.cc/zh-hk/history/8ez3kg4.html.

6. Taking the view that the whole of Hong Kong was Chinese territory, the PRC's position for many years was that the question of Hong Kong came into the category of unequal treaties left over from history, to be settled peacefully through negotiations when conditions were ripe, and that pending a settlement the status quo should be maintained. In March 1972, the Chinese government wrote to the Chairman of the UN Special Committee on the Situation with regard to the Implementation of the Declaration on the Granting of Independence to Colonial Countries and Peoples. The letter maintained that the settlement of the question of Hong Kong was a matter of China's sovereign right and that consequently Hong Kong should not be included in the list of colonial territories covered by the Declaration. See British Government (1984), op. cit., Introduction, para. 4.

7. The Basic Law, op. cit., Preamble, para. 1.

8. After 1949, the PRC Government required Hong Kong Chinese to travel to the Mainland on special papers and subsequently home-return permits (回鄉證), rather than British Hong Kong-issued passports.

9. G.B. Endacott (1964) *Government and People in Hong Kong, 1841–1962: A Constitutional History*, Hong Kong: Hong Kong University Press, p. 25.

10. The Hong Kong College of Medicine, founded in 1887 and renamed as such in 1907, was subsequently subsumed within the University of Hong Kong, established by Governor Frederick

Lugard in 1911 as a university to groom and train young elites for the new China and to educate them in British imperial values.

11. The Qing Government continued to keep a mandarin office in Hong Kong — within a fortress ('walled city') in Kowloon (九龍寨城) — until its officials were expelled by the British in 1899. However, the jurisdiction over this walled city was unclear and presumed not to belong to Britain, so much so that until its clearance in the early 1990s following the Sino-British agreement, it was a hotbed of drugs and various illegal activities, with its 40,000 inhabitants living in poor and unhygienic conditions.

12. Qi Pengfei (齊鵬飛) (n.d.) 'The origin of CCP's strategy of "temporarily keeping Hong Kong intact" after the establishment of New China' [in Chinese, 〈新中國成立後中共「暫時不動香港」戰略始末〉], *People's Net* (《人民網》), http://cpc.people.com.cn. From the CCP's point of view, keeping Hong Kong's position intact under the custody of British administration would enable China to deploy a more flexible strategy in defiance of US containment of the newly established Communist regime.

13. Hong Kong Government (1984b) *Green Paper: The Further Development of Representative Government in Hong Kong*, Hong Kong: Government Printer, Ch. II.

14. N. Miners (1991) *The Government and Politics of Hong Kong*, 5th edition, Hong Kong: Oxford University Press, p. 69.

15. R. Bickers (2013) 'Loose Ties that Bound: British Empire, Colonial Authority and Hong Kong', in R. Yep (ed) *Negotiating Autonomy in Greater China: Hong Kong and its Sovereign Before and After 1997*, Amsterdam: Nordic Institute of Asian Studies Press, p. 29–54.

16. From 1991 to 1995, a non-official deputy president was appointed by the Governor to preside over the LegCo on his behalf. From 1995, members of the LegCo elected their president amongst themselves.

17. The only restriction imposed was that under the *Royal Instructions*, the Governor could not, directly or indirectly, purchase for himself any such land without the special permission of the Crown given through the Secretary of State. See Legislative Council Library (2011a) *Royal Instructions*, dated 14 February 1917, as amended up to 12 May 1991, Instruction XXXI, in InfoPack No. LC03/2011-12, Hong Kong: Legislative Council.

18. Members of the ExCo were appointed at the Crown's pleasure as nominated by the Governor, who might, upon sufficient cause, suspend the exercise of function of any of them pending the Crown's confirmation.

19. These panels normally had an ExCo member or a more experienced appointed LegCo member as the convenor.

20. A.Y.C. King (1981) 'Administrative Absorption of Politics in Hong Kong: Emphasis on the Grass Roots Level', in A.Y.C. King and R.P.L. Lee (eds) *Social Life and Development in Hong Kong*, Hong Kong: Chinese University Press, pp. 127–146.

21. A.B.L. Cheung and P.C.W. Wong (2004) 'Who Advised the Hong Kong Government? The Politics of Absorption before and after 1997', *Asian Survey*, Vol. 44, No. 6, pp. 874–894. There were some 370 statutory and advisory bodies by the early 1980s.

22. S.K. Lau (1982b) *Society and Politics in Hong Kong*, Hong Kong: Chinese University Press.

23. N. Miners (1975) 'Hong Kong: A Case Study in Political Stability', *The Journal of Commonwealth and Comparative Politics*, Vol. 13, No. 1, pp. 26–39.

24. J. Rear (1971) 'One Brand of Politics', in K. Hopkins (ed) *Hong Kong: The Industrial Colony*, Hong Kong: Oxford University Press, pp. 55–139.

25. G.B. Endacott (1964), op. cit., p. 229.

26. A.Y.C. King (1981), op. cit., p. 130.

27. W.S. Law (2009), op. cit., pp. 28–29.

28. L.F. Goodstadt (2005) *Uneasy Partners: The Conflict Between Public Interest and Private Profit in Hong Kong*, Hong Kong: Hong Kong University Press, p. 6.

29. L.F. Goodstadt (2005), op. cit., pp. 9–12.

30. A notable example was the decision to build resettlement housing after the 1953 Christmas fire that left some 50,000 squatters homeless — a historic move which paved the way for expansion into a large-scale public housing programme in the 1970s. Primary education did not become free and compulsory until 1971. Social security, initially in the form of a public assistance scheme not mandated by law as entitlement, was also only introduced in 1971.

31. L.F. Goodstadt (2005), op. cit., pp. 12–13.

32. I. Scott (1989), op. cit.

33. R. Hughes (1968), op. cit.

34. Whether or not the real reason for failing to implement constitutional change was China's opposition to introducing Western-style party politics and elections into Hong Kong, as alleged by the British Government, the point remains that for a long time political options seemed to be unavailable as a solution to the government's legitimacy difficulties, and administrative reforms offered the only 'feasible' route to help ease these and other difficulties of governance. See British Government (1994) *White Paper: Representative Government in Hong Kong*, presented to the Parliament by the Secretary of State for Foreign and Commonwealth Affairs, 24 February, Hong Kong: Government Printer.

35. The Urban Council came into being first as the Sanitary Board (with three official and two unofficial members) in 1883 to deal with sanitation and hygiene. In 1936, it was renamed the Urban Council, and its responsibilities were extended to cover a wider range of public health matters. Shortly after the Second World War, the Council was reconstituted to comprise five officials and six appointed members, but without any elected members. The first post-War election (of two members) took place in 1952, and two more elected members were added in 1954 after the abortion of the 1948 Young Plan for more extensive constitutional reforms.

36. S.Y.S. Tsang (1988) *Democracy Shelved: Great Britain, China, and Attempts at Constitutional Reform in Hong Kong, 1945–1952*, Hong Kong: Oxford University Press. The Young Plan called for the transfer of some functions of internal administration (including urban services, education, social welfare, and town planning) to a new Municipal Council constituted with an elected majority returned by universal franchise.

37. Urban Council (1966) *Report of the Ad Hoc Committee on the Future Scope and Operation of the Urban Council*, August, Hong Kong: Government Printer; Urban Council Ad Hoc Committee (1969) *Report on the Reform of Local Government*, March, Hong Kong: Government Printer.

38. Hong Kong Government (1966) *Report of the Working Party on Local Administration*, November, Hong Kong: Government Printer.

39. *The New York Times* (1974) 'Hong Kong adopts a language lain', print archive, 24 March.

40. W.S. Law (羅永生) (2015) 'Decolonization in the Cold War: Comment on Hong Kong's Movement for Chinese as Official Language' [in Chinese, 〈冷戰中的解殖：香港「爭取中文成為法定語文運動」評析〉], *Thinking Hong Kong* (《思想香港》), Vol. 6, pp. 1–20, Hong Kong: Lingnan University, https://commons.ln.edu.hk/cgi/viewcontent.cgi?article=1053&context=thinkinghk.

www.nytimes.com/1974/03/24/archives/hong-kong-adopts-a-language-law-complications-for-officials.html.

41. See Y. Zhao (1997) 'Hong Kong: The Journey to a Bilingual Legal System', *Loyola of Los Angles International and Comparative Law Review*, Vol. 19, No. 2, https://digitalcommons.lmu.edu/ilr/vol19/iss2/3.

42. Alexander Grantham (1947–1957) had been a Hong Kong cadet before the War, and both Robert Black (1958–1964) and David Trench (1964–1971) had experience in the Hong Kong colonial government. All of them returned as Governor of Hong Kong following governorship postings in other British colonies (Fiji, Singapore, and the Solomon Islands, respectively).

43. The creation of a competitive Cadet Scheme to recruit fresh students with good education to serve as core administrators in overseas colonies (beginning with Hong Kong in the early 1860s and then other colonies in later years) was in line with the Northcote-Trevelyan reform of the British civil service at the time, which was inspired by recruitment through open competitive examinations in the Indian Civil Service.

44. H.J. Lethbridge (1978) *Hong Kong: Stability and Change*, Hong Kong: Oxford University Press, p. 32. A similar cadet practice was also adopted by the big British *hongs* like Jardines, Swire, and the Hong Kong and Shanghai Bank.

45. F.J.D. Lugard (1970) *Political Memoranda: Revision of the Instructions to Political Officers on Subjects Chiefly Political and Administrative, 1913–1918*, 3rd edition, London: Cass. Frederick Lugard was Governor of Hong Kong from 1907 to 1912 and later served in British colonies in Africa, notably Nigeria where he rose to become Governor-General (1914–1919).

46. Of course, such governance was not static over the years. Factors shaping the evolutionary process included: changes in world politics and the closer geopolitical environment; shifts in the mindset of successive generations of AOs recruited from a Britain which had seen its rise and decline as a cross-continental empire, its retreat from Asia and then east of the Suez Canal in the 1950s–1960s, and its repositioning within Europe; and the gradual recruitment since the late 1960s of local Chinese into the Administrative Service who were more attuned to the local culture.

47. S. Tsang (2007) *Governing Hong Kong: Administrative Officers from the Nineteenth Century to the Handover to China, 1862–1997*, London and New York: I.B. Tauris.

48. *Ibid.*, p. 188.

49. *Ibid.*, p. 190.

50. *Ibid.*, pp. 162, 188, and 193. Quoting an interviewee, Tsang defined the local people's expectation of good governance as 'a government that was basically efficient, fair, honest, paternalistic and yet non-intrusive in the lives of ordinary people' (p. 188).

51. L. Goodstadt (2005), op. cit., p. 13.

52. S. Tsang (2007), op. cit., p. 171. Hong Kong AOs often clashed with their counterparts in Britain from the 1980s in various matters, such as trade, Vietnamese refugees, implications of British nationality acts for Hong Kong, and defence cost agreements. The frequency and intensity of governments and ministers in London leaning on colonial Hong Kong varied, and more left-wing Labour governments tended to put more pressure on the colonial government (p. 178).

53. Patten set an example of political accountability by introducing his own Governor's Question Time in the LegCo. He actively built loose alliance with party groups and cultivated politicians and legislators within his larger schemes of politics, using the media for political messaging, in order to shore up the legitimacy of government actions.

54. A.B.L. Cheung (2001) 'Some are more neutral than others', *Hong Kong Mail*, 10 May.

55. See M.K. Chan (1997) 'The Legacy of the British Administration of Hong Kong: A View from Hong Kong', *The China Quarterly*, No. 151, pp. 567–582.

56. The Patten controversy blew away any such possibility. Anson Chan, Patten's CS (and head of the civil service), was considered by some in the pro-Beijing camp as being too close to him even though Chan tried to show her loyalty by emphasising her family's patriotic background. She announced in October 1996 that she would not seek the top post. In his memoirs more than a decade after reunification, Lu Ping (魯平), Director of the Hong Kong and Macao Affairs Office of the State Council from the late 1980s up to 1997, lamented that if there had been a deputy governor as originally envisaged, the final transition and the new administration would have proceeded much more smoothly. He remarked that Tung, as a businessman but not politician and a lone leader, had to depend on the cooperation of the inherited British-groomed civil service team. See Lu Ping (魯平) (2009) *Lu Ping's Oral Recollections on Hong Kong's Return* [in Chinese, 《魯平口述香港回歸》], Hong Kong: Joint Publishing (HK) (三聯出版), p. 105.

57. In an interview one year after reunification by the pro-Beijing newspaper *Wen Wei Po* (《文匯報》), Chan was reported as saying that she had pledged to President Jiang Zemin (江澤民) that she, together with all civil servants, would incessantly support the work of CE Tung Chee-hwa. See *Wen Wei Po* (1998) 'Anson Chan had pledged to President Jiang she would support Tung Chee-hwa' [in Chinese, 〈陳方安生曾向江主席保証支持董建華〉], 5 July.

58. In the final year towards reversion to Chinese sovereignty, rumour was rife that both CS Anson Chan and FS Donald Tsang might be replaced by more loyal pro-Beijing figures. In the event, both were retained in their original posts as were all other incumbent local Chinese Secretaries, including Peter Lai who occupied the more sensitive Secretary for Security post. There was no purging of the old guards, and the AOs expected they would continue to run the show under Tung's leadership.

59. Even in colonial times there were such precedent cases of appointing non-civil servants to Secretary posts, such as John Bremridge, a former Swire taipan, as FS in the early 1980s and James Blake, an engineer in private practice, as Secretary for Works in the early 1990s.

60. See G. Ure (2012) *Governors, Politics and the Colonial Office: Public Policy in Hong Kong, 1918–58*, Hong Kong: Hong Kong University Press, p. 2. Ure argues that both home and colonial government officials came from similar social backgrounds and shared common values.

61. N. Miners (1991), op. cit., p. 84. One can argue, of course, that since ExCo members were in effect nominated by the Governor with instruction to appoint from London, he would get like-minded people as his key advisers, and a situation where he would not listen to the advice of his hand-picked team would be unlikely. According to a retired senior government official, individual ExCo unofficial members with influence in London, such as British tycoons, might well have lobbied Whitehall in order to forestall any initiatives from the Governor perceived to threaten their business interests, but powerful Governors like MacLehose and Patten always got their way.

62. In the 1970s, Governor MacLehose and the then FCO had often disagreed about social reforms in the colony — see R. Yep and T.L. Lui (2010) 'Revisiting the golden era of MacLehose and the dynamics of social reforms', *China Information*, Vol. 24, No. 3, pp. 235–247.

63. J.D. Aberbach et al. (1981) *Bureaucrats and Politics in Western Democracies*, Cambridge, MA.: Harvard University Press.

64. J. Dimbleby (1997) *The Last Governor: Chris Patten and the Handover of Hong Kong*, London: Little, Brown and Company, p. 305. According to Dimbleby, Patten would not contemplate acceding to his CS's proposal and 'had been dismayed by her ill-judged attempt

in September 1995 to nobble the right of Hong Kong's newly elected politicians to introduce private member's bills, and by an earlier incident in which she had ordered a government bill to be withdrawn after it had been amended by LegCo (when she confided none too discreetly that her dubious decision had been taken to "teach the Democrats a lesson")' (pp. 354–355). Dimbleby had not interviewed Anson Chan for her side of the story.

65. Legislative Council (n.d.) *A Companion to the History, Rules and Practices of the Legislative Council of the Hong Kong Special Administrative Region*, Hong Kong: Legislative Council, Part I: 'An introduction to the Legislative Council, its history, organization and procedure', Ch. 1, www.legco.gov.hk/general/english/procedur/companion/chapter1_toc.html. Erskine May's (Clerk of the British House of Commons, 1871–1886) treatise on the law, privileges, proceedings, and usage of Parliament has remained an authoritative reference on parliamentary procedure in Hong Kong's LegCo.

66. The major powers and privileges conferred by the Ordinance covered privileges and immunities (notably freedom of speech and debate, immunity from legal proceedings, and freedom from arrest while in sitting) as well as evidence (notably the power to order attendance of witnesses, including power to issue warrant to compel attendance, and production of documents, and to examine witnesses on oath). Also, the LegCo can regulate admittance to precincts of its chamber, and the court cannot exercise jurisdiction in respect of acts of the legislature and its president or officers.

Chapter 2

1. Commission of Inquiry (presided by Justice Michael Hogan) (1967) *Kowloon Disturbances 1966: Report of Commission of Inquiry*, Hong Kong: Government Printer. One person died in the riots, dozens were injured, and over 1,800 people were arrested during the disturbances lasting from 4 to 8 April 1966. Hong Kong was in turbulent times throughout that period. A decade before the Star Ferry riots, the so-called 'Double Ten' riots occurred in Kowloon during 10–12 October 1956 when communist and KMT supporters clashed, with at least 60 people killed, some 400 seriously injured, and a large number of public and commercial buildings wrecked or damaged.

2. J. Cooper (1970) *Colony in Conflict: The Hong Kong Disturbances, May 1967–January 1968*, Hong Kong: Swindon Book Company; G.K.W. Cheung (2009) *Hong Kong's Watershed: The 1967 Riots*, Hong Kong: Hong Kong University Press; R. Bickers and R. Yep (2009) *May Days in Hong Kong: Riot and Emergency in 1967*, Hong Kong: Hong Kong University Press. A useful summary of the 1967 riots was published by The Foreign Correspondents Club (2017) 'Fifty years on: The riots that shook Hong Kong in 1967', 18 May, www.fcchk.org/correspondent/fifty-years-on-the-riots-that-shook-hong-kong-in-1967/.

3. By the time the riots subsided in December 1967, 51 people had been killed, of whom 15 died in bomb attacks, with some 830 people sustaining injuries, while about 5,000 people were arrested and nearly 2,000 of them were convicted.

4. A.A. Williams (1957) 'Administrative Adjustment of a Colonial Government to meet Constitutional Change', *Public Administration*, Vol. 35, No. 3, pp. 267–288. This article examined a similar system in colonial Singapore.

5. The Colonial Secretariat was organised into four divisions — general administration, finance, defence, and establishment. This practice of organising the Secretariat into several internal divisions to reflect groupings of functional departments was also common in other British colonies and ultimately formed the basis of ministerial demarcations once these colonies moved

to self-government and independence. See G.B. Endacott (1964), op. cit., pp. 221–222; R.L. Wettenhall (1976a) 'Modes of Ministerialization, Part I: Towards a Typology — The Australian Experience', *Public Administration*, Vol. 54, No. 1, pp. 1–20.

6. S. Tsang (2007), op. cit., p. 139.

7. Hong Kong Government (1974) *Annual Estimates of Expenditure and Revenue, 1974–75*, Hong Kong: Government Printer.

8. A. Rabushka (1979) *Hong Kong: A Study in Economic Freedom*, Chicago: University of Chicago Press, p. 83.

9. A.Y.C. King (1981), op. cit.

10. From the outset of the British acquisition of the New Territories via a 99-year lease under the Second Convention of Peking from 1 July 1898, the leased land was administered separately from the urban area, at first by an Assistant Superintendent of Police who was also the local magistrate. The Police Magistrate function continued for some years until the position was retitled as 'District Officer'. In 1910, a District Office New Territories was established, with two DOs in the early years, one for South and one for North. After the Second World War and into the 1960s, as the population increased rapidly and new towns were developed in the New Territories, the jurisdiction over the New Territories was gradually sub-divided into more offices, each headed by a DO under the oversight of a District Commissioner New Territories, who was later retitled Secretary for the New Territories after the McKinsey reforms in the mid-1970s.

11. I. Scott (1989), op. cit., p. 125.

12. As the then Deputy Secretary for Home Affairs claimed at a teach-in organised by the Current Affairs Committee of the University of Hong Kong Students' Union in April 1969: 'We have no general elections for the central government [referring to the government centre] and yet the general trends of government policy conform to the wishes of the mass of the people. [...] Our methods can certainly be improved, our thoughts thrown wider open, but we do have the essential ingredients of a democracy which has produced a general understanding of the people by the government and the government by the people' (quoted in J. Rear (1971), op. cit.).

13. Alastair Blake-Kerr, a former senior judge, was tasked with holding a Commission of Inquiry to investigate the Godber affair. Two reports were produced: A. Blake-Kerr (1973a) *First Report of the Commission of Inquiry under Sir Alastair Blake-Kerr*, Hong Kong: Government Printer; and A. Blake-Kerr (1973b) *Second Report of the Commission of Inquiry under Sir Alastair Blake-Kerr*, Hong Kong: Government Printer. MacLehose was the most critical intervening factor in a process of incremental reforms dating from his predecessor David Trench who strengthened the legal framework against corruption by amending section 10 of the Prevention of Corruption Ordinance in 1970, making any official who maintained a standard of living above that commensurate with the present or past official emoluments or was in control of pecuniary resources or property disproportionate to present or past official emoluments without satisfactory explanation guilty of an offence. Trench was, however, reluctant to set up an independent anti-corruption agency due to strong Police reservation. See R. Yep (葉健民) (2014) *Silent Revolution: A Century of Hong Kong's Collective Endeavour for Clean Government*, [in Chinese, 《靜默革命：香港廉政百年共業》], Hong Kong: Chung Hwa Book Company (中華書局).

14. There was a major challenge to the ICAC in the police confrontation of October 1977, forcing MacLehose to put a stop to actions on any corruption cases where investigations had not yet formally commenced then — known as the amnesty. While the amnesty had seriously shaken the morale of ICAC officers at the time, in hindsight it helped calm the unrest within the civil service, particularly in the Police Force, and eased the way for more targeting and effective ICAC investigations in the subsequent years.

15. As noted in A.Y.C. King (1980) 'An Institutional Response to Corruption: The ICAC of Hong Kong', in C.K. Leung et al. (eds), op. cit., p. 11.

16. For details of ICAC's achievements and recollections of the various challenges faced by it, see A.B.L. Cheung (張炳良) (2020) *Daring to Change the Sky: Extraordinary Years of Hong Kong's Anti-Corruption Pioneers* [in Chinese,《敢教日月換新天：香港反貪先鋒的崢嶸歲月》], Hong Kong: Chung Hwa Book Company (中華書局).

17. I. Scott (1989), op. cit., pp. 323–324.

18. According to the Transparency International's Corruption Perceptions Index 2019, available in July 2020, Hong Kong was ranked 16 out of 180 countries and jurisdictions, www.transparency.org/country/HKG#.

19. A.B.L Cheung (2008a) 'Evaluation of the Hong Kong Integrity System', in L. Huberts et al. (eds) *Local Integrity Systems: World Cities Fighting Corruption and Safeguarding Integrity*, The Hague: BJU Legal Publishers, pp. 105–115.

20. Jon Quah, an expert on comparative corruption studies, suggested that for an anti-corruption agency to be effective, it should fulfil six conditions, namely: it must be incorruptible; it must be independent from the police and from political control; there must be comprehensive anti-corruption legislation; it must have adequate staff and funding; it must enforce the anti-corruption laws impartially; and political will is crucial for minimising corruption. The ICAC seemed to have satisfied all these conditions. See J.S.T. Quah (2007) *Curbing Corruption in Asia: A Comparative Study of Six Countries*, Singapore: Eastern University Press by Marshall Cavendish.

21. According to Steve Tsang, 'MacLehose decided to take this novel approach partly because he felt a fresh look at the administration would be good for Hong Kong, and partly because he shared the Foreign Office's basic mistrust of the colonial government, which had been nicknamed "the republic of Hong Kong" during [David] Trench's governorship'. He added that MacLehose (himself from a diplomatic background) was keen not to be seen to have 'gone native' by his FCO colleagues. See S. Tsang (2007), op. cit., pp. 140–141.

22. McKinsey & Company (1973) *The Machinery of Government: A New Framework for Expanding Services*, Hong Kong: Government Printer.

23. By the time of the handover in 1997, the total number of Branches (retitled 'Bureaus' after the handover in accordance with the nomenclature of the Basic Law) had increased to 15 and now included: Broadcasting, Culture, and Sport; Constitutional Affairs; Civil Service; Economic Services; Financial Services; Education and Manpower; Health and Welfare; Home Affairs; Housing; Security; Planning, Environment, and Lands; Trade and Industry; Transport; Treasury; and Works.

24. See P. Harris (1988) *Hong Kong: A Study in Bureaucracy and Politics*, Hong Kong: Macmillan, pp. 135–141; Committee on the Civil Service (1968) *Report of the Committee on the Civil Service*, Vol. 1, 1966–1968, Cmnd 3638, London: HMSO.

25. R.L. Wettenhall (1976a), op. cit.; R.L. Wettenhall (1976b) 'Modes of Ministerialization, Part II: From Colony to State in the Twentieth Century', *Public Administration*, Vol. 54, No. 4, pp. 425–451.

26. S. Tsang (2007), op. cit., p. 146. My own experience as a civil servant in the late 1970s to early 1980s was that such innovative and rational 'McKinsey' style of submission and scrutiny was (at least most of time) superficial, as 'real' policy decisions and resource allocations were dictated ultimately by non-rational factors such as the preference of the Governor, the Secretary, or a department head with strong clout. Very often such top-down decisions were only

rationalised post hoc following the McKinsey template. Similar gaps between reform rhetoric and actual practice has existed in government reform initiatives in many countries and regions.

27. According to Alvin Rabushka who studied the system in the 1970s, the politics of budgeting at that time were played out through four main routes: seeking the approval by the Government Secretariat or ExCo of specific policy plans which favoured the department; screaming 'politics' to impress upon the government centre the political cost of inaction or insufficient services of the department; using the authority of technical specialist skills to bluff the Finance Branch on professional items; and establishing credibility and good relations with the Finance Branch. See A. Rabuska (1976) *Value For Money: The Hong Kong Budgetary Process*, Stanford: Hoover Institution Press, p. 136.

28. J. Yaxley (1988) *Financial Management Reforms in the Hong Kong Government*, speech delivered to the Hong Kong Branch of the International Fiscal Association, 14 November, Hong Kong.

29. N. Miners (1991), op cit., p. 91.

30. A. Gray and W.I. Jenkins (1985) *Administrative Politics in British Government*, Sussex: Wheatsheaf Books, Ch. 4.

31. N. Miners (1991), op. cit., p. 91.

32. I. Scott (1988) 'Generalists and Specialists', in I. Scott and J.P. Burns (eds) *The Hong Kong Civil Service and Its Future*, Hong Kong: Oxford University Press, pp. 17–49.

33. Hong Kong Government (1980) *Green Paper: A Pattern of District Administration in Hong Kong*, Hong Kong: Government Printer; Hong Kong Government (1981) *White Paper: District Administration in Hong Kong*, Hong Kong: Government Printer.

34. D. Akers-Jones (1984) *A Perspective of District Administration*, speech at the New Asia College Assembly, 17 February, Hong Kong: City and New Territories Administration; N. Miners (1975), op. cit., Ch. 12.

35. S.K. Lau (1982a) 'Local Administrative Reform in Hong Kong: Promises and Limitations', *Asian Survey*, Vol. 22, No. 9, pp. 858–873.

36. See, for example, R.J. Haynes (1980) *Organization Theory and Local Government*, London: George Allen & Unwin, Ch. III.

37. The 1983 National Audit Act confirmed the Comptroller and Auditor General (C&AG) as an Officer of the House of Commons and Head of the National Audit Office whose staff was no longer made up of civil servants. It gave the C&AG statutory power to produce VFM reports and enabled them to report to Parliament in a timely manner on discrete subjects. In Hong Kong, the Director of Audit was not made an officer of the LegCo but remained a public officer whose salary was directly specified by the Governor since 1979 instead of being part of the civil service pay structure.

38. See a detailed account in A.B.L. Cheung (2009a) 'Evaluating the Ombudsman System of Hong Kong: Towards Good Governance and Citizenship Enhancement', *Asia Pacific Law Review*, Vol. 17, No. 1, pp. 73–94.

39. Unlike the Audit Commission's regular VFM audit reports, which would be taken up by the LegCo's PAC formally, the Ombudsman's reports had not enjoyed such status. Under the present law, where a serious irregularity or injustice has taken place, the Ombudsman may decide to report to the CE, with a copy of the report laid before the LegCo.

40. R. Yeung (2008) *Moving Millions: The Commercial Success and Political Controversies of Hong Kong's Railways*, Hong Kong: Hong Kong University Press, pp. 68–72. The Japanese consortium was only given the contract to construct Hong Kong's first underground rail link,

with consideration at the time that an MTR Authority might be set up to manage the system once constructed. In the event, the MTRC was set up in 1975 to build and operate the underground railway system. It was fully owned by the government but otherwise run according to commercial prudence no different from a private enterprise. Indeed, should the government ask the MTRC to build and operate a subway link with return on investment below what was considered commercially viable, it had to provide 'full compensation' to the corporation under the Mass Transit Railway Ordinance.

41. Upon the electrification of the land rail, the KCRC was set up in 1982, modelled on the MTRC, to replace the Railway Department, the staff of which were dis-established from the civil service on favourable terms to become KCRC employees. Still, the KCRC was fully owned by the government until the two railway companies were merged in 2007 to become the present MTRC Limited.

42. See A. Barker (ed) (1982) *Quangos in Britain*, London: Macmillan; M. Cole (1998) 'Quasi-Government in Britain: The Origins, Persistence and Implications of the Term "Quango"', *Public Policy and Administration*, Vol. 13, No. 1, pp. 65–78.

43. The information about the 'golden handshake' payments amounting to HK$4 million was rumoured to have been leaked to the media by government directors who were unable to prevent the KCRC board from approving the payments. See R. Yeung (2008), op. cit., pp. 152–153.

Chapter 3

1. C. Hood (1991) 'A Public Management for All Seasons?' *Public Administration*, Vol. 69, No. 1, pp. 3–19; OECD (1995) *Governance in Transition: Public Management Reforms in OECD Countries*, Paris: OECD.

2. C. Hood and M. Jackson (1991) *Administrative Argument*, Aldershot: Dartmouth, p. 178.

3. OECD (1995), op. cit., p. 8.

4. A.B.L. Cheung (1999) 'Administrative Development in Hong Kong: Political Questions, Administrative Answers', in H.K. Wong and H.S. Chan (eds) *Handbook of Comparative Public Administration in the Asia-Pacific Basin*, New York: Marcel Dekker, pp. 219–252.

5. N. Panchami and P. Thomas (n.d.) *The Next Steps Initiative*, case study, London: Institute for Government, www.instituteforgovernment.org.uk/sites/default/files/case%20study%20next%20steps.pdf.

6. Finance Branch (1989) *Public Sector Reform*, February, Hong Kong: Finance Branch, p. 1.

7. See J.-E. Lane (2013) 'The Principal-Agent Approach to Politics: Policy Implementation and Public Policy-Making', *Open Journal of Political Science*, Vol. 3, No. 2, pp. 85–89, https://file.scirp.org/pdf/OJPS_2013042915421321.pdf.

8. A. Wildavsky (1964) *The Politics of the Budgetary Process*, Boston: Little, Brown.

9. In the past, internal 'provider' departments (like the Government Printer and Government Supplies Department) were allocated block budgets to cater for all the supply needs from user departments. The abolition of such block votes resulted in user departments being funded directly and having full control of their resources and purchase actions. Henceforth, provider departments had to bid for business from user departments.

10. A. Schick (1986) 'Macro-budgetary Adaptations to Fiscal Stress in Industrialized Democracies', *Public Administration Review*, Vol. 46, No. 2, pp. 124–134.

11. M. Hayllar (2005) 'Outsourcing: Enhancing Private Sector Involvement in Public Sector Services Provision in Hong Kong', in A.B.L. Cheung (ed) *Public Service Reform in East Asia: Reform Issues and Challenges in Japan, Korea, Singapore and Hong Kong*, Hong Kong: Chinese University Press, pp. 193–230.

12. Finance Branch (1995) *Practitioner's Guide: Management of Public Finances*, Hong Kong: Government Printer.

13. Efficiency Unit (1995) *Serving the Community*, Hong Kong: Government Printer, p. 43. Qualitative measures were used to monitor effectiveness — such as service trends and success rates to cover more strategic concerns, and response times and customer satisfaction levels to cover frontline service to the public. Quantitative measures were used to monitor efficiency — such as workload, costs, and productivity, and indicated overall performance to the community.

14. Civil Service Branch (1995) *Human Resource Management*, December, Hong Kong: Government Printer. It was stated that the government's aim was to 'establish a more open, flexible and caring management style so that staff will be motivated, developed and managed in a way they can and will give their best to support departments' mission' (p. 5).

15. Efficiency Unit (1995), op. cit., p. 41.

16. A.B.L. Cheung (2011) 'Performance Management in Hong Kong', in E.M. Berman (ed) *Public Administration in Southeast Asia*, London: CRC Francis & Taylor Group, pp. 295–314. An Audit Commission report in October 2005, for example, found that of the 3,262 performance measures reported by departments in the 2004–2005 financial year, only 11% related to effectiveness and 5% to efficiency. These findings underscored both the difficulties faced by government agencies in quantifying performance as well as the 'gaming' attitude of some bureaucrats. See Director of Audit (2005) 'Chapter 6: Performance measurement and reporting in the Government', *Report No. 45*, October, Hong Kong: Audit Commission.

17. Public management reforms among the developed countries of the OECD since the 1990s had often been driven by policy fashion rather than solid evidence about costs and impact, with significant over-claiming about best practices as acknowledged by the OECD itself. A good discussion can be found in OECD (2009) *Measuring Government Activity*, Paris: OECD.

18. N. Carter et al. (1992) *How Organizations Measure Success: The Use of Performance Indicators in Government*, London and New York: Routledge, p. 48.

19. See H. de Bruijin (2002) *Managing Performance in the Public Sector*, London and New York: Routledge, Table 1.1 and Ch. 2.

20. B. Ngoye et al. (2019) 'Assessing performance-use preferences through an institutional logics lens', *International Journal of Public Sector Management*, Vol. 32 No. 1, pp. 2–20.

21. J. Potter (1988) 'Consumerism and the Public Sector — How Well Does the Coat Fit?' *Public Administration*, Vol. 66, Issue 2, pp. 149–164.

22. A.B.L. Cheung (1996a), op. cit.; A.B.L. Cheung (1996b), op. cit.

23. A.B.L. Cheung (2005e) 'What's in a Pamphlet? Shortfalls and Paradoxical Flaws in Hong Kong's Performance Pledges', *Public Management Review*, Vol. 7, No. 3, pp. 341–366. An earlier study conducted by the EfU in 1998 also found that while customers seemed generally satisfied with departments' performances against their pledged standards and departments generally found the pledges useful for managing their operations and staff performance, less than two-thirds of the departments surveyed included all their services in the pledges and less than two-thirds of the customers surveyed thought the pledges had contributed significantly to service improvements. See Efficiency Unit (1998) *Survey on Performance Pledges*, August, Hong Kong, www.info.gov.hk/eu/english/pm/pm_ref/files/ppflyer.pdf (accessed in 2004, link no longer valid).

24. A.B.L. Cheung (2005e), op. cit., pp. 362–363.

25. W.D. Scott (1985) *The Delivery of Medical Services in Hospitals: A Report for the Hong Kong Government*, December, Hong Kong: Government Printer. As a result, the Medical and Health Department was broken up, with the medical services now under the Hospital Authority and a new Department of Health established to take over preventive health and clinic services.

26. A.B.L. Cheung (2002b) 'Modernizing Public Healthcare Governance in Hong Kong: A Case Study of Professional Power in New Public Management', *Public Management Review*, Vol. 4, No. 3, pp. 343–365.

27. Broadcasting Review Board (1985) *Report of the Broadcasting Review Board*, August, Hong Kong: Government Printer.

28. See a detailed account in A.B.L. Cheung (1997b) 'Reform in Search of Politics: The Case of Hong Kong's Aborted Attempt to Corporatise Public Broadcasting', *Asian Journal of Public Administration*, Vol. 19, No. 2, pp. 276–302.

29. See more analysis in A.B.L. Cheung (2006b) 'How Autonomous are Public Corporations in Hong Kong? The Case of the Airport Authority', *Public Organization Review: A Global Journal*, Vol. 6, pp. 221–236.

30. The Trading Fund Act of 1973 in Britain made possible the funding of certain government activities outside normal parliamentary supply, so that the enterprise concerned would not be dependent on annual budget appropriations for its expenditure. The Government Trading Funds Act of 1990 amended the 1973 law and provided greater flexibilities and enabling powers to trading funds, including that to borrow.

31. A.B.L. Cheung (1998b) 'The "Trading Fund" Reform in Hong Kong: Claims and Performance', *Public Administration and Policy*, Vol. 7, No. 2, pp. 105–123. If a government organisation staffed by civil servants could be allowed the same kind of financial liberalisation as a trading fund, then arguably that should be the general direction for all government departments and not just selected business-type agencies. This eventually became the trend for financial management reform under the new SAR regime and included envelope budgeting, efficiency-saving retention, and doing away with detailed line-item budgeting control.

32. C.H. Tung (1997) *Building Hong Kong For a New Era*, Address by the Chief Executive at the Provisional Legislative Council meeting, 8 October, Hong Kong: Printing Department, para. 151.

33. In 1998, GDP contracted by 5.1% in real terms according to the Economic Services Bureau (1999) *1999 Economic Prospects*, March, Hong Kong: Printing Department.

34. D. Tsang (1999) *The 1999–2000 Budget: Onward with New Strengths*, Speech by the Financial Secretary moving the Second Reading of the Appropriation Bill 1999 at the Legislative Council, 3 March, Hong Kong: Printing Department, para. 71.

35. D. Tsang (2000) *The 2000–01 Budget: Scaling New Heights*, Speech by the Financial Secretary moving the Second Reading of the Appropriation Bill 2000 at the Legislative Council, 8 March, Hong Kong: Printing Department, para. 119.

36. Civil Service Bureau (2003) *Civil Service-related Initiatives in the 2003 Policy Address*, Paper submitted to the Legislative Council Panel on Public Service, LC Paper No. CB(1)710/02-03(01), 13 January, Hong Kong: Legislative Council.

37. A.K.C. Leung (2003) *The 2003–04 Budget*, Speech by the Financial Secretary moving the Second Reading of the Appropriation Bill 2003 at the Legislative Council, 5 March, Hong Kong: Printer Department, para. 69.

38. A. Schick (1986), op. cit., pp. 124–134.

39. A.B.L. Cheung (2006a) 'Budgetary Reforms in the Two City States: Impact on Central Budget Agency in Hong Kong and Singapore', *International Review of Administrative Sciences*, Vol. 72, No. 3, pp. 341–361.

40. Meanwhile, due to the 'presidentialisation' of the CE's power especially after the introduction of the new ministerial system, the intervention and domination of the CE in macro-budgetary decisions has become more frequent in recent years, in strong contrast to the seldom-challenged supremacy of the colonial FS over fiscal and economic affairs along the tradition of the British Chancellor of the Exchequer.

41. D. Tsang (1999), op. cit., paras. 72–94.

42. The original target was 49%. Eventually only 24% of the shares were sold to private investors. The second phase of public offering was delayed because of the unfavourable economic and investment climate which could have prevented the government from achieving a good selling price. Afterwards, successive Administrations kept the government holding of MTRC Limited stock to around 76–77% of total shares.

43. A.K.C. Leung (2003), op. cit., para. 106.

44. H. Tang (2004) *The 2004–05 Budget*, Speech by the Financial Secretary moving the Second Reading of the Appropriation Bill 2004 at the Legislative Council, 10 March, Hong Kong: Printing Department, para. 93.

45. It was assumed that the MTRC could operate even more efficiently and profitably as a listed company regulated by listing rules, thus bringing better service to the consumers and improved investment income to the government as the majority shareholder. However, the reality is that the government has several conflicting roles in the MTRC — as a shareholder/investor, as the rail service and safety regulator, as the public transport fare gatekeeper, and as a funder/employer in some new railway projects (such as the XRL). The public and legislators have criticised the government severely for not imposing greater restraint over fare increases, failing to appreciate that the government is prevented to do so under listing rules whereby the majority shareholder's interests cannot override those of small shareholders (in this case mostly institutional investors who care the most about profits and dividends).

46. It was widely alleged that the Link-REIT put its short- to medium-term profitability first, upgrading and raising the rents of some well-located shopping malls in public housing estates, driving away small shops at the expense of local community customers, and selling those malls and carparks in less profitable locations to smaller investors who proved to be even more narrow-sighted and profit-driven. Today, the Link-REIT has extended its business to property development on the Mainland. Parties across the political spectrum have all viewed it as a greedy enterprise which ignores community concerns.

47. The independent review committee recommended in its March 2007 report that a new public broadcaster be constituted as a statutory body and funded primarily from the public purse to provide PSB that is genuinely universal, diverse, independent, and distinctive. It also proposed that the new public broadcaster be named Hong Kong Public Broadcasting Corporation. See Committee on Review of Public Service Broadcasting (2007) *Report on Review of Public Service Broadcasting in Hong Kong*, March, Hong Kong, www.cedb.gov.hk/ccib/eng/doc/Part%20I. pdf. However, the recommendations were rejected by both the RTHK staff as well as the Hong Kong Journalists Association. Eventually, in September 2009, the Tsang Administration decided to task RTHK to fulfil the mission as the new PSB, without changing its departmental nature. A charter, though, was subsequently issued, setting out the relationship between the government and the new RTHK, entrenching editorial independence arrangements. A broad-based board of advisers was established to enhance corporate governance and accountability.

48. E. Połońska and C. Backett (eds) (2019) *Public Service Broadcasting and Media Systems in Troubled European Democracies*, London: Palgrave Macmillan.

49. R. Reiter and T. Klenk (2019) 'The manifold meanings of "post-New Public Management" — a systematic literature review', *International Review of Administrative Sciences*, Vol. 85, No. 1, pp. 11–27.

50. For example, D.A. Harvey (2019) *Spaces of Global Capitalism*, London: Verso; M. Konings (2018) 'Against exceptionalism: the legitimacy of the neoliberal age', *Globalizations*, Vol. 15, No. 7, pp. 1007–1019; G. Gereffi (2014) 'Global Value Chains in a post-Washington Consensus World', *Review of International Political Economy*, Vol. 21, No. 1, pp. 9–37; T. Carroll et al. (2019) 'Power, leverage and marketization: the diffusion of neoliberalism from North to South and back again', *Globalizations*, Vol. 16, No. 6, Special Issue, pp. 771–777.

51. S.P. Osborne (2006) 'The New Public Governance?' *Public Management Review*, Vol. 8, No. 3, pp. 377–387; C. Pollitt and G. Bouckaert (2011) *Public Management Reform: A Comparative Analysis — New Public Management, Governance, and the Neo-Weberian State*, 3rd edition, Oxford: Oxford University Press.

52. See Efficiency Office (n.d.) *Our History*, Hong Kong: Efficiency Office, www.effo.gov.hk/en/index.html.

53. Efficiency Office (n.d.) *Past, Present and Prospective Public Sector Reform in Hong Kong*, Hong Kong: Efficiency Office, www.effo.gov.hk/en/doc/PSRHK(Eng)final.pdf.

54. Efficiency Office website information, www.effo.gov.hk/en/index.html.

55. The new PICO, established in April 2018, is responsible for policy research and innovation, co-ordination across bureaus and departments, enhancing public participation in policy formulation, and rendering assistance in co-ordination work for cross-bureau policies selected by the senior leadership of the government. It also provides secretariat support to the CE's new Council of Advisers on Innovation and Strategic Development. See Policy Innovation and Co-ordination Office (n.d.) *About Us*, Hong Kong, www.pico.gov.hk/en/about_us/PICO.html.

56. C. Hood (1996b), 'Exploring Variations in Public Management Reform of the 1980s', in H. Bekke et al. (eds) *Civil Service Systems in Comparative Perspective*, Bloomington: Indiana University Press, pp. 268–287.

57. C. Hood (1996a) 'Beyond "Progressivism": A New "Global Paradigm" in Public Management?' *International Journal of Public Administration*, Vol. 19, No. 2, pp. 151–178.

58. For example, a senior AO at the time, Simon Vickers, was concerned that 'the logic of this psycho-economic privatisation view taken to the extreme suggests that we cannot trust any public servant to do their work without a direct and complete financial incentive'. See S. Vickers (1990) *Hong Kong Country Paper — The Public and Private Delivery of Services in Hong Kong: Some Relevant Issues across the Spectrum*, Paper presented at the Pacific Economic Cooperation Conference, Kyoto, Japan, 11–20 October. Another senior AO, Patrick Hase, worried that 'if private sector management practices are to be treated as the sole form, [...] [t]here is a risk that the ethos of government will change, and certain virtues of the present system lost'. See P. Hase (1990) 'Review of E.S. Savas, *Privatization: The Key to Better Government*', *Asian Journal of Public Administration*, No. 1, pp. 119–129.

59. G.J. Ikenberry (1990) 'The International Spread of Privatization Policies: Inducements, Learning, and "Policy Bandwagoning"', in E.N. Suleiman and J. Waterbury (eds) *The Political Economy of Public Sector Reform and Privatization*, Boulder, CO: Westview Press, pp. 88–110; D. Dolowitz and D. Marsh (2000) 'Learning from Abroad: The Role of Policy Transfer in Contemporary Policy-Making', *Governance*, Vol. 13, No. 1, pp. 5–24.

60. Efforts in reconstituting policy management during the late 1980s were seen by some as 'recentralisation' within the government. See S.K. Lau (1987), op. cit., p. 33.

61. A.B.L. Cheung (1996a), op. cit.; A.B.L. Cheung (1996b), op. cit.

62. P. Dunleavy (1991) *Democracy, Bureaucracy and Public Choice: Economic Explanations in Political Science*, London: Harvester Wheatsheaf, Chs. 7–8. For more on budget-maximising, see W.A. Niskanan (1971) *Bureaucracy and Representative Government*, Chicago: Aldine-Atherton.

63. S. Huque et al. (1998) *The Civil Service in Hong Kong: Continuity and Change*, Hong Kong: Hong Kong University Press, pp. 146–149.

64. A.B.L. Cheung (1997c) 'Understanding Public-Sector Reforms: Global Trends and Diverse Agendas', *International Review of Administrative Sciences*, Vol. 63, No. 4, pp 435–457; A.B.L. Cheung (2005c) 'The Politics of Administrative Reforms in Asia: Paradigms and Legacies, Paths and Diversities', *Governance*, Vol. 18, No. 2, pp. 257–282.

65. For example, Britain was active in privatisation, but France and New Zealand opted for granting more autonomy to state-owned enterprises through means such as performance contracts. Countries like France and Germany focused on decentralisation to lower-level bodies, such as regions and communities, while the US was keen on deregulating private-sector activities.

66. S. Van de Walle et al. (2016) 'Introduction: public administration reforms in Europe', in G. Hammerschmid et al. (eds) *Public Administration Reforms in Europe*, Cheltenham: Edward Elgar, pp. 1–11.

67. A.B.L. Cheung (1996b), op. cit.

68. For example, E.S. Savas (1987) *Privatization: The Key to Better Government*, Chatham, NJ: Chatham House.

69. In March 1993, then US President Bill Clinton launched a plan to 'reinvent government', to change the culture of the federal bureaucracy away from complacency and entitlement towards initiative and empowerment. Then Vice President Al Gore was tasked with implementing this project and came up with the National Performance Review. See A. Gore, Jr. (1994) *National Performance Review*, Darby, PA: Diane Publishing; D. Osborne and T. Gaebler (1993) *Reinventing Government: How the Entrepreneurial Spirit is Transforming the Public Sector*, New York: Plume; OECD (1998) 'Government reinvention goes global', *Public Management Gazette*, No. 11, Paris: OECD.

70. S. Van de Walle et al. observed that in Europe, public administration reform programmes have usually been launched as 'grand visions, filled with hopes and dreams of real change' but actual reforms introduced often deviate from what was originally presented to the public and their effects differ substantially from what was intended. See S. Van de Walle et al. (2016), op. cit., p. 1.

71. T. Christensen and P. Laegreid (2001) 'New Public Management — Undermining Political Control?' in T. Christensen and P. Laegreid (eds) *New Public Management: The Transformation of Ideas and Practice*, Aldershot: Ashgate, pp. 93–121; J. Halligan (2007) 'Administrative Reforms in Westminster Democracies: The Long-term Results', *Journal for Comparative Government and European Policy*, Vol. 5, Nos. 3/4, pp. 524–539; G. Peters (2001) 'Administrative reform and political power in the United States', *Policy and Politics*, Vol. 29, No. 2, pp. 171–179.

72. A.B.L. Cheung (2020) 'Administrative Reform: Opportunities, Drivers and Barriers', in B.G. Peters and I. Thynne (ed) *Oxford Encyclopedia of Public Administration*, London: Oxford University Press, pp. 1–26, https://doi.org/10.1093/acrefore/9780190228637.013.1437.

73. J.G. March and J.P. Olsen (1983) 'Organizing Political Life: What Administrative Reorganization Tells Us about Government', *American Political Science Review*, Vol. 77, No. 2, pp. 281–296, quote at pp. 282–283.

74. A.B.L. Cheung (1999), op. cit.

75. K. Schedler and I. Proeller (2002) 'The New Public Management: A Perspective from Mainland Europe', in K. McLaughlin et al. (eds) *New Public Management: Current Trends and Future Prospects*, London: Routledge, pp. 164–180; A.B.L. Cheung (2006c) 'Reinventing Hong Kong's Public Service: Same NPM Reform, Different Contexts and Politics', *International Journal of Organizational Theory and Behaviour*, Vol. 9, No. 2, pp. 212–234, Table 3.

76. A.B.L. Cheung (2003) 'Public Service Reform in Singapore: Reinventing Government in a Global Age', in A.B.L. Cheung and I. Scott (eds) *Governance and Public Sector Reform in Asia: Paradigm Shifts or Business As Usual?* London: Routledge Curzon, pp. 138–162.

77. C. Hood (2002) 'Control, Bargains, and Cheating: The Politics of Public-Service Reform', *Journal of Public Administration Research and Theory*, Vol. 12, No. 3, pp. 309–332; C. Hood and M. Lodge (2006) *The Politics of Public Service Bargains: Reward, Competency, Loyalty and Blame*, Oxford: Oxford University Press.

Chapter 4

1. Hence the famous saying of Liao Chengzhi (廖承志), then Director of the State Council's Hong Kong and Macao Affairs Office, before a Chinese Manufacturers Association delegation from Hong Kong in November 1982: '馬照跑，舞照跳，換一面旗，換個總督' ('horse racing will continue, dancing parties will go on; [all that is required is] the change of flag and governor').

2. British Government (1984), op. cit., paras. 10–11.

3. Britain admitted in its White Paper on the Joint Declaration that: 'The choice is [...] between reversion of Hong Kong to China under agreed, legally binding international arrangements or reversion to China without such arrangements. This is not a choice which H.M. Government have sought to impose on the people of Hong Kong. *It is a choice imposed by the facts of Hong Kong's history*' (emphasis added); see British Government (1984), op. cit., para. 29.

4. It was suggested that even after Anson Chan was appointed as the first Chinese to head the civil service in the post of CS, her access to official documents should be limited on the grounds that she did not have formal 'Positive Vetting' clearance. See L. Goodstadt (2005), op. cit., p. 41.

5. The Basic Law Drafting Committee was established under the NPC in June 1985, comprising 36 members from relevant Mainland organs and 23 members from Hong Kong mostly notable figures (covering business, the professions, pro-Beijing organisations, and a few independents). In December 1985, a Basic Law Consultative Committee was constituted locally by the Drafting Committee to provide a platform for consulting the Hong Kong community during the course of deliberations and on the draft provisions of the Basic Law. There were altogether 180 members, some nominated by designated organisations and some invited directly by Drafting Committee members.

6. The first version (1986) contained the draft structure of the Basic Law. The second and third versions (versions 1 and 2 of 1987) respectively provided a Collection of Draft Provisions of the various Chapters prepared by the relevant Subgroups of the Drafting Committee, and the Draft Consolidated Texts of the Basic Law. The fourth and fifth versions (in 1988) were the pre-public Draft Basic Law and public Draft Basic Law (for solicitation of opinions), respectively. The sixth version (in 1989) was the Draft Basic Law agreed by the Standing Committee of the 7th NPC at its 6th meeting on 21 February 1989 for issue to the public for consultation. The seventh version (1990) was the final Draft Basic Law submitted to the NPCSC on 16 February 1990 and then to the 3rd plenary session of the 7th NPC on 4 April 1990.

7. Under the Basic Law, the Basic Law Committee (comprising both Mainland and Hong Kong members) must be consulted prior to the NPCSC giving an interpretation of any provisions of the Basic Law or before a bill for amendment of the Basic Law is made to the NPC.

8. Under the so-called 'through-train' arrangement, China would recognise all members of the LegCo serving the final term prior to the July 1997 handover, as well as pre-existing top officials and judges, and allow them to stay on after 30 June as the legislators, principal officials, and judges of the new SAR subject to certain procedural formalities. The only change would be the selection and appointment by Beijing of a new CE. The *Decision on the Method for the Formation of the First Government and the First Legislative Council of the Hong Kong Special Administrative Region*, passed by the NPC on 4 April 1990, provided that '[i]f the composition of the last Hong Kong Legislative Council before the establishment of the Hong Kong Special Administrative Region is in conformity with the relevant provisions of this Decision and the Basic Law [...], those of its members who uphold the Basic Law [...] and pledge allegiance to the Hong Kong Special Administrative Region [...], and who meet the requirements set forth in the Basic Law of the Region may, upon confirmation by the [SAR] Preparatory Committee, become members of the first Legislative Council of the Region' (para. 6).

9. Address by Deng to Basic Law Drafting Committee members on 16 April 1987. See X.P. Deng (鄧小平) (1993) *Selected Works of Deng Xiaoping* [in Chinese, 《鄧小平文選》], Vol. 3, Beijing: People's Press, p. 220.

10. Deng's remarks on maintaining prosperity and stability in Hong Kong when meeting the delegation of Hong Kong compatriots attending national day celebrations in Beijing on 3 October 1987. See X.P. Deng (1993), op. cit., p. 75.

11. S.K. Lau (1987), op. cit.

12. S.K. Lau (1987), op. cit., p. 39.

13. The colonial government did not allow any activities that would upset the delicate geopolitical status quo, such as overt KMT hostilities towards the CCP in the 1950s, as it would not be able to enjoy a comfortable time should Beijing decide to take back Hong Kong by military force or engage in active intervention into colonial Hong Kong's domestic affairs. The 1967 anti-British riots by local pro-Communists only came to an end because the CCP leadership decided not to support the overthrow of the colonial regime. Once Hong Kong entered the political transition, the British administration could not unilaterally implement any constitutional changes perceived by China as unduly upsetting political stability, or worse, seeking to pre-empt the latter's own political design for the post-1997 SAR.

14. District Boards had their most glorious days in the early 1980s when the LegCo was still a closed shop of government appointees. District Board members at that time were the only directly elected representatives of the community and enjoyed greater public respect and media attention than appointed legislators. However, as the LegCo subsequently opened up, elected district councillors began to lose their lustre. Though dressed up as part of representative government, District Boards were not the same as the district governments found in British locals or Mainland cities.

15. Hong Kong Government (1984b), op cit.; Hong Kong Government (1984c) *White Paper: The Further Development of Representative Government in Hong Kong*, November, Hong Kong: Government Printer.

16. C. Patten (1992) *Our Next Five Years: The Agenda For Hong Kong*, Address by the Governor to the Legislative Council, 7 October, Hong Kong: Government Printer.

17. Hong Kong Government (1984b), op. cit., Ch. I, para. 7.

18. *Ibid.*, p. 9.

19. When meeting the then Secretary for District Administration Donald Liao who visited Beijing in October 1985, the Director of the Hong Kong and Macao Affairs Office of the State Council, Ji Pengfei (姬鵬飛) (who also chaired the Basic Law Drafting Committee) emphasised the importance of 'convergence'. Soon afterwards, on 21 November 1985, Xu Jiatun (許家屯), Director of the Hong Kong Branch of the New China News Agency, China's de facto chief representative in Hong Kong, openly alleged that 'someone was not acting according to the text [of the document, implying the Sino-British Joint Declaration], and trying to turn Hong Kong into an independent or semi-independent political entity' ('有人不按本子辦事，要將香港成為獨立或半獨立實體'). See *Cheng Ming Magazine* (《爭鳴》雜誌) (1985), December issue.

20. Hong Kong Government (1984c), op. cit., p. 15.

21. Hong Kong Government (1987) *Green Paper: The 1987 Review of Developments in Representative Government*, May, Hong Kong: Government Printer, p. 41.

22. See Xu Jiatuan (許家屯) (1993) *Xu Jiatuan's Hong Kong Memoirs — First Part* [in Chinese,《許家屯香港回憶錄 [上] 》], Hong Kong: United Daily (Hong Kong) (香港聯合報有限公司), Ch. 6 (on controversies surrounding the future political system). Xu recalled that the Chinese government became wary of reported British attempts to achieve 'major changes within 13 years [in Hong Kong during the transition], then no change in 50 years [after 1997 as promised by China]' ('十三年大變，五十年不變').

23. Survey Office (1987) *Public Response to Green Paper: The 1987 Review of Developments on Representative Government: Report of the Survey Office*, October, Hong Kong: Government Printer. The consultant conducting polls on behalf of the Survey Office was accused of using dubious methodology to arrive at the conclusions that the majority supported the Green Paper proposals. See F. Ching (1987) 'How the survey dice were loaded', *South China Morning Post*, 6 November.

24. Hong Kong Government (1988) *White Paper: The Development of Representative Government: The Way Ahead*, February, Hong Kong: Government Printer, para. 22.

25. Hong Kong Government (1988), op. cit., para. 78.

26. In early 2012, the LegCo moved into a purpose-built Legislative Council Complex at Tamar next to the new Central Government Offices. The vacated Old Supreme Court Building was converted into the new CFA Building occupied from September 2015.

27. In September 1991, following the introduction of directly elected seats, a Deputy President, John Swaine (a government-appointed unofficial member), was appointed by Governor David Wilson to chair the sittings of the LegCo. The Governor remained president and member but absented himself from most of the sittings. In February 1993, Governor Chris Patten ceased to be a member and President of the LegCo. The presidency was handed over to a member (Andrew Wong) elected from among the unofficial members.

28. The Legislative Council Commission is a statutory body independent of the government. It is chaired by the President and consists of 12 Members. It is empowered to employ staff of the Legislative Council Secretariat and oversee its work, determine the organisation and administration of support services and facilities, and formulate and execute policies on their effective operation. As of 1 April 2020, there were 686 posts on the establishment of the Secretariat headed by the Secretary-General.

29. The nine New Functional Constituencies covered: (1) Agriculture, Fisheries, Mining, Energy, and Construction; (2) Textiles and Garment; (3) Manufacturing; (4) Import and Export; (5) Wholesale

and Retail; (6) Hotels and Catering; (7) Transport and Communication; (8) Financing, Insurance, Real Estate, and Business Services; and (9) Community, Social and Personal Services.

30. Because of the collapse of the 'through-train' arrangement, the Chinese government decided to set up a Preliminary Working Committee in March 1993, ahead of the Preparatory Committee, to make preparations according to the 'second stove' approach.

31. *Ming Pao* (《明報》) (2018) 'Britain advocated setting up Human Rights Commission but did not implement due to concern about China' [in Chinese, 〈英倡設人權委會，忌中方未推〉], 28 December.

32. There was an overlap of targets for political co-optation by both the British administration and Chinese government within the Hong Kong community during the late transition period. See A.B.L. Cheung and P.C.W. Wong (2004), op. cit.

33. According to the Basic Law (Annex I), the Election Committee initially consisted of 800 members, later expanded to 1,200, with a quarter of them from each of four categories, namely: (a) industrial, commercial, and financial sectors; (b) the professions; (c) labour, social services, religious, and other sectors; (d) members and representatives of political institutions (i.e., the LegCo, District Boards and Councils, the NPC, and the CPPCC National Committee). Details of the constitution of different sectors and how their members are elected (through sub-sector elections) are prescribed by local legislation. The franchise for electing members of the 2016 Election Committee which in turn elected the present CE in 2017, other than those ex-officio members, numbered around 246,440 among 38 sub-sectors. See Registration and Electoral Office (n.d.) '2016 Election Committee Sub-Sector Elections', Registration and Electoral Office website, www.elections.gov.hk/ecss2016/eng/figures.html.

34. B.C.H. Fong (2017b), op. cit.

35. The same Election Committee that elects the CE was also responsible for electing a small proportion of LegCo members up to 2004.

36. The debates on the appropriation bills for the 2012 to 2016 budgets (mainly during the 2012–2016 term of the LegCo) were subject to extended filibuster by opposition legislators moving huge numbers of Committee Stage Amendments prior to the Third Reading, resulting in prolonged scrutiny until as late as early June before the bills were passed, when provisional funds (usually applied for about two months from April until the approval of the annual budged) for the new fiscal year were almost exhausted.

37. The government would naturally be concerned that the pan-democrats might manage to win over half of the legislative seats in the September 2020 LegCo election given the rising anti-government sentiments since 2019 (that saw a landslide victory of pan-democratic candidates in the DC election in November, winning some 80% of the total number of seats on geographical 'first past the post' basis).

38. Under the Basic Law, any bills related to constitutional changes have to be passed by at least a two-thirds majority of the members of the LegCo.

39. For example, the views of late NPC deputy Wong Man-kong; see *Ming Pao* (《明報》) (2017) 'Not pressing to urge for Article 23 legislation this year, Wong Man-kong advocates removal of foreign judges' [in Chinese, 〈「不迫切」今年不提23條 王敏剛人大倡撤外籍法官〉], 9 March, p. A03. In 2012, former Secretary for Justice Elsie Leung criticised some foreign judges for lacking understanding of Chinese national sovereignty and only interpreting Basic Law provisions according to common law, as reported by *Oriental Daily* (《東方日報》) (2012) 'Elsie Leung criticized foreign judges for not familiar with Basic Law' [in Chinese, 〈梁愛詩批洋法官不熟基本法〉] 10 November, p. A3. Alan Hoo, a senior barrister and chairman of the Basic Law Institute,

echoed the views of Cheng Jie, associate professor of law at Tsinghua University, that CFA judges should all hold PRC passports and be HKPRs, as reported by *Sing Pao* (《成報》) (2012) 'Experts propose Hong Kong needs more Chinese judges to realize self-administration' [in Chinese,〈專家學者提出 體現港人治港 港需更多中國籍法官〉], 5 November, p. A05.

40. *South China Morning Post* (2018) 'Politics must be kept out of the appointment of senior judges', editorial, 6 May.

41. For example, over the nomination of judge Brett Kavanaugh to the Supreme Court from July to October 2018. See *The Guardian* (2019) 'Brett Kavanaugh', www.theguardian.com/us-news/brett-kavanaugh.

42. W. Zheng and E. Xie (2020) 'China upgrades Hong Kong affairs with new chief', *South China Morning Post*, 13 February.

43. The requirement that a CE candidate could not be a member of any political party was laid down in the election rules for selecting the first CE in 1996 through a Selection Committee established by the Hong Kong SAR Preparatory Committee. Subsequently, when the Chief Executive Election Ordinance was enacted locally in July 2001, in preparation for the election of the second-term CE, this restriction was retained with a small relaxation that a CE candidate could have a party affiliation which had to be removed upon election.

44. I. Scott (2010), op. cit., p. 51.

45. A.B.L. Cheung (1997a) 'Rebureaucratization of Politics in Hong Kong: Prospects after 1997', *Asian Survey*, Vol. 37, No. 8, pp. 720–737.

46. A.B.L. Cheung (2007a), op. cit.

47. A.B.L. Cheung and P.C.W. Wong (2004), op. cit.

48. See Chapter 11 for more discussion on the Medical Council reform in 2016. The government proposal, also in 2016, to introduce franchised taxis which could be booked online and with better facilities (including wheelchair accessibility), but properly regulated in fares as well as service and safety standards, was their response to the challenge posed by Uber. It was strongly opposed by the taxi industry in particular the large taxi operators, whose interests were voiced by the Transport constituency legislator. The current Carrie Lam Administration had initially decided to proceed with the proposal; however, it has been held in abeyance in light of unabated controversy within the LegCo.

49. The 2006 review focused mainly on (a) strengthening the role of the DCs in managing some district facilities by setting up a Facilities Management Committee under each DC; (b) creating a dedicated capital works block vote for improvement to district facilities and minor works; (c) enhancing communication between the government and DCs by setting up a Steering Committee on District Administration chaired by the Secretary for Home Affairs or the Permanent Secretary, requiring heads of departments to attend one DC meeting every 2–3 months, and hosting an annual CE-presided District Administration Summit; and (d) improving the support provided to DC members by increasing their honorarium and allowances. DCs were also encouraged to draw up plans on district development in partnership with other sectors. See Home Affairs Bureau (2006) *Consultation Document on Review on the Roles, Functions and Composition of District Council*, April, Hong Kong: Government Logistics Department, www.hab.gov.hk/file_manager/en/documents/references/papers_reports_others/District/Consultation_e.pdf.

50. In his address at the farewell ceremony for British rule on 30 June 1997, Governor Patten said: 'As British administration ends, we are, I believe, entitled to say that our own nation's contribution here was to provide the scaffolding that enabled the people of Hong Kong to

ascend. The rule of law. Clean and light-handed government. The values of a free society. The beginnings of representative government and democratic accountability. [...] No dependent territory has been left more prosperous, none with such a rich texture and fabric of civil society, professions, churches, newspapers, charities, civil servants of the highest probity and the most steadfast commitment to the public good.' See C. Patten (1997), op. cit.

51. The central government has become increasingly nervous about some of the more fundamental constitutional reforms and the rise of a party-government (which cannot be easily squared with the constitutional supremacy of the CCP throughout the whole of the PRC, including the Hong Kong SAR).

52. A.B.L. Cheung (2005b), op. cit.

53. For example, in the past, non-official members of the ExCo were groomed and recommended by top civil servants whom they held in deference and were willing to work with as loyal partners rather than political rivals.

54. Advisory bodies in the traditional mode lacked legitimacy in the new popular mood and were no longer an effective intermediary between government and society. See A.B.L. Cheung and P.C.W. Wong (2004), op. cit.; B.C.H. Fong (2018a) 'Advisory politics before and after 1997: In search of a new relationship between state, political society and civil society', in T.L. Lui et al. (eds) *Routledge Handbook of Contemporary Hong Kong*, London: Routledge, pp. 127–140.

55. Some of the members of the advisory committees and statutory bodies could still maintain an influence on government policy-making should they also be active in political parties and legislative politics.

56. See A.B.L. Cheung (2010b) 'In Search of Trust and Legitimacy: The Political Trajectory of Hong Kong as Part of China', *International Public Management Review*, Vol. 11, No. 2, pp. 38–63.

57. The Director of the Hong Kong and Macao Affairs Office, and the Directors of the Central Government's Liaison Office in Hong Kong SAR and Macao SAR, respectively, have always been members of the Central Coordination Group. After reorganisation into a Central Leading Group still chaired by Han Zheng, the Minister of Public Security and the Director of the enhanced Hong Kong and Macao Affairs Office of the State Council are now the deputy leaders of the Group.

58. Established in Beijing in December 2013, the Chinese Association of Hong Kong and Macao Studies has been headed by a retired Deputy Director of the Hong Kong and Macao Affairs Office of the State Council. Apart from institutional members, there are about 550 individual members, coming from Hong Kong, Macao, and the Mainland.

59. The establishment and scope of responsibilities of the Liaison Office were largely expanded in the aftermath of the 1 July 2003 mass protests which revealed a serious crisis of governance in the SAR and resulted in a comprehensive review of the central government's policies towards Hong Kong. Many local academics and commentators have all along suspected that the Liaison Office plays a significant role in coordinating different political and social forces within the pro-Beijing and pro-establishment camp, including the fielding of candidates for DC and LegCo elections and the mobilisation of community support for controversial policies of the SAR government. See, for example, S.S.H. Lo (2008) *The Dynamics of Beijing-Hong Kong Relations*, Hong Kong: Hong Kong University Press, pp. 10–11, 18–19; B.C.H. Fong (2017c), op. cit.

60. *Xinhuanet* (2020a) 'Central gov't agency, liaison office have power to supervise major affairs in HK: Spokesperson of liaison office', 17 April, Beijing, www.xinhuanet.com/english/2020-04/17/c_138986076.htm. Organisationally, the Hong Kong and Macao Affairs Office is one of the 'administrative offices' under the State Council to assist the Premier but without independent administrative functions. The Liaison Office is a 'dispatch agency' of the CPG (i.e., the State Council). It can be argued that State Council decisions and policies on Hong Kong would

not have been formulated without the active inputs of the two offices, and the State Council has the power of supervision over the SAR government. Under the Basic Law, the CE is held accountable to the CPG.

61. S.K. Lau (2002b) 'Tung Chee-hwa's Governing Strategy: The Shortfall in Politics', in S.K. Lau (ed) *The First Tung Chee-hwa Administration: The First Five Years of The Hong Kong Special Administrative Region*, Hong Kong: Chinese University Press, pp. 1–39; S.K. Lau (2007) 'In Search of a New Political Order', in Y.M. Yeung (ed) *The First Decade: The Hong Kong SAR in Retrospective and Introspective Perspectives*, Hong Kong: Chinese University Press, pp. 130–159. Lau, a political sociology professor at the Chinese University of Hong Kong, was considered a close adviser to the Hong Kong and Macao Affairs Office of the State Council during the 1980s–1990s. In the run-up to 1997, he was appointed as a Hong Kong Affairs Adviser and member of the Hong Kong SAR Preparatory Committee. In 2003, he was appointed as a member of the national committee of the CPPCC and served as Head of the Central Policy Unit of the SAR government from 2002 to 2012. He is currently one of the vice presidents of the Chinese Association of Hong Kong and Macao Studies.

62. S.K. Lau (劉兆佳) (2013b) *Hong Kong Politics After Reunification* [in Chinese, 《回歸後的香港政治》], Hong Kong: Commercial Press, pp. vii–viii.

63. S.K. Lau (劉兆佳) (2013a) *The Governance and New Regime Building of Hong Kong SAR Fifteen Years Since Reunification* [in Chinese, 《回歸十五年以來香港的特區管治及新政權建設》], Hong Kong: Commercial Press, p. 2. Lau mentioned that 'old' forces (those business and professional elites groomed by the British administration and who switched their loyalty to Beijing) and 'new' forces (traditional pro-Beijing patriotic forces and some new local elites groomed by Beijing during the transition) did not get on comfortably with each other within the pro-establishment camp, while the government elites (namely the senior civil servants) had been an inherited bureaucracy from British rule.

64. I. Scott (2000), op. cit.

65. Even a foreign academic who relied only on quick observations during short visits to Hong Kong and some secondary data could see that the governance system was dysfunctional. See P.W. Preston (2016), op. cit. Preston commented that 'the SAR government cannot command authority, the LegCo's status is in decline and social protest movements are in evidence but can only protest' (p. 140).

Chapter 5

1. Before 1997, both the British and Chinese governments paid high regard to the Hong Kong civil service for its efficiency and effectiveness and considered its stability an integral part of a smooth transfer of administration. In his final Policy Address in October 1996, Governor Chris Patten set out 16 benchmarks for assessing Hong Kong's success as an SAR under China's 'One Country, Two Systems' framework. Topping his list of benchmarks were questions related to the civil service: 'Is Hong Kong's Civil Service still professional and meritocratic? Are its key positions filled by individuals who command the confidence of their colleagues and the community and owe their appointments only to their own abilities?' See C. Patten (1996) *Hong Kong: Transition*, Address by the Governor at the opening of the 1996–97 session of the Legislative Council, 2 October, Hong Kong: Government Printer, para. 89.

2. S. Vickers (2001) '"More Colonial Again?" The Post-1997 Culture of Hong Kong's Governing Elite', *International Journal of Public Administration*, Vol. 24, No. 9, pp. 951–976 (quote at p. 951).

3. During his election campaign in late 1996, Tung asked the questions: 'Is our civil service too bogged down in the politics of our legislative process? Should they be devoting more time and energy to the formulation and efficient implementation of policies?' See C.H. Tung (1996) *Building a 21st Century Hong Kong Together*, Chief Executive Election Platform, 22 October, p. 5.

4. A.B.L. Cheung (1997a), op. cit., pp.

5. The president of the pro-Beijing FTU, Cheng Yiu-tong, for example, defended Tung's performance by saying that he had brought into the government only three personal staff and had been at the mercy of the bureaucracy. See *Ming Pao* (《明報》) (2001) 'Cheng Yiu-tong blasted government for lack of sense of crisis, pointing to weakness of CE and conflicting articulations among officials' [in Chinese, 〈鄭耀棠狠批政府缺危機感 指特首弱勢官員口徑不一〉], 7 October.

6. It was reported that when Anson Chan visited Beijing in September 2000 and had a meeting with the State Councillor in charge of Hong Kong affairs, Qian Qichen (錢其琛), Qian specifically asked her and the civil service she led to provide better support to Tung, in a disguised admonishment of her role as Tung's number two. *China Internet News* (《中國互聯網新聞》), 'Anson Chan Visited Qian Qichen' [in Chinese, 〈錢其琛會見陳方安生〉], 26 September, www.china.com.cn/chinese/2000/Oct/8369.htm. Chan decided to resign afterwards in January 2001.

7. See S.Y. Chung (2001) *Hong Kong's Journey to Reunification — Memoirs of Sze-yuen Chung*, Hong Kong: Chinese University Press, pp. 196–200 and 224–231.

8. J. Halligan (2007), op. cit.; B.A. Rockman (2001) 'Politics by Other Means: Administrative Reform in the United States', *International Review of Public Administration*, Vol. 6, No. 2, pp. 1–13.

9. C.H. Tung (2000) *The 2000 Policy Address: Serving the Community, Sharing Common Goals*, Policy address by the Chief Executive to the Legislative Council, 11 October, Hong Kong: Printing Department, paras. 112–113.

10. C.H. Tung (2001) *The 2001 Policy Address: Building on Our Strengths, Investing in Our Future*, Policy address by the Chief Executive to the Legislative Council, 10 October, Hong Kong: Printing Department, paras. 133–135.

11. See, for example, D. Rosenbloom (2008) 'The Politics-Administration Dichotomy in U.S. Historical Context', *Public Administration Review*, Vol. 68, No. 1, pp. 57–60; J.H. Svara (1998) 'The politics-administration dichotomy model as aberration', *Public Administration Review*, Vol. 58, No. 1, pp. 51–58; A. Heywood (2007) *Politics*, 3rd edition, Basingstoke: Palgrave.

12. The new system also had implications on the powers of the CS and FS. In colonial Hong Kong, these two officials, as the number two and three top officials under the Governor, coordinated other secretaries as gatekeepers to clear policy proposals before submission to the Governor-in-Council. The CS's policy leadership role was prominent because of their capacity as head of the civil service and of the Administrative Class from which secretaries were appointed. After the change, with the headship of the civil service unclear, the CS was left at the mercy of the CE who decided what to assign to them. To remedy this, a new Policy Committee was set up, co-chaired by the CS and FS, to provide 'a forum for considering policy proposals before they are submitted to ExCo, coordinating and harmonizing policy proposals which cut across different policy areas, and coordinating the timing for policies to be rolled out', so as to ensure better communication among ministers as well as policy coherence and consistency. See Constitutional Affairs Bureau (2003) *Twelve-month Report on the Implementation of the Accountability System for Principal Officials*, para. 20, www.cmab.gov.hk/upload/20040219153857/12mthreport-e.pdf. However, a strong-willed minister could always take their case directly to the CE, something that would not have happened in the colonial past.

13. Anson Chan was against the introduction of the POAS, and according to her interview by Cable TV in July 2007, she resigned when her advice was not listened to. See *Apple Daily* (《蘋果日報》) (2014) 'Anson Chan retired early in 2001 out of dissatisfaction with Tung Chee-hwa' [in Chinese, 〈不滿董建華2001年陳方安生提早退休〉], 30 April, https://hk.news.appledaily.com/local/realtime/article/20140430/52427995. As former AO-turned-minister Joseph Wong put it, 'Anson Chan, who used to be the de facto number two in the administration, regarded this proposal as a blunt act to remove her power and status, and no doubt it strengthened her resolve to leave the government'. See J.W.P. Wong (2013) 'Expanding and Destroying the Accountability System', in J.Y.S. Cheng (ed) *The Second Chief Executive of Hong Kong SAR: Evaluating the Tsang Years 2005–2012*, Hong Kong: City University of Hong Kong Press, pp. 31–58. Wong also mentioned that as a civil servant Donald Tsang did not favour the introduction of the new system.

14. Realising that the status quo was difficult to sustain, some senior AOs were resigned to the prospect of some form of political appointment. Instead of giving up the top portfolios entirely to outsiders, those mandarins with 'political' aspirations were prepared to retire from the civil service in order to join the CE's cabinet as political appointees.

15. The BBC television series 'Yes, Ministers' supplied satirical dramas on minister-bureaucrat interactions where the senior civil servants sought to defend the status quo at all costs and steered their minister towards their preferred course of action and away from options they detested using all kinds of skills and tricks, all in the name of taking orders from the minister.

16. J.W.P. Wong (2002) *Speech by the Secretary for the Civil Service at the Annual Dinner of the Oxford University Hong Kong Society*, 6 September, Hong Kong: Civil Service Bureau, www.info. gov.hk/gia/general/200209/06/0906251.htm.

17. *Ibid.*

18. Efficiency Unit (2004) *New Directions*, http://info.gov.hk/eu/english/history/history_mf/history_mf2002.html (accessed in May 2004, but the page has since been removed from the website).

19. Henry Tang was a former legislator, first appointed by the British administration in 1991 and then elected in 1995 to represent the Import and Export functional constituency. The other new ministers from outside the civil service were not political party members and had no background in elective politics (whether legislative or in DCs). Most were chosen by virtue of their personal expertise in the policy field concerned (e.g., the appointment of then Vice-Chancellor of The Chinese University of Hong Kong Arthur Li as Secretary for Education and Manpower; environmental expert Sarah Liao as Secretary for Environment, Planning and Lands; Hospital Authority chief executive and medical doctor Yeoh Eng-kiong as Secretary for Health and Welfare; and private sector Chief Financial Officer Fred Ma as Secretary for Financial Services and the Treasury). Patrick Ho, the new Secretary for Home Affairs had served on the Provisional Regional Council before (1997–1999) but only as an appointed member.

20. Permanent Secretaries are ranked and remunerated at D8 of the Directorate Scale, in principle at the same level as the politically appointed Secretaries whose remuneration is, however, paid on a 'total wage' basis (i.e., basic salaries plus fringe benefits) giving the false impression that the latter are higher paid.

21. Modern-day bureaucrats are no longer passive implementers of decisions but play an important though subtle (and at times behind-the-scenes) role in decision-making. See J.D. Aberbach et al. (1981), op. cit.

22. E.W.Y. Lee and R.L.K. Yeung (2017) 'The "Principal Officials Accountability System": Its underdevelopment as a system of ministerial government', *Asian Pacific Journal of Public Administration*, Vol. 39, No. 2, pp. 120–134 (quote at pp. 127–128).

23. W. Wong (2012) 'The Civil Service', in W.M. Lam et al. (eds) *Contemporary Hong Kong Government and Politics*, Hong Kong: Hong Kong University Press, pp. 87–100 (quote at pp. 94–95).

24. Indeed, many of those cases of sleaziness and maladministration exposed by Audit Commission and Ombudsman's investigations over the years did not necessarily result from the decisions of ministers, but rather stemmed from actions and practices down the line within the bureaucracy even though ultimate political accountability may rest with the ministers.

25. See J.P. Burns et al. (2012) 'Changing governance structures and the evolution of Public Service Bargains in Hong Kong', *International Review of Administrative Sciences*, Vol. 79, No. 1, pp. 131–148; J.P. Burns and W. Li (2015) 'The impact of external change on civil service values in post-colonial Hong Kong', *The China Quarterly*, No. 222, pp. 522–546. According to their interviews of both ex-ministers and senior civil servants (including permanent secretaries), Burns et al. observed that 'political neutrality was mostly valued by senior civil servants, while some outsider political appointees considered it a myth and an obstacle to civil servants exercising their vision' (p. 145). Furthermore, Burns and Li found that almost all senior civil servants interviewed agreed they should focus on long-term policy plans rather than short-term possibilities while political appointees were much less sure. Civil servants overwhelmingly agreed that the 'government works better if civil servants are politically neutral', but political appointees doubted this view (p. 536).

26. A good example of a competent non-expert is Gordon Brown, former British Prime Minister and Chancellor of the Exchequer, who studied history in university and worked as a lecturer in politics and as a journalist before being elected to the Parliament under the Labour ticket.

27. T. Bach et al. (2020) 'More delegation, more political control? Politicization of senior-level appointments in 18 European countries', *Public Policy and Administration*, Vol. 35, No. 1, pp. 3–23.

28. Quoted in J.A. Baker (2020) 'Public service needs to work with first-class political leadership for Singapore to succeed: PM Lee', *Channel New Asia*, 17 January, www.channelnewsasia.com/news/singapore/pm-lee-public-service-dinner-civil-political-leadership-12275234#cxrecs_s.

29. B.C.H. Fong (2014b) 'Ten Years of Political Appointments in Hong Kong: The Challenges and Prospects of Developing a Political Appointment System under a Semi-Democratic Regime, 2002–12', in J.Y.S. Cheng (ed) *New Tends of Political Participation in Hong Kong*, Hong Kong: City University of Hong Kong Press, pp. 67–103.

30. J.W.P. Wong (2013), op. cit., p. 37.

31. S.K. Lau (劉兆佳) (2013a), op. cit., pp. 121–134.

32. The POAS now covers the four categories of political appointees — (a) Principal Officials under the political appointment system (i.e., the Secretaries of Department and Directors of Bureau as defined in the Basic Law or, broadly speaking, the ministers); (b) Director of the Chief Executive's Office; (c) Under-Secretaries (i.e., Deputy Directors of Bureau); and (d) PAs.

33. This requirement was lifted when Patrick Nip, former Secretary for Constitutional Mainland Affairs of the current Carrie Lam Administration, was moved sideways to become SCS in April 2020. Nip was a former AO and Permanent Secretary of the Food and Health Bureau before he was appointed to the former ministerial post in July 2017 and thus had to leave the civil service.

34. Without any official clarification of relevant roles, the responsibilities of the SCS are even more ambiguous and confusing — could the SCS have full ministerial responsibility over civil service policy if the head of the civil service is de facto still the CS, a more senior minister under the CE? Ideally, the political officer in charge of civil service policy should either be the CE (in Britain

the Prime Minister has this responsibility, as assisted by another minister), and the most senior among Permanent Secretaries could be designated concurrently as Head of the Civil Service. In Britain, the top civil servant acts as the Head of the Civil Service and reports directly to the Prime Minister.

35. J. Uhr (1998) *Deliberative Democracy in Australia: The Changing Place of Parliament*, Cambridge: Cambridge University Press, p. 163.

36. G. Marshall (1986) *Constitutional Conventions: The Rules and Forms of Political Accountability*, reprinted edition, Oxford: Clarendon Press, especially Ch. IV 'Doctrine of Ministerial Responsibility'. For more on the application and development of individual ministerial accountability in Britain during the 1980s to 1990s, see D. Woodhouse (1994) *Ministers and Parliament: Accountability in Theory and Practice*, Oxford: Clarendon Press.

37. R. Mulgan (2012) 'Assessing Ministerial Responsibility in Australia', in K. Dowding and C. Lewis (eds) *Ministerial Careers and Accountability in the Australian Commonwealth Government*, Canberra, Australia: ANU E Press, pp. 177–193.

38. See, for example, C.Y. Cheung (2003) 'The Quest for Good Governance: Hong Kong's Principal Officials Accountability System', *China: An International Journal*, Vol. 1, No. 2, pp. 249–272.

39. SynergyNet (2002) *How to Take Governance Reform Forward: Accountability to Whom and How?* Hong Kong: SynergyNet, p. 26.

40. It was an incident that saw small investors dump low-valued or 'penny' stocks in more than 200 companies on 26 July 2002 after the Hong Kong Exchanges & Clearing Ltd (which ran the stock exchange) produced a consultation paper that suggested ways of handling de-listings of poorly performing stocks. That proposal caused 66 stocks to drop by more than 20%, with one dropping by 88%. In the event, the stock exchange withdrew its suggestion that shares should be de-listed if they fell below 50 cents for 30 days. Despite some calls for Ma to resign, CE Tung Chee-hwa defended him and said there was no direct correlation between the introduction of the accountability system and the incident.

41. Independent Expert Panel (2014) *Report of the Hong Kong Section of the Guangzhou-Shenzhen-Hong Kong Express Rail Link Independent Expert Panel*, December, www.gov.hk/en/theme/iep-xrl/pdf/IEP-report.pdf. See also A.B.L. Cheung (張炳良) (2018b) *An Unavoidable Reality — A Review of Transport Policies During My Five Years As Secretary* [in Chinese,《不能迴避的現實 —— 回顧任局長五年的運輸政策》], Hong Kong: Chung Hwa Book Company, pp. 140–141.

42. All serving civil servants that become political officials must first resign or retire from the civil service, except the SCS for the reason explained above.

43. Constitutionally, the CE only nominates ministerial Principal Officials who are then appointed by the CPG. It was rumoured that occasionally a candidate originally nominated by the CE-elect did not find favour with the central government. It is not known if the central government has ever, through any channel, imposed candidates of its preference on the CE for consideration and nomination.

44. Constitutional Affairs Bureau (2006) *Consultation Document on Further Development of the Political Appointment System*, Hong Kong: Government Logistics Department. Former SCS Joseph Wong commented that Tsang's game plan was that, armed with the new people-power to be cultivated by an enlarged political appointment layer, his administration would be able to override any objection from a legislature that did not have a government party or even one member who owed allegiance to him. See J.W.P. Wong (2013), op. cit., p. 35.

45. Even the CE's remuneration is less than that of an executive director of a big private company, not to mention a corporate chief executive officer whose income could easily be multiple times higher.

46. Since the introduction of the ministerial system in 2002, only five former legislators have served as ministers: Henry Tang (2002–2012), Anthony Cheung (2012–2017), Paul Chan (from 2012), Lau Kong-wah (2015–2020), and Law Chi-kwong (from 2017).

47. While the media and commentators would happily accept an AO (only a generalist) as being suitable for any policy portfolio, they would question an outsider's suitability should that person not come from a relevant professional background.

48. E.M. Wirsching (2018) *The Revolving Door for Political Elites: An Empirical Analysis of the Linkages between Government Officials' Professional Background and Financial Regulation*, paper submitted to 2018 OECD Global Anti-Corruption and Integrity Forum, Paris: OECD, www.oecd.org/corruption/integrity-forum/academic-papers/Wirsching.pdf.

49. D.Y.K. Tsang (2005b) *Campaign Speech for Chief Executive Election*, 3 June, www.donald-yktsang.com/press_speeches_e.html (last accessed in 2005; server link no longer exists).

50. Lam nominated Frank Chan, then Director of Electrical and Mechanical Services as Secretary for Transport and Housing, when she formed her first ministerial cabinet in 2017. In the April 2020 government reshuffling, she nominated his successor as director Alfred Sit as the new Secretary for Innovation and Technology, and Director of Immigration Erick Tsang as the new Secretary for Constitutional and Mainland Affairs.

51. J. Ho (2018) 'Behind a tall order: Goh Chok Tong reflects on succession and politics past and present', *Chanel News Asia*, 2 December, www.channelnewsasia.com/news/singapore/goh-chok-tong-succession-politics-tall-order-biography-10983670. See also S.H. Peh (2018) *Tall Order: The Goh Chok Tong Story*, Vol. 1, Singapore: World Scientific.

Chapter 6

1. As of December 2018, the civil service employed some 173,700 people or about 4.4% of Hong Kong's labour force. About 1,300 of them were directorate officers. Over 99% of the service are local officers and the gender ratio is roughly 5:3, male to female officers. See Information Services Department (2019b) *Hong Kong: The Facts — Civil Service*, September, www.gov.hk/en/about/abouthk/factsheets/docs/civil_service.pdf. The count of members of the civil service excludes judges, judicial officers, officers of the ICAC, and locally engaged staff working in overseas Hong Kong Economic and Trade Offices. The 12 general pay scales are: Directorate Pay Scale; Directorate (Legal) Pay Scale; Master Pay Scale; General Disciplined Service Pay Scales (Commander, Officer, and Rank and File); Police Pay Scale; ICAC Pay Scale; Model Scale I; Training Pay Scale; Technician Apprentice Pay Scale; and Craft Apprentice Pay Scale. Apart from the directorate officers, members of the disciplined services, and the manual and apprentice grades, the great majority of civil servants are remunerated according to the Master Pay Scale.

2. The Civil Service Bureau provides the 'headship' of the general grades while the heads of departmental grades are normally the heads of the specialist departments concerned. These heads of grades are responsible for policies on appointment, promotion, transfer, training, etc. in accordance with general civil service policy laid down by the Civil Service Bureau.

3. Civil Service Bureau (2009) *Civil Service Code*, 9 September, www.csb.gov.hk/english/admin/conduct/files/CSCode_e.pdf.

4. Under the Sino-British agreement in 1987 on the new civil service pension system, the Chinese government agreed to honour all pension payments due to serving civil servants. Apart from

extending the retirement age from 55 to 60, the new system allowed retirees to get a lump-sum gratuity of half of their calculated accrued pension, followed by monthly payments until passing, instead of one-quarter under the old system. It also gave those civil servants who left the service before retirement age but had served for at least 10 years an entitlement to deferred pension at their normal retirement age, whereas they would not receive any pension at all under the old system. See the detailed analysis of this system in A.B.L. Cheung (張炳良) (1987) 'Who are the Beneficiaries of the New Pension System? An Overall Appraisal of the Impact of the New Civil Service Pension System', [in Chinese, 〈誰是新長俸制度的受惠者？ 總評新公務員長俸制度的影響〉], *Ming Pao Monthly* (《明報月刊》), July.

5. In Hong Kong, employees and employers covered by the MPF system are both required to make regular mandatory contributions calculated at 5% of the employee's relevant income to an MPF scheme, subject to the minimum and maximum relevant income levels, presently set at HK$7,100 and HK$30,000, respectively, for a monthly paid employee. The government's contributions under the Civil Service Provident Fund (CSPF) Scheme, including mandatory and voluntary contributions, follow a refined progressive contribution rates schedule ranging from 5% to 25% depending on the years of service, with the disciplined services enjoying an additional special contribution from government of 5%. See Civil Service Bureau (2018a) *Key Features of the CSPF Scheme*, Hong Kong: Civil Service Bureau, www.csb.gov.hk/english/admin/retirement/421.html.

6. According to Article 103 of the Basic Law, the appointment and promotion of public servants shall be on the basis of their qualifications, experience, and ability. Hong Kong's previous system of recruitment, employment, assessment, discipline, training, and management for the public service, including special bodies for their appointment, pay, and conditions of service, shall be maintained, except for any provisions for privileged treatment of foreign nationals.

7. Namely the Secretaries, ICAC Commissioner, Director of Audit, Commissioner of Police, Director of Immigration, and Commissioner of Customs and Excise, all of whom are appointed by the CPG as 'Principal Officials'.

8. From the 1970s up to 1996, Oxford University offered a 9-month public administration programme for junior AOs. See J.W.P. Wong (2002), op. cit. In his speech, Wong mentioned that by so doing, 'the AO Grade does share a strong common value with [Oxford] university — elitism'. By the 2000s, such training in public administration for young AOs, after satisfactory completion of their first three-year contract, had expanded to other institutions in Britain and the US — including the London School of Economics and Political Science, University of California at Berkeley, Indiana University at Bloomington, and Syracuse University. Today, AOs promoted to Staff Grade C or above will be considered for full sponsorship to attend degree programmes or short-term executive development programmes run by distinguished overseas institutions, such as Harvard University, Stanford University, and INSEAD.

9. Today, directorate officers and AOs mainly attend programmes at the Chinese Academy of Governance, while senior officers at Master Pay Scale Point 45 or above join programmes at Tsinghua University or Peking University. Civil servants lower down the hierarchy are sent to other Mainland universities for similar programmes. For details, see Civil Service Bureau (2018b) *An Overview of Training and Development for Civil Servants*, paper submitted to the Legislative Council Panel on Public Service, May, Hong Kong: Legislative Council.

10. See Megaw Committee, Britain (1982) *Inquiry into Civil Service Pay*, London: HMSO, Vol. 1, Chs. 2–3.

11. In 1968, the colonial government reached a pay settlement agreement with the staff in the form of the *Statement of Principles and Aims of Civil Service Remuneration*, in which the former

accepted 'a duty and responsibility to maintain a civil service recognised as efficient and staffed by members whose conditions of service are regarded as fair both by themselves and by the public which they serve'. This is cited in Standing Commission on Civil Service Salaries and Conditions of Service (1979) *First Report on Principles and Practices Governing Civil Service Pay*, Hong Kong: Government Printer, p. 13.

12. For a detailed account and analysis, see A.B.L. Cheung (2005a) 'Civil Service Pay Reform in Hong Kong: Principles, Politics and Paradoxes', in A.B.L. Cheung (ed) *Public Service Reform in East Asia: Reform Issues and Challenges in Japan, Korea, Singapore and Hong Kong*, Hong Kong: Chinese University Press, pp. 157–192.

13. For the purpose of such surveys, the civil service was divided into three broad salary bands, and changes in pay and certain cash benefits enjoyed by employees within similar salary bands in selected private companies were assessed. Such broad banding has lasted until today. Gross PTIs for the three salary bands are first produced, based on information collected from private employers, and then adjusted by a reduction factor to take into account the value of annual increments at their payroll cost (expressed as a percentage of the total payroll cost) to produce net PTIs, which form the basis for pay adjustment decisions.

14. The Pay Survey and Research Unit of the Joint Secretariat serving the four pay advisory bodies conducts the annual pay trend surveys under the direction of a Pay Trend Survey Committee comprising staff members drawn from the four major staff councils, namely the Senior Civil Service Council, Model Scale 1 Staff Consultative Council, Police Force Council, and Disciplined Services Consultative Council.

15. Committee of Inquiry into the 1988 Civil Service Pay Adjustment and Related Matters (Burrett Committee) (1989) *Final Report*, March, Hong Kong: Government Printer, Chs. 5–6. According to its recommendations, pay level surveys should be based as far as possible on job-for-job comparisons. A number of 'marker' grades with identifiable functional counterparts in the private sector should be used as comparators. The pay of those grades not covered directly by the survey should be determined by internal pay comparisons.

16. L.J. Peter and P. Hull (1969) *The Peter Principle: Why Things Always Go Wrong*, New York: William Morrow & Company. Peter and Hull tried to address the problem of organisational incompetence and explained that everyone in a hierarchy would inevitably rise to their level of incompetence.

17. For example, following the 1988 Rennie Committee review of disciplined services pay, which recommended significant structural changes, upsetting existing pay relativities among various disciplined services, there was uproar from the staff associations concerned. The subsequent remedial pay revisions recommended by the newly established Standing Committee on Disciplined Services Salaries and Conditions of Service in 1990, in turn, were greeted with dismay when those services benefitting from the Rennie review found the post-1988 relativities being re-adjusted to their disadvantage. The Police Force was able to secure a pay package even better than their pre-Rennie position by arguing for a special status as the government's 'agency of last resort'.

18. OECD (1995), op. cit. Among OECD countries, 'there have been efforts [...] to gain tighter control over pay costs by changing the methods of determining general pay increase (e.g., elimination of indexing, reduction of the role of market comparison, removal of pay linkages among different groups of public servants) and the rules for individual pay progression (e.g., giving less weight to length of service as a criterion for pay progression)' (p. 58).

19. It was only at the end of 1998 that the new SAR government asked the Standing Commission to conduct a starting pay review for new recruits because of growing disparity in starting salary

between the civil service and the private sector in the wake of the Asian financial crisis. See Standing Commission on Civil Service Salaries and Conditions of Service (1999) *Report No. 36: Civil Service Starting Salaries Review 1999*, June, Hong Kong: Printing Department.

20. Specifically at the public forum on 'Civil Service Reform: A Balance between Stability and Flexibility?' jointly organised by the Centre for Comparative Public Management and Social Policy, City University of Hong Kong, and the Hong Kong Policy Research Institute on 13 May 1999 at the City University of Hong Kong. Lam later shared with the author that his bureau team had actually been exploring possible reform measures even prior to public pressure building up because it was felt that no major improvements had been made for many years given the need to focus on managing the 1997 handover and that Hong Kong was lagging behind the world trend.

21. Civil Service Bureau (1999a), *Civil Service into the 21st Century: Civil Service Reform Consultation Document*, March, Hong Kong: Printer Department, para. 1.6.

22. Civil Service Bureau (1999a), op. cit., Ch. 3.

23. Quoted in Civil Service Bureau (1999b) *Civil Service Reform Newsletter*, Issue No. 3, June, Hong Kong: Civil Service Bureau.

24. Task Force on Review of Civil Service Pay Policy and System (2002a) *Phase One Interim Report*, April, Hong Kong: Printing Department.

25. Task Force on Review of Civil Service Pay Policy and System (2002b) *Phase One Final Report*, September, Hong Kong: Printing Department.

26. OECD (2005) *Performance-related Pay Policies for Government Employees*, Paris: OECD.

27. G. Jeannot and P. Bezes (2016) 'Mapping the use of public management tools in European public administration', in G. Hammerschmid et al. (eds) *Public Administration Reforms in Europe: The View From The Top*, Cheltenham: Edward Elgar, pp. 219–230 (survey at p. 221).

28. Departments were instructed to strictly follow the requirements of the Civil Service Regulations, so that the annual salary increment would only be granted upon a conscious assessment of staff performance (covering conduct, diligence, and efficiency).

29. Civil Service Bureau (2016) *An Overview of the Civil Service: Establishment, Strength, Retirement, Resignation and Age Profile*, Paper for Panel on Public Service of the Legislative Council, 18 April, Hong Kong: Legislative Council.

30. Article 100 adopted the exact wording of a similar clause in Annex I of the 1984 Sino-British Joint Declaration. It seems highly likely that the Basic Law drafters had not anticipated the possibility of a serious economic downturn that would erode pay comparability between the civil service and the private sector. However, once written into the Basic Law, the provision has the effect of providing some kind of constitutional safeguard to the extent that civil servants might argue that in no way could their pay be reduced to a level lower than that prevailing at the time of the establishment of the SAR on 1 July 1997.

31. J. Hartman (2003) *Judgement on Lau Kwok Fai Barnard vs. Secretary for Justice and Government Park and Playground Keepers Union, Shum Man Lai and Leung Tat Wah vs. Secretary for Justice*, Constitutional and Administrative Law List Nos. 177 and 180 of 2002, Court of First Instance in the High Court of the Hong Kong Special Administrative Region, 10 June, para. 57.

32. Chief Justice Li, Mr Justice Bokhary PJ, Mr Justice Chan PJ, Mr Justice Ribeiro PJ, and Sir Anthony Mason NPJ (2005) *Judgement on Secretary for Justice (for and on behalf of the Government of Hong Kong SAR) v Lau Kwok Fai Bernard, The Government of Hong Kong SAR v Michael Reid Scott, and Secretary for Justice (for and on behalf of the Government of Hong*

Kong SAR) v Michael Reid Scott, FACV No. 15 of 2004, FACV No. 16 of 2004, and FACV No. 8 of 2005, 13 July, Court of Final Appeal of the Hong Kong Special Administrative Region, 13 July, para. 67. The court added that the Basic Law guaranteed the continuation of the 'special bodies', whatever they might be, responsible for public service pay and conditions of service.

33. Each of the four central councils comprises the Management Side and the Staff Side. Members of the Management Side come mainly from policy bureaus dealing with issues of staff concern whilst members of the Staff Side are all nominated by staff associations and unions. Meetings are held regularly to discuss issues of concern to staff. See Civil Service Bureau (n.d.) *Central Staff Consultative Councils*, www.csb.gov.hk/english/admin/relations/151.html.

34. D. Yue (2007) *Letter to all civil servants on 'Development of an Improved Civil Service Pay Adjustment Mechanism — Pay Level Survey'*, letter from the Secretary for the Civil Service, 24 April, Hong Kong: Civil Service Bureau, www.csb.gov.hk/textonly/english/letter/821.html.

35. C. Hood (2002), op. cit.

36. If middle-level managers were risk-averse, they might tend to play the 'nice boss' by adopting an egalitarian approach in determining performance rewards. Others might resent a performance-related pay system which entailed more administration, in terms of performance measurement documentation, more office politics and less staff trust.

37. OECD (1997) *Performance Pay Schemes for Public Sector Managers: An Evaluation of the Impacts*, Public Management Occasional Papers, No. 15, Paris: OECD.

38. Conceptually, Hong Kong might consider following Singapore's practice, by splitting civil service pay into two components — a stable basic pay element and a smaller variable pay element that is linked both to market fluctuations as measured by the regular pay reviews and to staff performance. Any variable pay arrangement need not be implemented across the whole civil service. A distinction could be made between senior (e.g., directorate) and junior ranks, with the latter given more fixed pay scales in recognition of their greater need for income stability. In Singapore, apart from the basic monthly salary, which follows a set of pay grades regularly reviewed to maintain market competitiveness, civil servants also have a '13th month' bonus, plus a 0.5 month variable bonus at mid-year, and another variable bonus of 0.5–1.0 month, depending on the country's economic performance that year. See Public Service Division, Prime Minister's Office (Singapore) (2018) 'Civil Service Year-End Payment 2018', press release, 23 November, www.psd.gov.sg/press-room/press-releases/civil-service-year-end-payment-2018.

39. Cabinet Office (2014) *Civil Service Reform Plan: Progress Report*, October, London: British Cabinet Office and Civil Service, https://assets.publishing.service.gov.uk/government/uploads/system/uploads/attachment_data/file/360637/Civil_Service_Reform_Plan_-_Progress_Report__web_.pdf.

Chapter 7

1. H.A. Kissinger (1979) *The White House Years*, New York: Little, Brown and Company, p. 39.

2. X. Wu et al. (2018) 'Policy Capacity: Conceptual Framework and Essential Components', in X. Wu et al. (eds) *Policy Capacity and Governance: Assessing Governmental Competences and Capabilities in Theory and Practice*, London: Palgrave Macmillan, pp. 1–25.

3. M. Painter and J. Pierre (2005) 'Unpacking Policy Capacity: Issues and Themes', in J. Pierre and M. Painter (eds) *Challenges to State Policy Capacity: Global Trends and Comparative Perspectives*, Basingstoke: Palgrave Macmillan, pp. 1–18 (quote at p. 2).

4. L. Weiss (1998) *The Myth of the Powerless State*, Ithaca, NY: Cornell University Press, p. 16.

5. C. Johnson (1982) *MITI and the Japanese Miracle*, Stanford: Stanford University Press.

6. R. Wade (1990) *Governing the Market: Economic Theory and the Role of Government in East Asian Industrialization*, Princeton, NJ: Princeton University Press. See also J. Unger and A. Chan (1995) 'China, corporatism, and the East Asian model', *The Australian Journal of Chinese Affairs*, No. 33, pp. 29–53.

7. P.B. Evans (1995) *Embedded Autonomy: States and Industrial Transformation*, Princeton, NJ: Princeton University Press; P.B. Evans (1989) 'Predatory, Developmental and Other Apparatuses: A Comparative Political Economy Perspective on the Third World State', *Sociological Forum*, No. 4, pp. 561–587.

8. T. Skocpol (1992) *Protecting Soldiers and Mothers: The Political Origins of Social Policy in the United States*, Cambridge, MA: Belknap Press of Harvard University Press; T. Skocpol (1985) 'Bringing the State Back In: Strategies of Analysis in Current Research', in P.B. Evans et al. (eds) *Bringing the State Back*, Cambridge: Cambridge University Press, pp. 3–37.

9. J. Migdal (1988) *Strong Societies and Weak States: State-Society Relations and State Capabilities in the Third World*, Princeton: Princeton University Press, p. 4.

10. G. Sørensen (1993) 'Democracy, Authoritarianism and State Strength', in G. Sørensen (ed), *Political Conditionality*, London: Frank Cass, pp. 6–34.

11. S.K. Steffensen (2000) 'The Weak State of Japan', in K.E. Brødsgaard and S. Young (eds), *State Capacity in East Asia: Japan, Taiwan, China and Vietnam*, New York: Oxford University Press, pp. 17–36; A. Khosla (2000) 'State and Economy: Some Observations and Inferences from the Japanese Experience', in K.E. Brødsgaard and S. Young (eds), op. cit., pp. 37–60.

12. L. Weiss (1998), op. cit. p. 39.

13. R.A.W. Rhodes (1997) *Understanding Governance: Policy Networks, Governance, Reflexivity and Accountability*, Buckingham: Open University Press. Rhodes expressed the new form of governance as 'a collection of interorganizational networks made up of governmental and societal actors with no sovereign actor able to steer or regulate' (p. 57).

14. E. Sørensen and J. Torfing (eds) (2008) *Theories of Democratic Network Governance*, Basingstoke: Palgrave.

15. G. Stoker (1998) 'Governance as Theory: Five Propositions', *International Journal of Social Sciences*, Vol. 50, No. 1, pp. 17–28; J. Pierre and G.B. Peters (2005) *Governance, Politics and the State*, Basingstoke, Hampshire: Macmillan.

16. C. Dunrose and K. Rummery (2006) 'Governance and Collaboration: Review Article', *Social Policy and Society*, Vol. 5, No. 2, p. 320. Emphasis is in the original.

17. J. Kooiman (1993) 'Governance and Governability: Using Complexity, Dynamics and Diversity', in J. Kooiman (ed) *Modern Governance: New Government-Society Interactions*, London: Sage, pp. 35–48.

18. K.E. Brødsgaard and S. Young (2000) 'Introduction: State Capacity in East Asia', in K.E. Brødsgaard and S. Young (eds), op. cit., pp. 1–16 (quotes at p. 3).

19. S. Bell and A. Hindmoor (2009) *Rethinking Governance: The Centrality of the State in Modern Society*, Melbourne: Cambridge University Press.

20. A.B.L. Cheung (2005d) 'State Capacity in Hong Kong, Singapore and Taiwan: Coping with Legitimation, Integration and Performance', in J. Pierre and M. Painter (eds) *Challenges to State Policy Capacity: Global Trends and Comparative Perspectives*, Basingstoke: Palgrave Macmillan, pp. 225–254.

21. S. Klein and C.S. Lee (2019) 'Towards a Dynamic Theory of Civil Society: The Politics of Forward and Backward Infiltration', *Sociological Theory*, Vol. 37, No. 1, pp. 62–88.

22. L.F. Goodstadt (2005), op. cit., p. 1. Appraising how Hong Kong transformed from a poor refugee community into one of the world's great cities 'against great odds' under British rule, Goodstadt describes how the colonial administration portrayed itself as creating a capitalist meritocracy that was superior to conventional democracy (pp. 11–13).

23. A.B.L. Cheung (2002a) 'The Changing Political System: Executive-led Government or "Disabled" Governance?' in S.K. Lau (ed) *The First Tung Chee-hwa Administration: The First Five Years of the Hong Kong Special Administrative Region*, Hong Kong: Chinese University Press, pp. 41–68.

24. A.B.L. Cheung (2005d), op. cit.

25. D.Y.K. Tsang (2005a) *Declaration Speech to Announce Chief Executive Candidacy*, 2 June, www.donald-yktsang.com/press_speeches _e_001.html (English version) or http://hm.people.com.cn/GB/42273/3438275.html (Chinese version). These links were originally accessed in June 2005, but they are now invalid.

26. Tsang appointed 153 non-official members (mainly professionals, academics, businessmen, politicians, and prominent labour and media personalities) to the Commission on Strategic Development (CSD). Looking upon the CSD as the most important advisory body, and pledging that his administration belonged to the people and would govern with people-based principles, he said he would expect the CSD to play a greater role in policy-making. Its members would join the government in exploring major issues related to long-term development. Views would also be canvassed by the CSD not when a policy was made but during the early stage of policy formulation. See Information Services Department (2005) 'Appointments to the Commission on Strategic Development', press release, 15 November, www.info.gov.hk/gia/general/200511/15/P200511150128.htm. In practice, however, there was scant evidence of the CSD's active involvement in policy-making, possibly due to resistance by political ministers and bureaucrats alike against outside intrusion into their policy turf.

27. D.Y.K. Tsang (2007b) *My Election Platform — Statement on Progression*, 2 February, Hong Kong: Donald Tsang Election Office. The ten relationships related to: development and conservation; democracy and governance; administration and legislature; rights and duties; rich and poor; large corporations and ordinary people; one country and two systems; central government and SAR; Hong Kong and the world; and progression and stagnation. The 'ten relationships' presentation is reminiscent of Mao Zedong's famous speech on 'The Ten Major Relationships' at the enlarged meeting of the CCP's Central Committee Politburo in 1956. Mao's stipulations at that time were geared towards resolving differences, enlarging unity, and pulling together all positive factors for building the new PRC, before political crackdowns on the 'Rightists' and other dissidents took over in the late 1950s that eventually led to widespread purges of cadres and the disastrous Cultural Revolution in the 1960s–1970s.

28. D.K.Y. Tsang (2007c) *The 2007–08 Policy Address: A New Direction for Hong Kong*, policy address by the Chief Executive to the Legislative Council, 10 October, Hong Kong: Government Logistics Department.

29. D.Y.K. Tsang (2008) *The 2008–09 Policy Address: Embracing New Challenges*, policy address by the Chief Executive to the Legislative Council, 15 October, Hong Kong: Government Logistics Department.

30. Based on the original single-package development approach under the Tung Administration, the government would, through tender, task the selected developer to finance, build, and manage government-specified arts and cultural venues and facilities in the WKCD, together with profit-making office and residential developments. There was strong opposition to this approach

mainly because of doubts concerning the property developer-led planning and financing models. Legislators, civil society, and art groups, as well as the general public, were highly critical, suspecting government-business collusion. After Tsang took over as CE in 2005, the original plan was overturned. A Consultative Committee on the Core Arts and Cultural Facilities of the WKCD, set up in April 2006, reconsidered the way forward. The government eventually decided to develop and manage the WKCD through a statutory West Kowloon Cultural District Authority injected with an upfront endowment of HK$21.6 billion for construction and operation, supplemented by revenue from commercial and residential developments to be granted by the Authority.

31. In July 2006, the government launched a public consultation on the introduction of a 5% flat-rate GST, the revenue from which, after deduction of administrative costs, would be mostly returned to the community as tax relief. However, it was opposed across the political spectrum in the LegCo. In December 2006, FS Henry Tang decided to withdraw the proposal citing lack of public support.

32. Based on a consultancy study, the government proposed to increase the toll charges of the government-owned Cross-Harbour Tunnel and Eastern Harbour Crossing for private cars, taxis, and motorcycles, with a reduction in charges by the still privately owned Western Harbour Crossing (under Build-Operate-Transfer, or BOT, franchise until 2023) through government compensation, in order to shift cross-harbour road traffic flow and alleviate congestion. The proposal was opposed by all major parties across the political spectrum, inducing the government to withdraw the motion to test the support within the LegCo twice (in January and March 2019). The Lam Administration has since decided not to pursue this plan.

33. T.R. Dye (2002) *Understanding Public Policy*, 10th edition, Upper Saddle River: Prentice-Hall, p. 1.

34. See N. Barr (2012) *Economics of the Welfare State*, 5th edition, Oxford: Oxford University Press, pp. 46–49.

35. H.D. Lasswell (1936) *Politics: Who Gets What, When, How*, New York: Whittlesey House.

36. C.E. Lindblom (1959) 'The Science of "Muddling Through"', *Public Administration Review*, Vol. 19, No. 2, pp. 79–88.

37. A.B.L. Cheung (2007b), op. cit.

38. A.B.L. Cheung and K.S. Louie (2000) 'Social Conflicts: 1975–1986', in S.K. Lau (ed) *Social Development and Political Change in Hong Kong*, Hong Kong: Chinese University Press, pp. 63–114.

39. While legislators do not have constitutional power to overturn a government policy decision, they can veto the allocation of public funds for policy implementation or refuse to support any enabling legislation. Thus, the government cannot entirely ignore legislators' views and demands. Given that the government does not possess any vote in the legislature, it has to cultivate pro-Beijing and pro-business parties, and some functional constituency legislators — the so-called pro-establishment camp — as allies vis-à-vis the pan-democratic opposition. In the process, policy concessions have become unavoidable.

40. E.W.Y. Lee et al. (2013) *Public Policymaking in Hong Kong: Civic Engagement and State-Society Relations in a Semi-Democracy*, London: Routledge.

41. A.B.L. Cheung and M.W.L. Wong (2006) 'Judicial Review and Policy Making in Hong Kong: Changing Interface Between the Legal and the Political', *Asia Pacific Journal of Public Administration*, Vol. 28, No. 2, pp. 117–141.

42. E. Chan and J. Chan (2017) 'Hong Kong 2007–2017: A backlash in civil society', *Asia Pacific Journal of Public Administration*, Vol. 39, No. 2, pp. 135–152. According to this study, in the

early post-1997 years, civil society groups were largely positioned as being in partnership with the government as the 'third sector' in providing services and promoting governance, while the civil society discourse in the second decade saw a shift towards social mobilisation and self-defence against the government, especially after the 2014 Occupy Central Campaign and Umbrella Movement, with new post-Umbrella groups proliferating in the professional sectors (such as Umbrella Parents, Progressive Lawyers, and Medecins Inspires) and local district communities (the 'district locals' such as Kwun Tong Locals, Shatin Locals, and Tuen Mun Locals). More recently, anti-extradition mobilisations have led to mass political confrontations characterised by violence, vandalism, and vigilante actions, in the name of fighting police brutality in suppressing the protests.

43. OECD (1996) *Building Policy Coherence: Tools and Tensions*, Public Management Occasional Papers No. 12, Paris: OECD, p. 12.

44. A.B.L. Cheung (2004) 'Strong Executive, Weak Policy Capacity: The Changing Environment of Policymaking in Hong Kong', *Asian Journal of Political Science*, Vol. 12, No. 1, pp. 1–30.

45. See, for example, N. Ma (馬嶽) (2017b) 'Weak State and Weak Society' [in Chinese, 〈弱國家和弱社會的蹉跎〉], *Ming Pao* (《明報》), 21 August. Concern was also expressed in E. Chan and J. Chan (2017), op. cit., who stated that '[w]hile some groups have taken it upon themselves to protect civil society, they unfortunately have turned towards and acted to exclude any outside groups' and cited the emergence of pro-independence groups as signals to the rise of 'bad' civil society that promotes hate and bigotry (p. 148).

46. E.W.Y. Lee et al. (2013), op. cit., pp. 10 and 131.

47. The extensive public consultation conducted on various options to increase land supply under the current Carrie Lam Administration is a case in point. Although the Task Force on Land Supply spent significant effort and patience when listening to stakeholders, holding townhall meetings, and participating in other public engagement activities, as well as undertaking opinion polls, the end result was that the polarisation of views among different sectors and political camps remained unchanged and as wide as ever. For details about the consultation, see Task Force on Land Supply (2018) *Striving for Multi-pronged Land Supply: Report of the Task Force on Land Supply*, December, Hong Kong: The Hong Kong Special Administrative Region Government.

48. A. Wesselink et al. (2014) 'Evidence and policy: Discourses, meanings and practices', *Policy Sciences*, Vol. 47, No. 4, pp. 339–344.

49. R. Hoppe (2005) 'Rethinking the puzzles of the science-policy nexus: From knowledge utilization and science technology studies to types of boundary arrangements', *Poiesis Prax*, Vol. 3, No. 3, pp. 199–215.

50. The term '3C' refers to the three Senior Secretaries (Chief Secretary for Administration, Financial Secretary, and Secretary for Justice) whose rank in Chinese is '司長', with the character '司' sounding like 'C' in English; hence the abbreviation of this meeting chaired by the CE as the '3C Meeting'.

51. See, for example, S. Virkar (2015) 'Globalization, the Internet, and the Nation-State: A Critical Analysis', in J.P. Sahlin (ed) *Social Media and the Transformation of Interaction in Society*, Hershey, PA: Information Science Reference (an imprint of IGI Global), pp. 51–66.

52. H. Margetts et al. (2015) *Political Turbulence: How Social Media Shape Collective Action*, Princeton: Princeton University Press.

53. Ministers did not always get their way because of resistance from their senior civil servants who might consider some policy ideas and measures not conducive to broader long-term public

interest or in adherence to fiscal prudence. This gave rise to minister-bureaucrat tension. See J.P. Burns and W. Li (2015), op. cit.; S.K. Lau (劉兆佳) (2013a), op. cit., pp. 121–127.

54. For example, C. Hood (1983) *The Tools of Government*, Hong Kong: Macmillan; H.A. de Bruijn and H.A.M. Hufen (1998) 'The traditional approach to policy instruments', in B.G. Peters and F.K.M. van Nispen (eds) *Public Policy Instruments: Evaluating the Tools of Public Administration*, Cheltenham: Edward Elgar, pp. 11–32; S.H. Linder and B.G. Peters (1998) 'The study of policy instruments: Four schools of thought', in B.G. Peters and F.K.M. van Nispen (eds), op. cit., pp. 33–45.

55. C. Hood (1983), op. cit. 'Nodality' refers to a store of information not available to others. Nowadays, it includes a good use of social media. 'Authority' refers to the possession of legal or official power to demand, forbid, guarantee, and adjudicate. 'Treasure' refers to money power. 'Organisation' refers to the possession of people and other physical inputs. The limit of each of these four categories of tools are, respectively, the government's credibility, fungibility, legal standing, and organisational capacity. Other studies, in a similar vein, have identified policy through advocacy, law, money, and action, respectively. See C. Althaus et al. (2013) *The Australian Policy Handbook*, 5th edition, Sydney: Allen & Unwin.

56. M. Howlett and M. Ramesh (1995) *Studying Public Policy: Policy Cycles and Policy Subsystems*, Toronto: Oxford University Press.

57. H.A. de Bruijn and H.A.M. Hufen (1998), op. cit.

58. C. Hood (1983), op. cit., p. 85.

59. P.M.P. Chan (2020) *The 2020–21 Budget*, Speech by the Financial Secretary moving the Second Reading of the Appropriation Bill 2020 at the Legislative Council, 26 February, para. 174.

60. Hong Kong Monetary Authority (2020) 'Exchange Fund Abridged Balance Sheet and Currency Board Account', press release, 29 April.

61. To improve roadside air quality and better protect public health, the Leung Administration announced in 2013 an incentive-cum-regulatory approach involving HK$11.7 billion to phase out some 82,000 pre-Euro IV diesel commercial vehicles. Eligible registered owners could apply for an ex-gratia payment of up to 33% of the average taxable values of new vehicles from March 2014 onwards.

62. Public housing rents are already maintained at a reasonably affordable level. Under the law passed in 2007, biennial reviews are conducted on the household income of tenants of public housing units (excluding those whose rent is paid by the government under the CSSA scheme). Depending on the increase or decrease compared to the last review, public housing rent is adjusted upwards or downwards. For any upward adjustment, it is capped by law at 10%. In addition, the Housing Authority operates a Rent Assistance Scheme to provide a 25–50% rent reduction to those tenants facing economic difficulties such as temporary unemployment.

63. The $6,000 scheme in 2011–2012 and the Caring and Sharing Scheme involved some HK$37 billion and HK$11 billion (estimated), respectively, plus administrative costs of HK$165 million (0.5%) and HK$311 million (2.8%), respectively.

64. That said, it is of course legitimate for the government to implement a social dividend scheme, such as that in Singapore and Macao, whereby every year the government would set aside an amount out of the annual fiscal surplus for distribution to all eligible citizens (such as HKPRs).

65. Information Services Department (2019a) 'FS announces measures to support enterprises and residents', press release, 15 August.

66. In terms of relief support, HK$5 billion was set aside to support transitional housing projects, while HK$1 billion was allocated to support small and medium enterprise (SME) expert marketing,

raising all payment rates of the Working Family Allowance and increasing the subsidy rate under the Public Transport Fare Subsidy Scheme. See C. Lam (2019) *The Chief Executive's 2019 Policy Address: Treasure Hong Kong: Our Home*, policy address by the Chief Executive to the Legislative Council, 16 October, Hong Kong: Government Logistics Department.

67. P.M.P. Chan (2020), op. cit., paras. 25–37; Chief Secretary for Administration's Office and various Bureaus (2020) *Item for Finance Committee*, Paper for discussion at Finance Committee, FCR(2020–21)2, April, Hong Kong: Legislative Council, para. 3. The two rounds of anti-epidemic support and relief measures were projected to result in a consolidated deficit of about HK$37.8 billion for 2019–2020 and about HK$139.1 billion for 2020–2021, accounting for 1.3% and 4.8% of GDP, respectively.

68. Under the present arrangement, the government can create non-directorate posts via delegated authority to heads of departments and permanent secretaries in charge of bureaus as 'Controlling Officers'. However, the authority over any change in the directorate establishment still rests with the Finance Committee of the LegCo (based on the recommendation of its Establishment Subcommittee).

69. D. Savoie (2010) *Power: Where Is It?* Montreal: McGill-Queen's University Press. According to Savoie, forces such as globalisation, the new media, the changing role of the courts in parliamentary democracies, the partisanship of political parties in shaping policy, and collapsing boundaries between governments and within government departments have all caused citizens to feel their countries are less democratic, so much so that power is leaving institutions and organisations and being distributed to powerful individuals in both the public and private sectors, who often push aside formal processes in order to drive change. Thus, power is getting more tangled and fluid, with both politicians and bureaucrats losing their grip. The new information age and social networks are further creating a new laissez-faire environment in politics, making it all the more difficult to locate who commands and who obeys.

Chapter 8

1. B. Jessop (1990) *State Theory: Putting Capitalist States in Their Place*, Cambridge: Polity Press. See also J. O'Connor (1973) *The Fiscal Crisis of the State*, New York: St. Martin's Press.

2. World Bank (1993) *The East Asian Economic Miracle: Economic Growth and Public Policy*, New York: Oxford University Press.

3. A.B.L. Cheung (2000b) 'New Interventionism in the Making: Interpreting State Interventions in Hong Kong after the Change of Sovereignty', *Journal of Contemporary China*, Vol. 9, No. 24, pp. 291–308.

4. R. Wade (1990), op. cit.

5. M. Friedman (1981) *Free to Choose*, Harmondsworth: Penguin Books, p. 54. The four basic duties of government according to Friedman are: protection from violence and invasion; protection from injustice or oppression; erection and maintenance of certain public works and certain public institutions; and protection of those members of the community who could not be regarded as 'responsible' individuals (detailed on pp. 47–53).

6. A. Rabushka (1979), op. cit., p. 83.

7. According to N. Monnery (2017) *Architect of Prosperity: Sir John Cowperthwaite and the Making of Hong Kong*, London: London Publishing Partnership.

8. Borrowing the concept of exclusionary corporatist state articulated in A. Stepan (1978) *The State and Society: Peru in Comparative Perspective*, Princeton, NJ: Princeton University Press.

9. G.B. Endacott (1964), op. cit., p. 244.

10. R. Wade (1990), op. cit.

11. Advisory Committee on Diversification (1979) *Report of the Advisory Committee on Diversification 1979*, Hong Kong: Government Printer. See also S. Haggard (1990) *Pathways from the Periphery: The Politics of Growth in the Newly Industrialising Countries*, Ithaca and London: Cornell University Press.

12. According to a US Central Intelligence Agency (CIA) report, then Prime Minister Lee Kuan Yew initiated in 1979 what was billed as Singapore's 'Second Industrialization' by making the country a high-technology manufacturing centre and a regional centre of the knowledge industries. Increases in wages were mandated in order to discourage low-skilled operations from locating in Singapore and to encourage existing low-wage manufacturers to upgrade their operations. Such increases averaged over 20% annually in 1979 and 1980 and about 16% in 1981. The Economic Development Board also took steps to spur capital- and technology-intensive investments. See Directorate of Intelligence, CIA (1982) *Singapore: Moving Ahead with the Second Industrial Revolution*, confidential report, May, approved for release on 10 July 2008, Washington, D.C.: CIA, p. 5, www.cia.gov/library/readingroom/docs/CIA-RDP83B00227R000100170001-0.pdf.

13. J.R. Schiffer (1983) *Anatomy of a Laissez-faire Government: The Hong Kong Growth Model Reconsidered*, Hong Kong: Centre of Urban Studies and Urban Planning, University of Hong Kong. He reckons that in terms of consumption, non-market factors accounted for more than 50% of a blue-collar household's normal expenditure. In production support, the government not only provided industry with infrastructure but also supplied it with a healthier, more educated and better housed workforce, hence making labour more productive and stable for capital.

14. J.R. Schiffer (1983), op. cit., pp. 31–32.

15. M. Friedman (1981), op. cit., p. 34.

16. L. Goodstadt (2005), op. cit.

17. B. Jessop and N.L. Shum (2000) 'An Entrepreneurial City in Action: Hong Kong's Emerging Strategies in and for (Inter)Urban Competition', *Urban Studies*, Vol. 37, No. 12, pp. 2287–2313.

18. H.J. Kwon (1998) 'Democracy and the Politics of Social Welfare: A Comparative Analysis of Welfare Systems in East Asia', in R. Goodman et al. (eds) *The East Asian Welfare Model: Welfare Orientalism and the State*, London: Routledge, pp. 27–74.

19. For example, F.G. Castles (1998) *Comparative Public Policy: Patterns of Post-war Transformation*, Cheltenham: Edward Elgar. Castles discovered that European public policy development did not evolved along uniform patterns. Cross-national patterns of social and economic policy outcomes were in a constant state of flux as they were shaped by a wide range of economic, social, cultural, political, and policy factors which all altered over time.

20. C. Jones (1993) 'The Pacific Challenge: Confucian Welfare States', in C. Jones (ed) *New Perspectives on the Welfare State in Europe*, London: Routledge, pp. 198–217.

21. M. Ramesh (1995) 'Social security in South Korea and Singapore: Explaining the differences', *Social Policy and Administration*, Vol. 29, No. 3, pp. 228–240; H.J. Kwon (1997) 'Beyond European welfare regimes: Comparative perspectives on East Asian welfare systems', *Journal of Social Policy*, Vol. 26, No. 4, pp. 467–484.

22. I. Holliday (2000) 'Productivist Welfare Capitalism: Social Policy in East Asia', *Political Studies*, Vol. 48, pp. 706–723.

23. A.B.L Cheung (2009b) 'Interpreting East Asian Social Policy Development: Paradigm Shift or Policy "Steadiness"?' in K.H. Mok and R. Forrest (eds) *Changing Governance and Public Policy in East Asia*, London and New York: Routledge, pp. 25–48.

24. *The Economist* (1997) 'The World Economy Survey', 20 September, p. 11 (based on statistics of the IMF).

25. C.S.S. Lo (1990) *Public Budgeting in Hong Kong: An Incremental Decision-making Approach*, Hong Kong: Writers' and Publishers' Cooperative, Ch. 2.

26. According to figures cited in Y.W. Sung (1986) 'Fiscal and Economic Policies in Hong Kong', in J.Y.S. Cheng (ed) *Hong Kong in Transition*, Hong Kong: Oxford University Press, Table 5.1.

27. *Ibid.*

28. P. Haddon-Cave (1984) 'Introduction [to the First Edition]: The Making of Some Aspects of Public Policy in Hong Kong', in D.G. Lethbridge (ed) *The Business Environment in Hong Kong*, 2nd edition, Hong Kong: Oxford University Press, pp. xiii–xx

29. H. Macleod (1992) 'My six months walking a financial tightrope', *South China Morning Post*, 9 February.

30. H. Macleod (1995) *The 1995–96 Budget*, Speech by the Financial Secretary moving the Second Reading of the Appropriation Bill 1995, 1 March, Hong Kong: Government Printer.

31. A.B.L. Cheung (2000b), op. cit.

32. Tung's popularity reached 67.7% in his third month in office (September 1997), the highest during his tenure as CE. HKUPOP (2019a), www.hkupop.hku.hk/chinese/popexpress/ce2017/cl/cecomparison/datatables.html.

33. C.H. Tung (1998) *The 1998 Policy Address: From Adversity to Opportunity*, policy address by the Chief Executive to the Legislative Council, 7 October, Hong Kong: Printing Department. The policy address mentioned strengthening government support for innovation and technological development by setting up an Applied Science and Technology Research Institute; establishing a HK$5 billion Innovation and Technology Fund and positioning Hong Kong as an Internet hub for the Asia Pacific Region; developing a world-class teleport at Chung Hom Kok to provide the best possible global satellite link; setting up a HK$100 million Film Development Fund; and establishing Hong Kong as an international centre for Chinese medicine.

34. C.H. Tung (2001), op. cit., para. 29.

35. A.K.C. Leung (2002) *The 2002–03 Budget*, Speech by the Financial Secretary moving the Second Reading of the Appropriation Bill 2002 at the Legislative Council, 6 March, Hong Kong: Printing Department, para. 42. Leung disagreed with the view that to maintain Hong Kong's economic freedom, the government should be passive and distance itself from the economy. He said that the government should have a clear vision of the direction of economic development and be a proactive market enabler. This role should include: maintaining an institutional framework conducive to market development; providing the infrastructure in which the private sector would not invest in; providing an appropriate environment and the resources required to raise the quality of human capital; securing more favourable market access for local enterprises; and taking appropriate measures to secure projects beneficial to the economy as a whole when the private sector is not ready to invest in them.

36. H. Tang (2004), op. cit., para. 7.

37. D.Y.K. Tsang (2006) 'Big Market, Small Government', press release by the Chief Executive, 18 September, Hong Kong: Chief Executive's Office, www.ceo.gov.hk/archive/2012/eng/press/oped.htm.

38. *Ibid.*

39. *Ibid.*

40. D.Y.K. Tsang (2007a) *Donald Tsang Election Platform: Policy Blueprint*, Hong Kong: Donald Tsang Election Office.

41. D.Y.K. Tsang (2007c), op. cit., p. 2.

42. *Ibid.*, p. 18.

43. Tsang elaborated his developmental goals by saying: 'I object to a dichotomy between the roles played by the Government and the market, whether it be a strong belief in the omnipotence of government intervention or a passionate support of the free market being sacrosanct. Both are sweeping generalizations. [...] The Government needs to balance the political, economic and social demands of different interest groups in the community, and to make progress while maintaining stability. It should take the lead at the policy-making level in certain areas such as promoting economic integration with the Mainland, taking forward cross-boundary infrastructure projects and making joint efforts to develop a world-class metropolis'. See D.Y.K. Tsang (2007c), op. cit., paras. 12–13.

44. D.Y.K. Tsang (2008), op. cit., para. 15.

45. The Competition Ordinance took full effect in December 2015.

46. K.C. Ng (2012) 'Finance chief John Tsang warns against ignoring Hong Kong's pillar industries', *South China Morning Post*, 31 December.

47. J.C.W. Tsang (2008) *The 2008–09 Budget*, Speech by the Financial Secretary moving the Second Reading of the Appropriation Bill 2008 at the Legislative Council, 27 February, Hong Kong: Printing Department, paras. 55–60.

48. Following the outbreak of the global financial crisis in 2008–2009, most developed economies as well as China embarked on QE measures, also known as large-scale asset purchases, as an expansionary monetary policy whereby a central bank bought predetermined amounts of government bonds or other financial assets from commercial banks and financial institutions, in order to stimulate the economy and increase liquidity. This helped raise the prices of those financial assets and lower their yield, while simultaneously lowering short-term interest rates and increasing the money supply. As a result, the property market in Hong Kong as well as other world cities entered a prolonged period of boom and bubble.

49. Four times the size of Hong Kong Science Park, the Hong Kong/Shenzhen Innovation and Technology Park will act as a key base for co-operation in I&T research to attract top-tier enterprises, research institutions, and higher education institutions from Hong Kong, Mainland cities, and the rest of the world. See the website of the Hong Kong Science and Technology Parks Corporation, www.hkstp.org/en/our-stories/our-footprint/hong-kong-shenzhen-innovation-and-technology-park/.

50. C.Y. Leung (2016) *The 2016 Policy Address: Innovate for the Economy, Improve Livelihood, Foster Harmony, Share Prosperity*, policy address by the Chief Executive to the Legislative Council, 13 January, Hong Kong: Printing Department, para. 77.

51. *Ibid.*, paras. 28 and 126. See also Information Services Department (2016a) 'Government Implements New Agriculture Policy', press release, 14 January, www.info.gov.hk/gia/general/201601/14/P201601140558.htm.

52. A.B.L. Cheung (張炳良) (2018a) *An Unavoidable Reality — A Review of Housing Policies During My Five Years As Secretary* [in Chinese, 《不能迴避的現實 —— 回顧任局長五年的房屋政策》], Hong Kong: Chung Hwa Book Company, Ch. 5.

53. During their campaigns for CE in 2012, both Leung Chun-ying and his rival Henry Tang committed to increasing elderly allowances. Upon being elected to office, Leung proceeded with the introduction of the Old Age Living Allowance in April 2013, to supplement the living expenses of elderly people aged 65 or above in need of financial support. It was during his term that an official poverty line was adopted by the government based on the recommendation of the Commission on Poverty chaired by his Chief Secretary for Administration Carrie Lam, announced in September 2013. The poverty line was defined as half of the median monthly household income of all domestic households in Hong Kong, prior to government intervention like tax and social benefits transfers. This calculation was based on the concept of relative poverty as opposed to absolute poverty expressed in terms of basic subsistence. Accordingly, Hong Kong's poor population in 2012 was found to be around 1.02 million (403,000 households), representing a poverty rate of 15.2%.

54. His compromise solution of mandating standard working hours was rejected by the trade unions. His proposal of a limited government funding injection to boost employers' ability to pay in the event of abolishing the existing 'offsetting' practice, with no retrospective effect, found ears on neither the labour nor employer sides.

55. Her Administration injected a total of HK$78 billion into I&T-related funds and increased funding for R&D in public universities.

56. Sustainable Lantau Office website, *Tomorrow Lantau Vision*, www.lantau.gov.hk/en/lantau-tomorrow-vision/index.html. The plan was first announced in Lam's 2018 policy address.

57. C. Lam (2017) *The Chief Executive's 2017 Policy Address: We Connect for Hope and Happiness*, policy address by the Chief Executive to the Legislative Council, 11 October, Hong Kong: Government Logistics Department, para. 35.

58. C. Lam (2018) *The Chief Executive's 2018 Policy Address: Striving Ahead, Rekindling Hopes*, policy address by the Chief Executive to the Legislative Council, 10 October, Hong Kong: Government Logistics Department, paras. 14–16.

59. At the beginning of her term, Lam set up task forces to further review eight key areas of education: professional development of teachers, curriculum arrangement, assessment system, vocational and professional education and training, self-financing post-secondary education, school-based management, parent education, and funding for university research and student hostels.

60. *China Daily* (2019a) 'Shenzhen surpasses HK in GDP', 28 February, www.chinadaily.com. cn/a/201902/28/WS5c7720fda3106c65c34ebd70.html. Hong Kong's GDP was cited as HK$2.845 trillion (equivalent to RMB¥2.4 trillion based on the average annual exchange rate) and Shenzhen's GDP as RMB¥2.422 trillion. However, per capita GDP in Hong Kong in 2018 was HK$381,870 (equal to RMB¥322,000), well above Shenzhen's RMB¥200,000. According to World Bank data, Hong Kong's nominal 2018 GDP was US$341.45 billion (HK$2,847.26 billion) which was equivalent to RMB¥2,593.61 billion according to the exchange rate on 31 August 2019. See World Bank (n.d.) *Hong Kong SAR, China*, https://data.worldbank.org/country/hong-kong-sar-china?view=chart.

61. For more on Hong Kong's participation in the Belt and Road Initiative, see the government's official Belt and Road Initiative website at www.beltandroad.gov.hk/participation.html. For more details of the Greater Bay Area Outline Development Plan and Hong Kong's involvement, see the government's official Greater Bay Area website at www.bayarea.gov.hk/en/home/index.html.

62. A.B.L. Cheung (2009b), op. cit.

63. M. Ramesh et al. (eds) (2010) *Reasserting the Public in Public Service*, Abingdon, Oxon: Routledge.

64. G. Majone (1997) 'From the Positive to the Regulatory State: Causes and Consequences of Changes in the Mode of Governance', *Journal of Public Policy*, Vol. 17, No. 2, pp. 139–167.

65. M. Mazzucato (2018) *The Entrepreneurial State: Debunking Public vs Private Sector Myths*, London: Penguin.

66. S.H. Linder and B.G. Peters (1998), op. cit.

67. M. Mazzucato (2018), op. cit.

68. According to the OECD, Chinese business coughed up 76% of the country's R&D expenditure in 2017. In Japan, businesses contributed 78% of R&D expenditure in 2017, while US businesses funded 62%. See OECD (n.d.) *Main Science and Technology Indicators*, https://stats.oecd.org/Index.aspx?DataSetCode=MSTI_PUB. China's R&D investment in 2017 reached RMB¥1,760.6 billion, 123 times higher than that in 1991 (i.e., an annual growth rate of 20.3% during the period concerned). See National Statistics Bureau (2018) 'Rapid advancement in science and technology, with outstanding achievement driven by innovation' [in Chinese, 〈科技進步日新月異 創新驅動成效突出〉], 12 September, Beijing: National Statistics Bureau, www.stats.gov.cn/ztjc/ztfx/ggkf40n/201809/t20180912_1622413.html.

Chapter 9

1. Economist Intelligence Unit (2020) 'Hong Kong', *The Economist*, https://country.eiu.com/hong-kong.

2. The Heritage Foundation (2020) *2020 Index of Economic Freedom*, www.heritage.org/index/ranking/; Z/Yen Group (2020) *The Global Financial Centres Index*, www.longfinance.net/programmes/financial-centre-futures/global-financial-centres-index/.

3. According to the Quacquarelli Symonds (QS) World University Rankings, four Hong Kong universities are in the world's top 50 — The University of Hong Kong (22), The Hong Kong University of Science and Technology (27), The Chinese University of Hong Kong (43) and The City University of Hong Kong (48). See Quacquarelli Symonds (QS) (2020) *QS World University Rankings 2021*, 10 June, www.topuniversities.com/university-rankings/world-university-rankings/2021.

4. K. Schwab (2019) *The Global Competitiveness Report 2019*, October, Cologny, Switzerland: World Economic Forum, www3.weforum.org/docs/WEF_TheGlobalCompetitivenessReport2019.pdf. According to this report, Hong Kong features in the top 10 of eight pillars (a record) and outperforms the OECD benchmark on every pillar. It ranks first on four pillars (the most of any economy): Macroeconomic stability (100), Health (100), Financial system (91.4), and Product market (81.6). It ranks third on Infrastructure (94.0) and Information and Communication Technology (ICT) adoption (89.4). Hong Kong's biggest weakness is its limited capability to innovate, with a score of 63.4 (26th), lagging considerably behind Singapore (13th).

5. Per capita GDP in 2018 for Britain, Germany, France, Canada, and Japan were US$42,962.4, US$47,615.7, US$41,469, US$46,234.4, and US$39,290.0, respectively. That of South Korea was much lower at US$31,380.1, while that of Singapore was much higher at US$64,581.9. See World Bank (n.d.), *GDP per capita (current US$)*, various economies, https://data.worldbank.org/indicator/NY.GDP.PCAP.CD.

6. OECD (2018) *For Good Measure: Advancing Research on Well-Being Metrics Beyond GDP*, Paris: OECD. It was also observed that much of the 'wealth' income is not produced assets but land or other ownership claims giving rise to rents (or 'exploitative rents'). See J.E. Stiglitz (2015)

'New theoretical perspectives on the distribution of income and wealth among individuals: Part I. The wealth residual', *NBER Working Paper*, No. 21189, www.nber.org/papers/w21189.

7. Vertical inequality measures inequality in income, consumption, and wealth among individuals, but it usually ignores systematic inequities among population groups and omits important non-income aspects. Horizontal inequalities look at inequalities among groups with shared characteristics, both in income and non-income dimensions, intra-household inequality, and the gender wealth gap.

8. Worldometer (n.d.) *Life Expectancy of the World Population* (data based on the latest United Nations Population Division estimates), www.worldometers.info/demographics/life-expectancy/; Hong Kong SAR Government (2017) '20 Years of Growth and Progress: The Facts', *20th Anniversary Fact Sheets Series*, Hong Kong: Information Services Department.

9. In 2018, Hong Kong was No. 1, followed by Singapore. See J.M Lee and W. Lu (2018) 'These Are the World's Healthiest Nations', *Bloomberg*, 19 September, www.bloomberg.com/news/articles/2018-09-19/u-s-near-bottom-of-health-index-hong-kong-and-singapore-at-top.

10. Task Force on Review of Self-financing Post-secondary Education (2018) *Review Report: Parallel Development, Promoting Diversity*, December, Hong Kong: Education Bureau, Introduction, para. 3.

11. Census and Statistics Department (2020d), *Wages and Labour Earnings*, Hong Kong: Census and Statistics Department, www.censtatd.gov.hk/hkstat/sub/so210.jsp.

12. TheGlobalEconomy.com (n.d.) *Hong Kong: Unemployment Rate* (based on World Bank figures), www.theglobaleconomy.com/Hong-Kong/Unemployment_rate/.

13. Census and Statistics Department (2020c) *Labour Statistics*, Hong Kong: Census and Statistics Department, www.censtatd.gov.hk/hkstat/sub/so30.jsp.

14. Census and Statistics Department (2020b), *Labour Force, Table 011: Unemployment Rate by Sex and Age*, Hong Kong: Census and Statistics Department, www.censtatd.gov.hk/hkstat/sub/sp200.jsp?tableID=011&ID=0&productType=8.

15. According to the World Bank's youth unemployment data (percentage of labour force in the 15–24 age range) based on International Labour Organisation estimates, Hong Kong's rate was 10.0% in 2019, comparing very favourably with the average of the OECD member countries (at 12.0%) and some individual developed economies (Australia 12.1%, Britain 11.3%, France 19.1%, Italy 29.3%, Spain 32.9%, and Sweden 17.8%, with only Germany and the US doing better at 5.4% and 8.5%, respectively). In East Asia, youth unemployment in Mainland China stood at 10.3%, while in Japan, South Korea, and Singapore it was 3.7%, 11.0%, and 9.3%, respectively. See World Bank (2020a) *Data: Unemployment youth, total*, https://data.world.bank.org/indicator/sl.uem.1524.zs. Taiwan's youth unemployment rate was 12.11% at end of 2019 according to Trading Economics (n.d.) *Taiwan Youth Unemployment Rate*, https://tradingeconomics.com/taiwan/youth-unemployment-rate#:~:text=Looking%20forward%2C%20we%20estimate%20Youth,according%20to%20our%20econometric%20models.

16. Hong Kong was ranked among the top 10 in 2017 (at 9th) but fell to 20th place in mid-2019, because of the changing international perceptions of the city due to the political unrest and escalating violence. See Economist Intelligence Unit (2017) 'Safe Cities Index 2017', November, London: *The Economist*, http://safecities.economist.com/safe-cities-index-2017; Economist Intelligence Unit (2019) 'Safe Cities Index 2019', August, London: *The Economist*, https://safecities.economist.com/wp-content/uploads/2019/08/Aug-5-ENG-NEC-Safe-Cities-2019-270x210-19-screen.pdf.

17. Henley & Partners Research Department (n.d.) *Henley & Partners Passport Index: 2020 Q2 Update*, www.henleypassportindex.com/passport-index. The PRC passport is ranked at 74th with visa-free entry to only 70 places.

18. To illustrate, on 11 June 2020, about 5 months after the outbreak of COVID-19, the total numbers of cases and deaths per million people were 148 and 0.5, respectively, comparing very favourably with Singapore (6,663, 4), New Zealand (301, 4), and South Korea (233, 5) which were generally regarded as high performers. Only Taiwan (19, 0.3) and Macao (69, 0) outperformed the city. Among the top worst performers were the US (6,245, 348) and Britain (4,275, 606). Mainland China's performance was striking (58, 3) even if allowing for its huge population as well as any under-reporting and under-estimation, as suspected by some critics. See Worldometer (2020) *Covid-19 Coronavirus Pandemic*, 11 June, www.worldometers.info/coronavirus/?utm_campaign=homeAdvegas1?%22#countries.

19. P.M.P Chan (2020), op. cit., para. 9. The IMF forecast in December 2019 was even more severe at -1.9%. See International Monetary Fund (2019) 'IMF Executive Board Concludes 2019 Article IV Consultation Discussions with People's Republic of China — Hong Kong Special Administrative Region', press release No. 19/485, 30 December.

20. See, for example, Census and Statistics Department (2020f) 'Quarterly business receipts indices for service industries for first quarter of 2020', press release, 9 June, Hong Kong.

21. A. Au (2020) 'Economic Situation in the First Quarter of 2020 and Latest GDP and Price Forecasts for 2020', press release, 15 May, Hong Kong: Information Services Department.

22. Census and Statistics Department (2020a), *Labour Force, Table 006: Labour Force, Unemployment and Underemployment*, Hong Kong: Census and Statistics Department, www.censtatd.gov.hk/hkstat/sub/sp200.jsp?tableID=006&ID=0&productType=8.

23. Such as the Anti-Epidemic Fund (amounting to some HK$150 billion in mid-2020) and the government 'bailout' of Hong Kong's flagship carrier Cathay Pacific Airline amounting to HK$29.25 billion announced on 9 June 2020 (HK$19.5 billion in preferential shares, warrants of up to a further HK$1.95 billion purchase of shares at a later date, and a HK$7.8 billion bridging loan).

24. S. Schiavo (2020) 'Covid-19 throws us into an unprecedented debt crisis, but it's one we can rise from', *European Network for Economic and Fiscal Policy Research*, 11 May; UN Department of Economic and Social Affairs (2020) *UN/DESA Policy Brief #72: COVID-19 and sovereign debt*, 14 May.

25. See, for example, T.L. Lui (2014) 'Fading Opportunities: Hong Kong in the context of regional integration', *China Perspectives*, No. 1, pp. 35–42; K.M. Lee et al. (2014) 'The New Paradox of Thrift: Financialisation, retirement protection, and income polarisation in Hong Kong', *China Perspectives*, No. 1, pp. 15–24.

26. Research Office of the Legislative Council Secretariat (2015) *Social mobility in Hong Kong*, Research Brief No. 2, Hong Kong: Legislative Council Research Division, pp. 1–12. According to the report, in terms of earnings mobility of the local workforce, 62.9% had no earnings mobility after 5 years of work (2003–2008) and 47.2% had no earnings mobility after 10 years of work (1998–2008) (54.1% for workers in the lowest income quintile). See also S.W. Chiu (趙永佳) and C.Y. Ip (葉仲茵) (2015) 'Social Mobility of Youth in Hong Kong: Objective Experiences and Subjective Perceptions' [in Chinese, 〈香港青年「下流」問題：客觀狀況與主觀感受〉], *Hong Kong and Macao Journal* [《港澳研究》], No. 3, pp. 65–74.

27. J. Helliwell et al. (2018) *World Happiness Report 2019*, New York: Sustainable Development Solutions Network, https://s3.amazonaws.com/happiness-report/2019/WHR19.pdf. This report

ranked 156 countries and jurisdictions by their happiness levels. The first World Happiness Report was published in April 2012 in support of the UN High Level Meeting on happiness and well-being.

28. The average price for a small residential unit surged by a total of 188% during 2006–2013, whereas the median monthly household income increased by 30% over the same period. This divergent trend contrasted with the earlier period between the 1980s and the mid-1990s, when the growth of median monthly household income closely matched the pace of housing price increases. See Research Office of the Legislative Council Secretariat (2015), op. cit.

29. For comparison purpose, from 2015 to the third quarter of 2016, overall housing prices in Hong Kong rose by 6%, whereas the corresponding increases in London, Sydney, and Vancouver were 18%, 19%, and 45%, respectively. See the analysis of this data in A.B.L. Cheung (張炳良) (2018a), op. cit., Ch. 5.

30. The US Federal Reserve's interest was lowered to 0.25% (effectively zero) in December 2008, which lasted until the end of 2015. The interest rate was raised slightly to 0.5% in December 2015, and then up to 0.75% in December 2016, which was slower than the market anticipated. It was only in 2017 that the rate of increase gradually picked up, reaching 2.5% by end of 2018. Since mid-2019, however, the Federal Reserve has cut the interest rate. In a recent move, it brought the interest rate down to near-zero (0–0.25%) and resumed QE measures in order to boost the US economy in the midst of the COVID-19 pandemic. A prolonged period of extra-low interest rates is expected globally.

31. According to Demographia's report on housing affordability, which covered 309 metropolitan housing markets (metropolitan areas) in eight countries (Australia, Canada, China [Hong Kong Only], Ireland, New Zealand, Singapore, Britain, and the US), Hong Kong was ranked as the least affordable in 2020, with an affordability ratio (i.e., the median house price divided by the median household income) of 20.8 (20.9 in 2019), followed by Vancouver (11.9) and Sydney (11.0). See Demographia (2020) *Media Release: 16th Annual Demographia International Housing Affordability Survey*, 20 January, http://demographia.com/dhimedia2020.pdf.

32. Information Services Department (2018a) '2016 Population By-census Thematic Report: Persons Living in Subdivided Units published', press release, 18 January, www.info.gov.hk/gia/general/201801/18/P2018011800595.htm. Sub-divided units refer to the small cubicles created within a single flat. These often have poor sanitation as well as limited toilet and cooking facilities.

33. Hong Kong Housing Authority (n.d.), *Number of Applications and Average Waiting Time for Public Rental Housing*, www.housingauthority.gov.hk/en/about-us/publications-and-statistics/prh-applications-average-waiting-time/index.html.

34. Transport and Housing Bureau (2014) *Long Term Housing Strategy 2014*, December, Hong Kong: Transport and Housing Bureau. Details of the formulation of the Long Term Housing Strategy and some analysis of this can be found in A.B.L. Cheung (2018a), op. cit., Ch. 4.

35. Education Bureau (n.d.) 'Government Expenditure on Education', *Figures and Statistics*, Hong Kong: Education Bureau, www.edb.gov.hk/en/about-edb/publications-stat/figures/gov-expenditure.html.

36. Task Force on Review of Self-financing Post-secondary Education (2018), op. cit., para. 2.18.

37. See K.C. Ng (2018) 'Hong Kong university graduates take home less pay than counterparts 30 years ago and one in six ends up in unskilled job, study finds', *South China Morning Post*, 18 December.

38. V. Vroom (1964) *Work and Motivation*, New York: Wiley. Expectancy theory explains that the performance of individuals is affected by how they consider the rewards they deserve compared to the rewards they are actually given.

39. K. Ohmae (2006) *M-shape Society: The Crisis and Business Opportunity of the Disappearance of the Middle Class* [Original in Japanese,《ロウアーミドルの衝撃》], 東京 [Tokyo]: 講談社 [Kodansha]. (There is no English translation. Chinese translation, 大前研一 (2006)《M型社會: 中產階級消失的危機與商機》, 台北市: 商周出版.)

40. OECD (2019) *Under Pressure: The Squeezed Middle Class*, Paris: OECD, www.oecd-ilibrary.org/docserver/689afed1-en.pdf?expires=1556088968&id=id&accname=oid014243&checksum=D179AD2C79957AC1C5B5A803C6EB562D.

41. C. Mudde (2017) *The Populist Radical Right: A Reader*, London and New York: Routledge.

42. Census and Statistics Department (2017b) *Hong Kong Population Projections, 2017–2066*, 8 September, Hong Kong: Census and Statistics Department.

43. Ibid. Please refer to the presentation slides of that reference, specifically slide 14, which can be found at www.censtatd.gov.hk/FileManager/EN/Content_1170/pop_proj_16based_slide.pdf. The overall dependency ratio refers to the number of persons aged under 15 and those aged 65 and above per 1,000 persons aged between 15 and 64. This ratio was 397 in 2016 and is projected to rise to 697 by 2036.

44. For a useful background history of the CPF issue, see Research Office of the Legislative Council Secretariat (2005) *Fact Sheet: Historical Development of Retirement Schemes in Hong Kong*, FS18/04-05, 19 July, Hong Kong: Legislative Council Research Division, www.legco.gov.hk/yr04-05/english/sec/library/0405fs18e.pdf.

45. Henry Tang (Liberal Party) and Lau Chin-shek (UDHK and Confederation of Trade Unions), respectively representing industry and labour within the LegCo at that time, joined hands in promoting the CPF option.

46. During the CPF and old age pension scheme debates in the early 1990s, even the FTU was not keen on the old age pension scheme idea as somehow Hong Kong employees preferred to keep their contributions to a retirement scheme within their own account to be withdrawn after retirement. They were against redistributing their retirement savings to others in the form of a uniform monthly pension payment.

47. Either Patten was too influenced by his social-market ideology or he deployed an old age pension scheme proposal (sounding more populist and 'socialist') to shift the public debate away from the CPF idea which he believed could create a channel easily manipulated by the post-1997 SAR government to siphon off a huge volume of centrally controlled funds from Hong Kong to risky investments on the Mainland (a reason cited during his closed-door discussion with the author in 1994 while the latter was chairman of the political group Meeting Point). The Mandatory Provident Fund Schemes Ordinance was passed by the LegCo on 27 July 1995. Legislators representing the business sector only reluctantly agreed to back the MPF legislation on the basis of an 'offsetting' mechanism being included to allow employers to offset part of their MPF contributory payments by amounts paid by them to make the mandatory long-service or severance payments to staff.

48. Although MPF fees and charges had come down since 2008 to 1.74 % in 2012, representing a 17% reduction, 'to the general public […] [it] is too little and too slow', in the words of the then Secretary for Financial Services and the Treasury, K.C. Chan. See Information Services Department (2012c) 'SFST's speech at the Asia Financial Consumer Protection Roundtable', press release, 14 December, www.info.gov.hk/gia/general/201212/14/P201212140555.htm. Following government intervention and other improvements made by the MPF Schemes Authority, the MPF System recorded a better return of 12.2% after fees and charges and annualised return of 4.1% since its inception in December 2000 (compared to –9.3% and 3.2%

respectively in 2018). See Hong Kong Mandatory Provident Fund Schemes Authority (2020) *Investment Performance of the MPF System in 2019*, February, p. 3.

49. For views and proposals from NGOs, see, for example, Hong Kong Council of Social Service (n.d.) T*he Elderly Pension Protection* [in Chinese, 《香港退休保障資訊網》], www.pension.org.hk/改革出路/改革強積金制度.

50. The Old Age Living Allowance was introduced in 2013 under the Social Security Allowance Scheme to supplement the living expenses of Hong Kong elderly persons aged 65 or above in need of financial support. It now comprises a normal and higher allowance, at HK$2,845 and HK$3,815, respectively (as at time of writing).

51. The Harvard Team (1999) *Improving Hong Kong's Health Care System: Why and For Whom?* April, Hong Kong: Health and Welfare Bureau.

52. The features of Certified Plans include: (a) guaranteed renewal up to the age of 100 regardless of change in the health conditions of the insured persons (i.e., without re-underwriting); (b) no limit on 'lifetime benefits'; (c) coverage extended to include unknown pre-existing conditions and day case surgical procedures (including endoscopy, etc.); (d) tax deduction for taxpayers who purchase Certified Plans for themselves and/or specified relatives; and (e) transparency of the premiums. For details, see Hong Kong Food and Health Bureau (n.d.) *Voluntary Health Insurance Scheme*, Hong Kong: Food and Health Bureau, www.vhis.gov.hk/en/.

53. L. Goodstadt (2013), op. cit.

54. *Ibid*., pp. 2–13.

55. See Task Force on Land Supply (2018) *Striving for Multi-pronged Land Supply*, December, Hong Kong: The Hong Kong Special Administrative Region Government. Labour shortage is partly due to the very restrictive labour importation scheme, which was implemented in Hong Kong following pressure from trade unions and major political parties. As at the end of 2019, there were only 5,637 imported workers in Hong Kong under the Supplementary Labour Scheme. See Labour Department (2020) *Annual Report 2019,* para. 5.40, www.labour.gov.hk/eng/public/iprd/2019/chapter5.html. However, the SAR government also introduced various Admission Schemes for Talent, Professionals, and Entrepreneurs to attract foreign and Mainland talent in specific fields and professions. See Immigration Department (n.d.) *Introduction of Admission Schemes for Talent, Professionals and Entrepreneurs*, Hong Kong: Immigration Department, www.immd.gov.hk/eng/useful_information/admission-schemes-talents-professionals-entrepreneurs.html. In comparison, the number of 'work permit' foreign construction workers in Singapore was 293,300, with a total foreign labour force (excluding foreign domestic helpers) reaching 1.165 million in December 2019. See Ministry of Manpower (n.d.) *Foreign workforce numbers*, Singapore: Ministry of Manpower, www.mom.gov.sg/documents-and-publications/foreign-workforce-numbers. At the end of 2019, Hong Kong had about 399,320 foreign domestic helpers compared to 261,800 in Singapore.

56. When calling for public support for a proposed mandatory waste charging scheme in November 2018, Secretary for Environment Wong Kam-sing said Hong Kong was already about 20 years behind Seoul and Taipei in starting such an arrangement. See P. Siu (2018) 'Hong Kong's environment chief Wong Kam-sing urges public to back waste charging scheme, saying city is 20 years behind Seoul and Taipei on issue', *South China Morning Post*, 4 November, www.scmp.com/news/hong-kong/health-environment/article/2171588/hong-kongs-environment-chief-wong-kam-sing-urges. Air quality has been a major concern. The Leung Administration released *A Clean Air Plan for Hong Kong* in March 2013 launching various measures to tackle air pollution from power plants, land and sea transport, and

non-road mobile machinery, as well as to strengthen collaboration with Guangdong Province to deal with regional pollution. In 2018, Hong Kong came 29th among the most liveable cities for Asian expatriates (compared to 11th in 2013) according to a survey of over 470 locations, partly due to its failure to address poor air quality (the top city was Singapore, ahead of Australian and Japanese cities). It dropped to 41st in 2019 and plummeted to 93rd in 2020. See Employment Conditions Abroad (ECA) International (2020) *Hong Kong plummets in expat liveability rankings*, 11 February, www.eca-international.com/news/february-2020/hong-kong-plummets-in-expat-liveability-rankings.

57. Hong Kong was ranked number 1 out of 100 cities in the 2017 Sustainable Cities Mobility Index compiled by Arcadis, a global design and consultancy firm based in Amsterdam. Only two other Asian cities were in the top 10 of the overall Index, Seoul and Singapore (ranking fourth and eighth, respectively). See Arcadis (2017) 'Sustainable Cities Mobility Index 2017', www.arcadis.com/media/8/B/8/%7B8B887B3A-F4C4-40AB-AFFD-08382CC593E5%7DSustainable%20Cities%20Mobility%20Index.pdf. Also, a 2018 global report by McKinsey & Company ranked Hong Kong as number 1 in urban transport, ahead of Singapore, Paris, Moscow, Seoul, New York, and London. See S.M. Knupfer et al. (2018) *Elements of Success: Urban Transportation Systems of 24 Global Cities*, New York: McKinsey & Company, www.mckinsey.com/~/media/McKinsey/Business%20Functions/Sustainability/Our%20Insights/Elements%20of%20success%20Urban%20transportation%20systems%20of%2024%20global%20cities/Urban-transportation-systems_e-versions.ashx.

58. Hong Kong received over 65 million visitor arrivals in 2018. See Hong Kong Tourism Board (2019) *Monthly Report — Visitor Arrival Statistics: December 2018*, https://partnernet.hktb.com/filemanager/intranet/pm/VisitorArrivalStatistics/ViS_Stat_E/VisE_2018/Tourism%20Statistics%2012%202018_R1.pdf. This number was among the highest across world cities. However, because of the political confrontations resulting in the protesters' disruption of the airport, public transport system, and even shopping malls, inbound tourism in the second half of 2019 was seriously affected. Visitor arrivals dropped by 14.2% to only 55.9 million for the whole of 2019. See Hong Kong Tourism Board (2020) *Monthly Report — Visitor Arrival Statistics: December 2019*, https://partnernet.hktb.com/filemanager/intranet/pm/VisitorArrivalStatistics/ViS_Stat_E/VisE_2019/Tourism%20Statistics%2012%202019.pdf.

59. Information Services Department (2018b) 'CE speaking to the media' [in Chinese, 〈行政長官北京會見傳媒談話全文〉], press release, 15 August, Hong Kong, www.info.gov.hk/gia/general/201808/15/P2018081500946.htm.

60. Innovation and Technology Bureau (2018) *Innovation Hong Kong*, September, Hong Kong: Government Logistics Department, p. 34.

61. *Ibid.*, p. 35.

62. StartmeupHK (n.d.) *Hong Kong's Startup Ecosystem: Going from Strength to Strength*, Hong Kong: InvestHK, www.startmeup.hk/about-us/hong-kongs-startup-ecosystem/. StartmeupHK is an initiative by InvestHK aimed at helping founders of innovative and scalable startups from overseas to set up or expand in Hong Kong. InvestHK is the government's department of foreign direct investment.

63. H.A. Simon (1947) *Administrative Behavior: A Study of Decision-Making Processes in Administrative Organization*, New York: Macmillan.

64. Some of the points in this section were first made by the author in A.B.L. Cheung (2017) 'Reflections on Governance in Hong Kong: Outside/Insider Perspectives', keynote presentation at the Serving the Evolving City Conference held by the Efficiency Unit, 12 January, Hong Kong.

65. Carrie Lam admitted in her 2017 inaugural policy address that there was a need to 'review existing legislation and regulations, so as to remove outdated provisions that impede the development of innovation and technology'. See C. Lam (2017), op. cit., para. 76.

66. For example, the government cannot even change the form used for fixed penalty tickets without first going to the LegCo to amend the schedule to the relevant legislation. Alteration of bus routes is also subject to the LegCo's annual negative vetting. Under negative vetting, a piece of subsidiary legislation has to be laid before the LegCo at the next sitting after it is published in the Government Gazette. No later than 28 days afterwards, the LegCo may amend the subsidiary legislation by resolution at a sitting. It may also, by passing a resolution, extend the scrutiny period by 21 days, or to the first sitting held after the 21st day from the original expiry day. Unless another date is provided, the subsidiary legislation commences on the date of its publication in the Gazette. Alternatively, if an ordinance which empowers the making of subsidiary legislation provides that the subsidiary legislation shall be subject to the approval of the LegCo, then formal passage must be sought before the subsidiary legislation comes into effect. This is known as positive vetting.

67. Within the government, there is tight restriction over the creation of additional posts to cater to new services and functions because of recurrent financial implications. Outside of the government, the LegCo's Finance Committee, which controls the directorate establishment, would cast suspicious and sceptical eyes over the creation of any directorate posts.

68. The top five political parties only scored an average support rating of 42.8% in April 2019, compared to 59.5% in August 1997, according to HKUPOP (2019d) *Rating of Top Ten Political Groups*, Hong Kong: HKUPOP, www.hkupop.hku.hk/chinese/popexpress/pgrating/topten1. html. After HKUPOP ceased to operate in July 2019, its original researchers have since privately run a new HKPORI to continue some of the polls (but not this one) using the same survey methodology. The credibility rating of the news media in general declined from 6.55 (out of 10) in September 1997 to 5.77 in January 2019 according to HKUPOP (2019b) *Credibility Rating of the Hong Kong News Media in General (9/1997–1/2019)*, Hong Kong: HKUPOP, www.hkupop.hku.hk/english/popexpress/press/nm_credibility/poll/MC_poll_chart.html. This rate dropped to 5.49 in March 2020 according to HKPORI (2020a) *Credibility Rating of the Hong Kong News Media (9/1997–2/2020)*, Hong Kong: PORI, www.pori.hk/pop-poll/media-performance/j016). In comparison, the former and incumbent Chief Justices have persistently obtained support ratings in the low to mid 60% until June 2019 according to HKUPOP (2010) *Rating of Chief Justice Andrew Li Kwok-nang*, Hong Kong: HKUPOP, www.hkupop.hku.hk/english/popexpress/judiciary/andrew/halfyr/datatables.html, and HKUPOP (2019c) *Rating of Chief Justice Geoffrey Ma Tao-li*, Hong Kong: HKUPOP, www.hkupop.hku.hk/english/popexpress/judiciary/geoffrey/halfyr/datatables.html). Chief Justice Geoffrey Ma's support rating has since dropped to around 57% from September 2019 according to HKPORI (2020b) *Rating of Chief Justice Geoffrey Ma Tao-li*, Hong Kong: PORI, www.pori.hk/pop-poll/rule-of-law-indicator/g001/rating).

69. C. Levett and S. Clarke (2019) 'Theresa May: a political obituary in five charts', *The Guardian*, 7 June. For comparison, the net approval rating of her predecessors was: –2% for David Cameron, –46% for Gordon Brown, –28% for Tony Blair, –17% for John Major, and +13% for Margaret Thatcher.

70. T.G. Schminke (2018) 'How (un)popular is French President Macron really?' *Europe Elects*, 5 December, https://europeelects.eu/2018/12/05/how-unpopular-is-french-president-macron-really/. Macron's popularity rebounded after he launched a national 'great debate' and made a series of significant policy concessions.

71. TVBS Poll Center (Taiwan) (2016) 'Approval ratings of eight years of President Ma Ying-jeo's administration' [in Chinese, 〈馬英九總統施政八年滿意度民調〉], June, https://cc.tvbs.com.tw/portal/file/poll_center/2017/20170602/0505041.pdf.

72. TVBS Poll Center (Taiwan) (2018) 'Approval ratings of President Tsai Ing-wen two years after inauguration' [in Chinese, 〈蔡英文總統就職兩年滿意度民調〉], May, https://cc.tvbs.com.tw/portal/file/poll_center/2018/20180516/27bcedb9362b32c82f7cc0c9e089b240.pdf; TVBS Poll Center (Taiwan) (2020) 'Approval ratings of President Tsai Ing-wen at second-term inauguration [in Chinese, 〈蔡英文總統連任就職滿意度民調〉], May, https://cc.tvbs.com.tw/portal/file/poll_center/2020/20200518/6fd57ec6489e3f7a2b78fb8d0e909a35.pdf.

73. A.B.L. Cheung (2010b), op. cit.

74. He argued that 'government need not be legitimated in Locke's sense to survive and even to manage a nation through major difficulties and into prosperity. It may suffice for government not to be generally distrusted.' See R. Hardin (1998) 'Trust in Government', in V. Braithwaite and M. Levi (eds) *Trust and Governance*, New York: Russell Sage Foundation, pp. 9–27, quote at p. 23.

75. For example, while opposition legislators and parties all blame the government for not doing enough to solve the housing supply and affordability problems, at the same time, they oppose any government plans on large-scale reclamation and resumption of land to build New Development Areas.

76. Distrust is a great weapon to derail unpopular policies and measures. As *The Economist* commented about the 'blame syndrome' in Britain after the outbreak of the global financial crisis, 'an excess of blame — blind and unthinking as it often seems — can be as dangerous as a deficit of it. Vitriolic blame can wreck morale in institutions [...]. It can inhibit decision-making and worthwhile risk-taking. And it can be both intellectually lazy and delusional. The wrong kind of blame reflects a false, dangerous simplification — and a false, childish hope.' See *The Economist* (2008) 'Bagehot: Heads must roll', 22 November, p. 64.

77. Edelman (2020) *Edelman Trust Barometer Global Report*, 19 January, www.edelman.com/sites/g/files/aatuss191/files/2020-01/2020%20Edelman%20Trust%20Barometer%20Global%20Report.pdf.

78. OECD and Korea Development Institute (2018) *Understanding the Drivers of Trust in Government Institutions in Korea*, Paris: OECD, Box 1.3, p. 27.

79. C. Goodsell (1994) *The Case for Bureaucracy: A Public Administration Polemic*, Chatham, NJ: Chatham House, pp. 77–78.

80. S.C. Craig (1993) *The Malevolent Leaders: Popular Discontent in America*, Boulder, CO: Westview.

Chapter 10

1. Zhao's wording in Chinese was '將來香港特別行政區實行民主化的政治制度，即你們所説的『民主治港』是理所當然的。' See *BBC News* (2014) 'Hong Kong University found Zhao Ziyang's letter promising democratic administration of Hong Kong' [in Chinese, 〈香港大學發現趙紫陽許諾民主治港信函〉], 14 January.

2. Among the anti-colonial student and social activists who formed the mainstay of the critical movement vis-à-vis British administration during the 1970s, independence was considered a non-starter, while return to China was not preferred by most locals because of the political turbulence and social and economic chaos on the Mainland at the time when the Cultural Revolution was tormenting the country, even though some young student activists fancied socialist ideals and embraced national identification with the PRC which was acclaimed as the New China.

3. The Period of Spring and Autumn was a period in Chinese history from approximately 771 to 476 BC, during the late Eastern Zhou Period which saw the demise of the Zhou Dynasty and before the Period of the Warring States (475–221 BC) when rival feudal states were at war. Eventually the Qin state conquered all the others to establish the new Qin Dynasty. While China was politically chaotic and unstable during these two periods (because of the absence of a central state power), multiple thoughts and philosophies, including those in literature and statecraft, flourished in competition for influence during inter-state rivalries and wars.

4. New pro-democracy political groups included Meeting Point, Hong Kong Affairs Society, and the Association for Democracy and People's Livelihood. Formed in early 1983 mainly by former student activists, Meeting Point was the first local political group to support Hong Kong's return to China in 1997 under the principle of 'democratic reunification' (民主回歸). After Tiananmen, some core members of these political groups, together with activists from some liberal trade unions and church organisations, formed UDHK in 1990 as the flagship pro-democracy party. UDHK, along with Meeting Point, scored landslide victories in the first direct election of geographical seats of the LegCo in 1991, securing 16 of the 18 seats. In 1994, UDHK and Meeting Point merged to form the Democratic Party of Hong Kong.

5. There was heated debate in the 1980s over a so-called 'legislature-led' system that the Chinese government believed to be contrary to the longstanding 'executive-led' system of Hong Kong. See *HK01* (2018) 'Executive-led is both principle and source of problem?' [in Chinese, 〈行政主導既是原則又是問題根源？〉], 21 March. *HK01* is a Hong Kong-based online news outlet.

6. Meeting Point Basic Law Committee and Information Centre (1988) *A Collection of Basic Law Commentaries* [in Chinese, 《基本法評論匯編》], internal reference, May, Hong Kong: Meeting Point.

7. In December 1985, an article appearing in the local pro-Beijing magazine *Wide Angle* (廣角鏡) outlined the features of a political structure rumoured to reflect Beijing's views. Under that proposal, a 100-person executive advisory council should, after seeking opinions from various sectors and then through democratic consultations and election, nominate a CE candidate to the central government for appointment. It emphasised the importance of achieving a centralised and stable government with high efficiency, to avoid party politics which would bring uncertainty and to prevent populist politics of direct elections that would lead to 'free lunch' welfare. See S.-F. Ku (古星輝) (1985) 'Preliminary suggestions on a blueprint for the future Basic Law' [in Chinese, 〈未來基本法藍圖芻議〉], *Wide Angle* (《廣角鏡》), December.

8. During the first consultation period, the Basic Law Consultative Committee received some 73,000 submissions.

9. Under this 'mainstream option', the first-term CE was to be selected by a 400-member Selection Committee while the second-term and third-term CE by an 800-member Election Committee. The LegCo would have 27% directly elected seats by universal suffrage in its first term, 37% in the second term, and 50% in the third and fourth terms. A referendum would be held during the period of the third-term CE to decide whether the fourth-term CE should be directly elected by universal suffrage and whether the fifth-term LegCo and beyond should be wholly elected by universal suffrage. If the referendum failed to endorse the transition to universal suffrage, then a similar referendum could be held every 10 years.

10. Looking back after three decades, Martin Lee now appreciates the 'mainstream' package of Louis Cha and Cha Chi-ming as full of wisdom and has lamented that should that option be accepted, Hong Kong would have already implemented democracy by universal suffrage. See *Hong Kong Economic Journal* (《信報》) (2018) 'Look backing at "double-Cha proposal" Martin Lee praises it as high wisdom' [in Chinese, 〈回首「雙查方案」李柱銘讚高智慧〉], 1 November.

11. Based on the author's personal discussion with Mainland members in the summer of 1988.

12. For a more detailed account of the discussions during this period, see N. Ma (馬嶽) (2012) *Oral History of Hong Kong's Democratic Movement during the Eighties* [in Chinese,《香港80年代民主運動口述歷史》], Hong Kong: City University of Hong Kong Press; S.H. Lo (1997) *The Politics of Democratization in Hong Kong*, London: Palgrave Macmillan.

13. Wen Wei Publishing Co. (文匯出版) (ed) (1990) *The Birth of the Basic Law* [in Chinese 《基本法的誕生》], Hong Kong: Wen Wei Publishing Co., pp. 127–130 (commentary of Xiao Weiyun). This book was an edited volume of recollections of Basic Law Drafting Committee members, relevant official documents and speeches, a brief history of the drafting process, and information relating to the meetings and activities of the Drafting Committee.

14. In line with the wording of the Chinese Government's Basic Policies regarding Hong Kong after 1997 as elaborated in Annex I of the 1984 Sino-British Joint Declaration, Article 45 of the Basic Law only stated that the CE 'shall be selected by election or through consultations held locally and be appointed by the Central People's Government'. Selection by consultations was actually ruled out during the consultation and drafting process of the Basic Law in the late 1980s. Thus, Annex I of the Basic Law prescribed the method for the election of the CE by a broadly representative Selection/Election Committee.

15. Local legislation was to stipulate: the delineation of geographical constituency boundaries; the delimitation of sectors and corporate bodies and allocation of seats for various functional constituencies; the voting methods for geographical and functional constituencies (including the introduction of 'proportional representation' for multi-member seats in the former); and the delimitation of sectors and corporate bodies and allocation of seats for the CE Election Committee.

16. The pro-democracy camp often referred to an article published by Lu Ping (魯平), then Director of the Hong Kong and Macao Affairs Office of the State Council, in the *People's Daily* overseas version (《人民日報》海外版) on 18 March 1993, which said: 'The Basic Law has made clear stipulations on the directly elected seats of the first three terms of the LegCo. As to how the legislature after the third term (after 2007) should be constituted, this is entirely up to Hong Kong to decide on its own, so long as it is passed by two-thirds of the legislators, agreed by the CE and reported to the NPCSC for record; it does not require the agreement of the central government. How Hong Kong should develop democracy in future is a matter *entirely within Hong Kong's autonomy*. The central government will not interfere.' (emphasis added) [in Chinese, 基本法對於前三屆立法會直選議席作了明確規定。至於第三屆以後[2007年以後]立法機關怎樣組成，將來完全由香港自己決定，只要有三分二立法會議員通過，行政長官同意，報全國人大常委會備案就可以，不必要中央政府同意。將來香港如何發展民主，完全是香港自治範圍內的事，中央政府不會干涉。]. This quote was cited by C. Ching (程翔) (2013) 'Electing Hong Kong's CE under one-party dictatorship' [in Chinese,〈一黨專政下的香港特首普選〉], *Hong Kong Economic Journal* (《信報》), 12 December.

17. By now pro-democracy political groups included the newly formed Article 45 Concern Group, which had transformed from the Article 23 Concern Group formed mostly by lawyers and professionals who led the campaign against Article 23 legislation. The Article 45 Concern Group won four seats in the 2004 LegCo election and later formed the Civic Party in 2006. Alan Leong, a leading legislator of the Civil Party, contested in the 2007 CE election (through the Election Committee) to challenge incumbent Donald Tsang.

18. On the same day that Tung delivered his 2004 policy address (7 January 2004) announcing consultation to be launched on constitutional development, the Hong Kong and Macau Affairs Office of the State Council took the unprecedented step of issuing a press statement pointing

out that the development of Hong Kong's political system related to the implementation of the 'One Country, Two Systems' policy and the Basic Law and touched upon the relationship between the central government and the SAR. It revealed that the SAR government had been requested to discuss the matter with the central government before deciding on the relevant working arrangements. For useful background details, see A.H.Y. Chen (2004) 'The Constitutional Controversy of Spring 2004', *Hong Kong Law Journal*, Vol. 34, No. 2, pp. 215–226.

19. Under the Basic Law, no proposals for reforming the existing methods of electing the CE and LegCo could have proceeded without Beijing's blessing. The NPCSC has the power to 'return' (i.e., invalidate) any SAR legislation if they consider it to not be in conformity with the provisions of the Basic Law regarding affairs within the responsibility of the Central Authorities or regarding the relationship between the Central Authorities and SAR (Article 17). Constitutional development in the SAR is considered a matter over which the central government has responsibility and authority.

20. NPCSC (2004a) *The Interpretation by the Standing Committee of the National People's Congress of Article 7 of Annex I and Article III of Annex II to the Basic Law of the Hong Kong Special Administrative Region of the People's Republic of China*, adopted at 8th Session of the Standing Committee of the 10th National People's Congress, 6 April, Beijing, www.basiclaw.gov. hk/en/basiclawtext/images/basiclawtext_doc18.pdf (in English). According to Albert H.Y. Chen, a University of Hong Kong law professor sitting on the Hong Kong Basic Law Committee of the NPCSC, the intervention of the NPCSC in April 2004 was clearly designed to halt the strong popular movement for further democratisation in Hong Kong by 2007 and 2008. The timing of the intervention was significant. In theory the central government could have waited until a fuller public consultation on political reform had been conducted by the SAR government. However, given that the SAR government had been perceived as a weak or even a 'lame-duck' administration since the 1 July 2003 mass protests, and given that the public sentiment in favour of universal suffrage was so strong, the central government probably weighed the costs and benefits of an early intervention against a later decision when public consultation showed a preponderance of opinion in favour of universal suffrage and expectations for its speedy introduction ran high. See A.H.Y. Chen (2004), op. cit.

21. NPCSC (2004b) *Decision of the Standing Committee of the National People's Congress on Issues relating to the Methods for Electing the Chief Executive of the Hong Kong Special Administrative Region in the Year 2007 and for Forming the Legislative Council of the Hong Kong Special Administrative Region in the Year 2008*, adopted at 9th Session of the Standing Committee of the 10th National People's Congress, 26 April, Beijing, www.basiclaw.gov.hk/en/materials/doc/2004_04_26_e.pdf (in English).

22. One would have thought that the CE, being accountable to the CPG, would not have ventured into encouraging a constitutional reform debate without Beijing's blessing. However, Beijing seemingly required both political and legal reassurance of its final say. Exercising its power to interpret the Basic Law provisions was one way for Beijing to ensure full control even if the pro-establishment parties or the SAR government might waver in the face of strong popular demand for universal suffrage.

23. In due fairness, suggesting a referendum was not a heresy in itself. Some jurisdictions allow holding a referendum as a legitimate means of resolving major political and policy disputes. The draft Basic Law issued for public consultation in February 1989 specifically provided for the use of a referendum on the universal suffrage issue during the period of the third-term CE and the fourth-term LegCo, subject to endorsement by a majority of all members of the LegCo, the consent of the CE, and the approval of the NPCSC, with the result being only valid if carried by more than 30% of eligible voters.

24. Such a 3-person makeup of the Task Force on Constitutional Development was followed by subsequent Administrations.

25. Task Force on Constitutional Development (2005) *The Fifth Report of the Constitutional Development Task Force: Package of Proposals for the Methods for Selecting the Chief Executive in 2007 and for Forming the Legislative Council in 2008*, October, Hong Kong: Constitutional Affairs Bureau.

26. Hoping to win the goodwill of the pan-democrats and break the ice between the pro-democracy camp and the central government, Tsang organised an official delegation tour by all the LegCo members to Guangdong province in September 2005 so that pan-democrats were able to make their historic Mainland visit (the first since 1989) and have direct dialogue with Guangdong party secretary Zhang Dejiang (張德江), then a CCP Politburo member (and subsequently Politburo standing committee member and Chairman of the 12th NPCSC during 2013–2018). At the meeting, radical pan-democrat Leung Kwok-hung ('Long Hair') and a few others even debated with Zhang on the 4 June Tiananmen issue.

27. A poll survey in late October 2005 showed that 58.8% of respondents accepted the government's proposals while 23.6% disapproved. See Public Policy Research Centre, Chinese University of Hong Kong (2005a) 'Findings of Public Opinion Survey on Constitutional Development' [in Chinese, 〈市民對政制發展意見調查結果〉], press release, 3 November, Hong Kong: Public Policy Research Centre of Hong Kong Institute of Asia-Pacific Studies, Chinese University of Hong Kong, www.cuhk.edu.hk/ipro/pressrelease/051103.htm. Even after a mass rally organised by the pan-democrats on 3 December 2005, public opinion polls showed 49.9% still accepted the proposal while 66% of the respondents opined that the government package should include a timetable for 'double universal suffrage'. See Public Policy Research Centre of the Chinese University of Hong Kong (2005b) 'Findings of Public Opinion Survey on Constitutional Development (Second Round)' [in Chinese, 〈市民對政制發展意見調查（第二次）結果〉], press release, 9 December, Hong Kong: Public Policy Research Centre of Hong Kong Institute of Asia-Pacific Studies, Chinese University of Hong Kong, www.cuhk.edu.hk/ipro/pressrelease/051209.htm.

28. At the last minute, in the week before the LegCo vote on the reform package, in order to secure sufficient votes, Tsang offered an improvement to the package by committing to phasing out government-appointed seats on the DCs — one-third or 34 seats in 2008 and the rest no later than 2016 — but even that did not induce the pan-democrats to change their minds. Lau Chin-shek, leader of the Confederation of Trade Unions and ex-Democratic Party member, was the only pan-democratic legislator who abstained instead of voting against the government proposal in the LegCo. See also A.H.Y. Chen (2005) 'The Fate of the Constitutional Reform Proposal of October 2005', *Hong Kong Law Journal*, Vol. 35, No. 3, pp. 537–543.

29. NPCSC (2007) *Decision of the Standing Committee of the National People's Congress on Issues relating to the Methods for Selecting the Chief Executive of the Hong Kong Special Administrative Region and for Forming the Legislative Council of the Hong Kong Special Administrative Region in the Year 2012 and on Issues relating to Universal Suffrage*, adopted at the 31st Session of the Standing Committee of the 10th National People's Congress, 29 December, Beijing.

30. If the CE was not elected by universal suffrage while the LegCo was formed fully by members directly elected by universal suffrage, the CE would suffer seriously from inferior legitimacy and might not be able to assert political power vis-à-vis the LegCo.

31. Constitutional and Mainland Affairs Bureau (2009) *Public Consultation on the Methods for Selecting the Chief Executive and for Forming the Legislative Council in 2012*, 18 November, Hong Kong: Government Logistics Department.

32. The five legislators who eventually resigned in January 2010 to make way for the so-called 'five-district referendum' were: Wong Yuk-man, Leung Kwok-hung, and Albert Chan (all from the League of Social Democrats), and Alan Leong and Tanya Chan (both from the Civic Party). Wong Yuk-man and Albert Chan later split from the League of Social Democrats to form People's Power.

33. Eventually, a total sum of HK$159 million in public expenditure was spent on the five by-elections. See Constitutional and Mainland Affairs Bureau (2010) 'Legislative Council By-election for the Five Geographical Constituencies', paper submitted to the Panel on Constitutional Affairs of the Legislative Council, LC Paper No. CB(2)889/09–10(03), February, Hong Kong: Legislative Council.

34. Information Services Department (2012b) '2012 Electoral Methods Package Published', press release, 14 April, www.news.gov.hk/isd/ebulletin/en/category/administration/100414/html/100414en01002.htm.

35. It was rumoured that the final decision to accept the Democratic Party's counter-proposal in order to achieve a deal and not to allow the radicals to dominate the pro-democracy camp was made at the highest level in Beijing, with Donald Tsang going very much out of his way to convince the central leadership of the need to have a breakthrough. In a mitigation letter submitted to the High Court in February 2017 in relation to the trial of Tsang for misconduct in public office, Wong Yan-lung, who served as Secretary for Justice under him, revealed the following: 'In June 2010, the original government proposal was losing support and hope was vanishing for it to be passed at LegCo. Time was running out. Whether to modify the package by incorporating a proposal of the Democratic Party (i.e., the additional 5 District Council Functional Constituency seats to be elected by over 3 million electorate, "the new DCFC election method") appeared to be the lynchpin. Without going into details again for confidentiality reasons, *I can again testify that the make-or-break moment was when Donald made the timely and difficult decision to revise the package by incorporating the new DCFC election method. It was an agonizing decision for him as he had to override certain internal opposition and to risk personal credibility and trust before the CPG.* As an insider, I know that decision was not a political manoeuvre but a selfless act for the sake of the long-term wellbeing of Hong Kong and the smooth transition toward universal suffrage.' (emphasis added) See the full text of the mitigation letter in English published in *CitizenNews* (《眾新聞》) (2017) 'Donald truly a "son of Hong Kong", Wong Yan-lung says', 20 February, www.hkcnews.com/article/1941/donald-truely-a-son-of-hong-kong-wong-yanlung-says.

36. The new seats were placed under the District Council (Second) Functional Constituency as there already existed a District Council Functional Constituency with one seat to be elected among all DC members, which the pro-establishment majority's candidate has always won.

37. During British rule, electoral reforms in the 1980s (for District Boards and LegCo) were all found unacceptable because of their incremental nature and rejected by the pro-democracy camp. However, because the government could command the majority of LegCo members (including those appointed by it), it was able to get its reform proposals passed. The only British administration electoral reform bill supported by some pro-democracy legislators (from the UDHK and Meeting Point which had by then announced their merger to become the Democratic Party) was the package introduced by Governor Chris Patten in 1992, which split the pro-democracy camp.

38. *Ming Pao* (《明報》) (2012) 'Leung hopes to join 2017 CE election by universal suffrage' [in Chinese, 〈梁盼參加2017特首普選〉], 25 March, Hong Kong, https://archive.is/20120719024512/http:/hk.news.yahoo.com/梁盼參加2017特首普選-032623212.html.

39. Information Services Department (2012a) 'Opening remarks by CE-elect', press release, 25 March, www.info.gov.hk/gia/general/201203/25/P201203250444.htm.

40. On 24 March 2013, Qiao Xiaoyang (喬曉陽), Director of the Hong Kong Basic Law Committee under the NPCSC, stated that CE candidates must be persons 'who love the country and love Hong Kong' and who do not insist on confronting the central government. Critics believed his comment implied screening out candidates from the pro-democracy camp. Then, on 22 November 2013, Li Fei (李飛), Qiao's successor, made similar remarks that the post of CE, who is accountable to the central government as well as to Hong Kong, 'must be taken up by a person who loves the country as well as Hong Kong — anyone opposed to the central government cannot [take it]'. See *People's Daily* (《人民日報》) (2013) 'NPCSC Deputy Secretary General and Hong Kong Basic Law Committee Director Li Fei pointed out: Chief Executive must be a person who loves the country and loves Hong Kong' [in Chinese, 〈人大常委會副秘書長兼香港基本法委員會主任李飛指出:行政長官須由愛國愛港人士擔任〉], Overseas Edition, 23 November, http://paper.people.com.cn/rmrbhwb/html/2013-11/23/content_1328915.htm.

41. A.H.Y. Chen (2018) 'The autonomy of Hong Kong under "One Country, Two Systems"', in T.L. Lui et al. (eds) *Routledge Handbook of Contemporary Hong Kong*, London: Routledge, pp. 33–51. As Beijing does not trust the pan-democrats and regards some of them as hostile forces (being influenced by foreign powers), it has been concerned that if entirely unrestricted elections by universal suffrage were introduced to elect the CE and all seats of the LegCo, these two most critical political institutions would be captured by the pan-democrats. This would pose a threat to the central government's comprehensive jurisdiction over the SAR and to national security.

42. In March 2013, Benny Tai was joined by Reverend Chu Yiu-ming and sociology academic Chan Kin-man as co-organisers of the now renamed 'Occupy Central with Love and Peace' campaign. By July 2014, the 'Occupy Central' movement had become a strong rallying force for democracy supporters and threatened to start occupying action in October. For some academic accounts on the Occupy Campaign and Umbrella Movement, and their modes of action, organisers, and participants, see E.W. Cheng and W.Y. Chan (2016) 'Explaining spontaneous occupation: antecedents, contingencies and spaces in the Umbrella Movement', *Social Movement Studies*, Vol. 16, No. 2, pp. 222–239; P.K. Hui and K.C. Lau (2015) '"Living in truth" versus realpolitik: Limitations and potentials of the Umbrella Movement', *Journal of Inter-Asia Cultural Studies*, Vol. 16, No. 3, pp. 348–366; H.T. Wong and S.D. Liu (2018) 'Cultural Activism during the Hong Kong Umbrella Movement', *Journal of Creative Communications*, Vol. 13, No. 2, pp. 157–165; W. Wong and M. Chu (2017) 'Rebel with a cause: Structural problems underlying the Umbrella Movement of Hong Kong and the role of the youth', *Asian Education and Development Studies*, Vol. 6, No. 4, pp. 343–353; K. Kong (2019) 'Human rights activist scholars and social change in Hong Kong: Reflections on the Umbrella Movement and beyond', *The International Journal of Human Rights*, Vol. 23, No. 6, pp. 899–914.

43. A pro-Beijing counter organisation, the Alliance for Peace and Democracy, launched a signature campaign during July–August 2014 which claimed to have collected over a million signatures against the Occupy Central movement.

44. Hong Kong Special Administrative Region Government (2013) *Let's Talk and Achieve Universal Suffrage — Method for Selecting the Chief Executive in 2017 and for Forming the Legislative Council in 2016: Consultative Document*, December, Hong Kong: Government Logistics Department. Issues related to the CE election in 2017 included the size and composition of the Nominating Committee, electorate base of the Nominating Committee, method for forming the Nominating Committee, procedures for the Nominating Committee to nominate candidates,

voting arrangements, and procedures for appointing CE, as well as the links with local legislation. Issues relating to formation of the LegCo in 2016 included the number of seats and composition of LegCo, composition and electorate base of functional constituencies, number of geographical constituencies, and number of seats in each geographical constituency.

45. The threshold for civic nomination was set at 1% of the registered voters. Political party nomination would require the nominating political party to have received 5% or more of the total valid votes in the last LegCo direct election. Under the Alliance's proposal, the nominating committee could not refuse to endorse any civic or political party nominees meeting the constitutional and legal requirements, such that they were not less than 40 years old and have no right of abode in any foreign country; however, it did not accept such political pre-conditions as 'love China, love Hong Kong' and 'no confrontations with Beijing'. The Alliance also demanded the abolition of the existing requirement under local law forbidding the CE to belong to any political party.

46. Hong Kong Special Administrative Region Government (2014) *Report by the Chief Executive of the Hong Kong Special Administrative Region to the Standing Committee of the National People's Congress on whether there is a need to amend the methods for selecting the Chief Executive of the Hong Kong Special Administrative Region in 2017 and for forming the Legislative Council of the Hong Kong Special Administrative Region in 2016*, July, Hong Kong: Government Logistics Department.

47. NPCSC (2014) *Decision of the Standing Committee of the National People's Congress on Issues Relating to the Selection of the Chief Executive of the Hong Kong Special Administrative Region by Universal Suffrage and on the Method for Forming the Legislative Council of the Hong Kong Special Administrative Region in the Year 2016*, adopted at the 10th Session of the Standing Committee of the 12th National People's Congress, 31 August, Beijing. This Decision formally determined, in response to the CE's report to it in July 2014, that the CE election by universal suffrage could be implemented starting from 2017 and set out conditions and a framework for such election.

48. It was branded the Umbrella Movement because the protesters used their umbrellas to confront police who then used tear gas to disperse the crowd on 18 September 2014, causing some injuries and making scenes of a mass rally of people holding umbrellas to fight for universal suffrage, which captured widespread international attention and sympathy. The pan-democrats subsequently adopted the yellow umbrella as the symbol of their campaign for true democracy.

49. For the nomination procedures and threshold, the government proposed to consider (i) whether there should be two stages, first 'members' recommendation' and then 'committee nomination'; (ii) whether the nomination threshold at the first stage should be 100 or 150 members of the Nominating Committee, with a cap on the number of nominees each member could recommend so as to provide sufficient choices for the whole Nominating Committee to consider at the committee nomination stage; and (iii) whether the CE candidates could be either those two or three nominees obtaining the highest number of endorsement of more than half of all the Nominating Committee members. See Hong Kong Special Administrative Region Government (2015a) *2017 Seize the Opportunity — Method for Selecting the Chief Executive by Universal Suffrage: Consultation Document*, January, Hong Kong: Government Logistics Department. At the same time, the Task Force on Constitutional Development also submitted, outside the 5-step process, the *Report on the Recent Community and Political Situation in Hong Kong* to the Hong Kong and Macao Affairs Office of the State Council (not openly disclosed).

50. The minor change was that a person obtaining recommendations jointly by 120 Nominating Committee members could enter the Committee nomination stage, with the requirement that

each Committee member may recommend only one person and each recommended person may obtain no more than 240 recommendations. See Hong Kong Special Administrative Region Government (2015b) *2017 Make it happen! Method for Selecting the Chief Executive by Universal Suffrage: Consultation Report and Proposals*, April, Hong Kong: Government Logistics Department.

51. At the Committee nomination stage, each member votes by secret ballot for at least two recommended persons seeking nomination. The three recommended persons who could obtain endorsement of more than half of all the members of the Nominating Committee and with the highest number of members' endorsement (or the two persons seeking nomination if only two such persons could meet these requirements) would become the candidates for the CE election by universal suffrage on a 'first past the post' basis.

52. According to a University of Hong Kong survey, 48% of the respondents supported the government's proposal while 38% opposed. See HKUPOP (2015b) *Survey on 2017 CE Election Proposal*, 15 June, Hong Kong: HKUPOP, www.hkupop.hku.hk/english/report/superSurvey2015/ppt.pdf. See also HKUPOP (2015a) *Joint-University Rolling Survey on 2017 Chief Executive Election Proposal*, Hong Kong: HKUPOP, www.hkupop.hku.hk/english/features/jointUrollingSurvey/. These polls jointly conducted by polling teams from the University of Hong Kong, Chinese University of Hong Kong, and Hong Kong Polytechnic University during April–June 2015, show a largely similar pattern of responses.

53. Before the final vote was to be cast, many pro-establishment legislators walked out of the LegCo chamber in confusion, led by a few leaders hoping to delay the vote procedurally to wait for one of their colleagues Lau Wong-fat, who had been ill and was rushing back to the LegCo. In the event, when voting took place, most pro-establishment legislators were not in the chamber while all 27 pan-democrats who had vowed to vote down the motion did so, resulting in the government motion being defeated by 8 for and 28 against, in stark contrast to the original expected outcome of 41 for and 28 against (still 6 votes short of the two-thirds majority of all members of the LegCo as required by the Basic Law). The voting results were portrayed by the international media as the government's reform package suffering a landslide defeat, much to the embarrassment of both the Leung Administration and the central government.

54. Information Services Department (2015) 'LegCo Vetoes Reform Package', press release, 18 June, www.news.gov.hk/en/categories/admin/html/2015/06/20150618_160738.shtml.

55. Information Services Department (2017) 'One man, one vote good for HK', press release, 5 July, www.news.gov.hk/en/categories/admin/html/2017/07/20170705_104516.shtml. Lam said that the launch of political reform discussions soon after assuming office might reignite social conflicts and stall economic progress; thus, she would have to wait for a favourable environment before doing so.

56. See, for example, K. Chung (2017) 'Xi "sent a reminder" to Hong Kong over Beijing's hard line on city', *South China Morning Post*, 16 December.

57. In the final transition years before the 1997 handover by the British, central government officials like Lu Ping had often emphasised the importance of maintaining Hong Kong as an 'economic city' and not turning it into a 'political city'. See C. Ching (程翔) (2015) 'In memory of Lo Ping: See what can be done by Hong Kong? Part II' [in Chinese, 〈憶魯平，看香港「怎麼辦」？（下）〉], *Pentoy* (《評台》), 21 May, www.pentoy.hk/憶魯平，看香港「怎麼辦」？-（下）/.

58. This would be akin to the bicameral system in Japan where both the (upper) House of Councillors and the (lower) House of Representatives are directly elected by universal suffrage, though with different geographical constituency boundaries and election methods.

59. In the aftermath of the landslide victory of pro-democracy and localist candidates in the DC elections in November 2019 in the heat of confrontations, the pan-democratic opposition was hoping to ride the popular outrage into securing a majority of seats in the LegCo election scheduled for September 2020, thus fundamentally redrawing the political landscape.

Chapter 11

1. T.R. Dye (1987) *Understanding Public Policy*, 2nd edition, Englewood Cliffs, NJ: Prentice-Hall, p. 2.

2. However, under Annex II (part II) of the Basic Law, government motions and legislation can be passed by a simple majority of all legislators present.

3. Typical subsectors based on individual franchise are in the professions (e.g., education and higher education, social welfare, legal, medical, health services, accountancy, engineering, architecture, surveying, etc.). Some legislators sitting on the Election Committee are also democratically elected.

4. Similar to some European systems, the use of proportional representation in geographical elections has given rise to the proliferation of parties and political groups as well as more intensive intra-party competition.

5. See, for example, W.C. Müller and K. Strøm (eds) (1999) *Policy, office, or votes? How political parties in Western Europe make hard decisions*, Cambridge: Cambridge University Press.

6. A. Lijphart (1999) *Patterns of Democracy: Government Forms and Performance in Thirty-six Countries*, New York: Routledge. See also J.-E. Lane and S. Ersson (2000) *The New Institutional Politics: Performance and Outcomes*, London: Routledge.

7. In the May 2019 general election, the Liberal-National coalition was able to secure a slight majority of federal parliamentary seats in Australia, thereby freeing it from relying on the independents for support in budget and confidence votes.

8. Federal government shutdowns took place from time to time in the US due to executive-legislative gridlock over the budget. The latest and longest one was the 2018–2019 government shutdown lasting 35 days (from 22 December 2018 until 25 January 2019) when the newly Democrat-controlled House of Representatives and Republican President Donald Trump could not agree on the 2019 appropriations bill due to an impasse over Trump's demand for US$5.7 billion in federal funds for a controversial US-Mexico 'border wall' pledged in his election campaign. Eventually Trump was forced to accept a stop-gap bill to reopen the government for three weeks to allow negotiations to take place for a bipartisan appropriations bill. On 15 February 2019, he opted for declaring a national emergency in order to bypass Congress and use military funding to build the wall.

9. Ji Pengfei (姬鵬飛) (1990) *Statement on The Basic Law of the Hong Kong Special Administrative Region of the People's Republic of China (Draft) and Related Documents* [in Chinese,《關於中華人民共和國香港特別行政區基本法（草案）及其有關文件的說明》], at the 3rd session of the 7th National People's Congress, 28 March, Beijing. These quotes are translated from the Chinese: '既保持原政治體制中行之有效的部分，又要循序漸進地逐步發展適合香港情況的民主制度' and '行政立法互相制衡、互相配合；司法獨立.'

10. See People's Republic of China Central People's Government (2007) *Forum to Commemorate the 10th Anniversary of the Implementation of the Basic Law of Hong Kong Special Administrative Region* [in Chinese,《紀念香港特別行政區基本法實施十週年座談會舉

行》], 6 June, Beijing: Central People's Government, http://big5.www.gov.cn/gate/big5/www.gov.cn/ldhd/2007-06/06/content_638628.htm.

11. For example, B.C.H. Fong (2018b), op. cit., p. 53.

12. *Ibid.*

13. N. Ma (2007a) *Political Development in Hong Kong: State, Political Society and Civil Society*, Hong Kong: Hong Kong University Press.

14. B.C.H. Fong (2018b), op. cit., p. 55.

15. B.C.H. Fong (2018b), op. cit. Fong suspected that for the central leaders, 'a strong ruling party [in Hong Kong] with mass support and deep roots in society would be difficult to control and might even nurture populist local politicians who can confront Beijing by mobilizing public support' (p. 58). This is why they preferred a non-partisan CE who would broker interests among different local political forces. See also N. Ma (2007b) 'Political Parties and Elections', in W.M. Lam et al. (eds) *Contemporary Hong Kong Politics: Governance in the Post-1997 Era*, Hong Kong: Hong Kong University Press, pp. 117–134.

16. The failure to pass the Government Reorganisation bill before June 2012 caused a major setback to incoming CE Leung Chun-ying who had pledged to extensively reorganise various bureaus in his election manifesto. The Copyright amendment bill was first introduced in mid-2011, but it was not moved for resumption of the second reading within the 2008–2012 legislative term because of the pan-democrats' threat to filibuster it. After some revisions of the original bill, resumption of the second reading was moved at the end of 2015 but again faced severe criticism by pan-democrats over the coverage of the bill, which they now suspected would unduly control the freedom to use information. The Medical Registration amendment bill was introduced in 2016 with the intent to increase the membership of the Medical Council so as to accommodate growing public demand for opening up the council to more lay participation. In the face of the medical profession's strong objection to the proposal, some legislators, including pan-democrats who originally supported the idea, turned around to criticise the bill. In all these cases, opposing legislators engaged in different filibuster tactics to prolong legislative proceedings so that the government was unable to proceed with the bills in order to make way for more pressing legislation including finance bills towards the end of the legislative term. A slightly watered-down Medical Registration amendment bill was only passed in March 2018 in the subsequent legislative term.

17. J. Blondel (1997) 'Introduction: Western European Cabinets in Comparative Perspective', in J. Blondel and F. Muller-Rommel (eds) *Cabinets in Western Europe*, 2nd edition, London: Macmillan and St. Martin's Press, pp. 1–17.

18. In the 1980s, Lydia Dunn was chairman of the Trade Development Council, Chung Sze-yuen was chairman of the newly constituted Hospital Authority, Allen Lee was chairman of the Hong Kong Productivity Council, and Maria Tam was chairman of the Transport Advisory Committee. In the 1990s, Rita Fan was chairman of the Education Commission and Rosanna Wong was chairman of the Housing Authority.

19. For example, Rita Fan, during her time as an ExCo member in 1989–1992, acted as if she was the government's spokesperson on the Vietnamese refugees and security issues, often crossing fire with the UN High Commissioner on Refugees on the question of resettlement of refugees in third countries and payment of costs to Hong Kong.

20. From the pro-establishment side, leading members from the DAB, FTU, Liberal Party (with only a short interruption), and later the BPA, New People's Party, and Heung Yee Kuk (that represents traditional rural interests) have always been appointed to the ExCo since 2002. From

the pan-democratic side, non-party affiliated individuals like Anthony Cheung and Anna Wu were appointed to the ExCo in November 2005 and January 2009, respectively. Cheung later became Secretary for Transport and Housing in the Leung Chun-ying Administration (2012–2017). Wu continued to serve on Leung's ExCo until June 2017. In Carrie Lam's ExCo, there is one non-official member with a pan-democratic background, Ronny Tong, a former legislator of the Civic Party who resigned from the party in June 2015 because of political differences.

21. In the most recent years, some individual non-official ExCo members from pro-establishment parties have occasionally expressed slightly different views from the government, but it is difficult for government to impose any strict 'collective responsibility' discipline because such members were considered crucial to be included in the ExCo in order to foster some semblance of pro-establishment solidarity.

22. After 1997, notable examples of ExCo non-official members heading major advisory and statutory bodies included: Rosanna Wong as chairman of the Housing Authority; Antony Leung as chairman of the Education Commission; Tam Yiu-chung, Leong Che-hung, and now Lam Ching-choi as chairman of the Elderly Commission; Laura Cha as chairman of University Grants Committee; Marvin Cheung as chairman of the AA; Anthony Cheung as chairman of the Consumer Council; Ron Arculli, Chow Chung-kong, and now Laura Cha as chairman of the Hong Kong Exchange; Anna Wu as chairman of the Mandatory Provident Fund Schemes Authority and then chairman of the Competition Commission; and Fanny Law as chairman of the Science Park Corporation.

23. It has been argued that prime ministers are only as powerful as their colleagues allow them to be. Even so, while ministers are given the opportunity to debate issues, with the goal of reaching an agreed cabinet position, it is for the prime minister, as chair of the cabinet, to summarise what the collective decision is, and this is recorded in the minutes by the cabinet secretariat. See House of Commons Political and Constitutional Reform Committee (2011) *Role and powers of the Prime Minister: Written Evidence*, London: British Parliament, p. 48 (written evidence submitted by Professor Martin Smith and Professor David Richards, Department of Politics, University of Sheffield) and p. 19 (written evidence submitted by Emeritus Professor George Jones, London School of Economics and Political Science, quoting from the Draft *Cabinet Manual*), https://publications.parliament.uk/pa/cm201012/cmselect/cmpolcon/writev/842/842.pdf.

24. G.W. Jones (1964) 'The Prime Minister's Power', *Parliamentary Affairs*, Vol. 18, No. 2, pp. 167–185.

25. G.W. Jones (2016) *The Power of the Prime Minister: 50 Years On*, London: The Constitution Society, p. 40.

26. Soon after former Liaison Office director Zhang Xiaoming assumed office in December 2012, he instructed that in public functions, where both Liaison Office and SAR officials of similar ranking are present (e.g., Liaison Office Director and the CE, a Liaison Office Deputy Director and the CS, a Liaison Office Department Head and a Policy Secretary, and so on), the latter should always come first. However, this was seldom observed by community organisations which often accorded a higher order of precedence to Liaison Office officials than even more senior-ranking SAR government officials present because of the perception that the former represented the central authority.

27. In his famous Jerusalem Prize acceptance speech in 2009, Haruki Murakami proclaimed: 'If there is a hard, high wall and an egg that breaks against it, no matter how right the wall or how wrong the egg, I will stand on the side of the egg. Why? Because each of us is an egg, a unique soul enclosed in a fragile egg. Each of us is confronting a high wall. The high wall is the system which forces us to do the things we would not ordinarily see fit to do as individuals.' Quoted

in S.L. Loney (2009) 'Murakami, in trademark obscurity, explains why he accepted Jerusalem award', *The Jerusalem Post*, 15 February, www.jpost.com/arts-and-culture/books/murakami-in-trademark-obscurity-explains-why-he-accepted-jerusalem-award.

Chapter 12

1. In March 1985, the 3rd Session of the 6th NPC officially defined 'One Country, Two Systems' as a basic national policy of China. See *Huaxia Jingwei Network* (《華夏經緯網》) (2017) 'Deng Xiaoping put forward "One Country, Two Systems"' [in Chinese, 〈鄧小平提出「一國兩制」〉], 22 November, www.huaxia.com/thpl/tbch/tbchwz/11/5546777.html. The same treatment was accorded to Macao which returned to Chinese rule in December 1999 after 442 years of Portuguese settlement and rule.

2. The decision to establish SEZs was made in 1979, as part of the new economic reform strategy. The locations chosen had to do with their close geographical proximity to Hong Kong, Macao, and Taiwan. Hainan Island was made a separate province and also given SEZ status in 1988.

3. Namely the Guangxi, Xinjiang, Tibet, Inner Mongolia, and Ningxia Autonomous Regions.

4. Y. Ghai (2013) 'Hong Kong's autonomy: Dialects of powers and institutions', in Y. Ghai and S. Woodman (eds) *Practising Self-Government: A Comparative Study of Autonomous Regions*, Cambridge: Cambridge University Press, pp. 315–348.

5. Since the establishment of the Hong Kong SAR in July 1997, no such request for garrison assistance has so far been made by the SAR government. In Macao, its SAR government requested assistance in disaster relief from the military garrison there in the aftermath of Typhoon Hato in August 2017.

6. This also applies to the Liaison Office of the CPG in Hong Kong.

7. Such office, known as the Office of the Government of the Hong Kong Special Administrative Region in Beijing (香港特別行政區政府駐北京辦事處) or Beijing Office for short, was duly set up in 1999. Later, Economic and Trade Offices were established in other major cities on the Mainland (namely, Guangzhou, Shanghai, Chengdu, and Wuhan), complemented by smaller liaison units in other cities. Under the supervision of the Constitutional and Mainland Affairs Bureau, their main functions are to promote Hong Kong's economic and trade interests. They also help to liaise with various Mainland government organisations and facilitate visits to the Mainland by SAR government officials. In addition, Hong Kong has established an Economic Trade and Cultural Office in Taipei under the aegis of this Bureau.

8. The *Letters Patent* (The Hong Kong Charter) of 1843 stipulated: 'And we do hereby grant and ordain, that the Governor for the time being, of the said Colony, with the advice of the said Legislative Council, shall have full power and authority to make and enact all such laws and Ordinances as may from time to time be required for the Peace, Order, and good Government of the said Colony of Hong-Kong: And that, in making all such laws and Ordinances, the said Governor shall exercise all such powers and authorities; and that the said Legislative Council shall conform to, and observe all such rules and regulations as We, with the advice of Our Privy Council, shall from time to time, make for his and their guidance therein: Provided, nevertheless, and We do hereby reserve to Ourselves, our Heirs and Successors, our and their right and authority to disallow any such Ordinances in the whole or in part, and to make and establish from time to time, with the advice and consent of Parliament, or with the advice of our or their Privy Council, all such Laws as may to Us, to them, appear necessary, for the Order, Peace, and good Government of our said Island and its Dependencies, as full as if these Presents had not

been made.' See Legislative Council Library (2011b) *Letters Patent*, InfoPack No. LC04/2011-12, Hong Kong: Legislative Council, www.legco.gov.hk/general/english/library/infopacks/yr11-12/1112infopacks-lc-04-e.pdf.

The *Royal Instructions* of 1896 to the Governor, for example, expressly required that the Governor shall not assent in the Crown's name to any ordinance for the divorce of persons. See Legislative Council Library (2011a), op. cit.

9. The electoral college for NPC deputies (known as Election Conference) comprises the sitting CE, members of the last-term Election Conference, present-term CPPCC National Committee members, and members of present-term CE Election Committee who are Chinese nationals. The Election Conference for the 2017 election consisted of 1,989 members. Under the election rules, candidates for NPC deputy must be HKPRs with Chinese nationality, of at least 18 years of age, and have obtained at least 10 nominations from members of the Election Conference.

10. At present, that deputy is Tam Yiu-chung, a former LegCo and ExCo member, former Chairman of the DAB, and former Vice-chairman of the FTU. Before him, from 2008 to 2018, it was Rita Fan, a former LegCo President.

11. There are now altogether 127 CPPCC members from Hong Kong at the national level. The CPPCC (known as the new CPPCC as opposed to the old CPPCC set up by the KMT government before the Communist takeover in 1949) functions as the unique political consultative system of the CCP-run government. Set up in September 1949 (even prior to the formal establishment of the PRC), it acted as the representative assembly to approve the PRC Constitution before the NPC was officially constituted in 1954. The designated sectors (known as 'circles') cover literature and art, science and technology, social sciences, economics, agriculture, education, sports, press and publication, and medicine and health. See National Committee of The Chinese People's Political Consultative Conference (2012) 'Composition of the CPPCC', 3 July, www.cppcc.gov.cn/zxww/2012/07/03/ARTI1341301498421103.shtml.

12. Donald Tsang was not so appointed because after he stepped down from the CE post he was investigated by the ICAC for alleged corruption practices. He was subsequently charged for misconduct in public office in October 2015 and found guilty by the High Court in February 2017. He appealed to the CFA which, on 26 June 2019, quashed his conviction but without ordering a retrial because he had meanwhile already served out his sentence.

13. For example, the SAR is authorised by the CPG to continue to maintain a shipping register and issue related certificates under its legislation, using the name 'Hong Kong, China'. It is responsible for various matters of civil aviation, including the provision of air traffic services within Hong Kong's flight information region. Acting under specific authorisation from the CPG, the SAR can renew or amend air services agreements and arrangements previously in force as well as negotiate and conclude new air services agreements and provisional arrangements.

14. Under the supervision of the Commerce and Economic Development Bureau, there are presently 13 Economic and Trade Offices in foreign countries, stationed in Bangkok, Jakarta, Singapore, Sydney, Tokyo, Brussels, London, Geneva, Berlin, New York, San Francisco, Washington, D.C., and Toronto. Additional Economic and Trade Offices are planned to be set up in Seoul, Mumbai, Moscow, and Dubai.

15. The exact wording in Article 5 of the Basic Law reads: 'The socialist system and policies shall not be practised in the Hong Kong Special Administrative Region, and the previous capitalist system and way of life shall remain unchanged for 50 years.' Regarding the '50 years no change' promise, Deng Xiaoping elaborated in 1987 that '[o]ur policy will remain unchanged for 50 years after Hong Kong returns to the motherland in 1997. [...] I have to add that after 50 years there will even be less necessity to change' and that '[though] by that time I will not be around, I believe

our successors will understand this reasoning'. (His original words in Chinese were '香港在一九九七年回到祖國以後五十年政策不變。 [...] 我還要説，五十年以後更沒有變的必要'，'那時候我不在了，但是相信我們的接班人會懂得這個道理的.') See Deng's speech at the meeting with members of the Hong Kong Basic Law Drafting Committee on 16 April 1987, in CCP Central Documents Editorial Committee (ed) (1993) *Selected Works of Deng Xiaoping — Vol. III* [in Chinese,《鄧小平文選》第三卷], October, Beijing: People's Press, pp. 215–222.

16. It was an open secret that the British administration in colonial Hong Kong would not allow any activities which might jeopardise stable relationship with Mainland China. Thus, a 1981 Taiwanese movie '皇天后土' (*The Coldest Winter in Peking*), which was anti-communist and highly critical and satirical of the Cultural Revolution, was banned from being shown in Hong Kong cinemas during the 1980s.

17. In the original Chinese: '井水不犯河水，河水不犯井水'. An accompanying articulation was '你走你的陽關道，我過我的獨木橋', literally meaning 'you walk on your own path, and we cross our own bridge'.

18. In 2018, there was a small debate as to whether the PRC Constitution would also apply in totality to Hong Kong, in which case it might not be legal for some local groups critical of CCP one-party rule, such as the Hong Kong Alliance in Support of Patriotic Democratic Movements in China (set up in May 1989 during the pro-democracy movement in Beijing) to embrace slogans like 'Down with one-party dictatorship'. Tam Yiu-chung, a Hong Kong member of the NPCSC, raised the question, but both the Hong Kong SAR government and central government officials shied from commenting at the time.

19. At the official ceremony commemorating the 20th anniversary of the establishment of the Hong Kong SAR and installation of the fifth SAR Government on 1 July 2017, President Xi Jinping once again emphasised that the central government would persist with the 'One Country, Two Systems' framework with neither distortion nor wavering, and would comprehensively and accurately implement it. His original words in Chinese were '中央貫徹 "一國兩制"方針堅持兩點，一是堅定不移，不會變、不動搖；二是全面準確，確保 "一國兩制"在香港的實踐不走樣、不變形，始終沿著正確方向前進.' See People Web (人民網), 'Official Ceremony Commemorating the 20th Anniversary of the Return of Hong Kong to the Motherland' [in Chinese, 〈香港回歸祖國20周年大會〉], http://live01.people.com.cn/zhibo/Myapp/Html/Member/html/201706/15_2575_595207dc21ee7_quan.html.

20. Article 22 prohibits any interference from government agencies and provincial and local authorities on the Mainland in the affairs which the SAR administers on its own. The CPG plays the role of guarantor and protector of the SAR, with the Hong Kong and Macao Affairs Office of the State Council assisting in this gatekeeping. At the same time, some provincial and local interests may well share the same aspirations of the Hong Kong SAR in terms of getting greater autonomy from and less direct control by the centre. See A.B.L. Cheung (1998a) 'From Colony to Special Administrative Region: Issues of Hong Kong's Autonomy within a Centralized Authoritarianistic State', *Verfassung und Recht in Übersee* [*Law and Politics in Africa, Asia and Latin America*], Vol. 31, No. 3, pp. 302–316. However, the rise of separatist politics in Hong Kong in recent years has certainly driven away regional sympathy towards Hong Kong's autonomy within the 'One Country' context. Sceptics also wonder if such factors are still effective the longer Hong Kong has gone past 1997 and the more it has become immersed and integrated into the national framework.

21. Various spatial, temporal, functional, hierarchical, and horizontal factors contribute to the prevalence of centrifugal forces in China in both traditional and modern times. The overall impact of the post-Mao reforms on central-local balances of power was neither straightforward

nor uniform. Although subnational governments have generally obtained a significantly expanded scope of discretion in the making and implementation of policy, the balance between centre and localities does not predominantly tilt towards the latter. See J. Chung (2016) *Centrifugal Empire: Central–Local Relations in China*, New York: Columbia University Press. Some have argued that local autonomy has always been a negotiated outcome in the PRC's political and administrative history and that such interactions should not be interpreted narrowly within a 'central controllers vs. local agents' compliance model but rather as coordination problems between central and local actors as co-agents. See L.C. Li (1997) 'Towards a Non-zero-sum Interactive Framework of Spatial Politics: The Case of Centre-Province in Contemporary China', *Political Studies*, Vol. 45, No. 1, pp. 49–65; L.C. Li (2010) 'Central-local Relations in the People's Republic of China: Trends, Processes and Impacts for Policy Implementation', *Public Administration and Development*, Vol. 30, No. 3, pp. 177–190.

22. A.H.Y. Chen (2018), op. cit.

23. On 4 November 2017, the NPCSC adopted the decision to add the new National Anthem Law to Annex III of the Basic Law. The SAR government then decided to apply this law locally by way of legislation, with the National Anthem Bill gazetted in January 2019. A total of 17 meetings were held by the relevant committee to scrutinise the bill. Amidst the controversy over extradition, the government did not proceed with the second reading of the bill before the LegCo's summer break as originally intended. Upon the eventual resumption of the second reading on 27 May 2020, pan-democrats staged protests and a filibuster. The legislation was finally passed on 4 June 2020 after heated and chaotic debates in the LegCo for over 50 hours.

24. References to 'subversion' and 'foreign political organisations' (not in the original Draft Basic Law) were added in the aftermath of the 1989 Tiananmen crackdown, when the strong local turnout in protest against Beijing caused some central government officials to worry that Hong Kong might be turned into a counter-revolutionary base of subversion.

25. Not only was the media concerned about the curtailment of press freedom, but academics worried about academic and research freedom and even librarians wondered if keeping books on Taiwan or Tibet 'independence' would constitute secession or treason. The proposed proscription mechanism for those organisations found to be connected to prohibited organisations on the Mainland, based simply on a certificate issued by the central government, further raised the alarm over the future of the rule of law and fair trial in the SAR. The wide discretionary powers proposed to be given to police officers to raid premises were also criticised.

26. Tung announced amendments on 5 July 2003, involving the deletion of those proposals to ban local groups whose Mainland counterparts are outlawed for threatening national security and to grant police powers to enter and search properties without court warrants, as well as the inclusion of a public-interest defence for disclosure of official secrets.

27. Article 23 legislation was not just a legislative disaster for Tung. It also opened the floodgate to political discontent as well as renewed demands for democratisation. The DAB was another major loser in the saga and was heavily penalised by voters in the subsequent DC elections in November 2003. The controversy also pointed to more deep-seated anxieties among Hong Kong people over their political future, as highlighted in another large-scale march on 1 July 2004 under the banner of 'Returning Power to the People'. For some assessments of the 1 July protests from multiple perspectives, see, for example, J.Y.S. Cheng (ed) (2005) *The July 1 Protest Rally: Interpreting a Historic Event*, Hong Kong: City University of Hong Kong Press.

28. Participants of the 1 July 2003 protests were mostly from educated and middle-class backgrounds. After that, this newfound middle-class professional activism attracted much more media and political attention and dominated the mainstream public discourse. The concern for

freedom and better governance further fuelled a strong middle-class demand for constitutional reform and democratisation. Later, in Tung's 2004 policy address, he specifically referred to the importance of engaging the middle class in policy consultation and formulation.

29. One practical way to proceed could have been to revive the 2003 revised bill with suitable modifications and start public consultation or use the Law Reform Commission route to secure more expert advice before taking any bill to the LegCo.

30. *Xinhuanet* (2020b) 'China Focus: Draft decision on HK national security legislation submitted to NPC', 22 May, www.xinhuanet.com/english/2020-05/22/c_139078396.htm; *Xinhuanet* (2020c) 'Highlights of China's decision on Hong Kong national security legislation', 28 May, www.xinhuanet.com/english/2020-05/28/c_139095813.htm. For an official English translation of the National Security Law for information, see Hong Kong Special Administrative Region Government (2020) *The Law of the People's Republic of China on Safeguarding National Security in the Hong Kong Special Administrative Region*, G.N. (E.) 72 of 2020, July, www.elegislation.gov.hk/fwddoc/hk/a406/eng_translation_(a406)_en.pdf.

31. A. Li (2020) 'China-enacted national security law must be consistent with Hong Kong legal principles', *South China Morning Post*, 2 June. See also G. Cheung (2020) 'Hong Kong's national security law must follow common law, former chief justices say', *South China Morning Post*, 2 June.

32. Under Article 27 of China's Legislation Law (立法法), a bill put on the agenda of an NPCSC session will in general be deliberated three times before being voted on. During the first deliberation, after a briefing by the bill's sponsor at a plenary session, preliminary deliberation will be conducted by divided group sessions. During the second deliberation, the NPC's Law Committee will brief the plenary session on the status of amendment and major issues in respect of the draft law, whereupon further deliberation will be conducted by divided group sessions. During the third deliberation, the Law Committee will give a report to the plenary session on the results of the deliberation on the draft law, whereupon deliberation on the amended draft law will be conducted by divided group sessions. If necessary, the NPCSC may convene a joint group session or a plenary session to discuss the major issues of the draft law. For the full unofficial English version available from the US Congressional Executive Commission on China, see National People's Congress (2013) *Legislation Law of the People's Republic of China*, www.cecc.gov/resources/legal-provisions/legislation-law-chinese-and-english-text#body-chinese.

33. NPCSC (1999) *The Interpretation by the Standing Committee of the National People's Congress of Articles 22(4) and 24(2)(3) of the Basic Law of the Hong Kong Special Administrative Region of the People's Republic of China*, adopted at the 10th Session of the Standing Committee of the 9th National People's Congress, 26 June, Beijing, www.basiclaw.gov.hk/en/basiclawtext/images/basiclawtext_doc17.pdf (in English). Soon after the 1997 transfer to SAR rule, Hong Kong faced the first social and legal challenge resulting from a large number of Mainland-born children of HKPRs claiming their right of abode in Hong Kong under Article 24 of the Basic Law. Many of them were of adult age and had either entered Hong Kong illegally or over-stayed their visas. In the *Ng Ka Ling* and *Chan Kam Nga* cases in 1999, the CFA ruled that all children born of HKPRs, irrespective of when they were born, had the right of abode in Hong Kong. The SAR government estimated this would mean allowing some 1.67 million such Mainland residents to migrate to Hong Kong over ten years, which would be beyond Hong Kong's capacity to cope with.

34. When Tung tendered his resignation from the CE post in March of 2005, two years before completing his second five-year term, there was the question as to whether the next CE should serve a new five-year term or just the remainder of Tung's second term, since neither the Basic Law nor the Chief Executive Election Ordinance clearly specified this. Upon request from Donald Tsang as Acting CE, the NPCSC interpreted the Basic Law provision to the effect

that the succeeding CE should fulfil the remainder of the resigning CE's original term. While some lawyers in Hong Kong did not agree with this interpretation, there was no strong reaction from the community.

35. FG Hemisphere Associates LLC (FG), a US company that was a creditor to the Democratic Republic of the Congo, wanted to seize US$102 million of the fees paid by China Railway Group to the Congo to satisfy debts the Congo owed to the company. The Congo government took its case to the Hong Kong court in 2010, which ruled in favour of FG, specifying that states do not have strict immunity in commercial proceedings. The Congo then applied to claim absolute state immunity from jurisdiction in Hong Kong, and the Court of First Instance accepted this claim of immunity. FG appealed, and the Court of Appeal reversed that decision. The Congo then appealed to CFA. See Research Office of the Legislative Council Secretariat (2012) *Fact Sheet: The decision by the Court of Final Appeal to seek an interpretation of the Basic Law from the Standing Committee of the National People's Congress regarding the controversy of state immunity raised in the debt litigation of the Democratic Republic of Congo*, FS17/11-12, 22 February, Hong Kong: Legislative Council Research Division, www.legco.gov.hk/yr11-12/english/sec/library/1112fs17-e.pdf. In accordance with Article 158, the CFA requested the NPCSC in June 2011 to interpret the relevant clauses in Articles 13 and 19 of the Basic Law. The NPCSC ruled that the Congo should have the right to diplomatic immunity. As this was more a legal point not affecting any Hong Kong interest, the interpretation did not raise any undue reaction. See NPCSC (2011) *Interpretation by the Standing Committee of the National People's Congress Regarding the First Paragraph of Article 13 and Article 19 of the Basic Law of the Hong Kong Special Administrative Region of the People's Republic of China*, adopted at the 22nd Meeting of the Standing Committee of the 11th National People's Congress, 26 August, Beijing, www.elegislation.gov.hk/hk/A114%21en.assist.pdf.

36. NPCSC (2016) *Interpretation of Article 104 of the Basic Law of the Hong Kong Special Administrative Region of the People's Republic of China by the Standing Committee of the National People's Congress*, adopted at the 24th Session of the Standing Committee of the 12th National People's Congress, 7 November, Beijing, www.basiclaw.gov.hk/en/basiclawtext/images/basiclawtext_doc25.pdf. Oath-taking by newly elected members of the LegCo was in the past only a matter of ritual, with at times attempts by a few radical legislators to make their political statement through the way the oath was recited. However, in the aftermath of the 2014 Occupy Central movement, some pan-democratic legislators, notably those with separatist tendencies, made use of the oath-taking in October 2016 for the new LegCo term to ridicule or otherwise deny allegiance to the PRC, or to add their own political aspirations in the wording of the oath. The SAR government then filed a judicial review application to ban them from retaking their oaths in order to assume office. While pending the High Court's judgment on the application, the NPCSC took the initiative to pass an interpretation of Article 104 of the Basic Law on 7 November 2018, whereby the CE, principal officials, and legislators must 'correctly, completely, and solemnly' swear (必須準確、完整、莊重地宣讀) a scripted oath, pledging allegiance to the Hong Kong SAR of the PRC. If legislators and others refuse to take the oath as such, purposefully read their own lines, or are 'not genuinely or solemnly' participating in the oath-taking, they would be deprived of their right to assume office and would not be allowed to retake the oath.

37. The NPCSC is widely believed by the public in Hong Kong to be state-directed, unlike an independent constitutional court in continental European countries such as France and Germany. The Basic Law Committee is the only organ where, with the presence of some Hong Kong members, any differences in legal understanding and practices between the two legal jurisdictions can be fully debated and resolved.

38. Information Office, State Council of the PRC (2014) *The Practice of the 'One Country, Two Systems' Policy in the Hong Kong Special Administrative Region*, 10 June, https://web. archive.org/web/20141008210149/http://news.xinhuanet.com/english/china/2014-06/10/ c_133396891.htm.

39. *Ibid.*, Foreword.

40. In the central government's parlance, 'Administrators' of the SAR included members of the SAR judiciary. This immediately caused grave concern among senior judges, particularly given the provision in the Basic Law that foreign judges from overseas common law jurisdictions could be invited to sit on the CFA (Article 82) (appointed as Non-Permanent Judges).

41. See J. Cheng (2009) 'The story of a new policy', *Hong Kong Journal*, Fall, www.hkbasiclaw. com/Hong%20Kong%20Journal/Cheng%20Jie%20article.htm. Cheng Jie (程潔), a law academic, was seconded to the NPCSC office to work on Hong Kong and Macau Basic Law issues during 2006–2007.

42. An academic critic explained the policy change as comprising three 'incorporation strategies' — namely, economic integration, political control (especially over the pace of constitutional reform), and national identity consolidation — all in pursuit of an assimilationist state-building nationalism on the part of Beijing. Such strategies to assimilate Hongkongers into one Chinese nation ironically backfired and led to the rise of a peripheral nationalism in Hong Kong and waves of localist counter-mobilisations. See B.C.H. Fong (2017c), op. cit.

43. An illustrative academic observation in this respect can be found in P.T.Y. Cheung (2017), op. cit. Peter Cheung reached a similar conclusion as Brian Fong (see previous footnote) that this tightening grip might engender even greater centrifugal tendencies among the Hong Kong people, especially the younger generations.

44. When explaining the need for such a co-location arrangement at the West Kowloon Terminus, the government detailed why alternative solutions explored were found impractical. Those options included: amending the Basic Law; introducing Mainland CIQ laws via inclusion in Annex III of the Basic Law; adding a co-location arrangement in separate stations for northbound and southbound trips; providing 'on-board' clearance (while the train is still running on the Mainland side between Futian Station in Shenzhen and the Hong Kong boundary within a very short span of about 10 minutes); and establishing a separate-location arrangement as in the present intercity through-train service between Hong Kong and Guangzhou East Station.

45. For a detailed account of the whole XRL saga, see A.B.L. Cheung (張炳良) (2018b), op. cit., Ch. 9.

46. NPCSC (2017) *Decision of the Standing Committee of the National People's Congress on Approving the Co-operation Arrangement between the Mainland and the Hong Kong Special Administrative Region on the Establishment of the Port at the West Kowloon Station of the Guangzhou-Shenzhen-Hong Kong Express Rail Link for Implementing Co-location Arrangement*, adopted at the 31st Session of the Standing Committee of the 12th National People's Congress, 27 December, Beijing, www.thb.gov.hk/eng/policy/transport/policy/colocation/ EN%20Decision%20(2%20Jan).pdf. See also Legislative Council (2017) *Co-operation Arrangement between the Mainland and the Hong Kong Special Administrative Region on the Establishment of the Port at the West Kowloon Station of the Guangzhou-Shenzhen-Hong Kong Express Rail Link for Implementing Co-location Arrangement*, CB(4)441/17-18(04), Hong Kong: Legislative Council, www.legco.gov.hk/yr17-18/english/panels/tp/papers/tpcb4-441- 4-e.pdf; Department of Justice, Transport and Housing Bureau, and Security Bureau (2017) *Customs, Immigration and Quarantine Arrangements of the Hong Kong Section of the Guangzhou-Shenzhen-Hong Kong Express Rail Link*, paper submitted to the Legislative Council, CB(2)1966/16-17(01), July, Hong Kong: Legislative Council.

47. Conceptually, if such mutual legislative approval was not forthcoming, the co-location arrangement would flop. In the event, the Guangzhou-Shenzhen-Hong Kong Express Rail Link (Co-location) Bill was passed by the LegCo on 14 June 2018, with the support of the pro-establishment camp.

48. Mutual arrangements exist between the US and some countries such as Canada in the form of border pre-clearance (before departure from the respective countries at their airports by border control officials of the other side), as well as between Britain and France in the mutual enforcement of CIQ laws and policing by British and French officials (together with the powers of arrest and detention according to their home country laws) in their designated 'control areas' inside the respective French and British stations of the Channel Train (known as Channel Fixed Link). See Secretary of State for Foreign and Commonwealth Affairs (1993) *Protocol between the Government of the United Kingdom of Great Britain and Northern Ireland and the Government of the French Republic Governing Frontier Controls and Policing, Co-operation in Criminal Justice, Public Safety and Mutual Assistance Relating to the Channel Fixed Link*, Treaty Series No. 70 (1993), Cm. 2366, London: HMSO. There is a local precedent arrangement as well. In July 2007, Hong Kong and the Mainland set up co-located checkpoints at the Shenzhen Bay boundary inside Shenzhen territory, where Hong Kong laws fully apply within the Hong Kong Port Area *as if* within SAR jurisdiction. The present West Kowloon station co-location arrangement differs from the Shenzhen Bay model because Hong Kong's civil and commercial laws still fully apply within the Mainland Port Area at that station.

49. A 'living constitution' is one that evolves, changes over time, and adapts to new circumstances, without being formally amended. The 'living constitution' school argues that the constitution has a dynamic meaning and that contemporaneous society should be taken into account when interpreting key constitutional phrases to keep up with rapid social, economic, technological, and international changes, as opposed to the views of the traditional and 'originalist' school. See, for example, D.A. Strauss (2010) *The Living Constitution*, Chicago: The University of Chicago Law School, www.law.uchicago.edu/news/living-constitution.

50. The Court of First Instance further held that upon a fair reading of the Basic Law establishing a broad framework for the exercise of a high degree of autonomy by Hong Kong, it is open to the legislature of Hong Kong to enact the relevant ordinance to provide that the Mainland Port Area in the West Kowloon Station shall be subject to the Mainland's jurisdiction and Mainland laws. See Court of First Instance, High Court of the Hong Special Administrative Region (2018) 'Constitutional and Administrative Law List No. 1160 of 2018', https://legalref.judiciary.hk/lrs/common/ju/ju_frame.jsp?DIS=119029&currpage=T.

51. The existing Fugitive Offenders Ordinance does not permit extradition between Hong Kong and the Mainland, or between Hong Kong and Taiwan or Macao, either by formal agreement similar to those treaties or agreements which Hong Kong has entered into with some countries, or in an ad hoc manner on a case-by-case basis in the absence of such an agreement. The proposed amendment would lift such restrictions. If passed, even in the absence of a formal agreement, new 'special surrender arrangements' would be introduced whereby the CE can first issue an authority to proceed with a surrender request from the other jurisdiction, with the evidence and circumstances of each case then examined by the holding of a committal hearing in open court, followed finally by the CE's consideration of a surrender order having regard to the court's committal decision and the circumstances of the case. See Security Bureau (2019) *Legislative Council Brief: Fugitive Offenders and Mutual Legal Assistance in Criminal Matters Legislation (Amendment) Bill 2019*, SBCR 1/2716/19, March, Hong Kong: Legislative Council.

52. For a good account of the extradition saga, see A.H.Y. Chen (2019a) 'A Commentary on the Fugitive Offenders and Mutual Legal Assistance in Criminal Matters Legislation (Amendment)

Bill 2019', *HKU Legal Scholarship Blog*, 3 May, Faculty of Law, University of Hong Kong; A.H.Y. Chen (2019b) 'A Perfect Storm: How the Proposed Law on Hong Kong-Mainland China Rendition was Aborted', *Verfassungsblog on Matters Constitutional*, 19 June, https://verfassungsblog.de/a-perfect-storm/.

53. Taken from Suzanne Collins (2014) *Hunger Games: Mockingjay*, New York: Scholastic. The phrase was ' "Fire is catching!" I am shouting now, determined he will not miss a word of it, "And if we burn, you burn with us!" '

54. R. Wodak (2015) *The Politics of Fear: What Right-Wing Populist Discourses Mean*, London: Sage.

55. On August 12, the day when operations at the Hong Kong International Airport came to a halt because of a mass sit-in by protesters, a spokesman for the Hong Kong and Macao Affairs Office warned that the serious violent crimes committed by radical protesters had begun to show the 'first signs of terrorism'. See *China Daily* (2019c) 'Signs of "terrorism" seen in HK unrest', 13 August, www.chinadaily.com.cn/cndy/2019-08/13/content_37501175.htm.

56. *China Daily* (2019b) 'Overriding task in Hong Kong is "to stop violence" ', 8 August, www.china daily.com.cn/a/201908/08/WS5d4b180ea310cf3e3556477f.html.

57. Only one such dialogue session was held on 25 September 2019, and this failed to quell social discontent because Lam was unable to offer any further reconciliation measures.

58. Among those supporting the idea of an independent inquiry were the former Chief Justice Andrew Li; religious, professional, and NGO leaders; and some former Secretaries, Under-Secretaries, and retired top civil servants.

59. *BBC News* (2019a) 'Hong Kong protests: President Xi warns of "bodies smashed" ', 14 October.

60. Independent Police Complaints Council (IPCC) (2020) *A Thematic Study by the IPCC on the Public Order Events arising from the Fugitive Offenders Bill since June 2019 and the Police Actions in Response*, Hong Kong: IPCC, www.ipcc.gov.hk/en/public_communications/ipcc_thematic_study_report.html, Ch. 4.

61. See *Ming Pao* (《明報》) (2020b) '350 arrested multiple times, 17-year old student 9 times' [In Chinese, 〈350人多次被捕 17歲生遭拘9次〉], 8 June.

62. See *Ming Pao* (《明報》) (2020a) '9000 arrested over anti-bill amendment, of whom 20% below adult age' [In Chinese, 〈反修例拘9000人 兩成未成年〉], 7 June.

63. J. Lam and Z. Ibrahim (eds) (2020) *Rebel City: Hong Kong's Year of Water and Fire*, Hong Kong and Singapore: South China Morning Post and World Scientific Publishing. In the beginning, the protests adopted the 'Be Water' strategy borrowed from Bruce Lee's philosophy, meaning be peaceful and leaderless.

64. This term refers to Beijing's policy of using economic means to shore up the Hong Kong SAR so as to help alleviate grievances of the middle class who, in its view, had become increasingly restless politically because of the economic slowdown which threatened their career opportunities and drove down their asset values.

65. The latest schemes in 2018 involved the issuing of residence cards, concomitant with certain social benefits, to those Hong Kong people resident in the Mainland for study or employment, and the inclusion of Hong Kong universities and researchers in accessing Mainland research funding. Facilitation measures cover the areas of education, employment, setting up business, and daily life matters. For details, refer to Constitutional and Mainland Affairs Bureau (n.d.), *Facilitation Measures for Hong Kong People*, www.cmab.gov.hk/en/issues/facilitation_measures.htm.

66. The CEPA is a free trade agreement concluded by the Mainland and Hong Kong signed on 29 June 2003, serving to open up huge markets for Hong Kong goods and services, thus

enhancing economic cooperation and integration. It has adopted a building block approach, by introducing liberalisation measures in different sectors by phases continually, as supported by regular supplements.

67. Foreign companies set up in Hong Kong can also benefit from the CEPA in accessing the Mainland market. However, setting up subsidiaries and professional practices in sectors already opened up would still require various permits or licences from provincial and local governments involving complicated procedures and additional requirements (sometimes as local protectionism), leading to the phenomenon of 'even though the big door is opened, the small doors have yet to open' (大門開了，小門未開). This is but expected. After all, many new businesses are emerging in China today, and Hong Kong companies setting up on the Mainland have to compete with them in expertise, efficiency, and cost, and cannot just rely on more favourable policies towards Hong Kong.

68. Since the 11th Five-Year Plan (2006–2010) of China approved by the 4th Session of the 10th NPC in March 2006, there has been a dedicated chapter in the Plan about the Hong Kong and Macao SARs.

69. '9+2' refers to nine neighbouring provinces and two municipalities (namely, Guangdong, Fujian, Jiangxi, Hunan, Guangxi, Hainan, Sichuan, Guizhou, and Yunnan provinces/regions, plus the Hong Kong and Macao SARs). The 9+2 Pan-Pearl River Delta Cooperation and Development Forum was started in June 2004 when Zhang Dejiang (張德江), retired NPCSC Chairman, was Party Secretary of Guangdong Province.

70. See State Council of the PRC (2019) *Outline Development Plan for the Guangdong-Hong Kong-Macao Greater Bay Area*, 18 February, Beijing (translated by the Hong Kong SAR government), www.bayarea.gov.hk/filemanager/en/share/pdf/Outline_Development_Plan.pdf. The Greater Bay Area comprises the two SARs of Hong Kong and Macao, and the nine cities of Guangzhou, Shenzhen, Zhuhai, Foshan, Huizhou, Dongguan, Zhongshan, Jiangmen, and Zhaoqing in Guangdong Province. Its total area is 56,000 sq. km. with a total population of around 70 million. Unlike other Bay Areas around the world (such as New York Bay, San Francisco Bay, and Tokyo Bay), there exist three different systems and legal jurisdictions among the eleven cities involved, posing challenges in addition to opportunities of regional integration.

71. The Hong Kong-Zhuhai-Macao Bridge was commissioned in October 2018. Built with capital injections from the three sides towards the construction of the main bridge-cum-tunnel, with each side also responsible for its own connecting road link to the main bridge, the whole bridge link is now the world's longest tunnel-cum-bridge. It takes only 45 minutes road journey between Zhuhai city and the Hong Kong International Airport in Chek Lap Kok compared to some 4 hours in the past. The XRL Hong Kong Section, connecting Hong Kong to the national high-speed rail grid, has reduced the journey time to Guangzhou (Guangzhou South Station) to only 46 minutes.

72. In 2017, Hong Kong accounted for 76% in overall cross-border RMB payments across the world, far ahead of London (6%) and Singapore (4%). See Research Office of the Legislative Council Secretariat (2018) *Financial Affairs: Offshore Renminbi Business in Hong Kong*, 28 February, Hong Kong: Legislative Council Research Division. According to the statistics in the '2019 RMB Internationalization Report' published by the People's Bank of China, Hong Kong's offshore RMB accounted for roughly half of the world's stock as at end-2018. See Information Services Department (2020) 'Written reply by the Acting Secretary for Financial Services and the Treasury, Joseph Chan, in the Legislative Council (on LCQ13: Offshore Renminbi businesses)', press release, 15 January.

73. Accepted as a founding member of AIIB, Hong Kong contributed US$10 million to its initial fund and geared its financial market towards extending infrastructure investment loans through consolidating its position as a key infrastructure financing centre in the region. An Infrastructure Financing Facilitation Office was established by the Hong Kong Monetary Authority in July 2016 with a mission to facilitate infrastructure investments and their financing.

74. Amid Hong Kong's political unrest in August 2019, the central government announced the plan to boost Shenzhen's growth into a new SEZ to carry out bolder reforms (including in the legal, financial, medical, and social sectors) as a model for other Chinese cities. This triggered speculation as to whether Beijing was planning to eventually use Shenzhen to replace Hong Kong. See P. Zhang (2019) 'Beijing unveils detailed reform plan to make Shenzhen model city for China and the world', *South China Morning Post*, 18 August; Y. Hinata (2019) 'China works to turn Shenzhen into the new Hong Kong', *Nikkei Asian Review*, 19 August, https://asia.nikkei.com/Spotlight/Hong-Kong-protests/China-works-to-turn-Shenzhen-into-the-new-Hong-Kong. See also W. Pesek (2014) 'No, Shanghai Can't Replace Hong Kong', *Bloomberg*, 30 September, www.bloomberg.com/opinion/articles/2014-09-30/no-shanghai-can-t-replace-hong-kong. Pesek took the view that businesses and capital fleeing Hong Kong would likely go to Singapore should the former's financial hub be at risk.

75. For a useful analysis, see Y.W. Sung (2018) 'Becoming part of one national economy: Maintaining two systems in the midst of the rise of China', in T.L. Lui et al. (eds), op. cit., pp. 66–85.

76. Karl Marx argued that the mode of production of material life determines the social, political, and intellectual life processes in general. It was not the consciousness of people that determined their being but, on the contrary, their social being that determined their consciousness. See K. Marx (1859/1993) *A Contribution to the Critique of Political Economy* (original in German, *Zur Kritik der Politischen Ökonomie*, translated by S.W. Ryazanskaya), Moscow: Progress Publishers, available online at www.marxists.org/archive/marx/works/1859/critique-pol-economy/index.htm.

77. The term 'existentialism' is used here to denote the sense of 'existence preceding essence' (as the philosophy of Existentialism argues) and the way of living in a social and historical context as 'average everydayness' perceived by people concerned. See J.P. Sartre (1947) *Existentialism*, New York: Philosophical Society; M. Heidegger (translated by J. Macquarie and E. Robinson) (1962/2001) *Being and Time*, Oxford: Blackwell.

78. See World Bank (n.d.) *GDP (current US$) – China, Hong Kong SAR, China*, https://data.worldbank.org/indicator/NY.GDP.MKTP.CD?locations=CN-HK&name_desc=false.

79. H. Lemahieu (2019) 'Five big takeaways from the 2019 Asia Power Index', *The Interpreter* (Lowry Institute), 29 May, www.lowyinstitute.org/the-interpreter/power-shifts-fevered-times-2019-asia-power-index. It was observed that 'under most scenarios, short of war, the US is unlikely to halt the narrowing power differential between itself and China'.

80. Such as the Capital Investment Entrant Scheme (2003–2015), Admission Scheme for Mainland Talents and Professionals (since 2003), Quality Migrant Admission Scheme (since 2006), Immigration Arrangements for Non-local Graduates (since 2008), and Technology Talent Admission Scheme (since 2018). For a list of various admission schemes and details, including those specifically for Mainland residents, see Immigration Department (n.d.) *Introduction of Admission Schemes for Talent, Professionals and Entrepreneurs*, www.immd.gov.hk/eng/useful_information/admission-schemes-talents-professionals-entrepreneurs.html#asmtp.

81. Whereas inter-marriages between Hongkongers and Mainlanders in the pre-1997 past were mostly cases of older-age Hong Kong working-class men marrying much younger Mainland women often from the rural areas, nowadays inter-marriages between educated

urban young people are becoming more common. Until the adoption of a 'zero quota' policy in 2012 by the Leung Chun-ying Administration, babies borne of Mainland (non-HKPR) parents in Hong Kong were automatically entitled to HKPR status. See Information Services Department (2012d) 'Government reaffirms its strict enforcement of the "zero quota" policy', press release, 28 December.

82. According to the University Grants Committee, there were some 6,750 Mainland students in publicly funded universities in Hong Kong in the 2007–2008 academic year. Over a decade later, in 2018–2019, the number had increased by more than 1.8 times to about 12,320. See University Grants Committee (n.d.) *Number of Mainland students in University Grants Committee-funded programmes by university and level of study, 2003/04 to 2016/17 academic years*, http://gia.info.gov.hk/general/201707/12/P2017071200689_263130_2_14998541 10454.pdf; University Grants Committee (2019) 'Internationalisation and Engagement with Mainland China', *Annual Report 2018–19*, www.ugc.edu.hk/eng/ugc/about/publications/report/AnnualRpt_2018-19.html, specifically Chart 2: Non-local Student Number of UGC-funded Programmes by Place of Origin, 2017/18 and 2018/19 on p. 58.

83. According to a report on 11 April 2019, up to then there were 10,433 Hong Kong secondary school graduates applying for places in Mainland higher education institutions during the academic year through various channels, of whom 3,511 joining a test-exempt admission scheme for Hong Kong students. See *Xinhuanet* (新華網) (2019) 'Statistics Show that the Number of Hong Kong Students Enrolling in Mainland Universities through the Test-free Enrollment Plan Increased by Nearly 10% this Year' [in Chinese, 〈數據顯示：今年通過免試招生計劃報讀內地高校的港生增長近一成〉] 11 April, www.xinhuanet.com/politics/2019-04/11/c_1124355664.htm (in Chinese).

84. Hong Kong Baptist University set up The Beijing Normal University-Hong Kong Baptist University United International College in Zhuhai in 2005, while the Chinese University of Hong Kong set up a branch campus in Shenzhen in 2014. The Hong Kong University of Science and Technology and the City University of Hong Kong have announced plans to set up campuses in Nansha and Dongguan, respectively, while the Hong Kong Polytechnic University is also exploring a venue for an offshore campus in the Greater Bay Area.

85. Hong Kong Tourism Board (2019), op. cit., Table 1. The number of Mainland arrivals in 2019 decreased to 43.7 million (-14.2%) because of the anti-Mainland atmosphere in Hong Kong during the political unrest in June 2019. The number was even lower by July 2020 (–86% compared to the corresponding period in 2019) because of the entry ban imposed after the COVID-19 epidemic outbreak. It is uncertain if the volume of Mainland visitor arrivals will return to the previous peak level should the disruptions caused by the epidemic and political unrest eventually subside.

86. Other major tourist cities in the world, like Venice and Barcelona, have also experienced similar anti-foreign tourist sentiments.

87. For example, Jiang Shigong (强世功), a Peking University law professor rumoured to have helped draft the 2014 White Paper, urges Hongkongers not to just pay attention to the central leaders' specific narrative about Hong Kong and Macao but also their overall narrative on China's historical positioning in the new era. See S.G. Jiang (2017a) 'The Centre's mode of governing Hong Kong wholly entering the Xi Jinping Era' [in Chinese, 〈中央治港全面進入「習近平時代」〉], *Ming Pao* (《明報》), 26 October. Tian Feilong (田飛龍), a law professor on the board of directors of the Chinese Association of Hong Kong and Macao Studies, suggested that 'One Country, Two Systems' has entered version 2.0, with these features: (1) governing Hong Kong according to law becoming an organic constituent of governing the country according

to law; (2) 'comprehensive jurisdiction' becoming a new legal basis of the centre's mode of governing Hong Kong; (3) an orderly democratisation of Hong Kong compatible with both the Basic Law and the national constitutional order; (4) integrative development of Hong Kong within China's new globalisation agenda; and (5) an organic integration of Hong Kong's high degree of autonomy with the centre's authority of comprehensive jurisdiction. See F.L. Tian (2017) 'One Country, Two Systems enters version "2.0"' [in Chinese, 〈一國兩制進入「2.0版」〉], *Ming Pao* (《明報》), 11 December.

88. This was a remark by Premier Li Keqiang (李克強) during a meeting with CE Leung Chun-ying on his annual duty-visit to Beijing. See *People's Daily* (《人民日報》) (2015) 'Li Keqiang Meets with Liang Zhenying and Cui Shi'an' [in Chinese, 〈李克強分別會見梁振英崔世安〉], 24 December, http://politics.people.com.cn/n1/2015/1224/c1024-27968435.html.

89. Hong Kong primarily belongs to Hong Kong people and to China, but at the same time, it should also belong to the world in much the same way as other global capitals like New York and London position themselves. As Jack Ma, founder of Alibaba, said during his speech at the 2018 conferment ceremony of the University of Hong Kong where he was awarded an honorary doctorate, 'Hong Kong [...] does not only belong to Hong Kong, Hong Kong does not only belong to China, it belongs to the world, it belongs to this century'. See J. Ma (2018) 'Speech presented in the 199th Congregation of The University of Hong Kong for the award Doctor of Social Sciences *honoris causa*', www4.hku.hk/hongrads/index.php/graduate_speech_detail/340/97.

90. Civic Exchange founder and former Under-Secretary for Environment Christine Loh and legal scholar Richard Cullen have advanced a similar point in their book by suggesting that with loyalty to China made clear, the capacity to contribute, as well as to lobby for Hong Kong's interests, is manifestly enhanced. See C. Loh and R. Cullen (2018) *No Third Person: Rewriting the Hong Kong Story*, Hong Kong: Abbreviated Press. Civic Exchange is an independent policy think-tank in Hong Kong.

91. It is a test of compatibility of different political traditions, administrative and legal systems; different laws and regulations, standards and procedures; and different policies and regulatory practices. It is a test of complementarity, so that integration would not add to 'zero-sum' suspicions and vicious rivalries. It is also a test of connectivity, in order to accord maximum convenience to people-to-people connection, whether physically or mentally, despite existing 'borders' and regulatory controls over information transfer.

Chapter 13

1. A 'Certificate of Identity' was for stateless residents, which would mean endless hurdles in applying for visas when travelling overseas.

2. British nationality had already undergone considerable changes since the 1960s. Before the passage of the Commonwealth Immigrants Act 1962, Citizens of the United Kingdom and Colonies enjoyed easy migration to Britain. Afterwards, except those with a close connection with the United Kingdom, all would be subject to immigration control and not automatically have a right of abode in Britain. The other categories of British nationality would not carry such status either simply based on nationality. The Immigration Act 1971 defined the concept of 'patriality' for the right of abode. The Nationality Act 1981 reclassified the Citizenship of the United Kingdom and Colonies into three categories: British citizenship; British Dependent Territories citizenship; and British Overseas citizenship.

3. Local Chinese could not use the Hong Kong-issued British passport at that time because the Chinese government regarded the Chinese population in Hong Kong as Chinese, not as British nationals. A home-return permit was issued to them instead via the state-run China Travel Service acting for the Mainland authorities.

4. R. Hughes (1968), op. cit.

5. Such Hong Kong residents acquiring British nationality had lost the automatic right to live in Britain even earlier as a result of the Commonwealth Immigrants Act 1962.

6. The silver standard was the basis of Hong Kong's monetary system until 1935 when, during a world silver crisis, the colonial government announced that the Hong Kong dollar would be taken off the silver standard and linked to the British pound instead at the rate of HK$16 to the pound. In June 1972, the British government decided to float the pound sterling. The Hong Kong dollar was then linked briefly to the US dollar. In November 1974, against a weakening US dollar, the Hong Kong dollar was allowed to float freely until 1983 when it was pegged to the US dollar again.

7. The colonial administration of Hong Kong had to strive for a separate voice within the British delegation because of opposite interests between the colony and the home government, the former defending free trade rights and the latter inclining towards protectionism. These trade conflicts were further aggravated when Britain attempted to enter the European Economic Community, which threatened to end Hong Kong's preferential access to the British market. See J. Fellows (2016) *The rhetoric of trade and decolonisation in Hong Kong, 1945–1984*, doctoral thesis, Hong Kong: Lingnan University, http://commons.ln.edu.hk/his_etd/9/. Hong Kong became a separate (91st) Contracting Party of GATT in April 1986 by virtue of the declarations of Britain and China over Hong Kong's full autonomy in its external commercial relations under Britain before 1997 and its SAR status afterwards in conducting its own economic and trade affairs in the name of 'Hong Kong, China'. Before that, GATT rules applied to Hong Kong as a dependent territory of Britain, and Hong Kong's interests were represented in the GATT from within the British delegation.

8. During the drafting process of the Basic Law, there was initial inclination on the part of the Chinese government to allow non-Chinese nationals who were HKPRs to be elected to the future SAR legislature in recognition of Hong Kong's cosmopolitan reality where many business and professional people held foreign nationality or had acquired the right of abode in a foreign country. This would be rather exceptional compared to either national or state/local legislatures in other sovereign countries. Later on, in order not to over-compromise on the principle of sovereignty, a cap was set in the final version of the Basic Law such that members with foreign nationality or right of abode overseas could not exceed 20% of the total membership of the LegCo.

9. T.H. Marshall (1992) *Citizenship and Social Class*, London: Pluto Press (monograph in 1950 based on his 1949 Lecture in Cambridge, reprinted in 1992). The civil aspect refers to the 'rights necessary for individual freedom' (freedom of speech, freedom of thoughts and faith, rule of law and rights to justice, property ownership, and so on). The political aspect refers to the 'right to participate in the exercise of political power, as member of a body invested with political authority or as an elector of the members of such a body' (the right to political representation, the right to vote and seeking electoral office, participation in political discourse, and so on). The social aspect refers to 'the whole range from the right to a modicum of economic welfare and security to the right to share to the full in the social heritage and to live the life of a civilised being according to the standards prevailing in the society' (the rights to welfare, healthcare, education, social benefits, cultural heritage, and so on).

10. Under Article 24 of the Basic Law, HKPRs shall include Chinese citizens born in Hong Kong; Chinese citizens who have ordinarily resided in Hong Kong for a continuous period of not less than seven years; and persons not of Chinese nationality who have entered Hong Kong with valid travel documents, have ordinarily resided in Hong Kong for a continuous period of not less than seven years, and have taken Hong Kong as their place of permanent residence (all whether before or after the establishment of the Hong Kong SAR).

11. See, for example, C.K. Lau (1997) *Hong Kong's Colonial Legacy*, Hong Kong: Chinese University Press, Ch. 1.

12. The implication was that up to 250,000 Hongkongers would be eligible for a full British passport. See British Government (n.d.) *British Nationality (Hong Kong) Act 1990*, www.opsi.gov.uk/ACTS/acts1990/ukpga_19900034_en_1.

13. NPC (1997) *Resolution of the Eighth National People's Congress at its Fifth Session on the Working Report of the Preparatory Committee for the Hong Kong Special Administrative Region of the National People's Congress*, adopted on 14 March, Beijing.

14. N.L. Sum (1995) 'More Than A War of Words: Identity, Politics and The Struggle for Dominance During the Recent Political Reform Period in Hong Kong', *Economy and Society*, Vol. 24, No. 1, pp. 67–100 (quote at p. 67).

15. E. Chan (2002) 'Beyond Pedagogy: Language and identity in post-colonial Hong Kong', *British Journal of Sociology of Education*, Vol. 23, No. 2, pp. 271–285.

16. Only those schools where teachers had been assessed as competent to teach in English and students as competent in learning in English were approved as English-medium schools. This meant that such schools gained in status and popularity given the great demand from parents for English-medium education for their children. The medium-of-instruction policy was fine-tuned in 2010 under the Donald Tsang Administration to provide more flexibility so that students can choose to learn through English upon meeting certain language criteria while schools are given more autonomy to offer English-medium classes. The new policy was in response to schools and parents who were concerned about the students' proficiency in English.

17. E. Chan (2000) 'Defining Fellow Compatriots as "Others" — National Identity in Hong Kong', *Government and Opposition*, Vol. 35, No. 4, pp. 499–519.

18. A. Fung (2001) 'What Makes the Local? A Brief Consideration of the Rejuvenation of Hong Kong Identity', *Cultural Studies*, Vol. 15, Nos. 3/4, pp. 591–601; A. Abbas (1997) *Hong Kong: Culture and the Politics of Disappearance*, Minneapolis, MN: University of Minnesota Press.

19. For example, legal professionals were prominent in the Article 45 Concern Group that championed the cause of universal suffrage and had, within less than a year, become the most popular political group in the city, outshining the Democratic Party. Lawyers, engineers, and academics were key members of the campaign to protect the harbour that forced the government to rethink its reclamation policy. Architects, artists, cultural critics, and academics were also involved in a campaign challenging the government's original plan to develop the WKCD project.

20. The core values proclaimed were: liberty, democracy, human rights, rule of law, fairness, social justice, peace and compassion, integrity and transparency, plurality, respect for individuals, and upholding professionalism. See Hong Kong Core Values campaign (n.d.) *Declaration*, https://web.archive.org/web/20040610052214/http://www.hkcorevalues.net:80/b5_declar.htm.

21. For example, the 2003 campaign against the reclamation of Victoria Harbour (seen as Hong Kong's natural heritage) and the rows in December 2006 over the demolition of the Star Ferry clock tower as well as in July 2007 over the removal of Queen's Pier in Central District.

22. D.Y.K. Tsang (2007c), op. cit., paras. 5, 10–17.

23. Speaking to the media in April 2016, Leung commented that his administration had solved the problem of inadequate obstetric services by abolishing the quota for Mainland mothers giving birth in Hong Kong hospitals and had improved the housing situation by introducing additional special stamp duties which had cut the number of Mainland buyers of Hong Kong properties. He said these showed the government put local interests first. See Information Services Department (2016b) 'HK interests top Gov't priority', press release, 5 April, www.news.gov.hk/en/categories/admin/html/2016/04/20160405_101940.shtml.

24. J.T. Hu (胡錦濤) (2007) 'Toast at Welcoming Dinner Hosted by the Government of the Hong Kong Special Administrative Region' [in Chinese, 〈胡錦濤在香港特別行政區政府歡迎晚宴上的講話〉], 30 June, Beijing: State Council of the People's Republic of China. His exact words, according to the official English translation, were: 'We should foster a strong sense of national identity among the young people in Hong Kong and promote exchanges between them and the young people of the Mainland so that they will carry forward the Hong Kong people's great tradition of "loving the motherland and loving Hong Kong".'

25. Curriculum Development Council (2012) *Moral and National Education Curriculum Guide (Primary 1 to Secondary 6)*, April, Hong Kong: Education Bureau. Following consultations, instead of only setting 'harmony, unity and the sentiment of caring for home and nation' as teaching objectives, the revised version embraced 'universal values' (such as democracy, rule of law, and human rights) so that students would learn to understand national development in both positive and negative aspects, as well as the difficulties and challenges facing China.

26. Scholarism leaders, together with leaders of the Federation of Students, turned the 'Occupy Central' rally in September 2014 into a protest movement surrounding the Tamar government offices and sabotaging government functions. They became the backbone of the rising separatist 'self-determination' radical extreme of the pan-democratic camp, imposing their political terms on the mainstream pan-democratic parties.

27. The SAR government had also introduced new arrangements in 2016 whereby any candidate standing for the LegCo election (later extended to DC elections and rural representative elections under the Heung Yee Kuk) could be disqualified by the Returning Officer if found to support independence and self-determination. Such 'disqualification' scrutiny has since been labelled by the pan-democrats and separatists as political repression.

28. The yellow colour, symbolising people's power, was used by pro-democrats in banners and ribbons during rallies and protests. Pro-establishment groups adopted the blue colour when they supported the Police by displaying blue ribbons, the corporate colour of the Hong Kong Police Force.

29. The Democratic Party does not officially support Hong Kong independence but seeks a maximum degree of self-determination under present PRC sovereignty, whereas the Civic Party considers its goal of 'internal self-determination' (內部自決) by Hong Kong people under the Basic Law not the same as Hong Kong independence though the Basic Law has to be amended to remove some unreasonable provisions. See Democratic Party (2017) *Standing on the Shoulder of Historical Giant: The Democratic Party's Review and Outlook on Hong Kong-Mainland China Relations* [in Chinese, 《站在歷史巨人的肩上 —— 民主黨對港中關係的回顧及展望》], 7 June, https://drive.google.com/file/d/0B1m5ziISS9RzN3JUOEZsQ09ObzQ/view; Civic Party (2016) *Practising Reform and Innovation, Reversing the Future: Ten Major Policy Programmes for 2016 Legislative Council Election* [in Chinese, 《實踐革新, 逆轉未來：2016 立法會選舉十大重點政策綱領》], https://2016.civicparty.hk//Uploads/document/doc/CP-Platform-chi.pdf. Another traditional but much smaller pan-democratic party, the Association for

Democracy and People's Livelihood, also championed internal self-determination but not Hong Kong independence. See Association for Democracy and People's Livelihood (2016) *Justice, Autonomy and Self-Rule: 30th Anniversary Declaration* [in Chinese, 《公義、自主、自治：民協三十週年宣言》], www.facebook.com/notes/民協-adpl/公義自主自治-民協三十週年宣言/10153686108020983/.

30. Demosistō (香港眾志) (2016) *Democratic Self-Determination Starts Here: Roadmap of Our Self-Determination Movement* [in Chinese, 《民主自決 此際起航 —— 我們的自決運動路線圖》], www.demosisto.hk/article/details/45.

31. The Hong Kong National Party was founded in 2016 by a few students who took part in the Occupy Central and Umbrella Movement protests. It claimed to have 30–50 members. Its leader Chan Ho-tin was disqualified by the Electoral Affairs Commission from taking part in the 2016 LegCo election for refusing to sign a 'confirmation form' to declare the understanding of Hong Kong being an inalienable part of China as stipulated in the Basic Law. In July 2018, the Hong Kong Police served the party convenor a notice under the Societies Ordinance to ban the party on national security grounds. The CE-in-Council upheld the Police's decision.

32. *Wen Wei Po* (《文匯報》) (2016) 'Xi Jinping: Hong Kong Independence not allowed' [in Chinese, 〈習近平：不容「港獨」〉], 22 November. The report was based on CE Leung Chun-ying's remarks after his meeting with President Xi Jinping during the Asia Pacific Economic Cooperation (APEC) Leaders' Summit in Peru. He relayed Xi's message that under the 'One Country, Two Systems' framework there was absolutely no room for 'Hong Kong independence', and that on cardinal issues of right and wrong involving the integrity of national sovereignty and territorial integrity, there was no room for any compromise (在一些大是大非的問題上，涉及到國家主權完整、領土完整，這些問題上是沒有任何妥協空間的).

33. C. Lam (2018), op. cit., para. 8.

34. J.C.W. Tsang (曾俊華) (2016) 'Localism not the same as Hong Kong Independence' [in Chinese, 〈本土不等於港獨〉], *Hong Kong Economic Journal* (《信報》), 29 July, www2.hkej.com/instantnews/current/article/1354927/曾俊華%3A本土不等於港獨.

35. A more moderate voice within the traditional pro-Beijing patriotic camp is that of Tsang Yuk-sing, DAB founding chairman and former President of the LegCo, who said in 2016 that localism was not the same as separatism and should not be cracked down upon (本土不同分離 盼勿打擊), according to a report in *Ming Pao* (《明報》) (2016) 'Tsang Yuk-sing: localism was not the same as separatism and should not be cracked down upon' [in Chinese, 〈曾鈺成：本土不同分離 盼勿打擊〉], 24 February, p. A03.

36. Other newly emerging 'patriotic' forces included: Voice of Loving Hong Kong (愛港之聲), All for Protecting Hong Kong (同心護港), Justice Alliance Party (正義聯盟黨), and Politihk Social Strategic (香港政研會).

37. The provision under the Education Ordinance that prohibited political discussion in Hong Kong schools ('political, subversive or tendentious activities, or propaganda in schools') was only abolished in 1990 in order to facilitate the promotion of civil education. Prior to the 1980s, the colonial administration had sought to delocalise the school curriculum by suppressing people's primary concerns and their local political collective identities. See W.W. Law (2004) 'Globalization and Citizenship Education in Hong Kong and Taiwan', *Comparative Education Review*, Vol. 48, No. 3, pp. 253–273.

38. See B.C.H. Fong (ed) (2017a) *Hong Kong Innovation Theory II: Thinking about Hong Kong's Future from the World* [in Chinese, 《香港革新論II：從世界思考香港前途》], Hong Kong: Chapter One Publishing (出一點文創), pp. 138–140; B.C.H. Fong (2017c), op. cit.

39. Things became worse during the 2019 extradition bill controversy where pan-democratic politicians went to the US and European countries to lobby their governments and legislators to voice objections to the bill, inducing Beijing to escalate the matter from SAR level to national level, rejecting foreign concerns about the legislation as undue interference with China's domestic affairs. In the ensuing political unrest, pan-democratic politicians and radical activists zealously campaigned for the passage of the Hong Kong Human Rights and Democracy Act by the US Congress, which will direct various departments to assess whether political developments in Hong Kong justify changing Hong Kong's unique treatment under US law. That Act was finally passed by the US Congress and signed into law by former President Donald Trump on 27 November 2019. As a response to the NPCSC's passage of a national security law for Hong Kong, effective from 1 July 2020, former President Trump stripped Hong Kong of its special status.

40. This in itself is a by-product of the current Chinese leadership under President Xi Jinping to pursue a fiercely nationalist line to further national interest and fulfil the 'China Dream' for the restoration of a strong China, not succumbing to pressures from the West.

41. B. Moffitt (2016) *The Global Rise of Populism: Performance, Political Style, and Representation*, Stanford, CA: Stanford University Press.

42. M. Lilla (2016) *The Shipwrecked Mind: On Political Reaction*, New York: New York Review of Books, p. xiv.

43. P. Mishra (2017) *Age of Anger: A History of the Present*, London: Penguin.

44. F. Fukuyama (2018a) 'Against Identity Politics: The New Tribalism and the Crisis of Democracy', *Foreign Affairs*, Vol. 97, No. 5, September/October, pp. 90–114.

45. J. Nilsson-Wright (2018) 'Nostalgia and Romanticism: Populism and the Rise of Identity Politics', *Global Asia*, Vol. 13, No. 3, September, pp. 48–63.

46. A.S.M. Ku (2018) 'Identity as politics: Contesting the local, the national and the global', in T.L. Lui et al. (eds), op. cit., pp. 451–461.

47. Local cultural studies scholar Law Wing-sang has further argued, from a post-colonial critical perspective, for an understanding of the continuous process of how the Chinese identity in Hong Kong has been constantly disembedded and reintegrated within the sites and channels where colonial power effectuated, creating mosaics of the local culture where such identity has been received, perceived, and experienced. See W.S. Law (2009), op. cit.

48. A. Fung (2001), op. cit. See also G. Matthew et al. (2008) *Hong Kong, China: Learning to Belong to a Nation*, London: Routledge.

49. C. Taylor (1992) *Multiculturalism and the 'Politics of Recognition'*, Princeton NJ: Princeton University Press.

50. S.H. Ng (2007) 'Biculturalism in Multicultural Hong Kong', *Journal of Psychology in Chinese Societies*, Vol. 8, p. 121–140. Ng alludes to the existence of the Chinese self and Western self in various combinations within the Hong Kong bicultural person — viz. Biculturals (where both selves are strong), Sino-centrics (strong Chinese self and weak Western self), Western-centrics (strong Western self and weak Chinese self), and Marginals (both selves are weak).

51. N. Ma (2015) 'The Rise of "Anti-China" sentiments in Hong Kong and the 2012 Legislative Council Elections', *The China Review*, Vol. 15, No. 1, pp. 39–66.

52. For example, C.P. Yew and K.W. Kwong (2014) 'Hong Kong identity on the rise', *Asian Survey*, Vol. 54, No. 6, pp. 1088–1112; B.C.H. Fong (2017c), op. cit.

53. C.K. Cha (2017) 'Discursive opportunity structures in post-handover Hong Kong localism: The China factor and beyond', *Chinese Journal of Communication*, Vol. 10, No. 4, pp. 413–432 (quote at p. 414).

54. In a way, Taiwan has undergone a similar dilemma, with people feeling the same anxiety and confusion. As Shih Shu-mei observed of the emergence of a complex Taiwanese psyche in the early 2000s, at a time when Taiwanese politics was heatedly defined by the pro-reunification versus pro-independence and 'de-Sinoisation' nexus, a paradox of ambiguity (of the economic and cultural) and clarity (of the political and national) prevailed as the political, economic, and cultural powers of Mainland China ascended. See S.M. Shih (2003) 'Globalization and the (in)significance of Taiwan', *Postcolonial Studies*, Vol. 6, No. 2, pp. 143–153.

55. According to a Chinese University study in August 2019, 57.7% of the participants in the anti-government protests were age 29 or younger, while more than 26% were between 20 and 24 years old — the biggest segment of the protest camp. A total of 73.8% of the protesters said they had received at least some tertiary education. See L.K. Sum (2019) 'Young, educated and middle class: First field study of Hong Kong protesters reveals demographic trends', *South China Morning Post*, 12 August.

56. C.Y.K. So (蘇鑰機) (2019) 'The feelings of people with diverse political inclinations and the youngsters as viewed from public opinion survey figures' [in Chinese, 〈從民調數字 看不同政見和年輕人的心聲〉], *Ming Pao* (《明報》), 27 September. The surveys were conducted by the School of Journalism and Communication of the Chinese University of Hong Kong for *Ming Pao*.

57. A recent academic critique also blames the crisis on the deteriorating quality of life and well-being in Hong Kong, especially among young generations, which contributes to such fear. See D.T.L. Shek (2020) 'Protests in Hong Kong (2019–2020): A Perspective Based on Quality of Life and Well-Being', *Applied Research Quality Life*, Vol. 15, pp. 619–635.

58. R. Wodak (2015), op. cit.

59. A.B.L. Cheung (2008b) 'Preface: Hong Kong's Role in Transforming China', in M. Chan (ed) *China's Hong Kong Transformed: Retrospect and Prospects Beyond the First Decade*, Hong Kong: City University of Hong Kong Press, pp. xi–xvii (discussion at p. xv).

Chapter 14

1. S.P. Huntington (1991) *The Third Wave: Democratization in the Late Twentieth Century*, Norman and London: University of Oklahoma Press.

2. M. Santora (2020), op. cit.

3. K. Manson (2020) 'Washington looks to Five Eyes to build anti-China coalition', *Financial Times*, 3 June. The 'Five Eyes' intelligence alliance, dating from the 1940s, comprises the US, Britain, Canada, Australia, and New Zealand. Recently, these countries have been working even closer to counter the rise of China. See also N. Barkin (2018) 'Five Eyes intelligence alliance builds coalition to counter China', *Reuters World News*, 12 October, www.reuters.com/article/us-china-fiveeyes-idUSKCN1MM0GH.

4. The 'Bamboo Curtain' (a parlance used to parallel the 'Iron Curtain' between the Soviet Bloc and North Atlantic Treaty Organisation in Europe) separated the communist states (namely, China, North Korea, and Vietnam) from the non-communist and largely pro-Western states of East and Southeast Asia during the Cold War.

5. The US Congress passed the Hong Kong Policy Act in 1992 to allow the US to continue to treat Hong Kong separately from China for matters concerning trade and economics after 1997. Under this Act, the US would fulfil its obligations to Hong Kong under international agreements regardless of whether the PRC is a participant of the particular agreement until the obligations are modified or terminated. Also, Hong Kong would continue to have access to 'sensitive technologies' so long as measures are in place to protect such technologies from improper use (implying transfer to the Mainland). The US President could change the way the relevant provisions are applied if they believe Hong Kong to be less autonomous as an SAR. See Office of the Law Revision Counsel (n.d.) *United States-Hong Kong Policy* (22 USC Ch. 66), Washington, D.C.: House of Representatives, http://uscode.house.gov/view. xhtml?path=/prelim@title22/chapter66&edition=prelim. Under the Trump Administration, the US stepped up strategic efforts (including a trade war) to contain China, moving from the previous Asia Re-balancing Strategy of the Obama Administration to the current Indo-Pacific Policy. In November 2019, a new Hong Kong Human Rights and Democracy Act was passed to enable sanctions to be imposed should the city's freedom, democracy, and autonomy come under assault. Following the implementation of the National Security Law from July 2020, the Trump Administration stripped Hong Kong of its special treatment under the Hong Kong Policy Act.

6. D. Marsh and J.C. Sharman (2009) 'Policy diffusion and policy transfer', *Policy Studies*, Vol. 30, No. 3, pp. 269–288; K. Holzinger and C. Knill (2005) 'Causes and conditions of cross-national policy convergence', *Journal of European Public Policy*, Vol. 12, No. 5, pp. 775–796; O. James and M. Lodge (2003) 'The Limitations of "Policy Transfer" and "Lesson Drawing" for Public Policy Research', *Political Studies Review*, Vol. 1, No. 2, pp. 179–193.

7. G.T. Allison (1980) *Public and private management: are they fundamentally alike in all unimportant respects?* Discussion Paper series No. 84, John F. Kennedy School of Government, Cambridge, MA: Harvard University.

8. The argument is that a 'horse' is a generic quality ('shape'), whereas a 'white horse' is a specific quality (in colour) which is unique and can be distinguished from the generic description as well as horses of other qualities/colours. Gongsun Long (325–250 BC) was a member of the School of Names (名家) of ancient Chinese philosophy during the Warring States Period. See discussion of Gongsun Long's philosophy (including his White Horse Discourse [白馬論]) in M. Bo (2019) *Semantic-Truth Approaches in Chinese Philosophy: A Unifying Pluralist Account*, Lantham and London: Lexington Books, Ch. 3.

9. C. Hood (2010) 'Can We? Administrative Limits Revisited', *Public Administration Review*, Vol. 70, No. 4, pp. 527–534. See also K. Yesilkagit (2010) 'The Limits of Administration: A Response to Christopher Hood', *Public Administration Review*, Vol. 70, No. 4, pp. 535–537; C. Hood (1976) *The Limits of Administration*, London: John Wiley & Sons.

10. This phrase has been mostly attributed to Tip O'Neill, a former Speaker of the US House of Representatives (1977–1987).

11. A.B.L. Cheung (2010a) 'Checks and Balance in China's Administrative Traditions: A Preliminary Assessment', in M. Painter and B.G. Peters (eds) *Tradition and Public Administration*, Hampshire: Palgrave Macmillan, pp. 31–43.

12. F. Fukuyama (1992) *The End of History and the Last Man*, London: Hamish Hamilton. For a critical review of Fukuyama's work, see L. Menand (2018) 'Francis Fukuyama Postpones the End of History', *The New Yorker*, 27 August, www.newyorker.com/magazine/2018/09/03/ francis-fukuyama-postpones-the-end-of-history.

13. The term 'Washington Consensus' was initially coined by John Williamson to describe a set of specific economic policy prescriptions constituting the 'standard' reform package promoted for crisis-wracked developing countries by Washington, D.C.-based institutions such as the IMF, World Bank, and the US Treasury Department. The term has since been used as a synonym for market fundamentalism and has become associated with neo-liberal policies in general. See J. Williamson (1989) 'What Washington Means by Policy Reform', in J. Williamson (ed) *Latin American Readjustment: How Much Has Happened*, Washington, D.C.: Institute for International Economics, pp. 7–20.

14. The World Bank labelled the East Asian economies of South Korea, Singapore, Taiwan, and Hong Kong a 'miracle' in 1993, which was quickly challenged the next year by Paul Krugman as 'The Myth of Asia's Miracle'. After the Asian financial crisis, some critics argued that there is evidence that these 'developmental state' strategies are not compatible with financial liberalisation and full integration into the open global economy. See World Bank (1993), op. cit.; P. Krugman (1994) 'The Myth of Asia's Miracle', *Foreign Affairs*, November/December; P.P. Masina (ed) (2002) *Rethinking Development in East Asia: From Illusory Miracle to Economic Crisis*, Nordic Institute of Asian Studies, Richmond, Surrey: Curzon Press.

15. K. Mahbubani (2008) *The New Asian Hemisphere: The Irresistible Shift of Global Power to the East*, New York: Public Affairs.

16. A.B.L. Cheung (2000a) 'Globalization versus Asian Values: Alternative paradigms in understanding governance and administration', *Asian Journal of Political Science*, Vol. 8, No. 2, pp. 1–15.

17. S.P. Huntington (1993) 'The Clash of Civilizations?' *Foreign Affairs*, Summer; S.P. Huntington (1996) *The Clash Of Civilizations and The Remaking Of World Order*, New York: Simon & Schuster.

18. J. Gray (1999) *False Dawn: The Delusions of Global Capitalism*, London: Granta Books.

19. J. Spence (1980) *To Change China: Western Advisers in China*, New York: Penguin Books.

20. For academic observations, see, for example, T. Christensen et al. (2008) 'Administrative Reform in China's Central Government: How Much "Learning from the West"?' *International Review of Administrative Sciences*, Vol. 74, No. 3, pp. 351–371. The authors of this study argue for a 'multi-causal' model to understanding administrative reform in China, where both internal (context) and external (imitation) factors are involved in the reform process, reflecting the flow of reform ideas and reinforcing the impact of technical and institutional pressures in strategies and policy choices.

21. This notion was quoted from Zhang Zhidong's (張之洞, 1837–1909) essay *Exhortation to Study* [in Chinese,《勸學篇》] in 1898. Zhang, a Grand Counsellor of the Qing court who rose to be Minister of Military Affairs in 1906, spoke for many Chinese scholar-officials at the time who believed that the Confucian style of learning should still be maintained as the basis of society when using Western learning for practical application in developing China's infrastructure, military and economy.

22. S.M. Lipset (1993) 'Pacific Divide: American Exceptionalism-Japanese Uniqueness', *International Journal of Public Opinion Research*, Vol. 5, No. 2, pp. 121–166 (quote at p. 160).

23. As Greg Sheridan put it: 'Asian values have an obviously political dimension but they are not just about politics. They have an obviously anti-Western tinge in the sense that they are often defined in contrast with the West, but that is not really what drives them either. They are much more to do with an internal Asian debate about the nature of the good life, about regional community, about the dynamics of modernization, about whether modernization means Westernization, about the civic dimensions of life, about the reconciliation of indigenous traditions with new

cosmopolitan dynamics, about the challenges of globalization.' See G. Sheridan (1999) *Asian Values, Western Dreams: Understanding the new Asia*, Sydney: Allen & Unwin, pp. 2–3. See also M.D. Barr (2004) *Cultural Politics and Asian Values: The Tepid War*, London: Routledge; J. Cauquelin et al. (eds) (2014) *Asian Values: Encounter with Diversity*, London: Routledge.

24. K. Mahbubani (2008), op. cit., p. 1.

25. G. Sheridan (1999), op. cit. p. 6.

26. G. Rachman (2017) *Easternization: Asia's Rise and America's Decline From Obama to Trump and Beyond*, New York: Other Press.

27. Inspired by Max Weber's famous explanation of the rise of Western capitalism with reference to Protestant ethics at the turn of the nineteenth century, some scholars had quite early on attempted to offer a cultural explanation of East Asian capitalism with reference to Confucian ethics. See, for example, S.G. Redding (1990) *The Spirit of Chinese Capitalism*, Berlin: de Gruyter.

28. See a preliminary discussion in A.B.L. Cheung (2013) 'Can There Be An Asian Model of Public Administration?' *Public Administration and Development*, Vol. 33, September, pp. 249–261.

29. P. Khanna (2019b) 'How Asia is Shaping the World's Future', *Asia Society*, 28 January, https://asiasociety.org/blog/asia/how-asia-shaping-worlds-future, reprinted from P. Khanna (2019a) *The Future Is Asian*, New York: Simon & Schuster.

30. D. Smith (2007) *The Dragon and the Elephant: China, India and the New World Order*, London: Profile Books.

31. See A.B.L. Cheung (2005c), op. cit.; A.B.L. Cheung (2012b) 'Public administration in East Asia: Legacies, trajectories and lessons', *International Review of Administrative Sciences*, Vol. 78, No. 2, pp. 209–216.

32. M.J. Moon and P. Ingraham (1998) 'Shaping Administrative Reform and Governance: An Examination of the Political Nexus Triads in Three Asian Countries', *Governance*, Vol. 11, No. 1, pp. 77–100. Even within public sector reform, despite all the rhetoric about devolution, partnership, and power-sharing, the actual decentralisation and power-shedding were of only limited significance. See A.B.L. Cheung and I. Scott (2003) 'Governance and Public Sector Reforms in Asia: Paradigms, Paradoxes and Dilemmas', in A.B.L. Cheung and I. Scott (eds) *Governance and Public Sector Reform in Asia: Paradigm Shifts or Business As Usual?* London: RoutledgeCurzon, pp. 1–24.

33. A.B.L. Cheung (2012a) 'One country, two experiences: administrative reforms in China and Hong Kong', *International Review of Administrative Sciences*, Vol. 78, No. 2, pp. 261–283.

34. According to the National Development and Reform Commission (國家發展及改革委員會) (2018) 'Press conference on the promotion of private sector investment' [in Chinese, 〈發改委舉行促進民間投資持續健康發展工作情況發佈會〉], 6 September, Beijing: The State Council Information Office of the People's Republic of China, www.scio.gov.cn/xwfbh/gbwxwfbh/xwfbh/fzggw/Document/1637294/1637294.htm.

35. Based on the World Bank's 2019 GDP data (available in mid-2020), China's GDP was 16.3% of the world's GDP (and 16.78% if inclusive of Hong Kong and Macao). That of the US was about 24.46%. See World Bank (n.d.) *GDP per Capita (current US$)*, various economies, https://data.worldbank.org/indicator/NY.GDP.MKTP.CD.

36. A.B.L. Cheung (2012a), op. cit. See also Z. Lan (2000) 'Understanding China's Administrative Reform', *Public Administration Quarterly*, Vol. 24, No. 1, pp. 437–468; Q. Wang (2010) 'Administrative Reform in China: Past, Present, and Future', *Southeast Review of Asian Studies*,

Vol. 32, No. 1, pp. 100–119; K. Yu (ed) (2010) *The Reform of Governance*, Leiden: Brill [a translated collection of articles in Chinese providing a glimpse of how scholars in China have been assessing their country's recent governmental history].

37. Y. Jing (2017) 'Creative Incrementalism: Governance Reforms in China Since 1978', *Chinese Political Science Review*, Vol. 2, No. 1, pp. 56–68.

38. Especially after Deng Xiaoping's famous southern inspection tour of 1992, spurring an unanticipated rapid process of marketisation and privatisation. The consolidation of a 'socialist market economy' was finally declared at the 14th CCP National Congress in November 1993. See K. Ngok and G. Zhu (2007) 'Marketization, Globalization and Administrative Reform in China: A Zigzag Road to a Promising Future', *International Review of Administrative Sciences*, Vol. 73, No. 2, pp. 217–233; A.B.L. Cheung (2012a), op. cit.

39. The collapse of the Soviet Union and its East European communist satellite states soon after the Tiananmen incident seems to have convinced the CCP leadership that had the pro-democracy movement not been suppressed, China might have faced a similar fate. See *Global Times* (2019) 'June 4 immunized China against turmoil', editorial, English edition, 3 June.

40. Some critics allege that state-owned enterprises have been allowed to unduly dominate the economy at the expense of private enterprises (國進民退, *guojin mintui*, meaning 'the state enterprises advance, the private sectors retreat'), with the state encouraging state-owned enterprises to consolidate, favouring them in regulation, and awarding them contracts and subsidies, and as a result crowding out other competitors, both domestic and foreign. See *The Economist* (2012) 'China's state capitalism: Not just tilting at windmills', 6 October.

41. The concept of the separation of party and state, written into the Political Report at the CCP's 13th National Congress in 1987, urged the party to only take part in major decisions and retreat from daily government operations. After Tiananmen, party committees were reinstated in government institutions, but it was still rare for officials to openly advocate the fusion of party and state apparatus. The importance of party committees in government organisations has since been rebounding, with the party secretary being in most cases the 'number 1 in-charge' (第一把手). The day after the 12th NPC closed on 20 March 2017, party authorities announced a further series of administrative restructuring geared towards subsuming State Council departments and functions under party organs. New central-level leading and working groups, merging party and state, have been set up to oversee ministries and other government organs. For a critical commentary, see W.W.L. Lam (2018) 'At China's "Two Sessions", Xi Jinping Restructures Party-state to Further Consolidate Power', *China Brief* (The Jamestown Foundation), Vol. 18, No. 5, 26 March.

42. In the US, the Trump Administration called China a 'revisionist power' with the intent to shape a world antithetical to US values and interests and to displace the US in the Indo-Pacific region. See The White House (2017) *National Security Strategy of the United States of America*, December, Washington, D.C. In a notable speech in October 2018, then US Vice-President Mike Pence said China had chosen 'economic aggression' when engaging with the world and 'debt diplomacy' to spread its influence, and that there was 'no doubt' that China was meddling in America's democracy. See M. Pence (2018) *Remarks on the Administration's Policy Towards China*, 4 October, Washington, D.C: Hudson Institute. During the COVID-19 pandemic, the US has criticised the World Health Organisation as being too trusting of and influenced by China. See J.C. Hernández (2020) 'Trump Slammed the W.H.O. Over Coronavirus. He's Not Alone', *The New York Times*, 8 April. Countering the US government's conspiracy theory, Zhao Suisheng has argued that China is a revisionist stakeholder, dissatisfied not with the fundamental rules of the post-War international order led by the US but rather its status in the hierarchy of that order. See S. Zhao (2018) 'A Revisionist Stakeholder: China and the Post-World War II World Order', *Journal of Contemporary China*, Vol. 27, No. 113, pp. 643–658.

43. J. Sachs (2019a) 'China is not the source of our economic problems — corporate greed is', *CNN*, 27 May, https://edition.cnn.com/2019/05/26/opinions/china-is-not-the-enemy-sachs/index.html.

44. J. Nye (1990) *Bound to Lead: The Changing Nature of American Power*, London: Basic Books.

45. C. Walker and J. Ludwig (2017) 'The Meaning of Sharp Power: How Authoritarian States Project Influence', *Foreign Affairs*, 16 November.

46. A. Graham (2015) 'The Thucydides Trap: Are the U.S. and China Headed for War?' *The Atlantic*, 24 September.

47. J.C. Ramo (2009) *The Beijing Consensus*, London: The Foreign Policy Centre.

48. D.A. Bell (2015) *The China Model: Political Meritocracy and the Limits of Democracy*, Princeton, NJ: Princeton University Press.

49. A. Nathan (2009) 'China since Tiananmen: Authoritarian Impermanence', *Journal of Democracy*, Vol. 20, No. 3, pp. 37–40. Nathan observed that 'the Chinese system as an authoritarianism [is] of a still poorly understood new type, one that mixes statism with entrepreneurship, political monopoly with individual liberty, personalist power with legal procedures, repression with responsiveness, policy uniformity with decentralized flexibility, and message control with a media circus' (p. 38).

50. See Y.Y. Ang (2018) 'The Real China Model: It's Not What You Think It Is', *Foreign Affairs*, 29 June. Ang suggests that there are a variety of images and interpretations of the 'China model' and that it is inaccurate and misleading to equate it with conventional authoritarianism. The 'real' China model, in her view, has been 'directed improvisation' with an adaptive governing system ever since Deng's time.

51. Such reconnections to China's ancient past are depicted as 'the China Order' by Wang Fei-ling who explains how the Chinese ideation and tradition of political governance and world order during the past imperial dynasties have shaped the CCP central state and determined its prospects. See F.L. Wang (2017), op. cit.

52. For example, S.G. Jiang (强世功), (2017b) 'Thought of Xi Jinping: The Re-Sinicization of Marxism' [in Chinese, 〈習近平思想：馬克斯主義的再次中國化〉], *Ming Pao* (《明報》), 30 October.

53. See E. Berglof (2018) 'Surprising findings in learning from China's incredible growth', commentary, *Channel News Asia*, 31 December.

54. S. Bell and A. Hindmoor (2009), op. cit., p. 1.

55. See, for example, *People's Daily* (《人民日報》) (2018) 'Comprehensively enhance the national capacity of governance and standard of governance' [in Chinese, 〈全面提高國家治理能力和治理水平〉], 2 March, http://paper.people.com.cn/rmrb/html/2018-03/02/nw.D110000renmrb_20180302_7-04.htm. This commentary called for deepening the structural reforms of party and state institutions, perfecting organisational systems and functions, scientific specifications, and efficiency and effectiveness.

56. R.I. Rotberg (2014) 'Good Governance Means Performance and Results', *Governance*, Vol. 27, No. 3, pp. 511–518. See also F. Fukuyama (2013a), op. cit.

57. The World Bank defines governance as 'the traditions and institutions by which authority in a country is exercised [which] includes the process by which governments are selected, monitored and replaced; the capacity of the government to effectively formulate and implement sound policies; and the respect of citizens and the state for the institutions that govern economic and social interactions among them'. See World Bank (2019) *Worldwide Governance Indicators 2018*, https://info.worldbank.org/governance/wgi/Home/Reports.

58. Asian Development Bank (1999) *Governance in Asia: From Crisis to Opportunity*, Manila: Asian Development Bank.

59. International Monetary Fund (IMF) (2005) *The IMF's Approach to Promoting Good Governance and Combating Corruption — A Guide*, 20 June.

60. UN Economic and Social Commission for Asia and the Pacific (UNESCAP) (2006) *What is Good Governance?* 24 December, Bangkok: UNESCAP.

61. M.S. Grindle (2002) 'Good Enough Governance: Poverty Reduction and Reform in Developing Countries', *Governance*, Vol. 17, No. 4, pp. 525–548.

62. E. Poluha and M. Rosendahl (2002) *Contesting 'Good' Governance: Crosscultural Perspectives on Representation, Accountability and Public Space*, London: Routledge.

63. D. Kaufmann and A. Kraay (2002) 'Growth Without Governance', *Economia*, Fall, https://sites.hks.harvard.edu/fs/pnorris/Acrobat/stm103%20articles/Kaufman%20and%20Kraay%20Nov2002.pdf; D. Kaufmann and A. Kraay (2003) 'Governance and Growth: Causality which way? Evidence for the World, in brief', February, http://siteresources.worldbank.org/INTWBIGOVANTCOR/Resources/growthgov_synth.pdf.

64. D. Kaufmann and A. Kraay (2002), op. cit.

65. F. Fukuyama (2013b) 'What is governance? Fukuyama replies', *The Governance Blog*, 30 April, https://governancejournal.wordpress.com/2013/04/30/1492/.

66. M. Andrews (2010) 'Good Government Means Different Things in Different Countries', *Governance*, Vol. 23, No. 1, pp. 7–35.

67. For example, U. Brand and N. Sekler (2009) 'Postneoliberalism: Catch-all word or valuable analytical and political concept? Aims of a beginning debate', *Development Dialogue*, January, pp. 5–15.

68. See *The Economist* (2019) 'Millennial socialism', 16 February. *The Economist* has noted that socialism is now back in fashion among the younger generations.

69. F. Fukuyama (2005) *State-Building: Governance and World Order in the Twenty-First Century*, London: Profile Books. Fukuyama examined 'stateness' from multiple dimensions — the functions, capabilities, and grounds for legitimacy of governments.

70. S.P. Huntington (1991), op. cit.

71. A. Tooze (2018) *Crashed: How a Decade of Financial Crises Changed the World*, New York: Viking.

72. See *The Economist* (2020) 'The state in the time of covid-19', 26 March.

73. OECD (2020) *OECD Economic Outlook*, Preliminary version, June, Paris: OECD, Ch. 1. The World Bank's baseline forecast envisioned a 5.2% contraction in global GDP in 2020 — the deepest global recession in eight decades, despite unprecedented policy support. See World Bank (2020b) *Global Economic Prospects*, June, https://documents1.worldbank.org/curated/en/502991591631723294/pdf/Global-Economic-Prospects-June-2020.pdf, p. xv.

74. For example, F. Fukuyama (2018a), op. cit.; F. Fukuyama (2018b) *Identity: The Demand for Dignity and the Politics of Resentment*, New York: Farrar, Straus and Giroux; P. Stephens (2018) 'Populism is the true legacy of the crisis', *Financial Times*, 31 August, p. 9.

75. See, for example, L. Hook (2018) 'Populism vs Paris', *Financial Times*, 3 December, p. 9.

76. *The Economist* (2017) 'Do social media threaten democracy?' 4 November, p. 11.

77. S.M. Zavattaro and L.A. Brainard (2019) 'Social media as micro-encounters: Millennial preferences as moderators of digital public value creation', *International Journal of Public Sector Management*, Vol. 32 No. 5, pp. 562–580.

78. See, for example, R. Krznaric (2019) 'Why we need to reinvent democracy for the long-term', *BBC News*, 19 March, www.bbc.com/future/story/20190318-can-we-reinvent-democracy-for-the-long-term.

79. In the words of late US Supreme Court Justice Felix Frankfurter, cited in J. Lepore (2020) 'The last time democracy almost died', *The New Yorker*, 27 January.

80. See M. Crozier et al. (1975) *The Crisis of Democracy: Report on the Governability of Democracies to the Trilateral Commission*, New York: New York University Press.

81. L. Diamond (2006) 'Promoting Democracy in Post-Conflict and Failed States: Lessons and Challenges', *Taiwan Journal of Democracy*, Vol. 2, No. 2, pp. 93–116. See also L. Diamond (2016) *In Search of Democracy*, London and New York: Routledge; L. Diamond (2019) *Ill Winds: Saving Democracy from Russian Rage, Chinese Ambition, and American Complacency*, New York: Penguin Press.

82. E. Luce (2019) 'Ill winds: Saving democracy from Russian rage, Chinese ambition, and American complacency, by Larry Diamond', book review, *Financial Times*, 24 June, www.ft.com/content/4a305392-90f6-11e9-aea1-2b1d33ac3271.

83. C. Crouch (2004) *Post-democracy*, Cambridge: Polity; F. Panizza (ed) (2005) *Populism and the Mirror of Democracy*, London: Verso; C. Muddle and C.R. Kaltwasser (2017) *Populism: A Very Short Introduction*, Oxford: Oxford University Press.

84. As commented recently in P. Stephens (2018), op. cit.: 'Many thought at the time that the collapse of communism would presage the permanent hegemony of open, liberal democracies. Instead, what really will puzzle the historians is why the ancien régime was so lazily complacent — complicit, rather — in its own demise.'

85. S.A. Ercan and J.-P. Gagnon (2014) 'The Crisis of Democracy: Which Crisis? Which Democracy?' *Democratic Theory*, Vol. 1, No. 2, pp. 1–10.

86. F. Fukuyama (2005), op. cit.

87. S. Levitsky and D. Ziblatt (2018) *How Democracies Die*, New York: Crown.

88. M. Gessen (2020) *Surviving Autocracy*, New York: Riverhead Books.

89. G. O'Donnell and P.C. Schmitter (1986) *Transitions from Authoritarian Rule: Tentative Conclusions About Uncertain Democracies*, Baltimore, MD: Johns Hopkins University Press; L. Diamond (2002) 'Thinking About Hybrid Regimes', *Journal of Democracy*, Vol. 13, No. 2, pp. 21–35.

90. For example, B.C.H. Fong (2013) 'State-Society Conflicts under Hong Kong's Hybrid Regime: Governing Coalition Building and Civil Society Challenges', *Asian Survey*, Vol. 53, No. 5, pp. 854–882; Y.H. Kwong (2018) 'Political Repression in a Sub-National Hybrid Regime: The PRC's Governing Strategies in Hong Kong, *Contemporary Politics*, Vol. 24, No. 4, pp. 361–378.

91. See such conceptualisation in A. Schedler (2006) *Electoral Authoritarianism: The Dynamics of Unfree Competition*, Boulder, CO: L. Rienner Publishers.

92. W. Case (2008) 'Hybrid politics and new competitiveness: Hong Kong's 2007 chief executive election', *East Asia*, Vol. 25, No. 4, pp. 365–388. For more on authoritarianism Singapore-style, see K.M. Nasir and B.S. Turner (2013) 'Governing as gardening: Reflections on soft authoritarianism in Singapore', *Citizenship Studies*, Vol. 17, Nos. 3–4, pp. 339–352.

93. B.C.H. Fong (2017b), op. cit.

Epilogue

1. According to the Cronyism Capitalism Index compiled by *The Economist*, Taiwan ranked among the top 10 based on crony sector wealth (7th in 2014 and 10th in 2016), ahead of China (inclusive of Hong Kong) (11th in both years). See *The Economist* (2016) 'Our crony-capitalism index: The party winds down', 7 May. The methodology of this index is, however, subject to certain limitations. One criticism is that it does not reflect the phenomenon of concealing fortunes common for cronies especially in some low-transparency economies.

2. R. Gramer (2020) 'Pompeo Emerges as Point Man in War of Words With China', *Foreign Policy*, 1 May.

3. It has been argued that 'radicalisation' can spread as people feel that justice and values are no longer respected by public authorities and those in power. The more they perceive exploitation, the greater their sense of moral force to take all necessary actions to defend their values and rights. See K. van den Bos (2018) *Why People Radicalize: How Unfairness Judgements are Used to Fuel Radical Beliefs, Extremist Behaviors, and Terrorism*, London: Oxford University Press.

4. J. Mai and W. Zheng (2019) 'China's Communist Party elite wrap up meeting with pledge to safeguard national security in Hong Kong', *South China Morning Post*, 1 November.

5. On 4 January 2020, the State Council replaced Wang Zhimin (王志民) with Luo Huining (駱惠寧) as Director of the Liaison Office in Hong Kong. In February 2020, the replacement of Zhang Xiaoming by Xia Baolong (夏寶龍) as the Director of the Hong Kong and Macao Affairs Office was announced, with Zhang retitled Executive Deputy Director. Both Luo and Xia are former provincial party chiefs (of Shanxi and Zhejiang province, respectively), and Xia is also a vice-chairman (and the then incumbent Secretary General) of the CPPCC. As part of a major organisational reshuffling to streamline coordination, Luo was concurrently made a Deputy Director of the Hong Kong and Macao Affairs Office which henceforth exercises leadership over the Liaison Office.

6. Fitch downgraded Hong Kong's credit rating from AA+ to AA on 5 September 2019 and then to AA– on 20 April 2020, while Moody's change their rating from Aa2 to Aa3 on 20 January 2020. Standard & Poor has not changed its rating from AA+, which was last set on 22 September 2017. See Trading Economics (n.d.) *Hong Kong — Credit Rating*, https://tradingeconomics.com/hong-kong/rating.

7. Francis Fukuyama is of the view that even though the pandemic originated in China and Beijing initially covered it up and allowed it to spread, China will benefit from the crisis, at least in relative terms, because 'other governments at first performed poorly and tried to cover it up, too, more visibly and with even deadlier consequences for their citizens. And at least Beijing has been able to regain control of the situation and is moving on to the next challenge, getting its economy back up to speed quickly and sustainably.' See F. Fukuyama (2020) 'The Pandemic and Political Order: It Takes a State', *Foreign Affairs*, July/August.

8. According to a local newspaper report: 'One year on, protesters are finding themselves at a crossroads, grappling with much that has changed in the pulse and purpose of their movement, and in the city itself. Their once formidable ranks have shrunk dramatically, the momentum lost.' Protesters whom the newspaper approached confessed to 'feeling lost, despondent even, and said they needed to see how the new national security law would unfold before planning their next steps'. See J. Lam (2020) 'Hong Kong protests: One year on, with the national security law looming, has the anti-government movement lost?' *South China Morning Post*, 8 June.

9. See *BBC News* (2019b) 'Do today's global protests have anything in common?' 22 October, www.bbc.com/news/world-50123743. This commentary examines mass protests from Lebanon to Chile, and from Spain (Barcelona) to Hong Kong over issues of inequality, corruption, and

political freedom, as well as across cities in Europe, Australia, and North America over climate change. Other sources focus on racial disparities and treatment. For example, the spread of Black Lives Matter protests in the US following the death of George Floyd in police hands in Minneapolis is a reckoning of deep-seated racism in American society. See *BBC News* (2020) 'George Floyd: Why are there huge protests in the US and around the world?' 11 June, www.bbc.co.uk/newsround/52813673.

10. J.D. Sachs (2019b) 'Why Rich Cities Rebel', *Project Syndicate*, 22 October, www.project-syndicate.org/commentary/explaining-social-protest-in-paris-hong-kong-santiago-by-jeffrey-d-sachs-2019-10.

11. C.Y. Chow (2019) 'Hong Kong risks being condemned to its own circle of hell', *South China Morning Post*, 2 November.

12. Beijing's move can be paradoxically interpreted, in a realist perspective, as its own way of breaking through the dead end in Hong Kong's political fate. See Zhang Xiaoming (張曉明) (2020) 'The stronger the national security bottom line, the greater the space for "One Country, Two Systems"' [In Chinese, 〈國家安全底線愈牢，「一國兩制」空間愈大〉], keynote speech at an online seminar hosted by the Hong Kong SAR government to mark the 30th anniversary of the promulgation of the Basic Law, 8 June, Hong Kong: Hong Kong and Macao Affairs Office of the State Council, Beijing, www.hmo.gov.cn/gab/bld/zxm/gzdt/202006/t20200608_21923.html. During his speech, Zhang, now Executive Deputy Director of the Office, suggested that dealing decisively with the 'destructive forces' under the new national security law for Hong Kong would safeguard and enlarge the space for the 'One Country, Two Systems' principle to be achieved, thereby ensuring that the NPC would support the governing model continuing beyond 2047, when it is due to expire.

13. Lau Siu-kai, a close advisor to the Hong Kong and Macao Affairs Office, also predicts that it is possible that following '50 years no change' (i.e., until 2047), the 'One Country, Two Systems' framework will continue in a modified form, with the Hong Kong Basic Law duly amended. The configuration of the post-2047 'One Country, Two Systems' model will become more and more apparent prior to that crucial date. See S.K. Lau (劉兆佳) (2020) *Thinking About the Future of Hong Kong under One Country, Two Systems* [In Chinese, 《思考香港一國兩制的未來》], Hong Kong: Commercial Press (商務印書館), p. xvi.

Postscript

1. *NPC Observer* (n.d.) 'Decision of the National People's Congress on Improving the Electoral System of the Hong Kong Special Administrative Region', https://npcobserver.com/legislation/npc-hong-kong-electoral-reform-decision/. According to the 1984 expression of Deng Xiaoping, the architect of the 'One Country, Two Systems' formula under which Hong Kong reverted to Chinese sovereignty in 1997: 'A patriot is one who respects the Chinese nation, sincerely supports the motherland's resumption of sovereignty over Hong Kong and wishes not to impair Hong Kong's prosperity and stability. [...] We don't demand that they be in favour of China's socialist system; we only ask them to love the motherland and Hong Kong.' This was quoted in *China Daily Hong Kong Edition* (2004) 'Why it's vital to recall what Deng said about HK', 20 February, www.chinadaily.com.cn/english/doc/2004-02/20/content_307613.htm.

2. *Xinhuanet* (2021) 'China's top legislature adopts amended annexes to HKSAR Basic Law', 30 March, www.xinhuanet.com/english/2021-03/30/c_139846350.htm. For additional information about the revamped electoral system, see Constitutional and Mainland Affairs

Bureau (n.d.) *Improve Electoral System, Ensure Patriots Administering Hong Kong*, from www.cmab.gov.hk/improvement/en/ceo-ele-committee/index.html.

3. For example, *Financial Times* (2020) 'The end of one country, two systems in Hong Kong', editorial, 2 July; J. Perlez (2020) 'One Country, Two Systems, No Future: The End of Hong Kong as We Know It', *Foreign Affairs*, September/October; N.J.P. Alsford (2020) 'Hong Kong: End of "one country, two systems" poses fresh challenges for Joe Biden', *The Conversation*, 17 November.

4. Democratic Party chairman Lo Kin-hei said the electoral changes were 'the biggest regression of the system since the handover'. See *The Wall Street Journal* (2021) 'China All but Ends Hong Kong Democracy With "Patriots Only" Rule', 11 March.

5. D. Rabb (2021) *Foreign Secretary statement on radical changes to Hong Kong's electoral system*, 13 March, London: Foreign, Commonwealth & Development Office.

6. Quoted in *NBC News* (2021) 'Hong Kong: G7 expresses 'grave concerns' over electoral changes', 13 March.

7. Article 1 of the Law of the People's Republic of China on Safeguarding National Security in the Hong Kong Special Administrative Region explains the legislative purpose in preventing, suppressing, and imposing punishment for the offences of secession, subversion, organisation, and perpetration of terrorist activities, and collusion with a foreign country or with external elements to endanger national security in relation to the Hong Kong SAR. See Hong Kong Special Administrative Region Government (2020), op. cit.

8. Under Article 55 of the national security law, this security office shall, upon approval by the CPG of a request made by Hong Kong SAR government or by the office itself, exercise jurisdiction over a case concerning offence endangering national security under this law, if: '(1) the case is complex due to the involvement of a foreign country or external elements, thus making it difficult for the SAR to exercise jurisdiction over the case; (2) a serious situation occurs where the SAR government is unable to effectively enforce the law; or (3) a major and imminent threat to national security has occurred'. One can imagine that in complex and more serious national security threats, where Beijing has less faith in the competence of the SAR government and judiciary to deal with them, the alternative mechanism within the Mainland's jurisdiction would be activated. This is beyond the original thinking of Article 23 legislation and does not apply to Macao as the other SAR.

9. P. Yiu and A. Katakam (2021) 'In one year, Hong Kong arrests 117 people under new security law', *Reuters*, 30 June, www.reuters.com/world/asia-pacific/one-year-hong-kong-arrests-117-people-under-new-security-law-2021-06-30/.

10. As of 1 April 2021, 129 civil servants have refused to sign the declaration pledging allegiance to the Basic Law. SCS Patrick Nip said that '[f]or those who still refused to comply, we will go through relevant procedures and ask them to resign'. See *The Standard* (2021) '129 civil servants refused to sign declaration, says Patrick Nip', 12 April, www.thestandard.com.hk/breaking-news/section/4/169395/129-civil-servants-refused-to-sign-declaration,-says-Patrick-Nip.

12. An indicator of such marginalisation is the removal of Hong Kong from the annual economic freedom index published by the Washington DC-based Heritage Foundation. Since the inception of the index in 1995, Hong Kong had been ranked as the No. 1 free economy in the world, only surpassed by Singapore in 2020. Now, Hong Kong, together with Macao, is ranked as part of China (which is rated No. 107 out of 178 economies in the 2021 ranking).

12. K. Leung (2021) 'Hong Kong leader Carrie Lam sets sights on "improving" city's education sector, its media, and training of civil servants after overhaul of electoral system', *South China*

Morning Post, 3 April, www.scmp.com/news/hong-kong/politics/article/3128243/hong-kong-leader-carrie-lam-sets-sights-improving-citys.

13. World Bank (2020c), *Worldwide Governance Indicators 2019*, https://info.worldbank.org/governance/wgi/Home/Reports.

14. P.M.P. Chan (2021) *The 2020–21 Budget*, Speech by the Financial Secretary moving the Second Reading of the Appropriation Bill 2021 at the Legislative Council, 24 February, Hong Kong: Government Logistics Department, paras. 10–11.

15. The 2021–2022 Budget forecasts a total deficit of HK$257.6 billion for 2020–2021 and a HK$101.6 billion deficit for 2021–2022, with this fiscal drain continuing until 2024–2025. Fiscal reserves will be drawn down from HK$902.7 billion in 2021 (as at 31 March) to HK$756.3 billion by 2025. See P.M.P. Chan (2021), op. cit., Appendix A, p. 7.

16. C. Dickens (1859/2016) *A Tale of Two Cities*, Macmillan Collector's Library imprint, London: Pan Macmillan, Ch. 1.

Bibliography

Abbas, A. (1997) *Hong Kong: Culture and the Politics of Disappearance*, Minneapolis MN: University of Minnesota Press.

Aberbach, J.D., R.D. Putnam, and B.A. Rockman (1981) *Bureaucrats and Politics in Western Democracies*, Cambridge, MA: Harvard University Press.

The Academy of Hong Kong Studies (2017) *Public Finance Civilian Report*, March, Hong Kong: Education University of Hong Kong. Retrieved 22 June 2020, from www.eduhk.hk/include_n/getrichfile.php?key=4fdbfd39f452215b3f432 1e1cccc5c8b&secid=50197&filename=ahks/SSDL/Public_Finance_Civilian_ Report.pdf.

Advisory Committee on Diversification (1979) *Report of the Advisory Committee on Diversification 1979*, Hong Kong: Government Printer.

Akers-Jones, D. (1984) *A Perspective of District Administration*, Speech at the New Asia College Assembly, 17 February, Hong Kong.

Allison, G.T. (1980) *Public and Private Management: Are They Fundamentally Alike in All Unimportant Respects?* Discussion Paper Series No. 84, John F. Kennedy School of Government, Cambridge, MA: Harvard University.

Alsford, N.J.P. (2020) 'Hong Kong: End of "One Country, Two Systems" Poses Fresh Challenges for Joe Biden', *The Conversation*, 17 November.

Althaus, C., P. Bridgman, and G. Davis (2013) *The Australian Policy Handbook*, 5th edition, Sydney: Allen & Unwin.

Andrews, M. (2010) 'Good Government Means Different Things in Different Countries', *Governance*, Vol. 23, No. 1, pp. 7–35.

Ang, Y.Y. (2018) 'The Real China Model: It's Not What You Think It Is', *Foreign Affairs*, 29 June. Retrieved 22 June 2020, from www.foreignaffairs.com/ articles/asia/2018-06-29/real-china-model.

Apple Daily (《蘋果日報》) (2014) 'Anson Chan Retired Early in 2001 Out of Dissatisfaction with Tung Chee-hwa' [in Chinese, 〈不滿董建華2001年陳方 安生提早退休〉], 30 April. Retrieved 22 July 2020, from https://hk.news. appledaily.com/local/realtime/article/20140430/52427995.

Arcadis (2017) 'Sustainable Cities Mobility Index 2017'. Retrieved 22 July 2020, from www.arcadis.com/media/8/B/8/%7B8B887B3A-F4C4-40AB-AFFD-08382CC593E5%7DSustainable%20Cities%20Mobility%20Index.pdf.

Asian Development Bank (1999) *Governance in Asia: From Crisis to Opportunity*, Manila: Asian Development Bank.

Association for Democracy and People's Livelihood (2016) *Justice, Autonomy and Self-Rule: 30th Anniversary Declaration* [in Chinese, 《公義、自主、自治：民協

三十週年宣言》]. Retrieved 22 July 2020, from www.facebook.com/notes/民協-adpl/公義自主自治-民協三十週年宣言/10153686108020983/.

Au, A. (2020) 'Economic Situation in the First Quarter of 2020 and Latest GDP and Price Forecasts for 2020', press release, 15 May, Hong Kong: Information Services Department. Retrieved 22 July 2020, from www.info.gov.hk/gia/general/202005/15/P2020051500447.htm.

Bach, T., G. Hammerschmid, and L. Löffler (2020) 'More Delegation, More Political Control? Politicization of Senior-level Appointments in 18 European Countries', *Public Policy and Administration*, Vol. 35, No. 1, pp. 3–23.

Baier, A. (1986) 'Trust and Anti-Trust', *Ethics*, No. 96, pp. 231–60.

Baker, J.A. (2020) 'Public Service Needs to Work with First-class Political Leadership for Singapore to Succeed: PM Lee', *Channel New Asia*, 17 January. Retrieved 22 July 2020, from www.channelnewsasia.com/news/singapore/pm-lee-public-service-dinner-civil-political-leadership-12275234#cxrecs_s/.

Barker, A. (ed) (1982) *Quangos in Britain*, London: Macmillan.

Barkin, N. (2018) 'Five Eyes Intelligence Alliance Builds Coalition to Counter China', *Reuters World News*, 12 October. Retrieved 22 July 2020, from www.reuters.com/article/us-china-fiveeyes-idUSKCN1MM0GH

Barr, M.D. (2004) *Cultural Politics and Asian Values: The Tepid War*, London: Routledge.

Barr, N. (2012) *Economics of the Welfare State*, 5th edition, Oxford: Oxford University Press.

BBC News (2014) 'Hong Kong University Found Zhao Ziyang's Letter Promising Democratic Administration of Hong Kong' [in Chinese, 〈香港大學發現趙紫陽許諾民主治港信函〉], 14 January. Retrieved 22 July 2020, from www.bbc.com/zhongwen/trad/china/2014/01/140109_hongkong_zhao_ziyang_letter.

BBC News (2019a) 'Hong Kong Protests: President Xi Warns of "Bodies Smashed"', 14 October. Retrieved 22 July 2020, from www.bbc.com/news/world-asia-china-50035229.

BBC News (2019b) 'Do Today's Global Protests Have Anything in Common?' 22 October. Retrieved 22 July 2020, from www.bbc.com/news/world-50123743.

BBC News (2020) 'George Floyd: Why are there Huge Protests in the US and Around the World?' 11 June. Retrieved 22 July 2020, from www.bbc.co.uk/newsround/52813673.

Bell, D.A. (2015) *The China Model: Political Meritocracy and the Limits of Democracy*, Princeton, NJ: Princeton University Press.

Bell, S. and A. Hindmoor (2009) *Rethinking Governance: The Centrality of the State in Modern Society*, Melbourne: Cambridge University Press.

Belt and Road Initiative (website) (2020) 'Hong Kong's Participation', Hong Kong: Hong Kong SAR Government. Retrieved 22 July 2020, from www.beltandroad.gov.hk/participation.html.

Berglof, E. (2018) 'Surprising Findings in Learning from China's Incredible Growth', commentary, *Channel News Asia*, 31 December.

Bickers, R. (2013) 'Loose Ties that Bound: British Empire, Colonial Authority and Hong Kong', in R. Yep (ed) *Negotiating Autonomy in Greater China: Hong Kong and its Sovereign Before and After 1997*, Amsterdam: Nordic Institute of Asian Studies Press, pp. 29–54.

Bickers, R. and R. Yep (2009) *May Days in Hong Kong: Riot and Emergency in 1967*, Hong Kong: Hong Kong University Press.

Blake-Kerr, A. (1973a) *First Report of the Commission of Inquiry under Sir Alastair Blake-Kerr*, Hong Kong: Government Printer.

Blake-Kerr, A. (1973b) *Second Report of the Commission of Inquiry under Sir Alastair Blake-Kerr*, Hong Kong: Government Printer.

Blondel, J. (1997) 'Introduction: Western European Cabinets in Comparative Perspective', in J. Blondel and F. Muller-Rommel (eds) *Cabinets in Western Europe*, 2nd edition, London: Macmillan and St. Martin's Press, pp. 1–17.

Bo, M. (2019) *Semantic-Truth Approaches in Chinese Philosophy: A Unifying Pluralist Account*, Lanham and London: Lexington Books.

Boas, T.C. (2007) 'Conceptualizing Continuity and Change: The Composite-Standard Model of Path Dependence', *Journal of Theoretical Politics*, Vol. 19, No. 1, pp. 33–54.

Bowe, A. (2018) *China's Overseas United Front Work: Background and Implications for the United States*, US-China Economic and Security Review Commission, Washington, D.C. Retrieved 22 July 2020, from www.uscc.gov/research/chinas-overseas-united-front-work-background-and-implications-united-states.

Bowring, P. (2018) 'A Slow Death for Hong Kong's Separate Identity in China', *South China Morning Post*, 24 October. Retrieved 22 July 2020, from www.scmp.com/comment/insight-opinion/hong-kong/article/2169948/slow-death-hong-kongs-separate-identity-china.

Bradsher, K. (2017) 'Once a Model City, Hong Kong is in Trouble', *The New York Times*, 29 June. Retrieved 22 July 2020, from www.nytimes.com/2017/06/29/world/asia/hong-kong-china-handover.html.

Brand, U. and N. Sekler (2009) 'Postneoliberalism: Catch-all Word or Valuable Analytical and Political Concept? Aims of a Beginning Debate', *Development Dialogue*, January, pp. 5–15.

British Government (1984) *White Paper: A Draft Agreement between the Government of the United Kingdom of Great Britain and Northern Ireland and the Government of the People's Republic of China on the Future of Hong Kong*, 26 September, Hong Kong: Government Printer (reproduced).

British Government (1994) *White Paper: Representative Government in Hong Kong*, Hong Kong: Government Printer.

British Government (n.d.) *British Nationality (Hong Kong) Act 1990*, London: British Government. Retrieved 22 July 2020, from www.opsi.gov.uk/ACTS/acts1990/ukpga_19900034_en_1.

Broadcasting Review Board (1985) *Report of the Broadcasting Review Board*, August, Hong Kong: Government Printer.

Brødsgaard, K.E. and S. Young (2000) 'Introduction: State Capacity in East Asia', in K.E. Brødsgaard and S. Young (eds) *State Capacity in East Asia: Japan, Taiwan, China and Vietnam*, New York: Oxford University Press, pp. 1–16.

Burns, J.P. (2004) *Government Capacity and the Hong Kong Civil Service*, Hong Kong: Oxford University Press.

Burns, J.P. and W. Li (2015) 'The Impact of External Change on Civil Service Values in Post-colonial Hong Kong', *The China Quarterly*, No. 222, pp. 522–546.

Burns, J.P., W. Li, and B.G Peter (2012) 'Changing Governance Structures and the Evolution of Public Service Bargains in Hong Kong', *International Review of Administrative Sciences*, Vol. 79, No. 1, pp. 131–148.

Bush, R.C. (2016) *Hong Kong in the Shadow of China: Living with the Leviathan*, Washington, D.C.: Brookings Institution Press.

Cabinet Office (2014) *Civil Service Reform Plan: Progress Report*, October, London: British Cabinet Office and Civil Service. Retrieved 22 July 2020, from https://assets.publishing.service.gov.uk/government/uploads/system/uploads/attachment_data/file/360637/Civil_Service_Reform_Plan_-_Progress_Report__web_.pdf.

Caporaso, J.A. and D.P. Levine (1992) *Theories of Political Economy*, New York: Cambridge University Press.

Cardenal, J.P., J. Kucharczyk, G. Mesežnikov, and G. Pleschová (2017) *Sharp Power: Rising Authoritarian Influence*, National Endowment for Democracy, International Forum for Democratic Studies, Washington, D.C. Retrieved 22 July 2020, from www.ned.org/sharp-power-rising-authoritarian-influence-forum-report/.

Carroll, T., J. Clifton, and D.S.L. Jarvis (2019) 'Power, Leverage and Marketization: The Diffusion of Neoliberalism from North to South and Back Again', *Globalizations*, Vol. 16, No. 6, Special Issue, pp. 771–777.

Carter, N., R. Klein, and P. Day (1992) *How Organizations Measure Success: The Use of Performance Indicators in Government*, London and New York: Routledge.

Case, W. (2008) 'Hybrid Politics and New Competitiveness: Hong Kong's 2007 Chief Executive Election', *East Asia*, Vol. 25, No. 4, pp. 365–388.

Castles, F.G. (1998) *Comparative Public Policy: Patterns of Post-war Transformation*, Cheltenham: Edward Elgar.

Cauquelin, J., P. Lim, and B. Mayer-König (eds) (2014) *Asian Values: Encounter with Diversity*, London: Routledge.

Census and Statistics Department (2002) *Hong Kong 2001 Population Census Main Report*, Hong Kong: Census and Statistics Department.

Census and Statistics Department (2017a) *Hong Kong 2016 Population By-census Thematic Report: Household Income Distribution in Hong Kong*, Hong Kong: Census and Statistics Department.

Census and Statistics Department (2017b) *Hong Kong Population Projections, 2017–2066*, 8 September, Hong Kong: Census and Statistics Department. Retrieved 22 July 2020, from www.censtatd.gov.hk/media_workers_corner/pc_rm/hkpp2017_2066/index.jsp.

Census and Statistics Department (2020a) *Labour Force, Table 006: Labour Force. Unemployment and Underemployment*, Hong Kong: Census and Statistics Department. Retrieved 22 July 2020, from www.censtatd.gov.hk/hkstat/sub/sp200.jsp?tableID=006&ID=0&productType=8.

Census and Statistics Department (2020b) *Labour Force, Table 011: Unemployment Rate by Sex and Age*, Hong Kong: Census and Statistics Department. Retrieved 22 July 2020, from www.censtatd.gov.hk/hkstat/sub/sp200.jsp?tableID=011&ID=0&productType=8.

Census and Statistics Department (2020c) *Labour Statistics*, Hong Kong: Census and Statistics Department. Retrieved 22 July 2020, from www.censtatd.gov.hk/hkstat/sub/so30.jsp.

Census and Statistics Department (2020d) *Wages and Labour Earnings*, Hong Kong: Census and Statistics Department. Retrieved 22 July 2020, from www.censtatd.gov.hk/hkstat/sub/so210.jsp.

Census and Statistics Department (2020e) *National Income,* 'Table 036: Gross Domestic Product (GDP) by Major Economic Activity — Percentage Contribution to GDP at Basic Prices', Hong Kong: Census and Statistics Department. Retrieved 22 July 2020, from www.censtatd.gov.hk/hkstat/sub/sp250.jsp?tableID=036&ID=0&productType=8.

Census and Statistics Department (2020f) 'Quarterly Business Receipts Indices for Service Industries for First Quarter of 2020', press release, 9 June, Hong Kong: Census and Statistics Department. Retrieved 22 July 2020, from www.censtatd.gov.hk/press_release/pressReleaseDetail.jsp?charsetID=1&pressRID=4646.

Census and Statistics Department (various years) *Hong Kong Annual Digest of Statistics*, Hong Kong: Census and Statistics Department

Cha, C.K. (2017) 'Discursive Opportunity Structures in Post-handover Hong Kong Localism: The China Factor and Beyond', *Chinese Journal of Communication*, Vol. 10, No. 4, pp. 413–432.

Chan, E. (2000) 'Defining Fellow Compatriots as "Others" — National Identity in Hong Kong', *Government and Opposition*, Vol. 35, No. 4, pp. 499–519.

Chan, E. (2002) 'Beyond Pedagogy: Language and Identity in Post-Colonial Hong Kong', *British Journal of Sociology of Education*, Vol. 23, No. 2, pp. 271–285.

Chan, E. and J. Chan (2017) 'Hong Kong 2007–2017: A Backlash in Civil Society', *Asia Pacific Journal of Public Administration*, Vol. 39, No. 2, pp. 135–152.

Chan, K.C. (陳冠中) (2005) *My Generation of Hongkongese* [in Chinese,《我這一代香港人》], Hong Kong: Oxford University Press.

Chan, M.K. (1997) 'The Legacy of the British Administration of Hong Kong: A View from Hong Kong', *The China Quarterly*, No. 151, pp. 567–582.

Chan, P.M.P. (2020) *The 2020–21 Budget,* Speech by the Financial Secretary moving the Second Reading of the Appropriation Bill 2020 at the Legislative Council, 26 February, Hong Kong. Retrieved 22 July 2020, from www.budget.gov.hk/2020/eng/pdf/e_budget_speech_2020-21.pdf.

Chan, P.M.P. (2021) *The 2021-22 Budget,* Speech by the Financial Secretary moving the Second Reading of the Appropriation Bill 2021 at the Legislative Council, 24 February, Hong Kong: Government Logistics Department.

Chen, A.H.Y. (2004) 'The Constitutional Controversy of Spring 2004', *Hong Kong Law Journal,* Vol. 34, No. 2, pp. 215–226.

Chen, A.H.Y. (2005) 'The Fate of the Constitutional Reform Proposal of October 2005', *Hong Kong Law Journal,* Vol. 35, No. 3, pp. 537–543.

Chen, A.H.Y. (2018) 'The Autonomy of Hong Kong under "One Country, Two Systems"', in T.L. Lui, S.W.K. Chiu, and R. Yep (eds) *Routledge Handbook of Contemporary Hong Kong,* London: Routledge, pp. 33–51.

Chen, A.H.Y. (2019a) 'A Commentary on the Fugitive Offenders and Mutual Legal Assistance in Criminal Matters Legislation (Amendment) Bill 2019', *HKU Legal Scholarship Blog,* 3 May, Faculty of Law, University of Hong Kong, Hong Kong.

Chen, A.H.Y. (2019b) 'A Perfect Storm: How the Proposed Law on Hong Kong-Mainland China Rendition was Aborted', *Verfassung's Blog on Matters Constitutional,* 19 June. Retrieved 22 July 2020, from https://verfassungsblog.de/a-perfect-storm/.

Chen, E. and R. Ng (2001) 'Economic Restructuring of Hong Kong on the Basis of Innovation and Technology', in S. Masuyama, D. Vandenbrink, and S.Y. Chia (eds) *Industrial Restructuring in East Asia: Towards the 21st Century,* Singapore and Tokyo: Institute of Southeast Asian Studies and Nomura Research Institute, pp. 209–238.

Cheng, E.W. and W.Y. Chan (2016) 'Explaining Spontaneous Occupation: Antecedents, Contingencies and Spaces in the Umbrella Movement', *Social Movement Studies,* Vol. 16, No. 2, pp. 222–239.

Cheng, J. (2009) 'The Story of a New Policy', *Hong Kong Journal,* Fall. Retrieved 22 July 2020, from www.hkbasiclaw.com/Hong%20Kong%20Journal/Cheng%20Jie%20article.htm.

Cheng, J.Y.S. (ed) (2005) *The July 1 Protest Rally: Interpreting a Historic Event,* Hong Kong: City University of Hong Kong Press.

Cheng Ming Magazine (《爭鳴》雜誌) (1985), December issue.

Cheung, A.B.L. (張炳良) (1987) 'Who are the Beneficiaries of the New Pension System? An Overall Appraisal of the Impact of the New Civil Service Pension System' [in Chinese, 〈誰是新長俸制度的受惠者？ 總評新公務員長俸制度的影響〉], *Ming Pao Monthly* (《明報月刊》), July.

Cheung, A.B.L. (1996a) 'Efficiency as the Rhetoric? Public Sector Reform in Hong Kong Explained', *International Review of Administrative Sciences,* Vol. 62, No. 1, pp. 31–47.

Cheung, A.B.L. (1996b) 'Public Sector Reform and the Re-legitimation of Public Bureaucratic Power: The Case of Hong Kong', *International Journal of Public Sector Management*, Vol. 9, No. 5/6, pp. 37–50.

Cheung, A.B.L. (1997a) 'Rebureaucratization of Politics in Hong Kong: Prospects after 1997', *Asian Survey*, Vol. 37, No. 8, pp. 720–737.

Cheung, A.B.L. (1997b) 'Reform in Search of Politics: The Case of Hong Kong's Aborted Attempt to Corporatise Public Broadcasting', *Asian Journal of Public Administration*, Vol. 19, No. 2, pp. 276–302.

Cheung, A.B.L. (1997c) 'Understanding Public-Sector Reforms: Global Trends and Diverse Agendas', *International Review of Administrative Sciences*, Vol. 63, No. 4, pp. 435–457.

Cheung, A.B.L. (1998a) 'From Colony to Special Administrative Region: Issues of Hong Kong's Autonomy within a Centralized Authoritarianistic State', *Verfassung und Recht in Übersee* [*Law and Politics in Africa, Asia and Latin America*], Vol. 31, No. 3, pp. 302–316.

Cheung, A.B.L. (1998b) 'The "Trading Fund" Reform in Hong Kong: Claims and Performance', *Public Administration and Policy*, Vol. 7, No. 2, pp. 105–123.

Cheung, A.B.L. (1999) 'Administrative Development in Hong Kong: Political Questions, Administrative Answers', in H.K. Wong and H.S. Chan (eds) *Handbook of Comparative Public Administration in the Asia-Pacific Basin*, New York: Marcel Dekker, pp. 219–252.

Cheung, A.B.L. (2000a) 'Globalization versus Asian Values: Alternative Paradigms in Understanding Governance and Administration', *Asian Journal of Political Science*, Vol. 8, No. 2, pp. 1–15.

Cheung, A.B.L. (2000b) 'New Interventionism in the Making: Interpreting State Interventions in Hong Kong after the Change of Sovereignty', *Journal of Contemporary China*, Vol. 9, No. 24, pp. 291–308.

Cheung, A.B.L. (2001) 'Some are More Neutral than Others', *Hong Kong Mail*, 10 May.

Cheung, A.B.L. (2002a) 'The Changing Political System: Executive-led Government or "Disabled" Governance?' in S.K. Lau (ed) *The First Tung Chee-hwa Administration: The First Five Years of the Hong Kong Special Administrative Region*, Hong Kong: Chinese University Press, pp. 41–68.

Cheung, A.B.L. (2002b) 'Modernizing Public Healthcare Governance in Hong Kong: A Case Study of Professional Power in New Public Management', *Public Management Review*, Vol. 4, No. 3, pp. 343–365.

Cheung, A.B.L. (2003) 'Public Service Reform in Singapore: Reinventing Government in a Global Age', in A.B.L. Cheung and I. Scott (eds) *Governance and Public Sector Reform in Asia: Paradigm Shifts or Business as Usual?* London: Routledge Curzon, pp. 138–162.

Cheung, A.B.L. (2004) 'Strong Executive, Weak Policy Capacity: The Changing Environment of Policymaking in Hong Kong', *Asian Journal of Political Science*, Vol. 12, No. 1, pp. 1–30.

Cheung, A.B.L. (2005a) 'Civil Service Pay Reform in Hong Kong: Principles, Politics and Paradoxes', in A.B.L. Cheung (ed) *Public Service Reform in East Asia: Reform Issues and Challenges in Japan, Korea, Singapore and Hong Kong*, Hong Kong: Chinese University Press, pp. 157–192.

Cheung, A.B.L. (2005b) 'Hong Kong's Post-1997 Institutional Crisis: Problems of Governance and Institutional Incompatibility', *Journal of East Asian Studies*, Vol. 5, No. 1, pp. 135–167.

Cheung, A.B.L. (2005c) 'The Politics of Administrative Reforms in Asia: Paradigms and Legacies, Paths and Diversities', *Governance*, Vol. 18, No. 2, pp. 257–282.

Cheung, A.B.L. (2005d) 'State Capacity in Hong Kong, Singapore and Taiwan: Coping with Legitimation, Integration and Performance', in J. Pierre and M. Painter (eds) *Challenges to State Policy Capacity: Global Trends and Comparative Perspectives*, Basingstoke: Palgrave Macmillan, pp. 225–254.

Cheung, A.B.L. (2005e) 'What's in a Pamphlet? Shortfalls and Paradoxical Flaws in Hong Kong's Performance Pledges', *Public Management Review*, Vol. 7, No. 3, pp. 341–366.

Cheung, A.B.L. (2006a) 'Budgetary Reforms in the Two City States: Impact on Central Budget Agency in Hong Kong and Singapore', *International Review of Administrative Sciences*, Vol. 72, No. 3, pp. 341–361.

Cheung, A.B.L. (2006b) 'How Autonomous are Public Corporations in Hong Kong? The Case of the Airport Authority', *Public Organization Review: A Global Journal*, Vol. 6, pp. 221–236.

Cheung, A.B.L. (2006c) 'Reinventing Hong Kong's Public Service: Same NPM Reform, Different Contexts and Politics', *International Journal of Organizational Theory and Behaviour*, Vol. 9, No. 2, pp. 212–234.

Cheung, A.B.L. (2007a) 'Executive-dominant Governance or Executive Power "Hollowed-out": The Political Quagmire of Hong Kong', *Asian Journal of Political Science*, Vol. 15, No. 1, pp. 17–38.

Cheung, A.B.L. (2007b) 'Policy Capacity in Post-1997 Hong Kong: Constrained Institutions Facing a Crowding and Differentiated Polity', *Asia Pacific Journal of Public Administration*, Vol. 29, No. 1, pp. 51–75.

Cheung, A.B.L. (2008a) 'Evaluation of the Hong Kong Integrity System', in L. Huberts, F. Anechiarico, and F.E. Six (eds) *Local Integrity Systems: World Cities Fighting Corruption and Safeguarding Integrity*, The Hague: BJU Legal Publishers, pp. 105–115.

Cheung, A.B.L. (2008b) 'Preface: Hong Kong's Role in Transforming China', in M. Chan (ed) *China's Hong Kong Transformed: Retrospect and Prospects Beyond the First Decade*, Hong Kong: City University of Hong Kong Press, pp. xi–xvii.

Cheung, A.B.L. (2009a) 'Evaluating the Ombudsman System of Hong Kong: Towards Good Governance and Citizenship Enhancement', *Asia Pacific Law Review*, Vol. 17, No. 1, pp. 73–94.

Cheung, A.B.L. (2009b) 'Interpreting East Asian Social Policy Development: Paradigm Shift or Policy "Steadiness"?' in K.H. Mok and R. Forrest (eds)

Changing Governance and Public Policy in East Asia, London and New York: Routledge, pp. 25–48.

Cheung, A.B.L. (2010a) 'Checks and Balance in China's Administrative Traditions: A Preliminary Assessment', in M. Painter and B.G. Peters (eds) *Tradition and Public Administration*, Hampshire: Palgrave Macmillan, pp. 31–43.

Cheung, A.B.L. (2010b) 'In Search of Trust and Legitimacy: The Political Trajectory of Hong Kong as Part of China', *International Public Management Review*, Vol. 11, No. 2, pp. 38–63.

Cheung, A.B.L. (2011) 'Performance Management in Hong Kong', in E.M. Berman (ed) *Public Administration in Southeast Asia*, London: CRC Francis & Taylor Group, pp. 295–314.

Cheung, A.B.L. (2012a) 'One Country, Two Experiences: Administrative Reforms in China and Hong Kong', *International Review of Administrative Sciences*, Vol. 78, No. 2, pp. 261–283.

Cheung, A.B.L. (2012b) 'Public Administration in East Asia: Legacies, Trajectories and Lessons', *International Review of Administrative Sciences*, Vol. 78, No. 2, pp. 209–216.

Cheung, A.B.L. (2013) 'Can There be an Asian Model of Public Administration?' *Public Administration and Development*, Vol. 33, September, pp. 249–261.

Cheung, A.B.L. (2017) 'Reflections on Governance in Hong Kong: Outside/Insider Perspectives', keynote presentation at the Serving the Evolving City Conference held by the Efficiency Unit, 12 January, Hong Kong.

Cheung, A.B.L. (張炳良) (2018a) *An Unavoidable Reality—A Review of Housing Policies During My Five Years As Secretary* [in Chinese, 《不能迴避的現實 — 回顧任局長五年的房屋政策》], Hong Kong: Chung Hwa Book Company.

Cheung, A.B.L. (張炳良) (2018b) *An Unavoidable Reality—A Review of Transport Policies During My Five Years As Secretary* [in Chinese, 《不能迴避的現實 — 回顧任局長五年的運輸政策》], Hong Kong: Chung Hwa Book Company.

Cheung, A.B.L. (張炳良) (2020) *Daring to Change the Sky: Extraordinary Years of Hong Kong's Anti-Corruption Pioneers* [in Chinese, 《敢教日月換新天：香港反貪先鋒的崢嶸歲月》], Hong Kong: Chung Hwa Book Company (中華書局).

Cheung, A.B.L. (2020) 'Administrative Reform: Opportunities, Drivers and Barriers', in B.G. Peters and I. Thynne (eds) *Oxford Encyclopedia of Public Administration*, London: Oxford University Press, pp. 1–26, https://doi.org/10.1093/acrefore/9780190228637.013.1437.

Cheung, A.B.L. and K.S. Louie (2000) 'Social Conflicts: 1975–1986', in S.K. Lau (ed) *Social Development and Political Change in Hong Kong*, Hong Kong: Chinese University Press, pp. 63–114.

Cheung, A.B.L. and I. Scott (2003) 'Governance and Public Sector Reforms in Asia: Paradigms, Paradoxes and Dilemmas', in A.B.L. Cheung and I. Scott (eds) *Governance and Public Sector Reform in Asia: Paradigm Shifts or Business As Usual?* London: Routledge Curzon, pp. 1–24.

Cheung, A.B.L. and M.W.L. Wong (2006) 'Judicial Review and Policy Making in Hong Kong: Changing Interface Between the Legal and the Political', *Asia Pacific Journal of Public Administration*, Vol. 28, No. 2, pp. 117–141.

Cheung, A.B.L. and P.C.W. Wong (2004) 'Who Advised the Hong Kong Government? The Politics of Absorption before and after 1997', *Asian Survey*, Vol. 44, No. 6, pp. 874–894.

Cheung, C.Y. (2003) 'The Quest for Good Governance: Hong Kong's Principal Officials Accountability System', *China: An International Journal*, Vol. 1, No. 2, pp. 249–272.

Cheung, G. (2020) 'Hong Kong's National Security Law Must Follow Common Law, Former Chief Justices Say', *South China Morning Post*, 2 June.

Cheung, G.K.W. (2009) *Hong Kong's Watershed: The 1967 Riots*, Hong Kong: Hong Kong University Press.

Cheung, P.T.Y. (2017) 'Beijing's Tightening Grip: Changing Mainland-Hong Kong Relations amid Integration and Confrontation', in B.C.H. Fong and T.L. Lui (eds) *Hong Kong 20 Years after the Handover: Emerging Social and Institutional Fractures after 1997*, London: Palgrave, pp. 255–286.

Chief Secretary for Administration's Office and various Bureaus (2020) *Item for Finance Committee*, Paper for discussion at Finance Committee, FCR (2020–21)2, 17 April, Hong Kong: Legislative Council. Retrieved 22 July 2020, from www.legco.gov.hk/yr19-20/english/fc/fc/papers/f20-02e.pdf.

China Daily (2019a) 'Shenzhen Surpasses HK in GDP', 28 February. Retrieved 22 July 2020, from www.chinadaily.com.cn/a/201902/28/WS5c7720fda3106c65c34ebd70.html.

China Daily (2019b) 'Overriding Task in Hong Kong is "to Stop Violence"', 8 August. Retrieved 22 July 2020, from www.chinadaily.com.cn/a/201908/08/WS5d4b180ea310cf3e3556477f.html.

China Daily (2019c) 'Signs of "Terrorism" Seen in HK Unrest', 13 August. Retrieved 22 July 2020, from www.chinadaily.com.cn/cndy/2019-08/13/content_37501175.htm.

China Daily Hong Kong Edition (2004) 'Why It's Vital to Recall What Deng Said about HK', 20 February. Retrieved 11 April 2020, from www.chinadaily.com.cn/english/doc/2004-02/20/content_307613.htm.

China Internet News (《中國互聯網新聞》) (2000) 'Anson Chan Visited Qian Qichen' [in Chinese, 〈錢其琛會見陳方安生〉], 26 September. Retrieved 22 July 2020, from www.china.com.cn/chinese/2000/Oct/8369.htm.

Chinese Communist Party, Central Documents Editorial Committee (ed) (1993) *Selected Works of Deng Xiaoping—Vol. III* [in Chinese, 《鄧小平文選》第三卷], Beijing: People's Press.

Ching, C. (程翔) (2013) 'Electing Hong Kong's CE under one-party dictatorship' [in Chinese, 〈一黨專政下的香港特首普選〉], *Hong Kong Economic Journal* (《信報》), 12 December.

Ching, C. (程翔) (2015) 'In Memory of Lo Ping: See What Can Be Done by Hong Kong? Part II' [in Chinese, 〈憶魯平，看香港「怎麼辦」？（下）〉], *Pentoy* (《評台》), 21 May. Retrieved 22 July 2020, from www.pentoy.hk/憶魯平，看香港「怎麼辦」？-（下）/.

Ching, F. (1987) 'How the Survey Dice Were Loaded', *South China Morning Post*, 6 November.

Chiu, S.W. (趙永佳) and C.Y. Ip (葉仲茵) (2015) 'Social Mobility of Youth in Hong Kong: Objective Experiences and Subjective Perceptions' [in Chinese 〈香港青年「下流」問題：客觀狀況與主觀感受〉], *Hong Kong and Macao Journal* [《港澳研究》], No. 3, pp. 65–74.

Chiu, S.W. and T. Lui (2009) *Hong Kong: Becoming a Chinese Global City*, London: Routledge.

Chou, B. (2015) 'New Bottle, Old Wine: China's Governance of Hong Kong in View of Its Policies in the Restive Borderlands', *Journal of Current Chinese Affairs*, Vol. 44, No. 4, pp. 177–209.

Chow, C.Y. (2019) 'Hong Kong Risks being Condemned to its Own Circle of Hell', *South China Morning Post*, 2 November. Retrieved 22 July 2020, from www.scmp.com/comment/opinion/article/3036064/hong-kong-risks-being-condemned-its-own-circle-hell.

Choy, C.K. (蔡子強) and S.L. Lau (劉細良) (1996) 'The Executive-Legislative Relations in Hong Kong Before 1997' [in Chinese, 〈九七回歸前夕的香港行政與立法關係〉], *Hong Kong Journal of Social Sciences* (《香港社會科學學報》), No. 8, Autumn, pp. 237–266.

Christensen, T. and P. Laegreid (2001) 'New Public Management—Undermining Political Control?' in T. Christensen and P. Laegreid (eds) *New Public Management: The Transformation of Ideas and Practice*, Aldershot: Ashgate, pp. 93–121.

Christensen, T., L. Dong, and M. Painter (2008) 'Administrative Reform in China's Central Government: How Much "Learning from the West"?' *International Review of Administrative Sciences*, Vol. 74, No. 3, pp. 351–371.

Chung, J. (2016) *Centrifugal Empire: Central-Local Relations in China*, New York: Columbia University Press.

Chung, K. (2017) 'Xi "Sent a Reminder" to Hong Kong over Beijing's Hard Line on City', *South China Morning Post*, 16 December.

Chung, S.Y. (2001) *Hong Kong's Journey to Reunification—Memoirs of Sze-yuen Chung*, Hong Kong: Chinese University Press.

CitizenNews (《眾新聞》) (2017) 'Donald Truly a "Son of Hong Kong", Wong Yan-lung says', 20 February. Retrieved 22 July 2020, from www.hkcnews.com/article/1941/donald-truely-a-son-of-hong-kong-wong-yanlung-says.

Civic Party (2016) *Practising Reform and Innovation, Reversing the Future: Ten Major Policy Programmes for 2016 Legislative Council Election* [in Chinese, 《實踐革新，逆轉未來：2016立法會選舉十大重點政策綱領》]. Retrieved 22 July 2020, from https://2016.civicparty.hk//Uploads/document/doc/CP-Platform-chi.pdf.

Civil Service Branch (1995) *Human Resource Management*, Hong Kong: Government Printer.

Civil Service Bureau (1999a) *Civil Service into the 21st Century: Civil Service Reform Consultation Document*, March, Hong Kong: Printer Department.

Civil Service Bureau (1999b) *Civil Service Reform Newsletter*, Issue No. 3, June, Hong Kong: Civil Service Bureau.

Civil Service Bureau (2003) *Civil Service-related Initiatives in the 2003 Policy Address*, Paper submitted to the Legislative Council Panel on Public Service, LC Paper No. CB(1)710/02-03(01), 13 January, Hong Kong: Legislative Council.

Civil Service Bureau (2009) *Civil Service Code*, 9 September, Hong Kong: Civil Service Bureau. Retrieved 22 July 2020, from www.csb.gov.hk/english/admin/conduct/files/CSCode_e.pdf.

Civil Service Bureau (2016) *An Overview of the Civil Service: Establishment, Strength, Retirement, Resignation and Age Profile*, Paper for Panel on Public Service of the Legislative Council, 18 April, Hong Kong: Legislative Council.

Civil Service Bureau (2018a) *Key Features of the CSPF Scheme*, Hong Kong: Civil Service Bureau. Retrieved 22 July 2020, from www.csb.gov.hk/english/admin/retirement/421.html.

Civil Service Bureau (2018b) *An Overview of Training and Development for Civil Servants*, Paper submitted to the Legislative Council panel on public service, May, Hong Kong: Civil Service Bureau. Retrieved 22 July 2020, from www.csb.gov.hk/english/admin/training/files/LCpaper_Overview_20190520_e.pdf.

Civil Service Bureau (n.d.) *Central Staff Consultative Councils*. Hong Kong: Civil Service Bureau. Retrieved 29 August 2021, from www.csb.gov.hk/english/admin/relations/151.html.

Cole, M. (1998) 'Quasi-Government in Britain: The Origins, Persistence and Implications of the Term "Quango"', *Public Policy and Administration*, Vol. 13, No. 1, pp. 65–78.

Collins, S. (2014) *Hunger Games: Mockingjay*, New York: Scholastic.

Commission of Inquiry (1967) *Kowloon Disturbances 1966: Report of Commission of Inquiry*, Hong Kong: Government Printer.

Committee of Inquiry into the 1988 Civil Service Pay Adjustment and Related Matters (Burrett Committee) (1989) *Final Report*, March, Hong Kong: Government Printer.

Committee on Review of Public Service Broadcasting (2007) *Report on Review of Public Service Broadcasting in Hong Kong*, March, Hong Kong, Retrieved 22 July 2020, from www.cedb.gov.hk/ccib/eng/doc/Part%20I.pdf

Committee on the Civil Service (1968) *Report of the Committee on the Civil Service*, Vol. 1, 1966–68, Cmnd 3638. London: Her Majesty's Stationery Office (HMSO).

Constitutional Affairs Bureau (2003) *Twelve-month Report on the Implementation of the Accountability System for Principal Officials*. Retrieved 22 July 2020, from www.cmab.gov.hk/upload/20040219153857/12mthreport-e.pdf.

Constitutional Affairs Bureau (2006) *Consultation Document on Further Development of the Political Appointment System*, Hong Kong: Government Logistics Department.

Constitutional and Mainland Affairs Bureau (2009) *Public Consultation on the Methods for Selecting the Chief Executive and for Forming the Legislative Council in 2012*, 18 November, Hong Kong: Government Logistics Department.

Constitutional and Mainland Affairs Bureau (2010) 'Legislative Council By-election for the Five Geographical Constituencies', Paper submitted to the Panel on Constitutional Affairs of the Legislative Council, LC Paper No. CB(2)889/09-10(03), February, Hong Kong: Legislative Council.

Constitutional and Mainland Affairs Bureau (2012) *Code for Officials under the Political Appointment System*, July, Hong Kong: Constitutional and Mainland Affairs Bureau. Retrieved 22 July 2020, from www.cmab.gov.hk/en/issues/PAO_Code_1.7.2012.pdf.

Constitutional and Mainland Affairs Bureau (2020) *Greater Bay Area*. Retrieved 22 July 2020, from www.bayarea.gov.hk/en/home/index.html.

Constitutional and Mainland Affairs Bureau (n.d.) *Facilitation Measures for Hong Kong People*, Hong Kong: Constitutional and Mainland Affairs Bureau. Retrieved 22 July 2020, from www.cmab.gov.hk/en/issues/facilitation_measures.htm.

Constitutional and Mainland Affairs Bureau (n.d.) *Improve Electoral System, Ensure Patriots Administering Hong Kong*, Hong Kong: Constitutional and Mainland Affairs Bureau. Retrieved 16 July 2021, from www.cmab.gov.hk/improvement/en/ceo-ele-committee/index.html.

Cooper, J. (1970) *Colony in Conflict: The Hong Kong Disturbances, May 1967–January 1968*, Hong Kong: Swindon Book Company.

Court of First Instance, High Court of the Hong Special Administrative Region (2018) 'Constitutional and Administrative Law List No. 1160 of 2018'. Retrieved 22 July 2020, from https://legalref.judiciary.hk/lrs/common/ju/ju_frame.jsp?DIS=119029&currpage=T.

Craig, S.C. (1993) *The Malevolent Leaders: Popular Discontent in America*, Boulder, CO: Westview.

Crouch, C. (2004) *Post-democracy*, Cambridge: Polity.

Crozier, M., S.P. Huntington, and J. Watanuki (1975) *The Crisis of Democracy: Report on the Governability of Democracies to the Trilateral Commission*, New York: New York University Press.

Curriculum Development Council (2012) *Moral and National Education Curriculum Guide (Primary 1 to Secondary 6)*, April, Hong Kong: Education Bureau.

Daily Headlines (《每日頭條》) (2017) 'Attempts by Republican Government to Recover Hong Kong' [in Chinese, 〈國民政府試圖收復香港始末〉], 26 July. Retrieved 22 July 2020, from https://kknews.cc/zh-hk/history/8ez3kg4.html.

de Bruijin, H. (2002) *Managing Performance in the Public Sector*, London and New York: Routledge.

de Bruijn, H.A. and H.A.M. Hufen (1998) 'The Traditional Approach to Policy Instruments', in B.G. Peters and F.K.M. van Nispen (eds) *Public Policy Instruments: Evaluating the Tools of Public Administration*, Cheltenham: Edward Elgar, pp. 11–32.

Democratic Party (2017) *Standing on the Shoulder of Historical Giant: The Democratic Party's Review and Outlook on Hong Kong-Mainland China Relations* [in Chinese, 《站在歷史巨人的肩上——民主黨對港中關係的回顧及展望》], 7 June. Retrieved 22 July 2020, from https://drive.google.com/file/d/0B1m5ziISS9RzN3JUOEZsQ09ObzQ/view.

Demographia (2020) *Media Release: 16th Annual Demographia International Housing Affordability Survey*, 20 January. Retrieved 22 July 2020, from http://demographia.com/dhimedia2020.pdf.

Demosistō (香港眾志) (2016) *Democratic Self-Determination Starts Here: Roadmap of Our Self-Determination Movement* [in Chinese, 《民主自決 此際起航——我們的自決運動路線圖》]. Retrieved 22 July 2020, from www.demosisto.hk/article/details/45.

Deng, X.P. (鄧小平) (1993) *Selected Works of Deng Xiaoping* [in Chinese, 《鄧小平文選》], Vol. 3, Beijing: People's Press,

Department of Justice, Transport and Housing Bureau, and Security Bureau (2017) *Customs, Immigration and Quarantine Arrangements of the Hong Kong Section of the Guangzhou-Shenzhen-Hong Kong Express Rail Link*, Paper submitted to the Legislative Council, CB(2)1966/16-17(01), July, Hong Kong: Legislative Council.

Diamond, L. (2002) 'Thinking About Hybrid Regimes', *Journal of Democracy*, Vol. 13, No. 2, pp. 21–35.

Diamond, L. (2006) 'Promoting Democracy in Post-Conflict and Failed States: Lessons and Challenges', *Taiwan Journal of Democracy*, Vol. 2, No. 2, pp. 93–116.

Diamond, L. (2016) *In Search of Democracy*, London and New York: Routledge.

Diamond, L. (2019) *Ill Winds: Saving Democracy from Russian Rage, Chinese Ambition, and American Complacency*, New York: Penguin Press.

Dickens, C. (1859/2016) *A Tale of Two Cities*, Macmillan Collector's Library imprint, London: Pan Macmillan.

Dimbleby, J. (1997) *The Last Governor: Chris Patten and the Handover of Hong Kong*, London: Little, Brown and Company.

Director of Audit (2005) 'Chapter 6: Performance Measurement and Reporting in the Government', *Report No. 45*, October, Hong Kong: Audit Commission.

Directorate of Intelligence, Central Intelligence Agency (CIA) (1982) *Singapore: Moving Ahead with the Second Industrial Revolution*, confidential report, May, approved for release on 10 July 2008, Washington, D.C.: CIA, Retrieved 22 July 2020, from www.cia.gov/library/readingroom/docs/CIA-RDP83B00227R000100170001-0.pdf.

Dolowitz, D. and D. Marsh (2000) 'Learning from Abroad: The Role of Policy Transfer in Contemporary Policy-Making', *Governance*, Vol. 13, No. 1, pp. 5–24.

Dowding, K. (2017) 'Australian Exceptionalism Reconsidered', *Australian Journal of Political Science*, Vol. 52, No. 2, pp. 165–182.

Dunleavy, P. (1991) *Democracy, Bureaucracy and Public Choice: Economic Explanations in Political Science*, London: Harvester Wheatsheaf.

Dunrose, C. and K. Rummery (2006) 'Governance and Collaboration: Review Article', *Social Policy and Society*, Vol. 5, No. 2, p. 320.

Dye, T.R. (1987) *Understanding Public Policy*, 6th edition, Englewood Cliffs, NJ: Prentice-Hall.

Dye, T.R. (2002) *Understanding Public Policy*, 10th edition, Upper Saddle River: Prentice-Hall.

Economic Services Bureau (1999) *1999 Economic Prospects*, Hong Kong: Printing Department.

The Economist (1997) 'The World Economy Survey', 20 September.

The Economist (2008) 'Bagehot: Heads must Roll', 22 November.

The Economist (2012) 'China's State Capitalism: Not Just Tilting at Windmills', 6 October.

The Economist (2013) 'Xi Jinping and the Chinese Dream', editorial, 4 May.

The Economist (2016) 'Our Crony-Capitalism Index: The Party Winds Down', 7 May.

The Economist (2017) 'Do Social Media Threaten Democracy?' 4 November.

The Economist (2019) 'Millennial Socialism', 16 February.

The Economist (2020) 'The State in the Time of Covid-19', 26 March.

Economist Intelligence Unit (2017) 'Safe Cities Index 2017', *The Economist*, November. Retrieved 22 July 2020, from http://safecities.economist.com/safe-cities-index-2017.

Economist Intelligence Unit (2019) 'Safe Cities Index 2019', *The Economist*, August. Retrieved 22 July 2020, from https://safecities.economist.com/wp-content/uploads/2019/08/Aug-5-ENG-NEC-Safe-Cities-2019-270x210-19-screen.pdf.

Economist Intelligence Unit (2020) 'Hong Kong', *The Economist*. Retrieved 9 June 2020, from https://country.eiu.com/hong-kong.

Edelman (2020) *Edelman Trust Barometer Global Report*, 19 January. Retrieved 22 July 2020, from www.edelman.com/sites/g/files/aatuss191/files/2020-01/2020%20Edelman%20Trust%20Barometer%20Global%20Report.pdf.

Education Bureau (n.d.) 'Government Expenditure on Education', *Figures and Statistics*, Hong Kong: Education Bureau. Retrieved 22 July 2020, from www.edb.gov.hk/en/about-edb/publications-stat/figures/gov-expenditure.html.

Efficiency Office (n.d.) *Our History*, Hong Kong: Efficiency Office. Retrieved 22 July 2020, from www.effo.gov.hk/en/index.html.

Efficiency Office (n.d.) *Past, Present and Prospective Public Sector Reform in Hong Kong*, Hong Kong: Efficiency Office. Retrieved 22 July 2020, from www.effo.gov.hk/en/doc/PSRHK(Eng)final.pdf.

Efficiency Unit (1995) *Serving the Community*, Hong Kong: Government Printer.

Efficiency Unit (1998) *Survey on Performance Pledges*. Retrieved 17 May 2004, from www.info.gov.hk/eu/english/pm/pm_ref/files/ppflyer.pdf.

Efficiency Unit (2004) *New Directions*. Retrieved 17 May 2004, from http://info.gov.hk/eu/english/history/history_mf/history_mf2002.html, link no longer available.

Employment Conditions Abroad International (2020) *Hong Kong Plummets in Expat Liveability Rankings*, 11 February. Retrieved 22 July 2020, from www.eca-international.com/news/february-2020/hong-kong-plummets-in-expat-liveability-rankings.

Endacott, G.B. (1964) *Government and People in Hong Kong, 1841–1962: A Constitutional History*, Hong Kong: Hong Kong University Press.

Ercan, S.A. and J.-P. Gagnon (2014) 'The Crisis of Democracy: Which Crisis? Which Democracy?' *Democratic Theory*, Vol. 1, No. 2, pp. 1–10.

Evans, P.B. (1989) 'Predatory, Developmental and Other Apparatuses: A Comparative Political Economy Perspective on the Third World State', *Sociological Forum*, No. 4, pp. 561–587.

Evans, P.B. (1995) *Embedded Autonomy: States and Industrial Transformation*, Princeton, NJ: Princeton University Press.

Fellows, J. (2016) *The Rhetoric of Trade and Decolonisation in Hong Kong, 1945–1984*, doctoral thesis, Hong Kong: Lingnan University. Retrieved 22 July 2020, from http://commons.ln.edu.hk/his_etd/9/.

Finance Branch (1989) *Public Sector Reform*, February, Hong Kong: Finance Branch.

Finance Branch (1995) *Practitioner's Guide: Management of Public Finances*, Hong Kong: Government Printer.

Financial Times (2020) 'The End of One Country, Two Systems in Hong Kong', editorial, 2 July. Retrieved 11 April 2021, from www.ft.com/content/5d3d7d2e-bba8-11ea-a05d-efc604854c3f.

Fong, B.C.H. (2013) 'State-Society Conflicts under Hong Kong's Hybrid Regime: Governing Coalition Building and Civil Society Challenges', *Asian Survey*, Vol. 53, No. 5, pp. 854–882.

Fong, B.C.H. (2014a) *Hong Kong's Governance under Chinese Sovereignty: The Failure of the State-business Alliance After 1997*, Abingdon, Oxon: Routledge.

Fong, B.C.H. (2014b) 'Ten Years of Political Appointments in Hong Kong: The Challenges and Prospects of Developing a Political Appointment System under a Semi-Democratic Regime, 2002–12', in J.Y.S. Cheng (ed) *New Tends of Political Participation in Hong Kong*, Hong Kong: City University of Hong Kong Press, pp. 67–103.

Fong, B.C.H. (方志恒) (ed) (2015) *Hong Kong Reformation Thesis* [in Chinese,《香港革新論：革新保港，民主自治，永續自治。為香港前途而戰》], Taipei: Azothbooks (漫遊者文化).

Fong, B.C.H. (方志恒) (ed) (2017a) *Hong Kong Innovation Theory II: Thinking about Hong Kong's Future from the World* [in Chinese,《香港革新論II：從世界思考香港前途》], Hong Kong: Chapter One Publishing (出一點文創).

Fong, B.C.H. (2017b) 'In-between Liberal Authoritarianism and Electoral Authoritarianism: Hong Kong's Democratization under Chinese Sovereignty, 1997–2016', *Democratization*, Vol. 24, No. 4, pp. 724–750.

Fong, B.C.H. (2017c) 'One Country, Two Nationalisms: Center-Periphery Relations between Mainland China and Hong Kong, 1997–2016', *Modern China*, Vol. 43, No. 5, pp. 523–556.

Fong, B.C.H. (2018a) 'Advisory Politics Before and After 1997: In Search of a New Relationship between State, Political Society and Civil Society', in T.L. Lui, S.W.K. Chiu, and R. Yep (eds) *Routledge Handbook of Contemporary Hong Kong*, London: Routledge, pp. 127–140.

Fong, B.C.H. (2018b) 'Executive-Legislative Disconnection in the HKSAR: Uneasy Partnership Between Chief Executives and Pro-Government Parties, 1997–2016', in B.C.H. Fong and T.L. Lui (eds) *Hong Kong 20 Years after the Handover: Emerging Social and Institutional Fractures After 1997*, London: Palgrave Macmillan, pp. 45–71.

The Foreign Correspondents' Club (2017) 'Fifty Years On: The Riots that Shook Hong Kong in 1967', 18 May, Hong Kong: The Foreign Correspondents' Club. Retrieved 22 July 2020, from www.fcchk.org/correspondent/fifty-years-on-the-riots-that-shook-hong-kong-in-1967/.

Friedman, M. (1981) *Free to Choose*, Harmondsworth: Penguin Books.

Fukuyama, F. (1992) *The End of History and the Last Man*, London: Hamish Hamilton.

Fukuyama, F. (2005) *State-Building: Governance and World Order in the Twenty-First Century*, London: Profile Books.

Fukuyama, F. (2013a) 'What is Governance?' *Governance*, Vol. 26, No. 3, pp. 347–368.

Fukuyama, F. (2013b) 'What is Governance? Fukuyama Replies', *The Governance Blog*, 30 April. Retrieved 22 July 2020, from https://governancejournal.wordpress.com/2013/04/30/1492/.

Fukuyama, F. (2018a) 'Against Identity Politics: The New Tribalism and the Crisis of Democracy', *Foreign Affairs*, Vo. 97, No. 5, September/October, pp. 90–114. Retrieved 22 July 2020, from www.foreignaffairs.com/articles/americas/2018-08-14/against-identity-politics-tribalism-francis-fukuyama.

Fukuyama, F. (2018b) *Identity: The Demand for Dignity and the Politics of Resentment*, New York: Farrar, Straus and Giroux.

Fukuyama, F. (2020) 'The Pandemic and Political Order: It Takes a State', *Foreign Affairs*, July/August. Retrieved 22 July 2020, from www.foreignaffairs.com/articles/world/2020-06-09/pandemic-and-political-order.

Fung, A. (2001) 'What Makes the Local? A Brief Consideration of the Rejuvenation of Hong Kong Identity', *Cultural Studies*, Vol. 15, Nos. 3/4, pp. 591–601.

Gereffi, G. (2014) 'Global Value Chains in a Post-Washington Consensus World', *Review of International Political Economy*, Vol. 21, No. 1, pp. 9–37.

Gessen, M. (2020) *Surviving Autocracy*, New York: Riverhead Books.

Ghai, Y. (2013) 'Hong Kong's Autonomy: Dialects of Powers and Institutions', in Y. Ghai and S. Woodman (eds) *Practising Self-Government: A Comparative Study of Autonomous Regions*, Cambridge: Cambridge University Press, pp. 315–348.

Global Times (2019) 'June 4 Immunized China Against Turmoil', editorial, English edition, 3 June.

GlobalEconomy.com (n.d.) *Hong Kong: Unemployment Rate*. Retrieved 22 July 2020, from www.theglobaleconomy.com/Hong-Kong/Unemployment_rate/.

Goodsell, C. (1994) *The Case for Bureaucracy: A Public Administration Polemic*, Chatham, NJ: Chatham House.

Goodstadt, L. (2005) *Uneasy Partners: The Conflict Between Public Interest and Private Profit in Hong Kong*, Hong Kong: Hong Kong University Press.

Goodstadt, L. (2013) *Poverty in the Midst of Affluence: How Hong Kong Mismanaged Its Prosperity*, revised edition, Hong Kong: Hong Kong University Press.

Goodstadt, L. (2018) *A City Mismanaged: Hong Kong's Struggle for Survival*, Hong Kong: Hong Kong University Press.

Gore, A., Jr. (1994) *National Performance Review*, Darby, PA: Diane Publishing.

Graham, A. (2015) 'The Thucydides Trap: Are the U.S. and China Headed for War?' *The Atlantic*, 24 September.

Gramer, R. (2020) 'Pompeo Emerges as Point Man in War of Words with China', *Foreign Policy*, 1 May.

Gray, A. and W.I. Jenkins (1985) *Administrative Politics in British Government*, Sussex: Wheatsheaf Books.

Gray, J. (1999) *False Dawn: The Delusions of Global Capitalism*, London: Granta Books.

Grindle, M.S. (2002) 'Good Enough Governance: Poverty Reduction and Reform in Developing Countries', *Governance*, Vol. 17, No. 4, pp. 525–548.

The Guardian (2019) 'Brett Kavanaugh'. Retrieved 22 July 2020, from www.theguardian.com/us-news/brett-kavanaugh.

Haddon-Cave, P. (1984) 'Introduction [to the 1st edition]: The Making of Some Aspects of Public Policy in Hong Kong', in D.G. Lethbridge (ed) *The Business Environment in Hong Kong*, 2nd edition, Hong Kong: Oxford University Press, pp. xiii–xx.

Haggard, S. (1990) *Pathways from the Periphery: The Politics of Growth in the Newly Industrialising Countries*, Ithaca and London: Cornell University Press.

Halligan, J. (2007) 'Administrative Reforms in Westminster Democracies: The Long-term Results', *Journal for Comparative Government and European Policy*, Vol. 5, No. 3/4, pp. 524–539.

Hardin, R. (1998) 'Trust in Government', in V. Braithwaite and M. Levi (eds) *Trust and Governance*, New York: Russell Sage Foundation, pp. 9–27.

Harris, P. (1988) *Hong Kong: A Study in Bureaucracy and Politics*, Hong Kong: Macmillan.

Hartman, J. (2003) *Judgement on Lau Kwok Fai Barnard vs. Secretary for Justice and Government Park and Playground Keepers Union, Shum Man Lai and Leung Tat Wah vs. Secretary for Justice*, Constitutional and Administrative Law List Nos. 177 and 180 of 2002, Court of First Instance in the High Court of the Hong Kong Special Administrative Region, 10 June.

The Harvard Team (1999) *Improving Hong Kong's Health Care System: Why and For Whom*, April, Hong Kong: Health and Welfare Bureau.

Harvey, D.A. (2019) *Spaces of Global Capitalism*, London: Verso.

Hase, P. (1990) 'Review of E.S. Savas, *Privatization: The Key to Better Government*', *Asian Journal of Public Administration*, No. 1, pp. 119–129.

Hayllar, M. (2005) 'Outsourcing: Enhancing Private Sector Involvement in Public Sector Services Provision in Hong Kong', in A.B.L. Cheung (ed) *Public Service Reform in East Asia: Reform Issues and Challenges in Japan, Korea, Singapore and Hong Kong*, Hong Kong: Chinese University Press, pp. 193–230.

Haynes, R.J. (1980) *Organization Theory and Local Government*, London: George Allen & Unwin.

Heidegger, M. (translated by J. Macquarie and E. Robinson) (1962/2001) *Being and Time*, Oxford: Blackwell.

Helliwell, J., R. Layard, and J. Sachs (2018) *World Happiness Report 2019*, New York: Sustainable Development Solutions Network.

Henley & Partners Research Department (n.d.) *Henley & Partners Passport Index: 2020 Q2 Update*. Retrieved 22 July 2020, from www.henleypassportindex.com/passport-index.

Heritage Foundation, The (2020) *2020 Index of Economic Freedom*. Retrieved 22 July 2020, from www.heritage.org/index/ranking/.

Hernández, J.C. (2020) 'Trump Slammed the W.H.O. Over Coronavirus. He's Not Alone', *The New York Times*, 8 April.

Heywood, A. (2007) *Politics*, 3rd edition, Basingstoke: Palgrave.

Hinata, Y. (2019) 'China Works to Turn Shenzhen into the New Hong Kong', *Nikkei Asian Review*, 19 August. Retrieved 22 July 2020, from https://asia.nikkei.com/Spotlight/Hong-Kong-protests/China-works-to-turn-Shenzhen-into-the-new-Hong-Kong.

HK01 (2018) 'Executive-led is both Principle and Source of Problem?' [in Chinese, 〈行政主導既是原則又是問題根源？〉], 21 March.

Ho, J. (2018) 'Behind a Tall Order: Goh Chok Tong Reflects on Succession and Politics Past and Present', *Chanel News Asia*, 2 December. Retrieved 22 July 2020, from www.channelnewsasia.com/news/singapore/goh-chok-tong-succession-politics-tall-order-biography-10983670.

Holliday, I. (2000) 'Productivist Welfare Capitalism: Social Policy in East Asia', *Political Studies*, Vol. 48, pp. 706–723.

Holzinger, K. and C. Knill (2005) 'Causes and Conditions of Cross-national Policy Convergence', *Journal of European Public Policy*, Vol. 12, No. 5, pp. 775–796.

Home Affairs Bureau (2006) *Consultation Document on Review on the Roles, Functions and Composition of District Council*, April, Hong Kong: Government Logistics Department, Retrieved 22 July 2020, from www.hab.gov.hk/file_manager/en/documents/references/papers_reports_others/District/Consultation_e.pdf.

Hong Kong Core Values campaign (n.d.) *Declaration*. Retrieved 22 July 2020, from https://web.archive.org/web/20040610052214/http://www.hkcorevalues.net:80/b5_declar.htm.

Hong Kong Council of Social Service (n.d.) *The Elderly Pension Protection* (in Chinese, 《香港退休保障資訊網》). Retrieved 22 July 2020, from www.pension.org.hk/改革出路/改革強積金制度.

Hong Kong Economic Journal (《信報》) (2018) 'Look Backing at "Double-Cha Proposal" Martin Lee Praises it as High Wisdom' [in Chinese, 〈回首「雙查方案」李柱銘讚高智慧〉], 1 November.

Hong Kong Food and Health Bureau (n.d.) *Voluntary Health Insurance Scheme*, Hong Kong: Food and Health Bureau. Retrieved 22 July 2020, from www.vhis.gov.hk/en/.

Hong Kong Government (1966) *Report of the Working Party on Local Administration*, Hong Kong: Government Printer.

Hong Kong Government (1974) *Annual Estimates of Expenditure and Revenue, 1974–75*, Hong Kong: Government Printer.

Hong Kong Government (1980) *Green Paper: A Pattern of District Administration in Hong Kong*, Hong Kong: Government Printer.

Hong Kong Government (1981) *White Paper: District Administration in Hong Kong*, Hong Kong: Government Printer.

Hong Kong Government (1984a) *Joint Declaration of the Government of the United Kingdom of Great Britain and Northern Ireland and the Government of the People's Republic of China on the Question of Hong Kong*. Hong Kong: now available from the Constitutional and Mainland Affairs Bureau. Retrieved 22 July 2020, from www.cmab.gov.hk/en/issues/jd2.htm.

Hong Kong Government (1984b) *Green Paper: The Further Development of Representative Government in Hong Kong*, Hong Kong: Government Printer.

Hong Kong Government (1984c) *White Paper: The Further Development of Representative Government in Hong Kong*, Hong Kong: Government Printer.

Hong Kong Government (1987) *Green Paper: The 1987 Review of Developments in Representative Government*, Hong Kong: Government Printer.

Hong Kong Government (1988) *White Paper: The Development of Representative Government: The Way Ahead*, Hong Kong: Government Printer.

Hong Kong Housing Authority (n.d.) *Number of Applications and Average Waiting Time for Public Rental Housing*. Retrieved 9 June 2020, from www.housingauthority.gov.hk/en/about-us/publications-and-statistics/prh-applications-average-waiting-time/index.html.

Hong Kong Mandatory Provident Fund Schemes Authority (2020) *Investment Performance of the MPF System in 2019*, February. Retrieved 22 July 2020, from www.mpfa.org.hk/eng/information_centre/publications/research_reports/files/Investment_Performance_of_the_MPF_System_in_2019-e.pdf.

Hong Kong Monetary Authority (2020) 'Exchange Fund Abridged Balance Sheet and Currency Board Account', press release, 29 April. Retrieved 22 July 2020, from www.hkma.gov.hk/eng/news-and-media/press-releases/2020/04/20200429-3/.

Hong Kong Public Opinion Research Institute (HKPORI) (2020a) *Credibility Rating of the Hong Kong News Media (9/1997–3/2020)*, Hong Kong: PORI. Retrieved 22 July 2020, from www.pori.hk/pop-poll/media-performance/j016.

Hong Kong Public Opinion Research Institute (HKPORI) (2020b) *Rating of Chief Justice Geoffrey Ma Tao-li*, Hong Kong: PORI. Retrieved 22 July 2020, from www.pori.hk/pop-poll/rule-of-law-indicator/g001/rating.

Hong Kong Public Opinion Research Institute (HKPORI) (n.d.) *People's Trust in the HKSAR Government*, Hong Kong: PORI. Retrieved 22 July 2020, from www.pori.hk/pop-poll/government-en/k001.html?lang=en.

Hong Kong Public Opinion Research Institute (HKPORI) (n.d.) *People's Trust in the Beijing Central Government*, Hong Kong: PORI. Retrieved 22 July 2020, from www.pori.hk/pop-poll/trust-and-confidence-indicators-en/k002.html?lang=en.

Hong Kong Public Opinion Research Institute (HKPORI) (n.d.) *Comparison between Ratings of Chris Patten, Tung Chee-hwa, Donald Tsang Yam-kuen, Leung Chun-ying and Carrie Lam*, Hong Kong: PORI. Retrieved 22 July 2020, from www.pori.hk/pop-poll/chief-executive-en/a-rating-combined.html?lang=en.

Hong Kong Public Opinion Research Institute (HKPORI) (n.d.) *Hypothetical Voting Results for Carrie Lam as the Chief Executive*, Hong Kong: PORI. Retrieved 22 July 2020, from www.pori.hk/pop-poll/chief-executive-en/a003-app.html?lang=en.

Hong Kong Public Opinion Research Institute (HKPORI) (n.d.) *Categorical Ethnic Identity: You would identify yourself as a Hongkonger/english/Chinese in Hong Kong/Hongkonger in China*, Hong Kong: PORI. Retrieved 22 July 2020, from www.pori.hk/pop-poll/ethnic-identity-en/q001.html?lang=en.

Hong Kong Science and Technology Parks Corporation (n.d.) *Hong Kong/Shenzhen Innovation and Technology Park*. Retrieved 22 July 2020, from www.hkstp.

org/en/our-stories/our-footprint/hong-kong-shenzhen-innovation-and-technology-park/.

Hong Kong Special Administrative Region Government (2013) *Let's Talk and Achieve Universal Suffrage—Method for Selecting the Chief Executive in 2017 and for Forming the Legislative Council in 2016: Consultative Document*, December, Hong Kong: Government Logistics Department.

Hong Kong Special Administrative Region Government (2014) *Report by the Chief Executive of the Hong Kong Special Administrative Region to the Standing Committee of the National People's Congress on Whether There is a Need to Amend the Methods for Selecting the Chief Executive of the Hong Kong Special Administrative Region in 2017 and for Forming the Legislative Council of the Hong Kong Special Administrative Region in 2016*, July, Hong Kong: Government Logistics Department.

Hong Kong Special Administrative Region Government (2015a) *2017 Seize the Opportunity—Method for Selecting the Chief Executive by Universal Suffrage: Consultation Document*, January, Hong Kong: Government Logistics Department.

Hong Kong Special Administrative Region Government (2015b) *2017 Make it Happen! Method for Selecting the Chief Executive by Universal Suffrage: Consultation Report and Proposals*, April, Hong Kong: Government Logistics Department.

Hong Kong Special Administrative Region Government (2017) '20 Years of Growth and Progress: The Facts', *20th Anniversary Fact Sheets Series*, Hong Kong: Information Services Department.

Hong Kong Special Administrative Region Government (2020) *The Law of the People's Republic of China on Safeguarding National Security in the Hong Kong Special Administrative Region*, G.N. (E.) 72 of 2020, July, Retrieved 22 July 2020, from www.elegislation.gov.hk/fwddoc/hk/a406/eng_translation_(a406)_en.pdf.

Hong Kong Special Administrative Region Government (n.d.) *Publication on the 15th Anniversary of Reunification*, Chapter 1. Retrieved June 2019, from www.basiclaw.gov.hk/en/publications/book/15anniversary_reunification_ch1_1.pdf.

Hong Kong Special Administrative Region Government (n.d.) *The Basic Law of the Hong Kong Special Administrative Region of the People's Republic of China*. Retrieved 22 July 2020, from www.basiclaw.gov.hk/en/basiclaw/index.html.

Hong Kong Tourism Board (2019) *Monthly Report—Visitor Arrival Statistics: December 2018*. Retrieved 22 July 2020, from https://partnernet.hktb.com/filemanager/intranet/pm/VisitorArrivalStatistics/ViS_Stat_E/VisE_2018/Tourism%20Statistics%2012%202018_R1.pdf.

Hong Kong Tourism Board (2020) *Monthly Report—Visitor Arrival Statistics: December 2019*. Retrieved 22 July 2020, from https://partnernet.hktb.com/

filemanager/intranet/pm/VisitorArrivalStatistics/ViS_Stat_E/VisE_2019/ Tourism%20Statistics%2012%202019.pdf.

Hood, C. (1976) *The Limits of Administration*, London: John Wiley & Sons.

Hood, C. (1983) *The Tools of Government*, Hong Kong: Macmillan.

Hood, C. (1991) 'A Public Management for All Seasons?' *Public Administration*, Vol. 69, No. 1, pp. 3–19.

Hood, C. (1996a) 'Beyond "Progressivism": A New "Global Paradigm" in Public Management?' *International Journal of Public Administration*, Vol. 19, No. 2, pp. 151–178.

Hood, C. (1996b) 'Exploring Variations in Public Management Reform of the 1980s', in H. Bekke, J.L. Perry, and T.A.J. Toonen (eds) *Civil Service Systems in Comparative Perspective*, Bloomington: Indiana University Press, pp. 268–287.

Hood, C. (2002) 'Control, Bargains, and Cheating: The Politics of Public-Service Reform', *Journal of Public Administration Research and Theory*, Vol. 12, No. 3, pp. 309–332.

Hood, C. (2010) 'Can We? Administrative Limits Revisited', *Public Administration Review*, Vol. 70, No. 4, pp. 527–534.

Hood, C. and M. Jackson (1991) *Administrative Argument*, Aldershot: Dartmouth.

Hood, C. and M. Lodge (2006) *The Politics of Public Service Bargains: Reward, Competency, Loyalty and Blame*, Oxford: Oxford University Press.

Hook, L. (2018) 'Populism vs Paris', *Financial Times*, 3 December.

Hopkins, K. (ed) (1971) *Hong Kong: The Industrial Colony: A Political, Social and Economic Survey*, Hong Kong: Oxford University Press.

Hoppe, R. (2005) 'Rethinking the Puzzles of the Science-Policy Nexus: From Knowledge Utilization and Science Technology Studies to Types of Boundary Arrangements', *Poiesis Prax*, Vol. 3, No. 3, pp. 199–215.

House of Commons Political and Constitutional Reform Committee (2011) *Role and Powers of the Prime Minister: Written Evidence*, London: British Parliament. Retrieved 22 July 2020, from https://publications.parliament.uk/ pa/cm201012/cmselect/cmpolcon/writev/842/842.pdf.

Howlett, M. and M. Ramesh (1995) *Studying Public Policy: Policy Cycles and Policy Subsystems*, Toronto: Oxford University Press.

Hu, J.T. (胡錦濤) (2007) 'Toast at Welcoming Dinner Hosted by the Government of the Hong Kong Special Administrative Region' [in Chinese, 〈胡錦濤在香港特別行政區政府歡迎晚宴上的講話〉], 30 June, Beijing: State Council of the People's Republic of China. Retrieved 22 July 2020, Retrieved from www.gov. cn/ldhd/2012-06/30/content_2174363.htm.

Huaxia Jingwei Network (《華夏經緯網》) (2017) 'Deng Xiaoping Put Forward "One Country, Two Systems"' [in Chinese, 〈鄧小平提出「一國兩制」〉], 22 November. Retrieved 22 July 2020, from www.huaxia.com/thpl/ tbch/tbchwz/11/5546777.html.

Hughes, R. (1968) *Hong Kong: Borrowed Place, Borrowed Time*, London: Andre Deutsch.

Hui, P.K. and K.C. Lau (2015) '"Living in Truth" versus Realpolitik: Limitations and Potentials of the Umbrella Movement', *Journal of Inter-Asia Cultural Studies*, Vol. 16, No. 3, pp. 348–366.

Humphrey, B. (2016) 'Russian Exceptionalism: A Comparative Perspective', *Politics in Central Europe*, Vol. 12, No. 1, pp. 9–20.

Huntington, S.P. (1991) *The Third Wave: Democratization in the Late Twentieth Century*, Norman: University of Oklahoma Press.

Huntington, S.P. (1993) 'The Clash of Civilizations?' *Foreign Affairs*, Summer.

Huntington, S.P. (1996) *The Clash of Civilizations and The Remaking of World Order*, New York: Simon & Schuster.

Huque, S., G. Lee, and A.B.L. Cheung (1998) *The Civil Service in Hong Kong: Continuity and Change*, Hong Kong: Hong Kong University Press.

Ikenberry, G.J. (1990) 'The International Spread of Privatization Policies: Inducements, Learning, and "Policy Bandwagoning"', in E.N. Suleiman and J. Waterburry (eds) *The Political Economy of Public Sector Reform and Privatization*, Boulder, CO: Westview Press, pp. 88–110.

Immigration Department (n.d.) *Introduction of Admission Schemes for Talent, Professionals and Entrepreneurs*, Hong Kong: Immigration Department. Retrieved 22 July 2020, from www.immd.gov.hk/eng/useful_information/admission-schemes-talents-professionals-entrepreneurs.html.

Independent Expert Panel (2014) *Report of the Hong Kong Section of the Guangzhou-Shenzhen-Hong Kong Express Rail Link Independent Expert Panel*, December. Retrieved 22 July 2020, from www.gov.hk/en/theme/iep-xrl/pdf/IEP-report.pdf.

Independent Police Complaints Council (IPCC) (2020) *A Thematic Study by the IPCC on the Public Order Events arising from the Fugitive Offenders Bill since June 2019 and the Police Actions in Response*, Hong Kong: IPCC. Retrieved 22 July 2020, from www.ipcc.gov.hk/en/public_communications/ipcc_thematic_study_report.html

Information Office, State Council of the People's Republic of China (2014) *The Practice of the 'One Country, Two Systems' Policy in the Hong Kong Special Administrative Region*, 10 June. Retrieved 22 July 2020, from https://web.archive.org/web/20141008210149/http://news.xinhuanet.com/english/china/2014-06/10/c_133396891.htm.

Information Services Department (2005) 'Appointments to the Commission on Strategic Development', press release, 15 November. Retrieved 22 July 2020, from www.info.gov.hk/gia/general/200511/15/P200511150128.htm.

Information Services Department (2012a) 'Opening Remarks by CE-elect', press release, 25 March. Retrieved 22 July 2020, from www.info.gov.hk/gia/general/201203/25/P201203250444.htm.

Information Services Department (2012b) '2012 Electoral Methods Package Published', press release, 14 April. Retrieved 22 July 2020, from www.news.gov.hk/isd/ebulletin/en/category/administration/100414/html/100414en01002.htm.

Information Services Department (2012c) 'SFST's Speech at the Asia Financial Consumer Protection Roundtable', press release, 14 December. Retrieved 22 July 2020, from www.info.gov.hk/gia/general/201212/14/P201212140555.htm.

Information Services Department (2012d) 'Government Reaffirms its Strict Enforcement of the "Zero Quota" Policy', press release, 28 December. Retrieved 22 July 2020, from www.info.gov.hk/gia/general/201212/28/P201212280415.htm.

Information Services Department (2015) 'LegCo Vetoes Reform Package', press release, 18 June. Retrieved 22 July 2020, from www.news.gov.hk/en/categories/admin/html/2015/06/20150618_160738.shtml.

Information Services Department (2016a) 'Government Implements New Agriculture Policy', press release, 14 January. Retrieved 22 July 2020, from www.info.gov.hk/gia/general/201601/14/P201601140558.htm.

Information Services Department (2016b) 'HK Interests Top Gov't Priority', press release, 5 April. Retrieved 22 July 2020, from www.news.gov.hk/en/categories/admin/html/2016/04/20160405_101940.shtml.

Information Services Department (2017) 'One Man, One Vote Good for HK', press release, 5 July. Retrieved 22 July 2020, from www.news.gov.hk/en/categories/admin/html/2017/07/20170705_104516.shtml.

Information Services Department (2018a) '2016 Population By-census Thematic Report: Persons Living in Subdivided Units published', press release, 18 January. Retrieved 22 July 2020, from www.info.gov.hk/gia/general/201801/18/P2018011800595.htm.

Information Services Department (2018b) 'CE Speaking to the Media' [in Chinese,〈行政長官北京會見傳媒談話全文〉], press release, 15 August. Retrieved 22 July 2020, from www.info.gov.hk/gia/general/201808/15/P2018081500946.htm.

Information Services Department (2019a) 'FS Announces Measures to Support Enterprises and Residents', press release, 15 August. Retrieved July 22 2020, from www.info.gov.hk/gia/general/201908/15/P2019081500648.htm.

Information Services Department (2019b) *Hong Kong: The Facts—Civil Service*, September. Retrieved 22 July 2020, from www.gov.hk/en/about/abouthk/factsheets/docs/civil_service.pdf.

Information Services Department (2020) 'Written Reply by the Acting Secretary for Financial Services and the Treasury, Joseph Chan, in the Legislative Council (on LCQ13: Offshore Renminbi Businesses)', press release, 15 January. Retrieved 22 July 2020, from www.info.gov.hk/gia/general/202001/15/P2020011500318.htm.

Innovation and Technology Bureau (2018) *Innovation Hong Kong*, September, Hong Kong: Government Logistics Department. Retrieved 22 July 2020, from www.itb.gov.hk/en/publications/InnovationHK.pdf.

International Monetary Fund (IMF) (2005) *The IMF's Approach to Promoting Good Governance and Combating Corruption—A Guide*, 20 June.

International Monetary Fund (IMF) (2019) 'IMF Executive Board Concludes 2019 Article IV Consultation Discussions with the People's Republic of China—Hong Kong Special Administrative Region', press release No. 19/485, 30 December. Retrieved 22 July 2020, from www.imf.org/en/News/Articles/2019/12/26/pr19485-hksar-imf-executive-board-concludes-2019-article-iv-consultation-discussions.

James, O. and M. Lodge (2003) 'The Limitations of "Policy Transfer" and "Lesson Drawing" for Public Policy Research', *Political Studies Review*, Vol. 1, No. 2, pp. 179–193.

Jeannot, G. and P. Bezes (2016) 'Mapping the Use of Public Management Tools in European Public Administration', in G. Hammerschmid, S. Van de Walle, R. Andrews, and P. Bezes (eds) *Public Administration Reforms in Europe: The View From The Top*, Cheltenham: Edward Elgar, pp. 219–230.

Jessop, B. (1990) *State Theory: Putting Capitalist States in Their Place*, Cambridge: Polity Press.

Jessop, B. and N.L. Shum (2000) 'An Entrepreneurial City in Action: Hong Kong's Emerging Strategies in and for (Inter)Urban Competition', *Urban Studies*, Vol. 37, No. 12, pp. 2287–2313.

Ji, P.F. (姬鵬飛) (1990) *Statement on The Basic Law of the Hong Kong Special Administrative Region of the People's Republic of China (Draft) and Related Documents* [in Chinese, 《關於中華人民共和國香港特別行政區基本法（草案）及其有關文件的說明》], at the 3rd Session of the 7th National People's Congress, 28 March, Beijing.

Jiang, S.G. (強世功) (2017a) 'The Centre's Mode of Governing Hong Kong Wholly Entering the Xi Jinping Era' [in Chinese, 〈中央治港全面進入「習近平時代」〉], *Ming Pao* (《明報》), 26 October.

Jiang, S.G. (強世功) (2017b) 'Thought of Xi Jinping: The Re-Sinicization of Marxism' [in Chinese, 〈習近平思想：馬克斯主義的再次中國化〉], *Ming Pao* (《明報》), 30 October.

Jing, Y. (2017) 'Creative Incrementalism: Governance Reforms in China Since 1978', *Chinese Political Science Review*, Vol. 2, No. 1, pp 56–68.

Johnson, C. (1982) *MITI and the Japanese Miracle*, Stanford: Stanford University Press.

Jones, C. (1993) 'The Pacific Challenge: Confucian Welfare States', in C. Jones (ed) *New Perspectives on the Welfare State in Europe*, London: Routledge, pp. 198–217.

Jones, G.W. (1964) 'The Prime Minister's Power', *Parliamentary Affairs*, Vol. 18, No. 2, pp. 167–185.

Jones, G.W. (2016) *The Power of the Prime Minister: 50 Years On*, London: The Constitution Society.

Kaufmann, D. and A. Kraay (2002) 'Growth Without Governance', *Economia*, Fall. Retrieved 22 July 2020, from https://sites.hks.harvard.edu/fs/pnorris/Acrobat/stm103%20articles/Kaufman%20and%20Kraay%20Nov2002.pdf.

Kaufmann, D. and A. Kraay (2003) 'Governance and Growth: Causality which way? Evidence for the World, in brief', February, Retrieved 22 July 2020, from http://siteresources.worldbank.org/INTWBIGOVANTCOR/Resources/growthgov_synth.pdf.

Khanna, P. (2019a) *The Future Is Asian*, New York: Simon & Schuster.

Khanna, P. (2019b) 'How Asia is Shaping the World's Future', *Asia Society*, 28 January. Retrieved 22 July 2020, from https://asiasociety.org/blog/asia/how-asia-shaping-worlds-future.

Khosla, A. (2000) 'State and Economy: Some Observations and Inferences from the Japanese Experience', in K.E. Brødsgaard and S. Young (eds) *State Capacity in East Asia: Japan, Taiwan, China and Vietnam*, New York: Oxford University Press, pp. 37–60.

King, A.Y.C. (1980) 'An Institutional Response to Corruption: The ICAC of Hong Kong', in C.K. Leung, J.W. Cushman, and G. Wang (eds) *Hong Kong: Dilemmas of Growth*, Hong Kong and Canberra: Centre of Asian Studies, University of Hong Kong and the Research School of Pacific Studies, Australia National University, pp. 115–142.

King, A.Y.C. (1981) 'Administrative Absorption of Politics in Hong Kong: Emphasis on the Grass Roots Level', in A.Y.C. King and R.P.L. Lee (eds) *Social Life and Development in Hong Kong*, Hong Kong: Chinese University Press, pp. 127–146.

King, A.Y.C. and R.P. Lee (eds) (1981) *Social Life and Development in Hong Kong*, Hong Kong: Chinese University Press.

Kissinger, H.A. (1979) *The White House Years*, New York: Little, Brown and Company.

Klein, S. and C.S. Lee (2019) 'Towards a Dynamic Theory of Civil Society: The Politics of Forward and Backward Infiltration', *Sociological Theory*, Vol. 37, No. 1, pp. 62–88.

Knupfer, S.M., V. Pokotilo, and J. Woetzel (2018) *Elements of Success: Urban Transportation Systems of 24 Global Cities*, New York: McKinsey & Company. Retrieved 22 July 2020, from www.mckinsey.com/~/media/McKinsey/Business%20Functions/Sustainability/Our%20Insights/Elements%20of%20success%20Urban%20transportation%20systems%20of%2024%20global%20cities/Urban-transportation-systems_e-versions.ashx.

Kong, K. (2019) 'Human Rights Activist Scholars and Social Change in Hong Kong: Reflections on the Umbrella Movement and Beyond', *The International Journal of Human Rights*, Vol. 23. No. 6, pp. 899–914.

Konings, M. (2018) 'Against Exceptionalism: The Legitimacy of the Neoliberal Age', *Globalizations*, Vol. 15, No. 7, pp. 1007–1019.

Kooiman, J. (1993) 'Governance and Governability: Using Complexity, Dynamics and Diversity', in J. Kooiman (ed) *Modern Governance: New Government-Society Interactions*, London: Sage, pp. 35–48.

Kraar, L. (1995) 'The Death of Hong Kong', *Fortune*, 26 June. Retrieved 22 July 2020, from https://money.cnn.com/magazines/fortune/fortune_archive/1995/06/26/203948/index.htm.

Krugman, P. (1994) 'The Myth of Asia's Miracle', *Foreign Affairs*, November/December.

Krznaric, R. (2019) 'Why we Need to Reinvent Democracy for the Long-term', *BBC News,* 19 March. Retrieved 22 July 2020, from www.bbc.com/future/story/20190318-can-we-reinvent-democracy-for-the-long-term.

Ku, A.S.M. (2018) 'Identity as Politics: Contesting the Local, the National and the Global', in T.L. Lui, S.W.K. Chiu, and R. Yep (eds) *Routledge Handbook of Contemporary Hong Kong*, London: Routledge, pp. 451–461.

Ku, S.F. (古星輝) (1985) 'Preliminary Suggestions on a Blueprint for the Future Basic Law' [in Chinese, 〈未來基本法藍圖芻議〉], *Wide Angle* (《廣角鏡》), December.

Kwon, H.J. (1997) 'Beyond European Welfare Regimes: Comparative Perspectives on East Asian Welfare Systems', *Journal of Social Policy*, Vol. 26, No. 4, pp. 467–784.

Kwon, H.J. (1998) 'Democracy and the Politics of Social Welfare: A Comparative Analysis of Welfare Systems in East Asia', in R. Goodman, G. White, and H.J. Kwon (eds) *The East Asian Welfare Model: Welfare Orientalism and the State*, London: Routledge, pp. 27–74.

Kwong, Y.H. (2018) 'Political Repression in a Sub-National Hybrid Regime: The PRC's Governing Strategies in Hong Kong', *Contemporary Politics*, Vol. 24, No. 4, pp. 361–378.

Labour Department (2020) *Annual Report 2019*. Retrieved on 22 July 2020, www.labour.gov.hk/eng/public/iprd/2019/chapter5.html

Lam, C. (2017) *The Chief Executive's 2017 Policy Address: We Connect for Hope and Happiness*, Policy address by the Chief Executive to the Legislative Council, 11 October, Hong Kong: Government Logistics Department. Retrieved 22 July 2020, from www.policyaddress.gov.hk/2017/eng/pdf/PA2017.pdf.

Lam, C. (2018) *The Chief Executive's 2018 Policy Address: Striving Ahead, Rekindling Hopes*, Policy address by the Chief Executive to the Legislative Council, 10 October, Hong Kong: Government Logistics Department. Retrieved 22 July 2020, from www.policyaddress.gov.hk/2018/eng/pdf/PA2018.pdf.

Lam, C. (2019) *The Chief Executive's 2019 Policy Address: Treasure Hong Kong: Our Home*, Policy address by the Chief Executive to the Legislative

Council, 16 October, Hong Kong: Government Logistics Department. Retrieved 22 July 2020, from www.policyaddress.gov.hk/2019/eng/pdf/ PA2019.pdf.

Lam, J. (2020) 'Hong Kong Protests: One Year On, with the National Security Law Looming, has the Anti-government Movement Lost?' *South China Morning Post*, 8 June.

Lam, J. and Z. Ibrahim (eds) (2020) *Rebel City: Hong Kong's Year of Water and Fire*, Hong Kong and Singapore: South China Morning Post and World Scientific Publishing.

Lam, W.M. and C.Y. Lam (2013) 'China's United Front Work in Civil Society: The Case of Hong Kong', *International Journal of China Studies*, Vol. 4, No. 3, pp. 301–325.

Lam, W.W.L. (2018) 'At China's "Two Sessions", Xi Jinping Restructures Party-state to Further Consolidate Power', *China Brief* (The Jamestown Foundation), Vol. 18, No. 5, 26 March. Retrieved 22 July 2020, from https://jamestown. org/wp-content/uploads/2018/03/PDF.pdf?x88024.

Lamont, M. and M. Fournier (1992) 'Introduction', in M. Lamont and M. Fournier (eds) *Cultivating Differences: Symbolic Boundaries and the Making of Inequality*, Chicago and London: University of Chicago Press, pp. 1–17.

Lan, Z. (2000) 'Understanding China's Administrative Reform', *Public Administration Quarterly*, Vol. 24, No. 1, pp. 437–468.

Lane, J.-E. (2013) 'The Principal-Agent Approach to Politics: Policy Implementation and Public Policy-Making', *Open Journal of Political Science*, Vol. 3, No. 2, pp. 85–89. Retrieved 22 July 2020, from https://file.scirp.org/ pdf/OJPS_2013042915421321.pdf.

Lane, J.-E. and S. Ersson (2000) *The New Institutional Politics: Performance and Outcomes*, London: Routledge.

Lasswell, H.D. (1936) *Politics: Who Gets What, When, How*, New York: Whittlesey House.

Lau, C.K. (1997) *Hong Kong's Colonial Legacy*, Hong Kong: Chinese University Press.

Lau, S.K. (1982a) 'Local Administrative Reform in Hong Kong: Promises and Limitations', *Asian Survey*, Vol. 22, No. 9, pp. 858–873.

Lau, S.K. (1982b) *Society and Politics in Hong Kong*, Hong Kong: Chinese University Press.

Lau, S.K. (1987) *Decolonization without Independence: The Unfinished Political Reforms of the Hong Kong Government*, Occasional Papers No. 19, Hong Kong: Centre for Hong Kong Studies, Chinese University of Hong Kong.

Lau, S.K. (1994) 'Hong Kong's "Ungovernability" in the Twilight of Colonial Rule', in Z.L. Lin and T.W. Robinson (eds) *The Chinese and Their Future: Beijing, Taipei, and Hong Kong*, Washington, D.C.: AEI Press, pp. 287–314.

Lau, S.K. (劉兆佳) (2000) 'The Executive-dominant System of Governance: Theory and Practice' [in Chinese, 〈行政主導的政治體制：設想與現實〉], in

S.K. Lau (ed) *Blueprint for the 21st Century Hong Kong* (《香港21世紀藍圖》), Hong Kong: Chinese University Press, pp. 1–36.

Lau, S.K. (2002a) 'Hong Kong's Partial Democracy under Stress', in Y.M. Yeung (ed) *New Challenges for Development and Modernization: Hong Kong and the Asia-Pacific Region in the New Millennium*, Hong Kong: Chinese University Press, pp. 181–205.

Lau, S.K. (2002b) 'Tung Chee-hwa's Governing Strategy: The Shortfall in Politics', in S.K. Lau (ed) *The First Tung Chee-hwa Administration: The First Five Years of The Hong Kong Special Administrative Region*, Hong Kong: Chinese University Press, pp. 1–39.

Lau, S.K. (2007) 'In Search of a New Political Order', in Y.M. Yeung (ed) *The First Decade: The Hong Kong SAR in Retrospective and Introspective Perspectives*, Hong Kong: Chinese University Press, pp. 130–159.

Lau, S.K. (劉兆佳) (2013a) *The Governance and New Regime Building of Hong Kong SAR Fifteen Years Since Reunification* [in Chinese,《回歸十五年以來香港的特區管治及新政權建設》], Hong Kong: Commercial Press (商務印書館).

Lau, S.K. (劉兆佳) (2013b) *Hong Kong Politics After Reunification* [in Chinese,《回歸後的香港政治》], Hong Kong: Commercial Press (商務印書館).

Lau, S.K. (劉兆佳) (2020) *Thinking About the Future of Hong Kong under One Country, Two Systems* [in Chinese,《思考香港一國兩制的未來》], Hong Kong: Commercial Press (商務印書館).

Law, W.S. (2009) *Collaborative Colonial Power: The Making of the Hong Kong Chinese*, Hong Kong: Hong Kong University Press.

Law, W.S. (羅永生) (2015) 'Decolonization in the Cold War: Comment on Hong Kong's Movement for Chinese as Official Language' [in Chinese,〈冷戰中的解殖: 香港「爭取中文成為法定語文運動」評析〉], *Thinking Hong Kong* (《思想香港》), Vol. 6, pp. 1–20.

Law, W.W. (2004) 'Globalization and Citizenship Education in Hong Kong and Taiwan', *Comparative Education Review*, Vol. 48, No. 3, pp. 253–273.

Lecours, A. and J. Dupré (2018) 'The Emergence and Transformation of Self-Determination Claims in Hong Kong and Catalonia: A Historical Institutionalist Perspective', *Ethnicities*, Vol. 20, No. 1, pp. 3–23.

Lee, E.W.Y. and R.L.K. Yeung (2017) 'The "Principal Officials Accountability System": Its Underdevelopment as a System of Ministerial Government', *Asian Pacific Journal of Public Administration*, Vol. 39, No. 2, pp. 120–134.

Lee, E.W.Y., E.Y.M. Chan, J.C.W. Chan, P.T.Y. Cheung, W.F. Lam, and W.M. Lam (2013) *Public Policymaking in Hong Kong: Civic Engagement and State-Society Relations in a Semi-Democracy*, London: Routledge.

Lee, J.M. and W. Lu (2018) 'These are the World's Healthiest Nations', *Bloomberg*, 19 September. Retrieved 22 July 2020, from www.bloomberg.com/news/articles/2018-09-19/u-s-near-bottom-of-health-index-hong-kong-and-singapore-at-top.

Lee, K.M., B.H.P. To, and K.M. Yu (2014) 'The New Paradox of Thrift: Financialisation, Retirement Protection, and Income Polarisation in Hong Kong', *China Perspectives*, No. 1, pp. 15–24.

Lee, P.K. (李彭廣) (2012) *Governing Hong Kong: Lessons from Disclosed British Archival Records* [in Chinese, 《管治香港：英國解密檔案的啟示》], Hong Kong: Oxford University Press.

Lee, W.Y. (1999) 'Governing Post-colonial Hong Kong: Institutional Incongruity, Governance Crisis and Authoritarianism', *Asian Survey*, Vol. 39, No. 6, pp. 940–959.

Legislative Council Library (2011a) *Royal Instructions*, InfoPack No. LC03/2011-12, Hong Kong: Legislative Council. Retrieved 22 July 2020, from www.legco.gov.hk/general/english/library/infopacks/yr11-12/1112infopacks-lc-03-e.pdf.

Legislative Council Library (2011b) *Letters Patent*, InfoPack No. LC04/2011-12, Hong Kong: Legislative Council. Retrieved 22 July 2020, from www.legco.gov.hk/general/english/library/infopacks/yr11-12/1112infopacks-lc-04-e.pdf.

Legislative Council (2017) *Co-operation Arrangement between the Mainland and the Hong Kong Special Administrative Region on the Establishment of the Port at the West Kowloon Station of the Guangzhou-Shenzhen-Hong Kong Express Rail Link for Implementing Co-location Arrangement*, CB(4)441/17-18(04), Hong Kong: Legislative Council. Retrieved 22 July 2020, from www.legco.gov.hk/yr17-18/english/panels/tp/papers/tpcb4-441-4-e.pdf.

Legislative Council (n.d.) *Changes in Membership of the Sixth Legislative Council (2016–2020)*, Hong Kong: Legislative Council. Retrieved 22 July 2020, from www.legco.gov.hk/general/english/members/yr16-20/notes.htm

Legislative Council (n.d.) *A Companion to the History, Rules and Practices of the Legislative Council of the Hong Kong Special Administrative Region*, Hong Kong: Legislative Council. Retrieved 22 July 2020, from www.legco.gov.hk/general/english/procedur/companion/chapter_1/chapter_1.html.

Lemahieu, H. (2019) 'Five Big Takeaways from the 2019 Asia Power Index', *The Interpreter* (Lowy Institute), 29 May. Retrieved 22 July 2020, from www.lowyinstitute.org/the-interpreter/power-shifts-fevered-times-2019-asia-power-index.

Lepore, J. (2020) 'The Last Time Democracy Almost Died', *The New Yorker*, 27 January.

Lethbridge, H.J. (1978) *Hong Kong: Stability and Change*, Hong Kong: Oxford University Press.

Leung, A.K.C. (2002) *The 2002–03 Budget*, Speech by the Financial Secretary moving the Second Reading of the Appropriation Bill 2002 at the Legislative Council, 6 March, Hong Kong: Printer Department.

Leung, A.K.C. (2003) *The 2003–04 Budget*, Speech by the Financial Secretary moving the Second Reading of the Appropriation Bill 2003 at the Legislative Council, 5 March, Hong Kong: Printer Department.

Leung, C.Y. (2016) *The 2016 Policy Address: Innovate for the Economy, Improve Livelihood, Foster Harmony, Share Prosperity*, Policy address by the Chief Executive to the Legislative Council, 13 January, Hong Kong.

Leung, C.K., J.W. Cushman, and G.W. Wang (eds) (1980) *Hong Kong: Dilemmas of Growth*, Hong Kong and Canberra: Centre of Asian Studies, University of Hong Kong, and the Research School of Pacific Studies, Australia National University, Canberra.

Leung, K. (2021) 'Hong Kong Leader Carrie Lam Sets Sights on "Improving" City's Education Sector, Its Media, and Training of Civil Servants after Overhaul of Electoral System', *South China Morning Post*, 3 April. Retrieved 5 April 2021, from www.scmp.com/news/hong-kong/politics/article/3128243/hong-kong-leader-carrie-lam-sets-sights-improving-citys.

Levett, C. and S. Clarke (2019) 'Theresa May: A Political Obituary in Five Charts', *The Guardian*, 7 June. Retrieved 22 July 2020, from www.theguardian.com/politics/2019/jun/07/theresa-may-a-political-obituary-in-five-charts.

Levitsky, S. and D. Ziblatt (2018) *How Democracies Die*, New York: Crown.

Li, A. (2020) 'China-enacted National Security Law must be Consistent with Hong Kong Legal Principles', *South China Morning Post*, 2 June.

Li, Chief Justice, Mr Justice Bokhary PJ, Mr Justice Chan PJ, Mr Justice Ribeiro PJ, and Sir Anthony Mason NPJ (2005) *Judgement on Secretary for Justice (for and on behalf of the Government of Hong Kong SAR) v Lau Kwok Fai Bernard, The Government of Hong Kong SAR v Michael Reid Scott, and Secretary for Justice (for and on behalf of the Government of Hong Kong SAR) v Michael Reid Scott*, FACV No. 15 of 2004, FACV No. 16 of 2004, and FACV No. 8 of 2005, 13 July, Court of Final Appeal of the Hong Kong Special Administrative Region.

Li, L.C. (1997) 'Towards a Non-zero-sum Interactive Framework of Spatial Politics: The Case of Centre-Province in Contemporary China', *Political Studies*, Vol. 45, No. 1, pp. 49–65.

Li, L.C. (2010) 'Central-local Relations in the People's Republic of China: Trends, Processes and Impacts for Policy Implementation', *Public Administration and Development*, Vol. 30, No. 3, pp. 177–190.

Lijphart, A. (1999) *Patterns of Democracy: Government Forms and Performance in Thirty-six Countries*, New York: Routledge.

Lilla, M. (2016) *The Shipwrecked Mind: On Political Reaction*, New York: New York Review of Books.

Lin, T., R.P. Lee, and U.E. Simonis (eds) (1979) *Hong Kong: Economic, Social and Political Studies in Development*, New York: M.E. Sharpe.

Lindblom, C.E. (1959) 'The Science of "Muddling Through"', *Public Administration Review*, Vol. 19, No. 2, pp. 79–88.

Linder, S.H. and B.G. Peters (1998) 'The Study of Policy Instruments: Four Schools of Thought', in B.G. Peters and F.K.M. van Nispen (eds) *Public*

Policy Instruments: Evaluating the Tools of Public Administration, Cheltenham: Edward Elgar, pp. 33–45.

Lipset, S.M. (1993) 'Pacific Divide: American Exceptionalism-Japanese Uniqueness', *International Journal of Public Opinion Research*, Vol. 5, No. 2, pp. 121–166.

Lipset, S.M. (1996) *American Exceptionalism: A Double-edged Sword*, New York: W.W. Norton.

Lo, C.S.S. (1990) *Public Budgeting in Hong Kong: An Incremental Decision-making Approach*, Hong Kong: Writers' and Publishers' Cooperative.

Lo, S.H. (1997) *The Politics of Democratization in Hong Kong*, London: Palgrave Macmillan.

Lo, S.S.H. (2008) *The Dynamics of Beijing-Hong Kong Relations*, Hong Kong: Hong Kong University Press.

Loh, C. and R. Cullen (2018) *No Third Person: Rewriting the Hong Kong Story*, Hong Kong: Abbreviated Press.

Loney, S.L. (2009) 'Murakami, in Trademark Obscurity, Explains Why He Accepted Jerusalem Award', *The Jerusalem Post*, 15 February. Retrieved on 22 July 2020, from www.jpost.com/arts-and-culture/books/murakami-in-trademark-obscurity-explains-why-he-accepted-jerusalem-award.

Louie, K. (2010) 'Introduction—Hong Kong on the Move: Creating Global Cultures', in K. Louie (ed) *Hong Kong Culture: Word and Image*, Hong Kong: Hong Kong University Press, pp. 1–8.

Lu Ping (魯平) (2009) *Lu Ping's Oral Recollections on Hong Kong's Return* [in Chinese, 《魯平口述香港回歸》], Hong Kong: Joint Publishing (HK) (三聯出版).

Luce, E. (2019) 'Ill Winds: Saving Democracy from Russian Rage, Chinese Ambition, and American Complacency, by Larry Diamond', book review, *Financial Times*, 24 June. Retrieved 22 July 2020, from www.ft.com/content/4a305392-90f6-11e9-aea1-2b1d33ac3271.

Lugard, F.J.D. (1970) *Political Memoranda: Revision of the Instructions to Political Officers on Subjects Chiefly Political and Administrative, 1913–1918*, 3rd edition, London: Cass.

Lui, T.L. (2014) 'Fading Opportunities: Hong Kong in the Context of Regional Integration', *China Perspectives*, No. 1, pp. 35–42.

Lui, T.L. and S.W.K. Chiu (2007) 'Governance Crisis in Post-1997 Hong Kong: A Political Economy Perspective', *The China Review*, Vol. 7, No. 2, pp. 1–34.

Ma, J. (2018) 'Speech presented in the 199th Congregation of The University of Hong Kong for the award Doctor of Social Sciences *honoris causa*'. Retrieved 22 July 2020, from www4.hku.hk/hongrads/index.php/graduate_speech_detail/340/97.

Ma, N. (2007a) *Political Development in Hong Kong: State, Political Society and Civil Society*, Hong Kong: Hong Kong University Press.

Ma, N. (2007b) 'Political Parties and Elections', in W.M. Lam, P.L.T. Lui, W. Wong, and I. Holliday (eds) *Contemporary Hong Kong Politics: Governance in the Post-1997 Era*, Hong Kong: Hong Kong University Press, pp. 117–134.

Ma, N. (2011) 'Value Changes and Legitimacy Crisis in Post-industrial Hong Kong', *Asian Survey*, Vol. 51, No. 4, pp. 683–712.

Ma, N. (馬嶽) (2012) *Oral History of Hong Kong's Democratic Movement during the Eighties* [in Chinese,《香港80年代民主運動口述歷史》], Hong Kong: City University of Hong Kong Press.

Ma, N. (2015) 'The Rise of "Anti-China" Sentiments in Hong Kong and the 2012 Legislative Council Elections', *The China Review*, Vol. 15, No. 1, pp. 39–66.

Ma, N. (2017a) 'From Executive Dominance to Fragmented Authority: An Institutional and Political Analysis', in B.C.H. Fong and T.L. Lui (eds) *Hong Kong 20 Years after the Handover: Emerging Social and Institutional Fractures after 1997*, London: Palgrave, pp. 21–43.

Ma, N. (馬嶽) (2017b) 'Weak State and Weak Society' [in Chinese,〈弱國家和弱社會的蹉跎〉], *Ming Pao* (《明報》), 21 August.

Macleod, H. (1992) 'My Six Months Walking a Financial Tightrope', *South China Morning Post*, 9 February.

Macleod, H. (1995) *The 1995–96 Budget*, Speech by the Financial Secretary moving the Second Reading of the Appropriation Bill 1995, 1 March, Hong Kong: Government Printer.

Mahbubani, K. (2008) *The New Asian Hemisphere: The Irresistible Shift of Global Power to the East*, New York: Public Affairs.

Mahoney, J. (2000) 'Path Dependence in Historical Sociology', *Theory and Society*, Vol. 29, No. 4, pp. 507–548.

Mai, J. and W. Zheng (2019) 'China's Communist Party Elite Wrap Up Meeting with Pledge to Safeguard National Security in Hong Kong', *South China Morning Post*, 1 November.

Majone, G. (1997) 'From the Positive to the Regulatory State: Causes and Consequences of Changes in the Mode of Governance', *Journal of Public Policy*, Vol. 17, No. 2, pp. 139–67.

Manavis, S. (2020) 'Covid-19 has Caused a Major Spike in Anti-Chinese and Anti-Semitic Hate Speech', *New Statesman*, 29 April. Retrieved 22 July 2020, from www.newstatesman.com/science-tech/social-media/2020/04/covid-19-coronavirus-anti-chinese-antisemitic-hate-speech-5g-conspiracy-theory.

Mann, M. (1984) 'The Autonomous Power of the State: Its Origins, Mechanisms, and Results', *European Journal of Sociology*, Vol. 25, No. 2, pp. 185–213.

Manson, K. (2020) 'Washington Looks to Five Eyes to Build Anti-China Coalition', *Financial Times*, 3 June.

March, J.G. and J.P. Olsen (1983) 'Organizing Political Life: What Administrative Reorganization Tells Us about Government', *American Political Science Review*, Vol. 77, No. 2, pp. 281–296.

Margetts, H., P. John, S. Hale, and T. Yasseri (2015) *Political Turbulence: How Social Media Shape Collective Action*, Princeton: Princeton University Press.

Marsh, D. and J.C. Sharman (2009) 'Policy Diffusion and Policy Transfer', *Policy Studies*, Vol. 30, No. 3, pp. 269–288.

Marshall, G. (1986) *Constitutional Conventions: The Rules and Forms of Political Accountability*, reprinted edition, Oxford: Clarendon Press.

Marshall, T.H. (1992) *Citizenship and Social Class*, London: Pluto Press.

Marx, K. (1859/1993) *A Contribution to the Critique of Political Economy* (original in German, *Zur Kritik der Politischen Ökonomie*, translated by S.W. Ryazanskaya), Moscow: Progress Publishers. Retrieved 22 July 2020, from www.marxists.org/archive/marx/works/1859/critique-pol-economy/index.htm.

Masina, P.P. (ed) (2002) *Rethinking Development in East Asia: From Illusory Miracle to Economic Crisis*, Nordic Institute of Asian Studies, Richmond, Surrey: Curzon Press.

Matsuda, N. (2003) 'Exceptionalism in Political Science: Japanese Politics, US Politics, and Supposed International Norms', *Electronic Journal of Contemporary Japanese Studies*, Vol. 3, Paper No. 4.

Matthew, G., E. Ma, and T.L. Lui (2008) *Hong Kong, China: Learning to Belong to a Nation*, London: Routledge.

Mazzucato, M. (2018) *The Entrepreneurial State: Debunking Public vs Private Sector Myths*, London: Penguin.

McKinsey & Company (1973) *The Machinery of Government: A New Framework for Expanding Services*, Hong Kong: Government Printer.

Meeting Point Basic Law Committee and Information Centre (1988) *A Collection of Basic Law Commentaries* [in Chinese,《基本法評論匯編》], May, Hong Kong: Meeting Point.

Megaw Committee, Britain (1982) *Inquiry into Civil Service Pay*. London: Her Majesty's Stationery Office (HMSO).

Menand, L. (2018) 'Francis Fukuyama Postpones the End of History', *The New Yorker*, 27 August. Retrieved 22 July 2020, from www.newyorker.com/magazine/2018/09/03/francis-fukuyama-postpones-the-end-of-history.

Migdal, J. (1988) *Strong Societies and Weak States: State-Society Relations and State Capabilities in the Third World*, Princeton: Princeton University Press.

Miners, N. (1975) 'Hong Kong: A Case Study in Political Stability', *The Journal of Commonwealth and Comparative Politics*, Vol. 13, No. 1, pp. 26–39.

Miners, N. (1991) *The Government and Politics of Hong Kong*, 5th edition, Hong Kong: Oxford University Press.

Ming Pao (《明報》) (2001) 'Cheng Yiu-tong Blasted Government for Lack of Sense of Crisis, Pointing to Weakness of CE and Conflicting Articulations among Officials' [in Chinese,〈鄭耀棠狠批政府缺危機感 指特首弱勢官員口徑不一〉], 7 October.

Ming Pao (《明報》) (2012) 'Leung Hopes to Join 2017 CE Election by Universal Suffrage' [in Chinese,〈梁盼參加2017特首普選〉], 25 March.

Retrieved 25 March 2012, from https://archive.is/20120719024512/http://hk.news.yahoo.com/梁盼參加2017特首普選-032623212.html.

Ming Pao (《明報》) (2016) 'Tsang Yuk-sing: Localism Was Not the Same as Separatism and Should Not Be Cracked Down Upon' [in Chinese, 〈曾鈺成：本土不同分離 盼勿打擊〉], 24 February, p. A03.

Ming Pao (《明報》) (2017) 'Not Pressing to Urge for Article 23 Legislation this Year, Wong Man-kong Advocates Removal of Foreign Judges' [in Chinese, 〈「不迫切」今年不提23條 王敏剛人大倡撤外籍法官〉], 9 March.

Ming Pao (《明報》) (2018) 'Britain Advocated Setting up Human Rights Commission but Did Not Implement due to Concern about China' [in Chinese, 〈英倡設人權委會，忌中方未推〉], 28 December.

Ming Pao (《明報》) (2020a) '9000 Arrested over Anti-Bill Amendment, of whom 20% below Adult Age' [in Chinese, 〈反修例拘9000人　兩成未成年〉], 7 June.

Ming Pao (《明報》) (2020b) '350 Arrested Multiple Times, 17-year-old Student 9 Times' [in Chinese, 〈350人多次被捕 17歲生遭拘9次〉], 8 June.

Ministry of Manpower (n.d.) *Foreign Workforce Numbers*, Singapore: Ministry of Manpower. Retrieved 22 July 2020, from www.mom.gov.sg/documents-and-publications/foreign-workforce-numbers.

Mishra, P. (2017) *Age of Anger: A History of the Present*, London: Penguin.

Moffitt, B. (2016) *The Global Rise of Populism: Performance, Political Style, and Representation*, Stanford, CA: Stanford University Press.

Monnery, N. (2017) *Architect of Prosperity: Sir John Cowperthwaite and the Making of Hong Kong*, London: London Publishing Partnership.

Moon, M.J. and P. Ingraham (1998) 'Shaping Administrative Reform and Governance: An Examination of the Political Nexus Triads in Three Asian Countries', *Governance*, Vol. 11, No. 1, pp. 77–100.

Mudde, C. (2017) *The Populist Radical Right: A Reader*, London and New York: Routledge.

Muddle, C. and C.R. Kaltwasser (2017) *Populism: A Very Short Introduction*, Oxford: Oxford University Press.

Mulgan, R. (2012) 'Assessing Ministerial Responsibility in Australia', in K. Dowding and C. Lewis (eds) *Ministerial Careers and Accountability in the Australian Commonwealth Government*, Canberra, Australia: ANU E Press, pp. 177–193.

Müller, W.C. and K. Strøm (eds) (1999) *Policy, Office, or Votes? How Political Parties in Western Europe Make Hard Decisions*, Cambridge: Cambridge University Press.

Nasir, K.M. and B.S. Turner (2013) 'Governing as Gardening: Reflections on Soft Authoritarianism in Singapore', *Citizenship Studies*, Vol. 17, Nos. 3–4, pp. 339–352.

Nathan, A. (2009) 'China since Tiananmen: Authoritarian Impermanence', *Journal of Democracy*, Vol. 20, No. 3, pp. 37–40.

National Committee of The Chinese People's Political Consultative Conference (CPPCC) (2012) 'Composition of the CPPCC', 3 July. Retrieved 22 July 2020, from www.cppcc.gov.cn/zxww/2012/07/03/ARTI1341301498421103.shtml.

National Development and Reform Commission (國家發展及改革委員會) (2018) 'Press Conference on the Promotion of Private Sector Investment' [in Chinese, 〈發改委舉行促進民間投資持續健康發展工作情況發佈會〉], 6 September, Beijing: The State Council Information Office of the People's Republic of China. Retrieved 22 July 2020, from www.scio.gov.cn/xwfbh/gbwxwfbh/xwfbh/fzggw/Document/1637294/1637294.htm.

National People's Congress (1990) *Decision of National People's Congress on the Method for the Formation of the First Government and First Legislative Council of the Hong Kong Special Administrative Region*, approved on 4 April, Beijing. Retrieved 22 July 2020, from www.elegislation.gov.hk/hk/capA202?xpid=ID_1438403581022_004.

National People's Congress (1997) *Resolution of the Eighth National People's Congress at its Fifth Session on the Working Report of the Preparatory Committee for the Hong Kong Special Administrative Region of the National People's Congress*, adopted on 14 March, Beijing. Retrieved 22 July 2020, from www.npc.gov.cn/zgrdw/npc/dbdhhy/content_5610.htm (in Chinese).

National People's Congress (2013) *Legislation Law of the People's Republic of China*, Unofficial English version available from the Congressional Executive Commission on China. Retrieved 22 July 2020, from www.cecc.gov/resources/legal-provisions/legislation-law-chinese-and-english-text#body-chinese.

National People's Congress Observer (n.d.) 'Decision of the National People's Congress on Improving the Electoral System of the Hong Kong Special Administrative Region'. Retrieved 11 April 2021, from https://npcobserver.com/legislation/npc-hong-kong-electoral-reform-decision/.

National People's Congress Standing Committee (NPCSC) (1999) *The Interpretation by the Standing Committee of the National People's Congress of Articles 22(4) and 24(2)(3) of the Basic Law of the Hong Kong Special Administrative Region of the People's Republic of China*, adopted at the 10th Session of the Standing Committee of the 9th National People's Congress, 26 June, Beijing. Retrieved 22 July 2020, from www.basiclaw.gov.hk/en/basiclawtext/images/basiclawtext_doc17.pdf.

National People's Congress Standing Committee (NPCSC) (2004a) *The Interpretation by the Standing Committee of the National People's Congress of Article 7 of Annex I and Article III of Annex II to the Basic Law of the Hong Kong Special Administrative Region of the People's Republic of China*, adopted at 8th Session of the Standing Committee of the 10th National People's Congress, 6 April, Beijing. Retrieved 22 July 2020, from www.basiclaw.gov.hk/en/basiclawtext/images/basiclawtext_doc18.pdf.

National People's Congress Standing Committee (NPCSC) (2004b) *Decision of the Standing Committee of the National People's Congress on Issues relating to the Methods for Electing the Chief Executive of the Hong Kong Special Administrative Region in the Year 2007 and for Forming the Legislative Council of the Hong Kong Special Administrative Region in the Year 2008*, adopted at 9th Session of the Standing Committee of the 10th National People's Congress, 26 April, Beijing, Retrieved 22 July 2020, from www.basiclaw.gov.hk/en/materials/doc/2004_04_26_e.pdf

National People's Congress Standing Committee (NPCSC) (2007) *Decision of the Standing Committee of the National People's Congress on Issues relating to the Methods for Selecting the Chief Executive of the Hong Kong Special Administrative Region and for Forming the Legislative Council of the Hong Kong Special Administrative Region in the Year 2012 and on Issues relating to Universal Suffrage*, adopted at the 31st Session of the Standing Committee of the 10th National People's Congress, 29 December, Beijing. Retrieved 22 July 2020, from www.elegislation.gov.hk/hk/capA211.

National People's Congress Standing Committee (NPCSC) (2011) *Interpretation by the Standing Committee of the National People's Congress Regarding the First Paragraph of Article 13 and Article 19 of the Basic Law of the Hong Kong Special Administrative Region of the People's Republic of China*, adopted at the 22nd Session of the Standing Committee of the 11th National People's Congress, 26 August, Beijing. Retrieved 22 July 2020, from www.elegislation.gov.hk/hk/A114%21en.assist.pdf.

National People's Congress Standing Committee (NPCSC) (2014) *Decision of the Standing Committee of the National People's Congress on Issues Relating to the Selection of the Chief Executive of the Hong Kong Special Administrative Region by Universal Suffrage and on the Method for Forming the Legislative Council of the Hong Kong Special Administrative Region in the Year 2016*, adopted at the 10th Session of the Standing Committee of the 12th National People's Congress, 31 August, Beijing. Retrieved 22 July 2020, from www.2017.gov.hk/filemanager/template/en/doc/20140831b.pdf.

National People's Congress Standing Committee (NPCSC) (2016) *Interpretation of Article 104 of the Basic Law of the Hong Kong Special Administrative Region of the People's Republic of China by the Standing Committee of the National People's Congress,* adopted at the 24th Session of the Standing Committee of the 12th National People's Congress, 7 November, Beijing. Retrieved 22 July 2020, from www.basiclaw.gov.hk/en/basiclawtext/images/basiclawtext_doc25.pdf.

National People's Congress Standing Committee (NPCSC) (2017) *Decision of the Standing Committee of the National People's Congress on Approving the Co-operation Arrangement between the Mainland and the Hong Kong Special Administrative Region on the Establishment of the Port at the West Kowloon Station of the Guangzhou-Shenzhen-Hong Kong Express Rail Link for Implementing Co-location Arrangement*, adopted at the 31st Session of the

Standing Committee of the 12th National People's Congress, 27 December, Beijing. Retrieved 22 July 2020, from www.thb.gov.hk/eng/policy/transport/policy/colocation/EN%20Decision%20(2%20Jan).pdf.

National Statistics Bureau (2018) 'Rapid Advancement in Science and Technology, with Outstanding Achievement Driven by Innovation' [in Chinese, 〈科技進步日新月異　創新驅動成效突出〉], 12 September, Beijing: National Statistics Bureau. Retrieved 22 July 2020, from www.stats.gov.cn/ztjc/ztfx/ggkf40n/201809/t20180912_1622413.html.

NBC News (2021) 'Hong Kong: G7 Expresses "Grave Concerns" Over Electoral Changes', 13 March.

The New York Times (1974) 'Hong Kong Adopts a Language Lain', 24 March. Retrieved 22 July 2020, from www.nytimes.com/1974/03/24/archives/hong-kong-adopts-a-language-law-complications-for-officials.html.

Ng, K.C. (2012) 'Finance Chief John Tsang Warns Against Ignoring Hong Kong's Pillar Industries', *South China Morning Post*, 31 December.

Ng, K.C. (2018) 'Hong Kong University Graduates Take Home Less Pay than Counterparts 30 Years Ago and One in Six Ends up in Unskilled Job, Study Finds', *South China Morning Post*, 18 December.

Ng, S.H. (2007) 'Biculturalism in Multicultural Hong Kong', *Journal of Psychology in Chinese Societies*, Vol. 8, pp. 121–140.

Ngok, K. and G. Zhu (2007) 'Marketization, Globalization and Administrative Reform in China: A Zigzag Road to a Promising Future', *International Review of Administrative Sciences*, Vol. 73, No. 2, pp. 217–233.

Ngoye, B., V. Sierra, and T. Ysa (2019) 'Assessing Performance-use Preferences through an Institutional Logics Lens', *International Journal of Public Sector Management*, Vol. 32, No. 1, pp. 2–20.

Nilsson-Wright, J. (2018) 'Nostalgia and Romanticism: Populism and the Rise of Identity Politics', *Global Asia*, Vol. 13, No. 3, pp. 48–63.

Niskanan, W.A. (1971) *Bureaucracy and Representative Government*, Chicago: Aldine-Atherton.

Nolte, G. and H.P. Aust (2013) 'European Exceptionalism?' *Global Constitutionalism*, Vol. 2, No. 3, pp. 407–436.

Nye, J. (1990) *Bound to Lead: The Changing Nature of American Power*, London: Basic Books.

O'Connor, J. (1973) *The Fiscal Crisis of the State*, New York: St. Martin's Press.

O'Donnell, G. and P.C. Schmitter (1986) *Transitions from Authoritarian Rule: Tentative Conclusions About Uncertain Democracies*, Baltimore, MD: Johns Hopkins University Press.

Office of the Law Revision Counsel (n.d.) *United States-Hong Kong Policy* (22 USC Ch. 66), Washington, D.C.: House of Representatives. Retrieved 22 July 2020, from https://uscode.house.gov/view.xhtml?path=/prelim@title22/chapter66&edition=prelim.

Ohmae, K. (2006) *M-shape Society: The Crisis and Business Opportunity of the Disappearance of the Middle Class* [Original in Japanese,《ロウアーミドルの衝撃》], 東京 [Tokyo]: 講談社 [Kodansha]. (There is no English translation. Chinese translation, 大前研一 (2006)《M型社會: 中產階級消失的危機與商機》, 台北: 商周出版.)

Organisation for Economic Cooperation and Development (OECD) (1995) *Governance in Transition: Public Management Reform in OECD Countries*, Paris: OECD.

Organisation for Economic Cooperation and Development (OECD) (1996) *Building Policy Coherence: Tools and Tensions*, Public Management Occasional Papers, No. 12, Paris: OECD.

Organisation for Economic Cooperation and Development (OECD) (1997) *Performance Pay Schemes for Public Sector Managers: An Evaluation of the Impacts*, Public Management Occasional Papers, No. 15, Paris: OECD.

Organisation for Economic Cooperation and Development (OECD) (1998) 'Government Reinvention Goes Global', *Public Management Gazette*, No. 11, Paris: OECD.

Organisation for Economic Cooperation and Development (OECD) (2005) *Performance-related Pay Policies for Government Employees*, Paris: OECD.

Organisation for Economic Cooperation and Development (OECD) (2009) *Measuring Government Activity*, Paris: OECD.

Organisation for Economic Cooperation and Development (OECD) (2017) *Trust and Public Policy: How Better Governance Can Help Rebuild Public Trust*, Paris: OECD

Organisation for Economic Cooperation and Development (OECD) (2018) *For Good Measure: Advancing Research on Well-Being Metrics Beyond GDP*, Paris: OECD.

Organisation for Economic Cooperation and Development (OECD) (2019) *Under Pressure: The Squeezed Middle Class*, Paris: OECD.

Organisation for Economic Cooperation and Development (OECD) (2020) *OECD Economic Outlook*, Preliminary version, June, Paris: OECD.

Organisation for Economic Cooperation and Development (OECD) (n.d.) *Main Science and Technology Indicators*, Paris: OECD. Retrieved 22 July 2020, from https://stats.oecd.org/Index.aspx?DataSetCode=MSTI_PUB.

Organisation for Economic Cooperation and Development (OECD) and Korea Development Institute (2018) *Understanding the Drivers of Trust in Government Institutions in Korea*, Paris: OECD.

Oriental Daily (《東方日報》) (2012) 'Elsie Leung Criticized Foreign Judges for Not Being Familiar with Basic Law' [in Chinese, 〈梁愛詩批洋法官不熟基本法〉], 10 November.

Osborne, D. and T. Gaebler (1993) *Reinventing Government: How the Entrepreneurial Spirit is Transforming the Public Sector*, New York: Plume.

Osborne, S.P. (2006) 'The New Public Governance?' *Public Management Review*, Vol. 8, No. 3, pp. 377–387.

Page, S.E. (2006) 'Path Dependence', *Quarterly Journal of Political Science*, Vol. 1, No. 1, pp. 87–115.

Painter, M. and J. Pierre (2005) 'Unpacking Policy Capacity: Issues and Themes', in J. Pierre and M. Painter (eds) *Challenges to State Policy Capacity: Global Trends and Comparative Perspectives*, Basingstoke: Palgrave Macmillan, pp. 1–18.

Panchami, N. and P. Thomas (n.d.) *The Next Steps Initiative*, case study, London: Institute for Government. Retrieved 22 July 2020, from www.instituteforgovernment.org.uk/sites/default/files/case%20study%20next%20steps.pdf.

Panizza, F. (ed) (2005) *Populism and the Mirror of Democracy*, London: Verso.

Patten, C. (1992) *Our Next Five Years: The Agenda for Hong Kong*, Address by the Governor to the Legislative Council, 7 October, Hong Kong: Government Printer.

Patten, C. (1996) *Hong Kong: Transition*, Address by the Governor at the opening of the 1996–97 Session of the Legislative Council, 2 October, Hong Kong: Government Printer.

Patten, C. (1997) 'Governor's Speech at the Farewell Ceremony of the Hong Kong Handover 1997', 30 June. Retrieved 22 July 2020, from www.american rhetoric.com/speeches/chrispattenhongkonghandoverceremony.htm.

Peh, S.H. (2018) *Tall Order: The Goh Chok Tong Story*, Singapore: World Scientific.

Pence, M. (2018) *Remarks on the Administration's Policy Towards China*, 4 October, Washington, D.C.: Hudson Institute. Retrieved 22 July 2020, from www.whitehouse.gov/briefings-statements/remarks-vice-president-pence-administrations-policy-toward-china/.

People's Daily (《人民日報》) (2013) 'NPCSC Deputy Secretary General and Hong Kong Basic Law Committee Director Li Fei pointed out: Chief Executive Must be a Person Who Loves the Country and Loves Hong Kong' [in Chinese, 〈人大常委會副秘書長兼香港基本法委員會主任李飛指出: 行政長官須由愛國愛港人士擔任〉], Overseas Edition, 23 November. Retrieved 22 July 2020, from http://paper.people.com.cn/rmrbhwb/html/2013-11/23/content_1328915.htm.

People's Daily (《人民日報》) (2015) 'Li Keqiang Meets with Liang Zhenying and Cui Shi'an' [in Chinese, 〈李克強分別會見梁振英崔世安〉], 24 December. Retrieved 22 July 2020, from http://politics.people.com.cn/n1/2015/1224/c1024-27968435.html.

People's Daily (《人民日報》) (2018) 'Comprehensively Enhance the National Capacity of Governance and Standard of Governance' [in Chinese, 〈全面提高國家治理能力和治理水平〉], 2 March. Retrieved 22 July 2020, from http://paper.people.com.cn/rmrb/html/2018-03/02/nw.D110000renmrb_20180302_7-04.htm.

People's Republic of China Central People's Government (2007) *Forum to Commemorate the 10th Anniversary of the Implementation of the Basic Law of Hong Kong Special Administrative Region* [in Chinese,《紀念香港特別行政區基本法實施十週年座談會舉行》], 6 June, Beijing: Central People's Government. Retrieved 22 July 2020, from http://big5.www.gov.cn/gate/big5/www.gov.cn/ldhd/2007-06/06/content_638628.htm.

People Web (人民網) (2017) 'Official Ceremony Commemorating the 20th Anniversary of the Return of Hong Kong to the Motherland' [in Chinese,〈香港回歸祖國20周年大會〉]. Retrieved 22 July 2020, from http://live01.people.com.cn/zhibo/Myapp/Html/Member/html/201706/15_2575_595207dc21ee7_quan.html.

Perlez, J. (2020) 'One Country, Two Systems, No Future: The End of Hong Kong as We Know It', *Foreign Affairs*, September/October.

Permanent Mission of the People's Republic of China to the United Nations (1981) 'Chairman Ye Jianying's Elaborations on Policy Concerning Return of Taiwan To Motherland and Peaceful Reunification', 30 September, New York: United Nations. Retrieved 22 July 2020, from www.china-un.org/eng/zt/twwt/t28922.htm.

Pesek, W. (2014) 'No, Shanghai Can't Replace Hong Kong', *Bloomberg*, 30 September. Retrieved 22 July 2020, from www.bloomberg.com/opinion/articles/2014-09-30/no-shanghai-can-t-replace-hong-kong.

Peters, B.G. (2001) 'Administrative Reform and Political Power in the United States', *Policy and Politics*, Vol. 29, No. 2, pp. 171–179.

Peter, L.J. and P. Hull (1969) *The Peter Principle: Why Things Always Go Wrong*, New York: William Morrow & Company.

Pierre, J. and B.G. Peters (2005) *Governance, Politics and the State*, Basingstoke, Hampshire: Macmillan.

Policy Innovation and Co-ordination Office (n.d.) *About Us*, Hong Kong: Policy Innovation and Co-ordination Office. Retrieved 22 July 2020, from www.pico.gov.hk/en/about_us/PICO.html.

Pollitt, C. and G. Bouckaert (2011) *Public Management Reform: A Comparative Analysis—New Public Management, Governance, and the Neo-Weberian State*, 3rd edition, Oxford: Oxford University Press.

Połońska, E. and C. Backett (eds) (2019) *Public Service Broadcasting and Media Systems in Troubled European Democracies*, London: Palgrave Macmillan.

Poluha, E. and M. Rosendahl (2002) *Contesting 'Good' Governance: Crosscultural Perspectives on Representation, Accountability and Public Space*, London: Routledge.

Potter, J. (1988) 'Consumerism and the Public Sector—How Well Does the Coat Fit?' *Public Administration*, Vol. 66, Issue 2, pp. 149–164.

Prasso, S. (2007) 'Oops! Hong Kong is Hardly Dead', *Fortune*, 9 July. Retrieved 22 July 2020, from http://archive.fortune.com/magazines/fortune/fortune_archive/2007/07/09/100122332/index.htm?postversion=2007062816.

Preston, P. (2016) *The Politics of China-Hong Kong Relations: Living with Distant Masters*, Northampton, MA: Edward Elgar.

Public Opinion Programme, University of Hong Kong (HKUPOP) (2010) *Rating of Chief Justice Andrew Li Kwok-nang*, Hong Kong: HKUPOP. Retrieved 22 July 2020, from www.hkupop.hku.hk/english/popexpress/judiciary/andrew/halfyr/datatables.html.

Public Opinion Programme, University of Hong Kong (2015a) *Joint-University Rolling Survey on 2017 Chief Executive Election Proposal*, Hong Kong: HKUPOP. Retrieved 22 July 2020, from www.hkupop.hku.hk/english/features/jointUrollingSurvey/.

Public Opinion Programme, University of Hong Kong (2015b) *Survey on 2017 CE Election Proposal*, 15 June, Hong Kong: HKUPOP. Retrieved 22 July 2020, from www.hkupop.hku.hk/english/report/superSurvey2015/ppt.pdf.

Public Opinion Programme, University of Hong Kong (2019a) *Comparison between Ratings of Chris Patten, Tung Chee-hwa, Donald Tsang Yam-kuen, Leung Chun-ying and Carrie Lam—Monthly Average*, Hong Kong: HKUPOP. Retrieved 22 July 2020, from www.hkupop.hku.hk/chinese/popexpress/ce2017/cl/cecomparison/datatables.html.

Public Opinion Programme, University of Hong Kong (2019b) *Credibility Rating of the Hong Kong News Media in General (9/1997–1/2019)*, Hong Kong: HKUPOP. Retrieved 22 July 2020, from www.hkupop.hku.hk/english/popexpress/press/nm_credibility/poll/MC_poll_chart.html.

Public Opinion Programme, University of Hong Kong (2019c) *Rating of Chief Justice Geoffrey Ma Tao-li*, Hong Kong: HKUPOP. Retrieved 22 July 2020, from www.hkupop.hku.hk/english/popexpress/judiciary/geoffrey/halfyr/datatables.html.

Public Opinion Programme, University of Hong Kong (2019d) *Rating of Top Ten Political Groups*, Hong Kong: HKUPOP. Retrieved 22 July 2020, from www.hkupop.hku.hk/chinese/popexpress/pgrating/topten1.html.

Public Opinion Programme, University of Hong Kong (HKUPOP) (n.d.) *People's Trust in the HKSAR Government*, Hong Kong: HKUPOP. Retrieved 22 July 2020, from www.hkupop.hku.hk/english/popexpress/trust/trusthkgov/index.html.

Public Opinion Programme, University of Hong Kong (HKUPOP) (n.d.) *People's Trust in the Beijing Central Government*, Hong Kong: HKUPOP. Retrieved 22 July 2020, from www.hkupop.hku.hk/english/popexpress/trust/trustchigov/halfyr/trustchigov_halfyr_chart.html.

Public Opinion Programme, University of Hong Kong (HKUPOP) (n.d.) *Ratings of various Chief Executives*, Hong Kong: HKUPOP. Retrieved 22 July 2020, from www.hkupop.hku.hk/english/popexpress/ce2017/cl/cecomparison/datatables.html.

Public Opinion Programme, University of Hong Kong (HKUPOP) (n.d.) *Hypothetical Voting on Carrie Lam as the Chief Executive*, Hong Kong:

HKUPOP. Retrieved 22 July 2020, from www.hkupop.hku.hk/english/popexpress/ce2017/vote/poll/cl_vote_chart.html.

Public Opinion Programme, University of Hong Kong (HKUPOP) (n.d.) *You would identify yourself as a Hongkonger/english/Chinese in Hong Kong/Hongkonger in China*, Hong Kong: HKUPOP. Retrieved 22 July 2020, from www.hkupop.hku.hk/english/popexpress/ethnic/eidentity/halfyr/datatables.html.

Public Policy Research Centre, Chinese University of Hong Kong (2005a) Findings of Public Opinion Survey on Constitutional Development [in Chinese, 〈市民對政制發展意見調查結果〉], press release, 3 November, Hong Kong: Public Policy Research Centre of Hong Kong Institute of Asia-Pacific Studies, Chinese University of Hong Kong. Retrieved 22 July 2020, from www.cuhk.edu.hk/ipro/pressrelease/051103.htm.

Public Policy Research Centre, Chinese University of Hong Kong (2005b) 'Findings of Second Public Opinion Survey on Constitutional Development' [in Chinese, 〈市民對政制發展意見調查（第二次）結果〉], press release, 9 December, Hong Kong: Public Policy Research Centre of Hong Kong Institute of Asia-Pacific Studies, Chinese University of Hong Kong. Retrieved 22 July 2020, from www.cuhk.edu.hk/ipro/pressrelease/051209.htm.

Public Service Division, Prime Minister's Office (Singapore) (2018) 'Civil Service Year-End Payment 2018', press release, 23 November. Retrieved 22 July 2020, from www.psd.gov.sg/press-room/press-releases/civil-service-year-end-payment-2018.

Qi Pengfei (齊鵬飛) (n.d.) 'The Origin of CCP's Strategy of "Temporarily Keeping Hong Kong Intact" after the Establishment of New China' [in Chinese, 〈新中國成立後中共「暫時不動香港」戰略始末〉], *People Web* (《人民網》). Retrieved 22 July 2020, from http://cpc.people.com.cn/BIG5/85037/8292161.html.

Quacquarelli Symonds (2020) *QS World University Rankings 2021*, 10 June. Retrieved 22 July 2020, from www.topuniversities.com/university-rankings/world-university-rankings/2021.

Quah, J.S.T. (2007) *Curbing Corruption in Asia: A Comparative Study of Six Countries*, Singapore: Eastern University Press by Marshall Cavendish.

Rabb, D. (2021) *Foreign Secretary Statement on Radical Changes to Hong Kong's Electoral System*, 13 March, London: Foreign, Commonwealth and Development Office.

Rabushka, A. (1976) *Value for Money: The Hong Kong Budgetary Process*, Stanford: Hoover Institution Press.

Rabushka, A. (1979) *Hong Kong: A Study in Economic Freedom*, Chicago: University of Chicago Press.

Rachman, G. (2017) *Easternization: Asia's Rise and America's Decline from Obama to Trump and Beyond*, New York: Other Press.

Ramesh, M. (1995) 'Social Security in South Korea and Singapore: Explaining the Differences', *Social Policy and Administration*, Vol. 29, No. 3, pp. 228–240.

Ramesh, M., E. Araral Jr., and X. Wu (eds) (2010) *Reasserting the Public in Public Service*, Abingdon, Oxon: Routledge.

Ramo, J.C. (2009) *The Beijing Consensus*, London: The Foreign Policy Centre.

Rating and Valuation Department (n.d.) *Property Market Statistics: Private Domestic Price Indices by Class (Territory wide) (since 1979)*, Hong Kong: The Hong Kong Special Administrative Region Government. Retrieved 22 July 2020, from www.rvd.gov.hk/en/property_market_statistics/index.html.

Rating and Valuation Department (n.d.) *Property Market Statistics: Private Domestic Rental Indices by Class (Territory wide) (since 1979)*, Hong Kong: The Hong Kong Special Administrative Region Government. Retrieved 22 July 2020, from www.rvd.gov.hk/en/property_market_statistics/index.html

Rear, J. (1971) 'One Brand of Politics', in K. Hopkins (ed) *Hong Kong: The Industrial Colony*, Hong Kong: Oxford University Press, pp. 55–139.

Redding, S.G. (1990) *The Spirit of Chinese Capitalism*, Berlin: de Gruyter.

Registration and Electoral Office (n.d.) '2016 Election Committee Sub-Sector Elections', Hong Kong: Registration and Electoral Office. Retrieved 22 July 2020, from www.elections.gov.hk/ecss2016/eng/figures.html.

Reiter, R. and T. Klenk (2019) 'The Manifold Meanings of "Post-New Public Management"—A Systematic Literature Review', *International Review of Administrative Sciences*, Vol. 85, No. 1, pp. 11–27.

Research Office of the Legislative Council Secretariat (2005) *Fact Sheet: Historical Development of Retirement Schemes in Hong Kong*, FS18/04-05, 19 July, Hong Kong: Legislative Council Research Division. Retrieved 22 July 2020, from www.legco.gov.hk/yr04-05/english/sec/library/0405fs18e.pdf.

Research Office of the Legislative Council Secretariat (2012) *Fact Sheet: The Decision by the Court of Final Appeal to Seek an Interpretation of the Basic Law from the Standing Committee of the National People's Congress Regarding the Controversy of State Immunity Raised in the Debt Litigation of the Democratic Republic of Congo*, FS17/11-12, 22 February, Hong Kong: Legislative Council Research Division. Retrieved 22 July 2020, from www.legco.gov.hk/yr11-12/english/sec/library/1112fs17-e.pdf.

Research Office of the Legislative Council Secretariat (2015) *Social Mobility in Hong Kong*, Research Brief No. 2, Hong Kong: Legislative Council Research Division. Retrieved 22 July 2020, from www.legco.gov.hk/research-publications/english/1415rb02-social-mobility-in-hong-kong-20150112-e.pdf.

Research Office of the Legislative Council Secretariat (2018) *Financial Affairs: Offshore Renminbi Business in Hong Kong*, 28 February, Hong Kong: Legislative Council Research Division. Retrieved 22 July 2020, from www.legco.gov.hk/research-publications/english/1718issh15-offshore-renminbi-business-in-hong-kong-20180228-e.pdf.

Rhodes, R.A.W. (1997) *Understanding Governance: Policy Networks, Governance, Reflexivity and Accountability*, Buckingham: Open University Press.

Rockman, B.A. (2001) 'Politics by Other Means: Administrative Reform in the United States', *International Review of Public Administration*, Vol. 6, No. 2, pp. 1–13.

Rogers, D.T. (1998) 'Exceptionalism', in A. Molhol and G.S. Wood (eds) *Imagined Histories: American Historians Interpret the Past*, Princeton, NJ: Princeton University Press, pp. 21–40.

Rosenbloom, D. (2008) 'The Politics-Administration Dichotomy in U.S. Historical Context', *Public Administration Review*, Vol. 68, No. 1, pp. 57–60.

Rotberg, R.I. (2014) 'Good Governance Means Performance and Results', *Governance*, Vol. 27, No. 3, pp. 511–518.

Sachs, J.D. (2019a) 'China Is Not the Source of Our Economic Problems—Corporate Greed Is', *CNN*, 27 May. Retrieved 22 July 2020, from https://edition.cnn.com/2019/05/26/opinions/china-is-not-the-enemy-sachs/index.html.

Sachs, J.D. (2019b) 'Why Rich Cities Rebel', *Project Syndicate*, 22 October. Retrieved 22 July 2020, from www.project-syndicate.org/commentary/explaining-social-protest-in-paris-hong-kong-santiago-by-jeffrey-d-sachs-2019-10?barrier=accesspaylog.

Santora, M. (2020) 'Pompeo Calls China's Ruling Party "Central Threat of Our Times"', *The New York Times*, 30 January.

Sartre, J.P. (1947) *Existentialism*, New York: Philosophical Society.

Savas, E.S. (1987) *Privatization: The Key to Better Government*, Chatham, NJ: Chatham House.

Savoie, D. (2010) *Power: Where Is It?* Montreal: McGill-Queen's University Press.

Schedler, A. (2006) *Electoral Authoritarianism: The Dynamics of Unfree Competition*, Boulder, CO: L. Rienner Publishers.

Schedler, K. and I. Proeller (2002) 'The New Public Management: A Perspective from Mainland Europe', in K. McLaughlin, S.P. Osborne, and E. Ferlie (eds) *New Public Management: Current Trends and Future Prospects*, London: Routledge, pp. 164–180.

Schiavo, S. (2020) 'Covid-19 Throws Us Into an Unprecedented Debt Crisis, But It's One We Can Rise From', *European Network for Economic and Fiscal Policy Research*, 11 May. Retrieved 22 July 2020, from www.econpol.eu/opinion_33.

Schick, A. (1986) 'Macro-budgetary Adaptations to Fiscal Stress in Industrialized Democracies', *Public Administration Review*, Vol. 46, No. 2, pp. 124–134.

Schiffer, J.R. (1983) *Anatomy of a Laissez-faire Government: The Hong Kong Growth Model Reconsidered*, Hong Kong: Centre of Urban Studies and Urban Planning, University of Hong Kong.

Schminke, T.G. (2018) 'How (un)popular is French President Macron Really?' *Europe Elects*, 5 December. Retrieved 22 July 2020, from https://europeelects.eu/2018/12/05/how-unpopular-is-french-president-macron-really/.

Schwab, K. (2019) *The Global Competitiveness Report 2019*, October, Cologny, Switzerland: World Economic Forum. Retrieved 22 July 2020, from www3.weforum.org/docs/WEF_TheGlobalCompetitivenessReport2019.pdf.

Scott, I. (1988) 'Generalists and Specialists', in I. Scott and J.P. Burns (eds) *The Hong Kong Civil Service and Its Future*, Hong Kong: Oxford University Press, pp. 17–49.

Scott, I. (1989) *Political Change and the Crisis of Legitimacy in Hong Kong*, Hong Kong: Oxford University Press.

Scott, I. (2000) 'The Disarticulation of Hong Kong's Post-1997 Political System', *The China Journal*, No. 43, pp. 29–53.

Scott, I. (2005) *Public Administration in Hong Kong: Regime Change and Its Impact on the Public Sector*, Singapore: Marshall Cavendish.

Scott, I. (2007) 'Legitimacy, Governance and Public Policy in Post-1997 Hong Kong', *Asia Pacific Journal of Public Administration*, Vol. 29, No. 1, pp. 29–49.

Scott, I. (2010) *Public Sector in Hong Kong*, Hong Kong: Hong Kong University Press.

Scott, I. (2017) '"One Country, Two Systems": The End of a Legitimating Ideology?' *Asia Pacific Journal of Public Administration*, Vol. 39, No. 2, pp. 83–99.

Scott, W.D. (1985) *The Delivery of Medical Services in Hospitals: A Report for the Hong Kong Government*, Hong Kong: Government Printer.

Secretary of State for Foreign and Commonwealth Affairs (1993) *Protocol between the Government of the United Kingdom of Great Britain and Northern Ireland and the Government of the French Republic Governing Frontier Controls and Policing, Co-operation in Criminal Justice, Public Safety and Mutual Assistance Relating to the Chanel Fixed Link*, Treaty Series No. 70 (1993), Cm. 2366, London: Her Majesty's Stationery Office (HMSO).

Security Bureau (2019) *Legislative Council Brief: Fugitive Offenders and Mutual Legal Assistance in Criminal Matters Legislation (Amendment) Bill 2019*, SBCR 1/2716/19, March, Hong Kong: Legislative Council.

Shek, D.T.L. (2020) 'Protests in Hong Kong (2019–2020): A Perspective Based on Quality of Life and Well-Being', *Applied Research Quality Life*, Vol. 15, pp. 619–635. Retrieved 22 July 2020, from https://doi.org/10.1007/s11482-020-09825-2.

Sheridan, G. (1999) *Asian Values, Western Dreams: Understanding the New Asia*, Sydney: Allen & Unwin.

Shih, S.M. (2003) 'Globalization and the (in)Significance of Taiwan', *Postcolonial Studies*, Vol. 6, No. 2, pp. 143–153.

Simon, H.A. (1947) *Administrative Behavior: A Study of Decision-Making Processes in Administrative Organization*, New York: Macmillan.

Sing, M. (2006) 'The Legitimacy Problem and Democratic Reform in Hong Kong', *Journal of Contemporary China*, Vol. 15, No. 48, pp. 517–532.

Sing Pao (《成報》) (2012) 'Experts Propose Hong Kong Needs More Chinese Judges to Realize Self-administration' [in Chinese, 〈專家學者提出 體現港人治港 港需更多中國籍法官〉], 5 November.

Siu, P. (2018) 'Hong Kong's Environment Chief Wong Kam-sing Urges Public to Back Waste Charging Scheme, Saying City Is 20 Years behind Seoul and Taipei on Issue', *South China Morning Post*, 4 November. Retrieved on 22 July 2020, from www.scmp.com/news/hong-kong/health-environment/article/2171588/hong-kongs-environment-chief-wong-kam-sing-urges.

Skocpol, T. (1985) 'Bringing the State Back In: Strategies of Analysis in Current Research', in P.B. Evans, D. Rueschemeyer, and T. Skocpol (eds) *Bringing the State Back*, Cambridge: Cambridge University Press, pp. 3–37.

Skocpol, T. (1992) *Protecting Soldiers and Mothers: The Political Origins of Social Policy in the United States*, Cambridge, MA: Belknap Press of Harvard University Press.

Smith, D. (2007) *The Dragon and the Elephant: China, India and the New World Order*, London: Profile Books.

So, C.Y.K. (蘇鑰機) (2019) 'The Feelings of People with Diverse Political Inclinations and the Youngsters as Viewed from Public Opinion Survey Figures' [in Chinese,〈從民調數字　看不同政見和年輕人的心聲〉], *Ming Pao* (《明報》), 27 September.

Sørensen, E. and J. Torfing (eds) (2008) *Theories of Democratic Network Governance*, Basingstoke: Palgrave.

Sørensen, G. (1993) 'Democracy, Authoritarianism and State Strength', in G. Sørensen (ed) *Political Conditionality*, London: Frank Cass, pp. 6–34.

South China Morning Post (2018) 'Politics Must be Kept Out of the Appointment of Senior Judges', editorial, 6 May.

Spence, J. (1980) *To Change China: Western Advisers in China*, New York: Penguin Books.

The Standard (2021) '129 Civil Servants Refused to Sign Declaration, Says Patrick Nip', 12 April. Retrieved 13 April 2021, from www.thestandard.com.hk/breaking-news/section/4/169395/129-civil-servants-refused-to-sign-declaration,-says-Patrick-Nip.

Standing Commission on Civil Service Salaries and Conditions of Service (1979) *First Report on Principles and Practices Governing Civil Service Pay*, Hong Kong: Government Printer.

Standing Commission on Civil Service Salaries and Conditions of Service (1988) *Review Committee on Disciplined Services Pay and Conditions of Service: Final Report*, October, Hong Kong: The Joint Secretariat for the Advisory Bodies on Civil Service and Judicial Salaries and Conditions of Service (JSSCS). Retrieved 22 July 2020, from www.jsscs.gov.hk/reports/en/rcds_fin/index.htm.

Standing Commission on Civil Service Salaries and Conditions of Service (1999) *Report No. 36: Civil Service Starting Salaries Review 1999*, June, Hong Kong: Printing Department.

StartmeupHK (n.d.) *Hong Kong's Startup Ecosystem: Going from Strength to Strength*, Hong Kong: InvestHK. Retrieved 22 July 2020, from www.startmeup.hk/about-us/hong-kongs-startup-ecosystem/.

State Council of the People's Republic of China (2019) *Outline Development Plan for the Guangdong-Hong Kong-Macao Greater Bay Area*, 18 February, Beijing (translated by the Hong Kong Special Administrative Region

Government). Retrieved 22 July 2020, from www.bayarea.gov.hk/filemanager/en/share/pdf/Outline_Development_Plan.pdf.

Steffensen, S.K. (2000) 'The Weak State of Japan', in K.E. Brødsgaard and S. Young (eds) *State Capacity in East Asia: Japan, Taiwan, China and Vietnam*, New York: Oxford University Press, pp. 17–36.

Steinmo, S. (2008) 'Historical Institutionalism', in D. Della Porta and M.J. Keating (eds) *Approaches and Methodologies in the Social Sciences: A Pluralist Perspective*, Cambridge, UK: Cambridge University Press, pp. 118–138.

Stepan, A. (1978) *The State and Society: Peru in Comparative Perspective*, Princeton NJ: Princeton University Press.

Stephens, P. (2018) 'Populism is the True Legacy of the Crisis', *Financial Times*, 31 August.

Stiglitz, J.E. (2015) 'New Theoretical Perspectives on the Distribution of Income and Wealth among Individuals: Part I — The Wealth Residual', *NBER Working Paper*, No. 21189. Retrieved 22 July 2020, from www.nber.org/papers/w21189.

Stoker, G. (1998) 'Governance as Theory: Five Propositions', *International Journal of Social Sciences*, Vol. 50, No. 1, pp. 17–28.

Strauss, D.A. (2010) *The Living Constitution*, Chicago: The University of Chicago Law School. Retrieved 22 July 2020, from www.law.uchicago.edu/news/living-constitution.

Sum, L.K. (2019) 'Young, Educated and Middle Class: First Field Study of Hong Kong Protesters Reveals Demographic Trends', *South China Morning Post*, 12 August.

Sum, N.L. (1995) 'More than a War of Words: Identity, Politics and the Struggle for Dominance during the Recent Political Reform Period in Hong Kong', *Economy and Society*, Vol. 24, No. 1, pp. 67–100.

Sung, Y.W. (1986) 'Fiscal and Economic Policies in Hong Kong', in J.Y.S. Cheng (ed) *Hong Kong in Transition*, Hong Kong: Oxford University Press, pp. 120–141.

Sung, Y.W. (2018) 'Becoming Part of One National Economy: Maintaining Two Systems in the Midst of the Rise of China', in T.L. Lui, S.W.K. Chiu, and R. Yep (eds) *Routledge Handbook of Contemporary Hong Kong*, London: Routledge, pp. 66–86.

Survey Office (1987) *Public Response to Green Paper: The 1987 Review of Developments on Representative Government: Report of the Survey Office*, Hong Kong: Government Printer.

Sustainable Lantau Office (n.d.) *Tomorrow Lantau Vision*, Hong Kong: Civil Engineering and Development Department. Retrieved 22 July 2020, from www.lantau.gov.hk/en/lantau-tomorrow-vision/index.html.

Svara, J.H. (1998) 'The Politics-Administration Dichotomy Model as Aberration', *Public Administration Review*, Vol. 58, No. 1, pp. 51–58.

SynergyNet (2002) *How to Take Governance Reform Forward: Accountability to Whom and How?* Hong Kong: SynergyNet.

Tang, H. (2003) *The 2003–04 Budget*, Speech by the Financial Secretary moving the Second Reading of the Appropriation Bill 2003 at the Legislative Council, 4 March, Hong Kong: Printer Department.

Tang, H. (2004) *The 2004–05 Budget*, Speech by the Financial Secretary moving the Second Reading of the Appropriation Bill 2004 at the Legislative Council, 10 March, Hong Kong: Printing Department.

Tang, J.T.H. (2008) 'Hong Kong's Continuing Search for a New Order: Political Stability in a Partial Democracy', in C. McGiffert and J.T.H. Tang (eds) *Hong Kong on the Move: 10 Years as the HKSAR*, Berkeley, CA: University of California, Berkeley, pp. 18–36.

Tao, J. (2006) 'A Confucian Way Out of the Paradox of Trust in Democracy?', Paper presented at an International Workshop on Governance for Harmony organised by the Governance in Asia Research Centre, City University of Hong Kong, 9–10 June, Hong Kong.

Task Force on Constitutional Development (2005) *The Fifth Report of the Constitutional Development Task Force: Package of Proposals for the Methods for Selecting the Chief Executive in 2007 and for Forming the Legislative Council in 2008*, October, Hong Kong: Constitutional Affairs Bureau.

Task Force on Land Supply (2018) *Striving for Multi-pronged Land Supply: Report of the Task Force on Land Supply*, December, Hong Kong: The Hong Kong Special Administrative Region Government. Retrieved 22 July 2020, from www.landforhongkong.hk/pdf/Report%20(Eng).pdf.

Task Force on Review of Civil Service Pay Policy and System (2002a) *Phase One Interim Report*, April, Hong Kong: Printing Department.

Task Force on Review of Civil Service Pay Policy and System (2002b) *Phase One Final Report*, September, Hong Kong: Printing Department.

Task Force on Review of Self-financing Post-secondary Education (2018) *Review Report: Parallel Development, Promoting Diversity*, December, Hong Kong: Education Bureau.

Taylor, C. (1992) *Multiculturalism and the 'Politics of Recognition'*, Princeton, NJ: Princeton University Press.

Tian, F.L. (田飛龍) (2017) 'One Country, Two Systems enters Version "2.0"' [in Chinese, 〈一國兩制進入「2.0版」〉], *Ming Pao* (《明報》), 11 December.

Tooze, A. (2018) *Crashed: How a Decade of Financial Crises Changed the World*, New York: Viking.

Trading Economics (n.d.) *Taiwan Youth Unemployment Rate*. Retrieved 22 July 2020, from https://tradingeconomics.com/taiwan/youth-unemployment-rate#:~:text=Looking%20forward%2C%20we%20estimate%20Youth,according%20to%20our%20econometric%20models.

Trading Economics (n.d.) *Hong Kong—Credit Rating*. Retrieved 22 July 2020, from https://tradingeconomics.com/hong-kong/rating.

Transparency International (n.d.) *Country Data: Corruption Perceptions Index*. Retrieved 22 July 2020, from www.transparency.org/en/countries/hong-kong.

Transport and Housing Bureau (2014) *Long Term Housing Strategy 2014*, December, Hong Kong: Transport and Housing Bureau.

Tsang, D.Y.K. (1999) *The 1999–2000 Budget: Onward with New Strengths*, Speech by the Financial Secretary moving the Second Reading of the Appropriation Bill 1999 at the Legislative Council, 3 March, Hong Kong: Printing Department.

Tsang, D.Y.K. (2000) *The 2000–01 Budget: Scaling New Heights*, Speech by the Financial Secretary moving the Second Reading of the Appropriation Bill 2000 at the Legislative Council, 8 March, Hong Kong: Printing Department.

Tsang, D.Y.K. (2005a) *Declaration Speech to Announce Chief Executive Candidacy*, 2 June. Retrieved June 2005, from www.donald-yktsang.com/press_speeches _e_001.html (English version) or http://hm.people.com.cn/GB/42273/3438275.html (Chinese version) (links no longer accessible).

Tsang, D.Y.K. (2005b) *Campaign Speech for Chief Executive Election*, 3 June. Retrieved 22 July 2020, from www.donald-yktsang.com/press_speeches_e.html.

Tsang, D.Y.K. (2006) 'Big Market, Small Government', press release, 18 September, Hong Kong: Chief Executive's Office. Retrieved 22 July 2020, from www.ceo.gov.hk/archive/2012/eng/press/oped.htm.

Tsang, D.Y.K. (2007a) *Donald Tsang Election Platform: Policy Blueprint*, Hong Kong: Donald Tsang Election Office.

Tsang, D.Y.K. (2007b) *My Election Platform—Statement on Progression*, 2 February, Hong Kong: Donald Tsang Election Office.

Tsang, D.Y.K. (2007c) *The 2007–08 Policy Address: A New Direction for Hong Kong*, Policy address by the Chief Executive to the Legislative Council, 10 October, Hong Kong: Government Logistics Department.

Tsang, DY.K. (2008) *The 2008–09 Policy Address: Embracing New Challenges*, Policy address by the Chief Executive to the Legislative Council, 15 October, Hong Kong: Government Logistics Department.

Tsang, J.C.W. (2008) *The 2008–09 Budget*, Speech by the Financial Secretary moving the Second Reading of the Appropriation Bill 2008, 27 February, Hong Kong: Government Logistics Department.

Tsang, J.C.W. (曾俊華) (2016) 'Localism not the Same as Hong Kong Independence' [in Chinese, 〈本土不等於港獨〉], *Hong Kong Economic Journal* (《信報》), 29 July. Retrieved 22 July 2020, from www2.hkej.com/instantnews/current/article/1354927/曾俊華%3A本土不等於港獨.

Tsang, S.Y.S. (1988) *Democracy Shelved: Great Britain, China, and Attempts at Constitutional Reform in Hong Kong, 1945–1952*, Hong Kong: Oxford University Press.

Tsang, S.Y.S. (2007) *Governing Hong Kong: Administrative Officers from the Nineteen Century to the Handover to China, 1862–1997*, London: I.B. Tauris.

Tung, C.H. (1996) *Building a 21st Century Hong Kong Together*, Chief Executive Election Platform, 22 October.

Tung, C.H. (1997) *Building Hong Kong For a New Era*, Address by the Chief Executive at the Provisional Legislative Council meeting, 8 October, Hong Kong: Printing Department.

Tung, C.H. (1998) *The 1998 Policy Address: From Adversity to Opportunity*, Policy address by the Chief Executive to the Legislative Council, 7 October, Hong Kong: Printing Department.

Tung, C.H. (2000) *The 2000 Policy Address: Serving the Community, Sharing Common Goals*, Policy address by the Chief Executive to the Legislative Council, 11 October, Hong Kong: Printing Department.

Tung, C.H. (2001) *The 2001 Policy Address: Building on Our Strengths, Investing in Our Future*, Policy address by the Chief Executive to the Legislative Council, 10 October, Hong Kong: Printing Department.

TVBS Poll Center (Taiwan) (2016) 'Approval Ratings of Eight years of President Ma Ying-jeo's Administration' [in Chinese, 〈馬英九總統施政八年滿意度民調〉], June. Retrieved 22 July 2020, from https://cc.tvbs.com.tw/portal/file/poll_center/2017/20170602/0505041.pdf.

TVBS Poll Center (Taiwan) (2018) 'Approval Ratings of President Tsai Ing-wen Two Years after inauguration' [in Chinese, 〈蔡英文總統就職兩年滿意度民調〉], May. Retrieved 22 July 2020, from https://cc.tvbs.com.tw/portal/file/poll_cen ter/2018/20180516/27bcedb9362b32c82f7cc0c9e089b240.pdf.

TVBS Poll Center (Taiwan) (2020) 'Approval Ratings of President Tsai Ing-wen at Second-Term Inauguration' [in Chinese, 〈蔡英文總統連任就職滿意度民調〉], May. Retrieved 22 July 2020, from https://cc.tvbs.com.tw/portal/file/poll_cen ter/2020/20200518/6fd57ec6489e3f7a2b78fb8d0e909a35.pdf.

Uhr, J. (1998) *Deliberative Democracy in Australia: The Changing Place of Parliament*, Cambridge: Cambridge University Press.

Unger, J. and A. Chan (1995) 'China, Corporatism, and the East Asian Model', *The Australian Journal of Chinese Affairs*, No. 33, pp. 29–53.

United Nations Department of Economic and Social Affairs (2020) *UN/DESA Policy Brief #72: COVID-19 and Sovereign Debt*, 14 May. Retrieved 22 July 2020, from www.un.org/development/desa/dpad/publication/un-desa-policy-brief-72-covid-19-and-sovereign-debt/.

United Nations Economic and Social Commission for Asia and the Pacific (UNESCAP) (2006) *What is Good Governance?* 24 December, Bangkok: UNESCAP.

University Grants Committee (2019) 'Internationalisation and Engagement with Mainland China', *Annual Report 2018–19*, Hong Kong: University Grants Committee.

University Grants Committee (n.d.) *Number of Mainland Students in University Grants Committee-funded Programmes by University and Level of Study, 2003/04 to 2016/17 Academic Years*, Hong Kong: University Grants Committee. Retrieved 22 July 2020, from http://gia.info.gov.hk/general/201707/12/P201 7071200689_263130_2_1499854110454.pdf.

Urban Council (1966) *Report of the Ad Hoc Committee on the Future Scope and Operation of the Urban Council*, Hong Kong: Government Printer.

Urban Council Ad Hoc Committee (1969) *Report on the Reform of Local Government*, Hong Kong: Government Printer.

Ure, G. (2012) *Governors, Politics and the Colonial Office: Public Policy in Hong Kong, 1918–58*, Hong Kong: Hong Kong University Press.

Uslaner, E.M. (2002) *The Moral Foundations of Trust*, Cambridge: Cambridge University Press.

van de Walle, S., G. Hammerschmid, R. Andrews, and P. Bezes (2016) 'Introduction: Public Administration Reforms in Europe', in G. Hammerschmid, S. Van de Walle, R. Andrews, and P. Bezes (eds) *Public Administration Reforms in Europe*, Cheltenham: Edward Elgar, pp. 1–11.

Van den Bos, K. (2018) *Why People Radicalize: How Unfairness Judgments are Used to Fuel Radical Beliefs, Extremist Behaviors, and Terrorism*, London: Oxford University Press.

Vickers, S. (1990) *Hong Kong Country Paper—The Public and Private Delivery of Services in Hong Kong: Some Relevant Issues across the Spectrum*, Paper presented at the Pacific Economic Cooperation Conference, Kyoto, Japan, 11–20 October.

Vickers, S. (2001) '"More Colonial Again?" The Post-1997 Culture of Hong Kong's Governing Elite', *International Journal of Public Administration*, Vol. 24, No. 9, pp. 951–976.

Virkar, S. (2015) 'Globalization, the Internet, and the Nation-State: A Critical Analysis', in J.P. Sahlin (ed) *Social Media and the Transformation of Interaction in Society*, Hershey, PA: Information Science Reference (an imprint of IGI Global), pp. 51–66.

Vroom, V. (1964) *Work and Motivation*, New York: Wiley.

Wade, R. (1990) *Governing the Market: Economic Theory and the Role of Government in East Asian Industrialization*, Princeton, NJ: Princeton University Press.

Walker, C. and J. Ludwig (2017) 'The Meaning of Sharp Power: How Authoritarian States Project Influence', *Foreign Affairs*, 16 November.

The Wall Street Journal (2021) 'China All but Ends Hong Kong Democracy With "Patriots Only" Rule', 11 March.

Wang, F.L. (2017) *The China Order: Centralia, World Empire, and the Nature of Chinese Power*, Albany, NY: State University of New York Press.

Wang, Q. (2010) 'Administrative Reform in China: Past, Present, and Future', *Southeast Review of Asian Studies*, Vol. 32, No. 1, pp. 100–119.

Weiss, L. (1998) *The Myth of the Powerless State*, Ithaca, NY: Cornell University Press.

Welsh, F. (1994) *A History of Hong Kong*, London: HarperCollins.

Wen Wei Po (《文匯報》) (1998) 'Anson Chan Had Pledged to President Jiang She Would Support Tung Chee-hwa' [in Chinese, 〈陳方安生曾向江主席保証支持董建華〉], 5 July.

Wen Wei Po (《文匯報》) (2016) 'Xi Jinping: Hong Kong Independence Not Allowed' [in Chinese, 〈習近平：不容「港獨」〉], 22 November.

Wen Wei Publishing Co. (ed) (1990) *The Birth of the Basic Law* [in Chinese,《基本法的誕生》], Hong Kong: Wen Wei Publishing Co. (文匯出版).

Wesselink, A., H. Colebatch, and W. Pearce (2014) 'Evidence and Policy: Discourses, Meanings and Practices', *Policy Sciences*, Vol. 47, No. 4, pp. 339–344.

Wettenhall, R.L. (1976a) 'Modes of Ministerialization, Part I: Towards a Typology — The Australian Experience', *Public Administration*, Vol. 54, No. 1, pp. 1–20.

Wettenhall, R.L. (1976b) 'Modes of Ministerialization, Part II: From Colony to State in the Twentieth Century', *Public Administration*, Vol. 54, No. 4, pp. 425–451.

The White House (2017) *National Security Strategy of the United States of America*, December, Washington, D.C. Retrieved 22 July 2020, from www.whitehouse.gov/wp-content/uploads/2017/12/NSS-Final-12-18-2017-0905-2.pdf.

Wildavsky, A. (1964) *The Politics of the Budgetary Process*, Boston: Little, Brown and Company.

Williams, A.A. (1957) 'Administrative Adjustment of a Colonial Government to meet Constitutional Change', *Public Administration*, Vol. 35, No. 3, pp. 267–288.

Williamson, J. (1989) 'What Washington Means by Policy Reform', in J. Williamson (ed) *Latin American Readjustment: How Much Has Happened*, Washington, D.C.: Institute for International Economics, pp. 7–20.

Wirsching, E.M. (2018) *The Revolving Door for Political Elites: An Empirical Analysis of the Linkages between Government Officials' Professional Background and Financial Regulation*, Paper submitted to the 2018 OECD Global Anti-Corruption and Integrity Forum, Paris: OECD. Retrieved 22 July 2020, from www.oecd.org/corruption/integrity-forum/academic-papers/Wirsching.pdf.

Wodak, R. (2015) *The Politics of Fear: What Right-Wing Populist Discourses Mean*, London: Sage.

Wong, H.T. and S.D. Liu (2018) 'Cultural Activism during the Hong Kong Umbrella Movement', *Journal of Creative Communications*, Vol. 13, No. 2, pp. 157–165.

Wong, J.W.P (2002) *Speech by the Secretary for the Civil Service at the Annual Dinner of the Oxford University Hong Kong Society*, 6 September, Hong Kong: Civil Service Bureau. Retrieved 22 July 2020, from www.info.gov.hk/gia/general/200209/06/0906251.htm.

Wong, J.W.P. (2013) 'Expanding and Destroying the Accountability System', in J.Y.S. Cheng (ed) *The Second Chief Executive of Hong Kong SAR: Evaluating the Tsang Years 2005–2012*, Hong Kong: City University of Hong Kong Press, pp. 31–58.

Wong, R. (2020) ' "This is the End of Hong Kong": Reactions Pour in as Beijing Proposes Security Law', *Hong Kong Free Press*, 22 May. Retrieved 22 July 2020, from https://hongkongfp.com/2020/05/22/this-is-the-end-of-hong-kong-reactions-pour-in-as-beijing-proposes-security-law/.

Wong, W. (2012) 'The Civil Service', in W.M. Lam, P.L.T. Lui, and W. Wong (eds) *Contemporary Hong Kong Government and Politics*, Hong Kong: Hong Kong University Press, pp. 87–100.

Wong, W. and M. Chu (2017) 'Rebel with a Cause: Structural Problems Underlying the Umbrella Movement of Hong Kong and the Role of the Youth', *Asian Education and Development Studies*, Vol. 6, No. 4, pp. 343–353.

Woodhouse, D. (1994) *Ministers and Parliament: Accountability in Theory and Practice*, Oxford: Clarendon Press.

Working Group on Overseas Community of the Basic Law Promotion Steering Committee (2012) 'Drafting and Promulgation of the Basic Law and Hong Kong's Reunification with the Motherland', in M.W.C. Tam (ed) *The Basic Law and Hong Kong: The 15th Anniversary of Reunification with the Motherland*, Hong Kong: Basic Law Promotion Steering Committee, Chapter 1. Retrieved 22 July 2020, from www.basiclaw.gov.hk/en/publications/book/15anniversary_reunification_ch1_1.pdf.

World Bank (1993) *The East Asian Economic Miracle: Economic Growth and Public Policy*, New York: Oxford University Press.

World Bank (2019) *Worldwide Governance Indicators 2018*. Retrieved 16 July 2021, from https://info.worldbank.org/governance/wgi/Home/Reports.

World Bank (2020a) *Data: Unemployment, Youth total*. Retrieved 22 July 2020, from https://data.worldbank.org/indicator/SL.UEM.1524.ZS.

World Bank (2020b) *Global Economic Prospects*, June. Retrieved 22 July 2020, from https://documents1.worldbank.org/curated/en/502991591631723294/pdf/Global-Economic-Prospects-June-2020.pdf.

World Bank (2020c) *Worldwide Governance Indicators 2019*. Retrieved 16 July 2021, from https://info.worldbank.org/governance/wgi/Home/Reports.

World Bank (n.d.) *GDP (current US$)*, various economies. Retrieved 22 July 2020, from https://data.worldbank.org/indicator/NY.GDP.MKTP.CD.

World Bank (n.d.) *GDP per Capita (current US$)*, various economies. Retrieved 22 July 2020, from https://data.worldbank.org/indicator/NY.GDP.PCAP.CD.

World Bank (n.d.) *GDP (current US$)—China, Hong Kong SAR, China*. Retrieved 22 July 2020, from https://data.worldbank.org/indicator/NY.GDP.MKTP.CD?locations=CN-HK&name_desc=false.

World Bank (n.d.) *Hong Kong SAR, China*. Retrieved on 22 July 2020, from https://data.worldbank.org/country/hong-kong-sar-china?view=chart.

World Health Organisation (WHO) (n.d.) *Naming the Coronavirus Disease (COVID-19) and the Virus that Causes it*, Geneva: WHO. Retrieved 22 July 2020, from www.who.int/emergencies/diseases/novel-coronavirus-2019/technical-guidance/naming-the-coronavirus-disease-(covid-2019)-and-the-virus-that-causes-it.

Worldometer (2020) *Covid-19 Coronavirus Pandemic*, 11 June. Retrieved 22 July 2020, from www.worldometers.info/coronavirus/?utm_campaign=homeAdvegas1?%22#countries.

Worldometer (n.d.) *Life Expectancy of the World Population*. Retrieved 9 June 2020, from www.worldometers.info/demographics/life-expectancy/.

Wu, X., M. Howlett, and M. Ramesh (2018) 'Policy Capacity: Conceptual Framework and Essential Components', in X. Wu, M. Howlett, and M. Ramesh (eds) *Policy Capacity and Governance: Assessing Governmental Competences and Capabilities in Theory and Practice*, London: Palgrave Macmillan, pp. 1–25.

Xinhuanet (新華網) (2019) 'Statistics Show that the Number of Hong Kong Students Enrolling in Mainland Universities through the Test-free Enrollment Plan Increased by Nearly 10% this Year' [in Chinese, 〈數據顯示：今年通過免試招生計劃報讀內地高校的港生增長近一成〉] 11 April. Retrieved 22 July 2020, from www.xinhuanet.com/politics/2019-04/11/c_1124355664.htm.

Xinhuanet (2020a) 'Central Gov't Agency, Liaison Office have Power to Supervise Major Affairs in HK: Spokesperson of Liaison Office', 17 April. Retrieved 22 July 2020, from www.xinhuanet.com/english/2020-04/17/c_138986076.htm.

Xinhuanet (2020b) 'China Focus: Draft Decision on HK National Security Legislation Submitted to NPC', 22 May. Retrieved 22 July 2020, from www.xinhuanet.com/english/2020-05/22/c_139078396.htm.

Xinhuanet (2020c) 'Highlights of China's Decision on Hong Kong National Security Legislation', 28 May. Retrieved 22 July 2020, from www.xinhuanet.com/english/2020-05/28/c_139095813.htm.

Xinhuanet (2021) 'China's Top Legislature Adopts Amended Annexes to HKSAR Basic Law', 30 March. Retrieved 11 April 2021, from www.xinhuanet.com/english/2021-03/30/c_139846350.htm.

Xinhuanet (n.d.) 'Chinese Dream—Special Report'. Retrieved 22 July 2020, from www.xinhuanet.com/english/special/chinesedream/.

Xu, J.T. (許家屯) (1993) *Xu Jiatuan's Hong Kong Memoirs—First Part* [in Chinese,《許家屯香港回憶錄　[上]》], Hong Kong: United Daily (Hong Kong) (香港聯合報).

Yam, J. (1999a) 'The Creation of the Linked Exchange Rate', *Viewpoint*, Hong Kong Monetary Authority, 4 November. Retrieved 22 July 2020, from www.hkma.gov.hk/eng/publications-and-research/reference-materials/viewpoint/19991104.shtml.

Yam, J. (1999b) 'Joseph Yam Recalls the Events of September 1983', Hong Kong: Hong Kong Monetary Authority. Retrieved 22 July 2020, from www.hkma.gov.hk/eng/news-and-media/insight/1999/11/19991104/.

Yaxley, J. (1988) *Financial Management Reforms in the Hong Kong Government*, Speech delivered to the Hong Kong Branch of the International Fiscal Association, 14 November, Hong Kong.

Yep, R. (葉健民) (2014) *Silent Revolution: A Century of Hong Kong's Collective Endeavour for Clean Government* [in Chinese, 《靜默革命：香港廉政百年共業》], Hong Kong: Chung Hwa Book Company (中華書局).

Yep, R. and T.L. Lui (2010) 'Revisiting the Golden Era of MacLehose and the Dynamics of Social Reforms', *China Information*, Vol. 24, No. 3, pp. 235–247.

Yesilkagit, K. (2010) 'The Limits of Administration: A Response to Christopher Hood', *Public Administration Review*, Vol. 70, No. 4, pp. 535–537.

Yeung, R. (2008) *Moving Millions: The Commercial Success and Political Controversies of Hong Kong's Railways*, Hong Kong: Hong Kong University Press.

Yew, C.P. and K.W. Kwong (2014) 'Hong Kong Identity on the Rise', *Asian Survey*, Vol. 54, No. 6, pp. 1088–1112.

Yiu, P. and A. Katakam (2021) 'In One Year, Hong Kong Arrests 117 People under New Security Law', *Reuters*, 30 June. Retrieved 16 July 2021, from www.reuters.com/world/asia-pacific/one-year-hong-kong-arrests-117-people-under-new-security-law-2021-06-30/.

Yu, K. (ed) (2010) *The Reform of Governance*, Leiden: Brill [a translated collection of original articles in Chinese].

Yue, D. (2007) *Letter to all Civil Servants on 'Development of an Improved Civil Service Pay Adjustment Mechanism—Pay Level Survey'*, Letter from the Secretary for the Civil Service, 24 April, Hong Kong: Civil Service Bureau. Retrieved 22 July 2020, from www.csb.gov.hk/textonly/english/letter/821.html.

Zavattaro, S.M. and L.A. Brainard (2019) 'Social Media as Micro-encounters: Millennial Preferences as Moderators of Digital Public Value Creation', *International Journal of Public Sector Management*, Vol. 32, No. 5, pp. 562–580.

Zhang, P. (2019) 'Beijing Unveils Detailed Reform Plan to Make Shenzhen Model City for China and the World', *South China Morning Post*, 18 August.

Zhang, X.M. (張曉明) (2020) 'The Stronger the National Security Bottom Line, the Greater the Space for "One Country, Two Systems"' [in Chinese, 〈國家安全底線愈牢，「一國兩制」空間愈大〉], Keynote speech at an online seminar hosted by the Hong Kong SAR government to mark the 30th anniversary of the promulgation of the Basic Law, 8 June, Hong Kong: Hong Kong and Macao Affairs Office of the State Council. Retrieved 22 July 2020, from www.hmo.gov.cn/gab/bld/zxm/gzdt/202006/t20200608_21923.html.

Zhao, S. (2018) 'A Revisionist Stakeholder: China and the Post-World War II World Order', *Journal of Contemporary China*, Vol. 27, No. 113, pp. 643–658.

Zhao, Y. (1997) 'Hong Kong: The Journey to a Bilingual Legal System', *Loyola of Los Angles International and Comparative Law Review*, Vol. 19, No. 2. Retrieved 22 July 2020, from https://digitalcommons.lmu.edu/ilr/vol19/iss2/3/.

Zheng, W. and E. Xie (2020) 'China Upgrades Hong Kong Affairs with New Chief', *South China Morning Post*, 13 February.

Z/Yen Group (2020) *The Global Financial Centres Index*. Retrieved 22 July 2020, from www.longfinance.net/programmes/financial-centre-futures/global-financial-centres-index/.